AN INSTITUTIONAL THEORY OF LAW

An Institutional Theory Of Law

Keeping Law in its Place

PETER MORTON

CLARENDON PRESS · OXFORD
1998

Oxford University Press, Great Clarendon Street, Oxford OX2 6DP

Oxford New York
Athens Auckland Bangkok Bogota Bombay
Buenos Aires Calcutta Cape Town Dar es Salaam
Delhi Florence Hong Kong Istanbul Karachi
Koala Lumpur Madras Madrid Melbourne
Mexico City Nairobi Paris Singapore
Taipei Tokyo Toronto Warsaw

and associated companies in
Berlin Ibadan

Oxford is a trade mark of Oxford University Press

Published in the United States
by Oxford University Press Inc., New York

British Library Cataloguing in Publication Data
Data available

Library of Congress Cataloging in Publication Data
Morton, Peter.
An institutional theory of law: keeping law in its place / Peter Morton.
p. cm.
Includes bibliographical references.
1. Law—Philosophy. 2. Jurisprudence. 3. Institutions (Philosophy) I. Title.
K355.M67 1997
340′.1—dc21 97–35700
ISBN 0–19–825825–9

Typeset by Vera A. Keep, Cheltenham
Printed in Great Britain
on acid-free paper by
Bookcraft Ltd., Midsomer Norton, Somerset

To Yvonne

PREFACE AND ACKNOWLEDGEMENTS

I embarked upon an institutional theory of law partly because of a dissatisfaction with accounts of the institutional nature of law in jurisprudential discussions. The starting point for the investigation was the insight that languages are essentially social, and that special languages, such as those of law or property, are not generated in some generalized social context, but that their words have uses and meanings in specific forms of life which are interrelated in highly distinctive ways. The first task was the identification of the very basic forms of human activity and association—which I have called institutional forms. The results of that preliminary enquiry into the atomic particulars of the institutional world are set out in Chapter 2. In the succeeding chapters I have attempted to demonstrate both the importance of employing these analytic tools if we would understand legal language and activity aright, and the dangers which may result from our neglect or misunderstanding of the institutional foundations of the law.

One initial positivist assumption had been that it would be possible to treat the institutional forms which underwrite legal language as neutral configurations of activity and association which could be identified in any age or clime. It was at a very late stage in the process of shortening and revising a draft I had submitted to Oxford University Press that I sensed the futility of trying to present the institutional forms of the legal field as neutral entities in the institutional world. I became aware of the central importance for analytic jurisprudence of making clear the ideological underpinning of the particular institutional forms which generate modern legal language with its emphasis on rights, and of the need to give prominence to the values of the democratic revolution of modern times. To the dismay of those with an interest in the rapid completion of the book it became clear that radical reorganisation and substantial rewriting was called for.

My thanks are due to Professor Michael McConville of Warwick University for his encouragement at the start of the investigation and to his colleague Dr Martin Warner for his comments on an early draft of the section on criminal law. I shall always be grateful for Richard Hart's guidance and help which was of decisive importance in ensuring the completion of the book. I must also acknowledge my profound indebtedness to Anna Rayne who has done so much to clarify the ideas and to amend the errors within a long, obscure, and imperfect script.

CONTENTS

ABBREVIATIONS

BP: beneficial position. A position held by an individual of entitlement to benefits, which is socially recognised.

CS: citizen and State

E: entitlement(s), which are transferrable beneficial positions.

I; interest(s), non-transferrable beneficial positions.

IE: interests and entitlements

LS(S): legal system(s). Each legal Practice possesses, in addition to its procedural rules, a set of norms. Together these make up its LS. These laws are maintained by the participants of the LS and govern their decision-making.

NP: normative product, the formal intended outcome of participation in a normative Practice. (A normative Practice is a procedure which makes possible the deliberate alteration of the norms of an associational form.) So a statute is the NP of a legislative Practice, and a judgment is the NP of a legal adjudicatory Practice.

SE: systematic exchange(s), exchanges between parties who decide to buy or sell in the light of their knowledge of the current rates of exchange for the sort of things which they possess.

ULP: the ultimate legislative Practice. The ULP constitutes the representative body within a democratic polity which has supreme authority to make laws (legal sovereignty) and to alter the constitution (political sovereignty).

1
Taking institutions seriously

An understanding of law—of the nature of its norms, of its structure, of its language and concepts—requires us to take very seriously the institutions which it inhabits. The laws of the land cannot be said to exist simply because they appear as prescriptive textual formulations, as paper rules in codes, statutes, law reports, and text-books. Like all social norms, laws have meaningful existence only insofar as they are recursively recreated within specific practices and activities. An institutional theory of law has at its core the idea that 'norms, aims and values are not organising and justificatory forces logically prior to social reality . . .; rather, they are systems of deliberation and control which are constituted through social action and interaction'.[1] A jurisprudence which deals with norms abstracted from those forms of life, that is, from their institutional foundations, will be incapable of providing a basis for the explication of legal concepts.

Many writers appear to have conceived of law as a structure of norms which, like a geodesic dome, is anchored to the ground only at certain points. Lip service may be paid to the importance of the institutions, but we can hardly be said to be treating institutions seriously if, while recognising the institutional character of law, we present the institutions as a mere backcloth or context for laws which are assumed to have their own independent, systematic existence.

One of the insights of postmodernism concerning the fundamental questions of religious belief has been the recognition that rationalists and fundamentalists share common ground: both positively, in the belief that it is possible to discover objective truths, and negatively, in the failure to acknowledge the crucial fact that our values and meanings have been constructed within the complicated forms of human life and activity. Similarly, in legal theory, natural lawyers and positivists in their shared search for objective knowledge of the law—putting their faith either in sovereign reason or in a rational sovereign—can both be accused of overlooking the important and inescapable fact that the very existence of law depends upon its involvement in complicated structures of human interaction.

Many writers today recognize that it is necessary to have regard for the institutional bases of law. Certainly, it is generally agreed that much conceptual analysis—exemplified in the works of Bentham, Austin,

Holland, Hohfeld, and Salmond—has involved a very questionable philosophy of language.[2] on the mistaken assumption that the concepts of law could be divorced from the language and activity of everyday life, many writers provided schematic definitions of legal terms, and accounts of their interrelationship, without reference to the activities, institutions, practices, attitudes, or beliefs of judges, lawyers, policemen, or citizens. The writers of works in which legal concepts were abstracted from the forms of life in which they exist appear to be dealing with a set of abstract logical counters. In presenting the legal system as a sphere of real human activity within which the law operates, they assumed that that system was readily understandable. Everyone was supposed to be sufficiently knowledgable about legislatures and courts. For such analysts the social realities of the context of law was a matter for investigation by political and social scientists.

The idea that languages emerge from the shared practices and patterns of meaningful human activity is now commonplace. The use of language is not only embedded in the concrete activities of everyday life, but also constitutive of them.[3] Few would disagree that to understand the language and concepts of a society it is necessary to understand its institutions. So if our objective is to understand a particular segment of the language of a society—such as the distinctive language of legal discourse—it is essential to investigate the structure and character of the patterns of human association and activity of which the language is an inextricable part, and which it may be said to construct. This book is a modest attempt to articulate and analyse the forms of life within which legal concepts live. Treating institutions seriously will provide a new perspective from which current legal theory can be appraised.

I: THE INSTITUTIONAL WORLD

The institutional world which we must try to understand and articulate is the immensely complicated world of social interaction: of innumerable human associations, activities, practices, norms, values, and meanings.

Clearly we cannot hope to understand the institutional products of social interaction, the 'things' of the institutional world—such as schools, banks, treaties, mortgages, and laws—by using the methods of investigation, or the conceptual apparatus, employed in the natural sciences. The methods of science will enable us neither to establish the existence or describe the structures of the objects of this world, nor to understand the manner in which they relate to each other. Even if many of these objects have phenomenal manifestations they cannot be understood simply in terms of those appearances—a court of law, bombed out of its courthouse, sits in a converted warehouse, the laws of the land are not to be identified with their documentary expressions. Clearly, many of the objects of this world are intangible; those objects would slip through the mesh of scientific enquiry.

However, the fact that the objects of this world are not amenable to empirical verification does not mean, as some realists have concluded, that they are illusory or metaphysical, nor that propositions in which they feature are meaningless.

The objects of this world, which exist in what Popper[4] called World 3, have autonomy from both World 1 (the material world) and World 2 (the world of subjective experience). World 3 includes all the products of the human mind, such as tools, institutions, and works of art. They yield up their secrets neither to the natural scientist nor to the psychologist.[5] They require a humanist rather than a reductionist understanding; in other words, they can be understood only in terms of the intersubjective meanings and ideas which sustain them and upon which their existence depends. The epistemological and ontological questions raised by our belief in the reality of this world and the objects in it have been widely discussed.[6]

In our everyday affairs we make factual statements about the objects of this world. We treat as an indisputable fact, for instance, that A is married, or that B has an overdraft, or that the next Olympic Games will be held in Sydney. Philosophers and social theorists have drawn attention to the ways in which institutional facts differ from facts about the physical world; they distinguish between institutional (or social) facts and 'brute facts'.[7]

Brute facts—such as facts about the existence of islands, plants, molecules, mountains, and storms—are accessible to our sense perceptions; the objects to which they refer have spatial positions and temporal duration, and they are in no way dependent for their existence upon human will, meaning, convention, or contrivance. These facts are all capable of verification by empirical methods.

By contrast, institutional facts—for instance the fact of A's marriage or of B's overdraft—cannot be established in this way. These facts all presuppose the existence of institutions—such as marriage ceremonies and banks—and can only be understood by reference to the norms, ideas, and meanings integral to the existence and the operation of the institutions. Meaningful assertions of the existence of institutional facts may be true or false, and their truth or falsity is judged by reference to a shared interpretation of the acts in the institutional world—acts, say, of borrowing, praying, selecting, appointing, and so on—and to shared understandings of the significance and meanings involved in the procedures and associational forms.

Although institutional facts involve phenomenal particulars, they cannot be reduced without remainder to brute facts. This is largely because the statements asserting institutional facts—about courts, enforcement agencies, or legal systems—presuppose norms and meanings, while brute facts do not. We cannot give a complete account of a transaction in which A lends B a book by describing only the objects, persons, and physical movements involved. Loans belong in the world of social interaction, and to understand such transactions we must grasp the point or meaning of what is done or said.

There is today perhaps little need to establish the case for the meaningfulness of statements about this world or for the reality or autonomy of the objects within it. Nevertheless, the character of the institutional world is such that we may question the possibility of achieving clear objective knowledge of it, for it confronts the observer with formidable problems.

The most striking feature of this world is its state of continuous change.[8] In the world of social interaction nothing stands still; new activities emerge as new techniques are developed and new inventions are made; old activities die out or are merged with others; practices are rendered obsolete; new procedures emerge or are instituted; relationships between agencies are renegotiated; and so forth. All objects in this world are, in differing ways, vulnerable to incremental change or subject to deliberate destruction and reform. The vocabulary of the types of changes in this Heraclitean world makes the vocabulary of geomorphological or biological change seem poverty-stricken.

Although the contingency of our social arrangements and the impermanence of the furniture of the institutional world requires emphasis, we must not exaggerate the rate of change. If we made the film recording too slow it would when replayed show society changing so rapidly that we would not be able to account for our sense of the stability of institutions, practices, and intersubjective meanings.[9] For only against a relatively secure institutional background is it possible to make meaningful judgments as to the truth or falsity of statements asserting institutional facts, to make judgments as to the propriety *of* social conduct, or to talk of a shared interpretation of the institutional world we inherit. Such judgments, made in the light of an interpretation of how things presently stand, are valid only for a particular moment of time.

So our understanding of this world depends upon both our experience of its relative stability and our awareness of its longer-term impermanence and contingency. It is the fact of the contingency of this world, of the never-ending processes of change, which explains, in part, why we cannot rely upon the language of everyday life alone to gain a faithful picture of the world in which we live. For linguistic changes seldom keep pace with institutional changes. Languages have the capacity to keep alive beliefs, concepts, and relationships which have been rendered obsolete by the incremental processes or deliberate reforms involving institutional change. Language may conceal—indeed, it may even be deliberately employed to conceal—reality.[10] Inappropriate but authoritative definitions may result in systematic distortion of the language employed in particular areas of human conduct.

Over the years the language used by members of a particular society may show a remarkable capacity for innovation and change. However, for the purpose of reflecting incremental and profound changes in institutional forms, language may prove less malleable, since it is often saddled with structures of terms which are difficult to replace, and are therefore contorted into new and unconformable use. This contortion is most apparent where we have to refer to authoritative written formulations which, being fixed, may fail to reflect the real world.

In order to analyse the contemporary world of social interaction, we need to achieve a different perspective, more reflective than that required of persons engaged in practical affairs.[11] If the unreflective operate successfully in the social world, this is no guarantee that they have an adequate theoretical understanding of that world. We cannot depend upon the deliverances of common sense or the understanding of the street-wise. Practical men and women may achieve their ends by making do with familiar linguistic resources, by ignoring inconsistencies, by fudging matters, and by relying on intuitions and tacit understandings which run counter to received or apparent meanings. They commonly say one thing and mean another, sometimes employing terms in a way which conduces to their pride in the exclusiveness of their group. The success which they achieve with their limited understanding may lead them to dismiss the urge to understand the social world more clearly as idle curiosity.

Leaving aside questions of the value of seeking a better theoretical understanding of this world, it is clear that those who do engage in that enterprise must choose carefully the apparatus to be employed in their attempt to articulate the world. That endeavour necessarily involves the identification of the component parts of the institutional world, and the description of the relationships between them.

Given the difficulties involved in the undertaking—difficulties stemming from the sheer range and complexity of the world itself, from the divergence between descriptions and the reality, and from the fact that our personal values may influence our perception—it is only to be expected that observers differ in their descriptions of the institutional world.[12] Some recognize objects which others exclude, and emphasize features which others relegate or ignore; they draw lines in different places, and so forth. The scope for disagreement about such matters is very great.

However, only those observers motivated by a desire to change the world—or to create a revolutionary consciousness—would deny that the best understanding of the features of this world will result from the account which does not impose itself on the world, but which faithfully maps its real divides and chasms, and highlights its most striking landmarks. Such an account will create a coherent picture of how things hang together, it will illuminate currently shared meanings and understandings, and provide an explanation—not merely an unsophisticated assumption that the human mind has a propensity to indulge in fetishes—of why ordinary languages generate mysteries and paradoxes. Above all, it will allow that the existence of institutional objects in a particular society is often a matter of degree.[13] Only in a completely static society with an unchanging language could it be otherwise. So an adequate interpretation of the institutional world must be, in one sense, a historical understanding, sensitive to the realities of growth and change, denudation and accretion; it must comprehend the ways in which the familiar objects of our world have come to possess locations, meanings, and relationships differing from those which they formerly possessed.

II: JURISPRUDENCE AND ITS INSTITUTIONAL FOUNDATIONS

However else it may be described, law is unquestionably institutional; we all have some familiarity with the major institutions of this distinctive segment of social life. Our objective is to achieve a better understanding of this domain, since an adequate understanding of the basic, identifiable forms of life within which laws must exist is essential in order to elucidate the law's central concepts, describe accurately its norms and structures, or draw the boundaries of the legal field. The target is to identify and give an account of the forms of life in which legal language is generated.[14] We must seek that articulation of reality which best expresses the real divides which confront us in everyday life, and which legal language may conceal and commentators may overlook.

A strong case can be made for the proposition that in the quest for an understanding of the social world, few of its features have proved more problematic, more productive of disputes and competing schools, than law.[15] Certainly, in investigating society's normative structures there has always been ample scope for confusion. In the ordinary language of many societies law constitutes one of the most ambiguous categories; it has been promiscuously employed to refer to norms of all sorts. Theorists have both welcomed and deplored this ambiguity. For those—specially in earlier times—who welcomed it, jurisprudence was the queen of social studies; [16] for those who deplored the ambiguity, the task of jurisprudence was to distinguish laws 'properly so called' from what were erroneously called laws. [17]

Among the reasons for the difficulties and confusions, the false starts and misplaced efforts in jurisprudence has been a mistaken assumption that the institutional context of the law is already well understood; a society's existing legal institutions are thought to be unproblematic and not in need of further investigation. Since the actual legal institutions of different societies are very differently structured, a study of the institutional context in one country could scarcely be expected to provide the foundation for a general theory of law.[18]

For the most part, natural lawyers and legal positivists were not interested in the law's foundations in social realities. Legal norms could be studied and understood in isolation, as norms deriving from reason, from higher norms, or from the will of the sovereign. The familiar institutions of the legal system were no more than a background—like the climate, geology, or the national characteristics of a people—against which the laws operated. Kelsen treated the law as a transcendent body of norms, unaffected by the realities of its institutional context, so that legal science needed no truck with social science.[19] Legal norms were not regarded as being anchored to forms of life, but were presented as logically distinct from the norms actually governing the activities of men and women in society. The only anchorage recognised in approaches of this sort was either a general form of association—the legal order or society in general—or such institutional monstrosities as the Austinian sovereign or the Kelsenian *grundnorm*.

If among the various schools of jurisprudence we find few signs of interest in the institutional world, what of the writers who have concentrated their efforts on investigating law in its social context? Can they be said to have increased our understanding of the law's institutional foundations? Few have deliberately sought such an understanding. For a variety of reasons, the identification of the basic forms of life in which legal language is generated and sustained has not featured prominently on the agenda of legal sociology; by contrast with the torrent of literature on law and society it constitutes a small trickle.

This has been due partly to the belief that a theoretical understanding of the language and concepts of the legal world—and hence of the institutional context—is a matter for legal theory rather than legal sociology. Given the pressing concerns involved in finding the facts, there will generally be a disinclination to defer investigation until satisfactory answers have been found to fundamental questions about the nature of law or society. Studies of law in society can proceed with working definitions of law and produce interesting insights and valuable information about aspects of its operation.[20]

A more principled objection is found in the idea that analytic studies will necessarily be narrow in scope and unhelpful. The very effort of disentangling laws from other social norms is sometimes regarded simply as reflecting the professional preoccupation of lawyers.[21] An investigation from this angle will, it is thought, provide at best a partial and distorted understanding of law in society. Lawyer's law, state law, may be important but it is only part of a much wider field of enquiry.

At one extreme this took the form of the exhilarating belief that virtually all the normative structures of society were part of society's legal resources, and that it was the task of jurisprudence to investigate the living law of that order.[22] The normative structures in society not normally regarded as being legal are undoubtedly of the greatest importance and deserve the most thorough investigation. The assumption that they are in some sense legal is ill-founded, resting as it does on little more than the ambiguity of the word 'law'.

The contribution of legal sociology to the theoretical understanding of the institutional world has been further diminished by writers with axes to grind; their articulations of the world are intended not to understand the phenomenon of law in its own terms, but to support their claims that our institutions stand in need of radical change.[23]

Legal sociology has failed to provide us with an adequate theoretical understanding of the manner in which law is related to its institutional foundations. Evidence of that failure is to be found in the rarely challenged commonplaces in the literature of law and society. I have in mind such assertions as: lawyer's law is state law; law is a means of social control; judges are officials; and law is the framework of society. The pervasiveness of such ill-considered generalities hinders institutional analysis.

Our starting point then must be the observation that jurisprudence today lacks a theory of social institutions. Even those writers who have explored aspects of law's institutional character have not considered that such a theory is required.[24] As a result, the apparatus employed to describe the institutional world is seldom more than that which common sense provides. Something more is required.

NOTES

1. MacCormick and Weinberger (1986: 26).
2. Postema (1986: 332).
3. Charles Taylor talks of the 'crashing truism' that language can only be maintained by being constantly renewed in action and speech (1985: 173–4). See also Gellner (1970: 191) and Giddens (1984: xvi).
4. Popper (1976: 180–7). See Dawkins (1976: ch. 11) for an attempt to construct a

unit of cultural transmission—the 'meme'—which is operative in human evolution.

5. See Hughes (1930: 95).
6. Most usefully in respect of law by MacCormick and Weinberger (1986), on whose work I have drawn freely in this section.
7. On 'brute facts' see Anscombe (1957: 62–72) and Searle (1969: 50–3) For an analysis of 'societal facts' see Mandelbaum (1955: 105–18). For a discussion of the distinction see White (1984: 2–10).
8. See Friedman (1990: 51) for illustrations of the rapidity of social change in modern times. This crucial fact of constant social change—in moral attitudes, knowledge, ideas, institutions, and language—is emphasized in the discussion of foundationalism in Ch. 9, below.
9. On the intersubjective meanings which are constitutive of the social matrix in which individuals live and act, see Taylor (1985: 36).
10. Nowhere more clearly evident than in the language of property; consider the fictions which have been necessary to make good the defects in the definition of ownership in modern codes; see Bolgar (1953: 204–19). See also Blakemore (1988) on the jargon of the French revolutionaries.
11. See Lienhardt (1966: 123) 'No social phenomenon can be adequately studied in the language and categories of thought in which peoples among whom it is found represent it to themselves.' Cf. Winch (1958) for whom the understanding of the agents themselves is decisive.
12. There have been many different approaches to the identification of institutional entities; contrast the wholly different institutions of Renner (1949), of Gurvitch (1947), and of Hauriou, in Jennings (1933: 68–85).
13. Whether law is a matter of degree or not is a matter of controversy; for Fuller (1963: 122–3) the existence of law was a matter of degree. Cf. Hart (1983: 10–12) against recognizing degrees of legality.
14. The distinctiveness of legal language will be a central preoccupation of institutional theory. Contrary to much contemporary opinion, legal language is not to be regarded as part of a continuum including moral and political languages. Cf. Shklar (1964: 3); see also Schurr (1968: 125) on law as a social phenomenon. For the view that legal language is fraudulently distinctive see F. S. Cohen (1935).
15. Oakeshott (1975: 181).
16. See Kelley (1991).
17. On the need to define 'law' because of the dangers arising from the abuse of words, capricious usages, and fustian definitions see Austin (1879) Lecture V.
18. On the difficulties of cultural comparisons see MacIntyre (1971: 15–32).
19. Kelsen (1973: xv) and (1934: 477–85). The total isolation of the ought—an epistemological category—as the only object of the pure science of law entails the exclusion of all institutional facts, since such facts can only be understood in terms of values and ideas. Institutions—which cannot be left out of account—are not reducible to norm structures. The reductionism which describes rights merely as the correlatives of duties, which describes the state and legal persons as fictions, cannot account for the identity of a legal system. See Raz (1979: 99).

20. Furthermore, the sociology of law is concerned with the contingent and the particular, requiring a wealth of detailed information and analysis of the features of a particular society: Raz (1979: 104).
21. On the earlier neglect of law by sociologists, see Schurr (1968: 5–8).
22. See Ehrlich (1936) for the view that law is not to be treated as a distinct category but is to be placed within a continuum of social norms. On which see Kelsen (1973: 24–8). See Allen (1958: 28–34) for a criticism of Megalomaniac Jurisprudence. On the approach of contemporary legal pluralists see Galanter (1981: 1).
23. 'Some Marxists have attached such importance to the preservation of a theoretical analysis conducive to the maximisation of consciousness and intensification of conflict that the original fidelity to the empirical science has been lost behind mindless repetition and hallowed rhetoric' Collins (1982: 7).
24. MacCormick and Weinberger (1986: 24–5). But see Gellner (1959: 231): 'If the meaning of terms is their use and context, then those contexts and the activities therein should be investigated seriously and without making the mistaken assumption that we already know enough about the world and society to identify the actual functioning of our use of words'.

2

Institutional Forms

Law is a social phenomenon. 'A legal system exists only if it is in force. . . . Normative systems are existing systems because of their impact on the behaviour of individuals, because of their role in the organisation of life.'[1] Laws are norms which are actually operative; they are not just propositions, or textual formulations. This reminder is for those who regard large stretches of legal history as an account of the vicissitudes of Roman law texts, rather than an investigation of the actual norms under which the subjects in the kingdoms, feifdoms, dukedoms, margravates, and towns of the Middle Ages were—as a matter of historical fact—entitled, compensated, coerced, and punished.[2] An epistemology which neglects the existence and reality of legal norms, and their connection with tangible threats and social dangers, is not an epistemology of law. Our knowledge of the law is knowledge of the actual. Our opinions about what the law ought to be, or what commentators say it is or was, is an entirely different matter.

It is a basic assumption of institutional theory that operative norms in social life are anchored to, and form part of, particular forms of life, and that we cannot properly understand the norms in isolation from those forms.[3] To understand legal norms we must first understand not only the forms of life in which laws are created and applied—hence the description of law as an 'institutionalized system'—but also of all the forms of life which constitute the necessary institutional context in which laws operate. For example, we must appreciate that the legal system cannot be understood as operating against a background of social interaction, but that it is necessarily a constitutive part of a distinct form of human association: a society defined in political terms.

A new start

In identifying the institutional foundations to which legal norms are anchored we must do more than merely examine the *institutions* of everyday life.[4] An institutional theory of law in the United Kingdom cannot hope to proceed by providing further and better particulars about the nature of such institutions as Parliament, the law courts, police forces, tribunals, penal institutions, the legal profession, law commissions, and so forth. Important though they may be in our practical affairs, we must recognize that, like the institutions of any other country, they are local products which have been shaped by particular historical circumstances;

that they differ from the institutions of other polities in their functions, their structures, and in the way in which they relate to one another. The analysis of particular institutions in other countries would scarcely provide us with the material for a general theory of law. At best, a comparative study of institutions will hammer home the lesson that we are not qualified by virtue of our familiarity with our own institutions to understand the institutions of any other country. The well documented vice of ethnocentrism in anthropological studies bears witness to the widespread tendency to embark on a description of the general with an apparatus suited only for the local.

Any approach to the institutional world, to the normative world, which makes a claim to generality must begin by identifying the most basic units of human life and activity—units which can be recognized in any culture or polity. I call these basic units *institutional forms.* They are the atomic particulars of the institutional world, being irreducible to more basic institutional elements.[5]

One of the reasons why we cannot rely on the familiar institutions of public life is their institutional complexity; many are compounded from a variety of more basic forms. So analysis will involve abstracting the basic forms from the institutions of everyday life: this is an important operation since a statement which is true of one constituent form of a particular institution may be untrue of another, yet they may well be made about the encompassing institution. For instance, a parliament will on analysis be seen to consist of, among other things, a legislative procedure and an organization. Failure to distinguish between the two forms has been a fertile source of confusion. Legal sovereignty, for example, attaches to the procedure but not to the organization.

Each institutional form is normatively structured, possessing its own particular types of norms. Analysis requires sensitivity to the different types of norms which are generated and sustained in each form. The nature of the relationships between the individuals involved will also differ from form to form. It is in the light of the nature of the different forms involved that social relationships must be understood. For example, the character of the relationships between members of society as a political unit is very widely misunderstood.

An institutional form is not just a symbol or classificatory label; each form exists as a stable phenomenon. They exist as distinct objects in Popper's World Three—as identifiable, bounded, configurations of human activity and association which have been thrown up in the course of social interaction. Of course they are not merely patterns of behaviour which can be described from an external point of view, but forms of life in which what is said and done can only be understood by reference to the norms and meanings which structure and animate them.[6]

The reality, and the substantial nature of the institutional forms upon which law depends require emphasis. We cannot hope to accommodate the forms within an analytical jurisprudence which conceives of a legal system as a normative structure to be studied in isolation, a jurisprudence in which the forms are reduced to norm contents.[7] These indispensable analytic primitives, in which norms are anchored, are complex objects; each is dependent upon natural conditions, resources, persons, actions, and meanings, as well as norms. Each has its own history and identity which changes in reaction to changing circumstances, and so its relationships to other forms also change.

The basic institutional forms may be divided into two types: the *associational* and the *practical*.[8] In the associational forms—Community, Society, Organization and Group—the emphasis is on norms which govern and unite the membership of the association, and define the relationships between the members. In the practical forms—Activity and Practice—the emphasis is on the character and structure of the norms involved in participatory activity undertaken for the achievement of certain objectives. Throughout this book capital letters are used to refer to the institutional forms.

I: THE ASSOCIATIONAL FORMS

A: Community

A Community can be described as a primordial associational form; it is the very earliest form of social life, although there do exist Communities which are accessible to us in modern times. Even if the reality of life in the ancient forms lies beyond our grasp, we can nevertheless assert with some confidence that some familiar pictures of that life are seriously distorted. For our purposes it is as important to see what such a form was *not* as to see what it was.

We can posit a self-sufficient, preliterate Community, innocent of markets, and relatively isolated from other Communities. The Community is homogeneous in that its members—possibly linked genetically—share the same goals, beliefs, and values. Although some Communities may be nomadic, many have subsisted within a fixed location bounded by natural geographical features. There is a naturalness about such a form in marked contrast to the artificiality of the associational form Society.

Our interest lies in the normative structure of such a form. There are few grounds for supposing, as many do, that such Communities possessed, or were structured by, social rules—or at any rate rules of the sort which operate within a Society.

Legalism, or the determination to describe the social world, and to approach its arguments and conflicts, in legal terms, has been one of the most crippling of all movements, in political science as in anthropology.[9] It may be one of legalism's subtlest victories that so many writers have so readily assumed the universality of social rules in all forms of association. There is a widespread assumption that, even in the earliest forms of human association, rules constituted a basic and essential category of social life; legalistic accounts of Communities are common.[10] In anthropological investigation the temptation to dress up norms as rules has proved strong. Yet the distortions which result from this assumption can be serious, for instance when the regular pursuit by Community members of subtle strategies is described as action in conformity with a set of rules; when practices of subsistence husbandry are translated into the language of individual property rights; or when the principles of particular practices and institutions—as worked out by observers but never expressed by the participants—are presented as rules.[11]

That Communities are not rule-governed does not mean that they are not normatively structured; rather we must assume that these forms of life will be positively saturated with norms. The norms will operate in all manner of associational units, and form an integral part of the practices or activities of a distinctive way of life. Accounts of life in Communities suggest that there is a great variety of different types of norm. Some of the norms of the Community can be said to be clear, and possibly even 'law-like', rules; many others have the character of customs, taboos, proverbs, superstitions, regularities, practices, techniques, rituals, rites, ceremonies, and so on.

By contrast with rules, Community norms are unlikely to be objectified and isolated as objects of attention which may have a history independent from the forms they structure.[12] The norms of early societies are spontaneously generated and, while they are operative, they are flexible and immediately responsive to change; should they cease to have relevance to the concerns of the Community they would, since they are stored only in the memories of the elders, drop out of sight without comment. Such norms stand in what has been called a 'quasi-homeostatic' balance with their associational forms. If the norms of a Community have this character then it is to be expected that in discourse about practical affairs, in the appraisal of conduct, the norm-concepts employed will be ambiguous, the classificatory systems highly fluid, and the distinction between the prescriptive and the descriptive of little consequence.

Something of the nature of the loose normative structure of a Community can be gleaned from a consideration of the institutions—commonly misdescribed as courts—in which serious questions of right and wrong in a Community are adjudicated. Studies of actual examples of normative Practices in tribal life—deliberative assemblies—must make us question the validity of the familiar social-rules-as-the-backbone-of-Community model. Observers of such forums in Communities which are accessible to us have noted that, in the process of righting wrongs, the participants do not proceed by setting out the rules which we might think ought to govern such matters. In their decision-making processes norms do not appear to have logical priority; the reasoning involved does not typically set out a rule as a major premiss. The norms are commonly implicit in the arguments put forward, and the reasoning—far removed from the familiar legal syllogism—may be full of what appear to be *non-sequiturs*.[13] We have evidence from widely different sources as to the character of the arbitral processes of such assemblies in which the norms of the Community are not articulated. If rules do not figure as a prime normative resource in the determination of the most important disputes in the Community's most august and only forum, are we not justified in supposing that they are unlikely to have greater obtrusiveness in the activities and conflicts of everyday life?

It is a characteristic of this institutional form that relationships between Community members are complex and close, even though they may regard themselves as members of families or clans rather than as members of a Community. Whatever the complicated structure of the Community as a whole, there will be, at various levels, a continuing concern about conduct, and a constant demand that members fulfil their allotted roles and recognize their responsibilities. We should, however, be alert to the possibility that in some cases such concerns may well be misstated if they are presented as demands for conformity to clear norms.

Within the Community sanctions are employed in response to actions by families and individuals who imperil safety, diminish resources, anger the gods, and so forth. Emphasis must be placed on the constraints, and the defined interpersonal relationships, which distinguish the Community from the non-deontological Group.

Communities may survive the emergence of Societies and States, existing in relative isolation within the territorial boundaries of a Society.[14] In modern conditions new Communities may emerge in ghettos or no-go areas, in the form of religious communes, bands of New Age travellers, and so forth. Although such associations display many of the *Gemeinschaft* characteristics of primordial Communities, they are always, in complicated ways, vulnerable to the enforcement Activity and rules of the Society in which they have emerged. They also differ from true Communities in that their members are often literate and are almost inevitably involved in market Practices.[15] The members of such Communities cannot fail to become aware of the general rules of Society; a Community located within a Society is always in tension with it, and questions as to which set of norms is to apply will need to be resolved. Studies of the impact of state laws on traditional Communities in the Third World underline the complications which attend a Community's existence within a Society, and its subjection to the governmental activities of the State.

B: Society

As an institutional form, Society is defined as an association of individuals who live within a territory with clearly defined boundaries, who are governed by a State, and subject to the same body of general social rules. [16]

Although, in non-institutional works, 'society' and 'state' are terms of great ambiguity, sometimes used interchangeably, in institutional theory Society and State are quite distinct forms. A State is an Organization, or more precisely an organizational complex, which exercises governmental powers over the individuals and other bodies within a defined area. A Society is no sort of Organization; rather, it is an association of individuals who are governed by a particular State.

A Society is thus a correlate of a State; it is a form of life which cannot be identified prior to the State's emergence. An imaginary social contract to initiate a State could not be made by *members* of a Society. Society, as an association of the governed, only emerges after the appearance of a particular type of State: the centralizing State. Associational forms making territorial claims in times before the emergence of States would have been types of Communities.

We need constantly to be reminded of the artificial nature of Society and of the wars by which peoples have been subjugated and the boundaries of political control fixed.[17] Superior physical force—the organized coercive power which can subjugate rebellious populations—is a necessary element in the emergence of this associational form.

We must certainly bear in mind the artificiality of both the form and its boundaries while emphasizing that the form is based on the fact of human settlement; one of the links between members of a Society is the fact of their living together within a geographically defined area: a country. All members make use of the country's natural resources and are variously involved in the forms of life which emerge within its boundaries. The territorial aspect of this form is of the essence; it is a condition which makes it possible to identify and locate many contemporary Societies by reference to a political map of the world.

In varying degrees members of a Society regard themselves as belonging to, and hailing from, a particular country. The land is theirs; members of Society are countrymen—significantly, a term having a certain quaintness today. For some members this tie is relatively weak; regional and local loyalties may far outweigh the sense of attachment to a country.

Those who would wax lyrical about members' ties to their native soil need to be reminded that the notion of citizenship—central to the idea of membership of Society—has its roots in urban life which, with its cosmopolitan dimensions, may be expected to diminish any sense of attachment to the land.

Now, a population identified by the fact of its settlement within a country's territorial boundaries, and which is subject to its laws, as a contingent fact will generally exhibit a great diversity of life-styles and attitudes. It may well be composed of individuals who speak different languages, practise different religions, have differing cultural affinities, come from different ethnic groups, and so forth.[18] So we cannot postulate for Society as we may for homogeneous Communities, a consensus—a body of shared beliefs and values—which functions as a normative social cement. Shared values, goals, and beliefs are the properties of Communities, Groups, and Organizations, not of Societies.[19] Even the description of Societies as nation states is tendentious as it connotes an aspiration to unity of nationhood—a condition of importance in times of war and emergency—in a form which is neither a Group nor an Organization but an entirely artificial collective. Nation-building is a deliberate effort to deny or diminish the heterogeneity which is the outstanding character of many Societies.

The tensions and conflicts arising from that heterogeneity cannot be resolved by the constraints of a contrived consensus. The only sort of social cement which will give any stability and coherence to a Society is the coercive power of the State. The entropy to which the artificial form Society is subject can only be held in check by a normative regime which must ultimately rely upon force.[20]

Social rules

All territorially limited political units require definition in terms of the control exercised by a central Organization: the State. For the recognition of the institutional form Society, however, something else is required: that the members of the association of the governed are also individually subject to normative control by way of general social rules. A Society is defined in terms of the subjection of its members to a normative regime of this sort.

Since they are a type of norm given a special meaning in institutional theory, an account must be given of certain aspects of social rules.[21] A general social rule is not simply a normative standard to be found in social interaction; it is the norm associated with, prescribing the conduct of the members of, a Society. Social rules are not factual statements about regularities of conduct, but prescriptions. Social rules—Society's rules—have limited application in that they do not apply to persons living beyond the boundaries of the country. A social rule will apply to all members of Society, unless it expressly excepts certain classes. It is of fundamental importance that the idea of the social rule carries with it—as many social prescriptions do not—the notion of individual equality.[22]

The social rules with which we are concerned prescribe standards of individual conduct; they may also regulate or constitute collective entities, but they are primarily norms to which the members are subject as individuals. In the light of this feature we must define the nature of the *centralizing State,* which is the correlative of a Society.[23] An indifferent State exercises its political power by imposing duties on collectives—on towns, villages, or regions—with little concern for the behaviour of individuals within these units. The centralizing State, by contrast, does show such concern and enacts, adopts, and enforces rules which apply, not to collectives, but to all their subjects as individuals. The governmental norms of the indifferent State may take the form of crude and general demands, decrees, and commands; those of the centralizing State are detailed and complicated social rules.

If Society is an artificial form, so too, in one way are its distinctive norms. There is no foundational consensus, no shared conceptions of the good from which they have been derived, or by which they can be judged. Social rules which are to apply to members in all parts of the country must therefore, to some extent, be imposed; they will cut across and displace naturally occurring, local, customary, Community norms, and conflict with the values of some Groups. In a heterogeneous Society the general rules enforced can scarcely be supposed to have emerged spontaneously; they must generally be somehow deliberately adopted or enacted. Also, as they cannot be taken to be in any way 'given' or 'understood', they must always be spelled out explicitly.[24]

Writing

It follows that Social rules are necessarily written rules; we could not identify Societies before the invention of writing,[25] before what Maine called 'the era of the codes'.[26] For only a written rule could possess the precision and fixity through time required by a social rule to be applied uniformly to all members of a widely dispersed Society.[27] The importance of writing is overlooked by writers who would treat Community norms as rules. There is nothing mysterious about the (true) dark sayings of common lawyers and the Historical School: that the law of a Community cannot be written down. When transcribed, the norms of a Community are transformed into norms of a wholly different type, whether or not there is any alteration in their content. Writing down laws inevitably abstracts the norms from their place in the various forms of life.

Prescriptive formulations in written documents have a sort of existence which might appear to undermine the claims of institutional theory that social norms have their existence only within forms of life. By virtue of the durability of the instruments in which rules are recorded, written laws appear to have an objective existence independent of human minds or activity. They appear to exist as laws by virtue of the mere fact that they are captured in the text of an authoritative code.

However, social rules, although written, can only exist within forms of life, and particularly within the practical form which I shall call *enforcement Activity*. In considering the existence of social rules realism is called for. Unless we believe in the unquestionable authority of the written text and all its provisions, we can distinguish between mere 'paper' rules and existent social rules. Social rules are those written rules which are actually applied and enforced.

If we make actual enforcement and application prerequisites of our recognition of social rules, then the picture of the associational form Society is enhanced. In view of the conflicts arising from the heterogeneity of its membership, the very existence of Society depends upon this Activity: that is, upon the persistence of deliberate attempts to secure conformity with its general social rules. Society is not defined only as an association of individuals subject to the power of a State; it is, by definition, also dependent upon the Activity in which the power of the State is specifically deployed to enforce a body of written rules. Enforcement Activity, which is defined as the enforcement of social rules, involves guaranteeing the authority of rules of entitlement as well as seeking conformity with, and ensuring punishment for, breaches of penal rules. The normative regime which founds Society is a regime of enforced social rules.

The sources of the rules are various. Societies do not depend on the existence of a formal code; nor, of course, are all social rules enacted. Although the social rules must be described as being imposed on the members, those rules need not necessarily emanate from, or be created by the State. It is only necessary that the State should enforce the rules. Many of the rules will, no doubt, have been created by the State in its role as lawgiver, but many must be described as being adopted by the State.[28] Thus, customary norms which are transformed into written rules by the courts may be said to be adopted by the State which enforces them.

At this point in the enquiry it is of little importance whether or not we call the social rules 'laws'. It is, however, important to recognize their character as the norms of a Society, and the fact that they are distinguishable from Community norms.

Each Society has its own distinctive collection of social rules, reflecting the conflicts and difficulties in the life of the Society in question. There are no grounds for treating this miscellaneous collection of social rules as though they formed a unified, coherent system of norms. Some rationalists have been tempted to write transnational codes, but the uniqueness of each country and the speed of change which each undergoes, render such an idea fanciful.

Sub-Societies

A sub-Society is located within a territory subject to a State; it has its own boundaries and its own regional or local government. Most importantly, its inhabitants are subject to social rules peculiar to that region, which constitute its property system, create local offences, and so forth. So the members of the sub-Society are subject to some rules which apply to all members of the larger Society and to other rules peculiar to the sub-Society. If all the rules of a territory under one local government differ from those in other territories subject to the same central State, we would recognize not a sub-Society but a Society with a dependent State. A population subject to a colonial government may thus constitute a Society.

Society is an unstructured association; it should never be described in terms of a command structure. We approach it from the bottom up: that is, from a consideration of the body of social rules which constitute and govern the relationships between the members of the association. So, the existence of a sub-Society within a Society makes the larger form less intense, as not all the social rules will apply to all the members.

Relationships between members

The members of a Society are individuals who are related to each other as citizens; that is, they need only be related in respect of their subjection to a State and to the regime of rules it enforces. Under the social rules they owe duties of respect to each other; they are subject to the same criminal laws and penal sanctions, are entitled to defined interests, and owe the same duties to the State. Ideally, the general social rules will be enforced regularly, in all areas, against all classes, and applied in courts to which all have access.

So the artificial form has many of the characteristics of the *Gesellschaft;* members do not share the same goals or values. Only a small Society can share the character of a Community.

If a Society is not a Community then neither is it an Organization. It is, as I have indicated, an unstructured form. There are no structural relationships between the members; whatever relative status they may have in other forms of life, as citizens they do not rank as superiors or inferiors. The members of a Society constitute an undifferentiated collection of individuals.[29] If there are castes or classes within one country who claim special privileges and immunities, and are subject to a body of rules different from that imposed on ordinary members and applied in different courts, then they might be regarded as forming non-territorial sub-Societies.

A Society does not constitute or reflect a particular way of life. Its social rules offer a framework of constraint in which different ways of life are pursued and innumerable competing forms of life emerge. The normative foundations of a Society are to be found only in the general social rules which have a formal charter and an official status. Its foundations are not constituted by all the social norms to be found within a territory. As a result, this associational form lacks the life and colour of the social milieu which is often presented as the institutional context of our laws.

Civil Society

Society as a basic institutional form is defined as the collective which is correlative with the centralizing State.[30] Its members are the individuals who are subject to general social rules enforced by the State. Civil Society is a very special institutional form; it may be regarded as a more refined version of Society. It is essentially a legal construct: it is the associational form Society as articulated from the legal point of view.[31] So, a civil Society depends for its existence not only upon a centralizing State but also upon effective legal Practices in which the relationships of members both to each other and to the State are legally defined. Within the legal Practices, the State takes on a new character: it is regarded as being incapable of relying upon its *de facto* power—in the eyes of the law the State is aboriginally a powerless Organization. Analysis of the nature of civil Society as a particular species of Society is only possible after analysing the legal Practices in which the legal point of view is generated.

C: Organization

The Organization is one of the basic institutional forms: an association of individuals, not territorially defined, whose members, subject to organizational control, co-operate in pursuit of the declared purposes of the Organization.[32] The purposes of an Organization are commonly expressed in an instituting charter. Their more detailed formulations are set out by those members of the Organization who are authorized by its norms to do so. In order to achieve an organized and co-operative pursuit of the objectives so declared, certain members of the Organization must be given power to make decisions, to draw up plans, and to lay down rules; they must be authorized to direct the activity of other members. Authority within the Organization is typically structured by specific—often named—normative positions within a hierarchy of control.[33]

The relationships between members of this associational structure are of a wholly different type from those found between members of a Society.

Not only are they structured in terms of organizational authority—being defined by the role of each individual within the Organization—but also they are coloured by the members' awareness that the activity of the Organization is directed towards the achievement of particular objectives.

Organizations aim to achieve goals and to that end they engage in Activities; organizational norms regulate the manner in which the Activities are pursued. It is important to appreciate that the objectives of Organizations, unlike those of Practices, are not to produce new social rules, nor to make other deliberate changes in the normative world. This may seem odd, since there are Organizations which appear to be instituted precisely to make laws, for instance a legislature, or a pressure group intent upon the reform of a particular law. However, it needs to be stressed that deliberate changes to the normative structure of Society, or of any other associational form, are generally to be made by way of a procedure, a Practice, and not by way of organized Activity. A legislature can be said to make laws only in the sense that its members—organizational members—are also participants in a legislative Practice. The organized ginger group may successfully influence the legislators, but it cannot change laws by the activities of its members alone. The importance of this distinction between Organization and Practice is highlighted by the confusions referred to above, which result from failure to distinguish between Parliament as an Organization, with its officers, and Parliament as a legislative Practice, with its participants.

Enforcement Activity, no matter how understated it may be, is a necessary feature of organizational association. Although rewards play an important motivating part in organizational life, discipline is essential.[34] It is maintained by the internal imposition of sanctions and constraints upon the members. It may even be that such Activity may be more obtrusive and persistent—and of greater importance—than enforcement Activity to which individuals as members of Society are subjected. A wide variety of norms, with differing degrees of normative force, can be identified within Organizations, ranging from normative standards, expressed as wide objectives, to general rules of entitlement and power, codes of conduct, minor office rules, and specific commands. The regulation of the Activities within the Organization is certainly not achieved by applying norms of only one type; the norms are not social rules.

Organizations, like Groups, must be regarded as existing within Society. Their norms operate at a different level from the rules of Society. So the status of a person within an Organization is distinct from his or her relative status as a member of Society. For the members of an Organization there is always an 'outside world', a 'civvy street' or private life, beyond the control of the Organization.[35] The essential controlling activity within the Organization, while giving normative force to its standards and rules, is itself subject to constraint and regulation imposed by the general rules of Society—that is, unless the Organization operates in secret.

Persons with authority over other members of the Organization are called *Officers*.

Organizations, like Societies, are manifestly artificial, and not 'natural' or 'moral' associations; for although Organizations are in part defined by their objectives, there need be no unity of purpose among the attitudes and values of all its members. Organizational purposes are not consensual in either origin or nature; they are the expressed objectives of members who are authorized by the rules of the Organization to formulate them. In other words, the purposes of the Organization are the purposes declared by officers or managers; they do not derive from the interests and wishes of the individual members. Morale-boosting exercises—attempts to instil loyalty to the Organization—may underline the practical importance attached to shared values, but they must not mislead us into thinking that consensus is a necessary feature of this form of association.

D: State

Of the importance of the State—one of the focal institutional forms of the political field—there can be no doubt. As an institutional form, to be analysed in terms of its normative structure, it is unproblematic. We have to examine the motives of those who have questioned the existence of one of the most obtrusive objects of the institutional world. The striking variety of different meanings given to the word 'state' in the political and social sciences results from the many different purposes and frameworks of belief evident in the works in which it has been defined.[36]

In institutional theory the State is an Organization which is—or claims to be—the most powerful body within the territory over which it exercises governmental powers.

The key to understanding the nature of the State is to appreciate its character as an Organization. It is an associational form, with a large and clearly defined membership, constituted and regulated by an immense variety of types of norms.[37] It is necessary to emphasize the variety of norms which structure this institutional form in order to stress its discreteness, reality, and life, and to counter suggestions that the State can somehow be reduced to a set of legal norms.[38] The State is a substantial, distinctive, institutional form with a life of its own; its norms can only be understood by reference to the conglomerate as a whole, and in the light of its many separate parts.

The State is today an immensely complex organizational structure made up of a number of separate Organizations. It is, however, a single unit—an Organization—and is not to be conceived of as a mere collection of Organizations. Though it involves many other forms—Practices and Activities—it must be defined in organizational terms: that is, as an associational form made up of many Organizations. The backbone of the State is its command structure; it is unified by control exercised over each of its constituent parts by a central executive, the managers of the Organization which is the State.

The various Organizations within the complex include the executive, the armed forces, enforcement agencies, government departments, and a host of bodies associated with them.[39] Clearly, it may be difficult to determine whether an agency is part, or an 'emanation', of the State. For the purposes of institutional theory, the only test is the extent to which they are, by express constitutive provisions, subject to executive control, i.e. the extent to which they are demonstrably within the overall organizational structure of the State. The difficulties of the agencies on the borderline need not be discussed here; our concern is with the central constituents of this form.

The dominance of the State which governs the population of a territory depends upon its continuous exercise of power. The power of the State is *de facto* power, it is nothing more mysterious than organizational power, whose foundation is the simple asymmetry of two against one. The State's ability to regulate, coerce, sanction, and protect the inhabitants of a country derives from its control of an organized membership with access to the resources they require. The armed forces inevitably hold a central position within the organizational structure of the State.[40]

The origins of the form of the State have been much debated.[41] Although monocausal explanations are to be treated with suspicion, it nonetheless seems likely that a Community which was protected by an organized body, capable of resisting external threats and preserving order, would be more likely to survive as an association and to retain its territory than unorganized Communities.

I have said that the power possessed by the State is *de facto* power; it is therefore no part of the definition of a State as an institutional form that it must be able to justify its exercise of power by reference to rules of succession, or conformity with moral norms, or any other standards or reasons which might appear to confer legitimacy. The State is identified simply as an organizational structure which as a matter of fact exercises governmental power over the peoples living within a territory.

We have seen that, unlike Societies, Organizations can have objectives; indeed, they are established precisely to achieve goals set out by the founders or managers. Some of the objectives of the State Organization are 'given': naturally, the State must secure and protect its dominant position within the territory and defend the inhabitants against external threats. Many other objectives are determined, and declared, by the executive. Which ends the State ought to pursue, and their order *of* priority, are the stuff of political debate. We must treat both the given and the declared objectives as operative norms which control and animate the Organization's activity. However, it is important that the objectives pursued by the State should not be ascribed to the form Society. To the extent that members of Society are organized, are subject to official direction in order to achieve certain ends, they cease to act as citizens and act instead as part of the State.

There is a clear distinction between membership of a Society and membership of a State. State membership is clearly defined; its attainment is commonly governed by procedures for appointment, co-option, selection, or election. The criteria defining membership of the various Organizations which make up the complex that we call the State are set out in the rules of the respective Organizations. The requirements of some executive offices are contained in constitutional provisions, for instance the rules of succession to the throne.

Although we may treat the State as a single institutional form, despite its structural complexity, an individual generally attains membership of the State by virtue of membership of one of its constituent Organizations. Therefore members of one part of the organizational complex may have no direct relationship with members of another part; the only necessary connection between them is that the Organizations of which they are members are all subject to formal executive control, that they are all ultimately concerned with the business of the State. Within each separate Organization of the State membership is highly structured; offices are defined and hierarchical positions are clearly established. As in all Organizations, members with powers over other members are defined as officers; *officials* are officers of State Organizations with power over ordinary citizens, i.e. non-members.

I have already indicated (*ante,* p. 18) that an important distinction must be made between different types of State, between different styles of governing a territory. At one end of the spectrum of government is the *indifferent State,* at the other is the *centralizing State.*

The indifferent State may be said to take the business of government less seriously. Its rulers, who may regard their power over the territory as that of dominium rather than imperium, are willing to delegate power—the chores of government—to magnates, local bodies, and communities; they reap the rewards of government without undue concern for the condition or conduct of the individual inhabitants.[42] Apologists for such a regime may stress that the ruler affords the territory protection from threats posed by other peoples or influences, and that the application of real power can achieve internal order.[43]

By contrast, the centralizing State is intolerant of divided allegiances and unwilling to delegate power to any bodies, regions, or magnates; the executive conceives itself to be responsible for all details of government. The crucial feature of the centralizing State is its view—shared by the citizens—that government involves responsibility for every individual citizen. Although not necessarily concerned with the welfare of citizens individually, the centralizing State attempts to control the conduct of all citizens by way of social rules. Government of this sort, whether it involves a view of the polity as a legalistic *Gesellschaft* or as an etatist *Gemeinschaft*, is inevitably bureaucratic. The emergence of such States in modern Europe is not unrelated to the growth of the market economy in which all citizens must participate individually.[44]

Dependent States

These are Organizations which exercise governmental power over a particular territory, but which are subject to a higher political power. Political dependence is defined, for our purposes, as control which is justified by reference to formal organizational norms; in other words, there must be express rules imposed by the central State which define both the limited competence of the local State and the control exercisable by the imperial, federal, or other superior power. Such rules may be said to prescribe the inclusion of the dependent State within the command structure of the State. So States are classed as dependent, not because of their economic reliance on other States, or the influence which other governments have on them, but because, as federal or colonial structures, they are formally subject to control.

E: Group

In institutional theory socially significant norms, norms which are not purely personal, are never footloose; they do not have a mere institutional context but are always anchored to—being generated by and sustained in—specific institutional forms. It is in the associational form of the Group that socially significant values, beliefs, and ideas—not always regarded as normative—have their habitation.[45] It is within Groups that we must locate the perduring values which we refer to as informing traditions and cultures, or constituting the conventional morality of a Society.

It is something of an innovation to define the Group as an associational form in axiological terms. Some explanation is clearly required, although only the briefest of sketches is possible here.[46] Understanding something of the character of Groups is particularly important if we would apprehend aright the artificial character of Society. For Society is most definitely not a Group.

As an associational form the Group may be described as resembling a fraternity, or fellowship, in which the members internalize, share, preserve, and communicate a distinctive and coherent set of beliefs, ideas, and values. The Group is the institutional matrix for those ideas and values. Writing may be essential for the existence of social rules, but values—operating as norms of a wholly different sort—are articulated, transmitted, and stored in a great variety of ways. In a Group many of the acts and engagements of members may themselves operate as communications to the others.[47] In Group life much is 'understood' or taken for granted. The values may be said to be kept alive not by any individual—though some may play a decisive role in changing them—but by the Group as a whole, in the myriad acts, communications, and commitments in the lives of the members. The uniformity of belief and values manifested in the authentic, unconstrained communications from so many personal sources allows a member to conceive of Group values and beliefs as a publicly accessible store—an objectively existing 'given'.[48]

Unlike the other associational forms, Organization and Society, a fraternity is not structured or sustained by a framework of rules or other deontological operators. The cement of this form is essentially the member's sense of belonging or allegiance to the Group; of sharing its values; a sense which is significant since membership involves degrees of commitment which cannot be divorced from awareness of being both influenced by, and constrained to act in accordance with, or to respect the values sustained by, the Group. The member's sense of participation in a fellowship is sustained by exposure to living proofs and embodiments of its values and by non-coercive communications of Group values.

These are general observations. Before setting out other aspects of this form it may be useful to give a tiny sample from the immense range of collectives which may be counted as Groups. They include: nations, many so-called communities, minorities, families, tribes, neighbourhoods, movements, tendencies, revivals, academic schools, coteries, dissidents, socialists, anarchists, right-wingers, libertarians, free-traders, Euro-sceptics, factions, estates, lawyers, doctors, New Age travellers, feminists, homosexual and lesbian communities, conservationists, lovers of this, friends of that, football fanatics, cricket enthusiasts, pigeon fanciers, gardeners, trainspotters, street gangs, and rock and roll enthusiasts.

A hopelessly heterogeneous collection! Such a miscellaneous list does little to clarify the notion of the Group as an institutional form. The collectives appear to range from small, easily defined fraternities, like realale drinkers or morris dancers, to ill-defined collectives of persons who may be linked only by tenuous geographical, genetic, or ideological links, like nations or conservatives with a small 'c'. They range from what may be regarded as reasonably respectable institutional forms to what are little more than the objects of terms of abuse. It might appear that the identification of a Group is nothing more than a matter of classification: an arbitrary lumping together of persons with common attitudes, origins, or beliefs. However, while it must be allowed that Groups may merge into, or overlap with, such classes, Groups as associational forms are substantial, significant, and important configurations in the social landscape: self-determining fraternities which cannot be reduced to mere classes of individuals.

A Group must have a membership which exhibits certain features. The essence of the Group as an associational form lies in the character of the membership. What is this character?

Group membership requires some degree of commitment by the individual to the values of the Group, an internalization marked by mastery of the language of the Group. Membership is to be judged by such things as the degree to which membership affects a person's allegiances, attitudes, aspirations, priorities, and beliefs.[49] Membership of a Group contributes to the identity or personality of the agent; it entails more than consciousness of being a member of a class having properties in common, or of having some sort of affinity with others.[50]

Of course this criterion of commitment as an index of membership is very vague; there are many degrees of commitment. In practice most Groups inevitably possess a huge penumbral membership of the less committed—the Laodiceans—whose membership is as doubtful as their beliefs are lukewarm.[51] Nevertheless, this open-endedness of the definition of the Group, this amorphousness, is itself of the profoundest significance; while it cannot be used to deny the reality or existence of Groups which have an inner core of the committed, it means that Groups lie beyond the cognitive grasp of disciplines, such as the quantitative sciences and the law, which depend upon precise definitions of the knowable.

So the actual size of a Group is seldom computable.[52] It is in any case complicated by the tendency of non-members to deal with stereotypes, and to assume a uniformity of commitment and belief to members and classes. In the absence of rules, of minimal standards, there can be no such conformity. Furthermore, there is a tendency to caricature central beliefs and values, to exaggerate the differences between other Groups and those to which we belong—a tendency to be expected of those who do not speak a particular Group language or share its beliefs.

In Group membership values which the member internalizes are for the most part not of his or her own discovery or devising, but are some sort of inherited structure; that structure is kept alive under the aegis of a community of interest and belief to which the member subscribes, and which the values inform and constitute. Group values acquire a degree of mind-independence by virtue of the fact that they are articulated and stored within the associational form.[53]

Groups perdure through time. They have a history: a constitutive history. Some may have suffered hardship and persecution, while others have a trouble-free growth. Both types of experience fortify beliefs and values, and shape Group language; for memories of sacrifice or rejection and proofs of lasting popularity can operate equally to reinforce the members' commitment to the values of the Group.[54]

Under the influence of juridical models of life in civil society, in which the citizen is an atomic individual governed by the rules of the Society, the Group as a significant form of life has been overlooked. Properly fearful of the potential tyranny of communitarian ideas, many cling to the notion of individual autonomy and the rationality of our personal election to adhere to certain values. However, more than many realize or admit, what we claim as our personal values are derived from, and sustained in, Group life. We live our lives in Groups; they rather than atomic individuals are the operative units of political, religious, artistic, intellectual, and family life.[55] Although Society and its general rules are a necessary framework for social life today, the Groups to which we belong have greater influence on our social behaviour, and provide more social cohesion, than any regulatory regime.

Since, unlike both Organization and Society, the Group possesses no regulatory norms, the conduct of members (in so far as it will be subject to the critical judgment of others) will be judged by reference to precedent models and general standards. Within the Group, although pressures are felt by, and may be exerted against, members, there is no enforcement Activity nor any significant coercive sanctions. Criticism of members will be, not that they have offended against or failed to conform to the minimal standards prescribed by rules, but that they have been disloyal, sinful, hypocritical, dishonourable, or insincere; that they have denied the truth, or failed to act in a way which was consistent with their beliefs, and so on.

Groups lack absolutely the formality which characterises all rule-governed forms. Groups are self-determining; they do not grow by enlistment or conscription; there are no prescribed conditions of membership, no formal admissions procedures, no initiation ceremonies; neither are there provisions for deliberately severing the links of association. An individual may be born into some Groups, for example a family, clan, tribe, or nation, but even then we need to remember that Group membership is active, and involves for mature members a continuing commitment to the values of the Group, engagement in its affairs, and communications with other members.

In the unstructured fraternity we find no specific roles or offices: no distinction between officers and other ranks, no vicars and sidesmen, no managers and labourers. Nor does Group membership directly bestow any individual entitlements and interests—socially recognized positions of benefit—either within the Group or outside of it. Members are to be graded only by reference to their levels of commitment, dedication, and influence.

As rules are not operative within the Group, there are no normative Practices for the creation of Group norms or the adjudication of conduct. However, a Group may sustain non-normative Practices which serve as means of affirming faith, symbolizing values, reaffirming ideas and beliefs, or playing out in socio-dramas the values of the Group. Resonant reiterations of Group values may also be found in stories and artefacts, works of art, and sacred texts.

As they are wholly unstructured and have no clear boundaries, Groups are highly fluid, never static. They respond to changes of circumstance with uncomplicated immediacy; they increase or diminish as, within the boundaries of Society, threats materialize, discoveries are made, opportunities beckon, or visions fade. Any Society will exhibit continually changing patterns of fraternity. It is this characteristic spontaneity and fluidity which enables such forms of life to be represented in terms of the growth and decay of organic forms.

In sketching the invertebrate anatomy of a Group, it is useful to visualize the form as having an essential nerve centre, a sort of axiological armature, in which authority is seen to reside. The focus provides the clearest articulation of the current framework of ideas, beliefs, and values It may consist of a text or corpus of works; or it may focus on the actions and thoughts of past exemplars, or present leaders, teachers, or activists. To that vital core members will, when challenged or in doubt, refer; and members will, when necessary represent the world and their attitudes towards it in the vocabulary of the Group. The members' ascription of authority to the central focus betokens a conception of the values of the Group as a funded reserve upon which they can draw, and enhances the sense of their objective existence.[56]

The language of the Group

Fraternity is never mute; it must always speak its name. The acts of the members are communications. Given their axiological axes, each Group inevitably develops its own language. The use of a nuanced language—which may be said to be constitutive of Group life—provides an index of a Group's existence. For if the beliefs, ideas, and values of the Group are to possess objectivity, if for a widely dispersed membership they are to exist as an available resource, they must be given public expression. As Groups are of many different types the manner in which the linguistic particularity of each is shown varies; thus the Group language may be a distinct natural language, as in the case of a nation or tribe; the Group may possess a particular vocabulary, as in fraternities arising out of professions or skills; or, in a class-conscious society, members may affect a particular accent or, where the Group has a regional foundation, maintain a distinct dialect. For a member of the Group, its language provides an articulation of the world or of some aspect of it.[57] For the outsider, the inflected usages in which the values of the Group are embodied are the clearest indication of the existence or membership of a Group. Deliberate attempts may be made to emphasize linguistic differences to foster an awareness of membership.[58] In stressing the importance of a particular language informing Group life, and of the ability to speak it as the *sine qua non* of membership, we can avoid the mysteries attending the postulation of a Group mind, and we can replace the inadequate notion of a consensus as a meeting of minds, as the agreement of individuals to a set of ideas, with a more potent index: mastery of the language of a fraternity.[59]

Changes in Group language reflect changes in Group life. The language of the Group, unconstrained and grounded in the acts and communications of members, lives and responds as circumstances change, as threats diminish, as ideas and fashions evolve, as past errors are recognized, and so forth. Current nuances and distinctions may be understood only by members with a knowledge of the Group's history.

The fertility of language generation within Group life may be contrasted with the manner in which languages are generated within the other associational forms: the State, Organizations, and Society. For in the life of such regulated structures the vocabulary will be far more limited; clearly, terms will be required for normatively defined positions—offices and roles, entitlements and interests—and for the association's rules and Practices, and so on. In such institutional forms the language is trapped by the rules. So if language is unquestionably constitutive of Group life, it is less obviously so for the other associational forms, for life in those forms may be said to be constituted less by language than by the constitutive and regulatory norms. The key to an adequate understanding of a rule-governed institution is to provide a realistic description of the rules and other normative standards actually in place, rather than to examine the language in which its life is lived and its business is conducted: the language may misrepresent the reality. There are significant differences between the internalization of values and beliefs of the Group and the internalization of the rules of a Society or Organization.[60]

To emphasize language is to highlight the fact that members see the world through the articulated frameworks of group ideas; that they establish their identities in part from such memberships. Members of a Society, *qua* members of a Society can be conceived of as isolated individuals. However, human life involves a sense of things shared and understood, as in a fraternity, and that sense is gained, not from our membership of a Society, but from our membership of a Group.[61]

Groups as institutional forms

It is necessary to recognize the Group as a distinct form of life: a form in which ideas and values which operate in social life have their being. The transmission of ideas, beliefs, and values is often considered in terms of cultures and traditions on which individuals draw. The location of contemporary complexes of ideas and values is invariably particular, being ascribed to churches, Organizations, nations, ghettos, schools of thought, and suchlike: institutional collectives which have little in common. However, in any consideration of the normative world, in looking at the axiological and normative dimension of social life, we require a separate general unit, which operates on a plane different from that of other rule-governed forms. What is needed is a basic form of life which is so general that in any institution or grouping, no matter how varied, we can recognize the same basic character. It must also be particular and precise enough to catch all the significant conflicting parties and elements in a tradition or culture. The fundamental assumption here is that values and ideas have a social location: that an individual is not influenced simply by one other, but by others who draw upon a distinctive social resource which resides, not in library shelves, art galleries, and museums, but in the communications of a fraternity.[62]

It is perhaps surprising to add the Group to the forms of the institutional world, as also the practical form Activity. In normative terms, the Group is the location for values, as Activity is for goals and objectives. Both Group and Activity being unstructured forms, they have no sanctions or coercive arrangements, and hence do not satisfy the normal requirements of institutions. Also, they are so amorphous as to be beneath the interest of those who would divide the social world into discrete and measurable constituents.

However, it is important to give some substance to the idea of the Group as a basic form and to differentiate it from other forms. Group membership only rarely coincides with membership of other forms, and relationships between Group members are qualitatively different from those between members of structures with regulatory regimes. Isolating the Group as a form clarifies the nature of the other forms such as Communities, Society, and Organization.

Communities differ from Groups in that the former are territorially based, and structured by complicated arrangements in which an array of norms and sanctions function to constrain the conduct of members. The self-determination enjoyed by members of the Group—who have absolute freedom of thought and conscience—is not shared by members of Communities, which claim to embody the values which all its members are expected to share. The fact that Community sanctions for non-conformity may be informal does not make them any less real. Neither do Groups, unlike Communities, provide an all-embracing normative framework which is embedded in a way of life related to subsistence and self-sufficiency. Typically, Groups exist within Society and therefore the Group can make no claim on the whole life of its members. Enthusiasts do sometimes make totalitarian claims, and may demand that Group commitment be extended to all aspects of social life. However, it is vital to appreciate that a member of one Group may simultaneously be a member of other Groups with incompatible values. The family man may at the same time be a Christian, a butcher, a vegetarian, a Fascist, and a pornographer.[63]

The problem caused by confusing Groups with other associational forms is particularly clear in the case of Society. The familiar conception of Society as a consensual body akin to a Group will be considered later (see *post*, p. 373). Here it suffices to contrast the two forms. Society is an artificial form, territorially defined, being a regulatory regime with a membership of great heterogeneity. By contrast, the Group is by definition a fraternal consensus, a self-determining form, with no regulatory structure, and united only in its members' commitment to its values.[64] I argue below that the dissensus of a pluralist Society should be seen, not as a matter of individual disagreement, but as a conflict between significant Groups.

Groups are the all-important units of political life. We cannot give an adequate description of the political scene without accounting for those Groups which are, from time to time, the focuses of rebellion, bigotry, hatred, and dissent, nor if we misrepresent the institutional location of the ideas and values which stimulate such powerful responses. Men take up arms, not for an idea, but for a shared idea.

Within a Society each Group has power over its members. It is real power, taking the form of influence rather than coercion. Within the Group heroes, saints, and other exemplars—those with the greatest knowledge, wisdom, or courage, or the sharpest style, which makes them appear worthy of emulation and respect—may have very great influence. We must not discount or underestimate that influential power.

The values and beliefs of the Group animate the members and, since Groups lack the capability to constrain or govern conduct, Groups may give rise to Organizations designed to promote and protect those values by means which the Groups lack. Such Organizations—rule-governed structures—which make calls upon Group members may become the focus of the Group. We can see this process at work when, for instance, a grass-roots religious movement becomes a church or a sect: then the personal experience of enlightenment is replaced by rites of initiation, and freedom of commitment is replaced by formal membership criteria. In the case of such Organizations we need, wherever possible, to distinguish the Group and its values from the Organization and its stated objectives and formal memberships. This task is easy enough if the Group generates an Organization to which only a few fanatics belong, whom the majority of Group members merely respect; it is less easy when the Organization claims to be the sole repository of Group values, and equates belief with membership. Even then the values must be seen to be anterior to the Organization, and commitment to them never a matter of conformity to rules; so a Group may continue to operate as an institutional form despite the existence of a rule-governed Organization which claims to serve its interests. The values are no doubt properly ascribed to the Organization, as being its values, but they are more importantly the values of the Group. We must not allow the power and distinctiveness of the rule-governed structure to distract out attention from the basic, more amorphous form which engendered the Organization.

Classes as non-institutional collectives

Associational forms must be distinguished from classes of human beings, which are non-institutional collectives. A class of persons is defined by reference to one or more objective, non-normative criteria. The classes of human beings which we create are no different from the classes into which we group material objects or other things. So we can create classes of persons over six feet tall; disabled persons; those in socio-economic class D, and so on. Unlike the institutional forms, classes are not a social 'given': we can arbitrarily select criteria to create new classes at will: onelegged Australian sheep-farmers. Classes involve articulations of the social world which are imposed according to the observer's concerns.

We select the criteria of class membership in order, for instance, to be able to enumerate its members; the criteria must obviously be precise enough to enable us to determine with certainty who falls within the class and who is excluded from it. We must be able to say of any person that he is, or is not, a member, without having to resort to spinning a coin or making a personal choice.[65] Classes can be arbitrarily specified: we might imagine a class of persons who are to benefit in some way; it could be made up of individuals with nothing in common except the fact that they were chosen by X. That criterion is clear, but we could not know in advance of X's selection which individuals would qualify as members of the class entitled to benefit. One of the objections to racist legislation is that the criteria of class membership which specify who is to be discriminated for or against cannot be objective, so the implementation of such policies inevitably confers a most objectionable power of selection upon officials.[66]

Classes lack an institutional character because the members do not share the same values—as they do in Groups—nor are they normatively linked together—as they are in the other associational forms. As class members they are only contingently subject to the same rules or norms. So classes must not be confused with Groups. It is but another instance of Hume's fork that we cannot infer from the fact that members satisfy the objective criteria of class membership any sort of Group membership. That is, from the fact that members satisfy the objective criteria of a class, we cannot assume that they therefore share the same values, attitudes, and beliefs, or have the commitments which characterise Group members.

All classes, being arbitrary articulations of the social world, are without influence. They are not fraternities because they lack any central armature of values; they are simply sets, such as all owners of R-registration cars. The members of a class may or course become a Group, sharing common values and interests, and conscious of their membership of a fraternity. So the members of the class—the owners of MG cars—may be easily recognizable as a Group having fraternal ties based on experience.

Classes and rules

It is important to understand the nature of classes because the concept of the social rule—a rule which sets out standards of conduct for members of Society—is only intelligible by reference to classes. It is part of the notion of the rule that it must specify the persons—the class—to whom it is to apply.[67] For it is obviously not the case that all general social rules apply to all members of Society: only the class of those who have committed a particular offence are to be subject to a specific sanction; only those who lack specified necessities are entitled to benefits, and so on. Social rules which apply in an all-or-nothing way are characterized by the inclusion of exceptions.[68]

In legal adjudication the drawing of lines and making of exceptions involves specifying classes of persons and objects. Legislators are also in the business of creating classes by their rule-making, of defining the criteria by which to determine whether persons are, or are not, liable, entitled, or empowered. A rule, in order to operate as such, should employ objective criteria; those criteria must be objectively ascertainable if only because the rule is to be enforced and applied by many different persons. Rules which set out vague criteria, specifying who is to act or be prevented from acting, may operate to empower officials to exercise discretion. It is well understood that norms of this sort may operate as power-conferring rules.[69]

Now, clearly framed social rules define classes, not Groups. Groups are, I shall argue, legally irrelevant (see *post*, p. 259). The making and application of rules depend on the definition of classes by means of criteria which are clear and objectively verifiable. The criteria of Group membership—

the complex of values, beliefs, and attitudes which an individual possesses and shares with others—cannot be employed in rule-making and application.[70] For Groups attract huge penumbral memberships and it may be difficult to decide whether those sympathetic to Group values are or are not members; and whether they are, or are not, subject to a rule.

The difficulty in determining Group membership arises from the fact that we have only indirect evidence of a person's beliefs and values. We may have ample evidence of the existence of the Group and its armature, but we cannot be sure how far its values have been internalized by any individual. Group membership is a subjective affair. Even extreme measures—torturing an individual in order to test his commitment—are notoriously unreliable, being likely to result in false confessions to avoid pain as frequently as they succeed in exposing the falsity of denials. As a result, a rule which attempts to treat members of a particular Group differently from other members of Society can scarcely operate as a rule since its application cannot be uniform or just. Norms which are not rules might operate, for instance, to license the persecution of suspected Group members.

Social rules which prescribe punishment must not make Group membership an offence—offences such as heresy, political non-conformity, and dissidence will be unknown in the ideal legal system. Just punishment requires norms of immense particularity and precision (see *post,* Ch. 4, p. 92). The business of extirpating heresy, or of changing beliefs and attitudes, requires a very different set of concepts from those such as rules, classes, offences, and punishment. The issue here, it should be noted, is not whether it is legitimate to harm persons for their heretical or non-conformist beliefs, but how we conceptualize that policy and its application. A prohibition against beliefs or values—undoubtedly some sort of norm—cannot be regarded as a legal rule, and harm inflicted under such a prohibition cannot constitute legal punishment.

The notion of general social rules prescribing conduct carries with it a neutral conception of the personality of the members of Society. The making and application of general rules encourages, and perhaps entails, a conception of the member as an atomic individual to be identified, made liable, benefited, or empowered by reference only to non-normative characteristics—as a member of a class. As an individual who is subject to the general rules of Society, the citizen is stripped of all his Group, Community, and Organizational ties—as also of all his other identifying physical features, dispositions, and history—and is identified only by reference to particular objective criteria as a member of a class. In a Society governed by general rules he is no more than a human possessing objective characteristics and doing verifiable acts.

II: THE PRACTICAL FORMS

A: Activity

An Activity is nothing more than an established behavioural pattern which is created when individuals or collectives pursue publicly recognizable objectives. An Activity is of course never constituted merely by the intention to do something, it is a generally observable configuration of human behaviour. The identity of the Activity depends on the nature of the ends which are pursued by the actors.[71] The defining goals are commonly everyday practical objectives, unlike the objectives pursued by participants in Practices, which are changes in the normative world. So the goal may be either the achievement of a physical state of affairs—as in the Activities of house-building, catching rabbits, collecting stamps, or keeping fit—or what we might call a change of mind—as in the Activities of educating, advising, propagandizing, or debating.

It will be apparent that, in the nature of things, many Activities will not be capable of clear delimitation: many will merge into other Activities, and some are merely steps towards further goals. We have considerable freedom as to the point at which, in the hierarchy of means and ends, we decide that a particular behavioural pattern, understood in the light of its goals, constitutes a distinct Activity. Nevertheless, some Activities have well established, clearly defined objectives, and have generated a body of knowledge as to the resources required and strategies to be followed.

I count the goal or objective as the central animating norm of this institutional form.[72] There may be no compulsion to reach one's goal; constraints will certainly exist if the achievement of the objective is conceived of as a duty. The goals are normative in the sense that the agent is aware of a standard which guides or governs his conduct in pursuing the goal. A commitment to achieving an objective does not always entail that the agent values the objective for its own sake; it is often merely a means to an end.[73]

In addition to the objectives, three other classes of norms can be recognized.[74] *Regulatory rules* may be said to be imposed on an Activity in the interests both of the actors and of others. As an Activity is a form of life within a Society, those undertaking the Activity are inevitably subject to the constraints of social control; the regulatory rules prescribe the goals which may be entertained in a Society, and govern the ways in which they may be reached. We are familiar with the safety, health, and environmental regulations which govern Activities such as farming, fishing, flying, and driving motor vehicles. However, the institutional character of Activities does not come from the fact that they appear as regulated patterns of activity within Society; the regulatory rules are neither necessary nor constitutive ingredients of an Activity.[75]

Directives or technical norms These prescribe what must be done in order to achieve success, for example recipes, directions, techniques, etc. Such technical norms are commonly formulated in the light of long experience. The force of these directions in guiding conduct rests upon the perception that they lay out the best, the simplest, the most economical ways of achieving the objective.[76]

Finally, there are what I call the *precepts of good Activity* which govern certain Activities. They consist of internally generated moral norms which can be said to ensure the integrity of an Activity; they guard against the achievement of goals in morally objectionable but economical ways. Thus there are good and bad ways of conducting research, giving professional advice, treating illness, enforcing laws, and so forth.

By definition, Activities—like Groups—do not involve interpersonal constraints. It is therefore questionable whether they count as institutional forms. They are, however, institutional forms in that Activities are structured by their objectives and precepts. The fact that the norms—the goals—may be set by the agent himself does not deprive them of their normative character as guiding and influencing a configuration of human activity. Activities are the locations for objectives as Groups are for values; both of these institutional forms lack a deontological element. Neither can be neglected if we would understand the nature of the freedoms which are claimed for individuals in political discourse.

Relationships between the actors engaging in an Activity are not normatively defined. That is, actors have only contingent normative relationships with other actors engaged in the same Activity, and then not by virtue of their engagement in the Activity alone. They may act individually in pursuit of their own goals, in loose co-operation with others, they may work for another under a contract, or they may, as members of an Organization, pursue the same goals within the organizational structure in co-operation with other members. Co-operation on a vast scale is required for Activities such as the building of pyramids or space ships which require immense organizational skills and structures.

Enforcement Activity, which I have already mentioned in relation to the associational forms Society and Organization, is intended to secure the conformity of members to the standards and rules of the associational form; it is considered in more detail below.

B: Practice

This is the most important of the institutional forms for the purposes of understanding the legal world. Of all the institutional forms, it is perhaps the one which most requires explanation. There follows a thumb-nail sketch of its main features: a fuller account is given in the description of each of the legal Practices in the following Chapters. I use the word 'Practice' to denote something very much more specific than a way of doing things which has become well established over the years.[77]

A Practice is a form of human activity, a procedure, which enables the achievement of an objective, some normative change, through specified moves and through compliance with certain conditions. The following concerns Practices which enable changes in the normative world, which I shall call normative Practices. These are distinct from the class of Practices —such as debates, games, rain-making ceremonies, rites, and rituals— which leave the normative world unchanged, and thus may be called non-normative Practices.

Normative Practices are procedures which make possible immediate and deliberate changes in the normative world. Participants in Practices alter the normative world by creating new rules, issuing orders, creating entitlements and other normative positions, conveying property, making contracts, appointing officers, and so on. In brief, Practices are the prescribed formal methods by which deliberate and immediate alterations can be made to an existing structure of entitlements, social rules, and normative relationships.[78] Examples of normative Practices are the procedures required for making mortgages, leases, contracts, wills, marriages, elections, coronations, appointments, and the procedures for legislating, for making administrative decisions, legal judgments, and so on.

Practices are important because in many circumstances they constitute the only means whereby such normative changes can be deliberately made. Practices do not just facilitate such normative changes, *they make them possible.*[79] Members of an associational form which lacked such normative Practices might be subject to *informal* normative direction, which could involve the arrogation of authority by a leader or junta. In the absence of both Practices and any such informal authority, changes in the normative world would depend on changes in social and physical conditions—consider the consequential normative changes which are caused by conquest, revolution, floods, or earthquakes—or the incremental changes by which customary norms are gradually eroded and new standards and institutions emerge.

In the terminology employed here, those taking part in a normative Practice are called *participants;* the precise steps of the procedure, the conditions to be satisfied, and the moves to be made in order to achieve a valid objective are here described as the *ground rules* of the Practice; and the change which the participants are able to make in the normative world, their immediate goal in participating, is called the *normative product* (NP) of the practice. NPs—such as statutes, contracts, or orders—can only be achieved by strict compliance with the procedural ground rules. NPs are either valid or invalid depending upon whether the participants have complied with all such requirements; they may be said to have Practice validity. The objectives of the participants in a Practice are thus unlike the ordinary objectives of actors in Activities, whose attainments are described in the language of success or failure, not in the language of validity.

Making deliberate changes in the normative world is a serious matter which is bound to give rise to countless problems: newly created rules, orders, and entitlements will be challenged; the capacity of the participants will be questioned; fraudulent claims to entitlements will be made; and so on. So the ground rules of the Practice may be regarded as attempts to deal with such problems in advance by making the validity of the NP conditional upon the conformity of the participants with a procedure which will, as far as possible, obviate the more obvious possibilities of carelessness, mistake, and fraud. Ground rules may incorporate provisions prescribing who has the capacity to participate; they may incorporate safeguards against the making of inadvertent changes, or against the improper or fraudulent use of the procedure; they may require that publicity be given to a transaction or that written evidence of it should be kept; or they may prescribe that, before binding normative changes are made, adequate investigation or consultation must be undertaken.

Practices exist *within* the associational forms—of Society, State, Organization, and Community—as the formal means for decision- and rule-making, and for the transacting of business by and on behalf of the members.[80] Many of the Practices of a Society are open to participation by all members, for example the Practices of contract or loan; but for some Practices, such as those of legislation, participation is only possible if an individual is authorized to participate by the rules of the associational form. Such capacity to participate, especially where it is limited to a few individuals, constitutes an important, and imperfectly understood, type of power.[81]

The idea of the Practice

In addition to the ground rules of the Practice, we must recognize what will here be called the idea of the Practice. This consists of the set of methodological values held by those who frame and maintain the ground rules of a particular Practice. They are the methodological values of normative change; that is, they are not the values of social justice by which the NPs of Practices may be appraised, but the standards by which we can judge the method or procedure by which a particular normative change is accomplished. Thus we may say of a procedure—or of the NP which is produced—that it is fair, just, democratic, expeditious, economical, rational; that it gives effect to, or reflects, the values placed on experience, expertise, or personal inspiration; that it instances the virtues of openness, or of confidentiality or secrecy and so forth. In most Practices the procedure—the ground rules—can be said to constitute, to some degree, a realization of such values.

Emphasis needs to be placed on the immense variety of Practices which make normative changes possible. The changes made by different Practices are of very different degrees of significance; thus, procedures by which a bet is laid or a car sold may affect but one or two individuals, whereas procedures for executive decision-making or parliamentary legislation affect an entire population; a conveyance of land is generally more important than a loan of the tractor needed to cultivate it.

Each Practice may be said to have its own idea, its own set of methodological values, which must be understood in the light of the type of changes it enables, the practical difficulties and constraints which exist, and the values held by those who prescribe the ground rules. We must not expect all Practices to share any particular set of methodological values; thus, the ground rules of a lottery are not designed to ensure the rationality of the outcome; fairness is irrelevant in the marriage ceremony; and the procedures for corporate decision-making in a trading corporation will not be expected to satisfy the criteria of democratic choice.

One reason for setting out the methodological values of Practices is to challenge the commonly held view that procedures are neutral recipes or protocols. The business of making normative changes affects the lives, opportunities and benefits of individuals, and is therefore a serious matter, often arousing powerful emotions. The methods devised to allow changes to be made generally reflects the sense of right of those who institute the Practices; indeed, some Practices may be designed to symbolize and promote such values. The rudimentary Practice whereby a Ruler makes decrees may be regarded as arbitrary by citizens, but it is clearly consonant with a positive value ascribed to the ruler's wisdom or inspiration.

Once we have identified the values—the idea of the Practice—then we can appraise the ground rules to see whether they are consistent with them. The recognition of the idea of a legal Practice—the methodological values of legal justice—is a matter of great importance. Demands for the reform of Practices arise from a perception that the existing ground rules do not conform to the idea. For instance, we may consider that the ground rules of contract are unfair, or that the legislative Practice is undemocratic, or that legal adjudication is unjust. Proposals for the reform of a Practice are designed to produce the best, or at any rate a better, method of making normative changes.

Practices are artifacts, always subject to criticism and open to change; their evolution or institution cannot be explained without reference to the demand that they should satisfy certain values. Although it would be hyperbolic to suggest that they have a life of their own, they are not merely footpaths; they are not composed of sets of secondary rules which just happen to have been laid down. Changes to a procedure come from two sources: either from the reforms of a legislature or—as is the case with a legal adjudicatory Practice—from the participants themselves. Where the participants develop and maintain the ground rules of their Practice the animating influence of the idea is particularly clear.

Every society has procedures which are outdated, involving the use of symbols and prescribing procedural steps which were appropriate for the realization of values no longer held, in conditions which no longer obtain. Such rituals, which may be accepted as the traditional or conventional methods of doing things, are survivals which scarcely qualify as Practices; they must be treated as exceptional. Also, of course, an enacted procedure which a legislator judged to be the best method of achieving a change may turn out to be wholly inappropriate.

There is a certain banality about the proposition that, within a particular culture, market, or political regime, we would expect to find a congruence between the methods of normative change employed and the wider values generally maintained. After all, the very nature of the procedures will colour our view of the regime itself. We would expect the legislative Practices of a commune to differ from those of a dictatorship, and neither would be appropriate for a theocracy. Each of these regimes has different procedures because they value different things. In order to understand the legislative Practices of different regimes, for example, we need to examine not just their institutional differences, but also the different frameworks of belief in terms of which the procedural differences are to be explained.

In other words, we must appreciate that a description of the Practices in the language of positivism will be inadequate and distorting. Certainly the positivists' account of Practice validity stops well short of a meaningful description. The validity of an NP depends upon conformity with ground rules, which are assuredly not value-free directives.

Now it must be admitted that concern to identify the methodological values, and demands that procedures should be designed to realize them, are peculiarly democratic preoccupations. A democratic polity breeds institutional variety and discrimination. This is not to suggest that all decision-making procedures should be democratic. Rather, there is a persistent demand that normative changes—the making of laws, contracts, decrees, regulations, judgments, and so forth—should be accomplished by the most appropriate methods. In institutional matters democracy takes as its maxim 'proper things in proper places'. The appropriateness of existing procedures is an important part of the democratic debate. Practices, under constant scrutiny, are subject to reform in the light of methodological values, and alternative Practices evolve or are instituted.

The democratic credentials of the preoccupation with institutional design is worthy of attention in face of the tendency to wonder at the emphasis which common lawyers have traditionally placed upon procedures. There is a cavalier attitude towards procedures among philosophers who consider that normative changes require little more than rational thought and expert calculation, rather than elaborate procedures; also among functionaries who accept the existence of procedures as neutral forms, as merely enacted or customary ways of doing things.

Practices are of especial importance in the institutional theory of law; it will be argued that it is in the process of applying general rules in the legal adjudicatory Practices of a Society that valid laws are created, and that it is within these forms that the distinctive language of the law is generated. Our understanding of these central forms of the legal field depends upon a clear apprehension of the idea by which they are animated.

III: INSTITUTIONAL STRUCTURES AND INSTITUTIONAL FIELDS

Institutional forms are the atomic particulars of the institutional world in the sense that they are not reducible to other institutional entities.

Of course, all institutional forms are related to other forms; they do not exist in isolation. Thus associational forms contain practical forms; Practices depend upon the existence of Activities; and Organizations and Groups exist within Societies. Many of the institutions of everyday language are what may be called institutional structures, being made up of instances of the basic forms which are combined in various ways. For instance, we can analyse the familiar institutions of marriage, property, the state, and the Bank of England into their constituent institutional forms. The links between the various components of an institution are generally strong, thus Practices will each belong to an associational form, e.g. the rites of the Church, or the procedures of Parliament. Smaller associational forms may exist within a larger one, as where Groups exist within a political party, or committees within a club.

At a higher level of generality we may recognize institutional fields. These fields of human activity are segments of social life, such as politics, religion, law, economics, and defence.[82] These fields are sometimes spoken of as institutions—we commonly find references to the 'institution of law'—and they may be referred to as worlds, domains, realms, sectors, spheres, provinces, or systems. Such general terms for significant segments of social life need to be sharply distinguished from the concept of the institutional form, because fields lack the coherence of the forms. It is a mistake to treat institutional fields—domains, provinces, or realms—as though they constituted singular undifferentiated forms of human activity.

An institutional field is regarded here simply as the bracketing together of an aggregate of different institutional forms; it embraces a variety of Organizations, Activities, Groups, or Practices within a Society, each of which stands in complicated interrelation to many others. So an institutional field must be analysed in terms of its constituent parts, the various instances of the institutional forms. In the religious field in this country, for example, we find unstructured *Activities* such as church-going, charitable works, evangelizing, theological study, prayer, and so on. There are *Organizations*, each possessing hierarchies, officers, and members, of which the Church of England, the Methodists, and the Salvation Army are examples. *Groups* also abound, such as the charismatic and ecumenical movements. Further, there are a variety of *Practices* such as services, and procedures for marriage, baptism, ordination, the appointment of bishops and so on. All of these different forms will exist within, and are inevitably related to, the *Society* in which they exist.

The constellation of particular institutional forms within a field involves an immense array of practical and normative interconnections—and sometimes conflicts—between the different forms. For forms do not exist in isolation: some are dependent upon others, some may be said to be symbiotic, and some are merely ancillary to more important forms. What we may call the practical ramifications within a field may be far-reaching and enormously complicated. So whatever coherence a field possesses is supplied by the interrelationships and interanimations between the forms of which it is composed. Undoubtedly, fields are not so structured that they can be regarded as having an institutional unity which makes it possible to attribute purposes or functions to them.[83]

Given the number and heterogeneity of the forms bracketed together within the field, and the manner in which they are directly or indirectly related to forms in other fields, there would clearly be little point in attempting to define field boundaries with any sort of precision. Institutional fields clearly cannot be presented as wholly discrete segments of social life—but neither are they merely aspects or dimensions of it. Boundaries to an institutional field can only roughly be drawn on the basis of decisions as to whether particular institutional forms are sufficiently closely related to those which are commonly regarded as being central to, or necessary for, the existence of the field. Many fields must be regarded as focusing upon one or more central institutional forms.

Although I have mentioned the fields of law, religion, and politics as familiar illustrations, we could decide to examine whatever field we choose: for instance, the nature of the institutional field of association football, or the wider field of sport, could be analysed into its constituent Practices, Organizations, Groups, and Activities.

Recognition of the nature of institutional forms and fields is particularly important in attempting to understand the phenomenon of law. For it is in the focal institutional forms of the field—the legal Practices—that legal language is generated and legal norms sustained. The implications of this for jurisprudence are far-reaching, for the autonomy of each of the Practices produces three legal domains, each with its own distinct character; a generalisation about the law which is true of one of them may be wholly or partly untrue of the others.

NOTES

1. Raz (1975: 126), reiterated in 979: 104).
2. 'The law that was first taught and studied in the West was not the prevailing law; it was the law contained in an ancient manuscript . . .' Berman (1977: 898). For an epistemology which appears to equate law with doctrine see Samuel (1994: ch. 4).
3. 'The meanings and norms implicit in . . . practices are not just in the minds of the actors but are out there in the practice themselves, practices which cannot be conceived as a set of individual actions, but which are essentially modes of social relation, of mutual action' Taylor (2978: 172).
4. The word 'institution' has been employed in a great variety of ways. Among the objects which have been said to be institutions are principles, concepts, language, and even humanity itself. Many definitions or descriptions do little more than describe practices of social interaction; see Scott (1995: 33): 'Institutions consist of cognitive, normative, and regulative structures and activities that provide stability and meaning to social behaviour.' See also Peil (1977: 17) 'an enduring complex of norms, roles, values and sanctions embracing a distinct segment of human life'. The *Dictionary of Sociology* (Abercrombie *et al.* eds. 1988: 124) describes institutions as 'social practices that are regularly and continuously repeated, are sanctioned and maintained by social norms and have a major significance in the social structure'. For a discussion of the concept see Eisenstaat (1968: 409–21). on the Romanist conception of a 'legal institution' see Sawyer (1965: 165–7). See also Douglas (1987: 46–53) and Wells (1970).
5 No claim is made here as to the value of the institutional forms as described here for other disciplines; anthropologists will, for instance, find little of value in the description of the form I have called Community. The basic forms are, as will become apparent, those which are required if we would understand the legal field of modern democratic societies.
6. Whatever the ontological status of the institutional forms may be, statements about them cannot be reduced to statements about individual actions and relations. Cf. the view of Jarvie (see Emmet and MacIntyre (eds.) 1970: 79)

'"Army" is merely a plural of soldier, and *all* statements about the army can be reduced to statements about particular soldiers comprising the army'.

7. The treatment of law as an autopoietic system, Teubner (1993: 25–46), will underplay the distinctiveness of the various forms which are to be found in the legal field. The institutional forms are—as points of reference, locations, objects to which attitudes are adopted—entities which cannot be left out of account. On autopoiesis theory see Cotterrell (1992: 65–70).
8. The distinction is not new; it was made by MacIver (1933: 12–17) and restated in MacIver and Page (1950: 15). The authors treat procedures as institutions and groups as associations. Sampford (1989: 194) distinguishes between (i) institutions which comprise relationships between pairs of people—as in the institutions of marriage, contract etc.—and (ii) those consisting of a web or matrix of social relationships between a set of persons in closer, more frequent, and more intense inter-connections with others of the set than with non-members.
9. Cf. Neil MacCormick's personal definition of legalism (1993: 143). For him legalism is not a vice but an appropriate concern with clear rules in matters of legal politics. The pejorative sense in which I use the term adverts to the inappropriateness of a preoccupation with clear rules in many areas of social interaction.
10. H. L. A. Hart's imagined pre-legal society is a regime of primary rules, restricting the use of violence etc.—rules 'which are always found in primitive societies of which we have knowledge' (1994: 91–9).
11. Bourdieu (1977).
12. Roberts (1979: 170) draws attention to groups which do not make use of normative propositions and are unable to cite examples of abstract norms which are applicable to their social lives.
13. See Goody (1986).
14. The ideal type of Community described here exists outside Society and beyond the reach of a centralizing state. All modern communities exist within Societies. On the variety of communities within Society see Cotterrell (1993: 336). For the suggestion that communities can be said to exist at different levels—state, neighbourhood, family—see Phillips (1993).
15. Contemporary forms of life which can also be recognized within pre-capitalist societies have been subtly transformed; see Abel (1982: 3).
16. As an institutional form Society is a construct differing markedly from the common-sense category employed by many jurists and sociologists; i.e. the association within the boundaries of the nation state; see Leach (1982: 41–3). It is to be sharply distinguished from social context or social life. For Ehrlich (1936: 26) societies could be described as containing the totality of all institutions and interactions within an association.
17. See Giddens (1985); Holsti (1991); Coser (1956); and Freedman (ed.) (1995).
18. The UK is an example of the artifice involved. On the subjugation of peoples and the resultant ineradicable tensions see Beresford (1993: ch. 16). See Kymlicka (1990: 231) on the significance of multi-lingualism; most countries are multi-nation states containing two or more linguistic communities. So if States are to promote culture or to enrich the language of society the ques-

tions arise: which language and whose culture? For institutional theory, heterogeneity is to be regarded as a fact of life, not as an objective; it would be wrong to treat value pluralism as an ideal to be actively promoted by the law.

19. Society as an institutional form is a purely formal collection of individuals: simply that class of persons upon whom membership has been conferred. Neither that association nor the polity in which it exists are to be understood in the idioms of teleology; it is not, for instance, a 'co-operative venture for human development'; Rawls (1971: 4). Nor should we look for any goal, or indeed any character common to all its members—not even their engagement in a practice; Oakeshott (1975: 122). Instead we must look for the establishment of certain institutional forms, made up from some of the members of Society only, which are necessary to sustain it; such forms as the State, enforcement Activity, the Group which is the legitimate opposition, etc.
20. See Balandier (1970: 36).
21. On rules in general see von Wright (1963: 1–16); Ross (1968); Hart (1994: 79–91); Twining and Miers (1982: ch. 3); Coval and Smith (1977).
22. Hart (1994: 161).
23. The centralizing State will be defined as a governmental Organization which prescribes and enforces social rules for the regulation of *individual* conduct. That is, its subjects are not primarily collectives—regions, towns, or villages—but individuals. The Society which is correlative with this State is an association of atomic individuals each of whom is directly subject to the State. The atomicity or modularity of individuals is the defining feature of the associational form Society which emerges with the centralizing State. See Taylor (1985: 187–210) for the view that the free atomic individual of the West is a product of a particular society and civilization. Civil Society is essentially a legal concept. A Community or Group would be an extra-legal association which could only be subjected to legal—as opposed to administrative— regulation by defining the members as class members.
24. Civil Society is essentially a legal concept and social rules are here defined as legal rules; they are the norms of the artificial form—Society—whose members are legal persons. On the important distinction between social rules which are enforced and employed in enforcement Activity and the legal rules employed by the judges in the legal Practices see *post*, pp. 116 and 201. Social rules are reflexes of the LS rules which may be regarded as being instutionalized 'good reasons'—see Toulmin (1950)—for the conclusions reached in legal arguments.
25. Goody (1986).
26. Maine (1905: 12–18).
27. In China the traditional distrust of explicit written codes of law has carried over to modern times. Where laws have been written, Chinese law-givers have adopted the tendency of paternalist administrators over the ages to endow the written formulations with an opacity which renders the provisions capable of any desired construction.
28. This must be qualified: in civil Societv the ULP and not the State is the legislator; see *post*. Ch. 7.
29. The distinctness, the equal worth, of the individual members is the defining

feature of the artificial form Society. However, any shared characteristics languages, beliefs, pursuits are contingent, local, and legally irrelevant.

30. A polity is not an associational form; it is simply the aggregate of institutional forms which are implicated in the governance of a Society. See *post*, p. 252.
31. See Gellner (1994: 5) 'Civil Society is that set of diverse non-governmental institutions which is strong enough to counterbalance the state and, while not preventing the state from fulfilling its role of keeper of the peace and arbiter between major interests, can nevertheless prevent it from dominating and atomising the rest of society'. For Gellner, civil Society is a sociological reality, an institutionally complex entity, exhibiting an individualistic moral order. This is obscuring; civil Society should be seen as essentially a legal concept. It is not a substantial association of the sort found in the discourse of moral philosophers or sociologists, but an artificial construct entailed in the language of legal adjudication; in the legal view of the world it is an irreducible form.
32. For an introduction to the vast literature on organizations and organization theory see Dawson (1996). Her definition is a useful starting-point for institutional theory: 'Organisations are defined as collections of people joining together in some formal association in order to achieve group or individual objectives.' (1996: xxii). See also Clegg (1990) and Scot (1995).
33. Authority in an organizational context is a very different thing from the authority which an individual has in a Practice, or in an Activity or Group—consideration which underlines the importance of identifying precisely the institutional forms in which a concept such as authority must be located if it is to be explicated. See Nowell-Smith (1978: 6–44).
34. It is very largely in these organizational forms, rather than in Society that we must locate Foucault's 'disciplinary society', his term for modern society: Cousins and Hussain (1984: 185).
35. Friedman (1990: 87).
36. In many contexts the State is regarded as encompassing the associational form Society; sometimes 'state' and 'constitution' are used interchangeably; see Lewis (1996: 7). See Quinton (1967: 6) on the importance of distinguishing the state from society. For a conceptual history see Skinner (1989); for over 150 different definitions see Titus (1931); and for observations on the emergence of the term see Oakeshott (1975: 196).
37. The State as an institutional form is an organizational structure, not an 'abstract conception' behind the men who possess power; it possesses not merely an assumed unity but a discoverable unity of command. Cf. John Chipman Gray (1931: 65).
38. See Kelsen (1973: 188) for the identification of the state as a juristic concept with the total legal order. Kelsen's concern about the hypostatization, and deification of the State was shared by many. See for example Duguit's denial of the personality of the state, on the ground that it postulates mysticism; Laski (1933: 55).
39. The character of the Organizations which constitute the State will vary with the nature of the polity. The inclusion of both legislative and legal Practices as parts of the State is common; although understandable, in view of the earlier

history of the state, it is to be deplored in any account of the democratic polity.

40. 'Sharply demarcated boundaries . . . are, in fact, achievements of the modern State, and war and military organisation have been central to the development of the State system that still provides the basic organising principle of human societies across the globe': Dandekes (1994: 110).
41. See Runciman (1986) on the variety of monocausal theories of the emergence of the state.
42. The distinction between the indifferent state and the centralizing state parallels a distinction between a society in which power is exercised and one in which rules are mutually accepted: Roberts (1979: 168, 183). Roberts observes that in many primitive regimes the operation of rules and the exercise of power are concurrent, closely interlinked functions.
43. The indifferent state, often personal in character, is not in a position to claim that, by virtue of its efforts alone, an ordered social life has been made possible for its peoples. It may attempt to justify its domination by proclaiming that it has conferred the blessings of a common culture, ideology language, or religion. Such factitious cultural unities as were proclaimed in the Holy Roman Empire of the Habsburgs and the Empires of Spain, France, Britain, and Holland were shattered by the emergence of nationalist centralist states. However, the democratic egalitarianism, with its cultural pluralism and religious scepticism, which underpinned the calls for independence, does little to establish the political identities of the new Societies. See Pagden (1995) .
44. For an analysis of the emergence of the state, the 'fundamental change in the institution of sovereignty that occurred in the nineteenth century', see Thomson (1994: ch. 1). She concludes that 'The territorial state's monopoly On violence is principally the result of interstate relations' (p. 147). The modern centralizing State would terminate competing authorities and divided allegiances: citizens are subjects of one state, one law. Although the impetus to achieve such undivided authority can be explained differently, it is also, if less obviously, a necessary feature of the democratic revolution. The emergence of the democratic polity possessing the undivided authority required to guarantee its egalitarian claims will entail profound institutional changes; in a civil Society the centralizing State loses all its aboriginal powers; so the erstwhile sovereign State gives way to a sovereign legislature, and the monopoly of punishment which was formerly ascribed to the Ruler becomes a monopoly enjoyed by the legal Practices. See *post*, Ch. 7, p. 261.
45. Values, defined as conceptions of the desirable, are to be regarded as normative operators in that, whether explicit or implicit, they influence the selection of ends, priorities, means, and modes. See Kluckholm's definition in Parsons and Shils (1951: 395).
46. The Groups described here as lacking any deontological framework, dependent only upon their axiological armatures and personal commitments are significantly different from the communities and the interacting social groups of sociology. See for instance Homans (1950); Giddens (1987: ch. 9); Coser (1956); Olson (1971); Gilbert (1989: 147). For a discussion of the necessity of

groups for the emergence of law see Honoré (1973). See also Sartre's distinction between a *group*, which is identified by the commitment of the members, and a *series*, in which the members show no such commitment; Cranston (1976: 220). The Group as an institutional form is perhaps somewhat closer to the 'thought collective' described in 1935 by Ludwick Fleck (1979). See also Sampford (1989: 210) for whom in groups, unlike institutions, there need be no social relationships between members; they are recognized when the subjective interests of individuals are perceived as being common interest, constituting a Group consciousness. Politically, the importance of Groups lies in the possibility that they may be mobilized into action.

47. On acts as communications see Lucas (1993: 8–9 and ch. 3); and Fletcher (1993).
48. Many values arise from our engagement in an Activity and will be reflected in the precepts of the Activity: see *post*, p. 38. On the shared assumptions and values of scientific investigation see Shapin (1994).
49. Religious Groups may, as cults, exercise a very powerful influence on members; few secular Groups have the same intensity or power. As public demonstration of commitment is especially important in religious life, the members of religious Groups are likely to engage in deontological activity so that a pristine Group may soon emerge as an Organization with its own structures and disciplines. The Group outlined here must not be equated with religious Groups; in some the commitment may not be conscious; realization of membership may dawn slowly. In Group life that which is understood, or assumed, may play a vastly important role.
50. Our membership of Groups gives us our sense of identity and self-esteem. So the growth of Group consciousness is linked to affirmation of the worth of Group members. On the importance of clarifying the unique qualities of the Group which operate to foster members' self-esteem see Herrenstein and Murray (1995). At the same time, membership of a Group may entail hostility to other Groups: 'Hostility between rival forms of life is inseparable from commitment': Nagel (1991).
51. Fleck drew a distinction between thought collectives whose membership is defined in terms of commitment—the true believers—and thought communities with a membership defined by more formal criteria. Thought collectives possessed an inner elite and masses on the peripheries: Douglas (1987: 14).
52. On the significance of this see *post*, p. 36.
53. Of the elements in World Three, Popper commented: '(i)t is one of the grave mistakes of contemporary philosophy not to see that these things—our offspring—though they are the products of our minds . . . also have an objective side' (1976: 195); see also Gellner (1964: 112).
54. The armature of the Group represents the contemporary interpretation of experience; the members draw on the resources of the past. So the cumulative value structures of the Group are always to be understood historically. For jurists, like Savigny and Puchta, who conceptualized the national group as a *Volksgeist*, history was the key to understanding the values underlying a Society's norms. As R. G. Collingwood maintained group membership is not just possession of a language, it is a shared experience.

55. We underestimate the extent to which the original thinker or artist depends on a range of intellectual and other social resources: see Douglas (1987: 16–17). The production of theory is a social process occurring within a tradition provided by a community of intellectuals; see Bourdieu (1988).
56. Groups are objectifies. They are the transmitters of unconsidered implications of experience, of understandings, of ways of proceeding not fully articulated. They transmit not only basic or express ideas but also the uncharted, untheorized implications of those ideas.
57. It has become a commonplace that our human experience is shaped by particular systems of representation with which we are familiar, that the language we use structures our experience. So the categories in which a Group articulates the human experience of even such basic elements as pain or sexual desire will shape the way in which the members see the world and themselves as desiring and suffering agents. See e.g. Winkler (1990); Foucault (1976). The epistemological implications of this insight have been explored by Barthes, Foucault, and Lacan.
58. Serbo-Croat being a notable example of a language employed deliberately to differentiate a national Group.
59. Sperber and Wilson (1989) argue that cognition depends upon a shared cognitive environment and shared domains of assumption about the world. The expectations shared by communicators and addressees coincide because, in communicating, both are looking for meanings which are most obviously relevant given their beliefs and interests. Groups may be said to provide ready-made cognitive environments; their armatures provide members with the criteria of relevance.
60. A Society is not a Group. Self-determination enables us to change our Group allegiances. This is not at all the case with social rules, which are imposed upon us; they are the norms of an artificial associational form—Society—of which we are members. Hart accounts for the internalization of social rules in terms of the use we make of rules. Though the rules reflect social values, they may not be values which we share, even though we may cite the rules to criticize others for breaches of them: Hart (1994:86–7).
61. This in no way leads to the postulation of a mysterious 'group mind'. Nevertheless, Groups do objectify coherent structures, embodying particular visions, worlds, and horizons, which we make our own. Wittgenstein maintained that our sense of ourselves derives, not from any 'mysterious ghost in the machine', but from the social realities of language and institution which we inherit and develop. Groups are among the most important of the social realities; it is their amorphous character which casts doubt on their real existence and contributes to their mystery.
62. 'Culture' and 'tradition' are general terms; like 'ways of life' or 'mentalities', they do not denote institutional forms but aggregates of overlapping and conflicting Groups and Activities in the nature of institutional fields. Cultures are thus composed of and kept alive by Groups; and the conflicts between Groups within a culture or tradition may be intense—contributing to the instability of cultural patterns. The general terms 'culture' and 'tradition' are of little value as explanatory devices. As individuals we are not committed to

cultures but to Groups which are the specific focuses for values. A person does not move from one culture to another but from one Group or set of Groups to another. On examination, what is called a culture may actually be the ethos of a Group; thus the *soi-disant* 'legal culture' of a country is no sort of common consciousness, but merely the ethos of its lawyers.

63. Much play is made with value pluralism as a feature of the social life of a democratic polity. For the view that many different and incompatible ways of life should be recognized as good in their own incompatible terms, see Raz (1994). The notion of 'a way of life', like that of a culture or a tradition, does not, however, do justice to the complexity of our commitments. For it is a feature of the human predicament—not only of that of the members of the bourgeois class—that, as individuals, we commonly find ourselves members of incompatible Groups and must find ways of living with their inconsistent values. Our commitments are inevitably messy, fragmented, and various, and disillusionment often results from discovering that no set of Groups to which we belong can sustain claims to absolute coherence or universal validity; however, it is theatrical to suppose that this should make us wish to leap into an extreme form of religious or political activism in which we will, by 'forsaking all others', achieve the coherence of commitment. It is the variety of disparate and not wholly consistent Groups to which we belong which makes it possible for us to choose to socialize in new forms, to alter our allegiances. We may be deeply committed to our Groups and embedded in our social roles—see Sandel (1984: 81–96)—but even if these memberships provide our constitutive attachments, no Group—whatever its claims—can pretend to totalitarian exclusiveness. See Kymlicka (1990: 215). Our consciousness of freedom depends on our awareness of other competing Groups; that is why, in the political field, all Groups must be respected.

64. Lacan emphasizes the manner in which humans are socialized by language. Our identity as citizens is instilled by society which enters us by way of language. So there is no neat division between self and social life. An autonomous individual is not influenced by society, but inhabited by it from the moment of the acquisition of language. See *London Review of Books* (Dec. 1990). However, it must be emphasized that we are socialized, not by the language of Society—which, after all, is the language of law—but by the languages of Groups into which we may be said to be born. It is profoundly important to note that each individual is heir to several Groups and becomes a member and speaker of their languages. Writers commonly overlook the subtleties of language use. 'Despite the fact that members of the same society often use the same language this is not necessarily a source of order and unity. Members of different groups within society will tend to use different words in describing the same situations, and even when they use the same terms the meaning will vary': Sampford (1989: 219). Man's ability to learn new languages, and to change Group allegiances, is of fundamental importance. We are not constrained to remain a member of any Group. See Carrithers (1994).

65. To recognize a class of things is to polarize and exclude. It involves drawing boundaries, an operation very different from that of grading. It is a big jump

from recognizing degrees of difference to creating a similarity class; Douglas (1987: 60).

66. E.g. the discretion exercised by the 3 Nazi doctors who decided which persons—tens of thousands—were disabled and thus qualified for euthanasia.
67. What Ihering called 'formal realisability' describes the degree to which a legal directive has the quality of rule-ness. The extreme case is 'a directive to an official which requires him to respond to the presence together of each of a list of easily distinguishable factual aspects of a situation by intervening in a determinate way'. A law prescribing the age for legal capacity would thus exhibit a high degree of formal realisability; Kennedy (1976: 1687).
68. The very idea of a social rule posits such equality: equality before the law. *Prima facie,* human beings who are the subjects of such rules should be treated alike; Hart (1994: 162). Equality is discussed in Benn and Peters (1959: ch. 5); Rawls (1958); Williams (1962); Westen (1981); Wilson (1966: Part III); and Hare (1963: 118–19). The democratic revolution (see *post,* Ch. 3) involves treating rules absolutely seriously. No doubt the *idea* that the rules should be applied without consideration of any conditions—class, status, gender, race—which are not spelled out in the rule has been understood from very early times. However, if rules are, as a matter of fact, to be treated seriously in this way then *certain institutional structures must be in place;* such structures have only been established in recent times. After all, a very high degree of legislative sophistication is required for equality to be honoured; it is essential that the rules themselves should specify all the relevant distinctions. Otherwise, as Plutarch maintained, equality means injustice.
69. Power-conferring norms do not impose duties or rights on those who are liable to have their position altered as a result of the power being exercised. Nor do rules which confer rights or impose duties on citizens confer powers on officials. However, if regulatory rules—which set standards to which citizens must conform—are drafted in wide or ambiguous terms, they may operate as norms conferring powers on those who are to apply and enforce them. Rules of this sort, which may be called Hayeckian horrors, breach the requirement that power-conferring norms must be fully deliberated in the light of the powers they confer. The courts may, or may not, declare and incorporate such regulatory rules. See Sartorious (1971) for a critique of Hart's distinction between primary and secondary rules.
70. Liberalism requires the 'absence, even prohibition of the use of any legal or governmental recognition of racial, religious, language, or cultural groups as corporate entities with standing in legal or governmental process, and a prohibition of the use of ethnic criteria of any type for discriminatory purposes, or conversely for special or favoured treatment'. M. Gordon quoted by Kymlicka (1992: 183). This is legalistic liberalism. The requirement in the legal Practices that Groups should be absolutely irrelevant does not have the same force in *governmental* activity: officials may legitimately be granted discretion to handle Group problems. In 1995 the Court of Appeal for the 6th Circuit of the USA upheld a Bill which barred protective rights for homosexuals and

lesbians on the ground that no law should either benefit or prohibit 'a group whose identity is defined by subjective characteristics'. Despite this consideration, in May 1996 the Supreme Court upheld the constitutionality of legislation to protect gay rights.

71. Activities are defined as something more than the pursuit of individually articulated targets and goals; they are patterns of conduct in pursuit of publicly recognizable objectives; they frequently involve understood methods of achieving ends.
72. Institutional forms are configurations, involving persons, communications, resources, and procedures, in which particular types of norms are to be recognized. So the Group is the prime location for values, and the Activity is the location for objectives, in addition to regulatory and technical rules: see von Wright (1963: 9). Organizations are the home of objectives and status and disciplinary norms; Communities possess a variety of norms; Society is governed only by legal rules. Practices are animated by their ideas and the ground rules.
73. Compare a group of keen anglers with a group of professional fishermen. Both are engaged in the same Activity; the former will possess the necessary commitment for Group membership, but this will not necessarily be the case among the professionals.
74. On the great variety of norms which may influence a man doing something as basic as catching a deer see Minogue (1978: 23).
75. On the distinction between regulatory and constitutive rules see Searle (1969: 33–42).
76. In some Activities the technical norms merge into Giddens' 'practical consciousness'; there may be ways of doing things successfully which cannot be articulated in the form of rules. See Giddens (1984: xxiii); also Oakeshott (1975: 91); and Hampshire (1960: 193). Some Activities are governed by what I shall call *precepts*. These are standards which are entailed or implicated in the objective of the Activity. They are not just optional technical directives which we can ignore if we choose and still achieve the goal: they are standards which, in a sense, define the Activity. So, for instance, scientific research must be characterized by standards of rigour, rationality, coherence, openness, verifiability, and so forth. On the precepts of enforcement and legal advice Activities see *post*, Ch. 4, p. 115 and fn. 114; and Ch. 5, p. 202.
77. The Practice of institutional theory is a procedure for the creation of normative changes. This distinct institutional form is clearly very different from the wider conceptions of practices as activities informed by constitutive norms. See e.g. Rawls (1955: 24); Runciman (1986); Oakeshott (1975: 55).
78. Practices are the most important element in the 'crucial activity of altering the world by creating new social relationships'; Leach (1982: 177). Luhmann (1985: 167) describes procedures as 'social systems of a special kind which are created for the selection of collectively binding decisions'.
79. We must treat with caution the suggestion that the law provides *facilities* enabling individuals to realize their wishes; Hart (1994: 27). Practices create new opportunities and stimulate wishes which can scarcely be entertained in

their absence; see Porn (1970; 52–3); Searle (1969: 3–42); and Rawls. (1955: 25).

80. It is important to emphasize that Practices are generally related to particular associational forms. That is, they are the norm-creating or norm-applying mechanisms, not of the normative world in general or of some social context, but of a particular association: say, a Community, Society, factory, school, or church. The Practices relate to a particular membership and may clarify the norms which the members create and employ; though the Practices of a Community may not perform this function.
81. The authority to create norms is a very special type of power which can only be understood in its institutional setting. It is a form of power which has been unduly neglected; a serious matter since capacity to participate in a Practice is a rather different sort of power from the ability to make another do what you want.
82. For an account of the fields of economics, law, and politics see Wells (1970).
83. Attempts to characterize a field in teleological terms are nowhere more evident than in discussions of the law—the legal field. See Pound (1922: ch. 3). The law has variously been said to have the end of promoting solidarity, of subjecting conduct to the governance of rules, of protecting rights, of promoting harmony, and of satisfying a maximum of wants with a minimum of friction.

3

The Institutional Theory of Law

To understand the nature of any normative phenomena it is essential to understand the forms of life in which the norms are, in various ways, implicated. For norms do not fully exist as paper formulations or as ideas in the minds of men and women: they exist as they are implicated in the perduring configurations of interaction in social life, i.e. in Societies, Communities, Organizations, and the practical forms of Activities and Practices. Of course norms do not exist only within forms of life. Many important rules and principles govern relationships *between* institutional forms; and some forms only can be understood if we understand how they are shaped by their relationships to other forms.

The existence of norms such as social rules does not call for a particular disposition on the part of individuals; that is, individuals need not necessarily adopt an internal attitude towards them. If particular social norms are seen to exist as an integral part of each form, in which individuals are engaged as members or agents, then it is simply by reason of their involvement in a particular form that its inhering norms will have relevance for them as members or agents. So, whatever may be the attitude of the individual, the norms of a street gang are relevant to a gang-member, just as recipes are relevant to a cook, and army regulations to a soldier, and laws to members of Society. We are caught up, sometimes involuntarily, in many forms of life, and through our involvement with those forms their constitutive and regulatory norms come to have relevance for us, whatever our attitude to the norms may be.[1]

The laws of a Society constitute a very clearly bounded set of norms; as a social phenomenon, the legal field stands out as a very distinctive segment of social life. To examine this phenomenon, and the distinctive language and concepts of lawyers, we need to identify the particular forms of life in which legal norms exist and legal language is generated. The concepts of law cannot be successfully explained without taking account of the institutional bases from which the concepts have emerged.

I: DEMOCRACY

The law which we are attempting to understand is *modern law:* law which exists in the forms of life engendered in modern democratic polities. The fundamental feature of the modernity of the forms of life in which law is generated is that in the evolution of each form, and in the manner in which they are related to other forms, they have been fundamentally influenced, shaped, and animated by the pervasive ideals of democratic legitimacy. Yet understanding of the democratic foundations of our contemporary legal norms and language is, in analytic jurisprudence, limited. It is generally agreed that the law constitutes a pillar of democracy—the rule of law is given pride of place—but it is less well understood that the location of the legal forms of life in a democratic polity determines the structures, the language, and the nature of the norms of contemporary law.[2] The results of this neglect, this failure to appreciate the crucially important democratic underpinnings of modern law, are, I believe, serious.

There is in jurisprudence an orthodoxy which assumes, or emphasizes, the continuity of law, if not the universality of its manifestations: *ubi societas ibi ius.* This orthodoxy gives no hint that modern law is a *qualitatively* different thing from the law of ancient Rome or mediaeval France.[3] For the purposes of institutional theory it is important that our law is seen to be a product of a revolution: that relatively recent democratic revolution in which personal, aristocratic, absolutist, or monarchical forms of government were in many countries displaced by the institutions of government by consent.

In the nature of things, much of the drama of revolution may have been absent from the legal field. If the political revolution has been endlessly advertised and celebrated, the revolutionary character of the changes wrought in the law have been concealed by their gradualness and complexity, by occasional retrograde developments, by the inertia of institutions and language, by the conservatism of lawyers, and so forth.[4] None the less, revolution there has been. This is not a revolution to which a date can be assigned; we can only point to the qualitative differences between the established structures of today and those existing in the past.[5]

So it is a central thesis of institutional theory that our law cannot be understood unless we pay attention to the relationships between contemporary legal forms and all the other forms of life *in a democracy.*[6] At a time when democracy is not a transitory social experiment, or an idealistic aspiration, but an established and enduring condition in which the relationships between the public forms of life can be fully realized, citizens become alert to the appearance of undemocratic tendencies, and acquire a sensitivity about the requirements of democratic legitimacy. It is in the light of the imperatives of democratic legitimacy that we must understand and describe the legal Practices in which law is generated. The ideal forms I shall be describing are those fit for a democratic polity.[7] The legal forms in existence today are of course imperfect; to the extent that they are imperfect they contribute to the legitimacy deficit of modern polities.

For practical reasons it is very important to achieve a sounder understanding of legal authority and political legitimacy than that which is gained from non-institutional approaches. Many observers of contemporary Western society have drawn attention to a widespread, and growing lack of respect for politics and law. The legitimacy deficit—which that disrespect may betoken—is unlikely to be reduced if some of the ambitious developments, institutional and otherwise, actively promoted by statesmen and lawyers, are realized. The failure to appreciate the inroads into legitimacy involved in some of these developments in the legal and political fields is partly attributable to a gross failure to appreciate the proper place of law in a democratic polity. Bad jurisprudence breeds bad politics, and *vice versa*. If our aim is to achieve democratic legitimacy, then the most damaging jurisprudence is that which nurtures law's imperial ambitions.

II: LEGAL PRACTICES: THE GENERATING MATRICES OF MODERN LAW

The forms of life in which legal norms are maintained and legal language generated in a democracy are a set of normative Practices which I shall call *legal Practices.* The generating matrices of our law are the autonomous Practices of the institutional form Society; that is, they are not Practices of the State. The legal field of a Society is not merely a collection of institutional forms all equally involved in the law; its core consists of these adjudicatory Practices by reference to which all the other forms in the legal field must be located.[8] It is their employment within the adjudicatory Practices which gives legal norms their distinctive character, rather than the fact that they form part of a coherent system of norms, or their relationship to official coercive power.[9]

Chapters 4, 5, and 7 analyse the nature of each of the three legal Practices—the penal, civil law, and public law Practices. By way of introduction it may be useful to make some general observations about the nature of all legal Practices, and to consider briefly some of the implications of a jurisprudence which takes such forms as its essential foundation.

To understand the legal Practices it is vital to understand that they cannot be reduced to sets of procedural and substantive rules. Practices are living, on-going forms of life, possessing at some points a physical embodiment as their existence depends on the availability of resources and facilities. Despite the fact that the Practices, as distinct institutional forms, may have to be abstracted from the complicated institutions of a formal system of judicature, they can be objectified as discrete entities with, in the terms of Popper's Third World, a real existence.

The temptation to equate the legal Practices with the institutions identified as courts of law must be resisted.[10] Among the reasons for insisting upon the distinction between courts and legal Practices is the ambiguity of the term 'court'. In addition, while we must certainly recognize that legal Practices exist within the adjudicatory activities of courts of law, in some systems the courts are charged with duties quite different from the legal adjudication of cases, and tribunals which are officially classed as falling outside the court system sometimes constitute part of the legal Practice. Practices differ from courts in that each legal Practice has an inherent, unbounded jurisdiction, whereas the jurisdiction of courts is frequently limited. Furthermore, in contrast to legal systems in which particular courts have authority to deal with penal, civil, and public law issues, each ideal legal Practice has authority to deal with issues arising in only one of these domains.[11]

Legal Practices are here described as adjudicatory Practices in which every normative product (NP) they create—that is, every express determination as to what is to be done about a dispute—must be *justified only by reference to rules.* The participants are empowered only to try questions which can be so determined and justified, that is, with justiciable issues. They will not be confronted with, for instance, conflicts calling for the exercise of academic, technical, political, or administrative judgment. The legal Practice must thus be distinguished from Practices in which decisions are made, perhaps with background reference to fixed standards and rules, but which are substantially justified by reasons other than those supplied by the norms. So legal Practices must be distinguished from Practices concerned with mediation, conciliation, or arbitration in which good reasons rather than rules justify the NPs.

The normative anatomy of each of the legal Practices consists of: (i) its normative products; (ii) the ground rules; (iii) the legal system; and (iv) its animating idea.

(i) Each legal Practice makes possible deliberate changes in the normative world; the changes which the participants in the Practice can make—its *normative products* (NPs)—consist of adjudicatory orders—the judgments—made by judges for punishment, remedy or declaration.

(ii) The *ground rules* of the Practice are primarily the rules governing the procedure to be followed. They set out the variety of steps to be taken and conditions to be satisfied to achieve a valid NP, that is, an NP with Practice validity.

(iii) In possessing ground rules and creating NPs legal Practices are similar to all other normative Practices. They differ from the others in that their NPs must be justified solely by reference to a system of rules. To this end the participants in each legal Practice maintain their own *legal system* —the LS (or plural LSS).[12]

(iv) What I call the *idea* of normative Practices was considered in the previous Chapter. It is in the light of the animating idea of each of the legal Practices that all their distinctive features must be understood. The methodological values of these Practices can be said to be the idea of legal justice. It is to legal justice that the judges in the ideal legal Practice must display a commitment; their sole objective must be to see that legal justice is done. Precisely what does legal justice mean in a democracy?

Over the years legal justice has had a rather bad press.[13] The iconography associated over the centuries with the cardinal virtue of Justitia has left in the popular consciousness an image of neutral detachment, wholly indifferent to the human cost of lawfully justified inequity. Although the contribution of legal justice to the rule of law has been readily admitted, the distance at which legal justice stands from conceptions of substantive social justice have rendered it an easy target for the irony of reformers.[14] Surely, it is said, principles compatible with the injustices and inequalities in society can be credited with little more than the promotion of the formal virtues of clarity, certainty, and order. For jurists such as Kelsen legal justice had no connection at all with justice, being in reality little more than the deontological truism that one should conform to the rules of law; an idea which is present in the very conception of the legal rule.[15]

However else it may be described, legal justice is a character which we ascribe to the decisions and acts resulting from the application of law. We say that legal justice is done if, in the process of adjudication, certain principles governing the application of rules have been complied with by judges.[16]

These principles of rule application in legal adjudication must be distinguished from the principles which, in the legal field of a democratic polity, should govern the wholly distinct Activity of the *enforcement* of rules outside the adjudicatory Practices. That Activity should be characterized by principles such as that the laws must be enforced regularly and consistently, and that—since enforcement Activity includes servicing the penal Practice—all pre-trial activities and procedures must be of a sort which will not prejudice the doing of legal justice in the Court.[17] The character of such principles, which may be called the *precepts of law enforcement,* stems largely from the fact that enforcement Activity is related to the legal Practices in which legal justice is administered. Remove the legal Practices, and we could introduce quite different principles of norm enforcement in a Society, emphasizing for example efficiency, sensitivity towards local feelings, compassion, and the like.

Neither must the principles of rule application be confused with the ground rules of the legal Practice itself, which are designed to secure procedural justice. The ground rules certainly prescribe the conditions in which legal justice may be done, but they are not themselves principles of legal justice. They determine the validity of the NP; they do not necessarily provide the criteria by which we measure whether a legal decision is just.

What then are the principles of legal justice? In earlier times legal justice entailed little more than respect for the rules. The written rules alone decided cases; the legal formulations stood alone as complete justifications. Legal justice involved the legalistic application of the rules *au pied de la lettre.* Legal rules are not guide-lines, but should be treated as strictly exclusionary reasons. Judges, being bound by the laws, must apply them with utter impartiality as the only justice with which they are concerned is that which is promoted by the rules themselves.[18]

In a democratic polity old attitudes are displaced, and there arises a need to amplify, to give a new dimension to the idea of legal justice. The change in emphasis in the idea of the legal Practice is necessary if the legal forms are to conduce to democratic legitimacy. The conception of legal justice which emerges—reflecting fundamental changes in the political context—is more than a refinement or extension of the old idea. The principles of legal justice in the new climate may well run counter to the ancient conception.

In a democracy legal justice has to be reconstructed around the basic principle of *respect for persons under the legal rules.* This requires that, in interpreting and applying the rules, the judges should be committed to showing the greatest respect for persons which the meaning of the established rules will allow. The old respect for the law simpliciter gives place to something quite different.[19] If this democratic principle entails equality before the law—we would scarcely be respecting persons if we did not follow the principle of formal justice and treat like cases like—it also provides the basis for developing criteria, *which will not he expressed in the enacted rules,* upon which the courts can distinguish between unlike cases and identify like cases. In the determination of conflicts between citizens, or between citizens and the State, the principle entails a conception of the person as a carrier of rights which are not just the entitlements of the market economy; and in criminal matters respect for the offender requires the finest distinction between degrees of guilt.

The idea of equality before the law, of the importance of treating like cases alike, may be recognized in pre-democratic conditions as a principle entailed in the impartial application of social rules.[20] However, such a principle is unlikely to be interpreted as an absolute when the power of the state is unquestioned, when aristocratic privilege is part of the order of nature, or where separate courts administer different laws for different classes. In the courts of a democracy the principle is not just treated more seriously, it is taken to the extreme.[21] The ways in which members of Society are to be treated unequally are no longer left to the discretion of magistrates but require specific sub-rules by judges declaring the law and by legislators enacting it. Such absolute equality before the law is a necessary ingredient in the establishment of the legitimate democratic polity. Any general perception of the significance and reality of the idea will require its continuous demonstration as an active principle; justice must be clearly seen to be done.[22]

A: Legal Practices are the sole guarantors of democracy

In the age of the masses in which, despite the rhetoric, the individual may easily be submerged, the principle of respect for persons is of paramount importance. No form of life other than a legal Practice can give this principle authenticity in a democracy; no other form can positively guarantee respect for every individual and achieve the detailed particularity demanded by equality.[23] Forms in which democratic representation is secured in the political process—electoral and legislative Practices which guarantee the individual's right to vote in elections and ensure the representation of all significant communities in political life—do nothing to secure substantial respect for every individual in a Society.[24] Certainly, in no other central form in a democratic polity is this principle of respect for individuals given priority; the State and the executive are concerned with the common good, and the major legislative Practices are not geared to considering individual grievances or protecting individual interests.

Many people might find it hard to accept that entitlement to equal respect and concern is a generally accepted principle by which activity in political and social life should ideally be governed.[25] While respect for persons is a fundamental principle animating the legal Practice, it is often irrelevant in other forms of life. Agents interacting in the various sectors of economic activity are not unprincipled, but this principle has little relevance for them; nor do men and women with commitments to family an friends always operate this principle in their private affairs. With regard to those they do not know or respect, their only concern is to avoid breaches of the law: those who forfeit our respect have no right to anything. The demand for equal respect is a powerful legal principle, appropriate for relationships *between citizens,* that is, between legal persons, but it is at best a contested moral principle in so far as it is claimed to apply to relationships between human beings engaged in private forms of life which are not constituted by the law, and within which the legal point of view is wholly irrelevant.[26]

The legal Practices are not just some of the forms which, in a democracy, are animated by this idea: they are the sole institutional locations in which it has any sort of significance.[27] It is the duty of judges to secure for the individual all his or her legal entitlements against other members of

Society and against the State. As that respect for individuals is a necessary feature of legitimacy, which no other body can secure, it is of central importance that the judges are committed to it and that the ground rules of their legal Practices are geared precisely to this objective.

This then is the animating idea, or the defining characteristic of the ideal legal Practices in a democratic polity. Not only are many of the features of the Practices to be explained by reference to the judges' commitment to this central idea, but also the benign influence which the law exerts upon other forms in the body politic will be proportionate to the degree to which the judges are true to it.[28]

B: The authority of the legal Practices

An absolute commitment to the principle of respect for persons, to the idea that the rules must be fashioned to secure legal justice for all members, confers *inherent* authority upon the participants in the legal Practices. Individual members of Society are unlikely to question the authority of a Practice which has no other end than to secure justice for them. They can recognize the legitimacy or authority of the Practice even though they may condemn as unjust the distribution of goods which results from the legally just application of the established rules. However, they can only be expected to recognize that authority if they have grounds for believing that the judges are not personally responsible for the substantive content of the rules which they apply.

In the penal Practice the citizen's recognition of the authority of the legal Practice depends upon constant demonstration of the judges' impartial concern to treat like cases alike, and to apply the principle of penal parsimony. The virtue of the penal Practice, with its concern for the accused, explains the universal acceptance of the fundamental principle that no one shall be punished except in a court of law—that is, under the principles of legal justice in which respect is shown for the humanity of the accused. In the civil law Practice recourse to the courts is voluntary, and the enforcement of rights optional. The authority of the courts may therefore be said to be reaffirmed by members each time they bring a case. In the public law Practice the court's concern to ensure that the State acts justly towards every individual citizen confers an authority which can scarcely be gainsaid.

So the authority of each legal Practice is not a vestige of the ruler's unlimited power which has been delegated to the courts neither is it a remit from the modern State, nor an authority conferred by the words of a written constitution. It is an inherent authority deriving from a perceived commitment by the judges to the principle of legal justice.

The exclusiveness of the idea

Legal justice, interpreted as respect for persons, will prove to be a jealous master: the judges' commitment to legal justice must be absolute and exclusive. This commitment excludes the possibility of judges claiming authority, by virtue of their participation in the Practice, to entertain any other objective, or to adopt any other ideas as to how the LS norms are to be applied.

For the pursuit of legal justice, the constant will to secure respect for persons under the law, will surely be obstructed if judges seek to reform the law and adopt the idioms of progress, or if they co-operate in the implementation of governmental policies. The pursuit of such objectives is incompatible with the doing of legal justice. The perception that judges are adopting an activist role will deprive citizens of confidence that they will at all times be treated equally under the law. The authority of the legal Practices will be undermined if judges stray beyond the confines of doing legal justice, partly because it entails that justice will not be done for all members of Society, and partly because citizens are aware that the participants in legal Practices are not necessarily qualified to tackle the problems of social reform.

In a Practice animated by an idea that legal justice amounts to little more than respect for rules of law, the potential authority of the participants will be limited only by the definition of what are to count as legal rules. The courts will have actual authority, conferred by the State, to administer the law in particular areas. They may be called upon to interpret the constitution—regarded as the fundamental law—or to fill in the gaps of widely drafted statutes, exercise administrative discretions, offer advisory opinions, and so forth.[29]

The natural jurisdiction of legal Practices in which the participants are committed to legal justice as respect for persons will extend to all areas of activity in which the LS rules impose duties and liabilities, and confer interests and entitlements, upon individuals. Any limitation of their natural authority, any attempt to oust the jurisdiction of the courts, will be strongly resisted by the courts. At the same time the judges' commitment will preclude them from determining any questions not directly involving vested individual rights. Even if the rules are unclear and cry out for authoritative interpretation, the courts will have no inherent authority to confer desirable social or economic rights, or to determine questions about the distribution of power, the relationships between public bodies, or any dispute about conflicts between general public interests.[30]

C: Declaratory Practices

Commitment to respect for individuals under the rules has a formative influence on the legal Practices. It will dominate the shape of these forms of life, dictate many of the requirements of the ground rules, and account for the distinctive character of the norms in the LS.

In particular, a commitment to legal justice confers authority on the judges to declare the law.[31] This is the authority to take a rule formulation which is relevant to a case, let us say a newly enacted rule, and where necessary to transform it into a norm, or set of norms, capable of being used for doing legal justice. In the LS of the Practice every norm, whether enacted or not, must be given sufficient precision and clarity to ensure that all persons can be confident of equal treatment under it. The process of incorporation, by which the judges take the legally relevant norm formulations and give them precision of this sort, defining terms and spelling out any exceptions, must be seen to transform ordinary social rule formulations. Such normative precision is not required for all social rules which are intended to regulate conduct.[32] By this process of transforming the rules and giving them minute detail judges create valid legal norms.

In institutional theory the law is defined as the set of rules for the doing of legal justice. The transformation of the norms under the principles of rule application deriving from the idea of legal justice gives a distinctive character to the laws. The rules declared are not merely those applicable to the instant case; the process of declaration sets out the conditions for the just treatment of all members of Society. The process of incorporating the norms into the LSS of the legal Practices must not be demeaned by describing the declaratory power as a power simply to interpret the rules; under the rules of precedent, it is necessarily a power to interpret and *reformulate* the legal norms. It involves constant, detailed amplification of the laws.

Within a democracy commitment to the principles of justice as respect for persons may be expected to result in an enlargement of their declaratory powers. The justification for exercising wider declaratory powers in such a quest obviates the need for any special conferral of power; there is no hint of arrogation in the declaration of laws in pursuit of legal justice. The growth of administrative law in common law jurisdictions provides a striking example of the process by which the declaratory powers of the courts may be gradually extended. Mandates conferring power on officials have increasingly been scrutinized as courts have gained understanding of and confidence in their inherent authority to enjoin the State to respect the interests of citizens. The doing of legal justice necessarily entails that courts have declaratory authority to transform the rules and make them fit for use in adjudication. The legal Practices of a democratic Society are identified by reference to their declaratory authority as the badge of their commitment to, and their animation by, the principles of legal justice.

D: Mute Practices

Unlike declaratory Practices, mute Practices are animated by an idea of legal justice which I have described as respect for rules. A mute Practice is an adjudicatory Practice in which the NPs can only be justified by the rules, perhaps in the form of a Code which is regarded as a fixed and comprehensive statement of the law. In their determination of cases the judges do not declare the law, they merely reiterate the formulations of the Code. As there is no doctrine of precedent—a necessary feature of a declaratory Practise—the law is wholly unaffected by the adjudication.[33] Each NP will be an independent application of the Code. Such determinations will inevitably require interpretation of the provisions of the Code, but the judges are not committed to any binding principles which will govern their interpretation: there is no principle of respect for persons. As justificatory resources, the formulations of the code are deemed to be entirely adequate, and may acquire the character of a sacred text. So the law, found in the words of the Code itself, consists of formulations existing independently of the Practice.

Given the inevitable gaps and ambiguities of the Code, the judge in a mute Practice, who is unconstrained by the interpretive declarations of other judges, will have very wide discretion. Under that discretion there may be uniform treatment of cases which are unlike, and cases which are alike may be treated differently. The inability of the judges in a mute Practice to elucidate the rules obstructs the single-minded pursuit of equality. In a changing world, members of a Society in which the legal Practices were mute would have an imperfect knowledge of their legal position.

The law applied by the participants in mute Practices consists of prescriptions which exist in the written formulations of the Code. The language—the categories of law—will be created by legislative rather than adjudicative activity. Since they cannot emerge from the exercise of a declaratory power, the only legally recognized entitlements of individuals will be those which are conferred and recognized by the legislators. Such Practices would not generate the language of legal rights.

III: A NEW CONCEPTION OF LAW

In a democracy jurisprudence must be foracentric; any analysis of legal language or account of the nature of legal norms must begin with an understanding of the forms of life—the three legal Practices—in which laws of a Society are generated.[34] These forms, which constitute the focus of the legal field, are declaratory, adjudicatory Practices animated by the idea of legal justice.

The insistence on the democratic foundations of modern law—a view which entails recognizing a discontinuity in the history of law—means that we cannot understand modern law by relying only on assumptions about its general character which may have been appropriate for pre-democratic law. Nevertheless, a number of such anachronistic assumptions and such a conception of law, are still commonly held as unremarkable strands in the orthodoxy of contemporary jurisprudence. If the social sciences have recognized the revolution wrought by the emergence of the market economy, and political science has recognized the break resulting from the democratic revolution, jurisprudence appears to cling to a conception of law which is timeless. An image of law appropriate for pre-democratic Societies and Communities underlies many of the questions posed and answers given; thus questions about authority, about legal validity, about the delimitation of the legal field, and the moral obligation to obey the law are discussed as though the only changes to legal systems since the Roman Republic were contingent changes in the social or political context or climate.

The failure of contemporary jurisprudence to grasp the significance of the historical changes which presaged a new stage of legal history—the era of modern law—is in part a consequence of a non-institutional view of law. Jurists ignore the crucially important, life-giving institutional forms; instead they start by abstracting the legal norms from their matrices and proceed to describe whatever structural features can be discovered in a normative system whose only contact with reality, with institutional facts, is that it is set against a general, undifferentiated *context* of social interaction in a nation state. If laws are enacted by legislatures, enforced by the police, applied by the courts, their existence requires only that they should be validated by other norms or, as the 'living law', be seen to be operative in the interactions of social life.

A: The image of the legal system

The novelty of the institutional approach is illustrated by the fact that institutional theory does not conceive of the laws of a democratic polity as a single system of rules. (I am not here referring to the usage under which a legal system denotes the general institutional background.) In institutional theory the law of a Society is seen to consist of *three* very distinct sets of norms, or systems in a very loose sense, each maintained in its separate legal Practice. Legal norms are defined as those formulations which are incorporated in the LSS of the three distinct Practices, each of which is animated by its own special idea of legal justice and which, in conse quence, generates norms of a different type from those of the other legal Practices. This precludes a conception of a Society's laws as forming a seamless web, or coherent system of uniform rules. It is important to recognize the very real differences between the three legal domains, each of which focuses on a distinct legal Practice. The crucially important relationships between the Practices, the various and subtle interconnections between these discrete forms, do not warrant the assumption that legal norms add up to a unified system.[35]

B: The regulatory function of law

Another set of assumptions which, from the institutional point of view, need to be challenged centre round the picture of the law as a regulatory mechanism.[36] The law is frequently envisaged as providing the normative framework of Society, as the social cement required to give it the necessary cohesion, and as the guarantor of order and stability. From such assumptions it would seem to follow that the purpose of the law must be to maintain order. One strand of this approach is the ready assumption that a Society's constitution, which provides the regulatory framework for political and governmental activity, is inherently a legal structure, that it is Society's most fundamental law. In constitutional, as in all other areas the beginning of wisdom is the differentiation between truly legal norms and what are called laws in the more liberal conceptions of the vulgar jurisprudence of everyday discourse.[37] The ideas accompanying the image of law as a regulatory mechanism—an image embedded in our language and consciousness—are a source of many fallacies and half-truths.

Provided that we do not define law as consisting of the norms of social control, we can recognize that the functions of social control, cohesion, and so forth can be achieved by means of non-legal norms, enforcement, and sanctions. Thus communities may be held together by their shared beliefs and values, their customary norms, and varied and diffuse methods of enforcement; dictatorships may secure social order by repressive measures involving ambiguous commands, and arbitrary enforcement by way of threats of savage, punitive, deterrent action.

Even within democratic Societies it is a commonplace that some areas of social life are best regulated by non-legal norms. The fact that such norms are not illegal does not make them legal. For instance, when questions arise about the distribution of goods or the regulation of Activities, there may be considerable debate about the advantages and disadvantages of adopting either legal or non-legal, i.e. administrative, regimes. Legislators have to choose whether to create legal interests and define legal wrongs; there are many perfectly legitimate non-legal methods of regulation.[38] In some areas which are presently within the legal field and subject to legal regulation there is much to be said for the introduction of non-legal regimes.

Regulatory norms are not *ipso facto* legal norms. There is a merely contingent relationship between legal norms and the regulatory function; our apprehension of that contingency will be lost if we conceive of the legal system as the central means of social control, and we will seriously misdescribe the law.

Of course no one can deny that many of the important regulatory norms in modern Societies are legal. However, they are legal, not because they are important and perform a regulatory function, but because they have been incorporated into the LSS of the legal Practices; in other words, because they have been transformed to meet the needs of justice. The reason why they appear in the LSS of the legal Practices is simply because the seriousness of many regulatory norms is underlined by the imposition of deterrent sanctions for their breach. The central principle of criminal law in a democratic polity is that all norms which prescribe punishments for members of Society are to be applied *only in the legal Practices*. It is the fact that they are required for the doing of legal justice to individuals which ensures that the regulatory norms of democratic polities are legal, rather than the fact that they function as a means of social control.

A natural consequence of the image of law as a regulatory system is the supposition that it is the business of the courts to regulate. However, it is not the duty of the participants in the adjudicatory legal Practices to engage in the regulation of social life. Legal Practices are not organs of government, neither is a system of judicature a department of State. The function of courts of law is to ensure legal justice by applying regulatory and other norms made elsewhere. That many of the norms they apply have a regulatory purpose does not confer on those empowered to apply them to individuals the authority to exercise social control. Yet the tendency to assume that courts should regulate, and that they should *enforce* the social rules, appears to be gathering momentum. There is a widespread belief that this is the function or purpose of the law—a dangerously mistaken perception of the law, and of the authority of legal Practices.

Perceptions of this sort contribute towards inflated ideas about the place of law in a modern Society. Law is dislocated from its peripheral role in the polity as it is urged to become a central pillar of government. In times when the executive is largely preoccupied with the trim of the ship of state in economic waters, and the legislature proves increasingly liberal or careless in its delegation or abdication of law-making powers to other bodies, it is understandable that the courts are increasingly seen as appropriate forums for the making of regulatory decisions.[39]

NOTES

1. This aspect of the internalization of rules is absent from Hart's account (1994: 88–91). Our involvement with others in a particular fonn of life entails a subjection to the norms of that form. It is scarcely necessary to say of officials, who after all are officials only by virtue of their membership of the State Organization, that they accept secondary rules which are constitutive of the State. Their attitudes are irrelevant. It is different for relatively independent aristocrats exercising power under a monarch.
2. On the connection between law and democratic institutions see MacCormick (1982a); Cotterrell (1989: ch. 4). See also Martin (1993: ch. 12). For an exploration of the idea that 'the law of modern democratic societies is a distinctive type of positive law' see Hall (1949: 85–100). Hall notes, pp. 28–9, that legal positivism had its origin in the monarchical state but flourished and gained wide acceptance in the Golden Age of liberalism.
3. The institutional theory of Law is concerned with the forms which develop after the revolution within a democratic polity. The forms of the classical world or mediaeval societies are irrelevant here, as are those characterized as legal by anthropologists studying traditional societies; see e.g. Pospisil (1971).
4. The transformation may have been partly concealed; Allen (1945: 253) describes the conflict between the fictions and the realities of the constitution—especially in relation to the functions of the Crown—as one of the more striking examples of the English faculty for adaptation.
5. The revolution is made up of many interrelated strands; the determination to treat seriously the ancient principle of equality before the law is accompanied by a shift away from the conception of the state as the personal property of the ruler, towards the view that it belongs to the people. Political authority then derives not from the ruling family but from a Society of free and equal agents recognized in law: see Beetham (1991: 128). What we might call a basic ideological shift in Society is possible only if the institutional framework—in which alone democratic principles can be realized—is established. Ackerman (1984) takes the New Deal to have constituted a more recent revolution, involving the rise of what he calls the 'activist state' and entailing a fundamental change in the legal institutional structures of the polity.
6. There can be little dissent from the proposition that democracy is an essentially contested concept. For a typology of contemporary competing versions of what a democracy means see Macpherson (1966: chs. 1–3). In institutional theory a democracy is defined as a polity in which institutional forms guarantee respect for both individuals and Groups, as it is only where these conditions are satisfied that government by consent is possible. Bernard Williams (1994) asks why all modern states profess some conception of

equality: 'The answer seems to be that in the modern world, which has largely rejected mythical or merely traditional sources of authority, only some conception of equal consideration for each citizen can fonn the basis of uncoerced and informed allegiance to a government.'

7. The democratic underpinnings of the transformation of the polity must be stressed. It is not enough to concentrate only on one form, the emergence of the centralizing State. The establishment of civil Society depends upon the emergence of a variety of forms, including the legal Practices and a sovereign legislative Practice: institutions which put the State in its place. The emerg ence of a new form of enforcement Activity governed by the precepts of legality is part of the general process. Weber's celebrated definition of the legal order—see Rheinstein (1954: 51)—'An order will be called legal if it is externally guaranteed by the probability that coercion to bring about con formity or avenge violation will be applied by a staff of people holding themselves ready for that purpose' is wholly inadequate for the under standing of the legal field in a democratic Society.
8. The emphasis on the legal Practices gives to the field a boundary very different from that which results from viewing law as a heterogeneous field of practices, a loose cluster of disparate skills, and a manageable compendium of institutions, mechanisms, and sources of known law for solving disputes, exercising power, or achieving security: Cotterrell (1995: 293). The change in perception of the law from that of a learned profession to that of a trouble shooting business operation inevitably makes the legal fundamentalism of institutional theory appear hopelessly implausible. In present conditions such lack of persuasiveness could be expected of any theory aiming to set out the logic of democratic legitimacy.
9. On the generation of principles of justice in the legal Practice see Mill (1962: 318): 'The greater part of the common maxims have come into use from the practice of the courts of justice which have been led to a more complete recognition and elaboration than was likely to suggest itself to others, of the rules necessary to enable them to fulfil the double function of inflicting punishment where due and awarding to each his right.' In similar vein, MacCormick (1993: 151) describes the law's ability to subject practical ques tions to more narrowly focused forms of argument than are available to unrestrained practical reason as one of the gifts of law to civilization.
10. On the concept of a 'court' see Shapiro (1981); Becker (1970); Raz (1970: 124); Cotterrell (1992: ch. 7). See also Golding (1978: 99) for an analysis of the concept of a 'trial'.
11. Emphasis must be placed on the institutional form, rather than the individuals who participate in it. Within a political culture, '(w)hat is important is not judges as such but almost by analogy with . . . the Queen in Parliament, judges in court . . .' Murphy (1994: 95).
12. The LS of a legal Practice consists of a set of rules, which may be described as institutionalized good reasons for conclusions of legal arguments; see Toul min (1950). In institutional terms the rules are the justifying reasons for the NPs of the Practice; as exclusionary reasons they must completely justify the NP; see penal Practice, *post,* Ch. 4. Legal rules must be placed within the

context of the legal Practice; statutory provisions are generally drafted with an eye to their use in the legal Practice.

13. On legal justice see Ross (1958: ch. 12); Perelman (1963: 11–28); Kelsen (1960: 15); Dowrick (1961: 176–204); MacCormick (1981b: 126); Stein and Shand (1974: 59-83); and Lyons (1993: ch. 2).
14. E.g. Anatole France on the majesty of the law, in Cohen (1950: 91). Legal Justice is commonly identified with legality. Although it is more than mere legality, and although it is defined as respect for persons, legal justice will often be in tension with conceptions of substantive justice. 'Justice is concerned with the content of the rules and too much commitment to procedural integrity may undo substantive justice' Selznick *et al.* (1969: 13–14).
15. Kelsen (1973: 14).
16. Legal justice is called formal justice; informal justice is defined by contrast with formal justice which is official, coercive, bureaucratic, centralized, and professional; see Abel (1982: II 2). Procedural formalism is characterized by passive judges, strict rules of evidence, and the use of legal counsel by both parties; Garth (1982: 184). in formal justice the emphasis is on the reliance upon rules to justify decisions.
17. See Rawls (1973: 235 43) on the importance of the precepts of legality.
18. Dowrick (1961: 184).
19. Although individualism can be traced back to Greek and early Christian origins, the institutional framework in which it is really significant is that of the democratic polity, a modern achievement. For Oakeshott (1933) the emergence of individualism was the pre-eminent event in modern European history. See White (1984: 175): 'The late birth of the idea of a right, which seems to have been unknown to the Greeks and possibly the Romans, as contrasted with what is right, may be partly due to the delayed, but now pronounced, prominence given to the individual.' See also Taylor (1985: 274) on the emergent modern view of persons as free agents, or equal right-bearers. It is the individual's status as a rights-bearer which sustains his or her identity. On the centrality of individualism in democratic thought see Lukes (1973); Sagan (1986); Friedrich (1974: 13–14); and Friedman (1990). Johnson (1992) sets out the fundamental democratic principles: in a democracy only individuals count; they count equally; and they count as agents. These may also be said to be the fundamental principles of the legal Practices committed to respect for persons, for the language of the modern law is the language of rights. However, individualism is not enough; in institutional theory democratic polities must combine respect for individuals, in law, with respect for Groups, in politics.
20. See Mcfarlane (1978) for the view that individualism was established in England in early times, and before the democratic revolution. However, the conditions for the realization of true isonomia—fair and equal treatment for all—call for resources and structures which only became available much later.
21. On the central importance of equality in a democracy see Raphael (1976: 142): 'A notion of equality of some sort must figure in any concept of justice, but it figures most prominently in the democratic concept of justice.' Although lipservice may have been paid to legal justice the penal system of 18th c.

England was chaotic: personal contacts and the discretion of magistrates and noblemen determined who lived and who died: Friedman (1990: 146). See also Hay *et al.* (1979); and Weber (1954: 353) who saw in England a court system and trial procedure which 'amounted until well into the modern age to a denial of justice to the economically weaker groups'. The essence of democratic justice is the seriousness with which rules are treated, which alone ensures that legal judgments can be made consistent.

22. A central pillar of democratic thought and practice is the equality of all members of Society. The principle that human beings are *prima facie* entitled to be treated equally is, for Hart, 'deeply embedded in modern man' (1994: 162). Where the laws are wholly opaque, inequality is consistent with outward respect for the law. However, that equality which is the logical consequence of following legal rules (Perelman 1963: 29–36) may be wholly out of place, as are also the rules, in situations where we require principles to guide us. There is no reason why we should, as Group members, treat people equally; if we do we will denigrate Groups, and fail to understand the identity of individuals as members of Groups.
23. Courts are the only place in which rights are respected and protected; Eisenberg (1988: 9). Equality of persons is an artificial *and entirely legal* conception; it is equality before the law which involves the protection of vested rights. Concern to enhance the well-being of individuals employing the language of equality is a political, not a legal, agenda.
24. Although, in the political field, the principle of equality finds expression in the general ideal of government by all the people—one man, one vote—this is a very limited, almost derisory recognition of equal worth: the processes of legislation are too complex to allow equal input from all individuals; see Raphael (1976: 155).
25. Not surprisingly, doubt has been expressed about the meaning of this *general* equality; see Christie (1982: 41) on the problems raised by Dworkin's 'absolute right to be treated as an equal, that is with equal concern and respect': Dworkin (1977: 31). To suppose that interaction in social life should generally be conducted in the language of rights is to misconstrue the legal principle of equality.
26. As an illustration of the way in which the purely legal principle of equality is pressed into service as a political end see Lukes (1973). His chapter 'Taking Equality and Liberty Seriously' asserts that 'the only way to realise the value of individualism is through a humane form of socialism'. Against this liberal foundationalism it must be stressed that the language and values of the law exist in one plane, and the values of our social life in another.
27. It is emphasized that there are in the democratic polity three legal Practices which are quite distinct forms, each the centre of a different domain. Each Practice operates with a different conception of legal justice.
28. The explanation for the distinctiveness of legal discourse is to be found in the commitment to legal justice. Cotterrell (1995: 51) asserts that there is little that is truly distinctive about the components of legal reasoning and legal analysis. Although the basic techniques of law are the same as those for other disciplines, its materials and concepts are all wholly distinct. We are

insufficiently aware of the borrowing by other discourses from the stock of legal terms and ideas. Jerome Hall (1949: 37) explains the technicality of legal language in terms of the sheer volume of facts, conditions, rules, and cases which can only be given legal significance by using general and common terms: the endless search for the one in many.

29. One reason why judges may refuse to offer advisory opinions is that they have authority only to apply laws when the rights of individuals are involved. They are expert in transforming the laws in order to do justice, not in interpreting general constitutional rules. Such rules call for principles of interpretation quite different from those required to ensure equality under the law.
30. Constitutional courts have a conferred authority; see *post*, Ch. 8.
31. For an account of how common law courts strove to establish that they had sole authority to declare the law of the land see Plucknett (1956: 328–41).
32. Standard maintenance rules: see *post*, p. 120.
33. Courts and Practices must always be distinguished. The legal Practice of a Society may have among its procedures a body of courts—of the greatest importance in dealing with the enormous volume of lesser offences—in which the law is not declared. Their ground rules are geared to the doing of legal justice; they apply laws which are subject to declaration in higher courts in which their NPs are appealable and their procedures are subject to review. Although individually mute, they must be counted as being part of the declaratory Practice. A mute Practice is one in which the application of the law in the courts is not subject to challenge except on grounds of corruption, or breach of natural justice. It is a model which, significantly, cannot be realized in practice, if only because the interpretation of enacted provisions cannot plausibly be said to be unimportant.
34. A non-foracentric approach to law will allow us to perceive the law as a policy instrument of centralized government; see e.g. Cotterrell (1995: 296). Instrumentalism has institutional implications.
35. For a study of various accounts of the normative structure of the legal system see Raz (1970).
36. Radbruch distinguished between law as regulation and law as a system of rights. The latter is the conception of modern democracies in which the regulatory function is incidental; in Eldridge (1971: 190). on regulatory functions in general see Cotterrell (1995: 279).
37. See *post*, Ch. 8 III on the non-legal constitution.
38. The proliferation of regulators and quangos with regulatory functions is an index of awareness of the pressing need to devise new forms of control.
39. Regulatory functions are manifestly undertaken by the European Court of Justice.

4
Criminal Law

Our investigation of the nature of criminal law starts, not with a definition of crime or criminality, but with an attempt to understand the nature of the institutional forms in which it exists. In particular, the character of the legal Practice in which a Society's criminal laws are interpreted and applied is examined. The job of the participants in this Practice is not just to interpret the law, but to order the punishment of members of Society. The character of the criminal law, the very shape and structure of the penal Practice, is determined by the awareness of the importance of, and the difficulties involved in, issuing orders of punishment.[1] The Practice of punishment cannot be understood merely by investigating the instruments and methods of punishment, the provisions of the penal code, the character of its judges, and so forth; it requires before all else an understanding of the very concept of punishment. I therefore attempt to clarify the more important aspects of this concept before examining the nature of the legal Practice in Section II, and the forms related to it in Section III. Some aspects of a theory of punishment are sketched in as the institutional investigation proceeds.

I: PUNISHMENT

A: Punishment in general

A necessity

Punishment is an evil, but a necessary evil. Its necessity is admitted neither by those who believe that, in any society, the existence of a system of punishment requires some moral justifications[2] nor by those who treat such a system as a contingent fact of life, for instance Christians who regard evil as the consequence of the Fall, or liberals who see it as a survival from a barbarous past.

I shall set out, without discussion, the thesis of the necessity of punishment. This maintains that, since we define institutions in terms of normative constraints and coercion, punishment—in its very broadest sense—is conceptually linked to the very possibility of a recognizable social life within associational forms.[3] or, more substantially, that activity involving the use of sanctions to maintain an associational form is essential if such a structure is to survive as a recognizable entity in a changing, competitive world.[4] An even more radical thesis maintains that the phenomenon of normative constraint, inevitably involving punitive elements, is necessary for the emergence of human consciousness.

The thesis of the necessity of punishment has an important place in the institutional analysis offered here. Its starting point is that, although we readily identify harms deliberately inflicted on individuals as evils which we would prefer did not exist, yet as social beings we cannot live without them, and the Society in which we live would not survive without them.[5] Punishment, broadly defined as the deliberate infliction of pain in response to wrong-doing, is more than a contingent fact of life: it is an integral, constitutive element of all human experience and social activity. In the face of the necessary implication of punishments in social life, the critiques of the law which regard the penal system as but one of the tools employed by a dominant class in an oppressive political structure must be seen to be based on a plausible reading of history which, however, fails to take account of institutional realities.

Punishment is an evil: its infliction involves harms suffered by members of an associational form.[6] The suffering is not the pain experienced by the over-sensitive individual; it is suffering which is recognized, and indeed intended, by other members. Accidental harms are never penal: the act of inflicting harm on a member of an associational form by way of punishment is deliberate; the person ordering punishment has an unequivocal intention to harm by way of reprobation.

As an evil, each individual punishment needs to be justified to other members of Society so that the inflictor can avoid blame, and the individual who is punished is deprived of grounds for objection or valid motives for revenge. It must also be emphasized that the justification is not an after-thought to a penal act, but an essential part of it; it may be said to be a criterion for the identification of the penal act. Punishment, a central term in the vocabulary of motives, must be defined by reference to the justification; punishment is defined as a justified act. So we recognize an act as a punishment by referring to the justification given, even if we do not approve of that justification.[7]

For punishment is a response to wrong-doing. The wrong-doing does not merely trigger, but justifies the penal response. So the punitive act is not just a response, it is a proper, justified counter-action. As there is a justificatory element in the response, the punishing agent is responding not just to a harm suffered but to wrong-doing.

The fact that the act to be punished is indeed a wrong is proved by reference to some norm, such as a command, a rule of law, a standard, or a principle.[8] Punishment is appropriate because, let us say: A disobeyed the officer's command; B broke the law; or C behaved disgracefully Then the norm by reference to which the wrong-doing is established will be used to justify the punishment.

So our identification of an act as punitive is conditional upon our recognition of the employment by the inflictor of a norm to justify the harms inflicted. We cannot hope to analyse and understand punishment as a social phenomenon unless we pay attention to the nature of the norms so employed. A great variety of norms may be implicated in acts of punishment; the taboos of a primitive community are wholly different from the sections of a penal Code or the commands of a sergeant-major. We need to pay attention to those differences. So it is simply not enough to say that the standard case of punishment is for the breach of a rule; it is necessary to identify the particular sort of rule which would be invoked to justify standard case punishment.[9] In seeking a general description or definition of punishment, which would embrace the punitive acts of gods, inquisitors, parents, referees, judges, military commanders, etc., the most we can say is that it is a harmful act justified by reference to a norm. Non-standard cases of punishment are best understood by analysing the types of norms which justify them, and the institutional forms in which such norms exist.

Punishment then must be defined in terms of its justifying norms. Proper analysis and understanding of the norms involved in punishment is only possible if we understand the institutional forms in which alone the norms exist. There is nothing simple about norms. They are not merely abstract, general, prescriptive formulations which can be assumed to operate in a general social context. In institutional theory social norms are always the norms of a particular form or institution: of a school, say or a factory, a family, or a Society.

In this Section, although reference is made to punishment generally, attention is concentrated on the norms of a particular associational form: Society. I argue that it is within the associational form, Society, that we must locate the paradigmatic acts of punishment against which all other varieties of penal action can be appraised and understood.[10]

The different sorts of norms used to justify punishments are employed with different degrees and types of justificatory force, as I hope to indicate in the following Section. They are employed in different ways, and do not all function in the same way in practical reasoning. Some norms are vague, and are employed in such a fashion that we can recognize only a small penal element in the harms inflicted, while others are so carefully framed that they allow us to talk of pure punishment. Vague norms may be said only partially to justify the penal acts; it will be necessary to provide reasons for the infliction of the pain in addition to the fact of the breach of a norm. By contrast, carefully framed rules may be said to provide a complete justification for punishment, so that no further reasons need be adduced.[11]

My concern is not with the standard case of punishment, but with the paradigmatic punishment, which I take to be a penal act for which a norm supplies a complete justification. In the paradigm case the justification of a particular punishment must be accepted by other members of the associational form to which the norm belongs. The inflictor need not justify the punishment to all the world, or to the members of other Societies, Communities, or Organizations. The punishment of a member of a Society will be completely justified when no other member of the Society is able to question or challenge its justice. This by no means requires that all members must be happy about it. They may challenge a punitive act on the ground that the justifying norm fails to show proper regard for humanity, common sense, established custom, expedience, policy, expense, and so on: however, they must still allow that these considerations have no connection with the justice of the infliction; that the norm, unsatisfactory as it may be, does indeed completely justify the punishment; that the punishment is legitimate.[12]

Complete justification which renders the punishment unchallengeable is only possible if a pre-existing rule clearly and precisely specifies both offence and sanction. There can be no complete justification for arbitrary or isolated punishment. Part of the complete justification is the fact that like cases have been treated alike. So it is part of the justification for punishing A that B, who previously committed the same offence was similarly punished, and that if C commits the same offence in the future he too will be similarly treated. Ideally, the justifying norm must itself justify every instance of punishment under it, leaving no scope for judicial discretion. Under a vaguely worded norm, though some punishments ordered may be difficult to challenge, many cases will lie on the borderline. Such a norm cannot be said to provide complete justification for punishments under it, for the important question of whether a borderline case should be punished will call for additional reasons to be taken into account, so that the person inflicting the punishment cannot rely on the norm alone.

The norm of a Society which achieves complete justification is a very special sort of penal norm, which has been refined over the centuries, and shaped by complicated political and legal developments. This is not the sort of norm which the wise ruler could, in the light of reason, work out for himself; nor could it be derived from a theory of punishment.

The justifying norm we seek is a legal rule. No other type of norm outside a legal Practice can provide a complete justification of punishment. Complete justification can only be given if the punishment is legally just. The charge of legal centrism which may be levelled against the assertion that the paradigm of the penal norm is a legal rule may be met, in part, by pointing out that we are concerned with punishment for breaches of the rules of the institutional form Society. Punitive activity in other associational forms cannot rely upon the legal Practices of a Society which alone can generate the ideal penal norms.

With respect to punishments inflicted within a Society, my aim is to specify the conditions necessary for the performance of the paradigmatic penal act, i.e. for the act which is purely penal in intention. The conditions for the performance of the purely penal act are to be found within, and only within, a mature legal system. In the light of this specification of the paradigmatic penal act, we can judge which penal acts are impure or ambiguous. For it is obvious that if we simply define the infliction of harm on an individual as 'a punishment' this could be used as a pretext for doing unjustified harm. Harms may be deliberately inflicted in order to achieve objectives which have nothing to do with sanctioning the breach of a norm. In such cases we must recognise that, while the acts may have had a penal element, they were not wholly punitive.

Those who have attempted to specify the conditions necessary to achieve a purely penal objective have experienced great difficulty partly because philosophers have not appreciated the distinctively legal character of an act of pure punishment: the fact that it depends upon the employment of a norm of the sort which only legal Practices can produce.[13] Furthermore, writers who have gone some way towards defining the paradigmatic penal act have either not tried, or have failed to persuade others that pure punishment must entail a complete justification. For it is widely felt that to justify the infliction of punishment on the sole ground that a social norm which promised punishment has been breached is somehow unsatisfactory.[14] The theory of punishment literature provides ample evidence of writers who seize upon objectives such as deterrence or rehabilitation, which are extraneous to the penal, and suggest that they represent something inherent in the penal act, in order to make good the deficit which those writers perceive in the account of pure punishment.[15] This is bad theory, and results in bad legal practice. The purely penal acts of the ideal legal Practice require no further, nor extraneous, justification.

The nature of the ideal penal norm is best illustrated by considering the stages, over a long period of human history, by which it could have emerged.[16]

B: The emergence of the ideal penal norm

Schematic histories have their uses. They are intended, not to provide a chart with which we can unravel the actual processes of change—historical reality is not an affair of stage-by-stage development—but, as gross reconstructions of past processes, to illuminate the origins and currency of a particular world-view. The reconstructed history of penal laws which follows is intended to illustrate the interrelationship of institution, norm, and concept which is crucial to the understanding of criminal law and its links with the quest for justice.

Stage 1: Community norms and punishment

We must begin our history of the ideal penal norm by considering the normative structure of early Communities. In Chapter 2 it was argued that the normative structure of early Communities was complex, that the norms implicated in the way of life of a homogeneous association are very varied in type, and that it is wrong to regard its means of social control as an Activity involving rules.

The present concern is to identify penal acts, and the norms used to justify them, within a Community. We must start by identifying all those acts by which harms are deliberately inflicted upon members—taking care to avoid substituting our notion of what constitutes harm for that which was entertained by the members. We must then distinguish between unprompted, initial harms and what we may call response harms. *Initial harms* are the product of hatred, greed, and the like, whereas *response harms* are—often justified—reactions to acts which are regarded as wrongs. It is useful to differentiate between two types of counteraction involved in response harms.

The first consists of acts in response to the breach of a *general social norm* which is regarded by all members as important for the continued existence of the Community. The breach of such a norm will be seen as threatening the Community and undermining its values. The seriousness of the norm breached is underlined by killing or visiting other harms upon the wrong-doer, or by a demand that the wrong should somehow be righted. The sanctions employed to protect the way of life of the Community in this way may be presented as propitiating the gods, cleansing the association or the wrong-doer, and so forth. No matter how odd the explanations for the infliction of harm might appear to us, they all demonstrate a belief that conformity to the norm is a matter of great importance for the well-being of the Community.

The penal element in such acts is undeniable: the harms constitute a response to the breach of the norm. However, as penal acts or punishments they may well be overdetermined and impure. For the frameworks of belief in which such acts are performed may defy simple penal characterization. The justification is not just that a norm has been breached: it may involve a requirement of propitiation and sacrifice, sometimes imposing no tangible penalty on the wrong-doer. The infliction of harms on members may also be regarded as a form of insurance against future calamities.

The second class of response harms are reactions to purely *personal insult and injury.*[17] The initial unprompted injury is to an individual or family but poses no danger to the Community. Such wrongs are not identified by reference to general norms but are articulated by the victim who will justify his counteraction in terms of requital and retribution.

As Communities may be very familiar with, and tolerant of, private disputes and squabbles, we may question the existence of general norms which prohibit all such personally damaging acts. If we are to find a penal element in this type of response—the infliction of harm, by way of self-help, upon the wrong-doer—we must be able to identify some general norm of conduct which justifies thc response. If we do assert the existence of such a norm, we run the risk of making clear what is vastly unclear, of constructing or imposing a general norm. The reason for the wrong-doing may well have been, not that X has breached a norm to love his neighbour but quite simply that X insulted or injured Y and Y does not like it. Y's claim that he is entitled to satisfaction for the wrong done to him is then entirely subjective.

At first glance we might suppose that where an individual seeks retribution for personal injury, we have a clear instance of penal intention: but are we justified in describing the intention in this way? Certainly we can recognize feelings of vengeance, of wanting to get one's own back However, it is incorrect to suppose that an intention to punish is the same as an intention to wreak vengeance. Punishment involves a common awareness of the seriousness of breaches of social norms, not merely a sense of personal injury. The idea of retribution for harms suffered or wrongs done—with its congeners of revenge, requital, or restitution—provides an insecure basis for identifying the penal act.[18] For many penal acts, defined as responses to breaches of a social norm, do not involve any sense of vengeance, and need not involve any actual harm to individuals which is perceived to warrant vengeance or requital.

Neither should we neglect the fact that the personal affairs of the protagonists may be very complicated. Harms deliberately inflicted may be the latest instalment of a long-running feud or vendetta and the intentions behind the purely tactical moves in these dangerous games may not be purely penal.

It follows that we must exercise caution in ascribing purely penal intentions to the members of early Communities. It is as inappropriate to suppose that we could identify a system of punishment in a Community as it is to suppose that its norms are a set of rules. This is precisely because the norms of early Communities are not of a sort which would, without more, justify punishment.

Although it is inappropriate to ascribe clear penal intentions to the members of early Communities, this does not detract from the fundamental importance of coercive and indeed penal *elements* in the many Activities by which the Community's way of life is maintained and survives. Rather, it is a reminder of the meaning of punishment, and of the fact that the institutional conditions in early Communities do not generally justify describing its coercive activity and norms in terms of crime and punishment.

Stage II: The indifferent State

The next stage in the history of the penal norm is marked by the appearance of a primitive form of State, which I call the indifferent State. This is an Organization possessing military power, which seeks to exercise control over a number of different Communities in a particular territory. The State, personified by a Chief, King, or Ruler, has no particular interest in regulating or administering the daily life of the members of Communities; the Ruler is concerned only to ensure their subjection to his will and the exaction of taxes and tribute. To the extent that the Communities are left undisturbed the lives of their members will continue to be governed by their customary norm structures. The existence of such a State does not entail a Society as its correlative; the forms of association of the subject peoples are Communities.

Within the crude political structure created by the emergence of the indifferent State, the Ruler will issue commands; they will be general commands applying to all subject Communities and their members. In our schematic history these alien commands constitute a new sort of norm, but one whose nature and operation—which may cut across the established rules, practices, and conventions of the Communities—is readily grasped by the members. It is immediately apparent that the commands are seriously intended, and must be obeyed on pain of fearful consequences. All the commands exist and have normative force by virtue of an Activity of enforcement in which, we may suppose, the State's warrior-officials are expert. There is no need for legislative procedures, or adjudicatory Practices in which commands are impartially applied.

There is indubitably a penal element in the enforcement of the Ruler's commands; any breach can lead to what may appropriately be called 'punitive action'. However, the response to wrong-doing or disobedience is marked by the absence of any sort of penal discrimination. If some wrong-doers can be conveniently picked out for punishment, they and their families will be used as examples; and where an individual responsible for an act of disobedience or defiance cannot be found, punitive action may instead be taken against an entire family, village, or Community. The fate of Lidice is the modern exemplar of such punitive action.[19]

In the relationship between an indifferent State and its subjects, much will be implicit. The Ruler's henchmen will be as ready to enforce implicit standards as his express commands. New rules will be discovered and invented in the process of enforcement, and harms will freely be inflicted for innominate offences of which the members ought to have known.[20] The Ruler has no need to promulgate a Code: his medium of government is terror and its norms are found in the universally shared understandings of those who live in subjection and fear.

The indiscriminate punitive response which meets every failure to obey the will of the Ruler has its practical justification in its deterrent effect. The infliction of punitive damage looks to the future rather than the past: those inflicting harms are teaching lessons which will not be forgotten. Every breach affords an opportunity to demonstrate the power of the Ruler and the absoluteness of his commands. The seriousness of the particular norm breached is immaterial, for every breach is an act of defiance. Harms are inflicted to signalize the consequences of disobedience. In this regime the gunman looms large, since the commands of the Ruler depend for their effectiveness upon a state of fear amongst the subject peoples.

We can hardly say that the norms of this regime—the general commands addressed to all subject Communities—adequately justify punishments; rather, they license an enforcement Activity in which the penal element jostles with other intentions and concerns. The norms, no matter how vaguely expressed, may be intended as absolute imperatives, and zealous conformity may be the necessary—but not a sufficient—way to avoid harm. Punitive acts are here politically motivated, intended to support, not a particular rule, but the State itself; they are justified less by reference to the rule breached than by the contempt shown for the State. Such penal action is far from being completely justified by a norm.[21]

Stage III: The centralizing State

Unlike the indifferent State, whose conception of government is the effective subjugation of Communities by terror, the centralizing State takes government seriously; this involves replacing Community norms by general rules applying to all individual members of Society. Only with the emergence of the centralizing State can we identify the institutional form Society.

The artificial general rules of a Society in this stage will be the written commands of a Sovereign, although it may be supposed that some of the general rules began life as Community customs and were adopted by the Sovereign. They are imperatives addressed to all members. Although they are intended seriously, the regulatory rules do not specify the punishments which are to be inflicted for their breach. At most they declare that unspecified punishment will follow upon a breach of the rules; members are adjured to obey the rules 'or else . . .'.

Social rules only exist if they are employed within the enforcement Activity of the Society. There is always the possibility that the commands of the Sovereign will be but paper rules. Since many of the general rules will run counter to the normative expectations of the now subdued Communities, their official enforcement will be necessary.

The rules we are considering here are, in Hart's terminology, primary rules. Hart's view was that primary rules do not logically require a sanction. This would be true if the rules could be said to exist as rules merely because they provided intelligible standards of conduct. However, social rules are not just ideas; to acquire normative force they must be anchored in an enforcement Activity which involves the use of sanctions. There is good sense in the Austinian view that for a command to exist those subject to it must be aware that sanctions will probably be applied for its breach.

Since it takes its governmental responsibilities seriously, we will assume that the State establishes Practices of adjudication. Let us suppose that the central element in the enforcement of the rules is a tribunal in which the breach of the rule is established and the punishment prescribed. The judges presiding over the tribunals are delegates of the Sovereign with unlimited magisterial powers to enforce the laws. The tribunals are thus emphatically part of the enforcement Activity, combining the functions of policing and judging—perhaps in addition to a range of other administrative functions. We may assume that some judges exercise their powers to order punishments wisely, while others are perceived to be arbitrary.

What is the penal element in the work of these tribunals? We will suppose that the judges give reasons for the punishments they order. In one sense the punishments are certainly justified by reference to the promulgated rule. The accused has disobeyed the prohibition or command; he or she is in breach of a duty and must be punished. However the amount or type of punishment inflicted cannot be justified by reference to the rule since the rules are silent on such matters. The accused is deserving of punishment, but we need to look beyond the rule in order to justify the penalty actually ordered. As the rule itself gives no guidance the response to the wrong-doing cannot be purely penal. The harms which judges order to be inflicted must be justified in other terms, as compensation, retribution, deterrence, the cleansing of Society, or economic advantage; in all cases the penalties can be justified as reaffirming the power and majesty of the law. To enthusiastic arbiters, for whom the commands of the Sovereign are sacred, every breach is equally serious because it shows disrespect for the will of the One who Must be Obeyed.

At this stage the Ruler himself does not treat the business of punishment seriously; he is willing to leave punishment to the judges. In a regime where the Ruler shows no interest in punishment, demanding only that his will should be obeyed at all times, the infliction of punishment is unlikely to be characterized by respect for persons. There is as yet no pressing need to treat like cases alike. Punishments are necessary; and arbitrary punishments may prove an effective instrument of government.

The rules of this regime of centralized government cannot provide complete justification for punishment. They operate as a licence to enforcers to punish, not as norms under which judges can do legal justice. The norms of the Ruler may have affinities with the norms which operate in the enforcement Activity of a homogeneous Society governed by a theocratic State in which imperatives derived from a text do not prescribe punishment with the precision required for legal justice.[22]

These rules are imperatives which do not prescribe punishments. This is a feature exhibited by moral rules. Social rules differ from moral rules in that they are enforced; they are necessarily part of an enforcement Activity. Moral rules have no such anchorage; a major objection to demands for the enforcement of morality is that the penalties which would be required would have to be arbitrarily assigned by judges. For the enforcement of morality within a Society to have any legitimacy, the penalties must be prescribed by a democratic legislature, and of course in that process the moral norms would acquire a legal character. Judges who today rightly disclaim authority to impose penalties for an enacted offence when the legislators have failed to do so can hardly claim the power to prescribe the penalties for an unenacted offence.[23]

Stage IV: The enactment of fixed penalties

The next stage in the development of the ideal penal norm also unfolds within a Society subject to a centralizing State, and in which adjudicatory Practices are well established. This stage is initiated by a public demand for justice, by an outcry against the arbitrariness of the penalties which officials have been inflicting in the exercise of their magisterial powers. The Ruler, being left in no doubt about the importance of treating the question of punishment seriously, realizes that governmental responsibilities cannot be discharged by issuing open-ended commands and trusting his delegate magistrates to attend to the details of penal enforcement. A framework of regulatory laws, even one founded on the dictates of natural law, is not sufficient alone to create a just Society. Punishment is clearly too important to be left to the judges.

So the pressing demand for justice is met by the promulgation of a code of laws whose prescriptions leave nothing to judicial discretion, and fix the penalty which will follow automatically when a person is found guilty of an offence. Judicial discretion is eliminated; the rules prescribing fixed penalties are absolute and unconditional. The officials enforcing the law—now mere functionaries—are presented with a comprehensive tariff, and the participants in the adjudicatory Practice are no longer concerned with enforcement Activity.

The penal laws of the Society are no longer simple imperatives addressed to all members; they now define both offence and sanction. The fixing of a penalty will often result in a much clearer definition of the offence for which it is prescribed. The laws are directions to officials, imposing on them a duty—rather than conferring upon them a power—to punish. Each penal rule can be regarded as a promise by the Ruler to Society: the infliction of the penalty fulfils that promise. Alternatively, the prescribed penalty is the exaction of a debt owed by an individual to Society by virtue of the commission of the offence. In the adjudicatory Practice an individual is punished, not because his act was such that he *deserves* punishment of a particular type or amount, but simply because that penalty had been promised for those who break that law.[24]

At this stage the important principle is established that the business of working out the appropriate punishment for each offence is a legislative and not a judicial function; it is a task to be undertaken by those who make the laws, not by those who apply or enforce them. As far as the enforcing officials are concerned, questions of desert, deterrence, and rehabilitation—reasons which might operate to justify a particular punishment—have all been predetermined by the legislator.

The type of norm created in response to the demand for justice constitutes an important advance towards the creation of a just penal system. If impartially applied, fixed-penalty rules ensure a high degree of univocality among the judges. The intention in fixing the penalties, in making them an essential part of the written law, is to ensure that like cases are treated alike. Their embodiment in the written law prescribes the like treatment of like cases—it is not necessary for one judge to find out how others are deciding those cases.

Although we are still a long way from the sort of norms which completely justify punishment, we must recognize that at this stage the penal intention of the judge in ordering punishment is pure. We have passed the stage in which the penal is just one of a variety of intentions behind an order. The judge's concern is now only to establish that the specified offence has been committed. For the rule operates as an exclusionary reason: it provides the only and, it is presumed, the adequate reason for ordering this type and amount of punishment. Any other reasons which might tempt the judge to order a punishment will be superfluous; he or she has no discretion and is under a duty to order the penalty prescribed. In the judicial discretion of the previous stage there were no restrictions on the sort of reasons which could be used to justify the punishment.

So the fixing of penalties is a step of crucial importance, for it is only with the enactment of fixed-penalty rules that the idea of equality before the law can gain currency. Under a system which allows judges unfettered discretion in enforcing imperatives, the inequalities of rank and status could, without challenge or comment, influence the choice of penalties. Where penalties are fixed, all those found guilty of an offence, whatever their social or financial status, must be treated alike. A written law which fixes the penalty to the offence makes any attempt by a judge to differentiate between classes of offenders immediately apparent. The only factors relevant to the ordering of punishment are those relating to the guilt of the accused.

The fact that innumerable ways may be found of avoiding the consequences of the fixed-penalty rule—ways of concealing guilt, or even, if guilt is manifest, of evading trial and punishment—does not detract from the fact that the fixed-penalty norms lay the foundations for the ideal of equality before the law. Henceforth the only legally relevant distinctions between persons are those expressly prescribed by written laws. Immunities and exceptions are to be spelled out by the legislator, not made at the discretion of the functionary judge. Otherwise the law—the command of the Ruler—will not mean what it says.

Furthermore, the promulgation of codes prescribing fixed penalties makes it possible to distinguish between Society's penal rules and all its other general norms. Of course no code will ever be complete; but in subsequent legislative instruments expressing the will of the Ruler the distinction between rules of law and mere exhortations and homily, between the legal and the moral duties of members of Society, can be made by means of the simple test: has a penalty been prescribed for failure to conform?

The logic of compensation—one of the central ideas of the civil law domain—is incompatible with the idea that fixed reparation for a specified type of injury is just. Instead, it dictates that reparation should be commensurate with the loss suffered by the plaintiff The simple tariffs of the earlier codes as to what is due in restitution are inadequate for the more complicated wrongs and losses of a market economy.

So we may suppose that the introduction and enforcement of fixed-penalty rules will gradually establish the boundary between what will eventually become the criminal and the civil law domains, and will differentiate the penal from the civil Practice, perhaps by way of the emergence of new—maybe unofficial—procedures in which plaintiffs privately ask to be given what is their due. In the previous stage, in which imperatives were enforced and judicial discretion was unlimited, the distinction between civil and criminal laws would have been of little consequence. After all, civil wrongs would be treated as wrongs; and, in the orders made to redress them, we would expect to find both penal and restitutionary elements.

So in this stage we may assume the existence of a distinct penal Practice—differentiated from the civil Practice—with established procedures in which safeguards are devised to avoid the wrongful conviction of the innocent. The Practice applying the fixed-penalty rules is, despite its deficit of justice, a legal Practice. Although it lacks full legitimacy, such a Practice is an important staging post on the road to legal justice.

Fixed-penalty rules are promulgated in order to make the infliction of harms in the name of Society more just. If consistently applied, they certainly eliminate the arbitrariness of judges. However, they are far from ideal penal norms, for they do not permit judges to take account of degrees of culpability. The mechanical application which such rules demand results in identical punishments being meted out in what are substantially unlike cases. Legislatively prescribed fixed penalties can be unjust in that they exclude the consideration of factors which members of Society would regard as rendering cases unlike.

Fixed-penalty rules are exceedingly blunt instruments and thus fail to provide adequate justification for the punishments inflicted.[25] Each penal order will, no doubt, be justified by reference to the rule; there will be proof of the commission of the act for which a punishment is prescribed. Yet while such mechanical justification—characterized by an absolute reliance upon the enacted rule—may satisfy the demands of legality, it fails to meet the more stringent requirements of the principle of respect for persons which is legal justice. Rule application is here necessarily unprincipled.

Stage V: Statutory maxima and judicial discretion

In the next stage the centralizing State is so well established that it appears to be part of a natural order, and there exists within Society a penal Practice which is completely differentiated from the civil legal Practice.

If the fixed-penalty rules remain on the statute book their defects can only be remedied by the unilateral action of the judges: that is, by their gradual arrogation of a discretion which allows them to treat the legislatively fixed penalty for a specified offence as a maximum, so that they can punish less serious instances of an offence more leniently than serious cases. Such an arrogation of power, while in no way representing a return to the bad old days in which punishments were ordered arbitrarily, would constitute a considerable increase in judicial power. No longer will judges, as mere functionaries, mechanically apply the law: now they will be actively concerned to see that justice is done in each case.

If in this schematic history the increase in judicial power is presented as an arrogation by the judges it is in order to suggest that the impetus derives from their commitment to legal justice. However, we should remember that this enlargement of judicial power may have been brought about partly by legislators who, aware of the defects of fixed penalties, enacted laws prescribing maximum penalties only. This stage, in which the judges have established, or have had conferred upon them, a discretionary power in the application of enacted rules which prescribe maximum punishments, marks a clear advance from the regime of fixed penalties and no judicial discretion.

We must suppose that in Stage V the enacted rules are applied in a mute Practice—a Practice in which the process of rule application does not in any way alter the written law.[26] Against this background the penal code, unaltered from its enactment, is the law. The formulations of the code exist as norms and acquire their character by virtue of the manner in which they are employed in a mute Practice. In such an institutional anchorage the law consists of norms which are sometimes unclear and operates to confer considerable power on the judges. So a lawyer advising a client will base predictions of the outcome of a particular case on his or her assessment of the personality and attitudes of the judge hearing it.

An enacted rule which specifies the offence and prescribes a maximum penalty, leaving it to the judges' discretion to determine the amount in each case, is not the ideal penal norm. This is because no rule can alone offer a complete justification for the punishment ordered. In justifying a particular penal order, the judge would have to provide reasons in addition to the rule. Although the justifying reasons ought to be generalizable, having equal force in all cases, there can be no guarantee that they will gain uniform acceptance in the Practice. We must accept that some reasons adduced by the judges may be no more than rationalizations. So there is a real possibility of serious anomalies in the penal orders issued by different judges at different times and places for similar offences. Judicial discretion does not conduce to the uniformity of decision-making.[27]

Stage VI: The generation of the ideal penal norm

The final stage sees the emergence of a declaratory Practice committed to legal justice; in such a Practice the participants declare and *reformulate* the legislated maximum-penalty rules as they incorporate them in their LS. In so doing they create norms which will completely justify punishments in Society. Only the briefest of accounts of this norm are given here; a full description of the norm and its institutional location is given in Sections II and III.

The declaratory character of the Practice is a consequence of the participants' commitment to legal justice; their authority to declare the law derives solely from their determination to do legal justice. As the norms of Stage V do not conduce to uniformity in sentencing—like cases will not be treated alike—they fail to do perfect justice. So it will be apparent that, if the demands of univocality and penal parsimony are to be met, both the penal order issued in every case and the rules declared to justify it must have precedential force. The reason behind a particular judgment which prescribes exactly the penalty for a less serious instance of the offence will be generalized. The reason—which should only relate to culpability—will found a sub-rule. Each judge will be bound to follow the properly made NPs of other judges in all like cases. So judicial discretion will slowly be whittled away and the law will appear as a set of sub-rules which judges will declare for each offence. Each sub-rule will fix a penalty appropriate for the degree of culpability in the commission of the offence.

Thus the ideal penal norm—the rule incorporated in the LS of the ideal penal Practice—is the product of the combined efforts of a legislative Practice and a penal legal Practice. The legislators decide upon the necessity of a general rule and prescribe the maximum punishment for its breach, while the judges applying the rule in the ideal penal Practice will reformulate it as a set of sub-rules with the detail and precision required to do legal justice.[28] In the ideal criminal rule the penalty is fixed, and judicial discretion plays a minor role in its application. Only such a rule, ensuring that like cases are treated alike in accordance with the principle of penal parsimony, can provide a complete justification for the punishment.

Judges cannot make ideal rules on their own nor can they take up and transform the deliverances of custom. The making of ideal penal rules depends absolutely upon the fact that the laws to be incorporated in the LS of the Practice have been enacted in a legislative Practice which has democratic credentials, which is the best possible procedure for judging the necessity of penal rules for the Society, and which, importantly, shows respect for the law. Perfect punishment, the pure punishment of wrong-doing in a Society—i.e. for breach of general social rules—is also legally just punishment. It requires something more than the enactment of clear positive laws and their application by impartial judges.

Further, the institutional apparatus needed to generate ideal penal rules requires our recognition that the laws exist, not as an enacted text or code, but as the precise rules declared and maintained in the LS of an ongoing Practice animated by the idea of legal justice. The ideal penal rule could never be found in a static code, no matter how detailed its provisions, because in a changing Society the legislature must constantly monitor and update the LS rules of the penal Practice. At the same time the participants in the penal Practice must be willing to recreate the laws in the interests of penal parsimony and in the light of changing ideas of what is relevant to the question of culpability. In other words, the ideal penal norms are necessarily the creation of forms of life animated by the desire for justice. They cannot be conceived of as existing apart from the legislative and adjudicatory Practices of a democratic polity. The jurisprudence of the criminal law—as for the law of the other domains—must be institutional.

The location of the penal system in a democratic polity, in which legislative and legal Practices have distinctive methodological values, has profound consequences for theory. Foundationalist theories justifying punishment in a democracy should be regarded only as articulating competing positions in the legislative debate. In a democracy punishment can only be justified by a well made norm; that is, a formal compromise, enacted after full deliberation and negotiation.[29] The laws are to be obeyed because they are thus well made, not because they conform to foundationalist criteria, or because disobedience could have a destabilizing effect.[30] The consequences of inflicting particular penalties, and the objectives which their infliction might achieve, neither add to nor detract from the justification provided by democratically agreed, legally applied rules. In the Practice of legislation, however, the participants employ such arguments. Of course in the making of penal laws, in the legislative Practice, we will expect such arguments to be employed; some participants will call for retribution, some will point to the impact of certain provisions on social life; many will declare their views about what punishment should signify or achieve, and so forth. All such arguments are strictly irrelevant in the decision-making of the legal Practice.

The naivety of this point of view is indicative of the extent to which our legislative and adjudicatory Practices fail to conform to the criteria of legitimacy. The recognition of these shortcomings, however, does nothing to enhance theorists' claims that they can provide the necessary foundations for us, nor does it license judicial activism.[31]

II: THE ANATOMY OF THE PENAL PRACTICE

The complete justification of penal acts can only be achieved within a legal Practice. In this Section the anatomy and character of an ideal Practice is described by examining the different classes of norms involved: 1. its idea, 2. the NPs which it creates, 3. the ground-rules which govern its procedure, and 4. the LS rules which are the laws to be applied.

A: The idea of the Practice: respect for persons

The penal Practice can only be understood in the light of its animating idea: the principle that, in applying the penal rules, respect must be shown for all persons equally.[32]

What precisely is the nature of that respect? It is a serious misrepresentation to suggest that the subject of the respect should be conceived of as a bearer of rights; that, in criminal matters, legal justice is a matter of taking citizens' rights seriously. The person to be respected—the accused—is not a bearer of rights but a person, standing under the threat of punishment; a human being, capable of suffering; a creature, vulnerable to feelings of shame, guilt, remorse, anger, loss, hope, and so forth. The respect due to him is a recognition of his humanity, of his vulnerability, not of his capacity to bear rights, nor of the rights he possesses.

It may seem perverse to maintain that in the penal Practice the accused is not a possessor of rights, and that the respect shown to him is not founded on an awareness of his rights. After all one can scarcely move in the world of criminal justice without stumbling over the rights of the accused. Despite their obtrusiveness in discourse about criminal justice, the rights of the defendant are not true rights—which are irrelevant in criminal adjudication—but instances of the enormous class of so-called rights which are no more than the correlatives of duties.[33] In criminal law those duties are set out in the ground rules of the Practice; they are not listed in the catalogue of interests and entitlements possessed by an individual. The ground rules of the penal Practice which impose the duties are part of a different picture; they constitute the elaboration of a conception of justice in an adjudicatory procedure by which a human being is liable to be ordered to be punished. It is because the judges respect that humanity, because they are conscious of the damage to the defendant which punishment can cause, that they prize fairness and articulate their own stringent duties to ensure justice. Whatever rights the defendant may be said to have must therefore be correlatives of duty, deriving from the respect due to them as human beings, rather than as legal persons. The defendant in a criminal case is a very different person from the legal person who litigates in the civil and public law Practices. The latter, after all, may be an artificial person, a bearer of rights without body, soul, or feelings. In criminal law we must conceive of the wrong-doer as a human agent, whose punishment is a necessary evil.

In a democratic polity the central strand of legal justice is the principle of respect for persons; in criminal law this must be understood as respect for individuals as human beings. The idea of the Practice is not to give to each his own, but to treat like cases alike and to ensure in every case that respect is shown for the accused as a human being. To emphasize rights may well be incompatible with the administration of criminal justice, for the safeguards embodied in the ground rules are intended to ensure that penal justice is done, not that rights are protected. The doing of legal justice by the application of Society's laws depends, it must be stressed, absolutely upon the establishment of a penal Practice. Perfect justice will be better promoted by improving institutional design—in the light of an understanding of the ideal forms of adjudication—rather than by the preaching the gospel of human rights. In the domain of criminal law the road to the *Rechtsstaat is* not paved with rights.

I have called the idea to which the participants are committed the animating idea. This element cannot be left out of any description of the law, because the demand for a complete justification of punishment—the aspiration to achieve a legal justice which involves principles of equality and penal parsimony—has a crucial impact, not on the content of the laws, but on their very character as legal norms. How can we explain the distinctive character of legal norms other than as the result of the age-long determination by judges, in applying the rules, to punish justly? A Practice in which primary rules were identified and applied by reference to secondary rules which were *not* framed according to the dictates of legal justice would have norms quite different from those of the criminal law with which we are familiar. For, as our schematic history makes clear, the legal norm is more than a legislative utterance, an independent imperative, or a sovereign's command. It is an enacted rule transformed by its application in adjudicatory processes dominated by the idea of legal justice. There is a lack of discrimination—and of explanatory power—in a positivism which fails to accord justice its rightful place in the business of punishing members of Society.

Commitment to legal justice, the essential feature of the legal Practice, is overlooked by those who treat the process by which rules are applied in the penal Practice as a matter of method or technique. That application is principled, involving something more than the expertise of legality; and its governing ideas surpass those commonly associated with 'the due process of law'.

Of course the actual penal Practice of any Society will, for a variety of reasons, never attain the ideal. Nevertheless, if we are to recognize a particular Practice as having a legal character, we must be able to recognize an aspiration on the part of the participants—a 'constant will'—to attain the ideal of justice. The ideal is unattainable: proximity to the ideal will vary from one Society's criminal system to another.

Only by reference to the ideal of legal justice can we analyse the nature of the norms involved in the legal Practice—the NPs, the ground rules, and the LS rules—and set out the requirements which these norms must satisfy, and understand the nature of judicial authority.

B: The normative product of the Practice

The normative product (or NP) of the penal Practice is an *order to punish.* It is something more than a determination of the guilt of the accused, as the Practice is more than an investigatory or deliberative agency. All aspects of the Practice must be understood in the light of its objective to punish, and to do so justly.[34]

The orders are penal; they command the imposition of physical harms or restraints, or normative disadvantages, upon the offender. They are intended to limit the offender's freedom, or to cause loss or pain to an individual.[35] The different types of punishment that may be ordered are those prescribed by the legislature. As the principles of legal justice give little guidance as to the type of harms which it is proper to inflict it can be no part of the judge's task to make the punishment fit the crime except insofar as he or she must choose between the various prescribed penalties.[36] What is to be regarded as appropriate punishment is clearly a question for the legislature—a question for positive law. The law's respect for persons may include in the range of prescribed harms some which we might personally regard as cruel or barbaric.

The orders are issued either to officials to inflict penalties or to the offender directly. An order to an official—to imprison, to hang, or to send to the galleys—gives rise to an organizational duty. Breach of that duty will be a matter for the organization; it is in no way co-ordinate with the duty breached by the offender.[37]

Orders issued to offenders directly will invariably be overseen by officials. They are either positive or negative: to pay a fine, undertake community work, observe a curfew, or stay within a prescribed place. Orders issued to offenders differ from orders in civil litigation, in that penal orders create a *new* obligation, expressed to be the punishment for an offence, whereas the civil order is intended to satisfy an *existing* (if often inchoate) duty arising from the injury done to the plaintiff.

Since the punishment ordered is not supervised directly by the judges, orders to either officials or the offender must prescribe exactly the type and amount of punishment, leaving no discretion to the official, nor doubt in the mind of the offender.[38]

The NPs are orders to punish at some future time. The NP of the penal Practice is not designed to ratify or justify past punishments, to indemnify or exculpate; it is intended to justify the punishment to be executed. We have no difficulty in distinguishing legal justice from Jedburgh justice, which proverbially involved hanging first and trying later.[39] We may suspect that this principle is infringed in cases where individuals are held in detention on remand and, upon conviction, are informed that the time spent in detention before trial will be taken into account in prescribing punishment.

An NP is not a memorandum written by the participants to themselves, but a formal statement commanding others to do something. It is an order to punish, not the punishment itself. Responsibility for executing the orders is imposed on officials. The electric chair, thumb-screws, canes, or gallows do not lie to the judge's hand. The image above the entrance to the court must be that of Justicia, not Castigatio.[40]

The NPs are orders of punishment, not orders of law enforcement. The participants have no authority to direct enforcement agencies to clamp down on certain forms of crime, or to attempt to assist them in their efforts; the judges' authority, deriving from their commitment to justice, is solely to order the punishment of criminals. So the penal Practice should not be regarded as part of a Society's enforcement Activity; it is often erroneously supposed that it is the function of the courts to *enforce* the laws. Judges *apply* the laws, using them as complete justifications for the punishments they order. The theory that punishment is to be justified by reference to, or proof of, its deterrent effect would place the penal Practice squarely within the Activity of enforcement.[41]

Although NPs are particular orders, they nevertheless contribute to, or recreate, the detailed LS rules. The orders of punishment issued by the participants may be said to reconstitute the sanction clauses of the LS rules. In prescribing an exact penalty for a particular offence the NP is either a new precedent, or it is controlled—i.e. bound—by the order made in a similar previous case. In the penal Practice the NPs do not create a rule by accumulating a number of cases for which the same punishments were prescribed: participants do not construct a rule by following a significant trend in the exercise of a discretion.

Ideally every NP would specify the punishment to be ordered for each offence, no matter how inferior the court imposing it. The fact that courts of summary jurisdiction do not set precedents may lead us to characterize their procedure as being less legal than that of the higher courts. The relatively minor character of the offences and punishments with which they deal allow the participants to trade off the demands for legal justice—with its notorious expense and delay—against speed and economy; however, that trade-off must be accompanied by adequate opportunities for defendants to appeal against conviction.[42]

The particular commands which the NPs constitute are not general rules but, if justice is to be done, they must be justified by reference to the LS rules which the judges recursively reconstitute. It is this feature which distinguishes the orders of a judge from those of an official, and from the NPs of legislators. In a court of law the justifying rule will ideally accompany the order, as a necessary part of the NP itself. For the NP is not just an order: it is a *justified order.* So it is the duty of the judge in a declaratory Practice to formulate the justifying rules in every case. The performance of this duty manifests the participants' commitment to legal justice.[43]

The order is justified by rules, not by reasons. However, if the order in a particular case constitutes a precedent, prescribing, in the interests of penal parsimony, a lesser punishment for an offence—because some hitherto unregarded circumstance is now judged to be relevant to the description of the act done—that will have to be spelt out as the sole reason for the variation; and in spelling it out the judge will redefine the offence clause of the LS rule. The emphasis must be on maintaining rules which exclude the exercise of discretion, i.e. of a discretion allowing penal orders to be justified by reference to reasons which are not relevant to, and do not affect the nature of, the act done.

The denial of judicial discretion, the exclusion of reasons and the reliance upon rules, makes the well made NP of a penal Practice the paradigm of penal intent.[44] The rule excludes the imposition of harm upon an individual for any other reason—for example to promote the public good, safeguard society, raise revenue, deter others, satisfy feelings of vengance, or put the offender out of circulation.[45] As the LS rule provides complete justification for inflicting the harm which the order prescribes, the NP is purely penal.

The penal Practice is not a legislative Practice; its ground rules are not intended to enact general rules for Society; each NP is a particular order, not a general rule. Nevertheless, in creating an NP judges must inevitably restate or reformulate the rules; thus they make new law. Their authority to make law derives from the imperative that they must completely justify their orders by reference to rules. They must spell out the rules which they refine to satisfy the demands of penal parsimony dictated by the principle of respect for persons.

Like the NPs of all normative Practices, orders of the ideal penal Practice are either *valid* or invalid. A penal order is valid if (a) the ground rules of the Practice have been complied with, and (b) the order is justified by the existing LS rules. The validity of the order is not determined by the extent to which it conforms to criteria of social justice, morality, or utility.[46]

I have said that the validity of an NP should be judged partly by its conformity to the ground rules; it is worth noting that this Practice validity of norms is distinguishable from the notion of the validity of a rule of law—a character determined by proof of the incorporation of the rule within the LS of a legal Practice. So a rule may be the NP of a legislative Practice and, if enacted in conformity with the ground rules of that Practice, it will also have Practice validity. On the other hand, if such a rule was not incorporated in the LS of the legal Practice, for whatever reason, it would not be a valid law.

Legal justice requires that there must be provision within the Practice for an appeal against an order, to allow individuals to challenge its validity. This requires some delay between the making of the order and its execution. That opportunity for legal challenge is obviously necessary because judges are not infallible and an executed order may inflict irreversible or uncompensable harm. A Practice committed to legal justice must take very seriously the possibility of inadvertent punishment of the innocent.[47]

The designation of an order as valid or invalid is given particular weight when an appeals procedure is established to determine finally the questions of whether the ground rules were obeyed, and the LS rules correctly applied. We might say that without an appeals procedure the question of the validity of an order would be to some extent academic. Certainly, any decision to undo a wrong or improper order could not legally determine validity, as it would have to be taken outside the Practice; the validity of a penal order can only be determined within the legal Practice.[48]

Quite apart from its validity or otherwise, the legal penal order is *authoritative*. It is authoritative because judges make their orders to officials, or know that officials will oversee their execution. Orders are authoritative because they will be carried out. The authority of an order does not derive from its validity, from the fact that it is legally unchallengeable, but from the judges' relationship to the officers of the organizational structure of the State. To consider the authority of orders we must switch our attention from the autonomous legal Practice to the organizational structure within which we might say that the judges occupy a superior position.[49]

The authority of the judges' orders, the fact that they will be executed, is an essential precondition for a legal Practice. The very legality of the Practice would be subverted if the judges' NPs lacked normative force and their orders were not consistently executed. The scrupulous care and concern for penal parsimony which characterizes the administration of legal justice would be difficult to maintain in a toothless Practice which lacked a trustworthy and effective machinery for the execution of judicial orders.

Validity is quite different from the authority of the order, and judges can therefore issue invalid but authoritative orders of punishment.[50] An order which is invalid—either because it fails to conform to the ground rules, or because the LS rules were wrongly applied—will, unless it is legally challenged by way of an appeal, be perfectly authoritative: it will be executed right or wrong.

C: The ground rules

The ground rules which regulate and structure the Practice enable participants to create just orders of punishment. They constitute the very core of the Practice, making it what it is: a rule-applying form.[51]

Rule application in a legal Practice is formal, by contrast with informal penal Practices such as Cadi courts, committees of public safety or revolutionary courts. However, the legal Practice is not just a formal rule-applying procedure; its ground rules are designed to secure legally just

NPs. The presence of the ground rules in the ideal legal Practice—indeed, of many actual Practice—would be difficult to understand without reference to the claims of justice. The formality has a moral purpose: a trial is not a mere ritual, the steps of a stately dance before an execution; nor is it designed to satisfy the demands of administrative convenience, or to project the majesty of the law. With their manifold safeguards against error and deceit, the ground rules signalize awareness of the seriousness of punishment and the imperatives of legal justice.

Legal justice cannot be administered by any well intentioned arbiter armed with a penal code and a manual of procedure. Legal justice is *essentially* institutional: it is only possible within the settled form of a legal Practice. This institutional form is irreducible; it cannot be represented as a mere set of procedural rules. Justice can only be achieved within an ongoing Practice which is inevitably structured and informed by a great variety of norms. So the ground rules must be seen, not as the fixed procedural rules of courts in a system of judicature devised by the executive, but as the norms of a continuously changing form of life.[52]

As they regulate and structure a living Practice, the ground rules consist of a great variety of sorts of norms. They are the products of experience, of continuing efforts to do legal justice in a particular set of local circumstances. The importance of experience in the gradual building up of the best ground rules for just punishment requires emphasis. For the ground rules of actual Practices cannot be rationally laid down in advance; they are fashioned to deal with the problems which litigation throws up. Also, and importantly, they are not all created by the participants; they are products of both deliberate institution and evolution. Many were created either when courts were first instituted in a Society or in subsequent legislative enactments.

Now, although judges do have authority to reform the ground rules of their legal Practice to ensure that they meet the needs of justice, problems attach to the exercise of this power.[53] In the first place, judges may be powerless to overturn legislated ground rules which stand in the way of justice. Also, given the normative force of established rules of their own devising, it may be impossible for a single judge, or even for a group of them, to initiate their reform. So, over the course of time, accretions to the ground rules may produce a body of procedural rules of enormous complexity and technicality, some of which have lost their original function. In such circumstances legislative intervention will clearly be required to remove the log-jam.

The role of the legislature in such fundamental matters as the reform of the penal Practice is a salutary reminder that legal Practices are not self-sustaining islands of legality. They are necessarily dependent upon other forms, and can only flourish within a constitution whose several parts are alive to the demands of justice. So, although it is imperative to treat the Practice as a discrete, autonomous form of life, it is equally important to stress its institutional connections.

There can be no doubt about the normative force of ground rules.[54] In a legal Practice that force derives internally from the commitment of the participants to the demands of legal justice, and externally from demands by members of Society that justice be done. A public outcry about a miscarriage of justice an be profoundly damaging. Although the knowledge that an appeal court can declare an order invalid might itself appear to encourage participants to conform to the ground rules, it is not the nullity of the order but the sense of having acted unjustly which provides the primary underlying sanction. For men of good will the sanction underlying the ground rules will be the cries of those unjustly punished.

The ground rules lay down the procedures which must be followed and the conditions which must be satisfied to create a valid NP. If questioned the validity of a NP will be determined by the appeal court; the appeal court thereby not only restates the LS rules, but also reaffirms the ground rules. The informally created judgments of, say, a Committee of Public Safety are neither valid nor invalid: they are not legal judgments to be appraised by reference to legal justice, but decisions—expeditiously made—to be judged by reference to moral or political standards.

Not all ground rules will prescribe conditions of validity for the NPs; nor will all breaches of procedural rules result in a declaration of the invalidity of the NP by the appeal court. Although the norms are manifestly of different degrees of importance, little useful purpose would be served in distinguishing between rules whose breach leads automatically to invalidity and the others. For there are many ways in which rules may be broken, and the concern of the appeal court must be to judge whether a particular breach was of a sort to deny justice to the accused. Only a misplaced legalism would endow a rule with such importance that *any* breach would automatically render the NP invalid.

The idea of legal justice has as a foundational maxim 'treat like cases alike'.[55] In itself the principle does not require that distinctive legal respect for persons, that penal parsimony, which the ground rules must promote—although it is obviously a necessary condition that, if respect is to be shown, it must be equal respect for all. In the ideal Practice the ground rules are intended to secure univocality, so that if the same case were adjudicated upon at different times, in different places, by different participants, then each participant judge would issue the same order of punishment, the one right legal answer. No actual Practice could hope to secure perfect univocality, but the aim must be there. It will not be achieved by Herculean efforts to establish the principles upon which the LS rules should be based—in criminal law the rules never run out—but only by maintaining the ground rules of a Practice which are devised to secure uniformity of treatment and guard against error.

Questions are sometimes raised about the status of the ground rules of the Practice, and difficulty still attends their accommodation within jurisprudential frameworks.[56] Are they laws or not? That they are legal norms of some sort seems to be undeniable, even if they are very different from criminal laws, the prohibitions of everyday life. If we would free ourselves from the scientific reductionism which Bentham attempted to stamp upon jurisprudence, in his attempt to make laws intelligible and clear by treating them as systems of uniform commands or imperatives, then we need to do more than acknowledge the variety of legal norms. We need to appreciate the vast range of norms in the legal field as they operate within, and between, the institutional forms. Only then can we appreciate their nature and recognize the pointlessness of questioning the status of the ground rules.

Institutional theory is realistic: the ground rules of an actual Practice must be those which actually operate on the minds and influence the conduct of the participants; they are never paper rules.

The ground rules of actual Practices will vary from Society to Society, but there are certain types of rules which must be present in a legal Practice. For justice to be done, every legal Practice must possess three classes of ground rules:

(i) basic procedural rules;
(ii) appeals procedures; and
(iii) norms of incorporation.

Basic procedural rules

The penal Practice consists of settled procedures which are designed as the safest way of establishing the guilt of the accused and the justest way of imposing the penalty. The procedures must therefore conform to principles of procedural justice of a very special sort, since in addition to being rational decision-making procedures they must also ensure that respect is shown for the individual accused.

The basic procedural rules govern *the trial,* the actual process of litigation. A trial is a drama with a beginning—'Silence in court!'—a middle—the complex process of adjudication—and an end—the issuing of the penal order. The Practice itself must be distinguished from the enforcement Activity which includes all pre-trial processes and negotiations. Although the norms governing pre-trial activity are not rules of the Practice, it is imperative that they also show respect for the integrity of the legal Practice.[57] A legal Practice serviced by an enforcement Activity without respect for law, in which enforcement was partial and arbitrary, would scarcely qualify as a legitimate Practice in which the NPs could be completely justified. The participants in the legal Practice must be able to assume that enforcers, as well as legislators, respect the law. Enforcement Activity and the penal Practice are mutually dependent; they have a symbiotic relationship.

Within the single penal Practice of a Society we need not expect to find just one procedure. Procedures in courts of limited jurisdictions may well differ from those of courts with unlimited powers; and those of a court of appeal will differ from both. However, the procedures in every court must satisfy the basic requirements of legal justice.

Although it is not possible to set out the precise rules common to all legal Practices, we can indicate what they must try to achieve. The rules must be framed to enable the facts to be established, and to exclude evidence of matters not relevant to the charge but which might influence the judgment of guilt. They must allow for the proper representation of the accused and for the fullest examination of conflicting evidence, and they must ensure high standards of judicial competence and impartiality.[58] They will also prescribe such matters as the order in which the trial must proceed, the roles of the various persons involved, and the authority of the judge to control the proceedings; and there must be rules compelling the attendance of the accused, witnesses, jurors, counsel, and so forth.

There are further general requirements to ensure that legal justice is done in all cases, such as that the Practice must be open and public and that every NP must be recorded. Such requirements may not be directly related to the validity of a particular NP, but they are important because they maintain the conditions in which the legitimacy of the Practice can be established. As norms governing the activity of the participants, these too will be counted among the ground rules of the Practice.

Whether the procedures should be adversarial or inquisitorial may appear to be a matter of choice; both have good claims to be suitable verification procedures. However, despite its limitations, the adversarial procedure has features which make it the natural and the only choice for a declaratory Practice. For inquisitorial procedures, whatever advantages they may have in finding the facts are ill suited to the tasks of rule-finding, rule-testing and reformulation which are crucially important functions of the participants in a declaratory legal Practice.[59] Adversarial procedures provide the opportunity to test the soundness of reasons adduced to excuse an act in order to determine whether they are of sufficient weight to require a redefinition of the offence. It is important to note that the adversaries do not just contest facts: they contest the law. Inquisitorial procedures—suited to a jurisprudence which conceives of the law as a text which will be unaffected by the process of rule-application—are found in Practices which do not engage in the continuous recursive restatement of the law.

The procedural ground rules may be defective in a number of ways, failing to conform to the dictates of reason or justice. A healthy penal Practice requires constant critical review and reform of specific procedures to ensure that they serve the ends of justice.[60] It is one of the important functions of the appeal court to ensure that the ground rules of the lower courts are observed, to reaffirm and restate them in every case, and, when it is necessary and possible, to reform them.

Procedures for appeal

The ideal Practice includes procedures enabling a defendant to appeal against a judgment.[61] Such appeal procedures are necessary for legal justice. An appeal is based on a claim that legal justice has not been done, that the NP is not justified by the legal rules, either because the procedures have not been correctly followed, or because the substantive law has been wrongly applied.

The legal Practice of a Society, it is emphasized, consists of all the procedures of litigation including those of appeal. Lower courts with their own procedures are linked by appeal procedures to higher courts. The appeal court is identified by its authority to pronounce upon the validity of the NP of the lower courts. There are many different courts, but only one legal penal Practice.[62] Within a Society different tiers of courts may employ different procedural rules, but they are all part of the same Practice insofar as they employ the same LS rules to justify their NPs. In checking the validity of an NP, ensuring that the ground rules of the courts of first instance are observed, the appeal courts contribute to the normative force of those rules.

Appellate judges do not just confirm or nullify the orders of the lower court they also clarify and reformulate the legal rules. Outside the Practice non-legal methods may be established by which miscarriages of justice can be rectified: pardons may be granted, remission awarded, compensation paid, and so forth. The exercise of such powers by the executive does nothing to refine the legal rules.

The undoubted pre-eminence of appeal courts in the restatement of the law must not blind us to the law-affirming and law-making authority of the lower courts. For the authority of the lower courts derives from the same source as that of the appeal courts: from the commitment of the judges to the idea of legal justlce.[63]

Norms of rule incorporation

Obviously the just application of rules depends upon the judges being able to identify the norms which can confidently be applied as the rules of law. Among the most important of the ground rules of the legal Practice are the norms which regulate the complex process by which the LS rules of the Practice are identified, declared, and maintained; in other words, the norms of incorporation.

One of the obscuring ideas of non-institutional jurisprudence is that a valid law should be identified by reference to a rule, or rules, of recognition. That approach fails to do justice to the complexity of the process by which judges incorporate LS rules. The norms which govern this process cannot be presented as a simple set of rules; they are norms of a great variety of types.[64]

The question of how judges should incorporate enacted laws involves questions of legitimacy; it has implications for both the authority of the judges and the relationship between the legal and legislative Practices. We will underestimate the importance of this complex process if we suppose that the judge's task of applying legislated rules can be described as little more than interpreting a text.

A mute Practice would require few norms of incorporation; its participants would require no more than an elementary rule of recognition, perhaps with some guidance as to how gaps and obscurities in the text are to be handled. Only in a declaratory Practice, in which the judges have authority to restate the law, are an array of detailed norms of incorporation required. The norms governing this process, not all of which can be categorized as procedural rules, will to a great extent have been created by the participants themselves.

The complexity of the incorporation process is worthy of note. The judges require guidance as to which legislative Practices are to be recognized; which of those legislative Practices are superior, and which inferior; and precisely which products of those Practices are valid. They will require canons of interpretation prescribing how to interpret ambiguous or vague provisions; they will need to know how new statutory provisions are to be accommodated within existing rules of the LS, and how repealing provisions are to operate. Guidelines will be needed about the extent to which gaps in the written laws can be filled in, and the treatment of inconsistent provisions. The participants' treatment of legislative provisions will send a clear signal to the legislators as to what is required from them in the way of respect for law.

With regard to any rules which are not legislative in origin judges must operate with an enormous number of principles and rules which make up the doctrine of precedent. In the penal Practice such rules will be required in cases involving enacted laws which have already been interpreted.

The *raison d'etre* of the norms of incorporation is to be found in the commitment to justice. In an ideal Practice the legislative formulations must be strictly interpreted; they must be limited in their operation so that judges punish no more than is absolutely necessary. The norms of incorporation—to be counted as ground rules of the Practice—must be framed in the light of the principles of penal parsimony, and designed to ensure that the rules incorporated represent the best and most recent decisions of the legislature.

A powerful influence on the norms of incorporation is the concern for the legitimacy of the Practice. In the ideal Practice it is clear that the judges have no authority to legislate, either to make new offences or to abolish old ones.[65] They can punish only for breach of an existing rule, and they cannot refuse to punish because they consider that a penal law is no longer necessary. Their NPs may be justified only by reference to clear and precise LS rules: principles play no part in the LS. However, any account of the norms governing the process of incorporation must consider understandings and principles as well as rules.

The norms of incorporation of the penal Practice are different from those of both the civil Practice and the public law Practice. The differences will be obscured by the suggestion that a legal system has only one rule of recognition which all officials employ.

D: The LS rules

We must begin with both a fanfare and a warning: a fanfare for the advent of perfect penal norms which give complete justification for punishment, and a warning that such ideal rules are unlikely to be consistently generated or applied within actual Practices.

The LS rules are the rules by which the participants in the penal Practice justify their orders of punishment. To be capable of providing a complete justification for those orders, all the LS rules must be legislative in origin (see *post*, p. 121).[66] The rules are enacted by legislators who judge them to be necessary for their Society. Although LS rules must originate as enacted rules, the LS does not consist only of these statutory formulations: as I suggested earlier, it is the job of the courts, in the process of incorporation, to transform them into ideal penal rules.

Unlike the ground rules of the Practice, the LS rules form a completely uniform set, all having the same structure. Every LS rule is composed of an offence clause and a sanction clause.

The *offence clause is* a precise act-description which specifies the offence. The LS rules define unlawful acts: they do not prescribe the duties of members of Society. That is, they do not declare what members ought to do, but describe *completed acts* which ought not to have been done. The acts defined will be voluntary acts, and are described in terms of the circumstances, intentions, and consequences attending them.

The offence clause defines a wrongful act, not a state of affairs, nor a characteristic which can be predicated of a person. Members of Society are not to be punished for their beliefs, their race or sex, or their membership of a Group; they are to be punished for something they have done. Punishment is a response to wrong-doing.[67]

The *sanction clause* defines the penalty to be imposed on those who commit the prohibited act. Unlike the raw enacted rule, the transformed LS rule will express the penalty, not as a possible maximum, but as a fixed amount to be imposed for the commission of the offence defined in its offence clause.

The two clauses form one single LS rule. The ideal rule will read: for the act x the fixed penalty is y. It is commonly thought, and not without reason, that criminal laws of the legal system are of two sorts, one defining offences, and the other prescribing the penalties.[68] On this view legal wrongs can be defined in isolation from legal penalties, the penal clause of the rule being no more than a postscript or addendum. Here, however, a legal offence is defined as a wrong which is defined and for which a specified penalty is prescribed in one and the same rule. The precise penalty is not left to be decided after the offence has been proved. The perfect legal norm leaves no judicial discretion as to the punishment to be ordered. Natural lawyers may claim to be able to spell out our social duties, but if they are prepared to leave punishment to positive law they cannot be said to be identifying legal offences.

If in every rule of the LS of the ideal penal Practice the offence clause and the sanction clause are inseparable, it follows that the diagnosis of wrong-doing and the prescription of punishment must be part of the same procedure; the trial judge who establishes the commission of an offence at the same time orders the prescribed penalty. An institutional arrangement whereby the guilt of the accused was determined at a different time, by different persons, under a procedure different from that employed for ordering his or her punishment, would clearly involve two separate Practices neither of which was committed to legal justice.[69] The Practice in which the guilt of the accused was established would not be concerned to restate or to clarify the enacted rules. As the norms it applied would not prescribe punishment, they would be imperatives laying down standards and duties to which members of Society must conform. The NP of such a Practice would be a decision only that the accused ought to be considered for punishment or treatment.

In such a system the sanctioning Practice, designed to make use of the experience and expertise of those familiar with the working of the criminal system, would likewise have no concern with legal justice. The discretion conferred on those ordering punishment would allow consideration of factors irrelevant to the actual commission of the offence. So the punishment ordered would be justified, not by a rule, but by other reasons, such as an argument that a particular course of treatment would benefit this deviant member of Society. The emphasis would be on the uniqueness of each offence and the circumstances of the offender, rather than on the principle that like offences should be treated alike.

This type of non-legal scheme could only be supported if there was evidence either that the infliction of harm on individuals in fact produced tangible benefits—to the offender, to others, or to society in general—or that there were clear advantages in refraining from punishing offenders and treating them in some other way. We would then have to be persuaded that such benefits outweighed the loss experienced by a Society which was deprived of the occasions upon which the law demonstrated its unyielding and scrupulous respect for persons. Given the elusiveness of the benefits which are supposed to result from punishments and treatments tailored to the individual wrong-doer, there is a strong case for the view that punishments are imposed only to signal the existence of general rules deemed necessary for Society's survival: the rules providing the framework within which we could, in every case, be satisfied that the punishments inflicted were just. Punishments imposed in the name of Society should be related to the requirements of legitimacy in a democratic polity, not to the strategies of social engineers. The two-stage scheme, reasonable though it might appear, betrays a fundamental failure to understand the nature and meaning of punishment.

The legislated rule is not the ideal penal norm. It may be addressed generally to members, defining an offence in general terms and laying down the maximum penalty. The legislature has decided that it is necessary to have a rule prohibiting or commanding members to do or refrain from doing something, and—as that imperative is to be treated seriously—it prescribes what it deems to be an appropriate range of penalties for its breach. Legislators can only legislate in such terms; they are incapable of prescribing the minute detail required for legal justice.

Yet such detail is essential. Clearly, not all instances of a given offence are of equal seriousness: some are serious while others may be relatively trivial. They are not all to be treated in the same way. This is a background assumption with which all must work; in prescribing a maximum penalty for the offence the legislator clearly intends, under the principle of penal parsimony, that lesser penalties should be imposed for less serious instances of the offence.

The common-sense view is that, faced with cases of differing degrees of seriousness, the judge, possessed of a discretion, will order punishment proportionate to the seriousness of the offence. However, legal justice claims no kinship with common sense; it requires that the punishment in every case is exactly and consistently proportionate, and leaves little discretion to the judge.[70]

Now, if A's commission of the offence is more serious than B's, in what ways are the cases unlike? Why is B deserving of less punishment than A?

Why would it be unjust to give them both the same treatment? In legal adjudication two cases can be said to be unlike because *the act* done in each case is different; because what A did is not the same as what B did.[71]

What makes the act different?[72] What reasons are relevant in deciding to treat one case differently from another? As far as those who would do justice are concerned, they are factors which alter the act-description of the offence. So the differences are to be found only in the intentions and circumstances existing before or at the time of the act; they are considera tions which can be used to explain or excuse the act in some degree.[73] The relevant factor is not something which merely qualifies an act, but is part of the very description of the act. We can see this when defences such as insanity, infancy, mistake, incapacity, or diminished responsibility are put forward. All these claim that the act committed did not constitute the offence; it was not the wrongful act described in the statutory offence clause. The defence redefines the act for which a penalty has been pre scribed.

In distinguishing between unlike cases, what is not relevant are circum stances which cannot be said to alter the character of the act.[74] So the unforeseeable consequences of the act, the accused's status, race, sex, family, commercial ties, and so forth, do not enter into the description of the act. Under the principle of the equality of persons such factors must be ignored. These things do not alter or excuse the act, and are therefore not relevant to the decision about whether the act is a more, or a less, serious instance of the statutory offence.[75]

Legislated rules might appear to define the act arbitrarily, specifying facts description which are generally regarded as irrelevant. The legislators might, for instance, enact that a particular class of persons is exempt and cannot be punished—in effect that its members cannot commit the act. In the ideal Practice, however, such statutory defences must be assumed never to be arbitrary; for enacted rules are taken to be the outcome of rational deliberation by legislators under conditions of procedural justice.

To describe a specified circumstance as a defence might encourage us to suppose that a person could commit the prohibited act but not be punished for it; that the accused was guilty but immune. This is not so. The person who successfully pleads a defence should be regarded as not having committed the act defined in the LS rule. His defence may appear to concede that he committed the offence as it is described *in the statute;* but the LS *rules,* the successful defence redefines the prohibited act, and generates a sub-rule. So if certain factors are present at the time of the offence the courts may recognize that the very nature of the act is different, for example that the act was not one of murder but of manslaughter.[76]

There are many different directions in which acts or offences can be redefined; at the time of the act we take into account: duress; the mental state, age, or malice of the accused; the type and amount of damage or injury intended; provocations and past wrongs suffered; the accused's good intention or pure heart; his conception of his duty or need; and so forth. In each of these directions we could qualify the wrongfulness of the offence.[77] We distinguish between acts which are wholly inexcusable, for which no excuses can be found, and those which are in different ways explicable or excusable. The ground rules of the Practice may be said to be designed to ensure that all such excuses can be aired.[78] Only the wholly inexcusable deserves the maximum penalty, the utmost rigour of the law.

It is for a court to decide which factors are relevant and which are not.[79] As knowledge has increased about the constraints and influences on human motivation and action, factors which had formerly been regarded as irrelevant are today regarded as capable of qualifying the act, of explaining conduct, and in some cases of reducing culpability. Courts now accept that certain states and conditions—allergies, blackouts, automatism, drunkenness, schizophrenia—must be regarded as rendering an act different from the offence specified. By contrast, good intentions—to enforce the law, or to relieve suffering—are said not to be relevant to the act description. Equally, religious or political beliefs do not excuse failure to perform civic duties.

The crucial point, however, is that these defences and excuses, no matter how novel, must be appraised at all times; herein lies the virtue of an adversarial procedure which, in the interests of penal parsimony, encourages pertinacious claims that acts are not what they seem to be. It is in the appraisal of such claims, in determining whether such states and intentions are to count—and to count in all like cases—that the courts possess inherent law-making authority. Unlike cases cannot be distinguished by reference to scientific criteria; relevant factors must be consonant with social attitudes and beliefs.[80] In their appraisal of the factors they hold to be relevant the courts may be said to refine the statutory formulation. Unless they are prepared to take account of the factors which, in the light of current knowledge, are relevant, they are not doing legal justice.

Irrelevant factors may speed the angels of mercy on their way—they may lead to calls for pardon, remission, alternative forms of punishment, and so on—but they have no place in the administration of legal justice.[81] Mercy tempers justice; its voice should be heard only after the law has spoken. There is ample evidence from many quarters that we need more effective procedures for tempering justice. A humane Society cannot allow that the just punishment of one individual should bring harm to others. Nevertheless those others, and the harms they may suffer, cannot be part of the legal calculation. The clearest possible distinction should be made between the legal order and merciful intervention.[82]

The dehumanization of the individual and the lack of discretion involved in the administration of justice have been subject to much criticism.[83] Those features should be prized, if only to free ourselves from the meretricious idea that punishments should serve a useful purpose, and that judges should exercise their discretion to achieve such a purpose.

The function of punishments in a Society is merely to signalize its absolute prohibitions and commands.[84] Punishments make mandatory those rules which operate within Society's boundaries, and are deemed necessary for its survival. From the legal point of view, the sole function of punishment is to make concrete the absolute rules; therefore, the purposes and policies which the rules are enacted to achieve are no concern of the judges.[85] They order punishments to underline the seriousness of the *rule*—thou shalt not smoke—not to co-operate with the enforcers' efforts to stop people from smoking. The judges' respect for persons involves recognition of the freedom not only to do whatever is not forbidden, but to disobey the law for which the punishment is prescribed. The legal person of the penal Practice is not an individual who ought to conform to all the standards and policies which laws are passed to promote. So the wrong-doer before the court is not to be treated as a delinquent, a deviant from normal patterns of human conduct; he or she is merely a person who has broken a rule, and committed an offence.

Conscious of the fact that punishments are harms, the judge's central concern is to minimize the amounts inflicted.[86] The suggestion that the deliberate infliction of harm confers a benefit on the person punished or on others is not borne out by the evidence; the idea that our systems of punishment should be designed to benefit anyone is profoundly misguided.[87] Such ideas are prevalent today. Unfortunately the effort to kill two birds with one stone—to punish justly, and at the same time to do something else—will assuredly divert us from the first and much more important target.[88] It needs to be emphasized that the aspiration to do legal justice—to order punishments which need no further justification— is one of the basic ingredients of political legitimacy.

III: THE PENAL PRACTICE IN CONTEXT

We cannot understand criminal law by concentrating solely upon the courts. The penal legal Practice—the focal institutional form of the domain of criminal law—simply could not exist without the co-operation of, and an understanding of its aspirations by, members of other institutional forms. In this Section the nature of both its dependence and its influence on those other forms is examined.

A: The State

The relationship of the penal Practice to the State—the governing organizational structure of a Society—is commonly misrepresented. In the early days of the State, authority to order punishments rested with the Ruler, the fount of justice. However, the business of punishing inevitably became a specialism which had to be undertaken by the Ruler's delegates, officials appointed possibly with a commission to do justice. That quest for justice prompts the emergence of the legal Practice, which gradually acquires independence from the State until, in its maturity, it becomes truly autonomous, ceasing to be an organ of the State—a mere department of government—even though its dependence upon support from the State is patent.

Courts rely absolutely upon the State for the execution of their orders. They also depend on the State to provide the material resources required for their effective operation. Court-rooms must be constructed, judges appointed, staff trained and put in place to see that all runs smoothly; such matters must be the responsibility of the executive, not of the judges.

However, this material dependence in no way detracts from the legal autonomy of the Practice, which springs from the commitment of the participants to the imperatives of justice. When judges are acting as participants within the Practice—when they are engaged in the process of adjudication—they can no longer be regarded as State officials or officers.[89] They are acting in a totally different capacity and exercising a different sort of power. As participants they must be deaf to any directions from the State as to the content of their judgments, since such directions would be inconsistent with the doing of penal justice. The independence of the judiciary is not the product of a constitutional provision; it derives from their adherence to the dictates of justice.

The judges' authority to punish may be said to derive from the very laws which they are empowered lo administer.[90] On being empowered to participate in the legal Practice, a judge is not given a general power to punish. A general magisterial, residual, power to punish for wrong-doing, which was in earlier times part of the conception of kingship, would entail a capacity to create new offences.[91] The judges' authority to punish is conferred only by those legislated rules which have been incorporated into the LS of the Practice; that is, the rules generated by the joint efforts of legislators and judges.

So the sanction clause of a criminal law not only specifies the penalty for an office, but is specific *authorization* for its infliction. A judge's only power, deriving from the sanction clause of the LS rule, is to punish the commission of specified offences. Each new statutory offence incorporated into the LS confers an additional specific authority. In the ideal Practice the ground rules will prescribe, in conformity with the demands of justice, that a statutory rule failing to specify the penalty for the offence which it defines cannot be incorporated in the LS because the legislature has not provided the necessary authorization for the judges to punish. It should also be remembered that the authority conferred by an enacted provision will be qualified by the consideration that judges are committed to penal parsimony. To be given a power to punish means to be given power to punish parsimoniously.

B: Society

Society, the correlative of the State, is the associational form upon which the legal penal Practice depends and which it must support.[92] With a jurisdiction which extends to the boundaries of the territory, the Practice maintains Society's penal laws. The penal Practice is the institutional form of the Society, not of the State; it punishes on behalf of the members of Society, not on behalf of the officers and officials of the State.

Society is an association of members who are subject to, and liable to be punished for, breaches of its laws. The penal laws of Society apply equally to all members, so that a class of members can be excepted from a general law only by being expressly singled out by the legislature as a class requiring different treatment. In the penal Practice there can be no discrimination between members of Society other than that prescribed by the LS rules.

As a basic constitutional principle, equality has a primary location in the penal Practice. Equality before the law is transparent. By contrast, equality as a principle upon which to base social—not legal—justice is a political ideal of extraordinary opacity. We may suspect that any intuitive appeal which may be claimed for equality as the foundation of social justice stems from conflating the political ideal with the imperative of democratic legitimacy which is equality before the law.

Now the members of Society who may be punished are not artificial legal persons but human beings: 'natural persons'. First among the considerations which lead to this conclusion is that the infliction of punishment on an artificial person may involve the punishment of the innocent: individuals with interests and entitlements in a joint venture represented by the artificial person. A second consideration is that as punishment involves suffering, loss, and deprivation of rights, there is no point in inflicting penalties on an entity which cannot suffer pain, or to whom an intention to harm could not be communicated.[93] The idea of punishment is that the person committing an offence is made to suffer for it. For an act to count as punishment the intention must be to cause suffering to a human being responsible for wrong-doing—a consideration which accounts for our apprehension that the whipping of trees, or church bells, or the execution of horses and sheep, for their implication in catastrophes may have been emotionally satisfying but was scarcely rational.[94] In cases of so-called corporate crime the aim must be to identify the individuals on whom responsibility can be pinned.

In order to describe the complicated way in which the penal Practice is related to Society we need to understand the nature of two ideal institutional forms, enforcement Activity and the legislative Practice, both of which are necessary parts of a civil Society which is defined in terms of its artificial rules.

Enforcement Activity

Enforcement Activity is part of the more general Activity of social control.[95] Associational forms cannot exist without some form of general activity which maintains their normative frameworks. Social control involves the maintenance, not just of rules, but all sorts of norms. Social norms are maintained in a great variety of different ways: by punishment, exhortation, criticism, education, propaganda, coercion, ostracism, and so on.[96] Norm formulations which are not so maintained are of no account.

Enforcement Activity is unquestionably part of, but should be distinguished from, other forms of social control. It is a distinct Activity whose objective is to secure conformity to the general social *rules* of a Society.[97] Although it is certainly a regulated Activity—there are right and wrong ways of engaging in it—it is not governed by validating ground rules; its outcomes are judged, not as valid or invalid, but in terms of effectiveness or success. As an institutional form, enforcement Activity is quite distinct from any normative Practice.

Although most members of Society may be more or less actively concerned to promote conformity to social rules, the Activity of enforcement in modern Societies is primarily the function of centralized agencies, the police and security forces.[98] The process of centralization was not merely the result of a utilitarian calculation as to the advantages which would accrue from it; it must be seen as part of the institutional revolution which accompanied the emergence of the democratic polity.

Whether the rules which are enforced are legal rules will depend upon the presence of a legal penal Practice within the Society. After all, enforcers might operate in a Society which lacks legal Practices, or in which the influence of the legal Practices is minimal; the norms they enforced might, for instance, be the commands of a dictator, lacking any legal character at all.

The defining objective of enforcement Activity is to ensure conformity to, or punishment under, the rules; it is wide-ranging. Some of its aspects are the subject-matter of criminology. Enforcement involves, among other things, preventing breaches of the law and promoting the virtues of conformity. In doing these things, enforcers may be encouraged to look beyond the rules to the policies which the rules were enacted to implement. Whatever other functions enforcers may have, whatever norms may guide their activities, our concern here is solely with their engagement in the enforcement of rules.

Ideally, enforcement Activity must be imbued with respect for the law; that is, the agents must pursue their objectives in conformity with the precepts of legality.[99] Only where the enforcers understand the relation in which their Activity stands to the penal Practice, and respect the values of that Practice, can we talk of a Society's system of criminal justice.[100] It is a primary function of the enforcers to service the legal Practice; they are charged with the responsibility of bringing before the courts for punishment those suspected of having committed an offence.[101] Prosecution is a responsibility which the State undertakes on behalf of Society. The administrative decision to send a person for trial is part of enforcement Activity.[102]

Much of enforcement Activity can be described as coercive; enforcers threaten legal action if members break laws. Importantly, the legal Practice is *not* coercive; participants do not threaten, they punish.

Now it is of fundamental importance that in a Society with a healthy penal Practice enforcement Activity will, so far as the infliction of punishment is concerned, be restricted to servicing the legal Practice. The enforcers will have no authority to punish whatsoever. Empowering officials to punish for minor offences will blur the distinction between Practice and Activity of enforcement. In a democratic polity punishment ought to be the monopoly of the participants in the penal Practice.[103]

How is this monopoly to be secured? Clearly, the participants in the penal practices appear to have limited authority to preserve their monopoly; their authority is restricted to the declaration of the law and the ordering of punishments. How can ordinary members of Society, or officials of the State, be dissuaded from taking the law into their own hands, and legislators from empowering them to do so? The answer must lie partly in the respect for law among members of Society, a respect based on a perception of the legitimacy of the penal Practice and the commitment of the judges to justice: on the belief that the legal Practice affords complete justification for punishments in the name of Society.

Although their authority is limited, the participants in the Practice can still play a part in preserving their monopoly, by resisting arguments that harms deliberately imposed on members of Society, whether by ordinary individuals or by officials, were excusable on the ground that they were done in support of the law itself.[104] At a time when there is a perception of rising crime rates, the argument that a law-enforcing intention is irrelevant in determining the guilt of someone who has harmed a member of Society may seem counter-intuitive to the law-abiding. However, because informal punishments lack justice, the intention to ensure conformity to the law ought never to exonerate punishment.

The recognition of the ideal of penal Practice standing apart from enforcement Activity is of great importance.[105] Yet there is a widespread view that the courts are part of a Society's enforcement Activity. Pressures are increasingly put on criminal courts to do things which lie quite beyond their authority.[106] They are adjured to co-operate ever more enthusiastic ally in efforts to counter the rising tide of crime: to deter criminals, to reform them, to wreak Society's vengeance upon them, and so forth. When judges yield to such pressures they undermine the legitimacy of the Practice, just as much as if they were to accede to demands in civil case that they should do social justice, or redistribute goods.

The distinction between the two institutional forms of enforcement Activity and the penal Practice cannot be overemphasized.[107] The maxim *nemo poena sine lege is* to be understood, not simply as requiring that punishments must be justified by reference to established rules, but that they must be justly—i.e. legally—inflicted. Here, ideally, the separation of powers must be absolute: enforcers should not punish; judges should not enforce. The distinction is important because we value justice. As with many distinctions and principles which are recognized to have constitutional significance, its foundations are imperfectly understood. The distinction can only be properly understood in terms of the ideal of legal justice.

The distinction between the two forms can be underlined by considering how the norms operating in the penal Practice differ from those employed in enforcement Activity.

Enforcement rules and Practice rules

Social norms must be tied to those distinctive configurations of human activity in which alone they can be said to exist. The institutional forms to which our criminal laws are anchored are the Practice of punishment and the Activity of enforcement.

Social rules, which are enforced in enforcement Activity, are of a wholly different type from the rules applied in the courts, the LS rules. The common assumption that judges apply the norms which regulate the lives of members of society is mistaken, and confusion results from the failure to distinguish between the two types of rule.

The account of the LS rule given in the previous Section pictures them as complicated, detailed, precise, and technical. Importantly, they are neither prohibitions or commands—rules rendering conduct non-optional —but rules defining acts which in the eyes of the law are inexcusable.[108] They owe their existence to their employment in the Practice, and their particular character to their incorporation in the LS. A valid, existent legal rule is defined as a rule which is actually incorporated in this form of life.

The norms which are enforced as social rules in enforcement Activity are of a different type from the LS rules of the penal Practice. In the first place, unlike the LS rules, the social rules are commands and prohibitions, imperatives addressed directly to the members of Society.[109] They are absolute rules governing the conduct of members. Their application is governed, not by the principles of legal justice, but by the precepts of legality. The norms of enforcement Activity can be said to exist as norms only to the extent that they are in fact operative within social life.[110] As the rules of a Society—artificial rules which apply to all members—they will be used to educate, inform, warn, and to justify coercive threats of legal action. For these are the rules used in that enforcement Activity which is necessary if a Society is to survive.

We cannot expect an exact correlation between the LS rules and the social rules, which are in one sense deductions from them, since we are dealing with two wholly different types of norm. Though both are derived from the same legislative formulations, they are very different.[111] As social rules, the legislative norms can be said to exist only in so far as they are employed to justify enforcement Activity; and, notoriously, the enforcement of the criminal law rules may be patchy and selective.[112] Enforcers may consistently discriminate against a particular class: members commonly assert that in enforcement Activity there is one law for the rich and another for the poor. Irregularities in enforcement may be due to lack of resources, racial bias, or law and order policies dictated by the executive or evolved by the enforcers.

By virtue of their institutional anchorage, the norms of enforcement differ from the norms of legal adjudication. For analytic jurisprudence matters are even more complicated; within the legal field of modern Societies we need to identify yet another type of norm which makes a claim to constitute the prescriptions of the criminal law, which I call legal advice rules.

Legal advice rules

These are neither the rules of the penal Practice nor those of enforcement Activity, but are related to both. They are located primarily in the professional Activity of lawyers.[113] They are the prescriptions set out by lawyers who are asked for information about the penal laws, or by academics in attempting to state the criminal law, of a Society.[114] In seeking the lawyer's advice, the law-abiding member of Society will want to know exactly what is forbidden and commanded by law, exactly what his legal duties are. Any legal advice given must be parasitic on the penal Practice. So the lawyer will need first to employ a rule of recognition to know what counts as a law. In the case of newly enacted provisions which have not yet been incorporated, the lawyer must then attempt to interpret the statute. In the criminal law domain, most of the norms set out in legal advice will be primary rules: commands and prohibitions. These rules are intended to guide the conduct of the member, so attention will be concentrated on the offence clause. The law-abiding citizen recognizes that they are absolute rules and therefore has no particular interest in the penalties prescribed; he is seldom going to calculate whether the prescribed punishment is such that it is worth risking the commission of an offence. At the back of the citizen's mind there may, in any event, be the belief that judges, in their discretion, decide what punishment to impose.

As an interpretation of the legislative formulation, the legal advice rule is a reflex of the LS rule. Even though the LS rule defines an offence, not a prohibition, we readily deduce from the fact that it is a punishable offence that the act is absolutely forbidden. The legal advice rule is not a simple reiteration of the LS rule, but a deduction from it. In translating the LS rules into workaday imperatives there will inevitably be some simplification or vulgarization In many cases the legislative utterance will be directly interpreted, more or less as a judge would do it but with less emphasis upon defences and excuses: simply stating as accurately as possible that which is prohibited or commanded.[115]

Reliance is placed upon such advice. For many, the legal advice rules are the law of the land. This, legally, is the position; upon this advice you would be justified in appraising the conduct of others from a legal point of view. These normative propositions are the law, the object of legal science.

In institutional terms, however, these legal advice norms, the black-letter law, are curious. Only weakly related to the institutional forms of the penal Practice and enforcement Activity, they lack self-confidence. We cannot be entirely sure of their status as existing norms. They are used as guides to behaviour, sure enough; and they will be so used because they may be employed in enforcement Activity: but only to the extent that they are so employed will they have status as existing norms. As the existence of the social rules depends upon their recursive recreation in enforcement Activity, we cannot simply suppose that a particular legal advice norm exists as a social rule at all. If an unrepealed legislative provision, or a rule of common law, is in fact a dead letter, it simply ceases to exist as a social rule. If the prohibition it states is consistently ignored, a member can do what it declares to be unlawful with impunity; the rule is defunct. One criterion for the existence of a social rule is use.[116] So the lawyer spelling out the legal advice rules may say that, from the strict legal point of view, a particular act is not permitted, but in practice it is not an offence here. Only technically, in the letter of the law, is there a prohibition.

By contrast, if the LS rule corresponding to the defunct social rule remains incorporated in the LS of the penal Practice, there is no question about its existence: it would be employed by the judges if enforcers sent for trial a person accused of an offence under the rule. As the judges lack authority to erase LS rules once incorporated, until it is repealed it will remain in the LS as a valid rule of law.[117] An LS rule is, of course, not a general social rule at all, and its validity does not depend upon use.

If we would understand the legal field aright we must understand these three different types of rule: social imperatives, LS rules, and legal advice rules. They will no doubt all be called laws. We will understand them only by understanding the institutional forms to which they are related.

Since social rules differ from LS rules, statements which are true of one type of rule may be untrue of another. Thus, for the social rules of enforcement Activity a predictive analysis is entirely appropriate.[118] The law is a fact. If a person is guilty of an offence certain predictable consequences will follow. The rules have existence and normative force to the extent that they are likely to be enforced. Taking a realistic view of the normative situation, we could say that an individual has an obligation by virtue of the fact that it can be predicted that he will be punished if he breaks the rule. The bad man demands a realistic assessment of the law, he wants to know how the rules are applied and his risk of being caught and punished. Of course, once the bad man has been caught and accused of an offence, his attention will focus on the LS rules; his concern will no longer be with the legal obligations to which he should have conformed, but with the punishment he may expect. The legal realists come into their own in describing social rules, but they cannot provide a satisfactory account of the LS rules.

It may be suggested that in jurisprudential analysis the emphasis commonly placed on the notion of legal duty or obligation is misleading.[119] It may cause us to overlook the different functions of different rules. Not all legal rules in the criminal law domain create obligations. To emphasize the analysis of obligation may mislead us into treating it as the fundamental category of criminal law, and lead us to believe that the only rules we need consider are those which create obligations. However, we need to recall that legal obligations, of the sort we associate with imperatives, are *not* the concern of the participants in the legal Practice applying LS rules. Duties have their place as articulative counters in statements employing the legal advice rules. The legal obligations to which we refer when dealing with legal advice rules cannot be explained in terms of predictions of judicial conduct, or in psychological terms. By contrast, for the obligations which we might, loosely but intelligibly, talk of as being entailed in the social rules of enforcement Activity, a predictive or psychological analysis might well be appropriate.

Standard maintenance norms

Brief mention must be made of a class of legislated norms employed in a form of enforcement Activity, but not generally incorporated in the LS of the legal Practice: standard maintenance norms.[120] They are standards, prescribed in general terms by the legislature, to advance policies in respect of public health, industrial safety, environmental amenity, and so forth, to which Organizations and other members must conform, or which they must attempt to achieve. Unlike penal rules, standard maintenance rules need not define offences but may set out general standards. Inspectorates may be set up to enforce the norms, and enforcement agencies will be given powers to negotiate with those failing to meet the general standards: to recommend action, to insist upon fulfilment, to monitor progress, and in any way to see that the standards are as far as possible achieved. The legislators may make it clear that they do not intend the inspectors to service the penal Practice, and much of the effort of the inspectors may be directed towards achieving standards without threatening legal action. In cases where punishment is prescribed in the statute as a last resort, it will be for the breach of a positive duty precisely defined either in the enactment or by the enforcement agencies.

Standard-maintenance is enforcement Activity of a special sort. We need to recognize that the legislated standards to be maintained are very different from the standards of conduct defined in the social rules which are the reflexes of the Practice LS rules. For standard-maintenance rules are not absolute; they do not define precise criteria of wrong-doing which merits punishment. Crucially, their formulation, enforcement, and application do not call for the observance of the imperatives of legal justice; and the enforcement agencies are not governed by the precepts of legality.[121]

These norms may be unsuitable for incorporation in the LS of the penal Practice because those subject to the standards are likely to be Organizations. I have argued that the infliction of punishments on artificial persons is irrational. Also, the attribution of responsibility to individuals within an Organization may be a matter of great difficulty. If responsibility can be fixed upon officers of the Organization as individuals, then punishment is possible if, and only if, as individuals they can be shown to be in breach of precise duties laid down by the law. The pressures on Organizations to conform to the standards will be largely extra-legal.

Certainly a *penal* Practice is not in the business of applying or enforcing standard-maintenance rules. Its business is to administer legal justice, not to enforce the law. Decisions as to whether adequate standards have been attained are not legal judgments. In dealing with such cases the so-called court of law must be seen to operate as a governmental agency engaged in administrative regulation.[122] That legislatures are prepared to confer such powers on courts of justice is understandable, but it shows a lack of respect for the law, deriving from misconceptions as to the law's character, and a failure to appreciate the importance of preserving the autonomy of the courts.

Evidence of failure to understand the central importance of preserving the autonomy of the penal Practice is found in the commentators' objections that standard-maintenance rules are not enforced in the manner of the LS rules, and misguidedly demand that they should be. The proper regulation of matters of environmental or general social importance is undoubtedly of major importance, and no doubt requires the backing of coercive force of the sort associated with legal execution. However, that pressing requirement does not justify undermining the legal Practice by empowering it to do a job for which it is ill adapted.

C: The legislative Practice

The ideal penal Practice of a democratic polity cannot operate with common law rules; its participants cannot call upon social customs or divine the intimations of the *Volksgeist* in order to replenish the LS. It is a requirement of justice that the rules of the LS must have their origin in a democratic legislative Practice.[123] We must not overlook the significance of the fact that, in common law jurisdictions, the power to punish for common law crimes has been deliberately abrogated or profoundly curtailed, and that today, in many jurisdictions, all the penal rules applied are legislated rules. This is a development which owes more to the quest for justice than to the inexorable growth of State power.

Our concern here is to examine the nature of the ideal legislative Practice and the relationship between the legal and the legislative Practices. The Legislative Practices of Society are discussed in Chapter 7, below. Here we concentrate on how Society's legislative Practice operates to produce penal laws.

We cannot theorize about the relationship between the legal and the legislative Practices without recourse to a theory of punishment. A theory of punishment imposed in the name of Society must emphasize the conceptual link between punishment and justification, and insist on the need for complete justification of those punishments.

We begin with the obvious: although a general system of punishments is necessary for Society to exist as an institutional form, that institutional truism can never be relied upon as an adequate justification for any individual punishment. In civil Society every punishment must be separately justified.[124]

In a Society no instance of punishment can be justified by good reasons produced *ad hoc*. Punishment is a response to wrong-doing, and for the wrong-doings of members in this association we need objective standards, established norms, by which wrong-doing can be identified. The only norm which can provide complete justification for an individual punishment is a legal norm which specifies both the offence and the penalty.

For a particular punishment to be completely justified, the rules must have been applied in conformity with the imperatives of legal justice. However, mere conformity to those imperatives in the application of the rules to the penal Practice, no matter how scrupulously undertaken, is clearly not sufficient. Let us suppose, for instance, that there are bad laws in the LS of the legal Practice: out-dated rules, universally condemned as being unnecessary, cruel, or iniquitous. Scrupulous concern to apply them according to the imperatives of legal justice is a threadbare justification for inflicting harms under them. At best we could say that the punishment was authorized by the law, that it was minimal and consistent with other punishments; that the offender had been punished because there existed a valid law which he had broken. However, it is simply not enough to claim that the rule has been long established and that the person punished knew, or ought to have known, of it. If the law is a bad law the judges have made the best of a bad job, but they have not done legal justice; they have ameliorated an injustice.

The observation that bad laws do not justify punishments would seem to suggest that if a punishment is to be completely justified, the rule applied must be a morally good law. We should, however, avoid the notion of the goodness or badness of laws and concentrate on the non-moral criteria which must be satisfied to achieve complete justification.

For a norm which can completely justify a punishment is not a law which is judged to be good by reference to the standards of critical morality, or utility.[125] The use of such critical standards to judge laws entails that we consider them to be either of universal application, or part of the mental furniture of every member of Society—including the one accused of an offence. That is simply not the case. We are punishing a member of Society; that artificial form is not founded on, and does not support, a moral code.[126] Those who have to be convinced of the completeness of the justification for punishment are not just the members of a particular Group—for whom the moral standards may be obvious and indisputable—but all the members of Society.

Clearly, complete justification for punishments could not be given by rules which are identified by purely formal criteria conventionally adopted by the courts. Conventionalism would suggest that the laws are identified by criteria which have been settled on for pragmatic reasons alone. The efforts of conventionalists to justify the legal infliction of punishments in terms of known laws and expectations are so inadequate that they can be relied upon to provoke foundationalist theories which strive to provide the laws with moral virtue.

To discover the criteria which penal laws applied by judges must satisfy—without allying ourselves to the cool indifference of the conventionalists, or the heated claims of the natural lawyers—we need to recall that we are dealing with civil Society and the punishment of its members; that it is an artificial and formal associational form; that the language of civil Society is the language of the law; and that its members are legal persons.

The criteria must be founded in democratic theory; a theory which demands that, in the polity, respect must be shown for all individuals and Groups. The ideal penal norms must possess a democratic pedigree, for the moral heterogeneity of Society must be accommodated. The laws must be recognized by all as being the valid laws of, as being right for, this particular association.

The only norms which could satisfy these demands of democratic legitimacy are those created in a legislative Practice designed to enable its participants to create valid judgments for Society. The legislative Practice of civil Society is not designed as an institution of executive decision-making—a War Cabinet—to achieve some predetermined end, but to produce, out of the chronic dissensus, laws which the member *qua* member cannot challenge.[127] Before examining the nature of this Practice, certain points require attention.

The norms which completely justify punishments are identified by their *source,* not their content.[128] Moral imperatives, prescriptions based on expert knowledge, and ultra-montane directives lack the imprimatur of democratic validity: none of these can claim the respect of all members, no matter how beneficial they might be.

Furthermore, *all* products of this Practice, by reason of the checks and scrutiny, deliberative rationality, and procedural justice involved in their creation, are equally justificatory no matter how bad we may judge some of them to be. In the first place we can rest assured that although some of its laws may be heartily detested, the Practice simply could not enact provisions condemning all blue-eyed baby boys to death. For it is part of the Practice's specification that powerful moral objections to a proposed law cannot be left out of the processes of scrutiny and deliberation. In actual Practices bad laws abound: the results of ill-judgment, changing circumstances, and so forth—a consideration which underlines the importance of insisting upon the contingency of all their products. However, the ill-judged law of the ideal Practice, no matter how wrong or ill advised, would have an absolute claim to our obedience and would provide complete justification for punishments authorized by it; and for the member of Society, as member, it must prevail over the most powerful moral reasons. Not, I hasten to add, because it is recognized as the *Law*—something sacred and the object of fear and veneration—but because it is the product of an institution designed to embody the virtues of democratic choice. The prudential reasons offered by natural lawyers for recognizing the validity of bad laws are useful in the real world because of the imperfections of the legislative Practice.

Society's laws produced in the ideal legislative Practice should not be considered as having been produced under the pragmatic conventions of legislation. The legitimate democratic legislative Practice is principled. It is an ideal form which is implicit in, and a condition for, the business of administering legal justice in a democratic polity. The courts' rule of recognition which accepts the products of the legislative Practice as valid laws would ideally be more than a historical accident, a political agreement. Its basis would be the demand for democratic law-making capable of producing the type of norms which completely justify judges' orders to punish members of Society.

Laws enacted in the ideal Practice which heeds the imperative of democracy and justice cannot be challenged by members of civil Society; they cannot on one hand claim membership and on the other deny that the laws of the ideal legislative Practice are the valid laws of the Society of which they are members. As members of Groups, individuals may not like them; but that is immaterial. For it is as a member of Society that an individual is subject to the rules and tried; as—we are often reminded—a decontextualized, dehumanized entity, not as a member of a Group. It is the dehumanized member who cannot challenge the statute's validity.

In a democratic Society it is not possible to prescribe—as foundationalists do—theoretical or moral limits for the criminal law. To do so is to stand on a different plane from that of legal discourse, and to pre-empt the judgment of Society, or more precisely of its legislators. We cannot suppose that the ideal penal law of a democratic polity has to conform with the dictates of liberalism: that the penal laws must be judged by their conformity with the harm principle, or that it should be subject to the constraints which our possession of human rights demands. We should require of theorists a modesty resulting from the recognition that their theoretical labours, are undertaken on behalf of a Group in competition with other Groups (whose language they may not understand), and can never represent the final word for the associational form Society. Foundationalism, in penal as in all other matters, is inherently incompatible with democracy.[129]

The ideal legislative Practice

In order to make ideal penal rules the legislative Practice must not only (a) be capable of producing the best judgments of what is necessary for Society, but also (b) have democratic legitimacy, and (c) show respect for the law.

Capable of producing the best judgments

The best judgments as to which normative restraints are necessary for Society can only be made by way of a settled procedure which allows for thorough deliberation and debate, and the most intense critical scrutiny of all proposals. Precisely what is the best way of proceeding must be worked out in the light of experience over the years.[130] Referendums, or the sampling of public opinion, can scarcely represent the best way of arriving at considered judgments about the necessity of particular norms, or about such detailed matters as the fixing of penalties for particular offences.[131]

In framing the rules which are to govern the members of a heterogeneous Society, the legislative Practice must conform to the requirements of the minimum conception of procedural justice, and take seriously the democratic imperative of respect for Groups. The legislators must have access to all the information which they require about all relevant factors and circumstances, and an opportunity for the fullest consideration of all competing views. As it is essential that the Practice be generally perceived as a forum in which the best, the most informed, judgments can be made, there must be, both within and outside the Practice, freedom to criticize and to promote unpopular or minority views.

Democratic legitimacy

Good legislative judgment as to the necessity of penal rules for Society can only be achieved in open, democratic conditions. The perception of the Practice as an agency which legislates according to the views of one dominant Group will undermine the claim that its laws are made in the name of Society[132] It is all too easy to ascribe to Society the judgments of a Group. In meeting the requirement that a judgment about the necessity of a penal rule really is a judgment of the Society, it is essential that the legislative Practice adequately represents the various Groups and interests within Society. The Practice should be so contrived that its legislative products—although they can never hope to gain the approval of all members of Society—will still be recognized as having a substantial claim to be the best possible outcomes which could be achieved in the circumstances.

Since, for obvious reasons, not all members of Society can participate in the Practice itself, it is essential that they should have some more general involvement in the process of law-making. At very least there must be regular elections in which all members vote for representatives with the capacity to participate in the legislative Practice.[133]

Respect for the law

A legislative Practice which is democratic and provides for the fullest deliberation and fact-finding may yet fail to produce well made penal laws. In order to do that legislators must also show respect for the law: a feature of the legislative Practice which can easily be overlooked. Legislatures, of course, do much more than enact penal statutes, and their multifarious activities may serve to conceal this particular *desideratum* which the participants in the legislative Practice must satisfy if they are to enact penal laws.

By respect for the law I mean that the participants legislate in the full knowledge of the nature of the penal Practice, with an understanding of what is entailed in its commitment to legal justice, and a proper respect for its authority and its limitations.

The requirement that legislators should respect the law will be satisfied only if (i) they exercise penal parsimony; (ii) they produce rules capable of direct incorporation; (iii) they take proper account of existing LS rules; and (iv) they actively engage in the continuous monitoring of the LS rules.

Penal parsimony

The effort to do legal justice to citizens will be subverted if the legislature shows a disposition to generosity in its enactment of penal sanctions.[134] The principle—nowhere more forcibly argued than in Bentham's jurisprudence—is that legislators must enact the fewest possible penal laws, and only where they can be shown to be absolutely necessary for the maintenance of Society or the implementation of policies which have been agreed upon.[135]

It will enact rules fit for incorporation

Legislators do not enact guidelines or principles but rules. If they are to show respect for the penal economy practised by the judges, the legislators must define offences with clarity, and prescribe for each the type and maximum amount of the penalty.[136] Their penal provisions must be sufficiently detailed to be capable of being incorporated.[137] As each rule must authorize the infliction of sanctions they will not be framed as simple prohibitions and commands—a constraint which operates against the ideal of codifiers who prize brevity, simplicity, and ease of access. A democratic legislative Practice making informed and impartial judgments leading to the promulgation of Society's penal norms would be going only part of the way to providing complete justification for punishments if the penalties were to be left in the discretion of the judges, to decide, or to be inflicted informally by enforcers.

New rules must be accommodated among the old

Legislation must be proposed and framed in the light of the existing rules of the LS. That is, there must be an awareness on the part of the legislators that a new enactment will effect existing norms; among other things they should attempt to avoid duplication of offences and penalties for the same act.[138]

This aspect of respect for law, which might be called fidelity to law, has an anti-rationalist tendency. Legislators appreciate that the best judgments of the necessity for particular new laws are not the products of deliberations starting from scratch, but that they will be based upon knowledge and experience of the working of the existing law. Any new rules enacted are understood to be additions to an existing structure. To some extent when legislators and judges refer to the existing values of Society they will be adverting to thc new values they hold to be implicit in the LS rules which have long been established.[139]

It will continuously monitor the law

An important proof of legislators' respect for law will be their constant review of the contents of the LS. The legislative function is not just a matter of making and unmaking laws; a legislature which is not continuously concerned to monitor the laws with a view to their affirmation, repeal, or reform will do little to ensure that all punishments in the name of Society are completely justified.

The reason lies in the Heraclitean insight that you cannot step into the same river twice; that Society faces new challenges and dangers from year to year; that old necessities pale into insignificance; and that allegiances, ideas, and attitudes change as generation succeeds generation.[140] We can too easily underestimate the speed, extent, and the revolutionary nature of the changes to which Societies are subject. In a changing world, penal provisions which may have been well made when enacted may rapidly become unnecessary.

If the courts apply obsolescent rules, even with scrupulous attention to the dictates of legal justice, the punishments inflicted will be unjustified. In such circumstances the doing of legal justice loses its point; the punishments are wrong. Yet the judges who must order the punishments have no authority to repeal or reform the penal rules in their LS.[141] That is a purely legislative task: the repeal or reform of the LS rules involves making judgments of necessity, which the courts cannot do, lacking both democratic credentials and procedures for making the best informed judgments. If the legal Practice is to preserve its legitimacy, the legislators must show their respect for the law by ensuring that judges are not put in a position which obliges them to legislate; they must not treat judges as junior partners in the legislative enterprise.

Outdated rules may remain in the LS for a long time without serious injustice being done if the rules are not enforced, so that those who offend against them are not brought before the courts for trial and punishment. Since legislatures are seldom as active as they should be, the good sense of enforcers is often heavily relied upon. Nevertheless, it is undesirable for a legislature to rely upon the pragmatic non-enforcement of such rules because the presence of unenforced laws in the LS will diminish respect for law, and because the enforcers could resume the enforcement of the rules, so that injustice would be done.

Tolerance for old laws may be encouraged by the views of the Historical School, founded on a conception of the associational form as a communion of members both past and present. Those views are wholly out of place if Society is viewed as an artificial form, a contemporary collective of legal persons.

Now the common-sense view of the relationship between the legislature and the courts is that the former make the rules and the latter apply them. Once rules are enacted they become established as the law of the land and that is that; the legislators bid farewell to their products at the factory gates. Their enactments may be terribly misconstrued or misapplied by the judges, but the legislators, short of passing a new statute, can do nothing.[142] When the rules are enacted and enter the statute book, the legislators are no longer involved in their existence.

Such a view, implicit in non-institutional jurisprudence, is clearly supported by proposals to enact codes and fundamental laws which are to be treated as timeless, free-standing imperatives. The view might be reinforced by a superficial reading of the doctrine of the separation of powers. Once a statute has been enacted the opinions of the legislators as to is meaning and interpretation are of no consequence, and the suggestion that legislators themselves might apply and enforce the laws would meet with the objection that they would, for various reasons, be incapable of doing legal justice. Legislators make laws; they do not apply them. However, the common-sense view, that the provisions of an ancient statute owe nothing to a newly elected legislature, is mistaken; it ignores the ongoing relationship between the legislators and the LS rules, and misrepresents the ideal relationship between the legislature and the courts. If penal justice is to be done, the rules to be applied must be regarded as *presently* necessary by those of our contemporaries who are in the best position to make such judgments.

The Austinian notion that the legislators tacitly approve of the customary and judge-made laws which they did not enact is, perhaps, not as weak as Hart suggested.[143] In respect of the criminal law—importantly, it does not have the same force in respect of civil and public laws—the tacit approval argument can be extended to laws enacted by previous legislatures. By not repealing old penal statutes the contemporary legislature must be taken to approve of their continued inclusion in the LS. Today's legislative Practice alone must bear the responsibility for the judgments of necessity which the rules embody; it must be regarded as giving its assent to every punishment prescribed in the LS rules.[144]

So a legislature is not just the *formal source* of law, losing all connection with a law once it has been incorporated in the LS of the Practice; it is a continuing authorizing source for all LS rules in the penal Practice. The penal laws are the laws of the Society for which the legislature speaks. If legislators are dedicated to the ideal of penal parsimony they must be regarded as actively subscribing to all LS rules. Such an attitude will be lacking in a legislature which enacts new penal rules according to political exigencies.

The notion of the tacit approval, or adoption by the legislators of the penal laws really makes sense only in an ideal world in which the participants in the legislative Practice have full knowledge of the existing laws. Of course, the plain fact that legislators do not have such knowledge is no objection to the assertion that, in the ideal Practice, they would show respect for the law by ensuring that all the LS rules can, today, be employed to justify punishments completely. The legislators' indifference will undermine the legitimacy of the courts. Generally, legislative Practices have fallen far short of the ideal; they have commonly shown, in discharging the legislative function, greater zeal in responding to mischiefs denounced by the media than in undertaking the politically unrewarding task of law reform. Only in recent times has the need for regular and constant monitoring of the penal laws been fully appreciated.[145]

The quest for legal justice in the penal Practices will be frustrated unless the source of its LS rules—the legislative Practice—is, in penal matters, sovereign. Given the need for the continuous review of all the LS rules against the criterion of present necessity, the legislative Practice cannot be bound by entrenched and unrepealable laws. Nor can its ground rules include the requirement that the validity of its NPs will be dependent upon conformity with some foundational blueprint.

As the legislative Practice must be both democratic and able to make the best judgments of necessity, the courts cannot recognize more than one Practice as speaking for Society. If other legislative Practices within a Society are empowered to pass penal laws, they must be subject to the same ultimate subscription and approval—in the singular democratic

Practice—to which all previously enacted laws are subject. The omnipotence of Society's legislative Practice, which alone can produce well made laws, is a condition necessary to support the judges' quest for legal justice: the quest can only succeed if the rules applied by the judges are capable of providing substantive justification for punishments. The doctrine of the sovereignty of Parliament is fundamentally inconsistent with the view that the criminal law is a text with normative potency which does not stem from the continuous subscription by the participants in an existing legislative Practice.

In modern polities legislatures are far from ideal; they are prevented from erasing some laws, and their judgments are overruled by the courts; the monitoring of the LS rules is low in the order of legislative priorities; and increasingly legislators are content to leave important issues to be decided by the courts.[146] Such considerations underline the fact that some of the greatest contributors to the legitimacy deficit of modern polities are badly designed, or badly functioning legislative Practices. We will find instances readily enough of Practices which are imperfectly representative, not properly informed, overworked, subject to the deformations of party politics, and so forth, as well as instances Of legislative assemblies which appear unconcerned with penal parsimony and lack proper respect for the law. Also, we do not have to look far to find constitution-makers and federalists with imperfect understanding of the nature and importance of legal justice in a democratic polity.

IV: CONCLUSION

Institutional theory presents a complicated picture of the nature and structure of the norms found in the criminal law domain. It replaces the simple picture of the law as a distinct code of rules, enforced and applied by different agencies within an ill-defined social context, with the complex interrelationship of the distinctive LS rules of the penal Practice, the imperatives of a non-punitive enforcement Activity, and the norms of a non-institutional text upon which the descriptions in legal advice are founded. In addition we must include among the norms of criminal law the ground rules, the NPs of the penal Practice, and its methodological values: the idea of legal justice. Standard-maintenance rules hover on the borders of the legal domain.

A non-institutional claim that the key to jurisprudence is the understanding that law is the union of the primary and secondary rules ignores the central importance of the institutional form: the legal penal Practice and its commitment to legal justice. Yet legal justice has a strong claim to be the key to modern jurisprudence. Only in a penal Practice animated by that idea can laws be generated; only that focus can produce a legal dimension of social control with its distinctive norms and categories.

The institutional character of the picture is all-important. For no legal Practice can be reduced to a set of procedural rules, and a principle of rule-application. Legal Practices have a life of their own as institutional forms which are irreducible elements in the legal field and which have complex, continuing relationships with other forms: with the State, Society, and the legislative Practice.

Although the dictates of legal justice are entirely consonant with the demand of the legal positivists that the law should be kept separate from morality, institutional theory parts company with positivism in claiming that legal justice provides the necessary index of law. In institutional theory a *legal obligation is* created, not by a merely formally accredited norm, but by a norm—a reflex of an LS rule—employed in enforcement Activity. The actual employment of the rule in enforcement Activity gives it a real existence as a social rule; but it is the fact that the rule is a reflex of the penal Practice rule which gives it its legal character.

Legal justice has its critics. The administration of legal justice with its limiting norms is perceived as an angular, dehumanizing mechanism, not infrequently making judgments which run counter to popular intuitions of what justice requires. Punishments ordered in the ideal Practice are seen to be inadequate by those in whom powerful feelings of vengeance or retribution are stimulated by criminal activity. They are perceived to be ineffective as deterrents, unsuited to the reformation or rehabilitation of wrong-doers, mechanical in their indifference to the social consequences of penal laws, and unjust in their refusal to make allowances for personal circumstances and histories. For some, the penal Practice is part of a repressive apparatus of social control established to promote the interests of a particular social class.

There have been many recommendations which appear to support moves away from legal justice in the process of adjudication; moves to reform the courts so that they can perform some of their supposed functions more effectively. However, any developments which would undermine the administration of legal justice must be resisted. If punishments must be meted out to members of Society, a heterogeneous associational form, within a legitimate polity, then legal justice, with its respect for persons, is imperative.

NOTES

1. Our understanding of the criminal law domain is commonly obscured by (a) an obsession with the criminal character and its salvation, and (b) the

imperfections of correctional institutions. Legal justice is concerned with neither. Although punishment is an embarrassment in the vocabulary of modern penology it is central to any understanding of the domain of criminal law. The difficulty that makes the punishment of those who commit crimes seem at odds with humane regard for them—Gross (1979: 457)—will not be experienced by those for whom punishment is necessary and for whom legal justice embodies respect for persons.

2. Hart (1959: 160); Hart (1968: 4 and 9).
3. On the importance of establishing a necessary link between crime, punishment, and justifying purposes of punishment see Duff (1986: 156).
4. A non-institutional approach to the criminal law domain, which ignores the institutional form civil Society, allows us to cast around for justifications for punishment in general. However, civil Society, in whose name punishment is carried out, is defined in terms of coercive norms: of prohibitions and commands which are not merely adjurations or exhortations. As members of Society we are committed to the punishments implied in its defining social rules. Any puzzlement about the justification for such punishments, about the right to punish, is thus unnecessary. Neither does it make sense to ascribe a purpose to the system of punishments in place, nor to worry about the fact that the sanctions which signalize, or are constitutive of, all prohibitions and commands are not achieving that purpose. Cf. Gross (1979: 300). Society's prohibitions are intentional; if we do not penalize breaches of rules we demonstrate that we really did not mean them to be prohibitions. See Lucas (1993: 99–100). See also Martin (1993: 223); the central characteristic of punishment is that it is conceived as a political legal institution. This location within a political system renders any search for a general justifying aim superfluous. .
5. As crime cannot be defined in the absence of punishment, it is curious to approach punishment as a means of crime-prevention. Punishment is a necessary element of social life, which cannot be rendered obsolete. In a democratic polity, prevention of crime is the business of non-punitive enforcement Activity. See *post*, p. 115.
6. For a critique of philosophies which characterize punishment as productive of pain see Martin (1993: 220–1). Generally, the execution of a penalty will involve unlawful acts, in that they impose losses and wrongs against which the law provides protection. The penalties are something more than the deprivation of rights. The harms and loss of rights can only be understood in their reprobative significance; the accompanying condemnation carries a stigma, over and above the facts of restraint or loss of rights. In civil Society punitive acts which are otherwise unlawful require legal justification; by contrast, acts of punishment in other institutional forms need only be permitted by law. The evils of the pains of punishment led Bentham to demand minimal legislation; Bentham (1970: 170). The human dimension of punishment involving pains suffered, needs emphasis. If penalties are imposed on artificial persons they may be effective, not because they stigmatize or cause pain to the artificial person, but because they adversely affect the IE of natural persons.

7. Consequentialist justifications for inflicting injuries or losses are not strictly punitive. They are justified by reference to past offences rather than effects. Punishment is for wrong-doing; it is a response to wrong-doing. 'If I am punishing you, it is not enough for me to have an appropriate justification, and be ready to give it *if* the question is raised. If you do not ask me, then I must tell you why I am doing it. I cannot punish you without your knowing. . . . The dialogues surrounding punishment not only occur naturally, but are constitutive of the concept.' Lucas (1993).
8. Johnson (1994) claims that most sets of moral rules are not adequate for the justification of say, decisions to punish. I argue that legal norms are fashioned, as non-arbitrary and binding norms, in order to provide a complete justification for punishment.
9. The standard case of punishment is described by Hart (1959: 161). Lucas talks of the individualized reasons for which punishment is imposed (1993: 89). Legal punishment is justified by a norm—a direction to judges to punish in all like cases—not just a reason.
10. The institutional form Society must be distinguished from the aggregate of forms which constitute what we may call social life (see *post*, Ch. 7). The scientific rationalism of the Enlightenment, which urged men to make social control more effective, was paralleled by a political revolution, in which reason was tempered by demands for justice. The former objectives operated in society, the latter in civil Society. So the emergence of Foucault's disciplinary society should be seen as the result of the application of rationalism to the pursuit of organizational objectives, to achieve success by the most effective means, rather than any desire to dominate. So changes in the legal penal system—the system of a Society—were a response to demands for legitimacy and justice rather than to demands to achieve social goals more economically. The disciplinary techniques employed in the forms of life in society must be contrasted with the punishments imposed in the name of Society: they belong to quite different forms. Foucault (1977: 117–84).
11. In a democratic Society punishment of the innocent is never an option; punishment must be completely justified, and this is only possible by reference to a legal norm. This excludes consideration of any *other reasons* for harming a citizen. The innocent could only be 'punished' by reference to some other reason; there could be no complete justification for it.
12. In a democracy questions about our duty to obey the law are related to questions about the grounds upon which laws may be challenged. A challenge to the validity of a law must be based, not on the moral content of the law, but on the procedural justice of its generation. For instance, we might object to defective procedures: to inadequate deliberation, failure to pay attention to certain inputs, failure to give due weight to particular views, and so forth—see Hampshire (1989). On procedural justice see Barry (1965: ch. VI). Our duty to obey arises, not because we must agree that the restrictions are morally good or rational, but because we simply cannot deny that the rules have been democratically well made. Cf. Hart (1955: 175); Soper (1987: 127–55); Rawls (1987: 85–6): our duty to obey stems from the fact that laws are generated, not in perfect, but in pure procedures.

13. Cf. Lucas (1993: 114): 'Many thinkers have reckoned punishment by legal authorities to be the only proper type of punishment and have often written such a requirement into their definitions. . . The requirements of due process are practical restrictions imposed on a developed legal system, not conceptual restrictions on the nature of punishment.' I would argue *contra* that, at least for a Society, punishment must be justified by legal norms generated in the legal Practices. Note Lucas's suggestion (p. 90) that there is a germ of a trial in the very concept of punishment.
14. Mabbot suggested that the 'only justification for punishing anyone is that he broke the law'. This was condemned by Mundle as being '(t)antamount to a refusal to discuss questions concerning the moral justification of punishment': Mundle (1969: 71). Although the process of *legislating* penal laws must give consideration to the views of those who believe that punishment should serve some social purpose, the *application* of the duly enacted laws must not.
15. For a splendid 'Which?' guide to Theories of Punishment: preventive, deterrent, reformative, and vindicative, see Lucas (1993: 92–3, and Appendix II, 280-5). For an attempt to steer a course between opposing theories of punishment see Primoretz (1987: 193–220). See also Martin (1993: 222–3) for a critique of the standard normative theories of the justification of punishment. Martin insists that the rationale of punishment depends upon its location within a political system.
16. The history of the penal norm may be regarded as an illustration of the movement identified by Weber from substantive to formal rationality; from punishments made on the basis of the special circumstances of each case to punishments under a general rule—the movement from reliance on reasons to justification by norms.
17. Unless they are recognized by all members, wrongs do not possess the objectivity required if they are to be dealt with on behalf of the Community as breaches of general norms.
18. Retributive theories of punishment, presupposing a degree of consensus, are appropriate for communities—for a society conceived as a Group rather than a heterogeneous form. Acts of revenge differ from punishment in that they are essentially personal and private: Lucas (1993: 88). The language of reprisal, revenge, and retribution is inappropriate for punishments legally meted out in civil Society: it is not the language of the rule of law. Unlike punishment under a rule, an isolated retributive act, officially administered, will always be challengeable. Imagine an instance of wrong-doing for which there are no precedents, and no rules, and which was committed in circumstances unlikely to recur. Whatever reasons are given to justify acts of retribution will be open to challenge. Unlike acts of revenge, which are essentially personal and private, retributive acts of reprisal may be official. In 1860 Lord Elgin was under pressure to inflict a reprobative act: to inculcate a lesson which would not be lost on the Manchu Dynasty and its subjects. The rightness of the action on which he settled, after much deliberation—the burning of the Summer Palace in Peking—will always remain a matter of controversy. The goal of substantial justice, including retributive balance, inevitably remains elusive: unlike the audit of legal justice within a Society.

19. The inhabitants of Lidice, a village in Czechoslovakia, were massacred in 1944 in reprisal for the assassination of the deputy leader of the SS. On scape-goating see Martin (1993: 241).
20. See Fuller (1958: 652) on the interpretation of Nazi law by administrators and officials.
21. In a system which allows Rulers and their henchmen to enforce their claims there is no compelling reason for adjudication to be rule-based: Roberts 1979: 179) Generally the serious application of rules will call for the interposition of adjudicatory Practices between the will of the commander and the execution of the commands. Under the regime of the indifferent State penal action, to signify that the Ruler must be obeyed, may well involve the punishment, whether deliberate or inadvertent, of the innocent; the indifferent State is collectivist in its calculations.
22. It is significant that theocratic regimes, in which sin is not distinguishable from crime, will have diffuse systems of enforcement Activity. For illustrations of some more extreme theocratic regimes of the past see Norman Cohn (1970).
23. For English judges, however, that principle appears to apply only to legislatively formulated offences; the House of Lords, as guardian of public morals, has proved capable of identifying new crimes and thus of prescribing the necessary penalties; see e.g. *Shaw* v. *DPP* [1961] 2 WLR 897. Cf. Lord Diplock in R v. *Knuller (Publishing) Ltd* [1972] 3 WLR 143.
24. A demonstration of the appropriateness of the penalty, or of the deserts of the offender, would commonly involve taking account of circumstances not relevant to the business of finding that the accused had committed the offence. Cf. Martin (1993: 220), who appears to think it necessary only that the rule should indicate some response, not that it should specify the sanction.
25. 'The practice of punishing all serious crimes with equal severity is now unknown in civilised societies, but such a radical departure from the prin ciples of proportionality has disappeared from the law only in recent times': Gross (1979: 464).
26. Mute Practices were clearly the ideal adjudicatory forms for codifiers of the law. Bentham was obsessed with the need to remove the power to make law from the judges; See Postema (1986: 267–86). French courts, which deliver terse judgments without giving reasons other than the provision of the code, might appear to be part of a mute Practice. However, they should be regarded as sub-Practices in the wider legal Practice in which the Court of Cassation makes new law. The LS of the French penal Practice consists of something more than the words of the penal code.
27. 'From the premises that justice fundamentally requires a uniform treatment of cases and that the law prescribes one way of dealing with them, we, are asked to conclude that justice in the administration of the law requires that officials follow the law. But this argument begs the question at issue which is whether the pattern of treatment prescribed by the law is identical (or even compatible) with the pattern required by justice. . . . The resemblances and differences between cases which the law tells us to consider are not necessarily the ones that justice says we may consider.' Lyons (1993: 29). The ideal

norm is a product of the commitment of the courts to legal justice; it is a refinement of the enacted law's distinctions. What are significant differences between cases will be the subject of the legal debate in the deliberative process.

28. For the view that many rules are the concretizations of principles, see MacCormick (1993: 147).
29. Foundationalist arguments—based on the values and beliefs of Groups—are of great importance in the legislative process. The validity of the NPs of the penal Practice are validated in part by the deliberations of the jury; they do not stand as representatives of a community but as individual members of Society with the duty of deliberating fully.
30. There is a line of thought from Acquinas to Finnis that obedience to the law, even bad law, is advisable lest worse should befall.
31. See Fish (1989).
32. There is a necessary connection between the emergence of the penal Practice and the democratic revolution, since part of that process is the increasing differentiation between the two Practices. The differentiation occurs because the two objectives—that of punishing offenders justly and that of protecting rights—are incompatible; a court cannot do both at the same time. The idea of the penal Practice therefore should not be expressed in terms of any purpose other than that of the doing of legal justice. Cf. Rawls (1973: 314) for whom 'the purpose of criminal law is to uphold basic natural duties which forbid us to injure other persons in their life or limb or to deprive them of their liberty and property, and punishments are to serve this end'. Inspectors and regulators may be given powers to impose fines, but those fines are generally imposed, not on individuals, but on corporations. The 'punishment' is then designed to deter delinquent corporations. The failure of a corporation to conform to standards involves wholly different considerations from the wrong-doing of individuals. Regulatory enforcement involving penalties does not call for treatment according to the dictates of legal justice.
33. It is stressed that attention is here concentrated solely on the penal Practice. In that Practice rights—other than those which ground an appeal against judgment—are wholly out of place. It is misleading to describe offences as violations of rights; this is not how, in the penal Practice, the wrongful act constituting an offence is described—even though an offence may involve damage to persons or property. Cf. Martin (1993: 225). However, within the criminal domain outside the Practice rights are of crucial importance for citizens who are subject to enforcement Activity; they need to have redress in the public law Practice for any unlawful official violation of their rights. See Griffith (1991: 151 97). The violation of rights by officials is not conceptualized in terms of offences.
34. All normative Practices create norms; courts are distinguished by their unique reliance on justification by rules. See Raz (1979: 107). Rule-applying agencies which do not create norms, such as the prison service, are organizational in character.
35. The modes of punishment do not include compensation or rehabilitation The penalties must depend upon the offence committed by the accused, not

the deserts of the victim or the character of the criminal. Cf. Martin (1993: 251-79). Any recompense or reform ordered must be in addition to, and separate from, the penalty.

36. If the humaneness of punishments in modern times is a cultural product—a product of the sensibilities of dominant Groups—the *types* of punishment which can be inflicted are the result of fully deliberated legislative choice. The only *desideratum* of legal justice is that, whatever the type prescribed, the punishments should be quantifiable—in terms of say a maximum of pain, infamy, time, or money—so that punishment ordered is proportionate to the degree of wrongness of the act.
37. Norms exist within distinct forms which are related to each other in complicated ways. To ignore the institutional forms and treat the unanchored rules as constituting a logical system leads to the pseudo-problems, such as the infinite regress of norms which arises in the definition of a delict. See Hart (1983: 170). For the view that the main task of jurisprudence—as opposed to sociology—is 'to find out the logical interdependence between various individual norms', and that 'logical analysis is therefore its chief method', see Timasheff (1974: 227).
38. Foucault (1977:194) describes the legal judgment as a pre-judgment; the real sentence begins when the offender is subject to the penal powers of the prison authorities. The legislative choice of the type of punishment, and the judicial judgment of the amount, should ideally be based on precise knowledge of the conditions prevailing in any disciplinary regime which may be involved .
39. The proverbial Jedburgh or Jeddart justice was apparently never an established practice. It derives from a hasty journalistic generalization following a single incident in which miscreants were first hanged and then tried: Encyclopedia Britannica, 15th edn., 1986.
40. There is the practical consideration that allowance must be made for the possibility of appeal.
41. On the deterrent theory see Lucas (1993: App. 2). Deterrence is an essential element in the penalties which are associated with the rules of standard maintenance. This is the approach of the indifferent State: see *ante*, p. 85.
42. The practical importance of such courts must not be underestimated: in the UK 90% of cases are heard by magistrates.
43. The style in which the judgment is couched, the language employed, is a product of the fact that judges have to formulate and declare a rule to justify the NP. They are engaged in the formulation and reformulation of rules to be applied by other judges; see Goodrich (1987: 117).
44. It is important to treat the Practice as a distinct form whose significance is appreciated by all. Such meanings are an essential element in any sociological understanding of the law; see Grace and Wilkinson (1')78: 252). The criminal court is understood to be the location of official reprobation and orders of punishment. The all-important penal intention is built into the Practice which is geared to the idea of just punishment. The judicial penal act is intended to harm in order to condemn wrong-doing; to demonstrate the absoluteness of the social norms. The consequences of executing the penal order are of less

importance. The punitive actions may be said to speak louder than prohibitory words. On the importance of the intention behind an act, see Lucas (1993: 88).

45. See Rawls' picture of an imaginary Practice of 'telishment' which is instituted to punish individuals wherever the judge is of the opinion that it would be in the best interest of society (1955: 11).
46. On the validity of rules see Hart (1994: 100-10); (1983: 359-60); Raz (1979: 146); Simmonds (1981: 24-36). The validity of an NP is enhanced by the careful deliberation by the jury, contributing to the democratic legitimacy of the penal Practice. The validity of legal rules has an institutional character; that is, it is not a purely legal calculation from rules, but the result of the process of incorporation. The institutional validity of the LS rules does not depend upon efficacy: that is a feature of social rules employed in enforcement Activity.
47. 'No issue has more vexed philosophic controversy than the justifiability of punishing the innocent' Gross (1979: 409).
48. The fact that the decision of one judge may be criticized by other judges in similar cases, that its validity and worth as a precedent may be questioned, does not prevent it from binding the accused. Pardons are of course granted under wholly different Practices.
49. A dissenting judgment may bolster a legal challenge but does nothing to undermine the authority of the NP.
50. Raz (1975: 135).
51. The autonomy of a Practice is related to the requirelnent that the validity of its NPs is the result of compliance with procedural rules, a process which neutralizes the personal element in decision-making; Luhman (1985: 135, 173). See also Watson (1977: 69). On the importance of procedural justice generally there is no more persuasive source than Stuart Hampshire's 'Innocence and Experience' (1989). It is significant that the principles governing the functioning of courts were not important in socialist states.
52. Hart's claim (1994: 98) that we have the heart of a legal system in the combination of primary and secondary rules gives little indication of the importance of the very special practical and associational forms within the legal field: see Joseph and Walker (1987: 155). The emergence of social rules, the rules of civil Society, depends upon tlle establishment of a set of institutional forms which are not just the products of long evolutionary developmental processes—Hall (1949: 45)—but are generated by democratic principles.
53. The English courts' claim to possess untrammelled power to regulate their own procedures—*Abse* v. *Smith* [1986] QB 536—must be read in the light of the need which arises for legislative intervention. The 1966 *Practice Statement* (Judicial Review) of the House of Lords clearly illustrates the reassertion of the inherent authority of the participants to alter the ground rules to conform with the demands of legal justice. See Paterson (1982: 146-51).
54. On the normative force of ground rules and the extent to which some are sanctioned see Evans (1981: 227-56). See also Hart (1982: 214): the wrongfulness of procedural acts must be distinguished from the invalidity of the NP.

55. See Stein and Shand (1974: chs. 3, 4); see also Lyons on formal justice (1993: ch. 2).
56. There have been difficulties in classifying ground rules, esp. the rules of precedent; see Zander (1985: 251) for references relating to the dispute about whether rules of precedent are 'laws' or 'rules of practice'.
57. The precepts of legality, see *post*, p. 146, fn. 99.
58. The fullest deliberation of the facts will be provided by a jury, 'a little parliament'. Its function in a democratic Practice is to deliver not the one right verdict but a well considered one. Although everything must be done to prove the facts, the penal Practice is not just a truth-certifying procedure. See Bankowski (1981: 266); Parker (1980: 96).
59. This point is considered more fully below in connection with the ground rules of the civil Practice, see *post*, p. 180. See the view of the Royal Commission on Criminal Justice (1993: 4): 'we ourselves doubt whether the fusion of the functions of investigation and prosecution and the direct involvement of the judges in both, are more likely to serve the interests of justice than a system in which the roles of police, prosecutors and judges are as far as possible kept separate and the judge who is responsible for the conduct of the trial is the arbiter of law but not of fact.'
60. The legislative reform of procedures is more likely to be undertaken by way of sporadic wholesale overhaul than regular monitoring and reform. There is, of course, an equal need for continuous regeneration of the rules by the participants in the penal Practice itself.
61. The emergence in England of the courts of criminal appeal as a distinct tier in the penal Practice was a slow and complex affair; see Kiralfy (1962: 128) for the beginnings of the process.
62. The differentiation of the penal Practice as it split off from the civil law Practice depends upon the unification of the criminal courts. The multiplicity of lesser courts are drawn into the Practice by way of appeals rather than judicial review. I have suggested that the process of unification is the result, not just of administrative rationalization, but of the perception that it is necessary for the achievement of legal justice. The powerful centripetal movement in the criminal law domain may be contrasted with the centrifugal tendencies of the civil law domain, i.e. the demands for alternative methods of adjudication and compensation.
63. An appeal court's affirmation of the reasoning of a lower court underlines the declaratory power of the lower court.
64. In view of its complexity and its employment by judges who are not officials, there is a degree of oversimplification in describing it as a rule conferring powers and imposing duties on officials; Raz (1970: 199).
65. The judges' lack of authority to legislate becomes clearer once the penal Practice is fully differentiated from the civil Practice. In the civil Practice the continuous development of the law through the process of litigation is of a qualitatively different sort from the refinement of statutory provisions in the penal Practice.
66. Non-statutory offences were formerly justified by reference to a common morality. 'There is no act which Christianity forbids that the law will not

reach, if it were otherwise Christianity would not be, as it has always been held to be, part of the law of England' *per* Best CJ in *Bird* v. *Holbrook* 1828. This represents a view of judicial authority of which traces linger to this day. In direct opposition to the view that the criminal law embodies the moral code of a Society, we must emphasize that most offences incorporated in the LS of the penal Practice are not the products of moral concern; 'a great many penal laws to be found in any modern legal system are enacted as measures of expediency to secure some policy of government evolved through a morally uncertain political process': Gross (1979: 382). See also Fuller (1971: 44): 'It would be grotesque indeed to select for the purposes of moral pedagogy many statutes in the books today.'

67. The LS rules prescribe punishments for single acts; they are not social rules (see below), nor are they recipes for the good life. It is generally agreed that penal laws cannot legitimately prescribe the punishment of an individual for being in a particular condition, or for leading a bad life. We would be inclined to say that penalties inflicted for holding certain religious beliefs, or having certain ethnic origins, were not punishments but instances of repression, persecution, or victimization. See Brennan (1968: 257); Plamenatz (1969: 173); Fuller (1964: 165-6); Hart (1968: 1813; Walzer (1970: 265). One implication of this is that the legislative Practices of Society must respect the law by defining specific offences rather than proscribing practices and activities. For breaches of this principle see Poulantzas (1978: 218).
68. Dias (1985: 338). It is important to differentiate between the domains of law, each of which focuses on a legal Practice. Although the norms of the penal Practice LS conform to Bentham's definition of a law, those in the LSS of the civil and public law Practices do not. The variety of norms in the different domains makes it impossible to describe all legal duties in terms of sanctions; Dias (1985: 236).
69. See the recommendations of Barbara Wootton (1963: 57). Her view that the 'primary objective of the criminal court is preventative rather than punitive' is subversive of democratic legitimacy. Wootton's concern was social hygiene: to cleanse society of the anti-social. See Gross (1979: 338-9). See also Duff's consideration (1986) of the possibility of 'diagnostic tribunals'. A disregard for the requirements of legal justice is apparent in the view that, although traditionally the work of the judge, the task of sentencing criminals is not an essential judicial function: Wade and Bradley (1985: 49).
70. The seriousness of an offence is not something which is given; it has to be decided. Because of the need to impose distinct penalties, because they are making sub-rules, when courts are making judgments about the seriousness of an act—a matter of degree—they are not involved in grading but in classifying. On grading see Urmson in Flew (ed.) (1966): significantly, he considers that 'right' and 'wrong' are not grading labels. See also Douglas (1987: 60).
71. For a useful analysis of the act see Gross (1979: 56): 'An act consists of events or states of affairs for which a person might be responsible according to the principles of responsibility that guide social judgments.'
72. It has been suggested that the principle of treating like cases alike is im-

possible to practise because of the difficulty of deciding which factual aspects of the case are relevant: Lyons (1993: 105). Although there is in general terms some truth in this, it is scarcely the case in criminal adjudication. For here the attention of the court is focused on an act, which is defined. The circumstances relevant to the commission of the act may well have been narrowed over a number of cases; they may be quite clear. The act is a familiar project, and a court will in a novel case be scrupulous in deciding whether the act done is similar to, or different from, other cases. The judge will spell out precisely which circumstances are relevant, and in doing so will have regard to the precedent which is being set.

73. The employment of *agents provocateurs* is clearly a relevant factor in the description of the act done.
74. To give undue weight to irrelevant factors will impede the impartial application of the law. Nevertheless I would claim that impartiality in the administration of legal justice itself entails that judges must in all cases be prepared to consider any *new* factors which might be relevant. On the impartial application of the law see Lyons (1993: 32-7).
75. The law is said to operate with a system of abstract rationality which decontextualizes, and insists on the equality of fault responsibility and voluntary action: Norrie (1983: 73). The dehumanization involved follows from the nature of the ideal penal norm and the way it is applied; justice excludes all features of individual identity and circumstance which are irrelevant.
76. The defences 'refine the wording of the offence'; they 'provide a more sophisticated account of the harm or evil sought to be prohibited': Robinson (1982: 209). However for Robinson the court's recognition of a justification does not redefine the act; the criminal act is done but justified (p. 214). Yet a crime is a *wrongful* act; if an act is justified it is not wrongful. On the view of Fletcher (1978: 178) that 'cases acknowledging that conduct is excused do not generate precedents that other people will rely on' see Hall (1982: 178) who insists that excuses are neither exceptions nor contradictions but additions to the rule.
77. Kant's assertion that to lie to a murderer in order to save anther's life is still a crime seems to underwrite a mistaken concept of a criminal wrong. A crime is to be defined not just as a neutral act but as a *wrongful* act. So the recognition of extenuating circumstances—which can be made express and are replicable—enables us to say that the act done, though it may have satisfied the act description of a widely drafted prohibitory rule, was in those circumstances not wrongful; it was in effect not the act which constitutes the offence. It is stressed that there is no logical requirement that the extenuating circumstances should be expressly stated in the rules. Justice requires only that exempting conditions recognized for the first time in one case, will be taken into account in the same way in all similar cases in future. Kant's approach illustrates that respect for rules which I call legality. Bentham provides us with a splendid illustration of legality applied in a badly drafted law: 'All who spill blood in the streets of Verona must die'. Applied literally, the physician who with the best of motives bleeds a patient in the street must be con-

demned to death. Recognition of a possible class of crimes of obedience indicates that, in exceptional circumstances, to follow the rules may itself be wrongful, or even criminal. See *Collision Regulations nnd Distress Signals Order* 1977, rule 2(b), which prescribes that if departure from the rules is essential to avoid imminent peril, no criminal liability arises.

78. A court committed to penal parsimony, to legal justice, and to respect for persons, will always be open to hearing new excuses; it is duty bound to deliberate on the possibility of distinguishing unlike cases. Given this commitment by the judges, we may wonder whether excuses in general stand in need of justification. See Hart (1968: 186-209).

79. These are matters for decision in the individual cases. Responsibility depends on beliefs and the knowledge available at a particular time. It is a matter upon which our intuition of the reality of free choice must be relied upon; see Gross (1979: 327). In view of this we can look again at the requirement of *mens rea*; it is not a conceptually necessary part of the criminal act; its absence is but an exculpating factor. See Martin (1993: 272). Although it is generally contrary to legal justice to punish those who do not act 'knowingly or willingly', it is nevertheless always open to the legislature to disallow this type of exculpating factor. Acceptable excuses are those which are agreed upon; but respect for persons is scarcely evident in crimes of strict liability.

80. Arguments based on the genetic inheritance of individuals would only be acceptable if it could be shown that all members of a class carrying a particular gene were unable to control their behaviour.

81. On which see Smith (1983) and Murphy and Hampton (1990). The ideal penal Practice is not a State agency. It is narrowly concerned with legally just punishment, not with enforcement Activity. What to do with a menace to society is to be decided not by judges but by those engaged in enforcement Activity; it involves political, ethical, and practical, rather than legal, questions. Detention or treatment which officials believe to be necessary for the public good must be closely scrutinized: the legality of the procedures would be a matter for the courts, but the discretion itself should be kept under review by a non-legal agency accountable to the Ultimate Legislative Practice (or ULP).

82. This does not mean that procedures for making decisions about the grant of pardons lie beyond the reach of judicial review. There could be well founded objections based on proof of arbitrary decision-making by the executive.

83. On the dehumanizing and decontextualizing of persons under the abstract rationality of the law, which assumes equality of responsibility and the voluntary action of the accused, see Norrie (1983: 73). For an account of the Islamic view that the Western practice of applying uniform rules and treating similar cases similarly is profoundly unjust see Rosen (1989). In Islamic legal thought justice requires a holistic analysis of the circumstances; decisions reflect notions of human well-being and harm.

84. The views set out here about punishment are broadly similar to those which Lucas calls vindicative (1993: 105). See also Feinberg (1')70: 95-118). The view that the function of punishment is to reaffirm social values (Lacey 1989: 193) must be seen to be foundationalist; the punishments do no more than reaffirm Society's penal norms. The notion that acts are also communications

has particular resonance here; the act of punishment constitutes one of the clearest and most basic of all communications between human beings in associational forms. The object of punishment is to reprobate, not to deter, prevent, or reform; nor is it as Hegel maintained, to annul the crime which would otherwise have been held valid, and to restore the right (1942: 69). Hart (1968: 234) calls this a piece of moral alchemy in which the two evils of moral wickedness and suffering are combined and transmuted into good.

85. Delinquency is a category employed in enforcement Activity, not in the penal Practice. In the interests of justice and legitimacy, it is imperative that the two forms be kept wholly separate. In the penal Practice the individual must be assumed to have autonomy and a free will—to be responsible—so that conditions which reduce that autonomy are recognized as excepting from criminal liability: Hart (1968). Foucault draws attention to the difference between the individual who is guilty at law, and the individual who is a deviant under a disciplinary regime. For Foucault the notion of the 'delinquent', which is the correlate of projects of reform or rehabilitation, is not a legal category. The punishments of law are not disciplinary or corrective, and do not rehabilitate or alter the person. To the detriment of just punishment, the penal Practice is infected with the categories of enforcement; in Foucault's words: 'normalising judgment has seeped into judicial judgment' (1977: 21).

86. The determination to minimize punishment is not something additional to legal justice; it is not a discretionary equity which tempers the legal mind. Penal parsimony is of the essence for a legal justice which has respect for persons.

87. The 'effectiveness' of legal punishment—however that is to be assessed—is not a matter for the judges. The imposition of a just penalty neither achieves nor is intended to achieve anything other than reprobation of the wrongdoing. Foucault (1977: 188) questions the effectiveness of disciplinary techniques. Many experts in the criminal justice system also feel that the impact of such techniques is marginal at best; see Friedman (1990: 138). In the case of punishment, as with other social institutions, the pursuit of one aim may be qualified by or provide an opportunity for the pursuit of another.

88. The problems of preserving order and containing lawless conduct are acute. The sheer volume of cases to be tried leads to routinization in the processing of cases—for example, to plea-bargaining: Freidman (1990: 139).

89. It is a commonplace to describe judges as officials, and courts as organs of the State. 'Judges are part of the machinery of authority within the State . . .' Griffith (1981: 190). See also Dworkin (1986: 355). However, in their judicial capacity, as participants in the penal Practice, judges are, it is emphasized, not officials. Within the democratic polity the doing of legal justice is never a State function. The autonomy of the legal Practice is easily overlooked, as for example in this definition of 'punishment': 'The word in its full and central sense may be defined as the infliction by some authority upon an offender of some penalty . . . for some offence against rules authorised by that authority' *Dictionary of Philosophy* (1979: 293). Yet the paradigm is of punishment ordered by judges who do *not* 'authorize the rules'.

90. They have an inherent authority to do legal justice, which involves authorlty to declare the law, to reform ground rules, to make valid NPs, etc. This authority derives from the rules, and is either direct or implicit. It is implicit, for instance, in the practical requirement that judges must have authority to keep order in court.
91. For Hobbes it 'belongeth to the office of the sovereign to make a right application of punishment and rewards': *Leviathan*, 228.
92. On the importance of distinguishing the artificial fonn Society from that of the Community, see *post*, Ch. 8. For a communitarian approach to criminal law see Lacey (1989).
93. See Arnold (1937) for illustrations of the way in which the corporation may be illegitimately personified.
94. On which see Evans (1987).
95. The dark saying that '(l)aw and social control are at the same time functionally related and conceptually distinct' (Kyggier 1976: 30) becomes clear if we pay attention to the different institutional forms involved: the legal Practice and enforcement Activity. On the difference between preventing a violation and punishing a violator, see Martin (1993: 219).
96. In addition to the use of deontological constraints, social control may be achieved by withholding resources, or by creating physical barriers, intervening in the markets, and so forth, with the intention of influencing behaviour, or denying, or allowing, citizens the opportunity to do certain things; see Porn (1970: 52 3).
97. In a non-legal regime the norms enforced will include principles as well as rules. In a polity in which law is equated with culture or ideology its norms are unlikely to have the clarity of legal rules. 'Many Chinese laws would appear to a Western observer to resemble statements of general principles and policies rather than a set of detailed rules': Li (1978: 42). The enforcement of communitarian norms may also involve education, rectification, and the remedial treahnent of offenders. See Li (1978: 87); also Teiwes (1976: 15-35). In earlier times communitarian enforcement was directed to sins as well as crimes. The maintenance of standards by regulatory inspectorates involves general norms, and a concern to prevent deviation in advance; see Kagan (1984: 37–64, Enforcement Activity which seeks to ensure conformity with legal rules is of a different character; it calls for centralized agencies whose personnel must have knowledge of the rules. Enforcement Activity is official; it is undertaken by State Organizations. The servicing of the penal Practice by the police and prosecution services is qualitatively different from efforts to secure conformity in the enforcement of community norms. Enforcement in a democratic polity is coercive; it is the enforcement of duties which a man not only ought but may be justly compelled to perform. Legal and extra-legal forms of social control co-exist; see Henry (1983: 21). If the form Society is constituted by enforcement Activity—the enforcement of legal social rules—the other institutional forms of our social life are replete with other controlling influences, activities, and Practices. The view that policing is relatively unimportant in the enforcement of law, Banton (1964: 127), seems to confuse the task of enforcing the legal rules of Society with the activity of ensuring

socially acceptable conduct, and securing conformity to norms in social life, upon which settled conditions depend.

98. Enforcement Activity in civil Society is limited to dealing with conduct which has failed to conform to the legal rules.

99. The precepts of legality include a wide range of norms, from the general principles of policing and prosecuting to such particulars as the Judges' Rules. On the practical difficulties which may be encountered in enforcement see Federico (1995: 233-42). It is important to preserve the distinction between the two forms involved in the domain of criminal law: the penal Practice and enforcement Activity. Postema (1986) draws attention to a possible conflict between two maxims of punishment: that every offender must be brought to trial, and that no one should be punished unfairly. Each is appropriate to a different form: the first is a precept of legality which applies only to enforcement Activity, while the second has relevance only in penal Practice.

100. Duff (1986: 192) refers to the possibility that 'a system of law which adhered strictly to the demands of autonomy and justice would be so ineffectual that it would simply ensure its own destruction'. The waters are muddied here by the ambiguity of 'system of law'. Strict adherence is precisely what is required of the healthy legal Practice; by contrast, the precepts of legality governing enforcement Activity will be subject to considerations of common sense, economy, and effectiveness. In keeping the peace—in enforcement Activity—autonomy and justice are not priorities, for enforcement Activity is not penal. The individual's worth will be respected in the penal Practice; his rights against officials involved in enforcement Activity are the concern of the Public Law Practice.

101. The Police Commission's 1828 description of the duties of the police was: the prevention of crime, the detection of criminals, and their punishment; Whittaker (1964: 88). On the different approaches to enforcement see Packer (1968).

102. The servicing of the penal Practice—the prosecution of offenders—is part of enforcement Activity; it is not a responsibility of the courts. Cf. Dworkin (1986: 224). See Edgeworth (1986: 134) on the ideological aspects of prosecution.

103. Enforcement Activity and legal punishment occur within the associational form Society. Punishments within disciplinary regimes of other associational forms—such as the Organizations of churches, armies, corporations, etc.—are a different matter, involving wholly distinct conceptual structures and activities. To regard such norms, or such activity, as part of the 'living law' is deplorable. They do not fall within the enforcement Activity of Society. The Practice claim to monopoly over Society's punishments must be qualified in that regulatory agencies have recently been given powers to order fines and payments which are enforceable by law. Over such regulatory agencies the courts have, at best, a power of review. To claim an appellate role would be to assume regulatory functions. Regulation of this sort is extremely important, but should not be regarded as a legal function.

104. The integrity of the penal Practice which claims the monopoly is of supreme

constitutional importance. It will be subverted if the courts countenance behaviour by officials which prejudices either basic human rights or the rule of law in order to bring criminals to justice, e.g. where evidence is obtained, or the defendant brought within the jurisdiction, by unlawful acts. See the dissenting views of Zander and Newbold on the recommendations of the *Report of the Royal Commission on Criminal Justice 1993* (at 233–5) regarding improper pre-trial procedures.

105. The Royal Commission on Criminal Justice was of the opinion that not only should courts be separated from the enforcement agencies but that the prosecution should be separate from the police, pp. 3–4.

106. Those pressures on the judges to solve social problems may go some way to explain why they so often misdescribe their legitimate authority. The view that judges are the key performers in the preservation of law and order is widely shared. 'In the criminal law the judges regard themselves as at least as much concerned as the executive with the preservation of law and order' Lord Devlin, in Griffiths (1981: 191). Smith (1985: 608) argues that in protecting the citizen against the State it is wrong for the courts to 'behave as an integral part of an institution whose principle purpose is the prevention of crime through the use of the criminal law'.

107. Packer's two different models of criminal system, the crime control model and the due process model (1968: 153–73) may be said to reflect the distinction between the two central institutional forms in the criminal domain.

108. Take as an instance Hart's characterization of criminal laws as making conduct non-optional. It is social rules which operate in this way, not the LS rules of the penal Practice.

109. Kelsen distinguishes between primary and secondary norms (1973: 61). The secondary norm, useful in the exposition of the law, prescribes the behaviour which the legal order endeavours to bring about in the primary norm—the only genuine legal norm—which stipulates the sanction. Codes are normally addressed to the people, but not always: see Paton and Derham (eds.) (1972: 312). The Great Code of punishments of the Ching Dynasty was a complex and sophisticated document addressed to officials: Kamenka and Tay (1978: 11).

110. They do not call for the existence of an internal attitude as Hart suggests (1994: 116). They are implicated, and acted upon, within an institutional form .

111. The *desiderata* which Fuller (1964: ch. 3) says rules should satisfy are appropriate for social rules, for the rules of enforcement Activity. The *desiderata* for the other norms in the legal field, the NPs, ground rules, and LS rules of the penal Practice, are somewhat different. Fuller's congruence between official action and express rules could be taken to indicate the connection between the norms of enforcement Activity and the LS rules. The importance of the close approximation of social rules to the LS rules is clear but, no matter how close, they are norms of different types. Social rules are not the same as, but deductions from the LS rules. The closeness of the match is called for under the precepts of legality. Cf. Raz (1975: 130).

112. For historical examples of partiality in law enforcement see Friedman (1993). For contemporary studies of the nature and problems of enforcement see Cotterrell (1992: 245-85). Pressures on the police to achieve efficiency targets and reduce crime-rate statistics may result in failure to record or prosecute offences. Patchy enforcement may lead to decriminalization by stealth: Society no longer reprobates, and victims are left to pursue their remedies at civil law.
113. Norms must always be anchored in their institutional forms. Legal advice rules, the rules of black-letter law, are located primarily in the professional Activity of lawyers. For the sake of simplicity I include the expository activity of academics within a general Activity of legal advice. The propositions which academics make about the law are identified by Ross (1958: chs. 1 and 2). He distinguishes between legal norms proper and doctrinal propositions about legal norms. Kelsen distinguishes prescriptive from descriptive norms (1973: 54-6); see Hart (1Y83: 286-95). Villa (1984: 260) recognizes two social practices 'which interact with each other; the practice of legal science . . . and the complex social practices which make up a legal system as a working order'. Such a distinction between legal advice Activity and the other forms in the legal field is useful; however, we must recognize the two major forms within what Villa calls the 'working legal order': the legal Practices and the enforcement Activity.
114. Legal advice Activity is a distinct institutional form. Like many other Activities, it is regulated: there are standards which must be observed. They are the *precepts of legal advice*. Like the precepts of legality they are based on respect for the law—concern for the integrity of the legal Practice. This is an exegetical Activity, attempting to set out precisely what the laws as social rules are. It includes academic legal science. Although professional legal advice Activity differs from academic Activity, the norms employed in the discourse of each share a common character and status. The 'descriptive' character of the norms of legal science is to be contrasted with the prescriptive force of the LS rules or the rules in enforcement Activity. Legal science, the concern of the academics, has in the nature of things different objectives, values, and standards from the Activity of professional lawyers. The educative function promotes the values of coherence, clarity, simplicity, exactness, and a greater emphasis on critical appraisal and demands for reform. Legal Advice is sought where the law is either not known at all, or is unclear. In this Activity there are no right answers; authoritative legal answers can only be supplied by the courts after deliberation. The lawyer may try to predict but, given the nature of legal deliberation, prediction cannot become a science; nor is it the task of legal science to make decisions which judges must make. See Kelsen (1934: 131). If I am right in tying the norms of legal advice to an Activity, then we must recognize that although the AI school may achieve useful results for legal science, they cannot take the place of the deliberations of the legal Practices. See Samuel (1994). This is simply because legitimate democratic procedures must aspire to achieve pure, not perfect, procedural justice, and therefore the decisions are almost by definition unpredictable. Legal science can order material with skill,

bringing out principles from which we can discern lines of possible development. However, given the miscellaneous character of legal material, there are always serious problems about the validity of that ordering and those principles. The rigour of computer operations can never remove the taint of foundationalism.

115. Arguments about legal science, legal reasoning, and conflicts between black-letter lawyers and sceptics or critics have their institutional context in legal advice Activity. Certainly, that appears to be the target of the critical legal studies movement. Arguments rage over how we should define the law in general, the law which could be set out for the uninitiated as a system, a body of knowledge. The concerns of academics and lawyers are not the concerns of judges and their LS rules, nor of enforcers and their social rules. Many academic arguments are essentially about the style in which we should set out the law for those who do not know what the law is. Theorists can easily take themselves too seriously, for legal advice can be given in various styles; a lawyer with a conventionalist approach may give good advice; the highly sceptical might also give practical advice of equal worth. The black-letter approach has virtues in some situations and realism in others; we ought, however, to question the motives of those who confuse legal advice with legal reform. Not every client, or law student, wants to be told what the law ought to be. Nor can academics pre-empt the outcomes of law generating in the legal and the legislative Practices of a democratic polity. We need to be aware of the concealed non-legal value choices that underlie the legal scholar's recommendations.

116. There is a point at which deviations from the rule remake the rule itself. Thus every act leads a double life, it constitutes conformity and becomes part of the societal process whereby action is defined': Unger (1976). This may be true of the norms employed in enforcement Activity, but is untrue of the LS rules. In the penal Practice the act is defined in fixed categories: the LS rules cannot be modified by behaviour.

117. For instance, blasphemy is on the statute books but is no longer prosecuted in the USA or the UK; see Levy (1992). Sociology certainly cannot deny the existence of a statute which has been forgotten, nor deny it legal validity as long as it meets the requirements of validity accepted by the legal system: Grace and Wilkinson (1978). Unenforced promulgated laws will not be part of enforcement Activity, nor will they be incorporated in the LS of the legal Practice. However, once they are incorporated they will remain in the LS until they are removed. See Li (1978: 20) for examples of enacted rules which are not enforced.

118. On the predictive account of legal obligation see Kelsen (1973: 171-4); for a critique of Austin's analysis of legal obligation see Hart (1994: 83-4). See Ross (1958: 38-58): 'Assertions concerning valid law are according to their real content a prediction of future social happenings' (p.49). A predictive account of our obligations is appropriate for those arising under laws which operate as social rules, which are the objects of enforcement Activity. For enforcement can, notoriously, be patchy; if there is no effort to enforce a social rule we can scarcely be said to have obligations under it. However, any such facts

about enforcement—of interest to the bad man or the social scientist—are clearly irrelevant to considerations of the existence of a rule which has been incorporated in the LS of the legal Practice.

119. See Dias (1985: 239-46) for a catalogue of duties of imperfect obligation. Strictly, no duties arising under social rules in the civil law domain are sanctioned or enforced.
120. On standard maintenance rules—'regulatory law'—see Cotterrell (1992: 257-69); Hawkins and Thomas (eds.) (1984); and Hawkins (1984).
121. In standard-maintenance there is no concern for legal justice, no respect for persons; the aim is to secure compliance with general standards. The regulatory Activity is governed by precepts of regulation, rather than by the precepts of legality which govern enforcement Activity. Strictly, this Activity lies outside, although obviously adjacent to, the legal domain. Inspectorates are extra-legal regimes; see *post*, Ch. 5. For the activity of standard-maintenance we need a different set of concepts.
122. The European Court of Justice hands down judgments about the conformity of member States to environmental standards. These are cases in which the Court sets and enforces those standards; matters which do not fall within the authority of a court of justice.
123. On the legislative foundations of all modern criminal systems, see *ante* p. 106. For Bentham's attack on judge-made law see Postema (1986: 275-86). See also Smith (1985: 608). For comments on the principles of interpretation of statutory provisions which might have penal implications see Cross (1995: 187) and Bennion (1992: 571-94). We must also recognize that most offences are designed to implement governmental policies, rather than to secure respect for generally accepted moral standards of conduct: Gross (1979: 382).
124. On the difference between justifying punishment in general and particular punishments see Hart (1959: 160) and (1968: 5-6).
125. The criminal laws of a Society consist of a miscellany of absolute commands and prohibitions. The notion that they have any factor in common is false. At best they are the products of a legislative Practice which is assumed to be in some way representative. In discussions of criminal law the predominance of technical crimes is commonly ignored; the moral wrong-doing in such offences as using non-metric units, or planting coconuts, is not immediately apparent. It is important to resist the idea that the criminal laws give expression to passions widely felt, or reflect some common moral sense. It is simply untrue that, as Durkheim claimed, crimes comprise acts universally condemned by members of each Society: Lukes and Scull (eds.) (1983: 42). Courts should be deaf to the *colère publique*. No doubt passions may run high over some offences, but any overview of our criminal law—the set of laws which prescribe penalties for acts—will reveal nothing more than a neutral miscellany of prohibited acts which have been agreed upon.
126. Society is a dissensus (see *post*, Ch. 7); there is thus no community basis for criminal law. Foundationalists, supposing otherwise, stress the values of the community. 'Punishment,' said Lord Denning in his evidence to the Royal Commission in 1953, 'is the emphatic denunciation by a community of a

crime.' For Hart, punishment is 'ratification of a morality which has been violated'. (1963: 63). The stronger the emotional response to the wrongdoing, the more likely it is to conjure up a community which is to be protected. It should be noted that a jury is not composed of representatives of a community; it has been described as a 'little Parliament', consisting of individuals who are to deliberate as fairly and fully as possible.

127. So it is stressed that the legislature produces morally neutral rules. It is not legislating a moral code but formulating prohibitions often attaching to policies. Therefore a statute can never be either pro-life or pro-choice.

128. Judges require clear rules to justify the NP. The justification for a punishment is always an enacted rule, never an explanatory reason. Soper (1984: 118) argues that officials must be able to show that the sanctions are not unfair and that they do this by reference to the public interest. See Griffith (1991: 274 82) for justification by judges in terms of public interest.

129. There can be no general theory which provides all the answers. Foundationalists play a supremely important role in providing arguments for Groups to use in the legislative debate; it is their claims of having discovered the only solutions which are to be ignored. The importance of accepting compromise, of recognizing the provisional nature of our laws, is overlooked by absolutists claiming to have final solutions: the consequences of such absolutism can be seen in the abortion debate in the USA. The institutional form we live in, Society, requires the acceptance of an ineradicable relativism in the political arena; it is our duty as citizens to recognize the dissensus, and hence to accept as law rules which we believe to be unjust. Civic relativism is the outcome of the struggle for religious toleration. Secular philosophies such as liberalism may make claims similar to those made by religious Groups, but the law cannot recognize them. The only possible positive outcomes for a dissensus are compromises. Foundationalists speak only for Groups. Even the universally accepted rule acquires its authority, not from our moral revulsion, but from the fact of its legitimate enactment. Joel Feinberg (1990) makes no claims to privilege liberal values; the criteria he employs are relevant and important to any debate about criminal law, but are not said to be decisive.

130. Coercion is necessary not merely for the existence of the associational form Society, but for the implementation of policies democratically agreed upon. Voluntary compliance with a joint venture would require that co-operation would be to each person's advantage; but some might find it to their advantage to defect from the joint strategy while inducing others to comply. So if collective action is to succeed, strategies fixed collectively must be coercively enforced. See Coleman (1988: 290).

131. In a democracy the question of what types of punishments are to be inflicted must be answered in the legislative Practice. They are questions of penal policy, which the judges have no inherent authority to decide. Famously, the Supreme Court in the USA determined that capital punishment was not 'cruel or barbaric'.

132. This was the view of the Marxists, for whom Parliament was no more than a committee of the ruling class.

133. The analysis here is of penal norms in a democratic polity. Only there can socially necessary inflictions of punishment have complete justification. The penalties imposed by a colonial power cannot; see Bryde (1976: 15-16).
134. When decisions about penalties are being determined in the legislature the *desideratum* of penal parsimony can only be maintained if there is a powerful opposition demanding respect for the law. The problem of over criminalization is serious. See Hall (1982: ch. 11) on the penalization of inadvertent behaviour. See also Fletcher (1978). However, this is a political not a legal problem. Legislative restraint should be called for by a legitimate opposition which demands respect for law. The failure of a legislative Practice to monitor criminal laws is a serious dereliction.
135. The suggestion that the minimum punishment sufficient to ensure against crime can be determined by reference to considered judgment in the community leaves the matter very uncertain; Gross (1979: 439). We need to substitute Society for the community, and to recognize that the legislative Practice of that Society is the only forum in which its collective judgments can be made. We are dealing with the practical judgments of a democracy, with questions which philosophy cannot answer.
136. Respect for the law means that the legislature confers power deliberately, not indirectly, by the statutory promulgation of a principle. What I have called a Hyeckian Horror is an enactment which, while purportedly imposing legal duties or conferring new rights or duties on citizens, in fact confers discretionary powers on judges or officials. Any such powers must be scrutinized and deliberated. Courts of law are inappropriate forums for legislative deliberation.
137. The judge does not require guidelines or a list of good reasons. There can be no incorporation of principles in the LS because principles do not decide cases. Offences must be precisely defined by the rules. The definition of a corrupt practice in a Ghanaian statute as: 'bribery, wilful oppression or extortion or any other act contrary to the public order or prejudicial to the economic or financial interests of the state' (Corrupt practices (Prevention) Act 1965, s. 9) exhibits an open texture comparable with Bentham's example of a bad law, see *ante*, fn. 77.
138. The ideal legislative Practice would have full knowledge of both long-established laws and the latest decisions and regulations. Only then could the democratic ideal that all laws are maintained by the ULP be asserted; see Martin (1993: 133).
139. Members of Society, having no general views, will take many of their moral standards wholesale from the written law. Where else is there so rich or authoritative a source in cases of doubt? See Beckman (1984: 29). Observers of traditional societies have sometimes cited the law as proof of the existence of customs; see Roberts (1979: ch. 2). 'Anything as straightforward as a community morality is nonsense at the top of a very high ladder'; Griffith (1979: 11). Equally, we may doubt the validity of Durkheim's assertion that crimes are universally condemned by the members of Society. They disturb the feelings which in any single society are to be found in every healthy conscience; Lukes and Scull (eds.) (1983: 42).
140. Acts formerly regarded as normal can subsequently be prohibited: slavery

was once an acceptable part of civilized life. Equally, punishable acts can cease to be prohibited: buggery is no longer a capital offence; gays can demonstrate publicly; abortion in some circumstances is now a right. See Friedman (1993).

141. Although a rule may be generally perceived as no longer necessary, the doctrine of *desuetudo* and the maxim *ratio legis cessante* pose dangers for judges; for if there is little doubt about the obsolescence of some rules, there will inevitably be far more borderline instances, opinions as to the necessity of which differ.
142. See Grace and Wilkinson (1978: 275).
143. See Hart (1994: 45–8).
144. The penal Code is not a sacred heirloom. Every law must be regarded as a contemporary choice, approved by the current legislature. Experience is important in deciding whether to retain or repeal a law. The unintended consequences of enactments may be such as to require their repeal. We must not let the fact that laws provide stability detract from the fact of their contingency. All laws can be repealed; all are provisional.
145. The monitoring of the criminal law is the duty of the executive accountable to the legislature.
146. See Fuller (1971: 155–7) for a consideration of the extent to which functions of government should be discharged through processes modelled on those of a court of law.
147. On the separation of law from morality see Cohen (1950).

5
Civil Law

I: THE CAPITALIST FOUNDATIONS OF CIVIL LAW

The civil law which governs relationships between members of a democratic Society, is generated in a legal adjudicatory Practice—the civil Practice—which occupies a central position among the institutional forms of capitalism. This legal Practice is an inextricable part of a market economy, so that the nature of the legal norms, the categories of law, and the institutional logic of the civil law domain must be understood in terms of the concepts and language of capitalism.[1] Capitalism is not a contingent background, or a mere context for the civil law; it is the necessary character of the Society in which civil law is generated. The idea of the legal Practice, the meaning of the legal justice it administers, can only be understood in the light of the engagement by every member of Society in certain capitalist Practices.

Although the legal civil Practice is located within the institutional structure of a capitalist Society, it must not be thought that its governing idea can be described as a capitalist ideology, as a doctrine about the manner in which goods should be distributed. The idea of the civil Practice is founded upon legal justice and legal rights, not upon conceptions of social justice. Legal justice and legal rights do indeed depend absolutely upon the engagement by members of Society in capitalist Practices, but because the law depends upon rules, the doing of legal justice—which involves the protection of legal rights—is wholly incompatible with the application of rules under the influence of ideas of social justice which stem from capitalist activity. The objective of participants in the legal Practice is to do legal justice, not to promote capitalism or ameliorate the social consequences of the working of the market economy.[2]

I take it to be a fundamental axiom of legitimacy that, although the law is central to democratic and capitalist forms of life, it can never, if it is to remain in its proper place, embrace foundational philosophies of social justice inspired by the values of democratic government or the market economy.

Our purpose is to understand the nature of Society as the associational form in which a civil law can be generated; we are not concerned to investigate the character of capitalism as a type of economic organization, or to consider its varieties. Among the range of institutional forms which are part of the capitalist system, we are concerned here only with those forms which create the conditions in which every individual member of Society is a person to whom respect must be shown in the market-place. In other words, we must concentrate on the catallactic dimension of capitalism, on the exchange Practices by which individuals transact business. These Practices make possible the acts of sale, purchase, loan, and so forth, and the creation of individual entitlements which need to be protected. Organizations and Activities associated with the production of goods are obviously essential preconditions for the emergence of universal Practices of systematic exchange; but it is in exchange Practices, not in Organizations and Activities, that the language of individual entitlement is generated.

A: The nature of the systematic exchange Society

Money is the badge or symbol of what I call the systematic exchange (or SE) Society: that is a Society whose members understand the logic of money and systematic exchange. It is an associational form in which *all* members rely upon the use of money, which functions as a medium of exchange, the unit of account, the standard of deferred payment and a store of value. Money is not an invention of Princes but a product of social interaction, emerging from particular Practices of exchange. Money is unlikely to result from unrelated, isolated, exchange transactions; its appearance is dependent upon the gradual establishment of extensive networks of systematically interrelated exchange transactions in which the values of objects exchanged can be calculated by reference to the 'rates of exchange' in the market-place. In an SE Society all members must necessarily participate in the Practice of systematic exchange; they must all buy and sell in accordance with valuations established in other exchange transactions. In short: they all use money.

In institutional theory attention is directed not towards money as a thing, as an object of ownership—which it is—but towards activity: the innumerable systematically interrelated transactions in which alone money exists. Money can all too easily be presented as just one more asset, co-ordinate with cars, shares, pictures, and land. It is emphasized that money is only part of, albeit an essential element within, particular patterns of human activity; that it exists only as an informing element within the catallactic segment of the social life of members of SE Society.

Beneficial position Practices

Universal familiarity with the use of money in systematic exchange transactions is necessary for the emergence, or institution, of a wide range of what I call *beneficial position Practices.* These are Practices which make it possible to create new, socially recognized, normative positions of benefit and entitlement. I have in mind Practices in which are created such things as leases, mortgages, loans trusts, wills, debts, contracts, bank deposits, partnerships, and so forth. Participation in these Practices is open to all members of Society. Indeed, many BP Practices play an essential part in the everyday life of members, all of whom must buy and sell, borrow and lend in order to acquire the goods needed to live. It is open to very few in the modern world to opt out of participation in the market-place, or to get by without the use of money.[3]

The necessary engagement by all members in exchange and other BP Practices, all of which depend upon the existence of money, is a feature of all modern Societies. They are all, no matter what the political ideology or economic policies of the State, SE Societies. Most Societies have their own currencies; except in troubled times, their members engage in market transactions in terms of that unit of account, employing that medium of exchange. No government has yet invented, or discovered, methods of distributing goods, or ways of co-ordinating economic activity, in which the use of money can be transcended; no Society can afford, as a Community may, to rely upon barter or the administrative distribution of goods.

There is ample evidence that in the course of history the emergence of SE Societies, in which all members use money and engage in systematic exchange transactions, has constituted a revolution. The revolutionary nature of monetary penetration can be seen most dramatically in Communities into which money and the Practices of systematic exchange have been introduced suddenly. In the history of Western Societies the complicated, gradual, episodic emergence and elaboration of systematic exchange Practices has no doubt served to obscure the nature of the revolution which has taken place, but revolution there has been.[4] For the development of extensive systematic exchange transactions not only alters the nature, it vastly increases the variety of types of entitlement which members may claim. Money makes possible, and is a necessary constituent of, new forms of social interaction; forms in which the world is articulated in ways hitherto inconceivable.[5] Since in a capitalist Society so many objects are capable of being employed in market transactions, its members, as participants in various Practices, adopt an arithmetic view of the world and divide or construct its constituent parts in terms of their value and acceptability in exchange transactions. Marx was at his most eloquent in describing the attitude of members of an SE Society in which every conceivable object, from a man's hope of eternal salvation to a woman's virtue, could be expressed in terms of its exchange value.

There is then a world of difference between an SE Society and a non-SE Community. Jurists and sociologists writing about law and society in modern times have sometimes failed to pay sufficient attention to the most important of all reciprocal actions: the interaction of members as participants in SE Practices. As members of Society, human beings, speaking the universal language of money, are related to each other primarily as participants in the SE Practices. From the institutional point of view SE activity is central to our understanding of the legal field. The establishment of SE Practices on a large scale allowing for—or perhaps condemning all members of Society to—an arithmetic view of the world, is arguably a necessary precondition for the appearance of civil law.

The persons of systematic exchange Society

Individualism constitutes a central strand in the world-view of SE Society members. Every member capable of engaging in market transactions is regarded in the market-place as distinct from, and equal to, all other members, whatever his or her status in traditional orderings of rank and privilege, and regardless of the position he or she may hold within any organization.[6]

Money allows for great precision and discrimination in social relationships. The needs, deserts, and wants of individuals can be precisely catered for; each individual can be rewarded for his or her individual efforts, and each individual's entitlement in a joint enterprise, or in indivisible property, can be calculated and realized in monetary terms. The use of money accustoms us to the idea that all individuals have a personal account in which we may itemize all the valuable things they own and possess. From one point of view, every man and woman in an SE Society is a merchant, and each is entitled to the things he or she has acquired by participation in SE activity. The egalitarianism of the market—in which all are free to participate in SE Practices—is of course wholly unaffected by the gross inequalities of wealth which result from the choices made by individuals as they participate in the market.[7] In an SE Society it will be generally agreed that because the advantages of allowing all members to participate in the systematic exchange and other BP Practices are so great, the exclusion of any class from the market must be exceptional and by way of deliberate prescription.

It may be natural to regard the membership of an SE Society as being, like the membership of a Community, composed of human beings. However, the operation of the principles of systematic exchange calls for a radical change in our conception of personality. The members of a Society dominated by SE transactions should be conceived of, not as human beings, but as catallactic nodes: separate accounts into and out of which property and money can be transferred. The persons involved, located at the intersection of impersonal relations of exchange, include not just human beings but other entities which, by virtue of their participation in SE transactions, cannot be overlooked. So among the players in what

Adam Smith called the 'great game' we must include artificial persons; entities which own property, owe money, possess separate accounts, and are able—through human agents—to take part in all types of BP Practices. Such artificial persons are irreducible; that is, their accounts and property entitlements cannot be ascribed to the individual human beings who are connected to them, either as agents or as the beneficiaries of their SE dealings. These beings are to be understood only according to the logic of SE activity, entities which it would be irrational for the law to refuse to recognize as persons to whom respect is due.

All human beings are capable of standing as catallactic nodes; it is in this way that they are to be regarded as members of the SE Society: as bearers of entitlements and interests.

Interests and Entitlements

In the market-place the person—the member of Society—is to be respected not for his or her human qualities and virtues but only because of his or her possession of marketable things. This must also be the attitude of the law.

In the language of the SE world we ascribe to members of Society two types of objects. The first type I call simply *entitlements* (E); these are transferable positions which are owned. The second type are *interests (I)* which are non-transferable; they are not owned but possessed by, and regarded as belonging to, the member.[8]

Each member of Society is conceived of as being the owner or possessor of a number of such IE. Though commonly referred to as the rights of individuals, such things are not legal rights, but the objects of the legal rights. So if we would understand the civil law and the legal rights it protects it is important to have a clear idea of the nature of these two types of objects. Interests and entitlements are the objects involved in SE transactions; they are objects over which disputes arise. It will be in the civil Practice that many of the disputes will be resolved, and the objects given their legal articulation.

Both interests and entitlements may be described as *socially recognized positions of entitlement to benefits.*[9] The benefits may be of almost any sort; there are a huge variety of advantages which individuals desire. If objects are to feature in SE transactions, they must yield benefits to someone. They must be things which it is better to have than not to have. The objects owned and possessed, the things which yield benefits, are socially recognized positions. So a statement that A owns or possesses an object—an IE—is never a brute fact; it does not denote a physical relationship to some material thing from which benefits flow, nor does it mean the actual receipt or enjoyment of benefits. Rather it asserts an *institutional fact;* that A has a defined *position* of entitlement, necessarily recognized by other members and involving duties of respect owed by them. That recognition is, it must be emphasized, not necessarily legal recognition.

As institutional objects, it is not possible adequately to describe interests of entitlements in purely normative terms. For instance, it is never enough to say of a piece of property that it is a bundle of rights and duties, as such a description ignores the fact that, as things in SE transactions, they are objects with an exchange value, related to the benefits they can produce, and which can be entered in the account of the person. In legal discourse the fact that the interest or entitlement has value may be taken as read, as a truism not worth commenting upon. However, the value of the object is not a contingent but a necessary quality which, if ignored, can lead to misdescription of the role of the law.

Both interests and entitlements are vulnerable: an owner or possessor may, in a variety of ways, be deprived for the benefits to which he is entitled by the actions of other members of Society. Other members may, in breach of their social duties of respect for entitlements, prevent the holder from enjoying the benefits to which he or she is entitled. In a competitive society members are regarded as being justified in striving to protect their property and in seeking restitution for any benefits of which they have been deprived.

II: THE CIVIL LAW PRACTICE

The legal Practice for the adjudication of disputes between members of a Society has capitalist foundations. However, the emergence of the Practice as an autonomous form is dependent upon changes not only in the economic but also in the legal and political fields. In the legal field of a democratic polity we can observe a process of differentiation by which, in the quest for more perfect justice, the penal Practice splits off from the all-purpose structures of legal adjudication and enforcement to achieve autonomy as a specialist body. This process, whereby the criminal courts assume the monopoly of power to punish in the name of Society, sets the civil law Practice free to concentrate upon working out the logic of civil justice.[10]

Although intimations of the imperatives of civil justice were noted in the tribunals of antiquity; although many of its claims have found eloquent expression down the centuries; and although, in a great variety of local courts, fair adjudication of disputes between individuals may have been achieved, the establishment of the conditions for the emergence of a unified civil law Practice, in which legal justice can be realized for all members of a Society, is a relatively recent achievement. The adjudicatory institutions—local, royal, ecclesiastic, aristocratic, manorial, and urban—

could never constitute a recognizable, unified institutional form: a legal Practice. It was in order to compensate for the heterogeneity of the courts that jurists, placing the emphasis on a substantial justice, sought to establish the unity of a Society's law, either in some comprehensive text or in the abiding customs of community life. A Practice, animated by the idea of legal justice as an absolute, capable of giving consistent protection to rights and of satisfying the needs of democratic legitimacy, can only be established through institutional developments in the political field.

The civil law of a Society can only be understood in terms of its generation within a Practice which is animated by the idea of justice.

A: The idea of the civil Practice

Legal justice is to be understood as respect for persons. As the animating idea of the civil law Practice, expressed in the Institutes of Justinian as 'the constant and perpetual will to give to each his own right', this respect is qualitatively different from the respect which must be shown in the penal Practice.[11] In setting out the idea of the civil Practice a precise account can be given of the individualism of the law, and of why the law's image of the legal person may be inappropriate when making practical judgments in other areas of social interaction. The law's individualism can only be understood by reminding ourselves of the nature of the Society in which the judges do legal justice: a democratic Society in which all members are engaged in SE Activity.

Legal persons

The persons for whom the courts guarantee respect are, I have suggested, essentially the players in the SE game: those who must be recognized as separate entities with the capacity to engage in SE transactions. It is this identification of the legal person as a player in the SE game which gives the respect shown to persons by the civil law its peculiar character. The persons who must be respected in SE activity include not only human beings but also artificial persons who are, after all, the most prominent players in the game. We should never overlook the fact that corporations are involved in a very considerable proportion of civil litigation.

In addition to ordinary artificial persons, there is no reason why the State should not be recognized as a person to be respected, insofar as its officials operate as agents who claim no special status for the State in their engagement in SE transactions with citizens. Nevertheless, relationships between the State and its citizens in SE transactions are often governed by special regimes. There is the added complication that, as a conglomerate, the State is made up of departments and agencies some of which are recognized as having a separate legal personality.

However, legal personality is not extended to informal collectives and classes, largely because they lack an economic identity. That is, they cannot normally be identified as having separate accounts in the transactions of the SE economy, nor do they own property or possess definable interests of the type which the law can recognize.[12]

The respect which the law extends to the legal person must be understood as a concern for the individual as the owner or possessor of an IE. In law persons are to be respected, not for what they are, but for what they possess. The courts are not concerned to compel others to respect persons in any other way than as owners and possessors. Persons are not to be respected for their personal qualities, character, social status, experience, or history, nor for their needs, desires, or deserts, but only for what they possess; that is, for the interests and entitlements which, as positions of benefit, they possess in the eyes of the law.

The court's protection can only be given in respect of those IE which a person presently, actually possesses.[13] The IEs protected must, we may say, be vested. Persons are respected for what they are recognized as possessing, not for those interests which they, or anyone else, consider that they ought to possess. So the respect due in law is limited to those possessions as they are defined by the rules in the LS of the civil Practice. The courts are obviously not concerned to protect IEs which are recognized by others but not by the law.[14] Such interests and entitlements are to be found in the extra-legal regimes existing within Society (see *post*, p. 167). The existence of such legally unrecognized IEs is of great importance, and worth noting here as a reminder of the fact that most IEs—and most BP Practices—now recognized by the law, are not the original creations of the courts or the legislature, but have a grass-roots origin, emerging out of the practices and customs of social life.

This conception of the person as a mere aggregate of IEs must be adopted by courts committed to doing legal justice, to treating like cases alike.[15] Here we have the very essence of the legal point of view. For the logic of legal justice which would have us treat like cases alike demands that we view persons as possessors of IE. If courts are to maintain the ideal of equality they must recognize the identity of the things which members possess. They must ensure that citizen A who possesses an x is treated in the same way as citizen B who possesses an identical x, no matter how different A otherwise may be from B. It is the law's employment of these categories of persons and their possessions which gives legal language its distinctive character. The moment you move away from this person-thing articulation you cease to use legal language; and any adjudication in terms other than these will not be legal adjudication.[16]

So the doing of legal justice involves a highly specific, market-oriented conception of the individual. The legal person is not an integrated personality; he is not a whole to be described by his aspirations, goals, or needs, nor by his relationships with others.[17] The courts are not concerned with a person's good, but with his or her goods. In the legal person we have the true atomic individual, a nucleus around which the IEs circle. In law the individual is not a unique being, for all are owners and possessors of the same kinds of things. The person is the sum of the IEs he or she possesses, and is to be respected only for those things.[18] So, from the legal point of view, members of Society confront each other as owners and possessors of things—defined positions of benefit—and in a court of law their claims to respect are determined solely by their possessions. An actionable wrong is not subjectively defined, but is treated as a wrong to an objectively identifiable thing to which duties of respect are owed. Although the law must indirectly recognize the involvement of men and women in forms of life which give meaning to their lives, in the eyes of the law individuals face each other as two-dimensional legal persons possessed of a limited range of economic and civil entitlements and interests.[19]

The two kinds of interests and entitlements

In a democratic Society members possess two sorts of interests and entitlements: *economic IE,* which are generated within SE activity, and *civil interests,* which are recognized as arising in social interaction outside SE activity. In other words, in the eyes of the law each member is regarded not only as a player in the SE game but also as a neighbour in a civil association, entitled to live his or her life without interference from others.

Economic interests and entitlements

It is not difficult to find a rationale for the law's protection of economic interests, both property entitlements and the non-transferable interests which are generated in SE activity.[20] The idea is that the players in the game, being possessed of vulnerable IE, must not be disadvantaged by the actions of others—as they would be if they were deprived of the possibility of receiving valuable benefits to which they are entitled. After all, the working of the SE system depends upon the expectations of all involved that the IEs which they individually possess and transfer are meaningful positions of benefit; that a person entitled to benefits will generally enjoy them and ought to be allowed to enjoy them. So a court of justice will reinforce the expectations of the market-place by clarifying the duties of respect which others owe to those proprietary IEs, and will where necessary employ its coercive power to ensure that individual losses are prevented or compensated. In a sphere of economic activity which depends upon, and stimulates, competition, legal protection will be limited to restraining and condemning acts which substantially reduce possible benefits to the owners of the IE. Judges do not and cannot attempt to restrain actions which, while affecting the market value of the position of benefit, do not directly obstruct the flow of benefits to the owner.

If courts are to recognize the economic IE they will have to oversee, and give clear formulations of, the ground rules of the BP Practices. So for example the courts may intervene to reform the Practices of contract, mortgage, or testation, and prescribe the conditions which must be satisfied for the IEs created by participants to be legally recognized. In the exercise of this power they will be giving effect to an idea of fairness; they must ensure that players do not cheat and that normative positions obtained by fraud, mistake, etc., are not recognized as valid. The 'sanction' which gives normative force to the ground rules so prescribed by the courts is the threat that the NPs will be declared invalid—a refusal to extend legal recognition to the IEs created.[21] Although the courts have played an important role in structuring and reforming BP Practices, the ground rules of many of them have been altered by legislative action.

Although courts lack the authority to regulate an Activity for the sake of the common good, they are empowered to clarify and reform ground rules of a set of BP Practices in the name of justice; their concern must be for legal propriety rather than economic efficiency or social justice. So equality before the law does not of itself license the courts to undo 'hard bargains' made in accord with the ground rules of the SE Practices kite-marked as fair.

Within the SE Society it is also the task of the courts to clarify the general distributive rules under which individuals can acquire IE, not by way of transactions but, for instance, by way of succession.

Civil interests

Civil interests are recognized as existing within the non-catallactic interactions of members. As they are personal and not capable of being transferred, they must be classed as interests, not entitlements. Although the legal person is conceived of as a player within SE activity, legal recognition of these purely personal interests may be regarded as being secondary to the recognition given to the economic IE.

Locke famously maintained that government is instituted to protect the rights of life, liberty, and property.[22] In institutional terms, liberty, being currently most at risk from the State, finds its protection in the public law Practice; and the protection of property is that which is given by the civil Practice to a member's SE entitlements; it is in the protection of personal, non-transferable interests that we can give meaning to Locke's right to life, as an individual entitlement to a personal space for the exercise and development of human capacities in a crowded world.

Although they may be in one sense secondary, in a democratic Society these civil interests constitute a supremely important class of possessions. They are interests in the integrity of the physical person, in the well-being, capabilities, reputation, and privacy of an individual.[23] For the most part, since they are defined in terms of human attributes and expectation, they can scarcely be attributed to an artificial person. There is something amiss when such 'rights' are claimed for a corporation, unless it can be shown that lack of respect for such an interest will adversely affect the competitive position of the corporation in the SE system.[24]

In the interests of legal justice the legal technique developed to protect economic IE is extended to deal with purely personal losses and injuries. That is, the losses, invasions, and injuries which the plaintiff can plead are expressed as harms to particular identifiable positions of benefit: distinct items or *things* which the person possesses.[25] Doing justice when an individual suffers wrongs by others requires that the interests are specified as institutionalized goods, as positions of benefit to which duties of respect are owed. In setting out common duties of respect for all, judges must specify the particular interest to which they relate. The courts do not protect A because she is scholarly, old, frail, and poor, but because she possesses discrete interests in specific conditions necessary for her well-being. We need not treat the 'thingness' of the interests too seriously; artificial though interests such as consortium in family relationships may be, they are simply ways of classifying the types of benefits which are to be protected.

Obviously the legal protection of personal interests requires a different rationale from that which can be given for the legal protection of property entitlements.[26] In some situations it is appropriate to recognize that the invasion of certain of these purely personal interests may indeed affect the position of a person in the 'great game', for instance where a personal injury may make finding a job more difficult, or where a blackened reputation entails commercial disadvantage. Indeed, many personal interests must in fairness be treated on the basis that injuries to them may disadvantage the victim member's engagement in SE activity and that compensation must be assessed accordingly.

However, it is emphasized that the rationale for the legal protection of personal interests is not to be found in the ethics of the market-place. The individual whose personal interests are to be respected is not just a game-player; the individuality which the law respects is that of the game-player who is also a human being, living as an associate *within a democratic Society;* a human being demanding the benefits of bodily integrity, and entitlements to pursue his or her goals undisturbed.[27] That each member of Society should be secured in such a position is of fundamental importance in a democracy, as the legitimacy of the polity is conditional upon the real voluntary consent of every citizen to the rules. The reality of that consent will be doubted it the autonomy of the citizen is not guaranteed. The citizen's freedoms are as much at risk from other members as from the State. Although criminal law goes some way to provide the conditions of individual autonomy, it has no concern with the rights of victims. So it is the function of the civil courts to demarcate and protect an area surrounding every single member in which each will be free to operate, and from which others can be excluded.[28] In defining the duties of respect owed, the courts must determine the boundaries of those areas within which each individual can claim privilege, and set the limits of the tolerances which must be allowed in social intercourse.[29]

So the rationale is to be found in the fundamental democratic tenet that each and every human life is of equal worth, every individual is equally worthy of respect. The personal interests which members are said to possess should be understood as the products of legal adjudication in a democratic Society in which every member counts as one. In such a Society every person is of equal worth, not just in the political field—where equality may take the form of a demand for an equal voice in such things as referendums or the election of representatives to public office—but in social interaction in all fields. This is a pervasive and substantial equality. In the eyes of the law all members of Society are to be equally respected, because all are possessed of the same catalogue of civil interests.

If this parity of worth is part of democratic doctrine—perhaps as a secular version of the ontological equality of Christian belief—we cannot expect to find universal recognition of the equal worth of members in the everyday transaction of social life. There is abundant evidence of an inconsistency between democratic ideals and our actual practices. This is true of so many of us, upon so many occasions, that it may be difficult to maintain that personal interests have a clear definition, or institutional existence, prior to, or apart from, their legal recognition. The principle of equal respect has true meaning and significance *only within the legal Practices* in which the interests are given definition and the general rules protecting them—coercively guaranteed—are prescribed to extend to all.[30] Such equality can be meaningful only to the extent that each individual is thought of as the owner of a set of basic interests identical to those possessed by all others. The moment our focus shifts from a consideration of the identical particulars which we own to a view of persons as integral wholes, we will be confronted by such ineluctable inequalities and incomparabilities as to render legal justice impossible.

I have said that a legal person is not an integrated personality; in considering his relationships to others, his good must be seen to be a set of goods.[31] So even if personal autonomy may plausibly be said to be the end of the civil law, in that the protection of a particular good is to be justified on the ground that it contributes towards the creation of conditions in which autonomy can meaningfully be predicated of individuals, it must be emphasized that the law is concerned only with those particulars in respect of which persons are equal.[32] The authority of the judges derives solely from the particulars; they are empowered to protect these things; they have no general warrant to promote or provide the conditions in which autonomy would be more fully realized.[33]

It is upon this idea of the equality of persons in respect of civil interests that the public law of the CS Practice depends; and it is upon this belief in the equal worth of every citizen that the rule of law must ultimately be founded.[34] As an inhibition upon arbitrary government, the rule of law could be honoured in a polity which yet denied the individualism of democracy. Its *raison d'etre is* not respect for rules but respect for persons.

The clearest manifestation of the democratic idea of equality is the law's treatment of *civil* interests. For although there must be equality in the law's treatment of the players in the SE system, in the eyes of members of Society it is bound to be overshadowed by the perception of the inequalities of distribution which are an ineradicable feature of market economies. So that with regard to our property entitlements it will always appear that some persons are more entitled to respect than others. However, in our civil interests we all possess an identical catalogue of goods.[35]

The limitations of legal justice

Legal justice is defined as respect for persons; in civil law it is to be understood as meaning neither more nor less than respect for the limited catalogue of economic and personal interests which are owned and possessed by members of the associational form Society.

The legal person recognized in the courts of civil law is a dehumanized being. In their social lives individuals are more than legal persons; that is, they are not just members of Society. They are members of other associational forms; they identify themselves as members of families, churches, corporations, clubs, groups, communities, and so forth, and appear as participants in a range of Activities and Practices. In their involvement in these forms within Society individuals assume special roles, hold positions of benefit and responsibility, possess powers and privileges, and are subject to liabilities and duties.[36]

The class of normative regimes, as I refer to all such activities and associations, is inescapably a most heterogeneous collection. Regimes appear in all shapes and sizes. They do not all correspond with the basic institutional forms; many consist of a set of forms relating to a particular Activity, constituting something in the nature of a field, such as the fields of horse-racing, medicine, athletics, or cinema. It is within the normative economies of these messy fields and forms that we find the institutional location for that rag-bag of norms which Austin called positive morality: a residual class of norms which has been unfairly represented. Many of the regimes originate spontaneously, emerging naturally out of the pursuit of certain goals in social life; others are deliberately instituted.[37] It is only to be expected that, unlike legal rules, the types of norms which will be employed within the regimes will be very varied; they will include standards, paradigms, principles, precepts, maxims, conventions, and understandings as well as rules, commands, taboos, recipes, and so forth. After all, these are the norms which regulate and structure not only the large, very loosely knit associational forms such as the scientific community, but also highly organized corporations and small family units.

Such regimes govern much of our social life; they are part of society with a small s. They are not part of Society, in that individuals are not involved in them as members of Society—they are not legal persons standing in legal relationships to one another—but as *subjects* of particular normative regimes.

All regimes within a polity are, of course, subject to ultimate legislative control. The State can be empowered to suppress them, or to regulate relationships between the members of associational forms and the conduct of those involved in Activities and Practices, insofar as such things are considered necessary for the public good. It is important to realize that even though regulation by means of legislation may result in the definition of new offences to be punished in the penal Practice, the regime will not thereby be transformed into a legal regime in which positions of benefit become legal rights, nor will other obligations and responsibilities take on the character of legal duties. It is also emphasized that because a regime is not illegal does not mean that it can be characterized as a legal entity constituted by legal norms. The structures of norms we are considering here must be recognized as extra-legal regimes.

Furthermore, the State may from time to time be empowered to create completely new regimes, as when it sets up administrative bodies to make authoritative decisions in particular areas of activity. In such State Practices the guidelines, principles, and policies which govern decision-making, and structure the exercise of discretions, are not legal norms: they will be neither declared in the legal Practice nor incorporated into its LS.

The nature and limitations of the authority of law courts over these administrative regimes is well understood. In addition to checking the validity of the powers of officials, the courts have authority to review the justice of the procedures by which the decisions are taken. However, as courts of law they have no authority to consider the merits of administrative decisions; they do not pronounce upon the rightness of the decisions: that is a matter for administrators. In exercising their powers of judicial review the judges protect the citizen's interest in fairness and preserve the integrity of the administrative discretion. (See *post*, p. 346.)

In the civil law Practice the participants should preserve precisely the same indifference to the regimes of social life; they should stand at a similar distance from the decisions made within the social regimes. If important regime matters are left undecided it is not for the courts to step into the breach. The authority of the courts extends only to the member of Society's interest in fairness, an interest in procedural rationality which can be recognized only in connection with the normative Practices of the regime. So in respect of social regimes the courts have an extremely limited authority: they have no power to recognize interests arising within normative structures of which they know nothing, or to adjudicate upon its internal disputes, or to regulate the conduct of subjects within the regime. Only the protection of the individual's interest in fairness enables the courts to intervene.

We must therefore recognize that within these regimes the courts lack the power to give to each his own. They have inadequate knowledge of the interests and entitlements arising as they are not masters of the language of the regime. In recognizing the autonomy of the regime, refusing to adjudicate on matters internal to it, the judges are not in breach of their judicial oath to do justice to all: they swear to do legal justice, and in these regimes legal justice is out of place. Subject to the protection of the interest in fairness which individuals have in respect of the NPs of a regime Practice, judges must respect the integrity of the nonlegal regime by preserving an Olympian detachment from its internal problems. For here the individualism of the law is out of place; equality before the law has no relevance; the language and the norms of the regimes are not those of the law; and any so-called rights are not legal in nature.[38]

The pressure upon the courts, as impartial arbiters, to do justice to the subjects of the regime may be considerable: the temptation to assist is strong, and precedents may suggest that the regime is ripe for legal development. However, the need for judicial indifference, for distancing the courts from the affairs of social regimes, is—for precisely the same reasons—as strong as it is in the case of the administrative Practices. For lawyers custom, like the past, is a foreign country; they do things differently there. The translation of alien customary ways into legal norms and rights has its analogue in the ethnocentric accounts which were given of the social arrangements of people in far-off lands by eighteenth-century travellers. Yet the consequences of the legal articulation of non-legal regimes are rather more serious, as the legal rules actively displace the seasoned and idiosyncratic norms of the regime and lead to the neglect of its informing moral principles. The effects of legalism, of bringing the apparatus required for legal justice to bear upon questions which require other articulations, has been well documented.[39] Legalism is not a vice of laymen alone; it can be found in the law itself, in the willingness to transmute all positions of benefit in non-legal regimes into legal rights. The legal reconstruction of regimes can destroy the pre-existing understandings and trust in ways which result in the impoverishment of social life and the debasement of political argument.[40]

Entitlements which are created in customary regimes and recognizable as valuable IEs of the market-place will, however, be protected by the law. Economic interests produced by commercial custom do not raise questions about the authority of the courts to intervene. The adoption of commercial customs into the common law by Lord Mansfield was, given the law's capitalist foundations, unexceptionable.

A prohibition enjoining the courts not to intervene in social regimes will not be found in any constitution, statute, or rule book. Interventionist judges will be guilty only of mistaking the nature of their authority and misapplying the principles of legal justice. However, this is a matter of great importance as improper legal intervention touches upon democratic legitimacy, since the transformation which will result from legal intervention in these forms of association—in which communitarian virtues thrive, relationships of trust are valued, and unique and meaningful roles are assumed—may entail a significant loss of opportunity and freedom.[41] The simplistic legal articulation of the relationships as rights and duties is destructive of the nuanced norms and inflected language of the forms of social life.

The decision whether to seek from the courts a declaration of their rights will of course lie in the hands of individual subjects. The majority may eschew such action; but where the courts are willing, the ominous possibility remains that disaffected persons, realizing that they stand to benefit, may pursue their claims for justice not as subjects but as members of Society claiming protection for their legal rights. The pursuit of self-interest in legal terms can alter the entire structure of the regime and the way in which the relationships between its subjects have hitherto been understood.[42]

The limited authority of the courts is likely to be obscured if we take the courts to be governmental agencies, or superior and expensive dispute-resolution agencies. Nor will those limitations be given prominence in a jurisprudence which fails to make a sharp distinction between legal and non-legal norms; examples are a jurisprudence which maintains that the rules of a club are legal rules, constituting a mini-legal system; or Bentham's jurisprudence, in which the admonishments of an usher and the commands of a mistress to a cook take their place alongside the Acts of Parliament as legal mandates. Take a close look at the institutional forms involved, examine the norms as they are employed within and between them, and the profound differences between legal and all other norms become clear. The approach of the legal pluralists who assume that regimes in industrial, commercial, familial, tribal, and other fields constitute the living law, even if it does not found a megalomaniac jurisprudence, will obscure the distinction between the legal and the extra-legal entailed by democratic legitimacy.

As any intervention will result in the making of substantially new and different rules, the regulation of a Society's regimes is manifestly a legislative matter—or more precisely: a matter for the legislature or its delegates. For a variety of reasons legislatures have tended to leave problems arising within social regimes to the courts, in particular because they are loth to deal with questions involving awkward moral, social, or political choices. In regimes within which self-regulation is difficult or inadequate non-legal Practices are needed whose participants are fully cognizant of the practices, understandings, norms, and values of the regime.

Warnings of the threats to legitimacy posed by the intervention of law courts in social regimes may be thought to come too late; the mapping of the legal rights of individuals in Organizations, in family life, medical care, and so forth proceeds apace. However, there is in some quarters a growing appreciation of the need for greater provision of non-legal Practices to deal with disputes and claims with greater flexibility outside the legal framework. It is a movement which, though often motivated by the need for expedition and economy, may also reflect the need to keep things in their proper places.

B: The NPs of the civil Practice

The normative product, or NP, of the civil Practice is a justified order to a legal person—the defendant—who, having had the opportunity to deny responsibility or liability, has been proved to have injured or threatened the IE of the plaintiff. The NP is an order to the defendant prescribing his or her duties arising as a result of injury or threat to the legally recognized IE of the plaintiff; it will order the defendant to give or give back certain goods, or to do or refrain from doing certain acts.[43]

A judge's refusal to make such an order when dismissing a case might not appear to be an NP of the Practice, as no new norm or order is issued. However, the judgment, which must be justified by a restatement of the LS rules, will, in its recursive recreation of the law, be just as important as any justification given for an NP which does constitute an order.

In the civil Practice an order to a defendant is the only type of order open to the judges. Orders are generally issued, not to officials, but to individual members of Society, and must therefore spell out exactly the members' duties, remedial or otherwise. For it is only upon breach of this order that further coercive or penal action may be taken. As the NP is a command of the court, not of the plaintiff, the duty imposed on the defendant is owed as much to the court as to the plaintiff.

The order against the defendant is justified by the fact that he has, in breach of the rules, threatened, or in some way been responsible for, injury or loss to the plaintiff, and that it lies within his power to prevent future injuries, or to make amends for those which he has caused. An NP ordering the defendant to do something when the plaintiff had proved no loss, injury, or threat, or was unable to show any connection between the defendant and his loss, would be wholly contrary to the idea of the Practice.

The normative product is a remedial not a penal order

Although it is coercively enforced the NP is not penal; it is ordered not to punish wrong-doing by the defendant but to compensate for the lack of respect exhibited for the plaintiff's IE.[44] It is a declaration of right. Although in the civil law Practice the relationship between two members has traditionally been expressed in terms of proof of wrong-doing or fault on the part of the defendant, the wrong-doing is not defined by reference to a sanction; and the duty imposed on the defendant is without punitive intent. For the concern of the judges is not to assess the seriousness of the defendant's breach of penal laws, but to rectify the position of a particular plaintiff. The LS norms of the Practice are not framed so as to justify punishments.

It follows that, in awarding punitive damages in civil cases, courts may be said to be acting beyond their authority, just as orders for the restitution of stolen goods made in a criminal trial constitute acts which are *dehors* the penal Practice.[45] The conferral of powers on judges in the penal Practice to order restitution is justified on the ground of convenience, but that reason is scarcely convincing when applied to the arrogation of power to award punitive damages in a civil Practice.

The intention behind all civil NPs is to give each man his due. An examination of the types of orders available to the courts shows clearly that the aim of the Practice involves preserving or restoring the status quo for the plaintiff. If, in a complicated world, the IEs of legal persons are to be respected and protected, the judges will have to make different and quite distinct types of orders to deal with different threats and harms. Among the more important remedies are: compensatory orders commanding the payment of money, orders to perform existing obligations or duties, injunctive orders prohibiting D from doing acts which are inconsistent with P's IE, and restitutionary orders requiring D to give back what belongs to P, or to repay money unjustly acquired. The remedial nature of these orders is patent; they are designed to restore the disturbed balance, or to prevent future disturbance.

The types of remedial orders which judges can make in their efforts to preserve the status quo are limited: they have no authority to tailor their orders for the good of society or the soul of the defendant. They cannot go beyond the narrow confines of the precise redress of an imbalance, defined in terms of specific entitlements and interests, between two parties. In the history of English law the constitutional implications of the emphasis on remedies should not be overlooked; it operated as an obstacle to the assumption of a more general magisterial power by the judges, serving to keep the courts in their proper place.

In a mature Practice we would expect the participants, aiming to do complete justice between the plaintiff and the defendant, to have the power to issue the whole range of possible remedial orders: *ubi ius ibi remedium*. Although all these types of orders must be available in the Practice as a whole, particular courts are empowered to make only some types of remedial orders.

Like any other NP, an order issued by participants in the civil Practice will be either valid or invalid. An order will be valid if, and only if, it was made in accordance with the prescribed procedure and it is justified by reference to the LS rules. A valid order is unassailable and must be obeyed. The possibility of legally challenging the validity of orders will depend on the existence of an established appeals procedure as part of the Practice. As I explained in the discussion of the penal Practice, an invalid NP of a legal Practice does not lack authority: although it can be successfully challenged, it will until then have undeniable authority.

The requirement that every NP must be challengeable by way of appeal within the Practice does not mean that the NP of a court of first instance is in any way provisional. Every NP of the Practice is intended to be absolute and perpetual, representing a final determination of the IEs of the parties, of what has happened, and what must now be done by the defendant. The NP is not a conditional resolution of a dispute dependent on subsequent revision or variation when, say, new facts emerge, new rules are legislated, or the parties do not find it satisfactory. It takes immediate effect as an authoritative order. The exacting and detailed ground rules are designed on the understanding that the NP of the ideal Practice ends the affair and that judges must get it right first time.[46]

The NP is an order which is coercively enforced by threats against the defendant's property or person. Its normative force does not depend on its acceptance by the defendant, nor on its validity—the knowledge that it accords with the law—but on the fact that judges can call upon officials to guarantee and oversee the execution of their commands.

In a democratic Society the Practice must operate not merely as a symbol of the equality of all members, but as the effective guarantor of all legal rights: a role which can only be sustained if the courts can call on State power. Within the *Gesellschaft* self-help and community action cannot be relied upon. Furthermore, if the judges in a large SE Society had to rely on the plaintiff and other members to ensure the enforcement of court orders then, for justice to be seen to be done, they would inevitably be drawn into involvement in enforcement Activity. The judges' access to State power spares the courts such preoccupations, so that judges need do no more than make remedial orders. The centralization of the law's sanctions is not a feature of the increasingly active and efficient State, but a practical condition required for the doing of legal justice, and a principled development. The law's dependence on State power must not be misunderstood. The coercive power of civil law courts is not another manifestation of State power, but represents a force employed in the name of Society to defend established individual rights.

A legal Practice is necessarily an efficacious Practice. The law must be defined in terms of effective coercive power, no matter how indirectly that power is related to the support of the social rules. For in the civil law of a democratic Society equality and freedom are not mere slogans but are fully realized under the law. An inefficacious Practice, the NPs of which could be ignored with impunity by defendants, would survive, if at all, not as a legal Practice but as an advice centre, outlining as an academic exercise what would happen if the courts had power, or setting out the rules which would justify acts of self-help by the plaintiff. The judges' awareness that law must be equated with efficacy influences their refusal to make orders which are unlikely to be effective, and perhaps also their disinclination to make merely declaratory orders, or to give advice on hypothetical cases. Their authority is essentially a power to command—a very different thing from a power to advise.

The necessity and significance of the coercive character of the legal Practice requires emphasis because it is the reliance upon that power, exercised in the cause of legal justice, which accounts for the nature of the NPs, ground rules, and LS rules of the Practice. Only in a Practice with this coercive capability will the language of legal rights be generated.[47]

It is important to appreciate not only the necessary connection of the civil law with State power, but the precise nature of that connection. In the civil law domain the norms which are sanctioned are not general rules, but court orders. The enforcement of such orders is at best indirect enforcement of the social rules. As social rules, the civil laws of a Society are the reflexes of those LS rules which justify coercive orders for the doing of legal justice. The norms of a defunct legal system are not legal norms; they lack legal character because they are not related to actual coercive power.

The NP is never simply an order: it is a justified order, carrying its justification on its back. The NP can be shown to be valid only if it can be justified by reference to the rules in the LS. It must not be justified by reasons, but by rules—even if the rules are newly minted by the judge. The LS rules of the civil Practice, no matter how comprehensive or detailed, could never provide the necessary justification for every NP. We must allow that frequently the rules run out. However, we can too easily misrepresent the institutional role of the civil Practice in Society if we concentrate solely on the hard cases—which admittedly constitute the overwhelming majority of cases heard, and which dominate jurisprudential discussions because of the exciting legislative issues which they raise.

To correct the bias which undue emphasis on the creative, law-declaring function of the judges may give to our perception of the Practice, we need to recall that the IE Practice operates to make available to all members the benefits of coercive legal assistance; that the Practice is not merely adjudicatory, it is *essentially* coercive. Its prime significance within a democratic Society is to guarantee legal rights. As a guarantor of individual rights and freedoms its *fundamental* role is not to resolve knotty legal problems—crucially important though that is—but to stand as a constant reminder to the recalcitrant that they can be compelled to do what is ruled to be right.

Of course the Practice's central function of coercion is scarcely reflected in the reports of the cases which it determines. It is a tribute to the efficacy of the legal Practice that the litigation of clear cases—which might be thought central to the successful operation of a Practice which guarantees the rights of members of Society—is relatively rare. If we can confidently predict the outcome of a clear-cut case, we would be sensible to deny P's claims only where we had good legal grounds to do so; and that would generally be where the rules were unclear or their application to the facts proved problematical. A court of justice is not a general dispute-resolving agency; nor is it instituted to give legal advice about clear cases: that is the job of the profession.

It is not wrong to go to court to test the law, but it is indefensible to attempt, by way of litigation, to change the law.[48] Generally, if the NP can be justified by the existing rules the legal Practice has no authority to create new rules to justify it.

C: The ground rules of the civil Practice

In legal history procedural rules tend to be overshadowed by the substantive rules of law. Yet they are of fundamental importance, making possible a form of life—a legal Practice—quite different from any other dispute-resolution agency. The ground rules of the legal Practice are the norms which make legal adjudication possible, so the very existence of the legal system depends upon them.

The normative structure formed by the ground rules of the adjudicative Practice is next set out in its ideal form. It is important to appreciate that the ground rules of actual legal Practices are always the result of experience; they represent the accumulated knowledge of the participants about the best procedures to follow in the adjudication of cases. Procedural compromises must be understood in the light of the problems raised by local circumstances, especially the presence of other institutional forms to which the legal Practice is related.

The formality which characterizes legal adjudication procedures are a product of the quest for legal justice. Formality is a necessary character of a legal Practice. It is of course also perfectly consistent with mere legality: ostentatious ritual and legal rhetoric may be employed in unjust regimes to promote an image of legitimate authority. However, whereas mere legality can be served perfectly well by a relatively informal style of adjudication, legal justice cannot; the formality which justice engenders is the consequence of a serious effort to ensure the consistent application of rules; to ensure that in every case all necessary steps are taken. Ideal ground rules must exclude, or minimize, the influence of irrational ele ments in legal adjudication.

Now the object of the ground rules may be said to be to render the NP unchallengeable. Within a democracy every order—executive, administrative, or legal—will be subject to challenge, and every order must be justified. So the ideal legal Practice of a democracy will be constituted by ground rules designed to ensure that every NP is completely justified by the law. The legitimacy of the legal Practice will be judged by the extent to which its procedures and processes in fact make that complete justification possible. For perfect justice is not to be achieved by selecting judges of profound wisdom but by establishing a carefully crafted body of ground rules which govern the manner in which they must proceed.[49]

Complete justification of legal NPs can only be achieved within *a declaratory Practice:* a Practice in which the law is perceived, not as a given, existing 'out there', but as being continuously generated and maintained in the Practice. It is in the light of the declaratory nature of the Practice that the ground rules of the ideal form must be understood. We are not dealing with the procedures and codes which govern the conduct of arbiters in mute Practices, who do no more than apply the rules which they are given, but with procedural rules for judges who are conscious of their continuous law-generating responsibilities.

A declaratory Practice, which alone can justify the NPs which it creates, will possess clusters of ground rules which are designed to ensure that:

1. the adjudicators are competent and impartial;
2. the questions for adjudication are legal questions;
3. all relevant information is presented and checked;
4. all the relevant laws are identified;
5. there is thorough deliberation about the application of the law; and
6. that it is possible to appeal against an invalid NP.

These specific objectives are requirements of legal rationality. A procedure which lacks any one of them cannot meet the demand for the complete justification of every NP—a demand which, in a democracy, must be satisfied.

Ensuring the competence and impartiality of the adjudicators

As the Practice has a declaratory function the judges must be competent to undertake this difficult and all-important task. Such competence is not just the ability to grasp complicated facts and understand the rules, nor to give fitting judgments. The essential requirement is competence to declare the law. Coke's celebrated response to James I when the latter claimed that he was qualified to sit in judgment upon his subjects stresses the artificial nature of the law and the difficulty of its interpretation.[50] Though this is frequently regarded as the self-interested pleading of a common lawyer, it reflects the real requirement that judges must be experienced lawyers, imbued with a knowledge of the uncertainty of the laws and skilled in the art of presenting the different readings which can be given to them.

Advocates require a like competence; they need training and experience in the art of presenting judges with variant readings of the law. It is through their training in this sort of advocacy in the legal Practice that judges acquire the experience necessary to enable them, on their elevation to the Bench, to declare the law.

The legitimacy of the Practice depends in part upon the perception of the judges' competence for this task—an awkward matter since such judgments can scarcely be those of the general public, but must be those of the professionals who alone can assess judicial competence. The criteria for assessing the competence of adjudicators cannot be reduced to a set of rules. It is enough if citizens are satisfied that the standards demanded are of the highest and that the methods of appointment are adequate to ensure the competence of those appointed.

The impartiality of the judges will be secured by ground rules, among the most prominent of which will be the familiar rules of natural justice: rules against bias and personal interest. Breaches of such rules will result in invalid NPs. In order that their particular judgments and declarations of the law should be seen to be based solely on the justification of the law itself, it is also necessary that judges should be immune from the influence of the State, and of any other Organization or person. The independence of the judiciary must be secured by norms external to the Practice itself.

Adjudication of legal questions only

The ideal legal Practice will possess a preliminary filtering process to ensure that the questions presented for determination are legal questions. There must be norms which prescribe the exclusion of disputes which require non-legal resolution. A legal question for adjudication in the legal Practice is essentially one which calls for a declaration of the law. It is in this sense that all cases are hard cases.[51]

Many disputes between members of Society call for relatively straightforward application of the law: when one party is reluctant to satisfy clear legal obligations. Such disputes call primarily for a demonstration of the coercive power of the law, a fundamentally important part of the administration of legal justice within Society. However, as such cases do not require the expertise and scrupulous consideration of a full legal hearing, they should ideally be filtered off to be dealt with in sub-Practices, as would trivial and minor matters.[52]

Similarly, questions to be decided not by reference to rules but by exercising discretion are not legal questions, even though individual interests are involved. Such polycentric questions call for discretionary judgment, weighing and balancing, arbitration and negotiation, rather than legal adjudication.

The authority and legitimacy of the Practice derives from its individualism. The justiciable questions are those which fall within the rights-based jurisdiction of the courts. The participants in the legal Practice are concerned only to see that individuals are respected. It is in filtering out the non-legal questions that the rules of *locus standi* play an important role. Adjudication upon the claims of interest groups and collectives—that is, on claims which are not based on the recognized individual IEs of the legal Practice—almost inevitably take on a political complexion.

The filtering procedure can never be an entirely separate preliminary stage. In some cases the legal character of the question is itself a most difficult matter which can be resolved only after careful deliberation of the facts and the law. The determination of preliminary questions as to what are, or are not, legal issues is a matter for the judges, and the ground rules which govern this stage are to be framed and clarified by the judges alone. This is a principle of great importance: positively, in that the judges can insist upon identifying questions of individual rights which the executive might wish to put beyond their reach; and negatively, in keeping the law pure and preserving the legitimacy of the legal Practice by excluding questions of a political nature.

All relevant information is to be presented

A crucially important body of ground rules is designed to ensure that all information relevant to the legal question is presented to the court; that the information is thoroughly checked so it can sensibly be relied upon as a basis for decision. These rures of evidence are designed as much to exclude irrelevant facts and circumstances as to ensure that all necessary information is presented. In order to establish the facts the court should have whatever authority is required to compel the attendance of witnesses, to discover documents, to administer oaths, and so forth.

Ground rules performing this function are of great importance, for if the information presented is false or inadequate the decision reached will be imperfectly justified and insecure. Legitimacy clearly demands the most rigorous discovery and verification procedures. At the same time it is clear that the discovery of the relevant facts can never be a scientific investigation, as it involves the interpretation of utterances and documents and the giving of significance to certain acts, events, and circumstances.

The identification of the law

There is an extensive and varied range of norms of incorporation, which govern a complicated process whereby the judges recognize the rules which they then declare in order to justify the NP of the Practice.[53]

Before embarking upon an institutional account of the rules of recognition, it is necessary to remind ourselves of the activity in which they are employed. These norms operate in the *legal debate* which precedes the judgment. That is, they are not simply rules employed by the judges: advocates must also abide by them in arguing for their variant readings of the law. The norms of incorporation are themselves always items in the legal debate; they are inevitably and constantly challenged. Such challenges—for instance questioning of the rules of implied repeal—are valuable in that they stimulate the restatement and clarification of the norms. In an ongoing Practice these norms will be malleable, although this does not render them less normative, nor are they mere guidelines for the exercise of judicial discretion.

In a democracy the malleability of the ground rules is attended by both possibilities and dangers. For these rules have the profoundest constitutional importance, which we will overlook if we regard them as merely describing traditional judicial practice. The pivotal place of the norms of incorporation is clear: they specify the sources of laws, they invest a legislature with sovereignty, preserve the integrity of the legal Practice, and make possible the nearest approach to complete justification for coercive acts.[54]

In the ideal legal Practice the norms of incorporation will of course be principled, not merely conventional or enacted. From the principles of democratic legitimacy we can work out what the central ground rules would be. In reviewing the norms actually in place in the legal Practices of different polities we may be able to distinguish between those compromises which have been dictated by practicality and those which indicate an imperfect understanding of democratic legitimacy. Many factors, quite external to particular Practices, may result in the use of ground rules which diverge from the ideal. However, it must be emphasized that the most serious threats may come from participants in the Practices who are unaware of the significance of the rules, or that apparently minor changes may have serious repercussions. The continuous testing and reformulation of the rules in the legal debate lays them open to one of the perennial dangers of the adversarial approach: the possibility that changes and restatements will be made which represent the triumph of advocacy over legitimacy.[55]

The norms of deliberation: the legal debate

A Practice in which the law must be declared requires a procedure to ensure that the fullest consideration is given to the law, to the facts, and to the way in which the law is to be applied to the facts. The procedure must be elaborated to ensure not only that a particular NP is given the most careful consideration, but also that the judge will be in the best possible position to declare the law of the land.[56] The manner in which judges deliberate should not be left to their discretion but must be prescribed for them. For these ground rules are not guidelines for the exercise of an individual or private skill; their purpose is to govern the conduct, within the legal Practice, of a public debate. The existence of *a procedure*—which, in the nature of things, must appear as an adversarial procedure—designed to ensure the fullest public deliberation, is a defining feature of a declaratory Practice.[57]

In a mute Practice the deliberative process might well be separated from fact- and law-finding. There, in neat and logical order, once the facts are found the judges could, in a separate operation, retire to their chambers and take time to consider how the provisions of the code should be applied. In a declaratory Practice the deliberative operation is an inextricable part of the process of finding the law and the facts. One result of this is that the ground rules governing the deliberative procedure are unlikely to be regarded as validating norms. The grounds of an appeal are likely to be, not that insufficient time, skill, and effort were exhibited in the process of deliberation, but that the facts were wrongly found and the law misapplied.[58] As a consequence the adversarial approach may be regarded simply as a style or mode of adjudication, rather than as a procedure which is necessary if law is to aspire to integrity.

At the heart of the demand for a thorough deliberative procedure—one which governs not a private judicial responsibility but a public debate—lies the recognition of the simple truth that two heads are better than one; that the deliberative law-making process is a co-operative effort involving all the other participants in the Practice; and it is because of their involvement that a structured procedure is called for.

In cases where laws and facts are shot through with uncertainty and doubt,[59] the adequate presentation of alternative readings and constructions, the research of the relevant legal material, the discovery of analogies, and so forth, call for the co-operative efforts of a large number of individuals. If the deliberation is to be adequate the methodological ideal is that each option should be given the best possible presentation.[60] Inadequate consideration of possible alternatives may result in decisions which could well have been different. The advocate, as a participant in the Practice, performs this function, not as an academic exercise, but with all the care of one who, in the concrete circumstances of the case, is professionally committed to articulate a particular option.[61]

No doubt it would be possible to present a court with a range of alternative readings of the law by a procedure which did not involve the drama of a forensic gladiatorial combat: but whether such a procedure would do justice to all the options is open to doubt. It is highly improbable that either a single judge or a collegiate bench—required to display impartiality—would present and criticize all the options as powerfully and rigorously as advocates are bound to do. The job of the judge is to select from the carefully articulated options presented that which most nearly conforms to the dictates of legal justice. The emergence of the Bar, composed of lawyers privileged to argue cases in courts of law, is an institutional reflection of the importance attached to the legal debate.

Now the nature of the deliberative procedure adopted is important for the legitimacy of the legal Practice. Practice legitimacy does not depend upon the conscientious manner in which the judge deliberates, but on the effectiveness of the set of norms which govern the public debate about the law and its possible applications. Only the intense scrutiny which results from an ordered and highly motivated public debate can satisfy the demands of procedural rationality in adjudication.[62]

A strict public deliberative procedure is necessary to ensure that the rules which immediately justify NPs are well made. The NP is not just an order, it is an order justified by the rules of law. In its generative declaration of the law, a court ought to show as much concern for the standards of procedural justice as is required of the legislative Practice in a democratic Society.[63] The fact that in the court of law the inarticulate majority vote of the legislature is replaced by the reported reasoned choice of the judge, must not conceal the fact that the legal debate itself—the pressing of the claims of all options under conditions of expert scrutiny—is the all-important legitimating requirement. For it is the legal debate which guarantees that the law will be well made: that the process of deliberation leading to the generation of the law is as thorough as possible.[64]

Where democratic legitimacy is at stake good law is not, as foundationalists suppose, right law.[65] No doubt an appellate court will commonly base its reversal of a lower court's decision on the ground that the reasons are bad; their critical approach will make it appear that the law is always striving towards an ideal.[66] However, the superiority of the appeal court's judgment lies, not in the fact that its judges are more likely to get the law right, but in the fact that they have the facilities to deliberate more fully than any other court.

In the deliberative process the debate will be focused. That is to say, all participants are committed to legal justice.[67] They seek the reading of the law most nearly in accord, not with the existing rules, but with the demands of legal justice. This is principled law generation, and the different points of view presented are concerned to ensure fidelity to established interests and entitlements of individuals. The principles governing the articulations offered are principles of legal justice, not of substantial justice. The Brandeis brief, which allows consideration of non-legal factors, constitutes a clear departure from these principles.[68]

It may be suggested that in common law jurisdictions the growth of the law, and the nature of the reasoning which we read in the law reports, would have been of a wholly different character if the reported judgments had in fact been entirely solo efforts by the 'oracles of the law'. As they would not have been subject to the constant encouragement of the advocates to generate new law, we would expect the judges to conceive of law as a given set of norms existing outside the Practice, and that their discretion would have been exercised in a very different way. However, since deliberation in the common law has always been a co-operative affair, the judges have been encouraged by the mode of debate to adopt more generous readings of the law, and have occasionally been influenced by forceful presentations of points of view which would not immediately spring to the judicial mind.[69] Since in the common law courts judges draw on the arguments of a legal debate they can, with real force, deny that they are legislating; for the debate they adjudicate has been solely about the legal options. It is a debate of a wholly different character from one in which political choices are canvassed.

Legal reasoning

The institutional context of the process of law generation and decision-making—the great co-operative effort involved in the creation of well made laws—is commonly ignored in studies devoted to legal reasoning, in which the judge appears as the legal analogue of the Kadi. The assumption often seems to be that, within his court, the judge sits alone in exercising his declaratory powers; that the debate which precedes judgment is nothing more than a forensic warming-up session.[70] True, the judge has the final authority; it is his judgment which is reported and is binding. However, he is not drawing on statute and case-law directly; he depends on particular readings of the law offered by the advocates. The judge's job is, in many cases, to select one of the carefully worked out alternative articulations. The judge may be a soloist, but the trial is a concerto.[71]

The study of legal reasoning which subjects the reported words of judges to close analysis is one of the most tedious of all academic labours. It may also be misleading since the reported judgments do not take account of the process by which the law is generated, the actual steps by which the conclusion was reached.[72] The judge's rationalizations will not always do justice to the institutional dimension of law-generation by public debate which ensures the rigorous testing of the alternatives. Our acceptance of the legitimacy of the NPs of a legal Practice should be based, not so much on the excellence of the judge's reasoning, as on the knowledge that, thanks to the debate, the deliberation in court has been as full and open as can be. The laws declared are valid, fit to be used in justification, not because they are substantively right, because they are thought to give the one right answer, but because they have been properly made in conditions of procedural legitimacy.[73] It is because they are procedurally legitimate that we can assume they will be substantively correct.[74]

The emphasis on procedural legitimacy rather than substantive propriety touches upon a fundamental point to which I shall return in Chapter 9. It is characteristic of the foundationalist approach to assume that the goodness of the law depends on the weight which we can give to the reasons adduced by the judges; that it is to be appraised by reference to its conformity with some overarching legal philosophy. The legal foundationalist believes that the judges ought to decide in accordance with a principled, defensible master-plan, and that it is the task of commentators to provide that plan for judicial guidance. In a democracy there is no such master-plan.

One of the virtues of the demand that the deliberation should take the form of a rigorous debate is that it does not assume that judges have, or should aspire to, superhuman powers. There is recognition of the limited nature of deliberation undertaken by one individual alone, and that all arbiters benefit from input by others and the stimulus of conflict. If the law generated by the judges is to have legitimacy the courts need to be established as the gaming cock-pits of the law: it is this competition which gives the courts the legitimacy of procedural rationality which we claim for the legislative Practices.[75]

Inherent in the establishment of an adversarial procedure is a view of law as something which could never be represented as a coherent, complete, or fixed text. The law of the declaratory Practice is seen as being continually made and remade. The apparently mystical conception of law of classical common law theory must be understood in the light of the institutional framework of law-generation.[76] The mystery of the law, its fuzziness, and the references to the common consciousness of the community on which it was based were not given prominence in order to privilege a professional caste; they were required in order to describe the nature of the law as it appears in the working of a particular tradition of adjudication. The adversarial procedure itself generates a conception of law which rationalists find difficult to accept. For them the ideal law would be clear and certain and would not need declaration.[77]

Appeals

The ideal legal Practice will contain a procedure enabling an individual to appeal against an NP of the Practice which directly affects his or her interests. It is an elementary principle of adjudicative procedural justice that, since mistakes can be made even when following the best procedures, there must be provision for an authoritative reconsideration of the decision. The appeal procedures enable the judges, where appropriate, to substitute new NPs for the original NPs.

So the ideal legal Practice will always have a two-tier structure. The appellate courts are not an optional extra for the well appointed legal Practice; they are a necessary, integral part of the legal Practice, which can be seen to perform various functions.

First, appeals procedures are, within a declaratory Practice, of especial importance as they add a further dimension to the deliberative process: they afford a further opportunity for considering particular points, examining options which have been ignored, and so forth. The declaratory function of the appeal courts is well understood.[78]

Secondly, appellate courts operate to monitor, clarify, and give normative force to the ground rules of the legal Practice itself. They have authority to annul NPs on procedural grounds, and to restate and reform the procedures followed by lower courts. They provide and restate the criteria by which the validity of legal NPs can be determined. Thus they clarify and restate the norms of incorporation, the norms governing the finding of facts, and they underline the importance of the filtering process. So the justification for the NPs of the appellate courts may consist of the declaration not merely of the LS rules, but also of the ground rules of the

Practice itself. The responsibility for ensuring the legitimacy of the Practice as a whole rests upon the appeal courts.

A legal appeal constitutes an authoritative appraisal of an NP ordered *within the Practice;* that is, of an NP made in conformity with the ground rules and justified by the LS rules. Appeals are thus internal matters; they will, of course, include appeals from mute sub-Practices which operate with the LS rules declared in superior courts.

In addition the courts have an inherent authority, founded upon the legally recognized interest in fairness which all citizens possess, to *review* the NPs and procedures of non-legal Practices which directly affect the interests and entitlements of individuals. The distinction between review and appeal will be reflected in the ground rules which make each possible.

Ground rules in general

(i) *The normative force of ground rules*

The normative force of the ground rules is unquestionable. These are not simply procedures recommended for good decisions; neither are they procedures traditionally followed by adjudicators, or the negotiable stages and conditions of an arbitral process. The most important ground rules—those specifying the conditions of validity for NPs—set out the imperatives which govern the conduct of those who undertake to do legal justice. Many different pressures conduce to compliance by participants with the ground rules: each judge's personal commitment to justice; the not inconsiderable threat of the censure of colleagues and confreres; the awareness of the appeal courts' power to invalidate NPs not made in conformity with the rules; and the dismal sanction of nullity which serves as a reminder of the pointless waste involved in presiding over a charade. In addition there is the real concern felt by the participants for the legitimacy of the Practice itself; and, embedded deep in the judicial consciousness, there is the folkloric memory of the infamy of corrupt judges, and the fate that some of them have suffered.[79]

It is sometimes asked whether such norms as the rules of precedent or the canons of statutory construction count as laws or not. Puzzlement about such norms will naturally arise in a non-foracentric jurisprudence which imagines the law to be a text. In institutional theory such norms are identifiable as ground rules of the legal Practice. Entirely distinct from the rules incorporated in the LS—the laws—they are constitutive of the civil Practice. Their place in the legal field is unquestionable.

(ii) *The complexity of the procedure*

The Practice is a complicated, rule-bound procedure for establishing the facts, and for the discovery, application, and declaration of the law. This is a normative Practice possessing both coercive and declaratory authority. If legal justice is to be done, if the law is to be declared in every case, then inevitably the ground rules must be complex, and must seem formal and technical to the layman.

In any appraisal of the virtue of a legal Practice there is but one criterion: its capability to deliver legal justice. In a Practice in which each case has value as a precedent there can be no compromise with considerations such as the cost or the efficiency of the procedure. Legal justice is notoriously slow and expensive. Given the importance attached to the public legal debate, the costs to the parties of a legal action are bound to be high.

The parties' potential liability to pay for their legal action involves a risk which turns participation in the process into a game which only the rich can play without jeopardizing their whole way of life. That risk is commonly seen as one of the most dangerously distorting factors in the administration of justice. The legitimacy of the Practice will clearly be undermined by a widely held belief that the doors of the courts are open only to the wealthy. As the threat of legal action may inhibit the freedom of action of the indigent, the law can serve the powerful as an instrument of domination: in a democratic polity this is a devastating denial of principle. A Practice which claims to guarantee equality yet which in its service to the citizens could be likened to the Ritz Hotel—open in theory to the rich and poor alike—stands as a monument of institutional hypocrisy.

Yet the courts themselves can do little to rectify their exclusiveness. Their task is to adjudicate cases brought before them, not to provide legal services; the judicial office is not instituted to offer cheap legal advice. The responsibility for ensuring access to courts must rest with the State—the State which provides the coercive force to guarantee our rights.

(iii) *Restraint in litigation*

The requirement that the courts should be accessible to all can very easily be misrepresented. The democratic ideal is not fulfilled by enabling every member in our Society to litigate freely on all matters of personal interest.[80] A proper understanding of the civil law Practice would make us qualify the requirement of access for all by requiring also restraint in litigation. Such restraint breaches no democratic ideals, and is of great importance if we are to preserve the integrity of the Practice—if law is to be kept in its place.

The courts themselves—unable to assist the necessitous—cannot always act effectively to deter the well-healed from unnecessary or inappropriate litigation.[81] Rules of *locus standi* and jurisdiction may not prevent unnecessary legal actions. There is a pressing need for restraint in litigation. Such restraint—primarily the responsibility of the legal profession—constitutes a true civility: a respect for the law which is based on a proper appreciation of the nature of the legal Practice as a beacon of justice. It is something more than the distaste of a professional caste for the ambulance-chasers who impair the dignity of a learned calling.

The only restraining factor in the popular mind is money. There is also a variety of popular misconceptions, and commonplaces open to misinterpretations, which runs counter to any awareness of the need for restraint. It is popularly thought that there is a legal answer to every dispute; that every man should have his day in court; that there is no Alsatia to which the King's writ does not run; that the courts are merely high-powered dispute-resolving agencies playing their part in the maintenance of social order; and so forth. Yet respect for the law is essential. Even where time and money are available, lawyers should be influenced by the principles of discrimination and respect for legal obligations.

Respect for the law, that civility which would urge restraint in litigation, is based on clear apprehension of the narrow scope of legal justice; on the understanding that many disputes are better dealt with by non-legal agencies of dispute resolution; that a legal articulation of a many-faceted problem may be distorting; and that, despite individual satisfaction with monetary awards, the remedies available from the courts may be inappropriate. The vice of legalism, which subjects all aspects of life to legal articulations, is profoundly damaging. There is a parallel between the idea that all our claims against our neighbours are legal, and the cynical view that all our values can be reduced to monetary terms. In view of the narrowness of the law's approach, the ideal is not that all disputes should be dealt with in inexpensive courts of justice, but that they should be determined in the most appropriate forums. There are many disputes for which the individualism of the law is out of place; they would be better resolved in another forum: in alternative dispute-resolution agencies (ADRs).[82] It may be suggested that until very recent times too little attention has been paid to the need for such agencies. The integrity of the legal Practice is to some extent dependent upon the existence of a range of ADRs in which the public has confidence.

If there is lack of restraint over what are best regarded as non-legal disputes, there is equally lack of respect in legal affairs. Respect for the law by members of Society should be based on a clear understanding of the nature of the legal Practice: that is, the understanding that, while its primary function is as a coercive body forcing the recalcitrant to show respect, it is also essentially a declaratory Practice. For the participants, the object of litigation is never simply to protect the plaintiff—the courts are not just debt-collectors—it is to declare the law. Every case is in the nature of a test case, a precedent. So when the law is clear and recalcitrance unlikely, litigation ought to be undertaken sparingly. A legal profession which encouraged legal challenges to clear moral and legal obligations, in the hope of finding a legal loop-hole on some technical point, would be showing scant respect for the law.

The importance of such restraint over unnecessary litigation in relatively clear cases is liable to be obscured by a jurisprudence which asserts that all laws are unclear, that all cases are hard cases, or that all laws which do not conform to some community morality are liable to be judicially reformed or repealed. Such a theoretical approach lends support to those who would embark on a deliberate programme of legislative reform by way of litigation. Neither the realists nor those who claim that law is integrity show proper concern for the integrity of the legal Practice.

The Practice is capable of preserving its integrity only in a Society in which the overly litigious individual is regarded as an oddity; it will be hard-pressed to do so where litigation has for many the appeal of a spectator sport, and for some the grip of an addiction. The responsibility for maintaining proper respect for the law must rest primarily with the legal profession. A profession demoralized by a jurisprudence which subverts the ideals of legal justice is likely to undermine the integrity of the Practice in the name of democracy and rights. The massive disrespect for lawyers which is apparent in some jurisdictions should be taken very seriously as a visible sign of the failure to keep law in its proper place in a democratic Society.[83]

(iv) *Preservation of Practice integrity*

Evidently, the internal rules of the civil Practice—those rules regulating procedure and prescribing conditions of validity—cannot guarantee the preservation of the clinical conditions required for the doing of legal justice. Additional protection for the civil Practice is required; this protection is given by the creation of criminal offences such as attempting to pervert the course of justice, perjury, and contempt of court, and by conferring civil and criminal immunity upon judges for anything said or done in their judicial capacity. Rules of this sort, which are not ground rules of the Practice, are of importance in establishing and maintaining the integrity and legitimacy of the Practice, and may be said to reflect the concern of members of Society to preserve the value of legality.

D: The LS rules of the civil Practice

The LS rules of the civil Practice represent the civil law of an SE Society. With greater authority than the norms of any other form of life, the LS is the ultimate reference point for all legal questions about the relationships between members of a Society. It consists of all the rules incorporated by the judges: rules created and transformed so that legal justice can be done. So the LS is a vast heterogeneous, unfinished collection of rules, constantly in need of restatement and reform. The civil law is never a written code; its norms are always the rules actually employed by the judges in an adjudicatory Practice.

Within the LS there are two major classes of rules: (a) the rules of entitlement which define the IE possessed by members, and (b) the rules of right which specify the duties of respect owed to those IE.[84]

The rules of entitlement

Within an SE Society, rules of entitlement prescribe who is entitled to which benefits. The function of these rules is not to prescribe duties—that is the role of the rules of right, or the rules of the criminal law—but to allocate valuable benefits, namely the interests and entitlements of members. The determination of how benefits are allocated is a necessary preliminary step in the doing of legal justice.

The rules of this large and important class cannot be presented as rules of conduct. As many writers have concentrated largely upon rules in some deontic mode—upon the mandatory, permissive, or power-conferring rules—the nature of the rules of entitlement has been somewhat neglected. Yet allocative rules which prescribe, not what members should, should not, or may do, but what things belong to them, are clearly of fundamental importance in an SE Society.

No doubt we can work out from the allocation of goods which the rules of entitlement prescribe many of the duties, liberties, and powers possessed by members in respect of their belongings. However, it is clear that we cannot perform the tasks of allocation and quantification by reference only to rules which regulate conduct. There is a logical priority about the rules which prescribe, for instance, that A is entitled to all the benefits of Blackacre, or to a third of the estate of B; to a monetary payment commensurate with some disability, or to a proportionate share in some enterprise. The proposition that William is entitled to a slice of cake is very different from an assertion that it is Ginger's duty to give it to him. William is entitled to the slice whether or not Ginger can meaningfully be said to have a duty to give it to him. Whether Ginger has, with respect to William's entitlement, any such duty to give clearly depends upon the circumstances.

The neglect of the allocative rules is partly due to the fact that circumstances giving rise to such duties are present in virtually all civil law cases; the plaintiff s cause is that the defendant has breached some duty, and the plaintiff's action is a demand that the defendant comply with it. Conflation of A's entitlement with B's duty is therefore almost inevitable in, say, a judgment that an employee is entitled to a particular sum which he has earned. From that assertion of entitlement we naturally assume that the employer has a duty to pay it. Nevertheless, the entitlement to a sum of money is analytically distinct from the employer's duty to pay it; unless the wages due are defined as being the duty of the employer, that duty does not logically follow from the statement of the worker's entitlement. In exceptional circumstances the duty to pay the worker may be imposed upon some other person. We may need to know the nature of the worker's entitlements for other purposes: to assess his tax liability, or to calculate the size of his estate upon his death; the rules by which we determine his entitlement will not be rules of conduct.

Although the rules which allocate benefits cannot be translated into an equivalent set of rules imposing duties on others, neither can they be presented as rules conferring permissions or powers on an owner or possessor. The nature of many IE renders the granting of a permission or the conferment of a power wholly irrelevant. Thus, if A has an interest under which he is entitled to £1,000 from the State, he does not need to be permitted or empowered to do anything. The allocation to A is of a sum of money, not of a power or permission to enjoy the money when he gets it. The rules simply quantify and locate the benefits.

Appreciation that allocative rules cannot be presented as deontic operators of command, prohibition, and permission has perhaps increased as schemes for the distribution of benefits and services by the State under social welfare policies have proliferated.[85] However, it has always been the case that all our private entitlements, arising from transactions between members of Society, are allocated under rules which prescribe who is entitled to what: rules which can be distinguished from, and are not reducible to, rules prescribing duties, liberties, and powers.

It is important to show that allocative rules cannot be reduced without remainder to rules of conduct in order to challenge the common assumption that, from the legal point of view, the things we own are no more than bundles of rights and privileges. The things we own are substantial; they certainly are not material objects but institutional positions of real social and economic benefits; but neither the socially recognized positions nor the benefits can be reduced to fascicles of legal rights. The distinction between IEs and the rights which attend them is central to an understanding of the nature of legal rights. There are two types of LS rules which perform an allocative function: general distributive rules, and the rules of the BP Practices.

IE created by general rules

Under general distributive rules members of Society are *automatically* entitled to positions of benefit: to both entitlements and interests. The member does not have to do anything, other than, in some cases, make a formal claim. A member will be recognized as the owner or possessor of IE if, by virtue of his condition or circumstances, he satisfies whatever criteria for entitlement the rules prescribe. Examples of such rules include rules of intestate succession under which, upon the death of a member, other members become entitled to parts of his estate; or the rules of social welfare legislation which provide, in the event of sickness, injury, unemployment, retirement, and so forth, that members become entitled to benefits.

Such general distributive rules have their source in either custom or legislation. Participants in the civil Practice, employing a rule of recognition, will adopt and clarify the social rules, giving them—as they appear as LS rules—a precision and authority they would otherwise lack.

IE created by beneficial Practices

The other major class of rules of entitlement to be found in the LS of the civil Practice are the rules of all the BP Practices which enable members of Society freely to create entitlements and interests, such as the IE created under trusts, leases, and mortgages. So the LS rules will include both the ground rules of the BP Practices—since the courts have to determine whether the NPs of the BP Practices are valid—and those BP Practice rules which define and limit the normative positions which can be created.

Now most BP Practices have emerged out of the voluntary interaction of members; they are maintained, and can only be said to exist, insofar as members actively create, recognize, and deal with the entitlements and interests which the Practices make possible. BP Practices do not exist simply because they have been given a legislative formulation, nor indeed because they receive legal recognition. Of course the fact of such legal recognition is of the greatest importance, for in considering the validity of IEs created deliberately by members, the judges have authority to clarify, supplement, and reform the ground rules of the BP Practices. Furthermore, they may reform the Practices to such an extent that a particular BP Practice may come to be regarded as an entirely legal creation.[86] Yet it needs to be stressed that such legal recognition is not wholly constitutive of BP Practices; in prescribing conditions of validity of IE, and in defining their nature and extent, the judges must be regarded as intervening, as exercising a supervisory role with respect to Practices which they did not create. The clarification of the ground rules of both BP and administrative Practices is a supremely important and somewhat neglected area of legitimate judicial legislation; it has perhaps greater prominence in the public law domain.

The imperfect LS

Although in the ideal legal Practice the rules of entitlement would be clear and comprehensive, for obvious reasons this will not and indeed cannot be the condition of the LS rules of any actual IE Practice in the modern world. There is simply too much in contemporary Society which is new and complex, too many developments which give rise to a range of unprecedented legal problems. The judges, who can clarify the nature of the new entitlements only as the contingencies of litigation dictate, therefore cannot hope to formulate all the necessary rules of entitlement. They are faced with the task of working out all the legal implications of the new types of Activity, new Practices, and new technology which result in the creation of all manner of new entitlements. They have to take account of both enactments which confer benefits, and those which limit and redefine the nature of benefits resulting from the ownership of material and other resources. In passing it may be noted that in formulating the rules of entitlement judges are sometimes hampered by obscure statutes and idiosyncratic legal categories.

The LS rules of entitlement are frequently unclear. Even so, awareness of the difficulties of decision-making which result from the manifest incompleteness of the LS of the actual civil Practice does not justify some of the exciting generalizations written about law by the postmodernists. For instance, we are told that it will never be possible to predict how a rule enunciated in relation to one set of facts will be applied to a later, and inevitably different set.[87] Assertions of this sort—of dubious truth in connection with penal rules or rules of right—are simply nonsensical if applied to those rules of entitlement which have been correctly applied without hesitation by members of Society innumerable times in the unique circumstances of their individual daily lives.

The judges have only the LS rules to authorize and guide them. Principles are not to be found among the norms of the LS. Judges are not subject to the guidance or control of an overall theory as to how beneficial positions ought to be distributed in a Society. Social justice is not legal justice; a theory of property is no part of the law. Social justice commonly involves advancing an ideal pattern of distribution. As the administration of legal justice depends upon the existence of LS rules which map the vested interests of members, the civil Practice is in no sense redistributive.

The rules of right

The rules of right are rules of conduct; they prescribe the duties of respect which other members owe to the possessor of interests and entitlements. Though it is possible to argue that, in a democracy, the respect for persons guaranteed in the civil Practice is ultimately based upon the Kantian idea of respect for persons as ends in themselves, for judges the respect is nothing more than respect for the things which an individual possesses.

The implications of respect being limited to the IEs actually owned are important. Such modest respect for individuals as only possessors of things makes irrelevant a person's station in life, individual worth, and needs. The civil Practice has no redistributive functions or authority. Social welfarism has established itself as a central strand in the conception of ideal democratic conditions, but is no part of the idea of the civil Practice. Provision for the underprivileged is a matter for political debate and negotiation, and the implementation of schemes for such provision is a matter of immense administrative difficulty. Such concerns are beyond the remit of judges, who are concerned only with specific individual claims to respect. Judges have no authority to ensure that each individual is provided with even the most minimal conditions of welfare; nor are they empowered to achieve any form of equality of opportunity.

In civil law respect for persons is ensured if all individuals fulfil their duties of respect for the IEs owned and possessed by a person under the existing laws. The remedies available to the judges clearly indicate the nature of the respect due; they are remedies designed to prevent future harms, or to restore the status quo. The availability of compensatory payments allows great flexibility in the effort to restore a balance which has been disturbed: a flexibility which carries with it the possibility of abuse. The rules of right in the LS prescribe the duties of respect; they set out the circumstances in which judicial orders can be made to compel a member to compensate for losses, restore property, perform obligations undertaken, refrain from acts which threaten injury, and the like.

The rules of right are enormously complicated and detailed; mostly they have been worked out by the courts.[88] In contrast to the criminal law, the civil law is essentially a product of adjudication. To a greater extent than is acknowledged, the great Codes of civil law all owed much to the experience of participants in adjudicatory Practices.[89] The rules of respect cover the entire range of IEs created in interaction in the SE system; they prescribe the duties owed to the IEs in property law, contract law, tort law, company law, commercial law, and so forth. In general terms, the duties of respect as they are recognized in the transactions of members in SE activity are gradually refined and clarified in an enormous variety of new situations. The LS is thus the repository of interests and entitlements and their attendant rights; its rules define not only the economic IEs but also the civil interests which are recognized as essential possessions of members of a civil Society.

The extensive rule-making activity of the judges in the civil Practice can avoid the charge that it is an illegitimate legislative activity only to the extent that the judges, making decisions on the basis of purely individual claims to rights, are prepared to ignore the wider social and political implications of their rule-formulation. Contrary to the views of some judges, their business is to map out the gardens of individual members, not to engage in town planning. Any law-making must be incremental, edging forward from past decisions about particular individual interests to determine the extent of those rights in new situations.

It is of great importance to insist that the LS consists of rules; its norms do not include doctrines or principles, which do not afford complete justification for the Practice NPs. The LS consists of norms which are incorporated as clear rules by the courts.

The LS has an enormous array of such rules, governing all aspects of social life in which legally recognized IE can be found. Although they prescribe duties, they do not define offences or prescribe conduct in general; they are rules of respect for the legal IE. It is because we can identify the IE recognized in law that we are able to distinguish the legal from the extra-legal regimes of a Society.

The nature of the LS rules

Common-sense jurisprudence would suggest that the norms of civil law are simply *social rules* taken up and applied by the courts; that, whether enacted or customary, they can have a legal character and status before they are declared by the courts. For institutional theory, however, the LS rules differ from social rules in civil law. The LS rules acquire their distinctive character as norms by virtue of their function of justifying NPs ordered in the process of adjudication; social rules do not perform this function.

Legal norms, differing from all other sorts of norms, must be seen to be *generated* in the form of life I have called the civil Practice and should be understood in terms of its idea and functions. We must take account of the fact that the Practice is, first, an adjudicatory Practice determining relationships between members of Society. Secondly, it is a *coercive* Practice: although its NPs are not issued with penal intent they are backed up by State force. Finally, it is a coercive Practice within a *democracy.* It may be the distinguishing mark of a democracy that the exercise of coercive power is always subject to challenge; that all agencies exercising power are held accountable and their claims to legitimacy rigorously tested. In a democracy the legitimacy of an institution can never be based on the acceptance of traditional forms, on civic inertia, an ingrained respect for ancient establishment, or a habit of obedience. Since democracy is a child of the Enlightenment, the legitimacy of the organs of a democratic polity must be demonstrable, provable, and rationally satisfying.

The coercive orders of judges in the civil Practice must be fully justified. In an ethically pluralist Society they clearly cannot be justified by reference to an ideology shared by all. Justification can only be satisfactorily achieved if each exercise of coercive power is justified by reference to norms of a very distinctive type: norms which are generated within an adjudicatory form of life.

It was suggested in Chapter 4 that the NPs of the penal Practice are completely justified only by legal norms of a very special sort, and that in the history of criminal law we witness the gradual emergence of such norms in the same way, the aim of judges in the civil Practice is to make their NPs *unchallengeable:* to provide a complete justification for each and every order that they make. They appreciate that such justification is provided only by norms of a very particular type; and the only norms which perform this function are *legal rules. So* the solution to Dworkin's question as to how we can justify the coercion of citizens, in the name of the law, is found within the very model of rules which he rejects.[90] Legal rules have a democratic significance: they are the only norms which can provide a complete justification for coercive action in the name of Society. To do this they must satisfy the requirements of legal justice.

Now many decision-making and adjudicatory Practices in a Society will justify their NPs by reference to good reasons: to practical considerations, policies, and principles. Those who exercise such power in a democracy are accountable, and the reasons they give to support their decisions are attempts to honour the trust placed in them. Since the participants in these Practices can rely on any sort of reasons and are not bound by rules, they are said to have a wide discretion. There is great virtue in the flexibility of such reasoned decision-making; and writers as different in their dispositions and objectives as Bentham and the American Realists have considered that legal adjudication ought to be of this sort.

Yet Practices of this sort, so useful and necessary in many areas of social life, simply cannot satisfy the overriding demand for respect for persons which the legal Practice must consistently satisfy. For in any non-legal Practices the principle of individual respect is always weighed against other factors, and the notion of honouring the underlying equality of the parties involved can never be more than a vague aspiration.

Complete justification of an NP must be based upon treating respect for persons as an absolute, which means that it is only possible in a Practice whose judges unwaveringly demonstrate equal respect for all. X can claim a coercive NP against Y because others in the same position as X have been able to claim the same protection. If we can recognize the same IE, we must allow the same respect and protection. Some writers make much of the uniqueness of cases, of the special factors which render one case unlike any other. However, if in one case involving a distinct IE an exception is made to a rule of respect, that decision must found a sub-rule, and stand as a precedent for all other like cases. When the rules run out the court must regard the case as not unique, but novel. The judge must justify his order by reference to a new rule which he must formulate, rather than by reference to principles to be given due consideration in the exercise of a judicial discretion in future similar cases.

The type of reasons which could properly justify a unique case are very different from those which would be adduced for a situation which recurs frequently in very different contexts. The calculations of the act utilitarian differ from those of the rule utilitarian. Recognition of the similarity of cases—which the legal articulation of IEs makes possible—requires that justification should be based upon binding rules which govern all like cases, rather than principles or weighty reasons which appeal to the judge in a particular case.

The objectivity of rules

The immunity of the NPs from challenge can only be secured if they are justified by reference to objective rules. An NP which is justified only by reference to reasons, policies, or principles, is clearly open to challenge by those who do not accept the force of the reasons, dislike the policies, and do not accord the same weight to the principles. In an ethically pluralist Society it is axiomatic that many will have subjective preferences different from those of the judges. In these circumstances, whatever authority the legal NPs possess might depend primarily on the fact that it is perceived to be backed by the force of the State. However, the ideal is to secure every individual's recognition of the authority of the rules irrespective of coercive power, and to justify NPs, not by subjective preferences, but by objective standards which only rules can supply.

Since they operate as exclusionary reasons, rules can confer objectivity on judgments. They do not require, but exclude as irrelevant, an array of factors which might, in isolated or unique cases, be considered to justify a decision. Rules—employed in a wholly different way from principles and policies—may be regarded as labour-saving devices, saving the judge from the effort of searching for reasons, weighing up principles, or considering all the circumstances.[91]

As the NP must be justified by rules, so any challenge to it must be based upon the validity of the rules; and the primary ground upon which rules may be challenged is that they are not well made. This means that the Practices and processes by which rules are created and formulated must satisfy the principles of democratic rationality in decision-making. Among other things, the participants in the legislative Practices, in which substantive decisions on political or moral matters are made, must properly consider all the evidence and respect all Groups; and the legal processes of law generation, i.e. the processes in which the judges formulate new laws, must not involve the determination of questions which cry out for negotiation, debate, and agreement on moral or political matters. The hegemonic tendency of the law is evident in the common assumption that many such problems are 'legal' problems, or at least that lawyers are somehow fitted to answer them.[92] Well made laws—as acceptable compromises, made in conformity with the procedural justice requirements of a democracy—are not open to challenge as they are the products of the best, and perhaps the only mechanisms in that Society for reaching agreement, or for formulating rules, to which all can subscribe. Rules which are so fashioned cannot be challenged by members of Society as to their content, only as to defects in their manufacture.

This consideration requires us to regard the rules of recognition in a new light. Now we can see that, ideally, such rules must embody the imperatives of democratic rationality. The rules of recognition are not merely the posited norms of a Practice; they are not pragmatic rules of thumb reflecting the institutional outcome of past power struggles. They should allow for the recognition only of those rules which are unchallengeable: that is, of rules which can completely justify the penal or coercive orders of the courts. Further, the criteria they employ must be ordered in terms of their democratic credentials—on which basis older statutes must give way to contemporary enactments, and case-law must always be inferior to the judgments of the democratic legislative Practice. Generally, the rule of recognition would exclude recognition of rules which, by virtue of their source, were not capable of completely justifying the NPs.

The rules as formulas

In its employment as a precise rule-formulation which is to be used to justify NPs without more, the LS rule will emerge as a fixed set of significant words. Reasons, policies, and principles can be expressed in a variety of different ways; their communication does not call for any particular form of words By contrast, an LS rule is a carefully drafted formula, more akin to a verse of poetry or a spell than to a homily or command. The products of legislative Practices are scrupulously selected words which have been agreed upon, often representing bitter compromises made, or treaties signed, between adherents of opposed and competing positions. The generation of new rules under the doctrine of precedent shows the same formulaic urge; the justification of the NP in a novel case derives, not from a reason, but from a new rule formulation. This formulaic quality is essential if the rules are to achieve objectivity. The legal rule, as a fixed formulation, mediates between the contestable policies, principles, and reasons—which may have influenced the creation of the rule—and the NP.

In the process of incorporation the declaration of law is the translation of words which express a norm-content into a rule-formulation. Thus the formulation by the court of a reported custom converts it into a set of rules: into formulations which can be used as complete justifications for making coercive orders in subsequent similar cases. Prior to such a legal declaration, customary norms operating in social life do not perform this function.

The rules are framed to draw lines between like and unlike cases; they specify classes of acts, persons, things, and events; they set out the conditions for their application and specify precisely the exceptions. Being embodied in a language which is necessary for rigorously justificatory norms they inevitably have a technical character. So the realization of the idea of legal justice entails the generation of detailed and often obscure norm.[93] To the dismay of democrats, justice is a serious obstacle to those who pursue the laudable goal of promulgating laws which are clear enough for everyone to understand.

The moral neutrality of the LS rules

Since we take it to be axiomatic that all political and moral ends are challengeable, the aim of creating an unchallengeable NP requires the justifying rules to be morally neutral. The process of incorporation of a particular rule may be regarded as the neutering or suppression of any political or moral goals which the law-makers had in mind when shepherding it through the processes of enactment. The judges must create and apply rules which are not expressions of a particular moral position, but which are objective and accepted as binding on all. Of course rules do not acquire this character merely from the use of particular linguistic forms. They can only be said to be objective if they are in fact consistently treated as such by the judges. Even the most legalistically drafted rules can be treated as embodying values and given a generous interpretation in the light of, say the teachings of a church, or the policies of a club or a company. Yet it must be insisted that Society is not a church, a club, or a company; and in the interpretation of its rules any political or moral objectives of either legislators or judges are irrelevant.

We know that many rules reach the statute book as the result of political activity by a committed Group. Once incorporated into the LS, such a rule may properly be notched up as a success for a particular Group; the law may be seen by its proponents as a norm which is central to the particular moral or political position which they espouse. However, from the legal point of view the norm which has to give a complete justification to an NP—even to those who oppose the values it is said to embody—must *never* be regarded as an expression of policy. It is no longer 'hot' or 'live': it is no longer morally charged, for now it is a law, a neutral legal norm with coercive force. The purposes, reasons, and objectives motivating its enactment do not figure as part of the rule.[94] The enacted law is a form of words authorizing coercive action in clearly specified circumstances.

So existing laws which specify the offences of murder and manslaughter must not be taken to enshrine the values of a pro-life group in the euthanasia debate. Nor would any law reform brought about by adherents of the 'freedom of choice' persuasion constitute a 'pro-freedom of choice' law: it will merely be a new rule in the statute book specifying the conditions under which persons can justly be punished; a rule altering the conditions of criminal or civil liability. Laws do not embody, or stand for, policy or moral principle.[95] There are notoriously enacted measures which fall far short of the demands of principle or policy which motivated the reform. The words which are incorporated must not be treated as though they were policy statements.

The moral significance which particular rules of law may have for us personally may be securely based on our knowledge of the history of their enactment, or it may be nothing more than a construct, or an inference. It is demonstrably a construct where, for instance, a law enacted to achieve one purpose is employed for another. Although we can claim knowledge of, or make plausible inferences about, the moral history of the rules, we must never confuse that knowledge, or those inferences, with the law. The inferences we may make, and the principles we may elicit from the judicial reasoning in the cases, is not the law. After all, they are not rules but principles, and as such they have neither more nor less legal significance than the moral or political principles we acquire from our membership of a religious or political Group. The fact that they have been unearthed from existing legal material does not endow them with a privileged status in any legislative debate.

In a democracy the judges of a coercive Practice are accountable, not on any formal occasion—at the end of a year, a term, or a session—but on the ordering of every single NP. Their NPs must be accounted for immediately and must be unchallengeable. That requirement can never be satisfied by reliance on persuasive advocacy based on principles, but only by the creation of, and reliance upon, an objective stock of rules. The distinctiveness of the legal rules, and of legal language, derives from the understanding that rules, and only rules, can provide complete justification. Thus the legal norm acquires its legal status, not from its conformity with moral standards, nor from its validation by a higher norm—as part of a system— but by reason of its suitability for use in justification.[96] The enacted rule will be regarded as law because it is a well made law—and as such can be employed to justify NPs—not because there is a higher norm which declares it valid.

III: THE CIVIL PRACTICE AND SOCIETY

The LS rules of the civil Practice stand at the centre of the civil law domain; obviously they are not the only rules operating within that domain—that is, they do not comprise all of the rules which we normally call the law. Although they are indeed norms which govern the interaction of men and women in the associational form Society they make up only a fraction of the prodigious mass of norms which govern the activities of social life.

Although the true civil law of a Society is constituted by the LS rules of the civil Practice, it differs from the legal system as portrayed in more orthodox theories: as a system of social rules which constitute a form of social control. For the LS is nothing more than a heterogeneous collection of rules which have been incorporated by judges to provide justification for those cases which have been litigated. As a system for the governance of social interaction the LS is manifestly incomplete. Given the dependence of the Practice upon litigation for the declaration of law, it is clear that there are large areas of legal uncertainty. The LS can tolerate very large gaps. The judges are not empowered to govern; they have no authority to prescribe and maintain a structure of social rules to govern all aspects of social life—an objective which *would* require a relatively comprehensive system of norms. Even in an ideal Practice the idea of maintaining an LS with pretensions to completeness—covering all possible causes of litigation—would be an absurdity, if only because every legal Practice exists within a rapidly changing Society.

The conceptions of law as an all-encompassing normative network, or as the essential normative structure of social life, or the description of law as *nomos* with all its implications of completeness, are conceptions inherited from the jurisprudence of a pre-democratic age.[97] In that jurisprudence laws are generated in, and inextricably part of, social interaction: a structure of norms which exists in the forms of social life outside the adjudicatory Practices. This view, which remains a powerful strand in modern orthodoxy, is both obscuring and undemocratic.

The idea that the law covers all aspects of social life, that it is an integral part of that life, carries with it the belief that the norms of the civil law ought to display a high degree of coherence. The coherence to be displayed would be that of a norm structure which provided effective regulation for the whole of social life and which would accordingly embody the moral values of that life. From this point of view the manifest gaps in the LS would seem superficial: they are but pages missing from a book, capable of being supplied by those who best understand the intimations of the narrative in which the central values of the community are reflected.

However, the legal system of institutional theory—that is, the LS of the legal Practice—is nothing more than a collection of morally neutral norms which, in particular cases, justify the exercise of coercive power in a democracy. Such a catalogue of rules is not intended to satisfy any *desiderata* of completeness or coherence which the romantic image of law may promote. Any coherence which the law is said to exhibit, any ends which it is said to pursue, will be a construction of the observer.

The judges' commitment to legal justice is incompatible with the ideal of securing coherence among the LS rules. Even in the ideal Practice, the judges are not concerned—as they would be in a theocracy—to ensure that the rules are conformable with any masterplan. This is not because they are declaring the law of a fragmented Society, but because—responsive to the imperatives of democracy—they are aware of the limits of their authority. The recognition of the essential heterogeneity of the norms of the LS is important. Not only do laws not constitute a seamless web, standing for or embodying some moral or political philosophy to which all subscribe; their designation as a 'system' is something of a misnomer. The jurisprudence which unthinkingly includes all society's structural rules in the field of the law not only distorts accounts of the legal field but, equally importantly, obscures the need for the proper appreciation of the nonlegal norms in social life; and, failing to allow for their proper treatment, it inhibits the development of the institutional forms in which they should properly be accommodated.

A: How the LS rules become social rules

The civil Practice is not a self-contained, isolated agency deciding cases according to the law; it is no sort of passport photograph slot-machine dispensing snapshots of justice to individual consumers. As a declaratory Practice committed to securing equal respect for all members, it has a necessary connection with social life. Its decisions are profoundly influential in governing the activities of members, including activities in which litigation is not contemplated. So, in a way the LS rules also operate as social rules. Yet if they are not framed as social rules by the judges how do they operate—in what manner do they exist—as norms in the social life of members of Society? The answer must be that they can operate only as reflexes of the LS rules.

The legal Practice is the focus of the civil law domain; its LS rules determine the extent of its boundaries. So we must exclude from the domain all social rules which are not reflexes of the LS rules. The rules excluded from the legal domain constitute a large class of extra-legal norms—some of which may well be legislative in origin—which govern relationships other than those in which legally recognized IEs are involved.

As reflexes of the LS rules the norms of civil law are employed to govern relationships between members in everyday life. They will be treated as regulatory rules: the do's and don'ts of everyday life. Although they are not officially enforced, many will operate as commands, prohibitions, or permissions.

In social life generally these norms are not used—as the LS rules are—to justify coercive orders; but they may well be used with coercive force, the threat of legal action providing an inducement to conform to them. In its social setting, outside the Practice, the civil law consists of those norms which can be used to justify threats of legal action. It is precisely this threat of legal action which makes it possible to ascribe a legal right—a predictive right—to a member (see *post,* Ch. 6).

If they are to be employed as social rules the LS rules need to be translated. In order to be understood by members generally they will need to be simplified, shorn of the detail and precision they acquire as LS rules.[98] Some may be translated into principles of conduct, in which case the purpose behind the rules may well be taken into account. In their use in social life something of the individualism of the Practice will be lost. Legal norms are employed in social life as guides and regulations, as a means of avoiding social dangers, of avoiding liability. Members may have no overriding concern with the respect they owe to others; they want only to avoid trouble.

B: Legal advice Activity: the legal profession

As a consequence of the judges' commitment to legal justice, the language and rules of the civil Practice are technical, the categories of legal thought artificial. Since the LS rules simply could not operate as social rules for laymen unversed in the language of the law the need for translation is obvious.

The *legal profession is* the medium through which the LS rules of the civil Practice become social rules operating in the Activities and lives of members of Society.[99] The importance of this mediatory function cannot be overestimated. The profession is a necessary element in the legal field; the very existence of the civil Practice may be said to depend upon the establishment of a legal profession. For if the legal rules are not communicated outwards by the professionals, if they are not in a form of intelligible reflexes which makes it possible for them to operate as social rules, recourse to the law would diminish, and the Practice would lose its authority as the LS rules diverged from the social rules.

In emphasizing the dependence of the civil Practice upon the attendant profession it is important to understand that the institutional form which services the Practice and translates its LS rules for laymen is not an Organization but an Activity, which I call the Activity of legal advice.[100] The objective of this Activity is to set out, or construct, the legal point of view for the benefit of members of Society. The Activity is one in which lawyers translate and explain the legal categories and rules; in which they rehearse or recapitulate cases which might be, or have been, determined by the judges in the IE Practice. Obviously, this Activity is logically dependent upon the existence of the Practice.

Of course, the work of the profession is not confined to the giving of legal advice; lawyers representing their clients act as participants in the civil Practice. However, although lawyers are commonly involved as participants, it is important to distinguish between the Practice and the Activity; between the authoritative rulings of judges and the advice of lawyers.

There is an institutional ambiguity in the notion of the legal profession. The failure to identify the different legal forms, the confusion of Practice and Activity, means that when the functions of the profession are described there is a tendency to ascribe to the profession functions which are only exercised by the Practice. This institutional ambiguity is increased if we pay undue attention to the organizational structures of a legal system, for both judges and lawyers may be members of the same professional Organization.

The legal point of view is generated by the courts, not by the profession in general. The courts do not merely adopt and apply the social rules which have been treated by the professionals. It is not the profession which transforms the social norms, generated in the life of members of SE Society, into legal rules; its members do not translate the vernacular of normative life into technical language, nor have they authority to convert the grass-roots Practices into legalized Practices. These developments are the province of the rule-making institutional forms: the legislature and the civil Practice. The profession lacks authority; it lacks coercive power; it is wholly parasitic on the civil Practice.

The popular supposition that the legal profession could generate the legal point of view derives from a jurisprudence which conceives of the law not as the LS of a coercive Practice, but as a text.[101] The law, not being anchored to any particular institutional form, is thought to exist as a system of rules which can be validated by reference to other rules, and given meaning by an interpretive community. From the view that the rules exist out there, as a text, it is plausible to suggest that the profession builds up the cultural legal ideology; that the profession's interpretation of the text has immediate and special significance.[102]

Today the Activity of the legal profession involves much more than the interpretation of the LS rules. In dealing with their clients' problems lawyers are asked to advise on non-legal matters; in particular on the meaning of the rules of extra-legal regimes. Some lawyers may acquire expertise in the handling of problems and disputes arising in such regimes, in recent times these have become the growth areas in the Activity of legal advice.[103] The great extension in the scope of the advisory activity of lawyers does much to conceal the boundaries of the legal domain; and our view of the law will be skewed or inflated if we take that professional Activity to be the central institutional form of the legal field. The manifold responsibilities assumed by lawyers in non-legal matters influence our conception of what is to be included in the legal field. In principle there is nothing objectionable about the extension of lawyers' concerns; these are, it is well understood, jobs which must be done. What is to be questioned is the support which such an extensive legal advice Activity seems to give to the more ambitious conceptions of law's empire.

NOTES

1. The relationship between the law and capitalism has generally been of greater interest to Marxists, who would see the end of the Law, than among writers who would uphold the Rule of Law. Among the former we may include Renner (1949) and Pashukanis (1978); for the latter see Commons (1924) and Posner (1963).
2. Cf. Posner (1963: 115); Burrows and Veljanowski (1981: 2–26).
3. Men and women who attempt to opt out of the market are found in collectives, groups, and communes. Though the individuals within these associations may neither engage in exchange transactions nor own property, yet the communes are rarely independent of the market.
4. The revolutionary changes which were introduced by capitalism have been variously interpreted by Marx (1990); Weber (1948); Tawney (1926). For an ingenious account of the derivation of some of our most fundamental concepts from market activity see Thomson (1961).
5. Georg Simmel's *The Philosophy of Money* (1978) is the most celebrated of all tributes to the virtues of money.
6. Individualism has complex religious, economic, and legal roots; see Macfarlane (1978). The individualism of modern Societies cannot be divorced from the market economy: Brittan (1995). For the connection between individualism and commodity exchange see Strathern (1989).
7. For an illustration of the inequalities endemic in participation in market transactions see Nozik (1974: 160–4).
8. The inalienability of some interests is a figure of speech. Interests are either logically non-transferable, such interests as freedom of speech, or they may be prescribed to be non-transferable, such as a licence to fish from a lake.

There is a lack of precision in locutions which suggest that we could alienate non-transferable interests such as the freedom from servitude. All such interests—the civil interests of civil law and the basic interests of public law— can be lost or destroyed. Prohibitions against subjecting oneself or others to servitude cannot strictly be achieved by rules which prohibit the alienation of interests. Cf. Calabresi and Melamed (1972: 1089–128).

9. The institutional nature of interests in both SE and legal Practices, in both the market-place and law court, must be emphasized; they are individually claimed entitlements to benefits which are afforded *social recognition;* that social recognition may be said to be constitutive of the interest. Here *esse est percipi*—that is, perception by the other members of some associational form—a point brought out in Rousseau's account of the emergence of property. Kant's account of 'mine' (Gregory 1963: 51) as that with which I am so connected that the use which another person makes of it, without my consent, is a wrong or injustice to me, needs to be supplemented by the requirement that other members of the associational form must also hold such use to be wrong. Social recognition may take time; what once constituted bribes can in the course of time become legal rights. As an institutional fact, an individual's socially recognized position of benefit, the interest is vastly different from the concept of the interest which is variously defined and explicated in political and legal theory. See Gray (1996: 223–8). The social or legal recognition clearly distinguishes the institutional fact which is the interest from subjectivist definitions such as that given by John Chipman Gray (1931: 18) who defines interest as an object of desire (a definition adopted in the 1922 American Restatement). For Pound (1943) interests were claims, demands, or expectations which people individually or collectively seek to satisfy. Nor is it simply an objective calculation of what is good for an individual. The interest here is defined in terms of entitlement; it is a socially recognized entitlement to benefits. The vested interest which is the institutional fact is thus a property rather than a desirable condition related to human flourishing.
10. The differentiation of the legal Practices—essential for legal justice—is blurred by introducing ideas of compensation into the penal Practice; cf. Martin (1993: 259). The inadequacy of compensation schemes for victims of criminal acts may be a gap in our social arrangements, but it is not one which should be filled by the penal Practice.
11. This definition of justice was given by Ulpian, the third-century Roman jurist; it appears in the first sentence of Justinian's Institutes.
12. Interests are belongings of individuals, things we own and possess. We own and possess them by virtue of social recognition: recognition of what all agree an individual is entitled to. This is important in considering the legitimacy of legal actions claiming protection for collective interests, the *actiones populares*. For such interests may well lack anything which could conceivably be called general social recognition. Within a Society, one Group's conception of their entitlements will almost inevitably conflict with that of another Group. Legal actions of this sort may well be motivated by desire to secure the legislation of regulatory norms; and their determination may involve questions of policy.

Group interests of another sort, i.e. rights we are supposed to possess individually by virtue of our membership of a Group, suffer from the difficulty of determining the membership of a Group. To appear as legal interests those entitled must be defined as a class. Any claim for the legal protection of such Group rights involves translating the Group into a class; and the criteria for inclusion in the class may well be a matter of dispute.

13. Legal persons have no basic right to the unfolding of the personality. On the Fundamental Law in Germany which confers such a right see Friedman (1990: 35). To purport to confer such a right may be said to be a mere reiteration of the legal justice principles: (a) that the law should not intrude in non-legal regimes of social life; and (b) that our civil and public law rights must be protected. Feinberg said: '(R)espect for persons . . . may simply be respect for their rights, so there cannot be one without the other; and what is called human dignity may simply be the recognisable capacity to assert claims. To respect a person then, or to think of him as possessed of human dignity, is to think of him as a potential maker of claims' (1980: 151). To treat the right to the unfolding of the personality as anything more than a reiteration of the principles of legal justice will justify the description of the provision as a Hayekian Horror: an enactment which, under the guise of imposing duties or conferring rights on citizens, confers discretions on judges or officials. See *ante*, Ch. 2, fn. 69.
14. Examples of such extra-legal SEs are found in commercial customs and community life; in the latter, for example, customary interests in land are given social recognition which, since they do not satisfy criteria laid down by statute, cannot be given legal recognition. As such entitlements are recognized in market transactions there is constant pressure on the courts to give them some sort of legal recognition.
15. In his social life the individual is a person of substance. So the highly artificial legal conception of the individual as a peg for a collection of interests and entitlements must be kept in its proper place: within the civil and public law Practices. Yet in much liberal theory the conception of the atomic individual generated in legal discourse is thought appropriate for social life. It is scarcely surprising that Marx should seize upon the legal person as accurately describing the human condition: the alienated individual of the nineteenth century; see McLellan (1975: 30). Furthermore, the legal person of the civil and public law Practices, the owner of rights, is not the same individual as the accused in a penal Practice. No such differentiation between the domains of law is made in Pashukanis's commodity exchange theory of law. See Collins (1982: 109). On the legal person in penal Practice see a*nte*, p. 94.
16. The distinctiveness of legal language stems, not from the law's preoccupation with rules, but from its intense individualism: its commitment to protect the IEs of individuals and to justify the NPs of the legal Practices, and, in the penal Practice, to offer respect for human vulnerability. We need to know exactly what we have and what others have. The distinctive language articulating legal persons, the offences they commit, and the rights they possess is necessarily a uniquely technical language. It does not form part of a continuum of other similar languages, but is generated only in the legal

Practices. It is, as political discourse is not, the language of justice. On the connection between technical language and legal justice see Hall (1949: 37). See also Hay *et al.* (1979), on the intensification of technicalities in legal discourse which followed from the desire to do justice under principles of penal parsimony: 'Its very inefficacy, its absurd formalism was part of its strength as ideology' (1979: 33).

17. Gluckman wrote that among the Barotse of Northern Rhodesia the 'litigant' 'comes to court not as a right and duty bearing person but in terms of his total social personality. . . . In administering the law the judges consider these total relationships, not only the relations between right and duty bearing units' (1953: 23).
18. For Althusser (1971), the autonomous individual, the figure of a free and responsible agent, is a product of the, law which is a set of institutions and practices founded in capitalist society. It is in coercive legal processes that the idea of the sovereign will of the individual is generated; it does not pre-date the law. The relationships of capitalism, based on ownership and possession of objects, depend on a conception of the individual as a subject in possession of a number of objects. There is great value in the Marxist insight that particular conceptions of individual identity and autonomy are generated within specific forms of life. However, it is wholly mistaken to pick out conceptions and language generated within the related forms of law and capitalism and to suppose that they dominate, or constitute, our consciousness to the exclusion of other determinants of identity and individuality which arise within other forms.
19. The atomic individual of liberal thought is essentially the person of the legal Practices; the person referred to in the language of the communitarians is embedded in the wholly different forms of social life. See Kymlicka (1990: 207). The two different conceptions belong to quite different institutional forms; they operate in different fields. To employ the liberal conception of the person in politics is detrimental to politics; to employ the communitarian conception in the legal field is to undermine the integrity of the legal Practises.
20. Just as some system of coercion and punishment is a necessary part of a Society, so money and private property are integral elements of the capitalist system upon which civil Society is founded. Private property no doubt presents us with the intellectual challenge of understanding its character, but it is supererogatory to seek a justification of such a system; unless the end of civil Society is contemplated, it is absurd to call for its abolition. Despite this, there is a flourishing literature of justification which goes well beyond the effort to understand its functions. Just as every particular punishment requires justification, so does every claim to ownership of an IE. The law is concerned only with the justification of particulars.
21. The sanction of invalidity of the NP is serious; although not penal, it certainly adds to the normative force of the rules; cf. Hart (1994: 33–5).
22. Locke (1956: 63–6).
23. See Birks (1996).
24. See Arnold (1937).

25. The objectification of a quality or attribute of a person is a product of the desire to maintain equality. It is a distinctly legal phenomenon. This must be the law's perception of a person and his properties. On the moral implications of treating an individual's attributes in the same way as we treat their external possessions see Walsh (1961).
26. However the reification of non-economic civil interests is necessary if the legitimacy of the polity is to be established, as this is the only way in which the individual can be respected as something more than a mere catallactic node. It is a phenomenon tied to the bifurcation of the civil from the penal Practice: a process of central importance in the movement to democratic legitimacy.
27. On the priority of social life see *post*, p. 255; the law recognizes the person as a private individual enjoying relationships in which confidence, trust, and secrecy are all important.
28. See Lomasky (1984: 45) for whom rights are 'an entitlement to moral space. By constituting boundaries that others must not transgress they accord to each right-holder a measure of sovereignty over his own life.' Legal rights are to be understood as having recognition not just in a general social context but in a democratic Society. The recognition of civil rights in the civil law Practice and of basic rights in the public law Practice is a logically necessary condition for any assertion of the legitimacy of the polity, because that legitimacy depends absolutely on the free acceptance of the laws by every individual member of Society. Men and women with no guarantee of a private area in which they could lead their own lives and develop their own ideas as to how to live could reasonably reject the authority of the law. Nagel (1991: 142–3). The justification for the protection of rights which depend 'on the nature of human life and the importance of preserving for each person a private area in which he can lead it and develop his personal relations with other individuals and his own conception of how to live' is to be found in 'the unanimity seeking conception of legitimacy' (p. 143). 'The guarantee of certain forms of inviolability is a straightforward condition of the legitimacy of a political system because anyone who does not enjoy that guarantee could reasonably reject its authority' (ibid.).
29. David Johnson (1994) maintains that the individualism of democracy depends upon a conception of the person as an agent. That view is embodied here in the rationale of legal civil rights; the natural person is not just a possessor of things but an agent. Agency is a centrally important element in right-holding; the person with rights must be capable of choice, of acting, of obeying social rules, of spending money, of transacting business. Artificial persons, with agents to act for them, do satisfy the requirement; they count as actors in the SE system.
30. Rights are generated in the legal Practices; it may be that their adoption in political discourse is a borrowing from that legal experience. Martin (1993: 170): 'An insistence on civil rights . . . will often lead to democratisation.'
31. Feminist writers refer to the legal conception of the individual as pre-social, in contrast with the person involved in the inevitable sociability of human life; see Lacey (1993: 207). The legal person is an artificial conception which

develops late; if it is indeed wholly distinct from any other conception, it is not pre-social.

32. The particulars are rights, which will be given identity as the civil Practice becomes differentiated from the penal practice. This is reflected in the change from the doing of right—*ius*—to the protection of rights, from adjudication in which human beings of ordinary discourse expect fairness, all things considered, to legal persons who demand to be protected in their rights: see Dagger (1989: 294–5).
33. 'The only idea behind the ideal of autonomy is that people should make their own lives': Raz (1994: 314). In the legal field autonomy is part of the idea of the legal Practices; but it does not feature as an item in the LSS of the Practices, as a norm against which other rules cannot prevail. In the CS Practice it is concretized as freedoms: interests which are not part of civil law. See *post*, p. 349.
34. 'Equality does derive its substantive content entirely from rights': Westen (1981). Equality is narrowly defined as equality of treatment under general rules; it simply means that the norms apply equally. This is a wholly different conception from that of equality in the distribution of goods other than civil rights. Although all citizens have an equal number of non-transferable interests—their civil and basic rights—they have unequal amounts of transferable entitlements. Legitimacy depends upon equality of interests, not equality of entitlements. Law is concerned only with established distributions of vested interests and entitlements, not with possible or desirable changes to the pattern.
35. Civil rights in private law, which are based on the idea of the legal person as owner, differ from the basic rights of public law; see *post*, p. 341. The latter are deductions from the axiom of the initially powerless State in the legitimate polity. The possessor of civil rights against other members is also entitled to basic rights against the State.
36. This is a very legalistic account of private life, with its confidences, understandings, and private constructs.
37. The large number of regulatory regimes with indeterminate limits and very varied normative components makes it difficult to map the boundaries between the legal and extra-legal. Where do we stop speaking of law and find ourselves simply describing social life? See Cotterrell (]995: 281). The enforcement of standard-maintenance rules has led to the appointment of regulators and the institution of inspectorates which are at certain points engaged in servicing the legal Practices.
38. See Aubert (1983: 78–9) for an account of a dispute involving theological questions about the meaning of Hell; since it involved the position of a Bishop—holding unorthodox opinions—it was referred to a constitutional lawyer. The resolution of disputes of this type within an Organization are clearly not legal matters; in respect of such an association the law's role is not to give advice, or to make any decision for the members, but merely to see that any decision made within the Church is procedurally just.
39. See Shklar (1964).
40. Jurgen Habermas considers that law as an instrument of policy can threaten

the structures of what he called the life world, the realm of spontaneous interaction and value formation in social life. See Pusey (1987: 105–10). For a discussion of other views which decry what Teubner has called the 'juridification of social spheres' see Cotterrell (1992: 289–91).

41. What may be suggested here is that the law can contribute to the diminution in the stock of trust; that the law's intervention is not merely a symptom but also a cause of decreasing trust. In certain areas of activity the introduction of legal controls, and reliance upon clear rules, diverts attention from the moral principles which ought to prevail. Durkheim drew attention to the importance for individuality of a society based on trust, contrasting it with a society without secrets under surveillance (1947). For a recent assertion of the importance of the level of trust inherent in society see Fukuyama (1995): a nation with a strong tradition of civil association and shared ethical habits will spend less time on crime, litigation, and state intervention.
42. Friedman (1990: 13) remarks that today there are fewer zones of immunity from law, fewer areas of life which are totally unregulated, totally beyond the potential reach of the law. He highlights the phenomenon of growing legalization which Habermas describes as 'the colonisation of personal life by the law'.
43. Other aspects of the NPs of legal Practices are explored in the discussion of the CS Practice, *post*, Ch. 8.
44. See Huber (1988).
45. For an assault on the integrity of the civil Practice see *Economist*, 9 Mar. 1991. The US Supreme Court declared that a jury's discretion to settle the amount of damages does not violate the due process clause of the constitution; in that case damages of $1.04 million were awarded of which $80,000 were punitive not compensatory. Consumer groups see punitive damages as an essential tool for *regulation;* business groups deplore it, arguing that damages should be compensatory. Regulatory fines may be useful in the control of activities, but the legal Practice is not the place to determine their extent.
46. The natural tendency to ascribe all declaratory power to the appeal courts may obscure the declaratory function of lower courts; the courts of first instance which are part of the legal Practice and also declare the law.
47. On legal rights see *post*, Ch. 6.
48. For a description of a liberal elite which cannot win elections and attempts to win lawsuits instead see Bork (1991)
49. In France the Court of Cassation has as an objective 'to maintain discipline among the judges', which reinforces the view of judges as functionaries in a government department. It may be a somewhat oblique way of preserving the ground rules, but it gives no hint of the court's declaratory functions.
50. Coke reports that he replied: 'God had allowed His Majesty excellent science and great endowments of nature, but His Majesty was not learned in the laws of his realm of England'. *Prohibitions del Roy* (1607) 12 Co. Rep. 63, 77 ER 1342.
51. On restraint in litigation see *post*, p. 186. The importance of such restraining norms is highlighted by Lawrence Friedman's description of the current belief in the USA that the right to go to court is totally unlimited; that everybody who has a claim or a claim to a claim can try his luck, the only

barriers being culture and cost (1990: 21). The filtering process includes the requirement that the plaintiff has to ask for a specific remedy; see the discussion on CS Practice, p. 316.

52. *Legal advice Activity* must be regarded as a separate institutional form (see *ante*, p. 117 on penal Practice). Like other Activities the way in which those engaged may proceed is regulated. Among the regulatory rules and standards are what may be called the precepts of legal advice; they have the same status as the precepts of legality which govern *enforcement Activity* (see *ante*, p. 114). Both Activities depend on a legal Practice; ideally, their precepts should also reflect the same respect for the law. The desirability of restraint in litigation will feature among the precepts of legal advice. Some legal advice precepts may overlap with the ground rules of the Practice, but strictly they are not Practice rules.
53. There are different rules of recognition for different Practices; see Hacker and Raz (eds.) (1977: ch. I).
54. The initial assumption is that a law exists which will answer the question; the reality will often be otherwise. So the creation of new norms may be necessary under norms of incorporation. Justification of the NP of the Practice is limited to the legal material available. It is this limitation which marks the difference between the law-making process within the debate in the courts and that found in a legislature.
55. Full institutional analysis of the rules of incorporation is not possible here.
56. The objective of the deliberation is to answer the narrow legal issue before the court; it is not a determination as to what, given all the circumstances, is to be done. To the legal question few considerations are relevant. This deliberation is of a special sort. On deliberation in general see Wiggins (1978). What Coke in the *Prohibitions del Roy* called the artificial reason of the law may be regarded as the reasonableness of the common law, a distinctive product of the legal debate in the cases. This is not at all an exotic form of reasoning, but a process which is to be understood in the light of the conventions governing legal debate, deliberation, and decision-making—a process which no individual can replicate.
57. See Golding (1978: 98–121).
58. It may be urged that defence lawyers were not in possession of, or did not do justice to the full facts, or that the arguments were not fully rehearsed, so that declaration was insecurely based.
59. The claims about the indeterminacy of the law made by the rule-and-fact sceptics in the US Realist School can be accepted without hesitation. There is what is virtually a conceptual link between the idea of a civil law case and the fact that the law has variant readings. We should treat seriously Llewellyn's demonstration of the different rules which could apply to govern the same case (1960). Although the Realists' claims were undeniable, however, they drew from them quite the wrong conclusions. See Cohen (1935). So too do all the disappointed absolutists, the left-wing radicals, and the Critical Legal Studies school. So, indeed, does Geny on revealing the huge uncertainties of codified law. Firmly within the tradition which spawned black-letter law, the tradition which prizes doctrine above procedure, they turn either to

foundationalism, the pursuit of some agenda for the common good, or to pragmatism, which is the antithesis of legal debate and deliberation, and which turns legal debate into political deliberation. The proper response should be the determination to ensure that the legal debate is as thorough and rigorous as it can be. Once we accept as a fact of life that there are huge tolerances in the legal material there is no need for cynicism. We can accept the democratic legitimacy of the decision reached, not because it is the result of a single individual's correct deduction from the rules or interpretation of the common good, but because it stands as a well considered, fully deliberated choice between the legally available options. One minor virtue of this approach is that it allows us to sidestep the tedious, jargon-ridden obscurities of postmodernist writers wrestling with the mysteries of legal reasoning.

60. Stanley Fish has described interpretation as a process of 'playing with the text where I am not trying to figure out what it means but trying to see what meanings it could be made to yield'. Quoted in Douzinas *et al.* (eds.) (1994: 83).
61. Golding (1978: 106–19) sets out justifications for the adversary system, which make no reference to the way in which that system allows for full deliberation of the law which will give the outcome legitimacy. Note the absurd suggestion to which he refers on p. 109 that the adversary system might one day be replaced by a laboratory technique. More valuable is Summer's comment on Golding's paper that the trial is intended not merely to discover the facts but to ensure accuracy in the application of the law, that the application of the law is itself the object of the debate. The system 'institutionalises suspension of judgment until all legal arguments are heard'. 'It is better that a judge hear vigorous opposing legal arguments as to the application of he law . . . than that the judge rely mainly on his assumed ability to carry on vigorous contrapuntal dialogue with himself' Summers (1978: 126).
62. If a legal ruling appears to illustrate the ascendancy of one person or set of interests over another the decision can be fully justified; it can withstand a challenge. The difference between a decision deliberated in conditions of procedural justice and an informal arbitrary act or command is the difference between justified action and arbitrary will. Cf. Fish (1989).
63. The inquisitorial approach to the administration of justice makes it likely that, despite respect for the separation of powers, judges will become involved in enforcement Activity. On the importance of keeping arbiters separate from the police and the prosecution service see the 1993 *Report of the Royal Commission on Criminal Justice, per* Runciman. Lon Fuller saw adversariness as a mode of proceeding crucial for the moral integrity of the enterprise of law. Philip Selznick has also emphasized the role of a system of institutionalized criticism in which the adversarial principle has a special place: see Schurr (1968: 55–6).
64. Warning against 'a mindless sort of authority worship', Lyons describes the positivists as employing a desiccated conception of legal authority: (1993: 47). The implication is that the authority of the law must be grounded in the congruence of the laws with some moral or utilitarian foundation. However, the unstated reason why judges unquestioningly regard themselves as bound

by legislation and judicial decisions is that those norms are well made. Laws have authority primarily because no other formulations could have been, in relation to the type of issues which face the court, as carefully considered. Dworkin (1987: 10) criticizes the orthodoxy that lawyers employ factual criteria to decide whether propositions of law are true or false. Yet the rule of recognition is designed to enable judges to decide, not whether propositions are true or false, but whether the norms are well made.

65. The position of the jury in the penal Practice underlines the point. They do not have to be right. They have above all to consider fully under clinical conditions what the verdict should be. They contribute to the legitimacy of the Practice. The NP must be fully deliberated. The emphasis on well made law, and the well made NP, renders a search for the single right answer unnecessary. Institutional theory clearly has no commitment to the determinacy condition; see Burton (1992: xi–xii).
66. 'To acknowledge the possibility of judicial error is to assume neither that the law provides a complete answer to any legal question, nor that when the law provides one it does so with logical exclusiveness. Judicial error may be the failure to follow the best legal arguments or the strongest legal reasons as is commonly assumed when judicial decisions are criticised on one legal ground or another' Lyons (1993: 45).
67. It is the nature of the legal debate which characterizes or differentiates law as a mode of argument; it is a debate within very carefully drawn boundaries. The relevance conventions are the accumulated wisdom of experience. The Practice ground rules structure the form of the argument; the arguments are based on conceptions of legal justice. Unchecked debate will allow the consideration of political, constitutional, and moral factors in addition to the legal material; see Martin (1993: 67). Postmodernist writers wish to blur the distinction between legal and political argument and discourse; see Goodrich (1987: 206). This completely ignores the location of legal arguments within courts having a clear *idea*. The methodological values of the law will render the type of deliberation required to produce its NPs wholly different from that involved in political decision-making.
68. The participants are sensitive to, and will be restricted to, the nature of the justificatory reasons—to the rules—which can be employed. Legal rules are not just institutionalized reasons; they are exclusionary reasons formulated in ways which make the doing of legal justice possible.
69. We overlook the significance of Milsom's observation that the common law is a product of the arguments presented and the decisions reached in individual cases, many of which involved juries: (1965: 149).
70. Although the deliberations of the courts have both moral and legal components (Burton 1992: 221–8), it is perhaps more important to pay attention to the collective nature of the deliberations.
71. Paterson (1982: 83) comments on significant aspects of the decision-making process in the House of Lords which are lost to posterity because the oral exchanges between judges and counsel are not reported: '. . . the pervasive influence of counsel's submissions, the pictures they paint, the baited analogies they proffer, the avenues they close in their arguments—all are left

neglected. Worst of all, the lack of proper transcripts helps to perpetuate the notion among academic scholars that the real work of the Law Lords and the only important aspects of appeals are the speeches produced at the end of the day. The concentration on the end product, to the exclusion of the process by which it was arrived at, is intellectually dangerous and academically unsound.'

72. For a challenge to the view that judicial decisions could only be legitimate if they follow statutory or constitutional provisions themselves legitimated by consent, see Kness (1989: 283–337).
73. Nor, *pace* Dworkin, are the participants all engaged in writing a chain novel: (1986: 228–38). They are adversaries giving variant readings of the law appropriate only for the instant case, no one of which is provably right, but all, derived from the legal material, claim to do legal justice.
74. According to Fish the formalist claim is that 'once a question has been posed as a legal question in proper form the answer to it will be generated by relations of entailment between that form and other forms in the system' (1993: 159). The claim of legal science to be able to provide the right answers to legal problems precisely where the legal material is inadequate to found a new rule is the besetting sin of foundationalism. The gaps are not filled with what is already there; they are filled by a specific, distinctive legislative effort, not by deduction. See Aubert (1983: 50) for the claim that legal scholarship has methods that meet the demands stipulated by the rule of law. Such methods of discovery cannot be substituted for the legal debate.
75. The debate is necessarily long and expensive; a factor in the filtering process.
76. See Eisenberg (1988: 157).
77. The surprise of the realists and of critical legal studies at the discovery of the indeterminacy of law, the discovery that the assumptions of legal discourse are incoherent and contradictory, is only explicable in the light of their subjection to the propaganda of an academic legal advice school preaching determinacy. To take the discovery as a licence for the advancement of a distasteful political vision (expressed in an appropriately graceless prose) shows a misunderstanding of legal adjudication and the needs of a democratic polity. In the legal history of the USA it is more interesting to speculate about the reasons for the establishment of an academic orthodoxy against which Realists reacted than about the motivation behind their voyage to discover the Old World. Admittedly, the conventions of legal debate were freer; but precisely why was there such faith in the black-letter law? Whence the generation of an orthodoxy which believed in the amplitude of the law and the possibility of employing purely deductive processes? For an example of the absurdity of such claims see Zane (1918). Clearly we have to examine the nature and development of academic legal advice Activity. Can we find German or French influences at work here? Was it the result of rationalism engendered by working with a written constitution? Or was it the dynamic of a federal polity? See J. C. Clark's thesis (1993) that the common law tradition was, due to political developments, given a wholly new reading in the American colonies in the 18th century. The common law always claimed to be grounded in natural law; and in their legal objections to

metropolitan measures the American colonists were increasingly forced to rely upon the deliverances of natural law. Such was the extent of this reliance that in effect they departed from a shared legal tradition.

78. 'Appeal court-itis' may be an affliction of academic legal advice Activity as the appeal courts appear to do most of the work of declaring the law. We must not overlook the contribution of the lower courts within a legal Practice; they too authoritatively declare the law in conditions conducive to full deliberation.
79. Darius, Emperor of Persia had a corrupt judge flayed; he ordered that the seat of judgment be covered with the skin to remind those who subsequently sat upon it of their duties.
80. See Friedman (1990: 18) on the widespread belief in the USA that all issues are justiciable.
81. The pleas for restraint in litigation are unlikely to be strengthened by the introduction of contingency-fee actions.
82. For an account of the popular, less formal courts in 19th-century England see Arthurs (1985).
83. See Shapiro (1995: 54-5) on the 'litigation explosion' in the USA.
84. This term is used by Salmond (1957: 261) following Ihering's definition of a right.
85. E.g. Lyons (1984: 45).
86. Bentham's view that property is entirely a legal creation misrepresents both the nature of economic activity in which property IEs are created, and the nature of the law's intervention in that field.
87. Goodrich (1986: 160).
88. The rules of right are not simple deductions from the nature of the IE, the object of the right; they are *decisions* as to what will be legally required in respect of a particular object, in particular circumstances. So we cannot deduce, but have to decide what follows from recognizing e.g. a right to marry; see Christie (1982: 40).
89. We should be mindful of the experience—the work of the Praetors—upon which Roman Law was founded; see Rodger (1995). It is paradoxical that Savigny, who asserted the importance of experience and history, nevertheless founded a school of Jurisprudence which prized conceptual consistency more than experience. See d'Entreves (1970: 96–7).
90. A question posed by Dworkin in *Taking Rights Seriously, p.* 15.
91. On rules as labour-saving devices see Raz (1975: 141).
92. This is particularly true of constitutional matters, since the constitution is commonly regarded as the fundamental law. So naturally those expert in its norms are lawyers. As a result, political choices about representation, devolution, and so forth, are argued to a great extent by lawyers; see e.g. Ganz (1994). Constitutional lawyers are at the forefront when demands are made for such innovations as a Bill of Rights and a written constitution.
93. Of course unnecessary obscurities must be avoided; there is a considerable degree of concordance between Bentham's requirements for legislation (1970) and Fuller's desiderata for law (1964). However, legal rules are not good rules because citizens can understand them but because lawyers can understand

them, and most importantly because they are well made and justify the decisions of the judges. Clarity is not the prime virtue of the legal rule; its virtue lies in providing a complete justifying reason for the NP.

94. The more precise the formulation of a rule, the less relevant do the purposes behind it, the reasons for its enactment, become 'Suppose the reason for creating a class of persons who lack capacity is the belief that immature people lack a faculty of free will. Setting the age of majority at 21 will incapacitate many but not all of those who lack this faculty. And it will incapacitate some who actually possess it. From the point of view of the purpose of the rules the combined over and under inclusiveness amounts not just to licensing but requiring official arbitrariness' Kennedy (1976: 1689). The specification of criteria other than the simple proof of age would entail the exercise of official discretion; it is here that the purpose of the rule becomes important. Where officials are authorized to exercise a discretion, i.e. where they must have regard to purposes, it is inappropriate for judges either to second-guess the official decisions or to crystalize the principles into rules—to declare them as laws.
95. However, consider the variety of claims about the purposes of the Race Relations Act 1968: see Twining and Miers (1982: 156). Although the Act does have several functions, its legal components are neutral; they confer powers on officials and rights on individuals, and create offences. So to the extent that its provisions are incorporated in the LSS of the legal Practices its rules are neutral. Formal 'legislative' utterances can of course be employed to exhort, as they were by Henry I or Charlemagne; or they may set out policy, in provisions which are not legal norms. It is important to stress that the NPs of legislative Practices are not *ipso facto* laws.
96. A rule performs its justificatory function because it has been deliberated as fully as possible; it has been enacted in the ULP and refined by the legal Practices. No one else can claim to have had more information about the rule's implications and consequences or to have paid respect to Groups or persons in the law-making process. Scrupulous deliberation can only be ensured if the procedures are formally regulated to meet such *desiderata*.
97. On the continuity of the tradition see Kelley (1991).
98. 'The civil code should be simple and clear like the laws of nature. . . . The individual will know the laws that govern him; he will be delivered from the subtleties and infinite complications that chicanery invents at his expense': P. Sagnac, quoted in Herman (1981: 188). The call for laws to be drafted in plain English ignores the expertise involved in technical matters. Concern for the man in the street must be met by the provision of access to expert legal advice.
99. For a useful review of the literature on the profession see Cotterrell (1992: ch. 6).
100. For institutional theory what is required is less a study of the Organizations than one of the Activity of legal advice. The Organizations—the guilds—are the most effective way of regulating the Activity. Emphasis on the associational forms of the profession can mislead. From the observation that the legal profession in Britain and on the continent has always been a political

body with varying religious, ethical, and political functions, we may go on to argue that law is therefore part of the social continuum in the political field (Goodrich 1987: 145). However, although the profession may well be a pressure group in the political field, legal advice Activity—by which the profession must be defined—simply does not lie in the political field at all. The emphasis must be on the practical form—the Activity; the profession must be seen as composed of actors in an Activity which is focused on the legal Practices. It is this focus which gives the discourse of the actors a distinctive character, wholly different from that of political discourse.

101. Typically, a Code giving support to the idea of law as a system of rules out there and a set of conventions—the means whereby the law can be applied. A foracentric jurisprudence will describe the existing rules of the LS, the rules in the form in which they have been incorporated.

102. For the view that the law is made by the general legal culture of a society see Friedman (1990: 197). It may be suggested that when we talk about a legal culture we are really talking, not about a set of ideas shared by the population at large, but about the ethos of a particular Group: the lawyers. Strictly, of course, the laws are generated not by this Group but in the legal Practices. Nevertheless, the Group—the actors in legal advice Activity—can alter the character of the law. Lawyers can exceed their brief, and in doing so they encourage judges to blur the boundaries of the legal domain and turn legal Practices into something else: mechanisms for social control, welfare amenities, government agencies, and so forth.

103. On the impact of recent developments which have diminished the autonomy of the profession see Cotterrell (1992: 197).

6
Legal rights

The language of civil law is above all a language of rights. It has proved to be a popular and wayward language, used extensively in politics and in philosophical discourse about the human condition unrelated to legal concerns. The ambiguity and overuse of the term 'right' in its various employments is notorious.[1] This ambiguity is as apparent in its legal usages as anywhere else. So varied are its uses in legal discourse that we cannot hope to understand its central meaning merely by investigating its manifold employments.

This chapter provides what may be called an institutional reconstruction of the legal right.[2] Normative concepts are generated within the specific institutional forms in which the norms are located. So the reconstruction of the legal right is to be achieved by locating the concept within the context of the generating civil law Practice. For we cannot hope to advance our understanding of the legal right merely by placing the term in some vague institutional context: for instance, against the backdrop of 'society', or within 'human interaction', 'social intercourse', in some 'sphere of discourse', or by importing something as ill-defined as a 'legal system' as an essential context.

The concept of the legal right could never have emerged simply from the general activity by which members of Society assert and protect their own interests. For legal rights do not denote the interests and entitlements which members own and possess: they denote special positions which the law confers upon the owners and possessors of the IE. The development of a language of legal rights depends on the emergence of a civil law Practice; a Practice whose overarching idea is the protection, by the use of force, of the interests and entitlements of members of Society.

The expression 'legal right' denotes an important and uniquely defined institutional fact.[3] As such, it must be distinguished from other institutional facts for which the term 'right' is also employed. It is an expression employed in the articulation of the legal point of view, and that point of view cannot be understood unless we grasp the nature of the legal Practice. The legal right is not some general notion of a claim which human beings may make in a vague legal context, it is a concept generated within distinctive legal forms of life.[4] Legal rights are institutional facts which exist within actual—and imagined—litigation. Remove the possibility of litigation from Society and legal rights would be wholly superfluous. Institutional analysis is concerned only with the right as an indispensable, uniquely defined concept. This institutional reconstruction of the legal right will lead us to discard all uses of the term for objects and relationships which are distinguishable from those institutional facts which are rights, and for which other terms are more appropriate.

A defining feature of the civil Practice is the normative product (NP)—an order issued to a defendant, D, to do, or refrain from doing something in favour of the plaintiff, P. That order is the means whereby the assistance of the law—guaranteed by the force of the State—is made available to P as a member of Society for the protection of his IE. Our starting point is P's legal right as it must be understood in this context. *In institutional theory P is said to have a legal right if, and only if, he is entitled to legal assistance to protect his IE, in the form of a specific NP ordered in his favour within the civil Practice.*[5]

The elucidation of the concept of the legal right in institutional terms will involve an examination of: (1) the legal right itself—the position of the right-holder, P; (2) the liability of D; (3) D's legal duties with respect to the right-holder's IE; and (4) the nature of the object of the legal right. Every one of these elements, and the relationships between them, has from time to time been misunderstood or misrepresented. The outlines of the relationships between these elements may be shown diagramatically:

The legal right

(1) *The right in P*

A power in P to get an NP ordered against D → (2) *Liability in D*: D's liability to have an NP ordered against him; arises on proof of D's responsibility for some harmful act in respect of P's IE.

↓ in respect of harm to ↓

(4) *The object of the right*

An interest or entitlement possessed or owned by P.

(from (2)) ↓ P may not exercise his right, but if he does: ↓

(3) *The duty in D*

The NP imposes a Practice duty on D which is coercively enforced.

← *Duty to act*

Imposed because the duty to do, not do, or give back exists under the LS rules.

↓ *Duty to compensate*

Imposed because of D's responsibility for P's loss of his IE.

A: The legal right in P

From the point of view of institutional theory P's right is an entitlement to legal assistance against a legal person, D. The assistance takes the form of a coercive order—the NP—issued at P's behest, commanding D to do or refrain from doing certain things. The remedial orders are of several types (see *ante*, p. 173). As there are different types of remedies we may say that there are different sorts of rights. A right to compensation is a different sort of entitlement from a right to specific performance. We need to attend to these differences, for there are dangers in generalizing from, say, the right to enforcement of a contractual duty, an example commonly used in jurisprudential discussion.

P's right—his entitlement to have an NP ordered against D in respect of P's IE—clearly arises only when D has actually harmed or threatened to harm P. Logically, a right to compensation arises only after P has suffered compensable loss for which D is responsible. There would be little point in P's requesting an order against D if D shows no sign of failing to fulfil his contractual obligations, or has no intention of creating a nuisance, or does not hold any of P's property. Coercive NPs are only required in circumstances where loss has been threatened or suffered. The precise degree of seriousness necessary for a threat to entitle P to legal assistance will be set out in the LS rules. Although inaccurate, the description of the remedial right given by nineteenth-century writers, as arising *ex delicto,* has the virtue of underlining the fact that P's right comes into existence only when certain circumstances have arisen.

Although P's legal right—which we may call the immediate right—arises only at a certain point, we can nevertheless assert, even before any damage is done, that if D were to do a certain act, or to cause loss, then P would be entitled to an NP. If D's action could in future, breach the duty of respect owed to P we might say that P would have an 'enforceable' right. In saying this we are not referring to a special sort of right distinguishable from the remedial right; we are predictively asserting a remedial legal right in P.

Now such predictive rights are an essential part of the legal articulation of the world; in setting out the legal point of view we want to know whether P would, if the need arose, have an entitlement to legal assistance.[6] In describing the world from the legal point of view these rights are central. The legal relationships which are expressed in terms of rights and duties between P and other members of Society are to be understood as being essentially the relationships between a plaintiff and a defendant in litigation. They are not relationships between actors in Activities or between members within associational forms. They are the interrelationships of the members as participants in a legal Practice.[7] In the language of the civil law the only rights we need recognize are remedial rights, whether immediate or predictive.

The 'primary' or antecedent right of jurisprudence requires redefinition as a predictive attribution of a future entitlement to legal assistance.[8] It does not, as is commonly supposed, denote a different sort of legal relationship from that which obtains when P *is* immediately so entitled. Remedial rights are not, as Holland asserted, 'merely part of the machinery provided by the State for the redress of injury done to the antecedent rights'.[9] In institutional theory the primary right is parasitic upon the recognition of a remedial right within the civil Practice; it does not exist prior to, or independently of, the remedial right.

A power

At least since the time of Hobbes and Spinoza writers have described a right as a sort of power.[10] P's legal right is a power which P may or may not exercise. On suffering an injury or being subjected to a serious threat—at that point prescribed by the LS rules—P can choose whether D should be coerced or not. Of course, up to that point P is entitled to take any other lawful action to encourage or compel D to do what is right. At this point, however—if the rules are clear—he also has undisputed power to call for legal assistance.

As a power, P's right must be deliberately exercised;[11] it is obviously not enough merely to entertain a desire, or signify an intention, to have an order made against D. Exactly how the power can be exercised will be laid down in the ground rules of the Practice. We can see how important this power is by reflecting that the very existence of the civil law depends upon its exercise by individual members over the course of time; rights are a fundamental part of the system of civil law.

Now it is important to recognize that P's power is essentially one of capacity, not of authority.[12] The distinction between these two forms of power has been largely neglected in jurisprudence, and also in political and social science. A person's *capacity* to change the norms stems from the fact that he is entitled to participate in a normative Practice. A person's *authority*—as, e.g., an officer or official—is an ability to affect the activity of others by issuing commands directly to them. Clearly the right-holder P, who can participate as plaintiff in the civil Practice, has capacity rather than authority: P will not normally be in a position effectively to issue commands to D.[13] Indeed it is precisely because he lacks this sort of power that he must have recourse to the law to get his due.

Yet there is an inclination, like Kant, to regard the power as an authority.[14] Hart uses the image of the right-holder gripping a chain binding another which he may pull if he chooses. 'The idea is that of one individual being given by the law exclusive control, more or less extensive, over another person's duty so that in the area of conduct covered by the duty the individual who has the right is a small-scale sovereign to whom the duty is owed.'[15]

However, we will seriously misdescribe P's position as a right-holder if we assert that he has authority or dominion over D. Although it is true that 'having a right entails having a moral justification for limiting the freedom of another person',[16] that must not be taken to mean that the right-holder can do the limiting. There will no doubt be justification for someone to restrict D's freedom, but although P has a legal right he does not necessarily have authority to restrict D's freedom himself. The very existence of a mature civil Practice involves a curtailment of P's ability to obtain redress by way of self-help. The criminal laws of a Society in which a civil Practice exists are unlikely to allow persons to take action against those who have committed a civil wrong. 'The point is not that the right-holder actually possesses the power to coerce others but that the use of force or the threat of force to secure compliance with the behaviour comprehended by the right would be appropriate.'[17] Within a Society it is a major function of the civil Practice to provide for the regulated and legitimate use of force to protect of members' entitlements.

In saying that P has a right, or a power to obtain an NP, we mean rather more than that he has a capacity to participate in the Practice; we mean that he has the power to get an NP ordered in protection of his IE. If a member who has been injured is deterred from conducting a legal action by the expense, we might think that in reality he lacks the power. Practical considerations of this sort do not however qualify the assertion of predictive rights: optional powers which will be recognized if certain circumstances are found. So our calculation of whether P has a right will be unaffected by the realities of the position which he might be in if he wanted to litigate.

Who may have a legal right?

Any member of Society with th e capacity to participate in the civil Practice as a plaintiff may be said to possess legal rights. The capacity to possess legal rights is prescribed by the ground rules of the Practice. Members of Society who are generally capable of exercising such a power may nevertheless be legally incapacitated; that is, the ground rules of the Practice might exclude a particular class of persons from participation. Then, although by virtue of their possession of IE social duties of respect will be owed to them, they will not have any legal rights.

It is not a defining condition of being a right-holder that an individual should be seeking legal assistance in respect of his own interests and entitlements. Provision may be made for another to exercise power on behalf of an individual incapable of acting in person. That other, and not the legal person, is then the right-holder, even though he is not entitled to the benefits of the IE in respect of which he sues D. The capacity to sue is not limited to entities with legal personality. Trustees, for example, may have no entitlements under the trust; they act on behalf of the beneficiaries. Legal persons are generally right-holders, but they need not be: the rights commonly ascribed to them are strictly the rights of their agents.[18]

The legal right can only be understood in its institutional setting. The concept of the right as a power is clearly a concept with a point. For a justified attribution of a right in P, whether immediate or predictive, is a significant institutional proposition. It is something more than a statement of D's duties of respect from P's point of view. It is a statement of P's entitlement to legal assistance.

B: The liability in D

If P has power to obtain legal assistance, in the form of a coercive order commanding D to do or refrain from doing something, then D's liability is simply the risk that P might exercise his power as a result of which D would be subjected to a coercive order. It is an essential feature of the legal right that P can choose whether to exercise his power. D's duties with respect to P's IE will not necessarily be enforced; it lies within P's power to have some of them enforced.

It must be insisted that D's liability is unaffected by the possibility that P may exercise his power and yet fail to get the order to which he is entitled; the liability is something more than the risk that D may have to appear as a defendant, or to pay costs. A statement about the possession of a legal predictive right is a calculation from the rules, a conclusion of law, unaffected by practical considerations.

This liability in D is the true correlative of the right in P. A statement that P has the power to get an NP ordered against D is logically equivalent to a statement of the liability in D to have an NP awarded against him at the behest of P. Though *duties* in D are, in some way, entailed in every right in P, they are not logical correlatives of P's power.

An *immunity* in D is a lack of liability to have an NP ordered against him in respect of acts which may affect the IE of others. A member injured by D who has an immunity has no entitlement to legal assistance. Immunities are thus exceptions, in that members whose IE are adversely affected by D will not be able to get legal redress. This does not mean that the duties of respect attending those IE do not exist, merely that only extra-legal protection of the IE is possible. So if it is prescribed that the State is not liable for damage to the IE of P, it does not follow that the State has no duties of respect towards P.

In institutional theory the liability arises at that point, prescribed by the ground rules of the Practice, when D's harm or threat to an IE entitles P to call for legal assistance. We can, of course, also recognize a *predictive liability* correlative to P's predictive right: if D were to breach a duty of respect then he would be liable at the moment when P becomes empowered.

Who is liable?

The liability is that of a legal person. Within the civil Practice only a legal person can be ordered by a judge to do what is right. For liability must include the possibility of being ordered to pay a sum of money by way of damages, to pay costs, and so on. The remedy of damages is a central feature of the civil Practice since, in a systematic exchange (SE) Society, private losses and injuries are quantifiable in monetary terms and considered to be reparable by the payment of money. So any person who is liable to be ordered to pay must own valuable assets in a separate, personal account. A human being who is legally incapable of owning property or money, who thus cannot possess a separate account, will, in the civil law Practice, be a non-person; he will lack legal personality. Given the condition of liability, that only the person responsible for the loss can be coerced into compensating for it, it follows that the liability of a legal person to pay must be limited to his account; his liability cannot be extended to the accounts of his friends and neighbours. The notional separate account or fund, from which alone payment may be ordered—i.e. which may be drawn on for the payment of damages—is an essential attribute of the legal person. Artificial persons have limited liability; they are essentially managed funds out of which any order to pay compensation to a member would be satisfied exclusively.

In the civil Practice an NP can be justified only if it is proved that D has acted or threatened to act inconsistently with P's IE. So the fundamental condition of liability is that D, who has a duty to respect P's IE, has threatened or caused, or is regarded as being responsible for, the loss of benefits to which P is entitled. The requirement that participants employ such a general principle specifying the necessary condition of liability is a defining feature of the Practice. Of course the precise extent of these duties, and of the criteria which the participants employ to determine responsibility, are difficult and contentious matters involving the notions of causation, foreseeability, remoteness, vicarious liability, agency, and so forth.[19] The circles of liability and responsibility will be differently drawn in the civil Practices of different Societies, but in all of them D must have been in a position, directly or indirectly, to cause or prevent losses to P.

The justification for imposing the coercive order may stress either of two ideas: it may indicate that D owes something to P or it may assert that

D is a wrong-doer, that every act inconsistent with P's IE is wrongful. The latter emphasis, more common in earlier times than it is today, will make the order appear to be a sanction, a civil version of the penalty which defines a criminal offence. In the ideal civil Practice, however, D is liable, not because he is a wrong-doer, but because he owes something to P. All questions of punishable wrong-doing are irrelevant. The idea of the Practice is merely to restore the balance between two individuals which has been disturbed.

C: The duties related to the legal right

To understand the duties of civil law, and the way in which these duties relate to legal rights, we need to anchor them securely to the form of life in which they are recognized and enforced. Rights, duties, and rules are not abstract counters in an unanchored conceptual network; they can only be understood in their institutional context. Thus it is not enough to treat the duties of civil law as being prescribed by the legal rules; we need to see precisely how those rules and duties are related to the coercive power of the civil Practice. Rules are commonly described simply as setting out duties as though they were unmediated by any enforcement activity.

> Rules prescribe behaviour and in so doing are said to impose 'duties' or 'obligations'. If we say Y has a duty to act in a certain way, we mean that there is a rule which leaves him no choice in the matter, that 'requires' it of him.[20]

If described in this way, the rules requiring us to do things seem to have a magical quality. Such statements elide the awkward but necessary business of the application and enforcement of rules; that is something which is understood or taken for granted. However, such elision suggests that there is a merely contingent relationship between a legal duty and its enforcement; and that suggestion is fundamentally mistaken. What is legally required of members is what the judges in the civil Practice can actually compel them to do.

An institutional examination of legal duties clearly shows that there are different types of duties all related to each other in complicated ways. Furthermore, although we can distinguish *legal* rights from other claims and interests which are also called rights, we may not be able to draw an equally clear line between duties which are legal and those which are not. Such considerations should weigh heavily with those who insist on the primacy of duty.[21] For the legal right cannot be reduced to the correlative of a duty prescribed by law.

In institutional theory we need to pay attention to three distinct but related types of legal duties:

(i) the duty created by the NP,
(ii) the duty arising on an injury or invasion, and
(iii) the duties of respect owed before such a breach.

The duty created by the NP

The duty most nearly related to P's right is created by, and derives its normative force from, a particular command of the participants in the civil Practice. The immediate legal right is related to a particular command to do right or to put right; not to a general rule which prescribes entitlements and duties.

Apart from the limited remedies of self-help permitted by the law, the only way in which the IE of members are protected, and duties are enforced, is by way of a particular command issued as an NP. The general rules of law are maintained and employed to justify these commands.

There is nothing problematic about the nature of this duty.[22] In any particular case the NP duty clearly needs to be spelled out with particularity, for it is a requirement of justice that if D is to be coerced into doing, or sanctioned for failing to do something, he must know precisely what is required of him. So D must be informed as to the exact amount which he must pay, what acts he must do or refrain from doing, what property he must restore to P and so forth.

Nor can there be any doubt as to the normative force of this duty; it is a command backed up by effective sanctions. Instances of failure to comply with the orders are relatively rare. The normativity of this duty may be underlined by the fact that the participants are reluctant to issue an order which cannot be enforced: ineffectiveness undermines legitimacy.

Can this NP duty be said to be owed to P? If the duty imposed is that which P has demanded, it is a specific duty ordered by the judges, so it may be said to be owed as much to them as to the plaintiff.

Obviously this is not a duty which arises automatically upon wrong-doing by D. It is a newly created order imposing a precise duty which did not exist prior to P's exercise of his power and the issuing of a valid NP. It is this duty which is legally enforced and no other. Whatever the rules say D should do, and whatever P may demand, until an NP is issued those prescriptions cannot be enforced; for the rules do not enforce themselves, and (let us assume) P lacks the physical power to compel D to meet his demands and may well be denied the authority to help himself. Since the duty comes into existence only with the creation of a valid NP, it is clearly not a correlative of P's right. On D's wrong-doing, P's right and D's correlative liability arise together; but the Practice duty with real normative force depends upon P's exercise of his power, which he may choose not to exercise.

Duties under the civil law operating as a body of social rules are not sanctioned and enforced. The duties which they impose are, as Austin put it, 'relative' not 'absolute'.[23] The only duties enforced in civil law are those prescribed by the particular commands of the participants in the IE Practice. By contrast criminal laws are enforced; specialized agencies prevent breaches of the law and ensure that offenders are prosecuted. There are no such agencies to secure obedience to the rules of right of the civil law.

The liability duty

This duty arises after D has actually injured or threatened P: that is, at that point when P may confidently be judged to have a legal right under the rules. Making the—often unrealistic—assumption that the rules are clear, it may be asserted that P has a right to an NP which will order D to do *x*. However, at this time no legal command has been issued to D; he is only liable to have a specific Practice duty imposed upon him. So if D fails to comply with his undoubted duty to do *x*, he will suffer no adverse legal consequences; he will not be in breach of an enforced legal duty. Nevertheless, D's legal duty is clear. His legal advisors, or indeed any objective observer with some knowledge of the rules and cases will be able to warn him of the nature and content of the NP to which he has made himself liable. Of course in many cases D's duty is necessarily inchoate or uncertain: the amount of compensation legally payable, or the precise nature of the performance which a court might order, may not be determinable without litigation.

Yet the knowledge that a duty exists may be profoundly influential; calculating that duty from the legal point of view is an important part of the lawyer's advisory function. So the liability duty has undoubted normative force through the threat of imposing of a specific Practice duty and its subsequent direct enforcement. The duty exists by reason of the not inconsiderable threat that P could, if he chose, exercise his power. P may prefer to assert a questionable authority to get what is his due; then debt-collectors, minders, and enforcers may be called upon. However, for most members of Society the only way in which the duties can be enforced is by calling for legal assistance; P must normally rely on the threat of legal action. In this sense we may regard P as being able to influence D's actions.

Predictive legal duties of respect

In considering the NP duty and the liability duty I have taken for granted the important fact that all duties in D are always in respect of IE. The duty we are concerned with here is one which can be asserted *before* D does an act which makes him liable to the exercise of P's right. These are duties which we would assert in describing the world from a disinterested legal point of view, the duties which will be set out in legal advice Activity. In order to consider the predictive legal duty, the duty which we identify quite apart from litigation, we need to understand the nature of the IE and their attendant duties of respect.

In an SE Society interests and entitlements are socially recognized positions of benefit, capable of existing as institutional realities—as positions of real benefit—quite apart from any legal recognition. Such entitlements to benefit entail duties of respect in that it would be inconsistent for us to recognize that a member was entitled to the benefits of that position without recognizing that we are under a duty not to interfere with his receipt of the benefits.[34] All IE are vulnerable, and for most there are many ways in which the flow of benefits can be interrupted; there are a myriad ways of acting inconsistently with our recognition of another's IE. There is a correspondingly large number of duties of respect. Though we may not normally think of these obligations as predictive, they have normative force in that their breach may result in undesirable consequences. For duties are never merely ideas as to how we ought to behave; they can only exist as an essential element within an institutional form in which they are given normative force.

For the most part, the IE owned within a Society are not constituted by the fact of their legal recognition. Furthermore, the notion of legal recognition of IE is not a simple matter. After all, it may amount to no more than a passing reference to the IE in legal reasoning, or a mention in some statutory formulation. The important point is that, while there may be some legal recognition of an IE, this does not necessarily mean that all the duties owed in respect of it will be enforced. The textbooks provide plenty of illustrations of non-enforceable duties, which may still be said to be legally recognized. The assertion that A possesses an interest or entitlement entails duties in others, but the legal recognition of an IE does not necessarily entail its legal protection.

What then are the legal duties of respect to which we refer in setting out the legal position without regard to litigation? They can only be understood if they are directly related to the coercive power of the Practice. From the legal point of view, when we talk of legal duties with regard to IE we are in effect predicting that they could be enforced in the Practice. Legal duties are predictive duties; they have their existence in the discourse of litigation.

To discover which of the duties of respect attending an IE constitute a legal duty, we must consult the rules of right of the Practice. From the past cases, and the rules which have been incorporated in the LS, we can predict which duties will be enforced. Those are the legal duties. Though it may appear to be a question of consulting the rules to see what duties they prescribe, the assertion of a legal duty is essentially a predictive judgment that a person in breach will be ordered by an NP to do, or refrain from doing, certain things.

For the normative force of this duty we must anticipate the consequences of its breach: if D breached the duty he would lay himself open to P's power to call for legal assistance, and would be liable to have a coercive order issued against him. P is not presently empowered to act, he has only a predictive right; D is not presently liable. So D's duty is only an 'enforceable' duty; it is not an enforced duty. D's breach has no other legal consequence than to make him liable to P exercising his power. The immediate sanction of breach of a predictive duty is the threat of a liability.

However, the identification of legal duties attending an IE is complicated by the nature of the remedies available to the participants in the civil Practice, in particular by the fact that the judges may be able to order a defendant to do no more than compensate for losses suffered by the plaintiff.[25]

Given the nature of the remedy of damages there are two possible approaches to the identification or individuation of predictive legal duties. On the first of these approaches we would say that D has a legal duty to do *x* because we can predict that not doing *x* will result in P acquiring the power to ensure that an NP is issued which orders D to do *x*, or to pay compensation, or both. This predictive legal duty is thus grounded in the threat of a complex liability. It exists as a legal duty because of that threat of the command to do an act or to compensate.

A narrower definition would require a strict correlation between the predictive right and the predictive duty. If P has a predictive right, a power to have a Practice duty imposed on D to do *x*, then D's present predictive duty must be the duty to do *x*. In other words, D's present predictive duty and the future enforced duty must have precisely the same content: that is, the doing of *x*. This means that where D owed a duty to P to do *x*, but where the only NP available against D was one which imposed a duty to pay compensation to P, then D's predictive legal duty would be no more than a duty to pay compensation for losses arising out of his not doing *x*; so P's predictive right would not be to the performance of the duty to do *x*, but simply a right to compensation for loss. On this approach D's duty to do *x* would be a duty of some sort, but it is not a clear legal duty. The legal duty is the duty which we can predict will be precisely and specifically enforced as a command.

All duties, the breach of which would result in an NP which could be either for the specific performance of *x* or for compensation, would be recognized as predictive duties to do *x*. Only those duties for whose breach compensation is the only remedy would we deny the status of a legal duty.

I shall adopt the narrower principle for the identification of legal duties; they are defined as those notional patterns of conduct in respect of an IE which, under the LS rules, are or could be the content of an NP order. Use of this principle will force us to revise our estimates of the number of legal duties that exist in respect of some IE, and to recognize that in some cases many of the specific duties of respect entailed in the IE are at best weak legal duties. For many IE there will be only one duty in D: to pay compensation for any loss for which he is responsible. Provided the acts prohibited by such duties do not constitute criminal offences, D is legally free to do them; even if they are counted as weak legal duties, they cannot be enforced in the legal Practice. If D does the acts prohibited or enjoined his liability amounts to nothing more than to pay compensation for damage; he cannot be ordered to do a specific act. Where the legally recognized IE supports nothing more than a right to compensation, as in many contract entitlements, it is clear that the legal recognition does not constitute the IE, nor does it determine or define the specific duties entailed in the IE. Those duties exist independently of, and may not be enforced by, the law.

There is thus a necessary connection between the legal duties which we recognize as arising under the rules and the particular legal duties imposed by the NPs of the Practice. All rule-prescribed duties may be said to be predictive command duties. The interrelationship between the two types of duty allows us to say that the judges, in issuing their commands, are underlining and enforcing a pre-existing legal duty. Members of Society work out their duties from the legal precedents, from their knowledge of the specific duties set out in the Practice NPs. For we should not forget that in the discourse of a declaratory Practice the rules and pre-existing duties are generalizations from a past series of command duties.

From the institutional point of view the legal duties of civil law have their existence, not by reason of their formulation as duties in statutes, nor by their general customary recognition or enforcement, but by virtue of the fact that we can predict that they will be enforced through commands issued by the participants in the Practice. We will not find legal duties in the 'living law' which lacks precise remedies and the structures needed for the systematic application of coercive power.[26]

Many of the rules of right are abstracts of previous Practice NPs. An enacted duty will be a legal duty only if it is articulated and enforced in the civil law Practice. For institutional theory the Practice enforcement is the *sine qua non* of its legal character.

The duties of the civil law are nothing other than duties to show respect for legal persons. They are not imposed to enhance the well-being of those who are to comply with them, or to promote the general welfare of Society. As the civil law Practice does not have regulatory functions, breaches of social duties which neither cause nor threaten significant loss to the IE of individuals are not sanctioned.

D: The object of the right

All legal rights have as their object an interest or entitlement (IE).[27] Some of the features of interests and entitlements have already been considered (see, *ante* p. 159). In the SE Society IE are institutional facts. I call relocatable positions of entitlement *entitlements* and non-relocatable positions *interests.*

A socially recognized position

An IE is not simply a claim or a condition, it is a socially recognized position of entitlement to specified benefits. As an institutional fact it depends for its existence upon the affirmative attitudes and actions of members of Society.[28] The members generally must believe, and act on the belief, that a particular individual can justifiably enjoy certain benefits; that they are rightfully and properly his to enjoy. A member may thus be entitled because he is, let us say, considered to deserve the benefits, or because he has purchased the position of entitlement, or simply because he is a member of Society, or because he holds a position as an official, husband, mortgagee, and so on.

The position which is the IE is normatively significant: the assertion that A owns or possesses a position of entitlement to certain benefits has normative implications; it means that other members may not curtail the benefits conferred by the entitlement. The normative significance of assertions with respect to many IE is related to the fact of the value and scarcity of benefits.

In describing the social recognition of IE, the emphasis must be placed upon the generally held belief of the propriety of a member's enjoyment of certain benefits; however, we must not ignore altogether some of the darker aspects of the recognition of entitlements in human history. We should remember that a sort of recognition may be exacted from members by force; we may find circumstances in which the acquiesence of members to the claims of a stranger have run counter to their privately held beliefs as to his entitlement. In a world in which original claims are notoriously based upon conquest and maintained by the sword, it cannot be supposed that social recognition involves nothing more sinister than the informal assent of the claimant's peers, or the resigned acquiesence of merry peasants to an ancient system of distribution. It is important then to allow that social recognition of IE is a complex matter and may involve in its origins, and for its maintenance, the use of force.

What the IE is not

In view of the range of characterizations given to the object of the right it is worth noting what the IE is not. As an entitlement to benefits it is never simply the actual enjoyment by a member of benefits; nor can the IE be defined as the benefits themselves. They are socially recognised entitlements, not simply objects which are desired, needed, deserved, or claimed. As entitlements they are never physical objects or complicated states of affairs; they are not human beings, or psychological facts such as a goal entertained by an individual. An entitlement is, it must be stressed, an institutional fact: something which is socially recognized as belonging to a member; it is part of his property; a position to which he is entitled.[29]

Benefits and norms

In an SE Society the crucially important feature of all IEs is that they are valuable things. It is useful to think of the owner or possessor of a particular IE as adding the value of that object to his personal account, and we may regard his enjoyment of the benefits as being a flow of money from it. The basic idea of the IE Practice—that of giving to each his due—involves looking at the object in respect of which the legal right is enforced as a valuable thing and translating its owner's entitlement to the benefits as an entitlement to a flow of money which must not be cut off or diminished by other members. The remedies of the legal Practice are designed to preserve the integrity of each member's personal account, to maintain the value of the items—the IEs—in that account and to recompense him for losses in respect of particular items.

So IE have primary significance in the allocation of benefits; each interest or entitlement specifies the valuable benefits to which its owner is entitled. It is important to emphasize the centrality of this allocation, which is sometimes overlooked in legal theory (see, *ante*, p. 189). A statement prescribing how benefits are to be allotted is a very different sort of statement from one prescribing the duties of respect owed by others to those to whom the benefits have been allotted.

Every IE is a normative position in that the assertion of its existence commits us to recognizing liberties and powers in the owner, and duties of respect in others. A merely nominal allotment of benefits to A where no one recognized any duties of respect could scarcely be regarded as giving A any sort of real entitlement; his position would be little different from that of a person who was in actual enjoyment of benefits, or one who made a claim to them.

In normative terms, an IE, as an allocation with its attendant duties of respect is a complex totality; but such a description can be misleading. To describe IE as a tangled cluster of Hohfeldian elements may result in the neglect, or elision, of the core of the IE: that is, of the allocation of the valuable benefits. For this allocative core cannot be reduced to, or translated into a catalogue of normative relationships involved in the entitlement.[30]

Legal rights in IE

Every legal right is possessed in respect of some IE. It is a fundamental ground rule of the Practice that possession of an IE recognized by law and in need of legal protection is essential if a person is to have *locus standi.* There is a necessary connection between the legal right and the IE in respect of which it is held. P will be assisted, not because he has a physical connection to land—because he lives there or needs it—but only because he possesses an entitlement to or in it.

Although there is a necessary connection between a legal right and an IE owned by an individual, it is not a simple logical connection. The IE are complex totalities capable of existing independently of the legal Practice. The protection of the law must always be seen as additional to the IE: the legal rights are not constitutive of it. So we should be aware of the dangers of describing pieces of property as nothing more than bundles of rights and duties. It is never possible from the nature of the IE logically to deduce the hedge of legal rights which an owner may have in respect of it. After all, in the civil Practice an IE may not be recognized at all; such IE may be found in extra-legal regimes. Even if it is in some sense recognized in the Practice it may be left partially or wholly unprotected. Legal recognition does not mean that all duties of respect will be regarded as enforceable.

To see why such IE are necessary if we are to ascribe a legal right to a person, we need to recall the nature and rationale of the legal assistance given in the civil Practice. The requirement that a plaintiff must possess an IE is inherent in the very idea of the Practice. The status quo which has been disturbed is articulated in terms of recognized IE; we can only work out what is due if we know what was owned by or belonged to the plaintiff. If NPs were ordered without reference to defined and vulnerable IEs—and proof of their injury or invasion—the Practice would have a very different character, operating perhaps as some sort of redistributive or regulatory agency. The doing of legal justice is dependent upon an articulation of the world as a place in which persons own or possess objects which are injured or threatened.

The independence of IE

Many IE exist independently of any legal right. They may be said to be antecedent to the right or any legal recognition in the IE Practice. The independence of economic IE, transferable pieces of property capable of being traded in the market place, is easily established. The independence of other civil interests is more problematic; for some interests exist only by reason of legal protection. If they are socially recognized positions of benefit, they have in fact been established and given their shape and definition only in the courts. Even so, the courts must treat them as distinct from the rights and duties used to protect them. The courts do not simply judge that B has been acting wrongfully towards A; for instance, he has offended by prying into A's private affairs. They approach the dispute by asserting a 'right to privacy': an interest difficult to define, but which may be described as the socially recognized entitlement to the real benefits which flow from the circumstance that other members may not know certain facts about us. The establishment of such an interest is important: otherwise the court could assume the role of a regulatory or redistributive agency. It is the loss of that position of benefit which has to be remedied. The plaintiff must claim in respect of some 'right' known to the law; that is, in respect of some interest which is legally recognized.

Working out the duties of respect

From our knowledge of the nature of an entitlement—a transferable piece of property—we can relatively easily work out many of the great variety of duties owed in respect of it. Interests are less easy. Nevertheless, the articulation of an interest as a distinct position of benefit makes it possible to work out, from its description in terms of benefits, the range of the duties which attend it. Legal reasoning in the civil law Practice does not proceed on the basis that B is prohibited from certain types of acts because they are offences. Rather, it is based on the establishing of an interest in respect of which some loss is suffered. The definition of the interest is necessary so that the participants can be seen to be doing legal justice; they do it by treating all like interests in the same way. An interest unique to A is of no interest in the Practice.

To see the world of social relationships in terms of persons as owners and possessors of IE is most decidedly an artificial view. The picture of each member as possessing a catalogue of valuable IE is a mercenary, market-oriented construct. Interests in family relationships illustrate the strangeness of this viewpoint: parents' entitlement to custody of a child, a child's entitlement to care and nurture, a husband's entitlement to consortium, a wife's entitlement to be maintained, and so forth. In articulating family life in terms of interests, as the legal point of view demands, we will be primarily concerned with claims to positions of benefits; concerned less with a family member's responsibilities, contributions, and duties than with the allocation of the benefits of family life to which each family member is entitled. We will in other words be concerned with just one facet of the position of each family member: as a separate account-holder.

To translate family relationships into the relationships subsisting between parties in litigation involves distortion and artifice.

The confusion of the right and the IE

One of the major obstacles to the understanding of legal rights is the usage which identifies the legal right with the object of the right. Such identification is found in laymen's language, lawyers' discourse, statutory formulations, declarations of human rights, and in legal theories which define rights as interests protected by law.

In many of these contexts the legal i.e. the primary or antecedent right, is equated with a legally recognized IE. The right-holder is regarded as the owner of the right which is the IE. If you own land you own a legal right; if you possess an interest in physical security you possess a human right. Lawyers talk of ownership of rights, title to rights, the vesting and divesting of rights, rights to shares in assets, and so on. All such locutions are entirely fitting if we use the word 'right' to denote an IE possessed by an individual, but they are scarcely appropriate when we are referring to the remedial rights of the civil Practice.

It would be absurd to challenge the legitimacy of usages which are so firmly established in legal language and thought. However, for an adequate theoretical understanding of the legal right it is of great importance to distinguish between the IE and any rights associated with it. We need to appreciate the metonymy involved in the designation of the IE as the right. Jurisprudentially, the target of criticism must be what has been called the beneficiary theory of legal rights.[31] This theory claims support from established usages; yet it is not necessary for analysts to respect usages which designate the IE as the right. The supposition, for instance, that they are bound to respect usages found in statutes is to misunderstand the nature and extent of legislative power.[32]

The beneficiary theory has the virtue of reminding us that the IE is a complex whole: an indispensable element in legal, political, and moral reasoning about rights. Its champions have made useful contributions to our understanding of some aspects of the object of the right. They have demonstrated that the right cannot be defined as the simple correlative of a duty; that its object is not a singular benefit from the performance of a duty.

Nevertheless, the theory not only misdescribes legal rights, it stands in the way of our understanding of the IE themselves. The assimilation of the legal right with the object of the right reflects the failure of jurisprudence to develop an adequate theory of property, failure to provide an adequate description of the *res* as a valuable object in an SE Society. It is unnecessary to interpose the notion of rights into an account of the objects we own and possess in an SE Society, and confusing to suggest that legal recognition converts the interests and entitlements into legal rights.[33] Our IE are best regarded as pre-legal institutional positions of benefit. Further, they can be so understood without reference to rights of any sort. The beneficiary theory concerns property and interests rather than rights; it describes the things we own and possess, not the rights to which we are entitled in respect of them.[34]

A further objection to this theory of the legal right is that it ignores the absolutely crucial relationship of legal rights to coercive force. The beneficiary theorists miss the point of the assertion of the legal right, and fail to recognize the circumstances in which a language of rights would emerge. This is because, in their concern for IEs alone, they underestimate the relationship between rights and the facts of justified coercion, that 'special congruity in the use of force or the threat of force', which characterizes legal rights. If all were to go swimmingly, say the theorists, although we would have no need for remedial rights we would still possess the more important primary or antecedent rights; in other words, we would still possess our IE which we could recognize as our legal rights. Yet in such Utopian conditions would not the concept of the legal right be wholly redundant? Secure in the possession of our IEs, we would have no need to claim from others what is ours. Members would certainly require a language to refer to the things they owned and possessed, but they simply would not need to develop a language of legal rights. It is only when other members of Society interfere with our IE that the need for a language of rights arises. Only in the troubled circumstances of the real world, in which we regard the use of force to protect our IEs as justified, where we need no longer rely on the disruptive and often ineffective contrivances of self-help, but can confidently call for the legal assistance of the coercive orders of the IE Practice, that we can say—with considerable point—that we possess legal rights.

Furthermore, the beneficiary theory which recognizes IE as the primary legal right cannot dispense with the secondary remedial right. Given the ambiguities associated with rights, and the variety of 'rights' which have been recognized, this may not seem serious. However, the application of Ockham's razor is appropriate here: there is simply no need to suppose that there are two different species of rights. So-called primary rights are nothing more than predictive remedial rights.

The interest as duty performance

One version of the benefit theory that a legal right is an interest protected by law defines the interest very narrowly. Some theorists have defined the interest as nothing more than the performance of a legal duty.[35] The benefits of such performances conduce to the well-being of the intended beneficiary and are legally recognized. We may say that the right-holder is better off for that performance by the person who owes him the duty. The duty may be negative, to refrain from entering A's land, or positive, to repair a motor vehicle. In such theories rights are regarded as duty-performance benefits protected by coercive legal commands.

In this theory the power to institute proceedings to enforce a duty is but contingently attached to the correlative legal right; the power to sue does not 'pertain to the essence of the conception of the legal right.[36] It follows that laws defining criminal offences, insofar as the performance of these negative duties produces a benefit for individuals, are to be regarded as conferring rights upon them even though they cannot sue for the enforcement of the duties.

This version of the benefit theory has been criticized on a number of different grounds: that it creates difficulties in delimiting the class of right-holders, that is, the persons who stand to benefit from the performance of a particular duty; that it obliterates the distinction between criminal and civil laws; and, more importantly, that the right defined as the correlative of a duty is quite simply redundant.[37] Given the indiscriminate use of the word 'right', the theory has at least the virtue of simplicity and coherence. However, it lacks explanatory power, and fails to accord with our intuition that the concept of the legal right has a point.

Au fond this is a theory which elucidates the concept of the legal right in terms of its relationship to benefits, but the description it offers of the relationship between the right-holder and benefits is defective. To demonstrate why, it is necessary to remind ourselves of the truism that people derive benefit, are regarded as being entitled to benefit, not just from performances or omissions by other persons, but in innumerable other ways from physical objects and circumstances. It would be odd to suggest that the benefits of a coal fire could only be described in terms of the duties of others to do or refrain from doing certain things. Such benefits deriving from things and circumstances are allocated to individuals; it makes good sense to say that the law assists us to realize these benefits in the only way available to the participants in the IE Practice; i.e. by issuing coercive orders to individuals. The judges will not assist our efforts to enjoy the pleasures of the fireside by sweeping our chimneys or fitting draught-excluders. The only protection they can give is against the detrimental actions of others, by enforcing legal duties of respect. The fact that these benefits are protected only by way of the coercive orders of the IE Practices must not lead us to suppose that the benefits to which the right-holder is entitled under the rules of entitlement are composed only of the performances of legal duties, or that the entitlement is to be defined as the sum of the benefits of such performances. It is of central importance for the analysis of legal rights to appreciate that rights are conferred in respect of our IE, as complex positions of entitlement to a wide range of benefits, not just to those benefits which may depend upon the performance of some specific duty.[38]

Proponents of the narrow benefit theory marginalize the object of the right, or even entirely elide it. So it is a major objection to this version of the right-as-interest theory that it fails to give an account of the object of the right: the IE.

The narrow benefit theory fails to provide an account of how the law determines when a member is to be given a legal right. The law creates rights and imposes duties for reasons other than the fact that a particular performance will benefit A. The law will assist A because he is the owner or possessor of an IE which is being adversely affected. So in any dispute A must establish not only the existence of, but also his title to, the IE. Yet the narrow benefit theory gives no indication of the nature of legal reasoning behind the conferral of rights. A has a right to exclude B from Blackacre, not because of some particular interest of A's, some special benefit he reaps from B's staying off his land, but because A is the owner of Blackacre. From the fact that A simply cannot enjoy the benefits of Blackacre if B trespasses on it, it does not follow that it is B's staying off the land which constitutes the benefits to which A is entitled. It is the entitlement to the real benefits of land as an economic asset which is protected. We work out duties of respect and decide upon the conferment of rights by referring to the object of the right, to the entire range of benefits allotted to the member. The primacy of the IE in reasoning about rights is not demonstrated by pointing out the advantages which flow from articulating interests in our practical reasoning, but by recognizing that the identification of the IE is an essential first step in the process of conferring remedial rights in the IE Practice.

NOTES

1. On the ambiguity of the right see Hohfeld (1965: 36); Samuel (1994: 285).
2. See Waldron (ed.) (1984); White (1984); Martin (1993); Summers (1987); Martin and Nickel (1980); Paul, Miller, and Paul (eds.) (1984).
3. Rights, and the interests they protect, give meaning to the notion of equality. A language of rights and IE is necessary for the idea of equality. Equal respect for persons entails seeking, not equality among persons as things in themselves, not equality of characteristics they have in common, but equality in respect of the *interests* they possess.
4. The only place in which legal rights are recognized and articulated is in the legal Practice. In institutional theory this is *not* recognition by the State. Claims recognized by a government, or in society, or in ethical codes and by other people will not be legal rights. Cf. Martin (1993: 51). Generally, recognition of rights in other forms of life are only significant because the rights are recognized and protected in legal Practices.

5. There is little that is new in this conventionalist account of the legal right. 'A person has a legal right, according to our abstract, conceptual account of legal practice if he has a right flowing from past political decisions, to win a law suit: Dworkin (1986: 152). The subjective right of continental jurisprudence, defined as the power to seek satisfaction of an interest recognized and protected by the legal system, is clearly conventionalist. See also Gray (1931: 18); the right is not the interest itself, but the means by which the enjoyment of the interest is secured.
6. On the predictive right see Terry (1924: 466 fn. 2). An owner of sheep, A, has a predictive right to security from B's vicious dog, even if B has no dog. The hypothetical nature of the right is clear. B owes no duty until he buys a dog. A nevertheless owns an entitlement, the object of rights, which may be violated in many different ways, and to which B can be said to owe duties of respect. Feinberg (1980: 43–4) analyses rights as existing when one is in a position to make a claim: 'To have a right is to have a claim to something and against someone, the recognition of which is called for by legal rules. . . .'
7. They are the relationships between members of a civil Society; i.e. between legal persons, not individuals in their social life.
8. On antecedent rights see Hohfeld (1964: 101): 'A multital primary right . . . should be carefully differentiated from the paucital secondary right . . . arising from the violation of the former.' See also Corbin, in Hall (ed.) (1938: 481). Primary rights do not arise from violation. See Salmond (1957: 124); Holland (1924: 47).
9. Holland (1924: 148).
10. The idea of the subjective right is said to be the work of William of Ockham; see McGrade (1980) and White (1984: 149). His analysis marks a turning point; the use of the word 'right' to refer to a standard or law defining a just or right relationship gives way to its employment to refer to a *faculty* or *power* belonging to the beneficiary of the relationship: Dagger (1989: 295). The individual changes from a person to whom *ius* applies to a legal person who is the owner of rights.
11. 'The State will not double up his fists for him, nor will it bring a suit for him in a court': Gray (1931: 21).
12. Capacity is here defined as the ability to participate in a Practice; it differs from a power to issue informal commands. Tax officials have authority; voters have capacity. Possession of a legal right entails a capacity to participate in a legal Practice as plaintiff. Capacities to participate in other Practices, such as those of contract or marriage, are interests which may be protected by rights. Capacities are positions of benefit, interests which are commonly called rights.
13. See Kelsen's account of the legal right (1973: 84).
14. Holland (1924: 85).
15. Hart (1982: 183).
16. *Ibid.* Relationships between members of civil Society are wholly neutral; there is no subordination or domination; there is equality before the law: an equality dependent upon a language of rights.

17. Kleinig (1978: 44). On execution see Pound (1922: 73). See also Nicholas (1962: 101) for the methods employed in Roman Law.
18. See White (1984: 73–92). Feinberg (1980: 167): '. . . that the sorts of beings who *can* have rights are precisely those who have (or can have) interests.' The central feature of the atomic individual in institutional theory is the ability to own or possess IE over which rights may be recognized. The IE are socially recognized positions of benefit ascribed to an individual. The IE ascribed to A may be protected by the agent B on A's behalf; B has *locus standi*. The benefits are not the agent's but A's. Beings or entities which cannot act for themselves can appear as owners and possessors only if agents are allowed to act for them. So an entity which is recognized as an object of ownership cannot itself be an owner or possessor; an owner cannot also be an agent for it; he cannot both be and not be entitled to benefits. Harms to x are harms to the owner. The atomic individual of the law is never a possession or object of ownership. It is not possible to be both owner of and agent for x at the same time. It is for the courts to decide whether to allow such representation, and hence such personality.
19. See Coleman (1988: 166–83) for observations on the morality of strict liability. Tort law is concerned with losses and the question as to who should bear the costs. A preoccupation with fault as an essential element in a just theory of torts has obscured other considerations. It is foundationalist to set out universal principles of fault liability from which we can draw the circles of responsibility. Decisions have to be made about responsibility in each case. To say that losses should lie with the victim unless there is a compelling reason for shifting it to another party (Holmes 1881: 76–7) is not a legal rule but may be regarded as a rule of thumb, a starting point; it is not a rule which can be used to decide cases. Coleman (1988: 183) suggests that once we consider cases we are likely to discover that in certain instances the strict liability rule is morally superior to the criterion of fault.
20. Benn and Peters (1959: 89). Such an approach to duties is that of legal advice Activity. Almost inevitably it will give rise to philosophical problems about the real existence of rights.
21. Kelsen (1973: 89) every rule of law necessarily lays down a right. See also Kockourek in Hall (ed.) (1938: 455 fn); 'A duty without a correlative claim, a right, is impossible and therefore unthinkable.' Greater caution is shown by Ginsberg (1965: 75) 'In general a right implies an obligation but it is not clear that a duty or obligation always confers a right.'
22. These duties are necessarily related to the right in P. See White (1984: 70) for the view that rights and duties are not correlatives.
23. Austin (1879) Lecture XVII.
24. The great variety of different ways in which we can interfere with an interest or entitlement is worth noting. Some interferences are licensed externalities. We need to pay attention not just to acts themselves but to the IE and the acts as seen from the point of view of the legal Practice.
25. Although compensation is central to the idea of giving each his due, it does not entail the possession of rights. Schemes for compensation in particular

areas of social life may well be administered by extra-legal administrative agencies.

26. Although invariably regarded as being legal duties, we may question whether statutory duties imposed, say, on officials are strictly legal duties; if they do not affect the IEs of individuals they may never be enforced in the penal, civil, or CS Practices. Their normative force comes, not from the law, but from sanctions operating within the organizational structures of the State.
27. Olivecrona (1939: 101) claims that in the case of patents there is no object of the right. This betrays a failure to recognize the IE as an institutional fact. The IE is a clear position of benefit, recognizable as something of value. The benefits of a patent are various and real, and the entitlement to them is vulnerable and requires legal protection.
28. Moral rights do not have such an object. Their logic is quite different. They are claims based on conceptions of human needs, autonomy, etc. Legal rights all protect an object as a belonging; it may be a very artificial construct. The significance of the IE as a distinct institutional fact cannot be overstressed. The insistence on their existence as institutional facts, that they are socially recognized positions of benefit (entitlement, not physical objects or mere utterances) may explain why rights create obligations. See Anscombe (1978) 318–23.
29. See also White (1984: 79–88) for an account of interests; on the 'murkiness' of interests see Gerwith (1984: 6). Salmond (1957: 261) describes interests as being the various elements of well-being such as life, liberty, health, reputation, and the use of material objects. In institutional theory an interest is a distinct possession; it is not murky, nor is it just an element of a person's well-being or an object of desire, but a thing: a socially recognized position of benefit valued by others.
30. See Cook (1964: 12) who criticizes Salmond's account of ownership of land, the fee simple, as being a right. It is, says Cook, a bundle of jural relationships. It is more than that: it is an IE, the object of legal rights; a valuable belonging which cannot be reduced without remainder to a bundle of legal relationships.
31. Waldron (ed.) (1984); MacCormick (1982b: 154–66).
32. Cf. MacCormick (1977: 192).
33. As an illustration of the way in which the IE can be confused with the right see Waldron (ed.) (1984: 10). The statement that a child in Somalia has a right to be fed does not necessarily entail that any specific person has a duty to feed, rather that the child has a socially recognized interest which is the ground for the assignment and allocation of duties. The interest in being fed is quite distinct from rights which the child might acquire and duties which might be imposed in law. Note that the social recognition of the interest must be the recognition of the inhabitants of Somalia.
34. Hart (1982). It is possible to argue that Roman lawyers did not generate a language of rights because the means of execution were very limited; there was great reliance on self-help. Nicholas (1962: 101). Gerwith (1978: 99) argues that, although Roman lawyers may not have made any direct appeal

To rights as such in the modern fashion, the nevertheless employed the basic concept without any express words for it: '(P)ersons might have and use the concept of a right without explicitly having a single word for it.' In institutional theory the establishment of the subjective right is dependent on the emergence of the centralizing State and the centralizing of enforcement Activity so that there is a clear distinction between official coercion and selfhelp. Only where official sanctions exist and can be relied on is an express word needed. Upon proof of an entitlement to legal assistance in respect of a defined IE we can deduce the predictive right in respect of our identical IE.

35. Bentham: see Postema (1986: 321).
36. Salmond (1957: 264).
37. On the redundancy of rights see Arnold (1978: 77–9). See also Hart (1982: 182) and Terry (1924: 461) for the view that the correspondent rights are of no practical importance.
38. See Coleman (1988: 35) who designates the legitimate interest as a right; calling it a right acts as a conceptual marker giving privileged status to the interest. Every privileged interest entails legitimate claims; the content of the claim is a function of the rules applied to them. The property and liability rules specify the content of rights by generating specific legitimate claims from them. Against this analysis it may be argued that all interests are legitimate as they are socially recognized. Some interests are hedged around with a thicket of rights, while others are very slightly protected, and some are not legally protected at all.

7

The ideal constitution of the democratic polity

I: LAW, DEMOCRACY, AND LEGITIMACY

The law of a democracy differs from the body of norms which may be called law within an absolutist regime.[1] In the latter a foracentric jurisprudence would be odd, and the idea of laws being the enactments of Society a figure of speech. The so-called law of a dictatorship and law in a democracy are not the same phenomenon in different political environments, but two qualitatively different types of norm structures and norms. In no domain of law is this more evident than in public law; and in no domain is it more important to understand the nature of the democratic polity.[2]

The democratic foundations of modern law, considered briefly in Chapter 3 and given passing reference in the investigation of the criminal and civil domains, require an institutional analysis. We can only understand the logic of democratic legitimacy by describing the basic institutional forms—Society, State, and the legislative and legal Practices—and the relationships between them. To set out an ideal elementary constitution for a democratic polity is a necessary preliminary to the investigation in Chapter 8 of the CS Practice in which the norms of public law are generated.

A: Legal Fundamentalism

An institutional investigation of the law is an attempt to understand the nature of the distinctive norms of the legal system in the light of the idea that norms—social constraints, standards, rules, principles—can only be understood as they operate within, and between, forms of life. The particular forms in which legal norms and language are generated are the adjudicatory Practices, those of criminal, civil, and public law, in which the controlling idea is that of individual legal justice.

From the investigation of criminal and civil law it will be obvious that such an approach results in an extremely narrow definition of laws as rules which are required for the doing of legal justice. As such they are quite distinct from a whole range of official and unofficial social norms which perform other functions and are not required for the doing of legal justice. The institutional approach may be described as leading to a legal fundamentalism which insists on the Importance of recognizing the difference between legal and non-legal norms, and the advantages of keeping the law free from impurity.

We can see varieties of legal fundamentalism in the work of the legal positivists who have consistently maintained the importance of distinguishing between legal and moral norms. In the face of objections that it is neither desirable nor possible to maintain any such clear distinction between law and morality, how have the fundamentalists justified their stance?[3]

Analytical positivists have relied largely on the modest claim that such an approach produces a truer picture of the legal field, that it sensitizes us to the real, qualitative differences which are found within the normative structures of society, and which can so easily be obscured by relying upon the unfocused lens employed by wider conceptions of law. The importance in practical matters of having a clear picture of the law was stressed, notably by Bentham, whose expository jurisprudence was essentially a prolegomenon to his censorial jurisprudence.[4] The legal positivist, in the spirit of Locke's philosopher, would perform the menial task of sweeping away the accumulated theoretical rubbish in order to give decision-makers a clearer picture of the issues confronting them.[5]

Such claims are reasonable and attractive, but the positivists' approach has been criticized on the ground that legal activity in any society simply does not exhibit such qualities of separateness and autonomy; that law lacks the clear and precise boundaries mapped by the positivists. In any case, say the critics, we have for all practical purposes a perfectly adequate grasp of what law is. The value of Bentham's work lay in his indefatigable labours to reform the law; just as there was no need for him to construct a moral philosophy to underwrite his legislative proposals, neither was an expository jurisprudence—which, after all, did violence to the ordinary language of legal discourse—necessary for his critical and practical purposes.[6]

B: Democracy is necessary for a pure theory of law

The real justification for legal fundamentalism—the insistence upon the strict separation of law from moral and political values and ends—lies in the support it gives to our allegiance to democratic forms of life. Law conceived and administered in such fundamentalist terms is, I suggest, a necessary element in the establishment of democratic legitimacy in Society. This jurisprudence is necessary to establish the conditions in which citizens can give voluntary obedience to, and recognition of, the authority of a State which exercises coercive power. Legal fundamentalism is an essential ingredient for a democracy; a democratic polity is a necessary condition for a pure theory of law.

The ultimate test of the virtue of any contemporary theory of law lies in the contribution it makes to the understanding and achievement of the *Rechtsstaat.* It does not lie in its descriptive range, its fidelity to the actuality of current practices, or its accommodation of the variety of concerns and functions which lawyers entertain and perform. I argue that writers who moralize or politicize the law contribute unwittingly towards a legitimacy deficit. Their efforts will be counterproductive, being liable to result in the emergence of conditions in which the ideals of the writers would be less likely of achievement. Bad jurispruence is a serious matter.

Now, even though the administration of the law should ideally be kept separate from political ideology, we cannot elucidate the concept of law in isolation from the political character of the polity in which it is enforced and applied. For the autonomy of law, the existence of the rule of law, is only possible within the political framework of a democracy. Democracy is for our purposes a given; as the condition upon which our identity as autonomous individuals depends, it presents us with the challenge of understanding its institutional logic, rather than that of justifying its ideas.[7] We live, we have our being, within democratic Societies; and the conditions there are, for us, unarguably better than those which we, with our democratic identities, would experience under non-democratic regimes.

The newness of democracy

Now it is of great importance to emphasize that democracy, not simply as an ideal or a transient social experiment, but as the reality of a settled political environment, an experienced condition in which we can in the light of experience begin to understand the nature of the central forms of life in which democratic ideals can be realized, is a product of relatively recent times; and that some of its principles and their implications are still not entirely clear.[8] Furthermore, it needs to be reiterated that a revolutionary change is involved in the establishment of Societies of a democratic character, as 'systems of civil, political and religious freedom'[9] grew out of, or overturned, absolutist and personal forms of government. For Dicey the problem facing the constitution makers of the nineteenth century was how to give the new constitutions which rested on the will of the people 'that permanence and stability which hitherto had been found only in monarchical and aristocratic states'.[10]

These political commonplaces are of the profoundest importance for jurisprudence. If the character of the legal field is determined by particular political conditions, then contemporary jurisprudence must have a different character than that appropriate for the era of monarchical regimes.

The legal field has not been immune from the revolutionary changes. Its structures had not merely to be repaired after being shaken by republican tremors: they all had to be provided with new foundations. Only an initial assumption of the total independence of law from the political substrate could lead us to suppose that there is, in jurisprudence, an unbroken tradition of legal theory on which we can draw and to whose older and wiser principles we should return. There is no such continuity, for the simple reason that the ancient tradition which Kelley has called 'Nomos' may have displayed communitarian virtues but was manifestly not democratic.[11] The conception of law as being in the very fabric of social life, in the particular customs and usages of the community—a conception which is appropriate for monarchical government—is an anachronism in modern democratic Societies. The paradigmatic law of democratic polities must be seen as a norm originating by way of enactment in a sovereign legislature. A law of this sort satisfies more clearly than laws from any other source the criteria of democratic legitimacy.

The appearance of legal positivism in Britain coincided with and reflected revolutionary political change.[12] It would be superficial to see this new jurisprudence as a response to the growing specialization of legal activity, or as the application of new scientific methods to legal phenomena, or as a revolt against the complacency of the common law.[13] It should be seen as an attempt to understand law-making and law application in a changed political world, in which new forms of life, animated by democratic ideas, are being worked out and established. The central tenet of positivism—the separation of law from morality or political ideology—expresses a condition which the law must fulfil if democratic legitimacy is to be attained.

So intimate a connection between the science of jurisprudence and democratic ideals was, however, not to the taste of the positivists. The jurisprudence of Bentham and Austin, writing before the Great Reform Act of 1832, gives no prominence to the needs of legitimacy, and denies any necessary connection between law and democracy. After all, it is perhaps easier to identify the commander as a despot than as the elusive sovereign body in a democracy. So too the positivists of the twentieth century, though profoundly concerned about questions of political legitimacy, have been inhibited from anchoring their jurisprudence to the *Rechtsstaat* by reason of their claims to transhistorical and transnational generality and scientific impartiality. In fact the basic picture which they draw of the law as an isolable, depoliticized activity, indifferent to the claims of religion or morality—is a most important contribution to our understanding of the legal field of the *Rechtsstaat*. However, proponents of a general theory of law which would provide the conceptual apparatus enabling us to recognize the legal system in ancient Babylon as in modern

China or the USA, or who would describe the transition from the pre-legal to the legal world in wholly neutral terms, would take exception to the suggestion that they were elucidating a concept of law appropriate only for modern democracies.[14]

We undermine the claims of the legal positivists to be setting out a truly general theory by showing that their language games are inapposite for the forms of life and normative structures of, say, ancient Egypt or mediaeval England. The attempt to translate into the language of the legal positivists the institutions, expressions, ideas, and activities involved in what the members of ancient societies may or may not have called law is yet one more instance of the insensitivity with which science approaches the social world.

Also, of course, it would be wholly contrary to the goal of a value-free analysis of law to allow that democratic forms of life with their inbuilt conceptions of legitimacy make up the social conditions on which the law depends.

Legal positivists, in allowing a connection between their concept of law and democracy, will only allow that a legal field in which the separation of law from morality is maintained is, at most, a condition without which the *Rechtsstaat* could not be maintained. Yet although such a system is necessary for the rule of law, it is also admitted to be compatible with the gross iniquities of manifestly undemocratic regimes. Fuller, certainly no positivist, wished to establish a connection between a legitimate state and a legal system which was imbued with an inner morality; but he could do little more than point to the historical record in which examples of their coincidence were found.[15]

For institutional theory, the fundamentalist image of law—of a set of legal Practices always aspiring towards autonomy, towards the separation of law from ideology—is the jurisprudence of democracy and of no other political condition. The legitimate state is as much a condition for the possibility of a pure theory as legal fundamentalism in practice, realized in the activity of the courts, is a necessary condition for the establishment of the truly legitimate democratic state. In order to establish this claim we need to look more closely at the idea of legitimacy itself.

C: Legitimacy

How are we to understand from the legal point of view this character of legitimacy which is ascribed to the political arrangements of democratic Societies as a term of recommendation? How is it to be recognized and measured?[16]

It will be generally agreed that the legitimacy of a State is not to be measured by the degree to which its activities conform to the absolute standards of substantial justice set out by the proponents of natural law, if only because there is no agreement as to what those standards are. Nor is legitimacy the sort of property with which positivistic social scientists would feel at ease, as something which can be observed and measured. We cannot take the degree to which citizens indicate their subjective approval for the State as the index of legitimacy. The Weberian approach has not survived the criticism of recent years.[17]

If it is not a question for social scientists, neither is it a question for lawyers. For legitimacy is not a property to be established by proving, as a lawyer might, that the exercise of power is justified by the established legal rules, by the Law. Democracy is, it must be emphasized, the child of revolution; this consideration rules out the possibility of justifying the exercise of power by an executive in a democracy by pointing to its lawful succession, or accession, to power. Democratic legitimacy has no genealogy; it is not a pedigree but a character, a reputation, which must be earned. We recognize it more as a continuing disposition to act justly than as a title to govern which can be established by reference to the rules of succession.[18] Democracy requires new and more complex power-conferring norms, shaped under a different conception of law. In some polities which have undergone a democratic revolutionary change, the old law, or the conception of law as an organic expression of the community, has been used to justify populist dictatorships, or to sustain a tiresome Jacobitism.

How then can legitimacy be recognized? In judging the democratic legitimacy of a Society we must first look at the degree to which the members give their uncoerced recognition to the authority of the coercive State.[19] Since it possesses vastly superior organizational force, the State can obviously secure a degree of conformity to its mandates by relying upon its raw coercive power. The problem for the democrat is how to contrive a climate in which the need for reliance on such threats is minimized; a climate in which conformity to the State's mandates can be accorded freely, and in which the claims of the State to coerce are seen to be justified.[20] In achieving this accord there must be no cakes and ale: no manipulation of citizens' attitudes by measures designed to purchase popularity and divert attention from the character of the State's power.

Crucially, we need to understand that the citizen's respect for the State which betokens legitimacy is conditional upon the State's demonstration of its respect both for individuals and for the Groups of which they are members. The members' assent to the exercise of State power is given only to the State which acts justly.[21]

Now it is quite unexceptionable to express something of the character of the legitimate State in terms of its concern for propriety, and the sensitivity it exhibits for the well-being of its citizens. For example, it is said that the legitimate State does not act in an arbitrary fashion, that it does not disappoint expectations, that it honours conventions, adopts principles, follows established rules, conforms to the rule of law, and acts in accordance with generally held ideas of equity and the public good.[22] However, such normative generalities will not do, as they do not indicate the real nature and the central importance of the respect which the State must show for individuals and their identifying Groups. Therein lies the key to legitimacy.

The institutional bases of legitimacy

The State's respect for individuals and Groups is not a matter of the personal attitudes of the rulers and officials; it is not a condition to be achieved by selecting from among the candidates for public office those who demonstrate a disposition to honour the constitution and the laws of the land.[23] It is imperative that the respect which the State must show for the citizen is substantially and irremovably built into procedures, governed by norms, and secured by a host of devices, so that it constitutes an integral part of the very process of government. The State's respect for the citizen must be prescribed as an abiding, all-encompassing obligation: as a pervasive condition of government, recognized and acted upon in every nook and cranny of governmental activity, so that even in the performance of its paramount duties to preserve order and defend its citizens the State will be condemned as behaving wrongly if it shows a lack of respect for individuals or Groups.[24] In the legitimate polity the State is not trusted to earn the citizen's respect; it is compelled at every turn to be respectful.

Looked at in this way, the character of democratic legitimacy cries out for an institutional treatment; that is, we need to anchor the norms of legitimacy, which guarantee respect for persons and Groups, to the established forms of life, to the particular subsisting configurations of activity and association of public life in which the norms have their domicile. Democratic legitimacy has an institutional logic; the norms of legitimacy are not free-floating maxims and principles unanchored to forms of life. It is within and between these forms of association and activity of the polity that we must locate the prescriptions which ensure respect for individuals and Groups.

At the same time it is important to recognize that this approach to legitimacy, with its emphasis on normative constraints, is not a recipe for a pervasive legalism. Although there must be specific and detailed prescriptions within the democratic constitution, the norms of legitimacy cannot be reduced to a system of legal rules. For they include general principles, ideas, and understandings which constitute, control, and animate particular institutional forms. So we cannot hope to construct the constitution for a democracy in the style of a code of law-like rules, or secure legitimate government by relying on the enforcement of such rules in the courts of law.

In institutional terms the achievement of democratic legitimacy is a matter of getting and keeping proper things in their proper places.[25] A central claim of institutional theory is that in modern polities law is not kept in its proper place, with grave consequences for democratic legitimacy.

II: THE INSTITUTIONAL FORMS OF A DEMOCRATIC POLITY

We will not proceed far in analysing legitimacy either by studying the particularities of actual institutions, or by generalizing about the norms which must govern the functions of government, legislature, and judiciary in a democratic polity.[26] We must examine the nature of the ideal institutional forms—ideals to which actual institutions should aspire—and the relationships between them, as though they were actual configurations of human association and activity.[27] Then, in setting out each of the ideal forms and seeing how they 'hang together' we will inevitably consider how they are all interdefined; we will see that each acquires its distinctive character by virtue of its relationships with the other ideal forms. A false description of the nature of the forms will lead to an imperfect understanding of the relationships between them.[28]

A: Civil Society

Society, the first form requiring to be unearthed, is somewhat elusive and very widely misrepresented. We may start by saying what it is not; distinguishing it from other things with which it is commonly confused. In the first place Society is not to be confused with a *polity*. A polity is not an institutional form at all. It is the overall arrangement of the political forms of life, a combination of the forms Society, State, and the legislative and legal Practices of Society.[29] As the polity is not an institutional form, its constitution, prescribing relationships between a miscellany of forms, displays none of the coherence of the rules of a club or the charter of a Corporation.

It is elementary that the Society must be distinguished from the *State* which, as an Organization or organizational conglomerate, is a wholly different associational form. The State's membership is determined in different ways, its officers and members being appointed, elected, etc., and their hierarchical relationships are of a quite different sort from those subsisting between members of Society. Yet the assimilation of Society and State is not uncommon, and takes a wide variety of forms; it is to be deplored as a potentially dangerous confusion. The co-opting of all members of Society into the State organizational structure is not a feature of the democratic polity.

Society is not to be confused with social life

Society is also not a mere non-institutional context, or general backdrop of social interaction against which political activity takes place, in which institutions are established and governmental functions discharged. Society is indisputably a distinct associational form with a defined membership, which is not merely a class membership.

So it is important to distinguish between civil Society and the totality of the great variety of forms of life found within it. By describing the forms as existing within Society I mean only that they are forms in which members of Society are also involved. Thus members of Society are involved in Organizations, Communities, Groups, Practices, and Activities of a private character; and any individual member can be involved in a large number of such different forms.

The form of association which is civil Society should not be considered as an aggregate or summation of all forms of social life within defined political boundaries. The aggregation of the forms of social life is no sort of associational form: a consideration central to the analysis of the democratic polity offered here. I refer to all the other forms taken together as constituting not a Society but a *society,* or as the social life of the members of a Society.[30] Before looking at the nature of social life (or society) more closely, certain aspects of the picture of civil Society must be examined.

Civil Society is a legal concept

The key to understanding civil Society lies in recognizing that it is a concept generated in the language of the legal Practices. Civil Society is the political unit of association as articulated from the legal point of view; it is a form in which the members are conceived of as legal persons— as owners and possessors of IE—and in which the only relationships between them are legal relationships.[31]A polity without legal Practices would not contain a civil Society.

However, this legal character should not make us doubt the reality of the form; from the legal point of view it is an association of foundational significance. For this is, after all, an associational form which is underwritten by the coercive power of the State.

In our dealings daily with our family, neighbours, business associates, workmates, fellow enthusiasts, fellow worshippers, etc., we do not ordinarily think of our relationships in legal terms, although we are well aware of the occasional need to switch to the language of law and to face other individuals as members of Society.

In distinguishing between the form Society, which is conceived of in legal terms, and society or social life in general, which we must describe in the languages generated by other forms of life, I am differentiating between the *public* and *private* aspects of human life in a democratic polity. The distinction between the language of the law and all other languages of social intercourse should be kept as clear as possible. The legally recognized associational form Society, for which the language is the language of the law, is not co-ordinate with the other forms in social life; it may be said to lie on another plane.[32]

We must avoid the temptation to treat the legal and artificial form Society as if it were in any sense a natural form—a mistake we can easily make in interpreting the Aristotelian dictum that man is by nature a political animal. It is safer to regard society—with a small 's'—as Rousseau's state of nature upon which the State was superimposed. Only after the State has appeared and legal Practices have been instituted will those subject to the State become—at another level, and from a different point of view—members of civil Society.

Membership

Civil Society is clearly an association of some formality and of limited scope; nevertheless, it is a real form with a clearly identifiable membership. The character of that membership is to be understood in terms of citizenship.[33] As civil Society is a form correlated with the State, an association of individuals governed by a particular State, citizenship entails the subjection of its members to both the governance of the State and the general rules of Society. It entails the protection of the member by the State from external and internal threats, and freedom of access, under the rules, to the resources and the forms of social life within the territorial boundaries.[34]

Membership of Society—citizenship—entails something wholly unnatural: absolute equality between members. Society is not an Organization, so within it there are no positions of superiority or inferiority. This is neither a brute fact nor an ought; it is simply how members are conceived in the language of the law. The basis of this equality lies in the fact that the members are in law all equally subject to the general rules of Society. From this consideration it follows that, within a democratic polity, each member must be characterized as a legal person. Precisely who is subject to the general rules is a legal question. It is for the courts to decide which individuals are members of Society, and how the general rules apply to them.[35] So the equality between the members of a Society is nothing more or less than equality before the law. The positive law frequently prescribes that one particular class is to be treated differently from another: this different treatment is recognized as an exception to the basic principle of the equality of all members.

If we are to give an account of Society which is consistent with the democratic ideal, the membership of a Society must be equated with legal personality: only within the legal Practices of the Society can we guarantee the respect for persons which—along with respect for Groups, lies at the heart of the democratic ideal.

Social life

The associational form, civil Society, with a membership consisting of legal persons, is a peculiarly dessicated form of life.[36] Its language is the language of law: a secular and technical language telling us nothing about the human condition. Unless we are intent on promoting nationalist causes, our membership of Society cannot give meaning to our lives.

It is important to preserve the distinction between civil Society, with its formal equality between members, and social life with its rampant and pervasive inequalities. We can all too easily suppose that references to social relationships generally, to all the different relationships which occur within the myriad forms of social life, are references to relationships between the members of the associational form Society. There is a strong temptation to give Society some substance, to endow it with something more than a legal character, to fill it out, and treat it as the totality of social interaction. However, the relationships between individuals within the particular forms of social life, their social standing, their activities and beliefs, are irrelevant in any characterization of individuals as members of Society—as legal persons.[37] Nevertheless it must be understood that every civil Society has its foundation in the rich and varied social life of its members. From the individual's point of view, his or her engagement in the substantive private forms of social life is more important than citizenship.[38] The involvement of individuals in the diverse forms of social life has a logical priority over their membership of Society, for it is in their member ship of Groups, communities, and Organizations, and their engagement as agents in Practices and Activities, that human beings establish their identity. The State is always an imposition on a basic social substrate, on existing ways of life; and it is only on the occasion of the emergence or imposition of the State that a population takes on a new character as subjects and, on the institution of legal Practices, as members of civil Society. Society is an artificial, political form. Every member of Society is first an associate and participant in the other forms of social life. If there were no such forms of life for members to engage in we would be dealing with an association of automatons.

So it is a necessary feature of membership of a Society that the members have a social life; that is, that they enter into, or find themselves caught up in, and speak the languages of, some of the many forms in the private sphere. Man's social life is not structured by, or restricted to, the rights and duties of citizenship and their relationships to the state. The understanding that the State is an intrusion finds expression in the residual principle of members' freedom to have a social life, and to enter into whatever forms of life they choose. The State does not constitute that social life; it can do no more than govern it and regulate its forms. Until it takes such action, all members involved in those forms of life are free.

The market economy and social life

The democratic polity we are describing is a modern structure, and the social life of members of Society is dominated by, and founded upon, their involvement in the Practices of a market economy.[39] All members of Society, as they buy and sell, use money as a unit of account, and so forth are willy-nilly participants in exchange Practices. We all understand the language of these Practices and articulate the world in the same way for market purposes. This universal involvement in the market is a more basic feature than industrialization, which some writers have regarded as the most influential social development of modern times.

Although all members of Society can be said to be members of a Group speaking the language of the market, it does not follow that we cite their involvement in the forms and values of the market as the basis for a consensus upon which we could build a political philosophy.[40] For the values of the market—the values of individualism, equality, and freedom—are formal and have limited application. They are valid for, or inherent in, the actual market Practices, but do not determine the choices and decisions we make as to whether, in particular circumstances, we should engage in any such transactions. Outside the market Practices they conflict with the values of many of the other forms of life with which we are involved. The consequences of permitting people to transact business with no regulation or assistance except that prescribed to ensure that the Practices were fair, may well be disastrous for the less successful. The central concern of much political philosophy has been to establish the values which would justify intervention in the market to secure greater social justice. There are irreconcilable differences of opinion about the character of the society, dependent on the market, which we should aim to create, and the manner in which the market should be regulated.

The dissensus in Society

Our social life requires regulation, not only in the market, but in all other areas of interaction. Here there will also be profound differences of opinion about the ends and values, to which we should give priority. We now live, it is said, in a multicultural, ethically pluralist society.

In attempting to establish the ends to which we should work, we cannot suppose that members of Society, either by virtue of their citizenship, their legal personality, or their engagement in the market, share the same most basic values.[41] Their membership of Society does not mean that, given the freedom to live a social life—with all that entails by way of entertaining incompatible ends and values—all share an unspoken consensus. The terms of association for Society require only subjection to its general rules and the governance of the State; they do not demand subscription to a tradition based on a history of its people constructed by a particular Group.[42]

From the fact that equality or freedom are implicit in both legal and market Practices, we cannot assume that they are fundamental values which should govern all our social life. The apparent conflict between these values in the works of those who theorize about the ideal conditions of social life is significant; for they do not conflict in the market or the legal context. The values of freedom and equality are the values of Society, not of society. Equality before the law in no way underwrites the ideal of equality as a principle of substantive justice.[43] Our social life in a democratic polity need not be governed by any such principles. Democratic societies can be, and indeed are, profoundly unequal and hugely regulated; but these inequalities and restraints do not represent an improper divergence from an ideal condition which can be deduced from our engagement in the forms of social life.[44]

It is axiomatic that the social life of individuals in a democratic polity will exhibit a persistent *dissensus:* there will be irreconcilable differences of opinion over many matters requiring moral and political judgment. The aspect of the dissensus most particularly to be recognized is the ongoing ideological conflict in the political sphere. This consists of fundamental disagreements about how social life, or particular aspects of it, should be articulated, conducted, reformed, and controlled; of disputes as to the values which those involved in social life should aspire; about the role of the State and the scope of legislative interference, and so forth.[45]

Despite the inevitability of dissensus in the social life of a democracy, it must be noted that when dangers such as war are real and imminent, incompatible differences between Groups may be set aside as the vast majority of the population determine to fight for the *status quo,* for the preservation of a particular polity and the ways of life it makes possible. Recollection of consensus created in such circumstances may lead some to assume that a Society thus united is the ideal context for political activity; that we should attempt to promote just such unity. However, in a democratic polity consensus is an unusual and temporary condition.

There is a certain naïvety in the disappointment felt when the sense of unity fostered in war disappears before the ink has dried on the instruments of armistice.

The dissensus lies between Groups

In an institutional account of the nature of the dissensus, it must not be seen as the competition between individuals, each holding firm to his personal moral and political opinions. Dissensus is not a personal affair arising from the incompatibility of the beliefs and commitments of Mr Laurel and Mr Hardy; nor is it a battle of the books or a clash of abstract ideas. To a greater extent than is appreciated, most individuals reading or maintaining a particular moral or political point of view will draw upon and gain sustenance from the resources of the Groups of which they are members.[46] There is certain unrealism in the idea that the individual, in a Cartesian mood, sits down and works out for himself alone the values he should maintain, and that in adhering to them he requires no stimulus, encouragement, or reinforcement from the experience of others.[47] In the political life of society the opinion of one individual, with the assent of no one but his cat, is of no consequence. What creates a dissensus is the wider conflict between significant Groups articulating influential positions to which members of Society may be drawn.[48] What counts are the associations we call parties, sororities, brotherhoods, bands of believers, schools, coteries, movements, tendencies, sects, and so forth which, through their members' experiences over many years, build up, maintain and communicate values and beliefs deeper and wider than those which could be achieved by any individual.[49]

So the ethical plurality which characterizes the membership of a democratic Society must be read as a competition between Groups for influence.[50] We must also recognize the great variety of such Groups, the incompatibility of their values, and the state of incomprehension which may exist between them, as when individuals feel that opponents are not speaking their language.[51] It is fanciful to suppose that over a whole range of fundamental issues in social life any general agreement could be found.

To appreciate something of the reality and significance of the dissensus in a democratic polity we should recall that the protracted and sometimes bloody struggles to establish religious toleration—continuing up to the present century—were an attempt to establish the propriety and normality of a dissensus. This was a struggle at the very heart of the democratic revolution. It should not be seen simply as a struggle between Organizations, between churches or between church and State; the claim for the legitimacy of dissent came from a variety of sects and movements, and found expression in the general demand for freedom of conscience. The importance of achieving respect for Groups within a polity cannot be overestimated: it is the only condition in which the notion ol the autonomous, self-determining individual can have meaning.

Although the incomprehension, distrust, and disdain of incompatible Groups is potentially divisive, we should never picture a dissensus as a state of war or conflict; it is not a condition of civic unrest.[52] It is not the antithesis of the peaceful consensus. Within the democratic polity competing value structures are accommodated, but they are not brought into line; the conflicts are not submerged. The achievement of religious toleration does not entail an ecumenical harmonisation of belief.[53] Yet if the dissensus of the democratic polity is to have this peaceful character it must be characterized by respect for all competing Groups. That respect requires not only that members of Groups are not disadvantaged or persecuted, but that their views are perceived to count in the political debate.

Further, and most importantly, the fundamental implication, of this respect is that Groups are unknown to the law and do not appear in the legal articulation of the world. The Group membership of the legal person is irrelevant; it neither qualifies for or debars from advantage or office, nor does it determine immunity from or liability for loss or punishment. The language of the law is strictly a language of classes, of sets defined by reference to objective, clear criteria of membership. The person protected by the law is an atomic individual, not a Group member.[54]

Given the profound disagreements about the regulation of social life—a potentially disruptive competition between influential Groups—it is clear that the most pressing need in a democratic polity is to devise the procedures whereby, in any decision-making and legislation which is going to affect all members of Society, respect must be shown for all the significant Groups of which the individuals are members. Respect for Groups must be the central feature of political life in a democratic polity; it is this ideal which will determine the nature of the legislative Practices of a Society.[55]

In the political field of a democratic polity there is no principle requiring us to respect individual opinions about political matters. Individualism is commonly out of place in politics and may lead to the employment of devices quite unfitted to allow for adequate deliberation and decision-making about what it is to be done. If referendums, for example, can usefully indicate the strength of Groups inadequately represented in the political process, they can scarcely be regarded as procedures in which proper understanding of all the circumstances can be reached or adequate consideration and respect be given to competing strategies or points of view.

Given that Society is an artificial form and not a natural Community, those who employ communitarian language about our social relationships must be taken to be members or founders of a Group within Society committed to a restatement of what they take to have been communitarian values, such as the value of consensus, respect for convention, involvement in local affairs, public service, concern for the disadvantaged and for neighbours, and so on; values which would probably not require such articulation in a Community. Hence the lack of resonance of locutions which refer to social life as a community, such as 'community service', 'community care', and the like.[56]

B: The State

The State is a very different type of associational form from that of Society (see *ante.* p. 23). It is an Organization, a conglomerate, with all that that means in terms of a hierarchical structure; it has a clearly defined membership of officials, officers, and ordinary members.[57] If a Society is to survive, the Organization which is the State must possess the capability of securing Society's borders against invasion, of subduing disruptive forces within the territory, and of enforcing the general rules against individuals. Its raw power—required for the discharge of all these functions—derives from the disciplined co-operation of its members. The centralizing State is a correlate of Society; the exercise of its power—particularly its enforcement of the general rules—being necessary for our recognition of the status of citizenship.

The composition of the State

In institutional theory the State is a distinct institutional form; it is not to be confused with the polity or with a general context of organized social interaction. As an associational form the State is essentially an organizational structure, that is: a conglomerate consisting of all departments, offices, and agencies which are directly subject to executive control. For present purposes the main importance of this is the exclusion from the State of both the legislative and legal Practices of the Society. Such Practices are part of the polity, not of the institutional form the State; their participants are not subject to executive control.[58]

Now the State is the apparatus of government and administration which is to be defined in terms of its power structure, not in terms of its functions. So questions of whether particular bodies are part of the State should be approached by considering the degree of executive control over their operations, rather than the type of services they may render, or the contribution they make to the discharge of what are perceived to be governmental functions.

The powers of the State

The democratic revolution entails a complete transformation of the State, which ceases to be the executive arm of the sovereign Ruler, entrusted with the well-being of citizens and with indeterminate powers to achieve the common good, and becomes an organizational structure whose every power is conferred by the Ultimate Legislative Practice, or ULP.[59] The revolution establishes the fundamental principle that the State is never sovereign; that its officers and of ficials can do only what they are specifically empowered to do. For in the new democratic polity the ULP is master. (See *post*, p. 267.)

In Chapter 8 the initial powerlessness of the State is presented as a necessary thesis for the participants in the legal Practices who would do legal justice.[60] However, the thesis is not limited to the legal point of view, but is of the widest constitutional significance. In a democracy those engaged in governmental and political activity must understand that the State can never rely upon good reasons, but only upon norms; that is, upon the specific powers conferred on it.

At a time when the hyperactive State is so obtrusive a reminder may be needed that all its powers must be severally and deliberately conferred by the ULP: that all State powers must have been assented to in the ultimate decision-making and deliberative body of Society. The State can act legitimately only when it can show that its powers have been so conferred or approved. So even the most basic and important State powers—to enforce laws, to defend the realm, to control the economy, and the like—depend upon conferment by the ULP. Insofar as any ancient powers have survived the revolution, they must be taken to have been assented to by the ULP.[61] The maintenance of the powers of the State by the ULP is the keystone of the democratic arch; this is the institutional manifestation of government by consent.

Although this principle is acted upon in the courts of law, it is in danger of being obscured by the rhetoric employed. The fundamental role of the ULP in conferring and maintaining the existing powers of government can easily be obscured by the claim that the State only has those powers which *'the Law'* allows. However, any appeal to 'the Law' as the source of State authority must reckon with the fact that even the oldest laws can be repealed.

To suppose that the State could derive its authority from 'the Law', conceived of simply as a set of established rules 'out there', confers a sacred character on the legal norms but gives us little reason to treat them seriously. Only when laws are seen to be norms to which our contemporaries have assented can we demand obedience to them. There is little force in the argument that we should recognize a particular norm operating to confer power because it has always been the law, or because our forebears regarded it as necessary, or because it is declared to be fundamental.[62] The suggestion that the power of the State derives in some sense from the law—a body of norms existing independently of the ULP—may well undercut the sovereignty of the ULP and confer extended authority upon judges to declare on any occasion what those powers are.

Any attempt to enshrine or contain State powers in unrepealable constitutional provisions is undemocratic; it deprives the contemporary ULP of its authority to determine the nature of the State to whose powers all members of Society are to be subject.

The exercise of power

The problem for democrats is to establish the conditions under which the State, despite its manifold accumulated powers, can be regarded as something other than an unjustified imposition on our ways of life. What are the conditions in which citizens can accept the commands of the State for reasons other than habit, or fear of its coercive power? In other words, what are the conditions in which State power can properly be recognized as authority?

The recognition that the powers of the State are conferred by the ULP goes some way to meet the democrat's concern to establish the legitimacy of the State. We gain some comfort from the fact that we are to be subject only to that authority which our representatives have conferred. However, an additional condition of legitimacy is that the powers conferred must always be exercised legitimately.[63] The legitimacy of a State depends on the respect which, in the exercise of its powers, it shows for *both* the individual members of Society *and* the Groups to which they belong. It depends upon a climate of mutual respect, in which the citizen respects the State and recognizes its authority precisely because the State respects the citizen.[64] We need not seek the grounds of the State's authority in any other quarter: it does not derive its authority from divine inspiration or favour; nor is legitimacy dependent on any title deriving from rules of succession or from a written constitution; nor is it a character dependent upon economic success or popular support.

The norms designed to secure that respect for individuals and Groups—which constraining norms are necessary as we cannot rely upon the goodwill of the State—are those which govern the relationships between the State and the other constitutional forms in the polity; so the State's respect for the individual is secured in the legal Practices, and its respect for Groups is secured in the norms governing its relationships with the ULP.

Respect for individuals

That the State is to be compelled to respect every individual citizen is the prime concern of the legal Practices of Society. In the penal Practice the punitive monopoly claimed by the participants entails the inability of officials to sanction State mandates penally; and in the public law Practice, the principles of *ultra vires* and fairness in administration are employed by the judges to justify their demands that officials respect the interests of individuals (see *post*, p. 347). Legislation initiated by the State and enacted in the ULP is transformed, in the process of incorporation, into rules for the doing of legal justice to individuals. It is therefore in the relationships between the State and the legal Practices that we must locate one of the central pillars of legitimacy: the rule of law. The effectiveness of the courts of law as a constraint on the State, compelling respect for persons, depends not only upon the independence of the judiciary, but also upon the existence of a powerful legitimate opposition (see *post*, p. 280).

Respect for Groups

The respect for individuals secured by the courts is a necessary but not a sufficient condition for legitimacy. The State must also show respect for Groups. The norms ensuring the State's respect for all significant Groups in social life are found primarily among the norms governing the relationships between the government and the ULP in which Groups are represented. Groups have no relevance in the associational form Society: that is, in the legal world. As they appear in our political life, as Groups whose values influence political choices and activities, they will appear primarily as they are represented in the ULP. The ground rules of the ULP are animated by the democratic imperative that in all legislation and decision-making, respect must be given to all the significant Groups of a Society.

So it is in the relationships between the executive and the legislature—possibly the trickiest and most sensitive of all interrelationships of the forms of life in a democratic polity—that we must locate the norms requiring the State to respect the Groups within a polity. This is an area of continuous movement, in which tensions will be experienced, express constitutional provisions may be ignored, and conventions emerge.[65]

Relationships between the government and the ULP may be spelled out in a written constitution as the relationships between the executive and legislative branches of the polity. Although they may appear prescribed and rule-bound, in a democratic polity such relationships must be seen to be principled, and the overarching principle must be the ultimacy of the ULP as the voice of Society. The norms governing relationships between the government and the ULP are, it must be emphasized, not legal norms;

the courts have no authority to articulate or to incorporate them in their LSS. This is not an area in which the rule of law is relevant; here the constraints must be constitutional and political rather than legal.

The State of the foundationalists

If the State is initially powerless, if every one of its powers must be conferred, it follows that we cannot, from a subjective conception of the functions of the State, specify the powers which it should possess.[66] We must regard specification by political theorists of the necessary powers of the State, or of the minimal powers which it can possess, as an attempt to pre-empt the judgment of the ULP as to the powers with which the State should be provided. Such pre-emptive specification of the constitutional powers is akin to the claims of foundationalists who, having a very clear idea of the functions of the law, demand that it conform to a masterplan which can be deduced from them.

From the fact that the State may be seen to possess certain necessary minimal functions and powers, it does not follow that it can legitimately perform *only* those basic functions. The advocates of the minimal State cannot question the legitimacy of the State whose powers the democratic ULP does in fact, maintain.[67] What a particular Group believes to be constitutionally right is never decisive of the legitimacy of institutions created and maintained by democratic consent. If a State has the support of the ULP, though we may question its conception of social justice, we cannot question the legitimacy of the powers conferred upon it.

The State must be capable of performing certain basic functions if civil Society is to exist: to defend the territory, preserve peace, and enforce general rules; however, that neither requires nor permits us to define the State in these terms. Such functions cannot be necessary elements in our definition of the legitimate State. This is because, in a democracy, State actions should never be justified in terms of necessity or needs, nor of functions or ends, but only by express authorization by the ULP. The sinister implications of the belief that State actions can be justified to the citizen by adducing *only* persuasive reasons are in no way removed by the rational demonstration that official action will conduce to liberal values, democratic ends, utility, or prosperity.

The legitimacy of the State is essentially a matter of the propriety of official conduct; this is not to be judged by reference to performance targets; that is, by reference to the State's ability to provide the conditions for economic progress, or guarantees of minimal welfare benefits.

Theories about the functions of government are of course a perfectly proper concern of political Groups; the theories will inevitably be related to conceptions of social justice about which there is no general agreement.[68] However, the ideal constitution will not embody any such conceptions of justice or such theories of the State; its elements will not be disposed to ensure the achievement of such Group values. Rather, the ideal constitution leaves governments free to attempt whatever radical social and political changes they advocate, without imposing the burden of making constitutional changes to implement them. The politicization of the constitution, the determination to ensure that it expressly embodies the values of a Group, will give it a rigidity wholly inconsistent with democratic politics and government.[69]

C: Government

The government is the controlling executive of the organizational complex, and is thus part of, but must be distinguished from, the State. As a distinct institutional form the government of a Society is a unique Organization. It is the nerve-centre of the State, with control of all its resources; its members initiate legislation, implement policies, regulate, and govern.

The government of a Society is a politically motivated Organization, making no claim to impartiality. Since it represents a dominant Group, or combination of Groups, with its hands on the levers of power, it is imperative that its powers should be conditional and limited: it must be compelled at all times to respect other Groups.

In the ideal constitution of a heterogeneous Society it is important that the politically motivated government should be seen to derive its authority only from the ULP; that it be wholly dependent on the ULP with no other independent legitimating source of power. The source of its power cannot derive from the rules—from the law or the constitution—but only from the empowering support of the living ULP.

Nor, importantly, does the authority of the government derive from the electorate. Its power comes from the true political sovereign: the ULP. The danger of the populist suggestion that authority to govern is conferred, or divested, by the electorate is that, while such a claim may appear to give the greatest possible respect to individuals, it undermines the respect for Groups, the recognition of whose worth lies at the core of democratic politics. Today the source of governmental authority is obscured by the naive democratic theory, embraced by a media geared to the discovery and analysis of the evidence of public opinion, and wedded to an assumption of the need for mandating electoral majorities.[70]

The populist assumption that governmental power is conferred by the people tends to obscure the conditional nature of *all* State power. It will override the assumption of the initially powerless State whose powers are created and maintained only by the ULP. The belief that the voters elect a board to manage the State plc can all too easily suggest that the State is a powerful independent bureaucratic machine. We need to stress the inextricable connection between the powers of the State and the authority of the government in order that both are recognized as being dependent upon the ULP.

Furthermore, in a world of rapidly changing circumstances and unforeseen contingencies the conferral of governmental power cannot always be reduced to the presentation of a simple choice between two or three possible parties. A government may, as a pragmatic solution to political stalemate, be contrived from a loose alliance of disparate Groups. As a body the electorate is incapable of the sophisticated deliberation and negotiation required in these situations. Judgments about the viability or competence of coalitions must be made by a body capable of something more than the simplest judgments.[71]

Were the conferral of governmental power reduced to a simple power of appointment in the electorate there would be little hope of recognizing the democratic condition: that the authority of the government is maintained, is continuously sustained, by the ULP. The ULP does not operate as an electoral college with a quinquennial grant of governmental power in its hands: it must be seen to sustain the government at all times, reconferring governmental power daily. So the assertion that the government's authority is founded upon the mandate of the people undermines the crucially important conditionality, the absolute contingency, of government power. For this power is subject at all times to the confidence of the ULP.

The government is answerable at all times to the ULP: not to some impartial arbitral board charged with protecting the public good, the constitution, or the law, but to the body upon which its life as a government depends. The recognition that the ULP confers all powers and that it is to the ULP that governments are answerable makes it unnecessary to do what populists demand: that is, to formulate constitutional limits on executive action or to empower courts to whom the State must answer.

Relationships between the executive and the ULP are manifestly complex and subtle, involving both conflict and co-operation. Against the fact that the ultimate control of government lies with the ULP not the people, we must remember that any government must possess a high degree of control and influence over the ULP. Otherwise, effective rule would be impossible: the government would be unable to take necessary and unpopular actions when irreconcilable differences between Groups, or changing circumstances, threatened the peace or prosperity of Society. Although in a democratic polity the legislature cannot be a rubber stamp, its members, while aware of their ultimate power to dismiss, must be prepared to accept a considerable degree of direction from the government.[72]

The recognition that the authority of government derives from the ULP may be expected to exert a beneficent influence on both the perception of political activity and its conduct. There is great virtue in acknowledging that a government is only a fallible party placed in a position of power; that it is a Group which holds its power under a revocable licence, rather than a fixed-term lease. It militates against the polarization which may infect the politics of a country in which the will of the people is regarded as a force to be reckoned with.[73] For a government, authorized only by the ULP, can make no serious claim to possess a mandate from the people; nor need it seek to discover or create a consensus or to implement its supposed demands. The party in power does not speak for the country, nor do its policies give effect to the will of the community. It can ignore the wisdom of psephological alchemists who would transmute statistics into the conditions of authority. The government—but one party among others competing for power—has no authority to govern without the confidence of the ULP; but it does have authority to make decisions which will score badly in opinion polls.

In the politics of democracy opposition to the government is not antagonism to the board of governors chosen by the people, nor is it defiance of the will of the electorate. Instead it is the proper and highly valued contestation of policies and powers by other Groups whose views must be respected.

D: The Ultimate Legislative Practice

The ULP, described here as an ideal form, is a living normative Practice. It is a perduring form of life in which human beings meet and interact in activities which are structured by norms; and it requires a location, resources, and facilities. The ULP is not merely a recipe for making laws, or the protocols of legislation; it is an institutional form, an entity, the dominant landmark in the polity—an object towards which citizens adopt attitudes.

In modern Societies, where social conditions change at an unprecedented rate, the legislative function of ensuring that the normative framework for social life is appropriate and effective becomes ever more important, and ever more difficult. As circumstances change, old laws and institutions are seen to need reform, and new forms of association and activity cry out for regulation.

The framing of laws without regard to the consequences is a simple exercise, but to make laws which effectively meet the needs of society calls for expertise and experience. The making of democratically valid laws, however, requires far more than expertise. It calls for co-operative action under procedures governed by the imperatives of legitimacy. The ULP emerges 'to ensure that the deliberative forces should prevail over the arbitrary';[74] to enable the making of laws which are democratically valid.

It is important to emphasize that this normative Practice is not merely a metropolitan law manufactory, but a unique institutional form with much wider significance: the voice of Society. For it is within this Practice, and only there, that Society can be said to have a voice. Yet only in a very qualified sense should this be considered the voice of the people. For this Practice makes possible the expression, not of the will of the people—no such thing exists—but of the assent of the people, which is a very different thing. Crucially, the function of ULP in a democratic polity is not merely to make laws but also to *maintain* them: it gives present authority to all existing social rules. It is the body to which all State institutions and officials are ultimately accountable.

Now the ULP, despite its wider significance as the voice of Society, is not an associational form. To talk of it as 'a legislature', or a 'legislative assembly' might suggest that it is. Its participants are related to each other only by their engagement in the Practice of law-making. Although they may combine with others in organized parties or loose coalitions for tactical reasons, and though groupings of them may share beliefs and attitudes, yet each participant acts in a (rather complicated) representational capacity as an independent agent who is a member of various Groups. There are acute difficulties in contriving systems for electing or selecting participants which ensure adequate representation of all significant Groups in the Society.

The ground rules of this Practice, the complicated procedures to be followed if valid laws are to be enacted, would have to be disentangled from a variety of different institutions in any actual contemporary polity. They will include the vetoes and assents of presidents and monarchs, who, it must be understood, may well be participants in the ULP. The ground rules will be complicated since they are devised, in the light of experience, to give effect to the overarching idea of the Practice. That idea is that the only laws which can legitimately be imposed upon Society are those created in the light of the fullest deliberation of the legislative proposals, with proper respect being shown to all significant Groups. For the ancient Goths, so the story goes,[75] wise decisions about matters important for the community were proposed when they were drunk, so as not to lack resolution, and debated when they were sober, so as not to lack discretion. The well made and valid law of the sprawling dissensus of the democratic polity is made in accordance with a procedure designed to ensure, among other things, that the views of all competing significant Groups are treated seriously.[76]

The electoral Practice

The legitimacy of the ULP depends upon its being perceived as the voice of contemporary Society: as the form in which all significant Groups are represented and in which, in the deliberation of projected policies, disparate and conflicting views are truly respected. The ULP is the central and sole forum for the artificial association Society. Its decision-making can be legitimate only if those with capacity to participate in the ULP in some way represent all other members of Society who, for practical reasons, cannot participate. The ULP therefore depends on the establishment of an electoral Practice designed to confer upon a limited number of persons capacity to participate in it.

If the legitimacy requirements of the ULP are to be satisfied, the electoral Practice must allow members of any Group to stand for election to the ULP, and not exclude any class of persons from participating in the election. It is necessary that elections be held at regular intervals, that candidates be free to publicize their policies, and that the electors should have complete freedom to vote for any candidate. It is well understood that a member's capacity to participate in the ULP is subject to reconsideration at each election.

The ground rules of an electoral Practice designed to meet these requirements may take a variety of forms; procedures for the final selection may be complicated. Given the variety of local circumstances it is not possible to stipulate in detail the nature of the ground rules. Electoral Practices are commonly the result of long experience.

Although the electoral Practice should ideally be regarded solely as the means of selecting members of the ULP, many Practices acquire a different significance. For instance, electors may regard themselves as voting for a government, rather than for the composition of a ULP which will authorize a government. Provisions may well be made for separate election to the ULP and to government. It may be considered that the democratic accountability of government is increased by the direct election of governmental officers. The effect of such direct participation by members of Society in the selection of government of course entails that the ULP is not sovereign. Governments appear to acquire authority from the people, and the State ceases to be a powerless entity dependent upon the ULP.

Satisfying the requirements for the electoral Practice of a true ULP in no way increases or diminishes the democratic credentials of governmental of fices or agencies which may be elected in a similar fashion. It does not render them more democratic, for their democratic legitimacy depends upon their accountability to the ULP. The belief that direct election to office has a validating effect on a government is linked to that article in the credo of innocence: that we all have a right to participate in government.

The ULP is not a State Practice

One of the most persistent misconceptions about democratic law making is that it is a function of the State: that the laws enacted are State laws, and that the legislative Practice is part of the structure of the State.[77] Against this it is important to emphasize that the ULP is the legislative Practice of a *Society.* Not being a department of State, its participants are not normally members of the State organization; nor are the laws it produces State laws. The demand for an autonomous legislative Practice, authorized by Society, is a central feature of the democratic revolution.

Yet traditional ways of thinking die hard; the ancient conception of the monarch combining the functions of ruler, judge, and law-giver[78] is reflected today in the doctrine of the separation of powers which provides that the three functions of government are discharged by three departments of the State. The imperatives of democracy, however, require autonomous, *non-governmental* adjudicatory and legislative Practices. No doubt it is knowledge of the working of actual legislative Practices, rather than intellectual inertia, which accounts for the description of the legislature as part of the State. For the degree of control actually exercised by governments over the legislative Practices makes their description as autonomous appear a shade idealistic.[79] Yet even in this sometimes unhealthy condition, the autonomy of the ULP will survive if it is understood to possess the ultimate power to overthrow a government. In any event we should recall that it is not the perduring State but temporary governments which exercise governmental control.

Even though, in modern conditions, good government calls for the enactment of a huge volume of government-initiated laws, legislation is never a capacity of the State. Except in conditions of emergency the State has no inherent power to legislate.[80] Any such inherent power would enable informal legislation. Then any procedures stipulated by the constitution would be, not constitutive of its legislative power, but merely limitations and qualifications of an aboriginal power. By contrast, in a democracy the ULP is a Practice which makes true law-making possible; it is constitutive of a power to legislate validly for Society.

For very good reasons, the State does possess legislative power in many different matters. However, these are never inherent powers, but are conferred by way of delegation under enactments of the ULP. Most of the State's legislative Practices will be prescribed and instituted by the ULP. Thus any surviving prerogative powers of legislation remain only by courtesy of the ULP; authority can be claimed for current prerogative legislative Practices, not because of their ancient origins, but because they have not been abolished by the ULP.

For institutional theory it is important to insist that the enactments of the ULP are not strictly laws. They only become legal norms upon their incorporation into the LSS of the legal Practices. Our ordinary usages clearly contribute to the obfuscating and widely held belief that all enactments are laws.[81] A foracentric view enables us to see that those normative products of the ULP which the courts lack the authority to incorporate—those which are not required for the doing of legal justice—have political, administrative, and constitutional rather than legal significance. We should include among the normative products of the ULP any expressions of its political sovereignty, for example its refusal to continue to recognize the authority of a government: which is scarcely a matter for legal adjudication.

Sovereignty

In the democratic polity the ULP is not just a legislature, not merely a form co-ordinate with judicial and executive forms: it is, I have suggested, the voice of Society. This is the animating idea of the legislative Practice. In this form we must locate the source of all State power; it maintains all Society's general rules, and is the apex of all its political activity. We may properly describe its pre-eminence among the institutional forms in the language of sovereignty; it is both legally and politically sovereign. That is, its NPs are recognized as having supremacy not only by the courts, but also by all who are involved in political life.[82]

The sovereign character of the ULP in a democratic polity rests on two claims.[83] The first is that no other individual or body within a Society can claim authority to speak about the state of contemporary social life and the aspirations of its dominant Groups; only the collective participants in the ULP have that authority, which they exercise in a representative capacity. The second claim is that, in a flourishing dissensus, only a law-making procedure devised as far as possible to ensure that proper respect is paid to all competing Groups could hope to enact laws which all members of society, however reluctantly, recognized as compelling their obedience, irrespective of the patent fact that the State has the power to compel such obedience.[84]

As the ULP is the only form which could colourably be said to be the voice of Society, there is little to recommend the suggestion that sovereignty could be divided: that ultimate authority could be shared with any Practice or agency which did not possess the representative character or procedural virtues of the ULP.[85]

We the people

Sovereignty does not rest with the people, for the people have no voice.[86] The Groups to which members belong make up a dissensus; our social life is a Babel of different tongues. Sovereignty must reside in the only institutional form which makes it possible to talk meaningfully about the voice of Society. To suggest that the electorate is the ultimate sovereign is to misunderstand the nature of democratic government. It is consistent with the pernicious assumption that the good law is the law which expresses the will of the majority; ignoring the imperative that all good laws must be deliberated fully, and drafted and enacted in the light of all the relevant evidence and under pressure from those who may disapprove of them. The mathematical approach—the counting of heads which has great attraction for the rationalists—shows no respect whatsoever for certain Groups.[87]

A similar lack of respect for Groups is found in the commonly held view that good democratic laws are laws embodying democratic principles.[88] That is, that good laws are created by legislators equipped with a blueprint designed to maximize the values of, say, freedom or personal autonomy. Further, as such values are self-evident, laws conforming with them can be enacted, and other laws repealed, with complete disregard for the benighted Groups which maintain quite different value-structures. Such a steamroller, in the livery of a liberal corporation, is regularly put on the road by those who misdescribe the ULP as a majoritarian monster.

Its products are settlements and compromises

The normative products, or NPs, of the ULP must be viewed as settlements and compromises negotiated by the participants under conditions in which the views of members of Groups opposed to them are given due weight; that is, in procedures which treat Groups seriously. It is in the light of this understanding that the ULP's products are negotiated compromises that participants in the legal Practices will construe as the enactments. From the legal point of view the statute to be incorporated and applied by the courts is never a piece of government legislation, but always an enactment of the ULP. It is not a government policy statement, but at best a vectored compromise upon whose exact words the legislators have agreed. The job of the court is to give effect to the agreement reached, not to further the assumed intentions of those who initiated the legislation. The literal rule of interpretation—scorned by those who fail to allow that statutory interpretation has an institutional context—reflects the sound democratic instincts of common law judges.

However, such a legalistic approach to the interpretation of statutes may be inappropriate for enactments on constitutional matters which do not directly impinge on individual rights. While such constitutional prescriptions must undoubtedly be read as settlements or compromises, to the extent that they were reached in circumstances wholly different from those of the present they require a less legalistic, more liberal interpretation, not by the courts, but by the officials and politicians who will apply them. The actual words employed are less important than the agreement reached.

To recognize the sovereignty of the ULP is to exclude the possibility of the promulgation of any fundamental law which is not open to repeal or renegotiation. Given the dissensus in a continuously changing society, the compromises reached in making a law declared to be fundamental at one point of time may vary considerably from those which would be reached in the ULP today. The objection to fundamental laws in a democratic polity is that they encourage a lack of respect for the Groups of present-day society. Those who would secure the democratic foundations by setting its fundamental laws in stone may be said to undermine them.

In stressing the autonomy of the ULP we must emphasize that it is indissolubly linked with, and is the focus of, the political activity of a society. Its participants are not elected bureaucrats or token representatives; they are not merely consultants or draftsmen for a government; nor are they guardians of the national conscience embodying the deliverances of the *Volksgeist* in statutory provisions. They are linked with, and profoundly sensitive to, the variety of conflicting political opinions and the range of concerns of people in all parts of society. The legitimacy of the ULP is conditional upon the perception by members of Society that the Groups to which they belong are being respected. This is a perception which is promoted by, but neither guaranteed by nor necessarily dependent upon a system of universal suffrage.

Process and Practice

The ULP must be placed within its context. We would give but a slanted and partial picture of law-making in a democratic Society if we concentrated only on the activity of the participants in the ULP. The ULP, standing at the apex of the political life of the Society, is part of a much wider process by which normative changes are brought about. The working of the ULP is dependent upon a much wider debate: on the informal, never-ending, unregulated conversation between competing Groups outside the Practice, which will in a variety of ways ultimately influence the decisions made within it. The variety and range of the types of activity which can be lumped together as part of, or related to, the process of legislation needs no elaboration. The process, constrained only by the need to preserve order, includes political activity of all types: from organized campaigns to informal bar-room arguments; from demonstrations and academic theorizing to the clearing of the ground which government departments undertake prior to laying legislative proposals before the participants in the ULP.

A ULP can only claim legitimacy if the political activity among the members of Society for which it legislates is unrestricted. One of the clearest indicators of a non-democratic polity is that citizens are fearful with reason about criticizing the State.

This is well understood. However, political freedoms are not enough, for the process leading to legislative change may be vitiated in more subtle ways. For instance, it is imperative that information relevant to all matters needing review and reform should not be withheld—as it can so easily be—by the State or by powerful interest groups. The public debate must be unbounded and informed. All the evidence necessary for rational decision-making in the ULP must be available at the grass roots. Yet movements for open government and for freedom of information are latecomers on the stage of democratic legitimacy; only now are the principles being worked out. If the public is often said to have a right to know, the normative structures required in this sensitive area cannot be articulated solely in terms of individual rights. We cannot expect movement towards more open government to be rapid in a polity in which the attacks in the legislative Practice upon one government's secretiveness or reserve come chiefly from an opposition which, as government-in-waiting, may fear the consequences of giving hostages to fortune.

The political climate in which the ULP operates is of fundamental importance. The justification for the sovereign status of the ULP—for the recognition of the legislative omnicompetence of the select few—is that only such a Practice can make it possible for the consent of the people to be expressed. In a democracy the people represented in the ULP are not just passive, law-abiding, constituents, but members of Society who, as members of Groups, are conscious of the contingency of all laws, and are engaged in the continuous criticism of those laws and of their administration.

E: The Legal Practices

The failure of many jurists to give due weight to the democratic foundations of law is paralleled by the failure of many political scientists to accord the law its proper place in a democracy. There is considerable disagreement about the meaning of the rule of law in both legal and political theory.[89]

An institutional approach is required to put law in its proper place: we must treat law, not as a function, nor as a system of norms, but as a set of Practices in which legal norms are generated and maintained. What is required is a clear understanding, not only of the three distinct forms—the penal, private, and public law Practices—but also of the manner in which they are related to the State, the ULP, Society, enforcement Activity, and the private forms of social life.[90]

The key to understanding the place of law in a democratic polity lies in what I have called the constitutive idea of the legal Practices: the idea of legal justice which is a commitment by the participants to respect, and to compel respect for, persons. The ground rules of the three Practices are all geared to this objective. In discussing the penal Practice I have argued that we can only understand the emergence, the differentiation, and the nature of the Practice in the light of the idea of legal justice, of showing respect for every offender. In the private and public law Practices judges are committed to compelling other members of Society and the State to respect the rights of every individual citizen.[91] Every member of Society is equal before the law. Private law apart, in a democratic polity the limited but necessary function of the courts is to ensure that any punishments inflicted on members, and any State interference with individual interests, must be justified by reference to laws enacted and maintained by the ULP and incorporated into the LSS of the legal Practices.

So if in the democratic polity the political field is dominated by the idea of respect for Groups, the legal field is dominated by the idea of respect for individuals.[92]

Why must the legal Practices be founded upon this idea of legal justice? Why in the ideal democratic polity, is it necessary that those who are governed be thought of as individuals with rights which must be respected? Can we not imagine a democratic polity in which, although there is freedom for all citizens to involve themselves in decision-making which affects them, and a strong tradition of such consistent involvement, there is no conception of the governed as being individual carriers of interests and entitlements to which rights attach?

Certainly, other theoretical approaches would give a very different account of the idea animating the activity of the courts. Thus *conventionalism is* primarily concerned with respect for rules. The laws are made elsewhere: it is the task of the courts to apply them if they satisfy the formal criteria for recognition. *Pragmatists* would deny that there is any animating idea at all, and hold that judges should not obscure matters by claiming to respect the rules, but openly declare the grounds upon which appropriate decisions are made. To the extent that realists are tempted to set out the guidelines for what is appropriate, they will be *foundationalists* (see *post,* Ch. 9). For such foundationalists the ideal judge would adjudicate and legislate in conformity with the principles of some doctrine or political philosophy. For them the idea of the law is an ideology, which may well give priority to the values of individualism.

The objection to all these ideas is that they are undemocratic. Though they are not compatible with each other, each can claim support from the actual activity of the courts, and for that reason each may have a certain plausibility. Yet if these ideas are realized in the courts there will be a legitimacy deficit. Each approach can be shown, in its own way, to undermine the inherent authority of the law; each puts law in the wrong place.

By contrast, legal Practices operating with the idea of legal justice—the idea of respect for persons—will be entirely democratic. Courts animated by this idea are essential to establish the conditions in which all citizens can give their uncoerced consent to the coercively supported laws.

Individualism

It is difficult to see how the citizen—as but one among millions—could fail to approve of the individualism of the law. In its adjudications the law does not simply demand respect for the plaintiffs who appear before the courts; its rules prescribe the respect due, in clearly specified circumstances, to every citizen in the territory. The participants in the legal Practices transform the laws; they turn them into rules for doing legal justice, and publicly declare them. In declaring law the courts have had the individual interests of every citizen in mind. For a court is not just an agency for ensuring that the particular aggrieved individual who appears before it is given satisfaction; courts are not dispute-resolution mechanisms. Crucially, they declare rules which entail the equality of all citizens, and upon which all citizens can rely. To describe courts as dispute-resolution agencies will create a climate in which litigation may become an addiction for those temperamentally inclined to confrontation.

Now the individualism and equality of the law are not optional or contingent values. They do not need justification, for they are values implicit in our way of life; we might say that they are part of our consciousness as members of a modern Society. We subscribe to these values, not because we have been persuaded by Christians or liberals that they are sacred, fundamental, or rational, but because we all necessarily engage in certain Practices which generate a language in which such values are implicit. That is, we are all members of a market economy, engaging in transactions of sale and purchase, in lending, giving credit, and so forth. We can only engage in these Practices as individuals: as free agents, making our own choices, and dealing with others who are also free to choose. Furthermore we have no choice about our engagement in these market transactions, it being almost impossible to opt out of what Adam Smith called 'the great game'. We all use money, employ the language of exchange values, and thus articulate the world in a way which includes the conception of all others as individuals equally forced to be free.

It is worth noting that, although all members of a Society speak the same catallactic language and articulate the world in the same way, the penetration of a monetary economy has notoriously destroyed traditional communities, and that one consequence of the engagement of all members in the market has been to foster the conditions of dissensus. The assumption that it would be possible to elaborate a philosophy, or set out a political agenda, based on the values of the market-place, which would have universal validity for all modern polities, is mistaken.[93] For, ignoring those theorists who would dispense with the market economy altogether, the central questions of political economy concern the degree to which the market should be regulated, and the extent to which we ought to reduce the gross inequalities resulting from engagement in its Practices. Policies which advocate either greater freedom for, or tighter control of, market transactions require philosophical justification which cannot be derived from the basic individualistic values implicit in the exchange Practices in which we all participate.[94] It is important to stress that the law does not give effect to any such market-inspired philosophy.[95]

What the law does is to take as its fundamental concern the individual who is the agent in the market-place, and to secure for him the respect to which he is entitled under the existing legal rules. The market requires regulation and support. The market Practices themselves merely assume that entitlements will be respected; they are limited forms of life with the objectives of creating interests, transferring property, and so forth, and their participants can do nothing to ensure that respect. It is in the legal Practices that the coercive power of the State is used to protect the individual; they are the only agencies in which respect for all holders of interests and entitlements can be guaranteed. The importance of the courts in establishing the foundations of capitalism has long been understood.

Now the legal person, as an individual with interests and entitlements, is a person of substance. This is perhaps not a conception which would be generated in a rule-applying agency in a non-market society. The legal person is something more than an individual who is recognized as being subject to a general rule equally with all others. For general rules can be roughly enforced and applied, and equality under the rules could be taken to mean equal liability rather than equal respect. Yet legal justice respects a person's interests and entitlements, and the courts' respect for them is scrupulous; the paradigm entitlement of the market is an entitlement upon which a precise monetary value can be placed.

Of course the interests and entitlements which the courts articulate and protect go well beyond the products of transactions in the market-place.[96] Nonetheless, all purely personal rights, or civil interests, must be understood as having the same logic as the entitlements of the market-place. Both right-holders and their rights have their genesis in our catallactic activity.

Why does this conception of the law as being animated by a respect for persons, as agents in the market, conform to the notion of democratic legitimacy? To see why, we need to remember that not one, but three legal Practices exist, performing quite different tasks.

Although the three Practices occupy adjacent areas of democratic space, questions of legitimacy do not feature prominently in the private law Practice, which is concerned to do justice between members of Society. In that Practice such questions will arise indirectly when the validity of enacted regulatory norms which affect the interests and entitlements of members may be challenged. Our concern here is primarily the legitimacy of the legal civil Practice itself. That legitimacy is prejudiced when its participants go beyond, or diverge from, their commitment to the respect of those members' interests and entitlements: for instance, if judges were to make punitive orders, or implement items of a political agenda.

In the penal and public law Practices the connection between legal justice and democratic legitimacy takes on a special significance.

In the democratic revolution the ruler or State undergoes a metamorphosis; from being a person or body, claiming as of right aboriginal, inherent, and sovereign powers limited only by custom and constitution, it becomes an Organization which, although possessed of the obvious *de facto* capability to compel, can claim as of right only those powers which have been conferred upon it by Society.[97] A State of this democratic character can be maintained only if there are legal Practices to restrain at every turn the inevitable tendency of the State, given its *de facto* power, to revert to a more absolutist character. Although government depends on the consent of the people, which can only be given by the ULP, that Practice is wholly unsuited for the continuous monitoring of the exercise of State powers. That monitoring must be achieved by examining individual claims of State injustice; it must be done in a court of law.

The individualism of the law plays an essential part in divesting Rulers of their formerly inherent powers.[98] This may be illustrated with reference to criminal law. In the absolutist or patriarchal polity the Ruler had an inherent power to punish; in the democratic polity the State has no punitive power whatsoever. Although the State must provide the resources required to punish and coerce, it is the participants in the penal Practice, committed to the individualism of legal justice, who have a monopoly of power to order punishment. The inflicting of punishment must be just; it can be neither informally nor officially administered. The rule of law, central to democratic legitimacy, entails that citizens should be secure from arbitrary penalties. In demanding, as they must, that the laws be well made the participants in the penal Practice recognize the sovereignty of the ULP. In penal matters, the doing of legal justice depends on the existence of a sovereign ULP, for only a legislative Practice of that character can enact laws which will, upon incorporation, completely justify an order to punish.

The connection between the individualism of legal justice and democratic legitimacy is perhaps even more clearly seen in the public law Practice. In compelling the State to respect every citizen, the courts legitimize the State. The legal Practice translates the general notion of consent to government into the recognition of the legitimacy of all its acts—that is, of those which are not legally challengable—affecting individual rights.

If the courts were to operate with only the conventionalist principle that the State must conform to established rules, they could scarcely be said to legitimate it. For then we could only say that there is conformity to the law; that the norms must be obeyed because they are the law. Once we inject the principle that the State must at every turn be compelled to act justly to the citizens, to respect every individual's rights, we can see, in the nature of the mandates which the courts incorporate, that the State will be required to conform to norms created in conditions in which the claims of all significant Groups have been weighed and individual rights have been respected. The norms to which the State must comply, and under which its powers are conferred, have democratic credentials which cannot be challenged. They are legally valid for that reason. There is something very much amiss in the view that the validity of legal norms is dependent upon their satisfying merely formal criteria.

Of course disputes and grievances arising in citizen-state relationships can all be dealt with in non-legal Practices that is, Practices which do not declare the law, which do not give primacy to rights of citizens, and which do not claim to do legal justice.[99] In such tribunals public law will be regarded as a distinct body of rules, quite separate from the rules of private law. No doubt many aggrieved citizens might be satisfied with their treatment under such arrangements. However, such agencies do nothing for the legitimacy of the State. They are State Practices concerned with the wrong-doing of the State, rather than with scrupulous regard for the rights of citizens. Liberals, perceiving something of a hiatus here, seek to fill it by promulgating a checklist of citizen's rights, a Bill of Rights; rights which may not feature in the mentality of the conventionalist or pragmatic tribunals. Such Bills constitute but another addition to the conception of the law 'out there' which haunts modern jurisprudence. They are examples of non-institutional solutions to institutional problems. They are intended to plug a hole in the adjudicative apparatus of the polity, as the doctrine of subsidiarity is introduced to remedy the deficiencies of undemocratic law-making Practices.

The legal Practices can only perform this legitimating function if they are autonomous, owing nothing to the State, not being departments of State, being neither subject to executive direction nor partners in framing and implementing government policy.[100] In their relationships with the ULP it must be clear that the courts cannot, without compromising their integrity, participate in making or reforming the law. They have inherent authority only to punish, to declare the law, and to check the validity of mandates created in State Practices. This they do by virtue of their concern for the rights of all individuals.

The ideal constitution and the law

The basic constitution of the democratic polity is an ideal structure seen from the legal point of view. The ideal institutional forms of the constitution are, in a sense, legally generated; they are constructed according to legal requirements. Starting with the idea of doing legal justice, we proceed to work out the character of the insititutional forms which must be established if justice is to be done. The exercise of power in a democracy must at all times be justified. In a particular Society such justification cannot be given by reference to a consciousness of right shared by all members, not because we can provide evidence of Society's ethical pluralism, but because in the doing of legal justice the values and beliefs of members of Society are irrelevant. Society is a legal concept, and an artificial form. So it is in the light of the law's indifference to the values of common or individual members, that we can imagine an ideal structure of forms which justify all acts limiting the freedom of members, or altering their conditions of life, against their will. The resulting constitution, in which State power is transformed into authority, prescribes the political arrangements in which the rule of law is possible.

However, although the ideal constitution set out here must conform to the specifications of a legal blueprint, although the forms must be defined from the legal point of view, it does not follow that the norms which structure the forms and govern their relationships are all legal norms. Legitimacy depends upon keeping law in its proper place. One of the most obscuring of the received ideas of modern times is the notion that a written constitution, which institutes and regulates the forms, must necessarily be a legal document and that its norms, or 'fundamental laws', are legal norms.[101]

F: The legitimate opposition

From the institutional point of view, which holds that norms exist only insofar as they are actually employed within forms of life, the picture of the ideal constitution as a working system to be described in terms of the interrelationships between the legally conceived forms of Society, State, ULP, and the legal Practices is incomplete. The assumption that these forms are the only necessary institutional components of a constitution is liable to be charged with the vice of formalism against which the realists inveigh. The establishment of a democracy requires something more than the institutions of legislative, adjudicatory, and executive power set out in the textbooks on constitutional law.

Democratic legitimacy requires a further associational form which, not being cognizable by the law, is naturally not included in the legally defined structure. This is a form which cannot be instituted by the founding fathers, and yet which is of absolutely fundamental importance. It is that Group within Society which I call the legitimate opposition.

The members of this Group are committed to the basic values of democracy and legitimacy, including the values of law. Since an understanding of such values and a familiarity with the vocabulary of democracy must be acquired, not being part of our natural endowment, it is obvious that not all members of Society will automatically become members of the Group. If the Group is to have significance there must be within a Society a strong commitment by a substantial number to those values.[102] Making use of their freedoms, the active members committed to the values may be expected to challenge at every turn and in all ways, the constitutional propriety of institutional interaction, the legality of executive and administrative action, and, importantly, they will make persistent demands for conformity with high standards of public morality by those engaged in public life.

This Group is wide and heterogeneous. Recruiting its members from all corners, it will embrace the disaffected as well as the politicians; those who favour and those who oppose the government of the day; those who are personally aggrieved as well as those who have a disinterested concern; influential members of the media and the unconnected man in the street.

It is of central importance to recognize that this unorganized, perpetually changing collection of members is a discrete institutional form: a Group.[103] Its diffuseness and uncertain boundaries are characteristics of all Groups. This Group has as strong a claim to individuality and reality as any other, since its armature is a value structure which has been extensively theorized and articulated. A democracy requires something more distinct than the conditions of open public debate, an informed electorate, a vigilant press, or a democratic climate. We need to isolate a distinct institutional form in order to emphasize not just the existence of a countervailing governmental force, but the coherence and continuity of an agenda of dissent and challenge which is built into the natural order of a democracy. The powerful influence exerted by the Group stems from the unchallengeable nature of central elements in its value structure. Individual protests are of little importance; there must be a history of challenge relying upon a ground-swell of support from those committed to the values. It is this Group which provides the eternal vigilance upon which our liberties rest.

The Group has a history: its members can draw on the experience of past events; they are aware of working within a tradition of continuous, active, and direct opposition to State injustice, a tradition embodying in precedent and symbol a refusal to accept at face value governmental professions of good intent, lawfulness, or bureaucratic rectitude.[104] Actions by the State which lack authority are directly opposed; this Group perceives of the State as existing only within the boundaries of its authority. There is a refusal to submit to the exercise of its unjustified raw power, no matter how carefully concealed by the cloak of formality. Group members draw confidence from the expressed values of the courts which the Group both supports and depends on.

The Group is not coincident with the political parties in opposition whose immediate objectives may be to oppose the policies of the government.[105] Nevertheless, concern for the democratic values of the Group are a vitally important aspect of political opposition; opposition parties have a responsibility to oppose vociferously any constitutional impropriety. The political opposition is sustained by, and itself supports, the Group. If it draws support from nationalists, its strength lies in its democratic values.

This Group is a *sine qua non* of legitimate democratic government. A polity in which there is no such Group is not a democracy. The claim to the term 'democratic' by Communist regimes was belied, not so much by the absence of any such Groups, as by an ideology which made them immoral and treasonable. The crucial importance of such a democratic opposition was overlooked by those who thought it possible to transplant a constitution based on the Westminster model to newly independent polities.[106]

Now the Group does not function merely as a watchdog challenging the State and ensuring the participation of citizens in an open, ongoing political debate about ends. Its major function within a democratic polity is to guarantee the norms of the constitution, to give them normative force, to electrify the constitutional grid.[107] There is little to support the belief that a source of power to ensure conformity to the constitution could be tapped within the various organs of the polity. Certainly, the courts cannot provide the necessary constraints against the State. Only an external force—the democratic opposition—can provide the sanctions and pressure for constitutional propriety. The significant Group transforms what might otherwise be aspirations, recipes, directives, or paper rules into norms which must be observed. It is impossible to overstate the importance of the Group in the normative world. Constitutional norms are not used and approved only between officials; they are norms in the public domain, observance of which is demanded by the Group. In Hart's terminology, the secondary rules are not merely accepted by officials, but must in a democratic polity be guaranteed by the democratic opposition.

The Group members pertinaciously question all laws and institutions. They keep alive the perpetual revolution which is democracy; they ensure the continuing renewal and renegotiation of its constitutional forms.[108] I have suggested that within a democracy all coercive action has to be completely justified. Coercive action for which there is no justificatory demand might just as well not be justified. Reasons need not be given; credentials need not be presented; no accounts need be made; the auditors need not be called in. A merely official recognition of the rules—the inter-departmental squabbles about the legality of acts—produces norms of a quite different sort. A democracy feeds upon the perpetual demand for justification; its State must be a justificatory State, answerable not merely to the legislative and adjudicatory Practices but ultimately to the democratic opposition. In the presence of such a Group the State must be constantly looking over its shoulder.

III: THE PRIORITY OF DEMOCRATIC LEGITIMACY

I take it to be axiomatic that democratic legitimacy matters, and that law plays a constitutive part in the achievement of the *Rechtsstaat. I* have suggested that the courts can only contribute to that achievement if they adhere to the ideals of legal justice; that is, if they are prepared to occupy a relatively modest position within the polity, consistent with their inherent authority.

Now the importance of legitimacy is questioned by those writers who claim that the familiar attempts to establish a link between law and democratic legitimacy are disingenuous; that the trappings of legitimacy are systematically employed to obscure the fact of exploitation. Admittedly, well-founded attacks have been mounted from the left against conventionalist positions; for instance, against the views of formalists whose notion of legitimacy appears to be little more than the disposition of officials to abide by the rules.

Much of the appeal of radical theories lies in the skill and forcefulness with which they describe the injustices of contemporary society, which is characterized by the universal engagement of its members in market transactions. There is no doubt that we benefit from reminders of the coexistence of privilege and poverty, and of the extent of social conditions which must shame the liberal conscience. Few can be unaware of the apparent indifference of the law to present injustices, and the support which the law, while opening its doors to all, offers mainly to the rich and powerful. If radical theory selects the softest of soft targets the critiques cannot be ignored—though we may have doubts about the accuracy of analyses which betray a romantic inclination to perceive conspiracy in the workings of a hidden hand and overestimate the communitarian virtues of earlier and happier forms of social life.

Nor can we dismiss the conceptions of substantive justice which underwrite the radicals' demands for the reform of the law to ameliorate the conditions of the less advantaged; except, perhaps, insofar as they advocate distributive arrangements which are wholly incompatible with any market activity.

Radical critics of our imperfect democratic societies are, however, not to be judged by the accuracy of their portraits of contemporary misery, or the virtue of their conceptions of social justice, but by the worth of their suggestions for restructuring the forms of life of political and legal activity. The criteria for judging such proposals must be the criteria of legitimacy. For whatever changes in man's social conditions may be possible, we cannot realistically assume the demise of the dissensus or the disappearance of the need for organized coercive force. So the question must be whether the proposed institutional changes would operate to secure the recognition by all those subject to coercive power that its exercise is justified, not in general but on every particular occasion. Equally, we must enquire of more modest proposals for restructuring our institutional forms: would the restructured forms operate to reduce, or to increase, the existing legitimacy deficit? For while we must resign ourselves to perpetual disagreement about substantial justice, there is a fundamental requirement that we must agree about the nature of the forms of life by which we are governed.

Radical critics of capitalist society are disinclined to provide details of the forms of life which should replace the, admittedly imperfect, institutions of a democratic polity. After all, they are faced with the impossibility of knowledge about imaginary forms of life, so that any hypotheses about the language and consciousness which the forms would generate will be the product of innocence rather than experience. However, we can draw on the bitter experience of those who have been governed by rulers who ignored the imperatives of democratic legitimacy.[109] That experience must surely convince us of the importance of democratic legitimacy and the need to secure the rule of law.

NOTES

1. See Hall (1949: 7).
2. We should define a democracy in terms of the institutional forms, rather than in terms of subscription to general principles of individual autonomy. The forms will be those of a unitary polity, not of a federation. Although federations are practical solutions to intractable political problems, they do not represent the ideal polities to which post-imperial states should converge; cf. Pagden (1995).
3. The conception of the law as a closed system, having internal coherence, has been employed to legitimize the legal profession, legal and political institutions, and to buttress the academics' claim to expert knowledge, and to

persuade citizens that they inhabit a normatively ordered environment free from arbitrariness and uncontrolled discretion. See Cotterrell (1993: 175).

4. See Postema (1986: 306–7).
5. Locke (1894) describes the modest role of the philosopher engaged 'in clearing the ground a little and removing some of the rubbish that lies in the way to knowledge' in 'The Epistle to the Reader' which prefaces his *Essay Concerning Human Understanding*.
6. Toulmin (1961: 196).
7. See Raz (1994: 62) on Rawls' failure to define a democratic society. See also Rorty (1994) for the view that democracy does not need a philosophical justification. On the democratic revolution see Beetham (1991: 87). It is the requirement of mass legitimation which makes the decisive point of difference from the traditional order in which the right to express consent was located in the privileged or propertied sections of society. 'The criteria of public good [is] to be found not in some special wisdom, revelation or expert knowledge but in what the people, freely organised determines it to be, either directly or through their representatives.'
8. 'It was only with the Benthamite principle of utility . . . accompanied by the introduction of party reform that modernity began to make itself felt. That at last the relics of the idea of fundamental law gave way before the realisation that there was nothing to hinder the possessors of power from using it to promote their own interests and that how to do so successfully is the art of politics' Gough (1955: 191). See also Postema (1986: 3–4) on the conditions in which classical common law theory emerged.
9. Fisher (1936: vi).
10. Dicey, quoted in Cotterrell (1989: 117).
11 Kelley (1991)
12. For a warning to beware of nostalgia, that contemporary problems require new institutions and new relationships, see Griffith (1979: 1–21): 'The particular set of relationships between the legislature, the executive and the judiciary which happened to emerge in the 17th century and which suited the conditions of the 18th and early 19th centuries do not represent some ideal balance.' Against this it may be argued that the central forms, standing in certain relationships to each other, are necessary features of every legitimate democratic polity. Today it is clear that additional and quite other forms are badly needed to undertake the tasks for which the central forms are ill-suited. It is as mistaken to think that the central forms can, without such supplementation, evolve and develop to meet new challenges and changing conditions without suffering a loss of legitimacy, as it is that other institutions could be devised to supplant the central forms.
13. The rise of legal positivism accompanied the political securing of the well ordered bourgeois state: Norrie (1993: 3).
14. Kelsen (1973: 19); Hart (1994: 91–9). On the appropriateness of positivism for both monarchical and democratic times see Hall (1949).
15. Fuller (1964: ch. IV).
16. On legitimacy see Taylor (1985); Beetham (1991); Habermas (1973); Barker (1990); Schaar (1981). For the view that the State maintains its legitimacy by

using social services to maintain the marginal Groups in Society see O'Connor (1973: 70).

17. Nor is economic success to be taken as an index of legitimacy: cf. Gray (1996: 44). This is a criterion by which governments are to be judged, not polities. See also Gellner (1964: 33).
18. Although Charles II was recognized as the legitimate monarch by the Convention Parliament in 1668 even 'without the ceremony or solemnity of a proclamation', the words of the Bill of Rights suggest that if his successor James II had lost his title by a constructive act of abdication, he had lost all legitimate claims to govern by his failure to respect 'ancient rights and liberties'.
19. Though I speak here of the legitimacy of the State, the condition is also the character of a polity as a whole in which there is a proper interrelation of various forms; each of the forms has legitimacy insofar as it occupies its rightful place within the overall polity. There is virtue in Lipset's distinction between legitimacy and effectiveness (1958: 86). A polity can be legitimate; it is hardly appropriate to talk of its effectiveness. Effectiveness is a criterion for a form such as a government; an ineffective government can be removed. Judgments about a government's failure to deliver the goods, to fulfil certain functions, or to meet demands and achieve targets are not judgments about its legitimacy. A State lacks legitimacy if the government depends on its *de facto* power, its superior knowledge and expertise, rather than norms which confer powers.
20. Nagel's views are interesting: 'The pure ideal of political legitimacy is that the use of state power should be capable of being authorised by each citizen' (1991: 9). This calls for unanimous agreement, for 'if there are citizens who can legitimately object to the way state power is used against them or in their name, the state is not legitimate . . . (T)he search for legitimacy is a search for unanimity . . . not about everything but about the controlling framework within which the more controversial decisions are made.' (1991: 33). That unanimity must be found in the recognition of the suitability of the central forms and of the appropriate relationships between them. The member of Society is described here as being subject to the general rules. The citizen's allegiance to the State and moral obligation to obey those rules depends on the legitimacy of the State. See Martin (1993: 185–217) on allegiance. In a non-democratic polity additional or other grounds—such as an oath of allegiance, or considerations of the public good—would be required to support a moral duty.
21. Our obligation to obey the law stems from, *inter alia,* our belief in the unchallengeable propriety of the procedures by which decisions are made, not from our participation in voting Practices which leads others to believe that we will accept the outcome: cf. Singer (1973: 52).
22. Taylor maintains that legitimacy depends upon the existence of a 'common form of life' and that the neutral State undermines the shared sense of the common good which is required if citizens are to accept the sacrifices demanded by the welfare state. Citizens can recognize those demands as legitimate only where there is a common form of life. Given that welfare

policies are contestable, that the demands they entail are not constant, that the extent of the sacrifices we are required to make—and the benefits we may receive—depends upon the government of the day and the urgency of other calls on resources, we cannot talk of a general perception of legitimacy but only of the legitimacy of each separate demand, which we accept because each demand has been democratically agreed. See Kymlicka (1990: 224).

23. See Fuller (1971: 96) who reflects on the complexity of modern constitutions and 'their tragic dependence on the integrity, judgment and insight of those who must interpret and administer them'.
24. For an account of the criteria by which the legitimacy of enforcement of standard-maintenance rules can be appraised see Baldwin (1995). The legitimacy of the Activity is to be judged by the degree to which the actors conform to their legislative mandate, are accountable, respect due process, make use of expertise, and prove efficient.
25. Proper words in their proper places was honest John Dryden's prescription for good prose. The feeling of appropriateness of institutions fulfilling their proper functions within the polity must mean that operating in concert they are seen to conduce to the freedom and security of the individual. In a democracy the Platonic notion of justice may be adapted to apply to institutions rather than individuals. The idea that there is an institutional logic of democratic legitimacy requires no doubt more secure foundations than I have given here. For the view that 'there is no reason why the liberal project of devising a *modus vivendi* for people who hold to incommensurably different conceptions and values should everywhere be best achieved by the adoption of liberal institutions' see Gray (1996: vii); this position is elaborated in Gray (1995).
26. Rawls' just constitution, to be adopted after the parties to the original position have adopted the principles of justice, is described as 'a system for the constitutional powers of government and the basic rights of citizens': Rawls (1971: 196). The powers of government are conferred by the ULP, not the constitutional act or a blueprint of justice. Rawls' non-institutional approach to the political arrangements of a democratic polity leads directly to two dangerous principles: (a) the entrenchment of individual rights, and (b) the principle of equal participation—all citizens have an equal right to take part in and determine the laws (p. 221). See *post*, Ch. 8. Emphasis on these principles will displace the legal Practices from their legitimate place in the ideal constitution.
27. Any discussion of authority in a democracy must refer to the legitimacy of the Practices by which norms are created, and the nature of the capacity of participants. Attitudes to such Practices are a crucial component. The exercise of charismatic authority is not related to any normative Practice. Authority is accorded to persons, especially those whose views we detest, because of the citizens' confidence in the rationality of the Practice. The authority of a determination not reached under conditions of procedural justice is slight. Cf. Winch (1967: 105–6) for the view, later disowned, that authority is accorded by those who believe that what is ordered is the right thing to do.

See also Freidrich (1958: 28–48) for whom authority depends upon a capacity which is not defined in terms of a Practice.

28. See Martin (1993: 172): 'The intellectual challenge of attempting to justify political practices and institutions typically arises in view of the fact that these things characterised as they are, have a logic of their own, a systematic interplay which must be captured and taken into account.' Yet Martin's account of democratic institutions describes principles rather than forms: universal franchise, contested voting, and majority rule (1993: 172). We need to look at institutional forms: the electoral Practice and the legislative Practice. Identifying the forms allows us to see the structure of the constitution. The constitution consists of interrelated forms with their inhering ideas, rather than local institutions which operate under principles.
29. Gellner (1994: 5) defines civil society as 'the set of diverse non-governmental institutions which is strong enough to counterbalance the state, and while not preventing the state from fulfilling its role of keeper of the peace and arbitrator among major interests, can nevertheless prevent it from dominating and atomising the rest of society'. Civil Society is a single institutional form which must be distinguished from the other forms of social life and from the legal and legislative Practices which are the countervailing forms to the State. Gellner confuses the form—Society—for the institutions which make its appearance possible. Civil Society is not active; it is not a form to be reckoned with. The forms upon which it depends—creating the conditions for its recognition—are active. Civil Society is a legal construct, rather than a sociological fact. See Gray (1996: 314–20) for a civil society which is equated with the polity.
30. On the extra-legal regimes of social life see Ch. 5, above. Jurgen Habermas refers to the 'life world', the realm of spontaneous interaction and value formation in social life; see Cotterrell (1995: 303). Sampford (1989: 223) sketches in a non-systematic theory of society. He provides a description not of Society but of social life, and goes on to discuss the unsystematic nature of law, saying that it is appropriate for the unsystematic society he has depicted. While we certainly need to stress the unsystematic nature of law it should be noted that the language of law is not the language of social life. Law has no place in the social milieu except insofar as, within the extra-legal regimes, regulation is introduced and legally recognized IE are created.
31. The atomic individuals of civil Society are generated by the methodological individualism of the law. They are as out of place in social life as are collectives in the law. Much of the debate in political philosophy about the individual stems from the feeling that atomic individual of liberal thought has no social life. On that debate see Lukes (1970: 76–114).
32. The language of the law is not the language of a fraternity seeking a better world. Cf. Dworkin (1986: 413) for whom law aims 'to lay principles over practice to show the best route to a better future, keeping the right faith with the past. It is . . . a fraternal attitude, an expression of how we are united in community, though divided in project, interest and conviction.' Nagel (1991: 3) talks of the familiar problem of reconciling the standpoint of the collective with the standpoint of the individual: 'My claim is that the problem of

designing institutions that do justice to the equal importance of all persons without making unacceptable demands on individuals has not been solved' (p. 5). However, the identification of what is unacceptable is always a matter for democratic agreement; it is not a discoverable property.

33. Members of civil Society are defined simply as individuals subject to the law In the eyes of the law members are autonomous and free. They possess freedoms but do not have a general right to freedom. See Clark (1978) for reference to 'disputes in philosophy as to whether there should be an area of life in which one has an inherent right to freedom'.
34. The democratic revolution transformed political allegiance; the subject who had sworn personal allegiance to a sovereign is now regarded as owing duties to the impersonal State; see Skinner (1989: 123).
35. This appears to conflict with my assertion that membership is a matter for the executive (see *post*, Ch. 8). Of course the conferral of powers on judges to decide such matters may well be a good public relations exercise in the international scene where fundamental human rights are regarded very highly. 'It is not a fundamental human right of an alien to enter Canada. It is a privilege. It is a matter of domestic policy' *per* McKenzie King, *Re Hanna* (1937) 21 WWR (NS) 400.
36. Communitarians mistakenly suppose that Group or Community values can be ascribed to Society. A democratic Society is no sort of community; see *post*, Ch. 9. Disillusionment with the emptiness in secular Societies is widespread; see Kepel (1994). However, the characterless civil Society needs to be highlighted to emphasize the need for involvement in, and reliance upon, other associational forms. There must be an understanding that our identities come, not from the polity, but from the forms within social life; forms which do not aspire to govern our public lives. Civil Society depends on the sharpest separation between the public and the private. The Islamic approach is to turn Society into a private form; the American dream is to seek one's identity in the public form.
37. The atomicity of liberalism; see Taylor (1985: 187-210); Gauthier (1992: 151–64).
38. Private life consists of relationships and conditions which are not subject to legal articulation. The private life of citizens is a correlative of the powerless State. The priority of the personal, of a private life, may be said to be recognized by the law. Unless the norms of law have been created to govern or limit the forms of private life, those forms remain secret, confidential, private; neither the State nor anyone else has authority to intervene in those structures. We need to stress the confidentiality upon which Organizations, families, and other associational forms depend. Any justified intrusion into private life and activity must be agreed upon in the ULP. The confidentiality of private life, in all its many forms, must be contrasted with the openness and publicity of the law.
39. The legitimacy of the State does not depend upon its creating favourable economic conditions, providing benefits, or redistributing goods. The State ceases to be seen as an imposition only when it is conceived of as an initially powerless Organization upon which all its powers were conferred; its

legitimacy is established by its conformity to the rule of law. There is no aboriginal duty on the State to provide anything. Although welfare provision is now generally regarded as a fundamental duty of the State, the existence and extent of that duty remain politically controversial. It is not a defining function of the state or government. It is no doubt cold comfort for the needy that from the legal point of view 'everyone matters as much as everyone else' (Nagel 1991: 64); the needs of individuals are not a matter of legal concern. Legal equality is very different from Christian and other moral ideas of equality of persons. The welfare approach is, like the Christian approach, a Group valuation. The legal point of view does not embrace such Group valuations; the courts are concerned with guaranteeing the vested interests of legal persons, not with meeting the needs of the indigent.

40. The assumption that the principle of equality before the law justifies welfare and egalitarian policies has an analogue in the assumption that the principles inherent in market transactions validate right-wing policies. For a demonstration that there is no connection between the economics of the market-place and right-wing politics see Brittan (1995). The market is the economy of free men, provides the foundations for the civil Society, and generates the individualism of modern democracies; however, given the impact of social problems and the urgency of needs, social and economic policies clearly cannot be deduced from market principles alone. Importantly, the law embodies neither a particular economic theory or an egalitarian philosophy.

41. While emphasizing the pluralism of contemporary societies, Rawls (1987: 4) asserts the existence of a common culture consisting of principles accepted by all as valid. See also Raz (1994: 64). For institutional theory the wholly imaginary construct of the common culture must be replaced by something much more precise, i.e. the armature of the Group which I have called the legitimate opposition. See *post*, p. 280.

42. On efforts to construct cultural entities see Anderson (1991); Hobsbawm (1990); Deletant and Hanak (eds.) (1988). Some right-wing politicians lay great store by a cultural or political homogeneity which they equate with ethnic homogeneity. The idea of the English character must be set against the condescension of English historians to the Welsh, Scots, and Irish, who are also members of the Civil Society in the UK; see Beresford (1993: 215–51). We may question John Gray's assertion that 'in a democratic age civil society must rest on common membership of a national culture' (1995b). Although injustice has historically generated a consciousness of the cultural or religious identity of the oppressed, it does not follow that the just polity depends on such identity. Against the disturbing disaffection of some minorities within democratic polities we should remind ourselves of the dangers of a conception of Society which promotes policies of *Blut und Boden*. See also Gellner (1994: 106) for the view that the individualist or modular character of human identity makes nationalism, the political embodiment of cultural identity,

unavoidable. 'The modularity of man . . . has two principle corollaries; it makes possible Civil Society, the existence of countervailing and plural political associations and economic institutions . . .; and it also makes mandatory the strength of ethnic identity arising from the fact that man is no longer tied to a specific social niche, but is instead linked to a culturally defined pool.' The law treats the individual as an impersonal entity, and must do so, yet it does not follow that the citizen seeks his identity in nationalism. We are not born and socialized as legal persons; we must find our social niche in the innumerable forms of life which structure our private activities and concerns .

43. As Isaiah Berlin has often pointed out, equality is merely one value competing with others for the allegiance of individuals.
44. The subtlest of all foundationalisms is promulgated by writers who prize personal autonomy, value pluralism and equality, and assert their primary political importance in democracies. They must be seen as liberal values—the values of a Group; it is imperative in a democracy that Groups who do not place primacy on these values should also be respected.
45. See Chambliss and Seidman (1982) on the perpetual conflict in society and the importance of the dominant elites. See also Alasdair Maclntyre (1985: 53) for the view that 'modern politics is civil war carried on by other means'. For an eloquent account of the cultural diversity of modern societies see Gray (1995: 153).
46. 'Almost all the opinions we have are taken by authority and upon credit': Montaigne. The institutional dimensions of social life cannot be accommodated by individualistic philosophers. Cf. Elster (1990) who is opposed to all structural and functional explanations of social institutions and historical change. Institutions operate and change only through individual desires beliefs and actions. Yet, paradoxically, it is individualism rampant which provides the axioms upon which we may construct the ideal constitution made up of irreducible institutional forms operating with ideas which are not individually generated or determined. Our concept of legal justice is institutional in origin: the result of experience of many, not the insight of one or two individuals .
47. On the difficulties accompanying epistemic individualism—the idea that we should doubt anything except what we have established for ourselves: see Coady (1992).
48. Rawls pays attention to the differences between individuals, asserting that the 'Plurality of distinct persons with separate systems of ends is an essential feature of modern societies': Rawls (1971: 29). For a different emphasis on the dissensus see Raz (1994: 170–91). Multiculturalism 'recognises that cultural groups are not susceptible to reductive analysis in terms of individual actions': ibid. 178.
49. Group consciousness is both heightened and weakened in the modern world. Due to new technology, media, communications networks, etc., Groups can more readily communicate, criticize, and act. However, any heightening of consciousness may be offset by greater awareness of alternative sources of commitment.

50. For an attack on the pluralist metaphysic see Barry (1965: Chs. 14 and 15).
51. Sampford's description of the social *mêlée* depicts the collision of different languages and frameworks of action: as though football is being played under different codes in one game. Social peace and stability result from frustrated and inconclusive conflict between groups (1989: 205–10). In looking at the conflict from the point of view of the constitution we should con centrate on conflicts over the existing social rules: normative and legislative conflicts upon which Adam Smith's 'Impartial Spectator' can offer no opinion. This is a focused dissensus, part of the process of legislation.
52. Activists who use terror, violence, or coercive threats to attain their ends include animal-rights extremists, Muslim fundamentalists, the anti-abortion lobby in the USA, and activists who would stifle discussion on euthanasia.
53. The tolerance is of mutually incompatible, wholly antagonistic views. Compromises may result in the weakening of a Group which must accept the painful circumstances of being out of date, wrong, or derided as inferior. Thus, as Nagel (1991) points out, legal recognition of homosexual marriage would entail the passing away of the current type of marriage whose exclusive heterosexuality is part of its essence. Groups are commonly linguistic and pose formidable problems; see Kymlicka (1990: 231).
54. If, as Critical Legal Studies claim, law is an oppressive mechanism whereby holders of power legitimate their domination—law being an expression, not of the common good, but of elites defined by race, gender, or class prestige—they should be reminded of its concern for procedural justice and individual rights. See Thompson (1975: ch. 10). The law is blind to Group membership.
55. Respect for Groups is to be embedded in electoral Practices. See Barker (1990: 141); voting is only meaningful if the electoral system appears to give due weight to most significant parties.
56. '[T]he values of community are often postulated *ex cathedra* by judicial elites or legal philosophers. The link between the idea of community and mechanisms for democratic expression of the interests, values and judgments of the regulated population seems often obscure or even non-existent': Cotterrell (1995: 321). For a contemporary view of communitarian values see Etzione (1995). We can agree that such values are shared by the members of a Group, but must insist that the community which they structure is imaginary.
57. *Officials* are defined as members of the State with power over citizens; *officers* have power over members of the State.
58. Cf. Miliband (1969), who includes both legislature and the judiciary in the State. Legitimacy is compromised if either is regarded as part of the State, subject to the executive control of govermnent.
59. The historical antecedents of a long established State apparatus and the nature of constitutional institutions contribute to the view of the State, not as empowered by the ULP, but as having an independent existence and exercising powers and acquiring more power as time goes by. Etatism—a survival of the medieval notion of governance—may be defined as a failure to recognize the fundamental transformation of the State. On this view, the State in modern times has not been transformed, but it is merely subject to greater democratic controls. The transformation is from the State as a reference to the

governmental status of the secular Prince, to the State as an impersonal distinct institutional form. See Skinner (1989: 91).

60. The powerless State is essentially a legal conception. It is interesting that writers stress the abstractness of the State and that Kelsen deprives the State as a juristic entity of all substance (1973: 188–9).
61. Established in pre-democratic conditions as the inherent powers of Princes; what Bacon called their 'garlands of prerogative powers' were not conferred, but arose from the necessities of government. Today such anomalous powers have been reconferred and repealed by countless statutes. Although the law today envisages the powerless State, it must still acknowledge the powers and immunities previously recognized at common law and which have survived.
62. For the view that the law and the constitution are maintained by the ULP, see *post*, Ch. 8, p. 329. Contrast the conveyancers' approach to the constitution, which assumes that the polity derives its legitimacy from some creative act: an initial treaty, contract, or plebiscite, in the same way that a contract or title is created by a legal act. See Ridley (1988): 'In constitutional theory a governmental order derives its legitimacy from the constituant act which establishes it.'
63. The justification for State acts is not that the government achieves what we think is right, whether economic targets or the protection of internationally recognized human rights. That is foundationalist. The justification must be that the State exercises its powers in the right way; that it shows respect for individuals and Groups. This condition cannot be established merely because the State relies upon good reasons and inherent powers; it can only be achieved if the State can prove the precise conferment or valid creation of power.
64. 'Authority represents a two way process; a claim to be obeyed and a recognition that this claim is morally right' Finer (1970: 30–1). Citizens of a legitimate state will believe in the moral right to issue commands and accept a moral duty to obey them.
65. Tensions exist in the US where the executive is free from legislative control. It has been suggested that in recent years there has been a *coup d'état:* a usurpation of power by the legislature, especially over foreign policy, resulting in an enfeebled government. See Draper (1990).
66. On recommendations for a neutral State, or for an interventionist or perfectionist State, see Kymlicka (1990: 218). These can never be constitutional specifications as to the character of the ideal State in a polity; they are but contemporary instances of the ancient genre known as advice to princes. Furthermore, the economic constraints upon Governments are less determined than is often suggested; we need the reminder that governmental expenditure on welfare benefits is not a matter for economic theory but for democratic choice.
67. See Nozick (1974: ch. 7) for the view that the minimal state is the most extensive that can be justified. The new right project of restoring the minimalist state has been condemned by Gray as an exercise in anachronism and illusion. However, Gray's insistence (1996: 44) that the legitimacy of the State

depends upon its securing concrete results for the citizens confuses government—which must produce results or perish—either with the State, which is the organizational tool of government, or with the polity.

68. Even Locke's view that the State is instituted for the protection of rights can become a foundationalist charter. The function of the State is assumed to be the protection of rights: something which is inconsistent with the principles of the democratic revolution. Members of Society, in the ULP, decide what the State can and cannot do; what its functions and purposes are. In any case the protection of rights is for the legal Practices, not for the State. The State will be given powers in order to maintain the conditions in which a civil Society can survive. In a democracy the State's existence is justified to the members of Society, not by reference to the rights of citizens, but by the enacted power-conferring laws of the ULP.
69. The absence of a written constitution gives the British constitutional practice 'a revolutionary quality, and enables us to entertain the hope of bringing about social transformations without the agony and prolonged crises experienced by less fortunate nations': Bevan (1961: 100). In the USA the New Deal entailed constitutional changes which rejigged the legal Practices; see Ackerman (1984). Note the observation of Stone (1995: 225): 'In France and Germany, at least, the making of public policy and the development of constitutional law are often one and the same thing.' Policy should not be argued in terms of the constitution; nor should constitutional developments be shaped in the light of policy considerations.
70. Cf. Riker (1982) who emphasizes the fact that governments are divested by the people. The people vote in an election precisely to remove a government or to affirm it in office; they have ultimate control. Voters exercise a veto which can restrain official tyranny, and are thus guardians of liberty. Voting helps to reduce coercion by increasing the cost to legislators of their removal from office. Liberty is maximized when coercion is minimized.
71. In the Netherlands the norm is of coalition government; its authority stems from agreement, not from the people directly: Kate and Koppen (1995: 373–4).
72. During the Fourth Republic France was notorious for the many changes of government. De Gaulle responded to this by devising means to secure a stable and stronger executive, increasing the powers of the President.
73. Polarization was nowhere more evident than in Fascist theory and practice. For the Fascists the purpose of the State was to maximize the coherence and unity of forces in social life. Significantly: 'to the Fascists, as to Ihering, powerlessness is the state's mortal sin for which there is no absolution' Jones (1956: 282). The State is above the law.
74. Mr Justice Brandies in *Whitney* v. *California* (1927) 274 US 357. In Rawls' view the ideal legislative process involves attaining certain objectives: 'In the ideal procedure the decision reached is not a compromise, a bargain struck between opposing parties trying to advance their ends . . . [it is] an attempt to find the best policy as defined by the principles of justice.' (1971: 357). Upon which Barry comments that if people do not behave in the ideal way, if they

support legislation on the basis of self-interest rather than justice, then all is lost (1973: 137).

75. Lawrence Sterne's *Tristram Shandy* (1967: 420). In the twentieth century in Great Britain the contributions of the three estates were: the Crown gave direction and force; the Aristocracy provided stability; and the Commons ensured that grievances were not overlooked.
76. Democracies need agreed procedures for making reasonable, not the best or right, decisions. We accept the decisions not because they are the best, but because they are the best compromises which can be reached; because they are seen to be decided fairly.
77. 'The State is the supreme law making and enforcing agency for society': Beetham (1991: 121). The prevailing view is that Parliament's function is not to legislate; that is for the government. In institutional terms we must distinguish between the government, which initiates legislation, the State, which is the instrument of government, and the legislative Practice, which alone can be said to create laws. Parliament is not part of the State. Federal structures encourage the idea that legislation is essentially a function of government. It is to be hoped that acceptance and endorsement of the law provide legitimacy which cannot be derived from the processes of its making. It is important to keep legislative functions separate from the executive. See Poulantzas (1978: 220) on the dangers which arise when it becomes difficult to distinguish executive acts from legislative acts. The blurring of function is reflected in the appearance of 'ill-defined wrong-doing', as opposed to clearly specified offences. 'For the punishable offence laid down by a universal and general Act of Parliament we are moving towards the suspicious circumstance whose contours are administratively defined by supple, malleable and particularist regulation'.
78. 'Eighteenth century jurists portrayed monarchs and enlightened despots as absolute law givers and judges as their personal spokesmen': Lenhoff (1949: 312)
79. The reality of the executive's supremacy over the legislature may appear to transcend Parliament's theoretical sovereignty, giving rise to the spectre of an 'elective dictatorship'. See Griffith and Ryle (1989: 6) for the views of statesmen that Parliament is but a talking-shop. Unsurprisingly, the influence wielded by Eurosceptic backbenchers on government action—clear proof of the sovereignty of Parliament—has been criticized often with suggestions that the pressure is improper.
80. The Case of Proclamations (1611) 12 Co Rep 63.
81. Legislation may be effective even though it is not incorporated or capable of incorporation. The assumption that enactments are laws by virtue of their enactment, is widespread. Failure to distinguish between social rules and those of the LSS, both of which are called laws, can result in a damaging legalism.
82. Sovereignty should never be ascribed to the State: but it often is. Ivor Jennings (1933: 70) ascribed this view to Dicey. Legal sovereignty can be ascribed only to the Practice of legislation. In British constitutional theory sovereignty is an attribute of 'the Queen in Parliament'; this is obscure, but correct, for this is

the ULP. It is an ascription to a Practice which was transformed in the democratic revolution. The sovereignty of the ULP is clearly not Blackstone's 'absolute despotic power which must in all governments reside somewhere' for, by definition, the power of the ULP is not despotic; the procedures are designed precisely to avoid the arbitrary.

83. The Diceyan conception of the sovereign has been attacked often enough; see Craig (1990b). Locke makes the all-important link between sovereignty and democratic consent. The legislative is the 'supreme power of the common wealth', without which 'the law could not have that which is absolutely necessary to its being a law, the consent of society, over whom nobody can have power to make law but by their own consent and by authority received from them' Locke (1956) ch. XI, 'Of the Nature of Legislative Power'.

84. It is important that the ULP is perceived by the population as speaking for Society, that all significant Groups are represented, and that it is not a majoritarian monster. Among the peoples of a territory subject to general rules enforced by the State, where such a perception is wholly lacking federal structures may be a solution. The ULP is the central institution of the unitary polity. The acceptance of the authority of the ULP, the analogue of the habit of obedience, must characterize Groups rather than individuals, in the sense that no significant Group can claim to be wholly ignored.

85. Commentators have noted the loss of political sovereignty of the UK Parliament. A vast range of matters has slipped from its grasp, so that Parliament is now just one piece in the jigsaw of institutions which control our affairs. The failure of parliamentarians to resist these movements is notable.

86. See Crick (1964: 59–63) on the sovereignty of the people. For an assertion of such sovereignty see Ridley (1988). Cf. Karl Popper: 'A theory of democracy is emphatically not a theory of the rule of the people, but rather the rule of law that postulates the bloodless dismissal of the government by popular vote' (*Economist* 21 Aug. 1988, 25). In opposition to Locke, who said 'the people retain supreme power to remove or alter the legislature', Blackstone declared that this would undermine 'all positive laws whatsoever before enacted'. John Austin regarded the electorate as sovereign, Parliament holding its powers on trust; and Dicey had no doubt that political sovereignty rested with the people. However, to deny that sovereignty can be ascribed to the people is not to deny that the authority of the ULP stems from the people. 'We the people' is the rhetoric of revolution; see Beetham (1991: 128). The 1789 version of the French *Declaration of the Rights of Man* which says that the 'Nation is essentially the source of all sovereignty' is to be preferred to the 1793 version which asserts that 'sovereignty resides in the people'. Note Art. 21 of the *Declaration of Human Rights:* 'The will of the people shall be the basis of the authority of government.' In institutional terms 'the people' would be the members of Society. Society as an associational form is never a sovereign body capable of any expression of will. As an associational form it is more like a neutral class of legal persons: those subject to government. Influence on government is exerted not by Society but by other associational forms, Organizations and Groups.

87. The ULP, accepted as a public forum giving respect to all significant Groups,

will fail to satisfy the demands of social choice theorists. For voting systems which satisfy the requirements of procedural fairness necessary for democratic choice will produce arbitrary social choices, in the sense that the outcomes cannot be directly related to the preferences of members of Society: Riker (1982). So no claim can be made that the ULP produces the best, most favoured outcomes; only that *for a particular Society* it is the outcome which could not have been better deliberated. The acceptability of its products depends not on their correctness but, in part, on their contingency: on the fact that they can always be repealed, as can any law-making by the courts.

88. It is never enough to demonstrate the goodness of a law, decision, or measure. For a critique of the politics of the common good see Kymlicka (1990: 206–8).
89. See Raz (1979: ch. 11). Reactions to Dicey's account of the Rule of Law have been varied. The rule of law is often regarded as a concept of open-texture lending itself to a wide range of interpretations; de Smith and Brazier (1989: 18).
90. Enforcement Activity is one of the institutional forms transformed by the democratic revolution. In the democratic polity, since the Activity services the legal Practices for the whole of Society, it must now be governed by the precepts of legality; it becomes transformed into a new form of life in which any punitive capability is absent. The transformation is evidenced by the growth of State enforcement agencies, whose objective is to apprehend criminals rather than to influence behaviour. See Gellner (1983: 4): 'The state exists where specialised order enforcing agencies, such as police forces and courts, have separated out from the rest of social life. They are the State.'
91. Dworkin (1986: 95) describes pragmatism as the belief 'that judges do and should make whatever decisions seem to them best for the community's future'. The pragmatism advocated by Posner (1995), which allows freedom in adjudication, must be distinguished from the so-called pragmatism which would employ this freedom for the implementation of a political agenda.
92. Shapiro's suggestion that the legitimacy of the courts is always in doubt involves seeing the courts as dispute-resolving agencies and ignores the judges' commitment to legal justice. See Cotterrell (1992: 210).
93. Durkheim's organic solidarity is based on the requirements of the exchange society- society's moral code stems from the needs of the market-place: Giddens (1978).
94. That human beings are solely motivated by self-interest is a foundationalist assumption; the legal person, or the member of Society, is not a self-interested individual. Barry (1989) attacks the account of justice which draws on the economists' analysis of bargaining and assumes the universality of self-interest.
95. See Paton and Derham (1972: 110).
96. See *ante*, p. 164 on the civil rights protected in the IE Practice.
97. The powerless State is a necessary legal axiom for the derivation of all our basic Public law rights; see *post*, on the CS Practice. After the democratic revolution the centralizing State, despite its increased potential to control due to improved methods and technological advances, paradoxically becomes powerless in the eyes of the law. Though the State's claim to sovereignty

includes the possession of a monopoly of punishment, it can in fact no longer punish; that is the job of the legal Practice. Expressions such as 'the sovereign state' conceal such a transformation.

98. The view that the common law courts played a central role in secularizing the Crown, in refusing to accept the claims that central authority was sacred, should be qualified by the more important consideration that their recognition of the sovereignty of Parliament was part of the democratic revolution.

99. Cotterrell (1995: 278) on sites of adjudication outside formal court structures; some of these regulatory agencies are commonly regarded as being within the legal system. See also Aubert (1983: 134–41).

100. Courts are not departments of State; cf. Bankowski and Mungham (1976: 114) and Dworkin (1986: 11). Since in pre-democratic times the administration of justice was one of the prerogatives of the Crown it was natural that judges were perceived to be part of the governmental system: see Maitland (1908: 530–9). In medieval England there was no real separation of law and politics; the judges were part of the governmental system itself. C. 20 writers have not moved far from this perception: the courts are variously described as: the legal arm of government, a branch of the administration, departments of government, and 'indisputably agencies of State power'. We must not be misled by the formal titles, descriptions, origins, and dependence in asserting the autonomy of the legal Practices. Autonomy is established to the extent to which governmental agencies become concerned with justice. The *Conseil d'Etat,* which begins life as a government department, acquires autonomy, and the title of its head, *Commisaire du Gouvernement,* becomes a misnomer.

101. A Bill or Charter of Rights is almost by definition a legal document.

102. The wider meaning of the constitution 'comprehends the normative attitudes held by the people towards government, their conception of how power ought to be regulated, of what it is proper to do and not to do': Bogdanor (ed.) (1988: 3). I suggest that the constitution is to be supported by something far less diffuse than a sentient population; constitutional matters require the critical attentions of an intelligent, informed, and committed Group: the legitimate opposition. Habermas talks of the emergence of the opposition in Germany in terms *of* 'constitutional patriotism', an important development which he regards as a profoundly heartening sign for Germany. It is noteable that in the late C. 17 'patriot' referred to one who had the courage to take a principled stand against his government: see Dietz (1989: 183).

103. In constitutional matters it is supremely important to recognize institutional forms rather than principles; in place of a common, or political culture we must put an active Group. Rawls suggested (1971: Part III) that the principles of justice required to be maintained in the moral consciousness of citizens. In his later work (1993) he requires 'overlapping consensuses' from different political perspectives. Something far more influential and defined is required: a Group committed to the constitutional armature, with a

significant membership and considerable influence; an opposition which is understood to be beneficial.

104. It is important to emphasize that it is the Group of a particular polity; that its members, as members of a specific Society, uphold specific local values; this is no universalist democracy league.

105. To some degree the Group transcends the dissensus. Its values are truly democratic. Of course most Group members will also be members of other Groups in the political arena; this may cause tensions within individual minds. We ought not to expect the values of the legitimate opposition to coincide with those of partisan political Groups of which we are also members.

106. Federalism aims to create 'a system of government to encompass different and conflicting political traditions and to devise a separation of powers between a central government and a series of religious or ethnic groups whose self interest and identity alike preclude them from finding satisfaction under a centralised system': George Boyce, in Bosco (1991: 118). A federation, defined as an association of polities each with its own institutional forms but subject to federal controls, provides no clear focus for the formation of a Group which is identifiable as a legitimate opposition. The objections, challenges, and claims will not be about locally generated values and institutions but legalistic questions about breaches of federal rules. The suggestion that in a federal structure constitutional objections stem from a common culture is even less convincing than the suggestion of a common culture in a unitary State.

107. It may be difficult to know what the constitution says. 'The potential of a written constitution to serve as a source of fragmentation and disintegration is nowhere more savagely illustrated than in the carnage of the US Civil War. For ultimately that fratricidal struggle was over two views of one constitutional document': Murphy (1993: 9).

108. The dangers of populism are to be avoided, not by the elevation of a set of values which all are deemed to share, but by the activity and influence of a Group—the loyal opposition—committed to democratic legitimacy. We may regard the Group as an elite with special knowledge of the complex armature of democratic values; a Group which speaks the constitutional language of that Society.

109. See Hampshire (1989). The communitarian association to which some Marxist adherents of Critical Legal Studies look forward lacks credibility. Accounts of it suffer from lack of information about the institutional structures, and the form of association which would emerge with the withering away of the state. See Price (1989: 271-301). It is, says Price, puzzling that a movement claiming to identify with the interests of the vulnerable should find individual rights and the rule of law objectionable.

8
Public Law

Although public law has ancient roots, its emergence as a distinct and extensive body of law is a relatively recent phemomenon. Of the three domains of law it has proved the most resistant to theory.[1] The study of public law is notable less for the controversies it has generated than for the imperfect understanding of the nature of law which is exhibited, and the inflated claims and false expectations which have been the result. One need not search far to discover that the investigation of a subject-matter of such central importance, and which cries out for a clear grasp of the nature of law, has been hampered by the commentators' reliance upon common-sense conceptions of law which are little more than the deliverances of folk jurisprudence. The intuition, and indeed the celebration, of the importance of the rule of law has been accompanied by an imperfect understanding of the legal norms which are to rule, and the manner in which that is possible.

The assumption of folk jurisprudence that what is officially promulgated is law, and the rationalists' faith in the virtue of the rule-book, have in the twentieth century both been reinforced by the appearance of many written constitutions which were expected at a stroke to provide the fundamental law for each society. The commonplace that provisions of written constitutions may be nothing more than the empty rhetoric of constitutional legality has not dented this faith. The jurisprudence which identifies the promulgated words of a constitution with the law of that country continues to thrive; for in countries in which written constitutions have been long established they are appealed to as legal instruments, and their success is taken to be evidence of the power of law. Although the formalism of many nineteenth-century accounts of constitutional structures has given way to more realistic descriptions of the normative structures actually in place, there is still only limited understanding of the conceptual network by which the quite distinct legal dimension of the actual norms of constitutional life can be apprehended.

To understand the structures by which governmental power is distributed and controlled, an institutional analysis is required; the norms of public law must, at all times be understood, not as sacred words or documentary formulations, but as operative norms, constantly being recreated, within specific institutional forms. Only an institutional approach will allow us to see exactly where the law fits in to constitutional life; in particular it will enable us to understand the limits of the law and the nature of the courts' authority.

I: THE PUBLIC LAW DOMAIN

In institutional theory the public law domain is focused on the CS Practice: an adjudicatory Practice in which disputes between citizens and State are determined, and the law governing citizen-State relationships is declared.[2] The commitment of its participants to ensuring that the State acts justly towards individual citizens endows this Practice with an unchallengeable, inherent authority to declare the law.

We may regard this institutional form, animated by the principles of legal justice, as the *generating matrix* of the public law of a Society. It generates both its language, particularly the categories of public law rights, and the distinctive norms of public law. The constitutional life of a Society is governed by countless norms of all sorts; clearly not all of them are legal. The legal norms are those which are employed by the courts of justice.

All norms have existence and meaning only in their actual uses within particular forms of life. The norms of the LS of this legal Practice have a distinctive character as they are employed by judges to justify their decisions. In their employment in the quest for legal justice the norms are subtly transformed. They acquire the status of valid legal norms, their validity being dependent upon the fact that, certain conditions and criteria were satisfied in their making.

A foracentric jurisprudence is only desirable if the courts of law, generating the legal norms, are animated by democratic principles. Such a jurisprudence will have much to recommend it once we are alerted to the fact that the courts are the *only institutions* within a democracy in which the principle of the individual worth of every citizen can be fully and consistently realized.

These principles are of crucial importance. A foracentric jurisprudence which defines courts as adjudicative bodies with no need to conform to the principles of legal justice has little to recommend it. For what may be called a *court,* whose declarations are to count as laws, may be merely a general dispute-resolution agency having powers, arrogated or conferred, to determine all sorts of disputes and promiscuously to declare the laws of the land. Though such a court may be said to show concern for the rules, it need not be subject to any constraint in their application.

Being unconstrained by the principles of legal justice, such a court might well acquire a clear legislative capacity. In their celebrated dicta about the substantial power of those authorized to interpret the law, neither Hobbes nor Bishop Hoadly make any reference to such principles of justice.[3] So the power they ascribe to those who interpret the law is of a different type from the power possessed by judges in courts of justice. For in the ideal legal Practice the judges, aware of the constraints implicit in the task of interpreting laws in accordance with the principles of legal justice, can truthfully declare their incapacity to legislate.

The legitimacy of courts in which legal justice is not the animating principle will rest on the public perception of the virtues of individual judges rather than the goodness of the institutional design of the Practice; it will depend on respect for the knowledge, experience, impartiality, and *gravitas* of the judges, rather than on an appreciation of the constant institutional will to secure respect for individuals.

For analytical jurisprudence a foracentric approach is justified by the fact that the rules incorporated by a court of justice, committed to uphold the rights of citizens, will have a different character from all other norms. Legal justice impresses the norms employed in its service with a special stamp. By contrast, there is no reason why the laws declared by a Practice committed to legality rather than to legal justice should differ from other customary or enacted norms. The declared norms would suffer no transformation; they would not be fashioned into that uniform style in which alone legal justice can be done. In a Practice of mere legality the only thing which would mark out legal from other norms would be the fact of their statement by the court; they would be laws only because they had received the imprimatur of judicial approval: an unsatisfactory foundation for our jurisprudential definition of the legal norm.

A foracentric jurisprudence centred upon the legal CS Practice obviously leaves us with a very narrowly delimited public law domain. It will embrace most of what is called administrative law, but exclude a large part of what is regarded as constitutional law. The benefits of thus narrowing the area of the law are many. The cause of democratic legitimacy is served not only by putting law in its proper place and achieving a better understanding of its authority but also, and most importantly, by treating non-legal normative structures with greater respect.[4] Much is to be gained by freeing such non-legal norms from the clutches of legalism, and in making it clear that many norms should ideally be applied and enforced in political forms and contexts in which it would be inappropriate to adopt the methods and style of the law.

A: It is centred on the legal CS Practice

In a foracentric jurisprudence our understanding of the law will depend entirely upon an understanding of the forums—the legal Practices—in which the law is generated. In this section I examine the character and normative anatomy of the CS Practice as an ideal institutional form.

A relatively recent development

The CS Practice—the youngest of the legal Practice—is a product of a well established democratic polity. Its emergence in the present century as a distinct form of life differentiated from the other legal Practices reflects the recent establishment of democracy as an achieved condition of civic life, in which, to however limited an extent, substance is given to claims to provide democratic government. It is in the establishment of political institutions in which democratic ideals are realized, rather than in the patent fact of the increasing power and activity of the State, that we find the conditions for the emergence of the CS Practice.[5] After all, there is no shortage of methods—not calling for the articulation of individual rights—for handling the problems resulting from the intervention of the State in the lives of its subjects. So the emergence of the legal CS Practice must be seen as part of wider democratic developments; as part of the movement to work out, and make real, the rights of citizens in the new democratic polity.[6]

The establishment of substantial conditions of democracy is surprisingly recent. Under the influence of Whig historians it is easy to misread the significance of some landmarks of British constitutional history; for instance, to see in the civil war, or in the Glorious Revolution of 1688, a significance in the march towards the triumph of democracy which they cannot bear. However, we do not have to embark on revisionist history of the seventeenth and eighteenth centuries to bring forward to more recent times the date at which democratic forms are firmly established. The secularization of politics and the political reforms, which were necessary to give any sort of credence to the claims that true democratic foundations had been established, were part of the history of the last century.[7] Not until recent times could the common law doctrine of Parliamentary sovereignty be supported on the basis that Parliament could claim democratic legitimacy. For the enactments of Parliament could not easily have been presented as the authentic expression of democratic consent until the franchise was extended to all but the manifestly incapable, and Parliament's inefficient legislative procedures had been subjected to radical reform.

So it is in the context of these recent institutional developments that we are able to trace the emergence and growth of the new legal Practice in the UK over the past hundred years.[8] It is a fascinating process in which the judges have gradually worked out the distinctive principles of legal justice governing relationships between citizen and State, elaborated the special procedural rules which make its administration possible, and attained a fuller understanding of the nature and extent of the court's authority to control the State.

This Practice was not deliberately instituted. It emerged as a new institutional form by splitting off from the established legal Practices. Only very gradually was the new legal CS Practice differentiated from the criminal and the civil Practices, until it reached a point at which it could colourably be said to have become a discrete form of life. Its origins within, links with, and dependence upon the older Practices underlie Dicey's observation in 1875 that, 'the constitution is the result of the ordinary law of the land'.[9] As he was writing before the clear emergence of the new CS Practice we can see in his work the recognition of an increasingly important area of law which, unlike the domains of criminal and civil law, lacked the clear and cohesive focal point of a legal Practice.

Today a system of judicature in which no distinct set of administrative and constitutional courts have been instituted helps to obscure the nature of the institutional revolution which the common law has witnessed. In the UK we need to recognize, not just a new area of law served by ordinary courts, but the existence of a real, complex, and distinct legal Practice upon which the domain is focused.[10]

Related to other legal Practices

Although the CS Practice is divorced from the other legal Practices, the nature of its connection with them is important. Separate and distinct, it must nevertheless be seen as a Practice exactly co-ordinate with, and dependent upon, the other legal Practices. The importance of this dependence was not lost on Dicey. What the legal CS Practice shares with the other legal Practices, making its courts in Dicey's word 'ordinary', is its individualism: its commitment to the principles of legal justice. It is precisely because the CS Practice is committed to legal justice that it cannot function in isolation from the other Practices. For doing legal justice in public law means that the judges have to depend upon, carry over, and borrow from the articulations which the other Practices provide, and at some points to employ the standards they maintain. Its specialist function does not isolate it from the other legal Practices.

Because it is connected in this way I shall call the ideal legal CS Practice an *embedded* Practice: embedded in the existing law and having its foundations in a view of the world, deriving from an unremitting individualism, which is maintained by the other two Practices. An embedded Practice is thus to be contrasted with a *detached* CS Practice, exemplified by the French *Conseil d'Etat*, the Italian *TARS*, and in many constitutional courts. Detached CS Practices, which are unrelated to and separate from the civil and criminal law, are specialist tribunals: partly in that the body of rules they administer is distinct, and partly in that they may be regarded as part of the State organization. Under the doctrine of the separation of powers it is understood that the adjudicative authority of such a Practice covers executive and administrative questions which are not matters which should be the concern of the judiciary.[11]

However, the fundamental difference between embedded and detached Practices lies in their different animating ideas. The principles employed by the participants applying rules in a detached Practice are those of *legality,* not of legal justice. The 'constant will' of the judges is not to secure respect for persons, but conformity of institutions, officers, and officials to the established rules and standards of good administration. Constitutional and bureaucratic rectitude is the watchword.[12]

By contrast, the animating idea of the embedded Practice is that of legal justice; and the foundations upon which justice can be achieved are to be found in the law maintained by the other Practices.[13] In other words, the individual to be respected by the State—the citizen—is none other than the legal person of the civil law Practice. He or she is a person of substance; an owner and possessor of legal rights. The defining feature of the embedded Practice lies in the court's understanding that it is this legal person—not a mere subject, one of the masses, a statistical unit, or a human being who has suffered ill-usage at the hands of the state—who is to be respected. Thus the virtue of this CS Practice is not that it ensures the State's conformity to the rules, but that it demands respect for the rights of individuals. It is the extreme individualism of the Practice, its commitment to legal justice, which is its defining feature and its crowning glory.

Generates public law rights

The significance of this adoption of the legal person, lock, stock, and barrel, from the civil Practice needs to be spelled out. If the legal person is to be given respect by the State it will become apparent that, in the very special circumstances of citizen-state relationships, special and particular principles of legal justice will need to be applied. The most important consequence of the application of these particular principles of legal justice is not just that the legal CS Practice recognizes the legal person and secures respect for his or her ordinary rights as they are recognized in the civil law Practice, but that *it is committed to the crucially important task of working out a completely new set of public law rights for this well endowed person.* To him who has civil law rights shall also be given public law rights.[14]

Now the set of public law rights generated by the embedded legal CS Practice are of fundamental constitutional importance: they are the rights which, under the rule of law, all citizens will possess against the State. Being deductions from the legal principles of justice, they can be worked out and realized only within an embedded Practice. The significance of this is examined below in the section on public law rights.

II: THE ANATOMY OF THE CS PRACTICE

To understand the normative anatomy of the ideal legal Practice, all its different types of norms must be analysed: those which structure it (its idea and ground rules); those which it creates (the normative products, or NPs); and those which it employs to justify its orders (the LS rules). Noninstitutional jurisprudence, which regards law as being applied by unproblematic courts, treats the law as a system or hierarchy of rules or norms, as a union of primary or secondary rules. As a result it not only fails to discriminate between different types of norms, but ignores some altogether. To give an adequate explication of the concept of law it is important to distinguish between the classes of norms found in the operation of the legal Practice.

A: The idea of the Practice

The fundamental norm of every legal Practice is its idea; its commitment to the doing of legal justice. In the CS Practice the principle of legal justice is simply that *the State must show respect for legal persons.* So the central concern of the Practice is to secure respect for the rights of persons; not necessarily to protect them, but to ensure that the State treats them with proper respect and consideration. It is possible to treat this as an operative norm within the legal field only if we tie it to an institutional form. For this is not merely a free-floating principle, which may or may not influence the behaviour of individual judges; it is an idea which is embodied in a legal Practice.[15]

The fact that it is the State, rather than other legal persons, which must show respect raises particular problems. For the State is, by comparison with other members of Society, patently in a specially favoured position. Not only can it make irresistable demands for obedience by virtue of its *de facto* organizational power, it also has the capacity, given the recognized legislative Practices subject to its direction, to acquire powers enabling it to confer and abridge rights and to impose liabilities and duties. In respect of all these powers, *de facto* or *de jure,* the legal Practice stands firm in its determination that the State must at all times act justly. It will not permit the State to rely upon its brute power, and demands that it must, in the exercise of all its conferred powers, show respect for legal persons.

The idea of this Practice is not to advance legality or to safeguard constitutional principles, but to pursue individual justice. The emphasis is not on rules but on rights. In demanding respect for the individual, judges must of course require the State to respect the legal norms; but this demand for conformity to the legal norms is not a matter of mannerly legality but of justice. As justice is the watchword we need to appreciate that the embedded CS Practice has not emerged in order to maintain a balance between the State and the citizen; its participants are not to be perceived as impartial arbiters giving their expert interpretation of the rules which structure and control the activities of those engaged in the difficult art of government.[16] The embedded CS Practice should be regarded as an intensely partisan institution, wholly dedicated to the cause of individual justice, which in pursuit of that goal plays a vital role in the democratic polity. Thus in the public law domain the image of justice with scales and blindfold, symbolizing impartiality, should be replaced by an image of the guardian of the citizen—of Themis or the Archangel Michael—standing vigilant against the State and prepared to intervene with the sword on behalf of the oppressed.[17]

The CS Practice may be said to be institutionally suspicious of the State. In a democracy every coercive act is open to challenge; the courts are the primary locations for those challenges. There is no room for trust in the legal articulation of citizen-State relationships. Trust, an ingredient of many extra-legal regimes, has no place in this legal regime.[18]

The powerless State

To maintain this partisan stance the participants in the embedded Practice must adopt something in the nature of a legal—wholly unhistorical—axiom: that the State, whatever its *defacto* power, is powerless; that it has originally no authority to interfere in any way with the interests of the citizen. From the legal point of view the actual power of the State, that obvious capability for irresistible coercion possessed by a vast organization, is invisible. Lacking any general original authority, the State must whenever it interferes with a citizen's rights, be able to prove that it has been given the requisite authority.[19] It possesses no inherent power, only that which is conferred. So it is doubtful whether we can ever regard the State as being on the same footing as a citizen. As an Organization, the State even requires to have powers conferred in order to transact business in the market-place.[20]

However, in a dangerous and uncertain world the State must be allowed some inherent powers to deal with emergencies; powers to which no rational arbiters could object. Yet the occasions which call for the exercise of such powers are rare, and the exceptional inherent powers—which have in many polities, for the removal of doubt, been supplanted by similar statutory powers—can be ignored. In times of peace, our starting point must be that the State, in the eyes of the law, has no more primordial substance than a legal person; it is nothing more than a formal peg upon which powers can be hung.

How, in a democracy, can this powerless State justify, as justify it must, to the satisfaction of the judges, any interference with the rights of citizens? *Reasons* alone can never completely justify; although they can explain, excuse, extenuate, or support what has been projected or done, they can never confer any authority on the State. It is never a justification, in the eyes of the law, to demonstrate that action was taken to further some desirable goal or policy. Giving reasons to an aggrieved citizen might be a politic or civil response, but it can scarcely be construed as showing respect for a legal person. The necessary respect is shown only by the State's production of its credentials. In attempting to justify its actions by reasons only the State might be said to be taking its authority for granted, for this would not justify an exercise of its lawful authority, only an exercise of its *de facto* power.

In meeting the challenges which, in a democracy, will be made to all official actions, reasons operate as *political*, but not as legal justifications. They are obviously the all-important staple of political debate. In a heterogeneous Society reasons for State action will never meet with universal approval, no matter how compelling they might appear. In political discourse the authority or power of the State is taken for granted. For instance, when proposals are put forward for the implementation of a new policy, the legislators, aware of practical constraints, proceed on the basis of the can-do State; the task of the executive is to ensure, by means of power-conferring legislation, that the State can lawfully do what is proposed.

Power-conferring norms

The State can only interfere justifiably with a citizen's rights if a well made *norm* confers on it a power to do so. The well made norm is the only reason which the courts can accept; it alone supplies the complete justification which justice demands.

It is a unifying principle of the penal and the CS Practices that harm, or loss of freedom suffered by members of Society—legal persons—can be justified only by reference to a well made norm.[21] Legal norms are always justificatory in purpose. A complete justification can be given only if the justifying norms are of a particular character. I have argued *(ante,* Ch. 4) that the emergence of the idea of just punishment depends upon the gradual evolution of a particular type of penal norm. One of the prime concerns of the institutional theory of law is to examine the character of the legal norms, acts in conformity with which are beyond challenge. It is characteristic of foundationalism (see *post,* Ch. 9) to attempt to justify the coercion of members of Society by offering reasons, or setting out standards and principles, none of which are capable of affording complete justification for particular acts. Foundationalists—notably disinterested in the analysis of norms and norm structures—ignore the importance of ensuring that the norms which confer powers to punish or interfere with citizens' rights must be of a sort which can completely justify.

The distinction between justifying reasons and legal norms provides the basis for explicating the nature of civic authority and the distinction between power and authority. In the legal field civic authority may be understood as legally recognized power which is conferred under properly made norms. Authority is not a character resulting from popular consent; nor does it stem from superior rationality or expert knowledge. It can be recognized only where power—capacity to make norms, or power to command or do certain things—has been conferred under norms of a special type.

Chains of authority[22]

The primary norms which the courts recognize as justifying State interference with citizens' rights are provisions in statutes which have been fully deliberated within the ULP, and which are beyond question well made. Under the doctrine of sovereignty, such enactments of the ULP can confer on the State power to abridge or destroy any individual interests whatsoever, therefore the courts have no authority to protect the rights of citizens against such norms. It is in the ULP that the *reasons* for empowering the State to act have been canvassed and considered. Confronted by a statute, the court cannot question the reasons which prompted its enactment; neither can they review the procedure in the ULP.

However, damage to an individual's interests commonly results from action which is not immediately authorized by an Act of Parliament. Between the policy of the statute and its execution the interposition of officers and officials is necessary. When we question the authority of the particular official who directly affects an individual's rights, we can often trace a *chain of authority* back to the enabling Act: a chain in which power is delegated, decisions are made, and actions under them are authorized.

The importance of these chains of authority must not be underestimated. For in making the various links of these chains the law demands that the State respect the interests of the citizen. Although the law is powerless against an enactment of the sovereign, it is by no means powerless against the norms of any subordinate authority. Courts of law have authority to declare whether such norms are valid; and the manner in which they do this is worthy of note.

The empowering norms in any chain of authority recognized by the courts will all be legal norms, to be declared legally valid by the courts. Both Bentham and Kelsen, in their different ways, made it clear that not all norms possessing legal validity were general rules; they could also be particular commands.[23] As there was a certain oddity in calling all such commands 'laws' Bentham labelled them 'legal mandates'. Such a wide conception of law—of little significance in penal and civil law—certainly has its place in the public law domain where many justiciable questions involve just such power-conferring norms which are not general rules.

It is a commonplace of positivist jurisprudence that the validity of an inferior norm may be determined by checking it against a superior validating norm. To take a familiar example: the by-laws of a local council are valid because they have been passed under regulations created by a Minister empowered to make such regulations by an Act of Parliament. Yet that account of the concretization of norms gives us a very incomplete account of the manner in which the inferior power-conferring norms are legally validated. It is an account of legalistic validity only.

In the actual business of administration the chains of authority may be complicated and not entirely clear. To bring out the legal principles involved we need to employ a schematic model in which each link in the chain involves the production of an inferior empowering norm. In institutional terms we must regard each of the procedures by which a particular norm in the chain is made as being a separate Practice, no matter how simple or rudimentary that form may be. Each inferior norm is to be treated as though it were the NP of a separate normative Practice.

It is by checking the procedural justness of each such separate State Practice that the courts ensure respect for the interests of Groups and individuals. For the validity of the normative product of any such Practice is never dependent merely upon conformity to the higher norm.[24] Its validity is not, as the positivists suggest, judged solely by its legality, but is dependent upon satisfying the demands of legal justice. That is, the courts will demand that the ground rules of each of the Practices must ensure that, whenever possible, the interests of citizens are not ignored. Each inferior norm must be shown to be well made, conforming to the requirements of rational decision-making in a democracy.[25]

Procedural propriety, then, is not just a matter of conformity with the rules of a fixed procedure. A decision which will affect individual rights, or the creation of a power-conferring norm, will be held invalid if the procedure by which it was created fails to show respect for Groups or persons. The well made power-conferring norm, or the decision affecting individual rights, must never be arbitrary; the method by which they are created must exhibit procedural justice.[26] Not only do the courts have authority to insert additional safeguards into the enacted procedures, they may also introduce conditions into processes of informal decision-making, by prescribing what are in effect the mandatory ground rules of a rudimentary Practice to ensure that citizens' interests are not neglected. This they will do in the name of justice and fairness.

In reviewing the legal validity of decisions and norms the courts must of course avoid making judgments about their substantive merits: about the strength of the reasons used to support them. Their concern is solely to assure themselves that the norms are properly made. The courts will only take note of the reasons given where they appear to signal arbitrariness or irrationality in the decision-making process.[27]

The individualism of the law

The principles of legal justice, which together I have called the animating idea of the Practice, govern the application of norms in a legal Practice. In the Practice, adhesion to these principles does not mean that the judges have a generalized bias in favour of citizens' rights, but that they have an unwavering commitment to the business of securing respect for them. In the CS Practice legal justice is an imperative; the norms must at all times be interpreted and recreated in conformity with the principle of respect for individuals. So not only will the enactments of the ULP be construed so as to minimize the authority to interfere with individual rights, but also the inferior norms made under those statutes must be created in conditions of procedural justice.

The idea of legal justice can only be worked out within an ongoing Practice. The principles of legal justice, as worked out in the embedded CS Practice, provide us with a restatement of the rule of law. The benefits of being ruled by laws and not by men can accrue only if the laws satisfy the requirements of legal justice; that is, when the legal norms are capable of providing complete justification for all State actions. To be of value the rule of law must not simply reaffirm in general terms the principle of the equality of all citizens; that equality must be realized in a legal Practice which exhibits the constant will, and the confidence, to ensure that the State never rides rough-shod over the interests of citizens.[28]

The idea of legal justice gives us an intuitively satisfying explanation of the authority of courts of law in their exercise of a rights-based jurisdiction; it enables us to grasp the character of legal norms; and it provides a basis upon which to understand the notion of the authority of the State. A value-free positivism, with its emphasis on legality, will lack any sort of explanatory power. It is difficult to see, for instance, how we could explain the development of administrative law in the USA or the UK without reference to the principles of legal justice.

The charge against the legal positivists is that although they emphasize the importance of clear legal norms, they fail to recognize the signal importance of the principles required for their just application. For these are principles which operate to transform the norms themselves. A court adjudicating with nothing more than a principle of legality, unperturbed by the fact that the norms to be applied are not well made, is like a pianist playing a badly tuned piano: though the score is faithfully followed, the music grates. Such are the dissonances of mere legality.[29]

Legitimation

A Practice which reviews the procedural justice of all State norm-creating and decision-making Practices exerts a benificent influence in the democratic polity. In signifying their approval of the procedures followed, the courts effectively legitimate State action; in effect, they declare that official acts done in accordance with the legal norms are completely justified.[30]

The notion of legitimation by the courts loses its force if the courts require only that officials conform to the rules, without abusing or exceeding the powers set out in the rules. Apart from the, admittedly significant, advantage that citizens may then be in a better position to predict how officials will act, there is no particular virtue in being subject to State action under declared general rules.[31] What advantage is there in knowing one's position if the rules are arbitrarily made and the decision-making procedures lack justice? The certainty which precise rules provide is, more likely to be produced by a legal Practice committed to legal justice than by one concerned only with formal legality. For legality is surprisingly tolerant of broadly framed rules and wide discretions. The type of detailed and clear norms which enhance predictability are created in legal Practices committed to legal justice.

The State as a legal concept

The preoccupation of the participants in the CS Practice with justice leads them to view the State as nothing more than a locus of legal power. Although aware of its brute power, they recognize only its authority; as judges of legal questions, they are concerned only with its authority to affect the rights of individuals. Equally they are concerned with the duties of the State only insofar as individual citizens' rights require their performance; for the legal CS Practice is not a constitutional court; it lacks regulatory authority.

For the participants in the legal Practice the State is necessarily an associational form: State powers are conferred on particular bodies and individuals who are defined by reference to their place within the organizational complex. However, in the eyes of the law the State is not so much a substantial institutional form, a complicated conglomerate divided and subdivided into innumerable component parts, as a peg upon which the ULP may hang governmental powers. The picture of the State created by the courts is of an associational form serving as nothing more than an essential context for the innumerable chains of authority which they investigate. It is not a many-chambered castle, but a single generalized location.

In the eyes of the law the State is an undivided entity; the citizen is on every occasion related to the State rather than to some part of it. Judges do not need to conceptualize the State beyond accepting it as the associational form which is the context for the chains of authority. It is by no means surprising that the State is not regarded as a legal category. Actions against the State are brought against particular officials and departments; there are many points at which the conglomerate can be attacked.

The law's indifference to sociological truths about the State, its concern only with the norms in the chains, is reflected in Kelsen's analyis.[32] In the eyes of the law the State has neither history nor substance. Clearly the legal Practice generates a concept of the State which is wholly different from any of the great variety of definitions entertained in the social and political sciences. This is certainly not the State with which the social contract was agreed. Given the minimalist conception of the State required in legal adjudication, there is no need for judges to theorize about its structure or functions.

Yet it must be emphasized that in treating the State in this way there is no intention to reduce it to a set of norms, or in any way to question its reality as an institutional fact. It means only that, within the form of life which is the CS Practice, any attributes of the State other than its legal powers are an irrelevance—a serious irrelevance in that some attributes of the State must be excluded from consideration in the process of adjudication. What the State does or can do cannot justify official action.

The diffuseness of State powers

The State's legal powers lie not at its core but in its extremities. In the eyes of the law the State possesses legal power only when its acts can be completely justified by legally valid norms. The completion of all the steps in a chain of authority is generally necessary for the creation of such a justifying norm. Until such end-products are created the State possesses no power to interfere with the rights of citizens. Although its officers have lawful authority to create such power, the State itself cannot be said to possess power until the final norms in the chain are created. The lawful power of the State exists in its fingertips.

The process of concretization must be seen, not as a process by which existing State power is *refined,* but in which, at the very end of the chain, State power is *created.* The law has no interest in the ability of the State to acquire power, only in its actual lawful power. Thus strictly the State has no power at that point when Parliament confers capacity on a Minister to decide on a course of action, or to create norms, in respect of an activity affecting citizens, apart from cases in which an enabling statute confers on a Minister a discretionary power which can be exercised informally.

The fact that the State's power to affect citizens' rights only comes into existence when the interference can be justified by a well made norm tends to be obscured by our usages. One of the most familiar is the assertion that Parliament delegates power to a body or a Minister, which implies that Parliament already possesses power as a sort of essence which it can dilute and ladle out to its delegates. Folk jurisprudence is replete with such misunderstandings of the logic of legal power.

The diffuseness of State power is a corollary of the principle that the participants in the CS Practice will recognize State powers only if the norms creating the power are well made.

Precisely the same principle of necessary norm-creation will be employed by judges in recognizing the *enacted rights* of citizens. Such rights are never conferred by norms which operate only as general standards, principles, or expressions of contemporary perceptions of human needs. If the enacted rights are to be legally protected they must be proved just as rigorously to have been vested in individuals by reference to well made, precise norms of conferral. For it must be remembered that the individual to be respected in the CS Practice is not primarily a human being[33]—who can claim with good reason and by reference to express statutory or constitutional formulations why he or she should be respected in particular ways—but a legal person in clear possession of well defined, vested legal rights. It is in the light of this legal requirement that the partisanship of the Practice must be understood.[34]

B: The NPs of the CS Practice

The product of this normative Practice is *either* an order, with its justification, made by a judge on behalf of the citizen against the State *or* a refusal to make an order, with its justification. Every NP of the Practice must be regarded as consisting of two parts: the order or refusal, and the justification.

The order

The order against the State which is either issued or refused by the court will have been formulated with precision before the hearing commences. This is an order to which the plaintiff claims to be entitled as of right; the object of the hearing is to determine whether or not the order claimed should be issued. So the order, the normative product, is not something which emerges, or is hit upon during the course of the deliberations, as a fitting or appropriate response to State wrong-doing. The question for the judge is never the politicians' question: what is to be done? It is the legal question: do the judges approve or disapprove of the order demanded by the plaintiff. They are called upon to give a yea or a nay in a zero-sum game. The legal argument turns upon whether this particular order can be completely justified by the legal norms.

The clarification before the hearing of the question to be determined distinguishes a legal Practice from a dispute-resolution agency; in the latter the nature of the final decision may well be subject to argument and negotiation. In the legal Practice there are no plaints for unspecified assistance; what the plaintiff claims is a right to have a particular order issued in respect of his interests. He bases his claim on the fact that such orders have been issued in previous similar cases.

The plaintiff in an action against the State is not free to seek what he considers to be the appropriate action, but must select from a limited number of types of orders or remedies, which he can claim as of right. The types of remedies available to him are limited by a number of factors.

The first limiting factor is that the order must be capable of being completely justified. This general requirement means that the order must be justifiable by reference to the legal norms in the LS. This will exclude any demand for an order justifiable only by good reasons, rather than norms. So the courts may not make administrative orders to provide facilities for members of Society, or orders justified only by reference to some dimension of the common good. For this the State would require express authorization by a statute. For a court to make such orders would appear to make it a part of the State Organization, and its order would surely conflict with the concept of the powerless State.

Secondly the order must be capable of binding the State. Although there are in theory no bounds to the legal liability of the State to respect citizen's interests, clear exceptions may be prescribed. The ULP may grant the State immunity from legal action by way of a particular type of order, or in respect of the exercise of its powers in certain areas of activity. The jurisdiction of the court may be ousted by direct prescription without more; or, more subtly, by the institution of extra-legal regimes which make no provision for appeal to the courts.

Neither does it lie within the authority of this Practice to issue penal orders against officials. The idea of punishing the State is, after all, decidedly odd. All official offences must be tried under the ground rules of the penal Practice. It is no part of the authority of this Practice—or indeed of the penal Practice—to regulate and control the administration.

The operative part of the NPs of the legal Practice is necessarily an order selected from an established catalogue of possible orders. The orders which are appropriate to ensure respect for citizens rights include: those which are declaratory of the illegality of acts or the invalidity of norms and decisions; orders which prohibit or command acts; orders which command the restitution of things wrongfully taken; and orders of compensation for loss wrongfully suffered.

The justification

The normative product of the CS Practice includes not only an order against the State, but also and *essentially* a justification for it. The validity of the NP depends upon the fact that it is completely justified. No matter what the outcome, whether an order is made or not, the lengthy deliberation leading to it will have been precisely about whether it can be justified in law. The public justification is a component of the NP of a CS Practice: not something additional to the judgment, but an essential ingredient of every legal decision.

Ideally the justification will be given by the binding norms found in the LS of the Practice. The norms having been transformed in order to perform this function must be clear and precise. The justification cannot rely upon the interests of the State, policies, or principles; as general standards, these operate merely as factors to be weighed. The law must be clear; where it is unclear it is the job of the courts to clarify the new norms, which can then be used to justify. The *'ratio decidendi' is* a splendidly ambiguous phrase, but it should be understood to refer to that part of the judgment which expresses the formulated legal norms, rather than the reasons which influenced their formulation.

The requirement that the order must be *completely justified* entails that the courts have authority to declare the law. This is because the general rules themselves—the norms of custom, the provisions of a statute or code—will rarely provide the complete justification required for an order to be issued in the particular circumstances of the case. It is because they are seeking complete justification in every case that judges must engage in a legislative effort. Their refined formulations of new sub-rules and norms become part of the LS of the Practice. The justificatory component of the NP is therefore of the greatest significance, and constitutes a vitally important contribution to the normative resources of Society.

The declaratory function distinguishes the legal Practice from other tribunals or agencies, which may provide other reasons for the solution to a problem. Judges are not merely performing the useful function of resolving conflicts which have arisen in social interaction in setting out the legal position, they are adding detail to the map of the legal world.

The finality, validity, and authority of the NP

The NP is a legal product, with all that that entails of finality and authority. In considering this character of the NP it is important to keep the two parts of the NP separate.

The order itself is final and not open to renegotiation by either the State or the citizen; and it is so unshakeable because it is completely justified. A legal challenge can of course be made that the order is not justified: that is, the order is appealable. Unless and until it is successfully appealed against, however, the order is authoritative even though it could be predicted that it would be declared defective in an appeal court. Non-legal challenges to a valid order are calls for the legal norms to be changed. Such challenges often unfairly take the form of a call for a change in the legal Practice or of its participants.

The justification given for the order—the declaration of the law—sets out the valid legal norms. Obviously, from time to time the laws are wrongly declared. They may be correctly declared either in an appeal or, importantly, when a later case overrules an1l earlier judgment. However, the finding that the original order was not completely justified does not, under the doctrine of *res judicata,* affect its authority.

The normative force of the order

In both the penal and the private law Practices the normative force of the NPs is unproblematic; the courts can, without compromising their independence, rely upon State agencies to enforce their orders. By contrast, the judges in the CS Practice, issuing orders against the State, cannot rely upon the organizational power of the State.

Yet, as legal norms, the NPs of the CS Practice must be guaranteed by some real force. For norms will lack a legal character if they are not perceived by both citizens and officials to be absolute. There is little to commend a jurisprudence in which paper rules or ineffective orders count as valid legal norms. The legal rights of citizens are realized rights, actual possessions; they can only be real if they are guaranteed. Those rights cannot be secured by the judgments of a mere impartial arbiter armed with a Bill of Rights. Who then can be relied upon to ensure conformity by the State? It is clear that reliance cannot be placed upon the State itself. Few would have confidence in such a system of self-regulation by the State; and there is little merit in the suggestion that the necessary constraints would be guaranteed by one department regulating another.

We must look outside the State altogether to find the institutional force which guarantees the binding, absolute character of public law. We will find it in the pressure exerted by the legitimate opposition (see *ante,* p. 280. This institutional form, central to the existence of a democratic polity, poses a real and ever-present danger to a State tempted to exceed its lawful powers. The courts issue their imperative NPs against the background of perpetual vigilance by this Group, and the commitment of its members to ensure that justice is not ignored.

C: The ground rules of the CS Practice

If the court is to be in a position to order the State to act justly towards individual citizens, the ground rules of the CS Practice will need to prescribe the conditions to be satisfied and the steps to be taken to ensure that the methods of fact-finding, law discovery, deliberation, and declaration are the very best possible. Structuring the legal Practice, the ground rules may be said to make possible the doing of legal justice in citizen–State relationships.

Many of the ground rules common to all legal Practices have been examined in the sections on the penal and the private law Practices above. The emphasis here is on aspects of importance in examining the ground rules of the legal Practice in the public law domain.

For convenience the ground rules are divided into three major clusters:
(i). norms of procedural justice;
(ii). norms of Practice integrity; and
(iii). norms of incorporation.

The procedural justice of the Practice

Since its aim is to do legal justice, the legal Practice must be perceived to be a paragon of procedural justice. Its basic norms must give effect to the time-honoured principles of natural justice. The ground rules must prescribe that everything possible is done to ensure the citizen a full and fair hearing—among other things, that he or she is properly represented, and is given time and opportunity effectively to challenge the State. Rules will also be needed to ensure that the judges are competent and unbiassed.

Among the mass of procedural rules which accumulate over time within the Practice there will be some which prescribe how proceedings are to be initiated and conducted, the remedies which are available, and how they may be applied for. Not only will there be basic rules of evidence to ensure that the facts are properly found, but also special rules taking into account the privileged position of the State. For it is hardly likely that a bureaucracy will voluntarily impart information which it would prefer to keep hidden. Rules are needed to allow for the treatment of obstructive officials; for the compelling of witnesses, the discovery of documents, and the administration of oaths; and there must also be provisions governing the court's reaction to claims by the State that the doing of justice in a particular case would prejudice national security.

Provision must be made for appeals against the NPs of lower courts, in order that errors made at first instance can be rectified. I have indicated above that an appeals procedure is an integral part of any legal Practice (see *ante*, p. 184). An appeals tier is necessary not only to secure justice in each case brought by the citizen, but also to ensure that the law which is declared has been given the fullest consideration. The deliberative and declaratory functions of the appellate courts are of particular importance.[35]

Generally, for reasons given above, the deliberative process by which a decision is reached as to whether the order claimed by the citizen is justified will be adversarial in character (see *ante*, p. 180). The open legal debate is important: it ensures that all possible readings of the law can be presented and that the judge-made norms will be well made. Those who believe that the aim of the legal Practice should be legality rather than legal justice will find much to recommend in an inquisitorial procedure.

Only in the light of the court's submission to the imperatives of procedural justice can the partisanship of the court be understood. I have emphasized this partisanship in order to counter the suggestion that the courts of public law are instituted in order to hold the balance between the citizen and the State; that it lies within the judicial office to weigh the interests of the State against the rights of the citizen. Such an approach ignores the commitment to legal justice which holds the citizen's rights as inviolable against all State action except that which is justified by reference to a well made legal mandate. However we may view such an approach, there must be no suggestion that the commitment to legal justice entails a disposition to bend the rules of procedure in order to give an advantage to the citizen in his challenge to the State. The ground rules of the legal Practice are scrupulously designed to ensure the impartial judgment of legal issues. The courts are concerned only that a citizen's rights established under the law are, unless express power has been conferred to override them, sacrosanct.

Practice integrity rules

A profoundly important set of ground rules defines the scope of the courts' authority. In effect, they prescribe what the courts can and cannot do while preserving its integrity—and hence its legitimacy—in a democratic polity. The norms are necessary if the participants are to perform their democratic function of securing the liberty and equality of individual citizens. The discharge of this function is conditional upon the absolute autonomy of the Practice; that autonomy will be compromised if, in addition to doing legal justice, the courts perform other functions.

The ground rules of the CS Practice give meaning to the separation of powers by imposing internally prescribed institutional constraints on the activity of the courts. The independence of the Practice from the legislature is secured under the norms of incorporation. Its independence from the executive is achieved by the insistence that administrative or political matters lie beyond the authority of the courts. The rules are designed to prevent judges from being asked to make administrative decisions, or to determine issues which ought to be settled in the political arena.[36]

Of particular importance in preserving the integrity of the Practice are the rules of *locus standi,* which specify the citizens who have capacity to participate in the Practice.[37] The principle is that only a citizen whose individual interests have been, or may be, directly affected has the necessary capacity. The judges do not hold the doors of the court open to all with grievances against the State. The courts exercise a rights-based jurisdiction. If the courts were allowed to determine an *actio popularis,* this would inevitably extend the functions of the court and involve consideration of matters other than those necessary for legal justice.

For those who perceive the Practice in terms of legality rather than legal justice, rules of standing are not based on principle but are merely maxims of prudence; they constitute a useful filter to prevent the courts from being swamped by more cases than they could possibly handle. From that viewpoint the ancient rules may well appear at times to impede the court's willingness, or even duty, to decide a whole range of issues which cry out for determination. When the court's authority to determine such cases is challenged, the answer is often that it derives from the need to uphold the rule of law. However, reliance upon a reading of the rule of law as demanding at all times the conformity of the State to the rules does nothing to promote the integrity of the legal Practice.[38]

The logic of appeals

An appeal may be defined generally as a second hearing in which the participants in the appellate Practice have authority: (i) to confirm or replace a prior determination; and (ii) to examine and substitute the justificatory reasons given for the order issued. An appellate order does more than alter the order or confirm the validity of the earlier order; it must always involve a full reconsideration of the *rationale* of the NP. That is, it involves a deliberative procedure in which the merits of the case, the grounds of the decision, and the reasons adduced in its support are reconsidered so that the final order will be more securely justified. So an appeal against the NP of a court of law involves the reconsideration of those justificatory reasons. It is a re-checking of, and a new declaration of the law. In the zero-sum game played by the participants in the legal Practice, the order issued by the lower court will be either affirmed or refused by the higher court.

The appeal court is authorized only to hear appeals from NPs created within the CS Practice: to consider challenges to orders which have been justified solely by reference to legal norms. It has no authority to hear appeals from normative Practices which justify their NPs with general standards or reasons, that is, non-legal material. The appraisal of such reasons does not lie within the special competence or knowledge of the judges; their deliberative procedure is not geared to decide on the wisdom of such decisions. The judges have, we say, no authority to examine the merits of an administrative decision. Any such power would have to be conferred. This inability, of course, has nothing to do with the training or intelligence of the judges; it is a question of institutional competence. In hearing such an appeal they would be issuing orders which could not be completely justified.

However, Practices external to the legal Practice, of which State Practices constitute the largest class, are nevertheless subject to its authority. Where the legal rights of individuals may be adversely affected by a decision made by participants in a non-legal Practice who have justified their NP by producing good reasons, the courts have inherent authority to *review* the decision. The review is concerned, not with the soundness of the supporting reasons, but with the justice of the procedure by which the NP was created. Quite without regard to the justifying reasons, the court will judge whether the decision was legally valid or not. Review by the participants in the legal Practice determines only the validity or otherwise of the NP which has been challenged. The judges' authority is limited to deciding whether the Practices are procedurally just: whether the NPs were well made.

Judicial review maintains the rule of law among the institutional forms of extra-legal regimes. In a democracy the courts' authority to review cases is a correlative of the citizen's public law interest in just administration (see *post*, p. 347). By sitting in judgment on the operation of the State Practices the courts in no way become involved in the business of the State; they do not thereby become part of the governing apparatus. Their concern is with the rights of citizens rather than the good behaviour of the State.

In the light of this understanding of the nature of the legal Practice NP we can provide an ideal reconstruction of the concepts of a 'judicial' hearing or office, and of a 'justiciable' issue.[39] They are concepts to be understood by reference to the idea of legal justice and the authority which accompanies the commitment to it. The judicial office is the capacity of a participant in a Practice in which the norms of law are used to justify completely the NP; in which the NP is supported only by legal norms. A justiciable claim, issue, or question is one in which individual rights are at risk. Neither of the terms can be adequately explicated in isolation from the legal Practice and its commitment to justice; what is justiciable is a question which can be decided by reference to the rules of law and the judicial office, or judicial action, involves the activity of doing legal justice.

The ground rules defining the types of question upon which the courts may adjudicate and the type of justification which they must produce are of central importance in preserving the integrity of the CS Practice.

Threats to the integrity of the Practice

Although we can work out ground rules to preserve the Practice of the ideal court, we must recognize that actual courts have inevitably to make compromises. There are today powerful and persistent pressures on the courts to depart from the strict standards prescribed by the ground rules of integrity. There are pressures to dispense with the rules of *locus standi,* to justify decisions not solely by rules but by reasons; pressures to adopt a purposive approach to legislation, to take account of the social consequences of their judgments. In yielding to such pressures the courts produce NPs which, however attractive, cannot claim to be completely justified. One consequence of this is the increased likelihood that the judgments will be challenged; for reasons do not have the finality of rules. In hearing an appeal against an incompletely justified NP of the lower courts, an appeal court—unless it is vigilant to preserve the integrity of the Practice—will assume the character of a constitutional court, whose members may not perceive themselves to be the modest defenders of individual rights, but guardians of the sacred flame of democratic liberalism. In that exalted office, they may not be unduly worried about making judgments on political matters. In that case they cannot rely upon the inherent authority of judges as participants in a legal Practice, but must rely upon an authority—given plausibility by misreading the rule of law—which they possess by virtue of being guardians of the constitution; they claim a licence to judge impartially between political arguments to which the legal norms give no sort of answers. Although the loss of integrity of the Practice may have its compensations for judges in their increased power, for the democratic polity it constitutes a profoundly damaging development.[40]

The norms of incorporation

The formidable miscellany of norms governing the discovery and declaration of the law in the CS Practice are little different from those governing the IE Practice. However, the commitment of the participants in the CS Practice to legal justice, their role as partisans of the citizen's cause against the State, does result in differences.

One of the main differences is that many of the norms which will require to be declared will not be general rules but particular legal mandates: the commands, directions, and decisions of administrators within the chains of authority. The primary concern of the courts will be to ensure that the mandates have been created in conditions of procedural justice. They will be concerned to see that procedures prescribed by the legislature have been followed, and prepared to add to them in the interests of justice.

When the rules or mandates are ambiguous and need interpretation the courts will presume against any intention on the part of the legislature to interfere with individual rights. It is constitutionally important that judges adhere to the literal rule of interpretation.[41]

The absolute autonomy required for the courts to protect the interests of individual citizens dictates that the participants must never act as partners either in the business of the State or the legislative process. They will not make administrative decisions or pronounce upon the merits of decisions already made; nor will they attempt to fill the gaps in statutes.

The courts have authority to deal only with rules which touch upon the interests and rights of individual citizens. The LS of the Practice is not a constitutional handbook but a most detailed compendium of the position of the citizen *vis-a-vis* the State.

D: The legal system of the CS Practice

The LS of the legal CS Practice is a very distinctive body of law; it contains the laws—all the valid legal norms—of the public law domain. These are the norms employed by the judges to justify their NPs. The LS of the CS Practice is a heterogeneous collection of norms, and differs from the LSS of the civil and penal Practices. The norms required to justify completely an order of punishment, or those required to do civil justice, are of a different type from those required to justify an order against the State.

The LS of this Practice consists of nothing more than the norms necessary to define the rights of individuals and the powers of the State. The participants in the Practice, committed to ensuring that justice prevails in relationships between citizen and the State, can be said to overlay a diagram showing the individual rights of members of Society with a transparency upon which the presently existing pattern of State power is drawn.

The rights of the citizen

As this is an *embedded* Practice, in addition to the norms relevant to the definition of all public law rights (see *post*, p. 339), the LS will include the norms defining all the rights of private law. It is worth noting that most of norms defining rights will not be enacted but will be found in the reports of the cases prescribing the duties of respect owed to the possessors of legally recognized interests.

Statutory provisions which directly confer or limit the rights of citizens will, as well made norms, be included in the LS. Any enacted or promulgated norms attempting to create legally recognized interests must, if they are to be incorporated, provide clear criteria by which it can be determined whether or not an individual is possessed of an interest.

The powers of the State

The other major class of norms consists of the variety of legal mandates by which power is conferred on the State to remove or abridge the rights of individual citizens. I have suggested (see *ante*, p. 314) that State power of this sort lies in its extremities; that while in some instances such power may be directly conferred under a statute, it is more commonly only validly created at the end of a process of concretization. So the LS of the Practice will include the mandates in all the chains which the judges have declared to be valid. Such a collection of validated norms provides a detailed and comprehensive map of the powers of the State. The particularity of these norms incorporated into the LS is worthy of note. The LS is by no means simply a collection of general rules.

The ULP may confer many powers on the State, but the courts have authority only to declare the norms defining powers to affect the rights of citizens. The strict rules of *locus standi* reflect the limits of the declaratory authority of a court of justice. If the integrity of the Practice is to be preserved, the participants must honour the principle that norms can only be incorporated and declared by the courts if they are relevant to establishing the validity of the links in a chain of authority leading from an actual intervention in, or threat to, the rights of individual citizens. Courts of justice are thus not concerned with breaches of norms which are *not* relevant to the validity of the chains of authority.

Although the courts' protection of the individual is of central constitutional importance, their reliance on rules of standing which limit their jurisdiction means that many norms of great constitutional importance will not be incorporated in the LS and will thus be excluded from the legal domain. The constitution is not an inherently legal structure.

The principles of legal justice are not part of the LS

The interpretation and declaration of the enacted norms is governed by the principles of legal justice. However, judges do not directly use these principles to justify their NPs. For that purpose they must employ the incorporated legal norms which have, with great care, been precisely formulated. The principles of justice are not legal norms of this sort; they are not LS rules but ultra-legal principles operating to generate the ground rules of the Practice. They are to be respected as principles. There are dangers in supposing that, in order to promote certain values, the prin ciples should be formulated as rules; that they too should be declared by the courts, or given legislative expression.

III: THE LAW AND THE CONSTITUTION

The shortcomings of actual constitutional arrangements and the virtues of imaginary constitutions have occupied the minds of men since early times, but there was until recently little concern about the precise role of law in those arrangements. Under the legal pluralism of pre-democratic times law was allowed to have a most pervasive presence andinfluence.[42]

Only with the emergence of democratic polities does law become self-conscious. Then questions will be raised about its place, either as a distinct set of norms or as an area of activity, within the increasingly complex constitutional arrangements.[43] The doctrine of the separation of powers gives law—or at least the judicial arm of government—a specific role. The doctrine of legislative sovereignty led some legal positivists to challenge the old pluralist assumption that all important operative norms were legal rules; John Austin was prepared to relegate constitutional law to a place outside the province of jurisprudence altogether.[44]

Austinian jurisprudence emphasized the sovereign who could not be bound. This may have inhibited, but could not prevent, the growth of the general perception of the legal character of constitutional norms and the appearance of public law as an academic discipline. The awkward question of the precise role of law—and thus, for the conscientious, of the concept or definition of law itself—in the constitution of a secular polity remains controversial; notwithstanding, there are relatively few doubts about the centrality of law. This position seems to have been put beyond question by the promulgation of so many written constitutions, perceived to express the fundamental laws of their respective Societies.

Today few would question the view that the constitution of a democratic polity has a legal framework, or that constitutional activity is governed primarily by legal norms.[45] This view, implicit in commentaries upon both written and unwritten constitutions, does not of course mean that any particular constitutional structure will be entirely legal; it may possess non-legal norms. There is, particularly in the UK, acceptance of the importance of the unenacted norms: the conventions of the constitution. However, although these are regarded as having an important role, it is nevertheless regarded as a supporting role: the lubricant for the machine, or the flesh on the legal bones. In coming to terms with conventions, it seems that commentators' views of the fundamentally legal nature of the constitution have been reinforced.

Within the orthodoxy which sees constitutions as legal structures two schools can be identified. One defines the legal norms of the constitution narrowly, as those which are applied or enforced by the courts of law. The other takes the constitutional structure as a whole and prefers to identify the legal rules by referring to the rule or recognition employed by politicians, officers, and officials. If our aim is to describe the constitution as whole, to explain how it works, to demonstrate the range of activity involved, and to trace its recent developments, the non-foracentric approach wins hands down. However, if our objective is to draw a clear line between the constitutional and the legal, or the unconstitutional and the illegal, in order to understand a divide reflected in our usages, then the foracentric approach is more fruitful.[46] In throwing into relief the role of the courts in the maintenance of the rule of law, it obviates the need to hypostatize the constitutional rules themselves as being in some way an active force within the polity.

A: The constitution as a non-legal structure

Contrary to the prevailing orthodoxy, the constitution must, from the point of view of institutional theory, be regarded as *essentially* a non-legal structure; the variety of forms of life in and between which its norms operate make up a non-legal regime. The only norms of this regime which are legal are those which happen to have been transformed into legal norms because they are necessary for the doing of legal justice to individual citizens; in other words: the only legal norms are those found in the LS of the CS Practice. The law occupies a place not at the centre but at the side of the regime.

Institutional theory does not call for a redefinition of the constitution. It is generally agreed that a constitution is that normative structure which constitutes, regulates, and controls the distribution of power within a polity.[47] It is indeed a fundamentally important framework which must possess systematic coherence. The norms operate to structure and control the great variety of forms of life in political and governmental activity, and form part of the language of that activity.

Some of the confusion which has arisen over the nature of constitutions may be resolved by distinguishing between institutional forms and institutional fields.[48] It needs to be emphasized that a constitution is not the normative framework of an associational form; it clearly does not consist of the norms of the civil Society, for these are all to be found in the LSS of the legal Practices. Although it will include them, it is clearly something more than the structuring norms of the Organization which is the State. A constitution is the body of norms that structures a polity which is not a form but an institutional field. The internal relationships between the governmental and political forms in the field are inevitably very varied and subject to change, and field boundaries cannot be precisely charted.

Constitutional norms can be said to exist only insofar as they are in fact operative: that is, to the extent that they are actually employed as guides, constraints, and ideals. They do not exist by virtue of the fact of their formulation within a constitution or a statute. This is a dictate of realism which commentators sometimes ignore. It does not, however, mean that we must exclude from the constitution any political ideals or aspirations to which the founding fathers may have given expression. It is the determination to treat a written constitution as a legal instrument which makes commentators treat with condescension the inclusion within its Articles of norms of aspiration and principle.[49]

For institutional theory norms must not only be operative, but must also be anchored to, and understood in the light of their connection with, the institutions in which they exist. Constitutional norms exist in the vast array of forms in the political and governmental activity of a polity. Our understanding of the normative structure depends upon our understanding of those institutional forms which have inherent authority to declare and change the norms; for these are the forms in which the constitution is maintained.

The necessity for concentrating on the dominant forms—the forms in which authority resides—arises from the fact that a constitution is an *artificial* structure; its parts require constant authoritative renewal and control in a rapidly changing world. There is no room for constitutional sentimentality. A constitution is not an emergent, crescive, customary collection of norms to be honoured for its antiquity and wisdom; neither, in institutional terms, does it consist of a collection of co-ordinate institutions achieving a homeostatic balance. For the constitution of a polity is inevitably full of rifts and tensions; it is a structure in which constraints are imposed upon institutions and persons in areas of life in which power is constantly contested, arrogated, and abdicated. Such artificiality, so obvious in the promulgation of written constitutions, is no less a feature of the traditional unwritten constitution.

The constitution under investigation is that of a democracy; a constitution which has a foundation, however distant, in the ideals of the legitimate democratic constitution. In that ideal the State clearly has no inherent authority to maintain the constitution; only the ULP and the legal Practices have that authority.

The authority of the legal Practice is, as I have indicated, very limited indeed. The legal CS Practice has inherent authority to declare only those constitutional laws which are found in the chains of authority by which the rights of citizens are affected.[50] Though it might be thought that the authority to investigate the chains of authority opens up virtually the whole of the constitution to judicial review, the court of justice in fact has a very limited view of the overall structure and, on many constitutional matters, has no authority at all.[51]

Once the fundamental question has been resolved as to which formulations are to count as sovereign utterances—as Acts of Parliament which represent the voice of Society—the courts have no authority to pronounce on the constitutional propriety of any acts or arrangements which are antecedent to, or involved in, the production of those final formulations which have the consent of Society.

For the courts, a statute represents a cut-off point beyond which they cannot go in investigating the validity of the norms in the chain of authority. They therefore have no authority to decide who, under current norms, should control the ULP, to prescribe its procedures, to review the rules which say who should initiate legislation, or to define the role of the President, the Monarch, or the Prime Minister; and so forth. Nor do they have authority to declare the law on matters which are not relevant to the validity of norms in the chains of authority. For instance, they cannot pronounce on the composition of the executive, or of government departments; on relationships between the Executive and Parliament, between the provinces and federal government, or between local and central government.[52] Nor can they intervene in non-legal regimes in which disputes about party structures and discipline arise. Thus, once it was established that the laws of England were to be made only by the King or Queen in Parliament, the propriety of stripping the monarchy of its powers was no concern of the law. If that was a crucially important political issue it was never a legal question.

B: The enforcement of the constitution

The Authority of the ULP

As legal norms make up only a fraction of the constitution, it is important to give an institutional location to the non-legal norms, which are the major structural elements in the constitution.[53] The institutional form in which they are maintained is the ULP; for these are political rather than legal norms, and are thus subject to political not legal interpretation.

A constitution is a real normative structure, not a paper formulation; it is a structure made up of the norms which are actually employed.[54] Whatever appearance of stability may be conveyed by written provisions, the real constitution is in a continuous state of flux. It is continually recreated, re-enacted, and revalidated as its norms are actually employed as guides and constraints. In that process of continuous constitutional creation the ULP operates as the ultimate authoritative form. Operative constitutional norms structure and control the great variety of the forms of life in political and governmental activity. Although they are applied, interpreted, and enforced within these forms, they are only given final and authoritative statement in the decisions of the ULP.[54a] How does the ULP perform this function? And what is the nature of the norms it maintains?

The nature of constitutional norms

Bearing in mind the variety of institutions in which constitutional norms operate it will be obvious that they cannot all be rules: it is mere legalism to suppose that they are, or should be. Within the varied forms of political life we must expect to find a wide spectrum of different types of norms: ranging from the strictest of rules to attenuated understandings about the propriety of conduct; from principles of democratic legitimacy to departmental regulations. Of course, the norms also derive from many different sources. Most obviously, there are an enormous number of enacted norms—constitutional, statutory, and other provisions—by which bodies and agencies are to be instituted and regulated. It is important to add that such statutory provisions do not possess a legal character by virtue of their enactment.[55]

Of no less importance in a comprehensive and realistic account of the constitution is the great variety of unenacted norms which guide and constrain. Among the unenacted norms are the most fundamental of all operative norms: the *principles of democratic legitimacy.*

One charge against many orthodox commentators is that they fail to recognize that these principles are *operative norms* of the constitution. The narrow technical approach of lawyers expounding the rules of democratic constitutions results in the principles being treated, not as internal components of the machine itself, but as something separate: as part of the ethos, or the ideological background, of the constitution.[56] Yet the principles are not merely contextual beliefs or values; they must be seen as the defining, operative norms of the democratic constitution. Although they are not always spelled out in constitutional instruments they are the necessary, constitutive norms of a democracy; they are norms which must be maintained by the ULP.

What then are the fundamental principles? It is the virtue of institutional theory that by identifying the ideal forms of life within a democratic polity we can give the principles a clear institutional statement. In accord with the doctrine of the separation of powers they can be presented as the interlinked basic principles of the sovereignty of the ULP, the original powerlessness of the State, and the independence of the judiciary.

In the working of any actual constitution these principles may not always appear to be fully operative. Working institutional structures inevitably fall short of the ideal: the judges may not be independent, the ULP may not be sovereign, the State may not be powerless.[57] Nevertheless, these principles, appearing as intimations of what is involved in the idea of government by consent be found to operate in the reactions to the many constitutional issues which arise. After all, we have powerful intuitions that legal justice requires absolute judicial independence, that the consent of the people must be obtained for the making of new laws, and that the State must be subject to the law.[58] These democratic intuitions surface time and again in practical affairs: the lack of a sovereign legislature leads to persistent calls for more stringent requirements of consent on important issues; the ousting of the jurisdiction of the courts is met with principled objections; Ministers who claim wide discretionary powers are condemned; the impropriety of judicial legislation is generally admitted; the inability of the legislative Practice to control the executive is perceived to be wrong in principle; and so forth.

Yet democracy represents the triumph of pragmatism; its hallmark is the surprising but emphatic denial that the ideal could ever provide the sole guide in practical affairs.[59] This pragmatism applies as much to constitutions as to any other normative systems in the polity. The principles of democratic legitimacy are not rules; they are not absolutes enforceable as legally binding rules, but must be weighed against other principles. In a wicked world of mischiefs and failures compromises with the ideal may be necessary, and institutions which manifestly do not conform to the ideal may have to be maintained.

Within a democracy the extent to which practical circumstances require principles to be compromised is a burning political question; the answer will not be found in either legal rules or constitutional theory. For the ideal does not coincide with the possible. Structural foundationalism, which would present us with the ideal constitution and proscribe compromise, would prefer to give constitutional norms the fixity and certainty of legal rules.

The mere fact that democrats recognize the necessity for compromise does not affect their commitment to the ideal constitutional standards. We all understand that pragmatism is never enough; that the principles must remain in the background as operative norms in decision-making and legislation if our polity is to have a democratic character. In a democracy where we choose just how democratic our constitution should be, we are prepared to accept its compromises only on the understanding that existing constitutional provisions are corrigible and are only contingently in place.[60]

Political enforcement of constitutional norms

The legal cast of mind typically regards the enforcement of many constitutional norms as problematic: it measures them against legal norms backed by legal authority and looks for some sort of sanction. Commentators certainly do not completely overlook the processes of political enforcement—references will be found to government climb-downs, broken careers, and the like; but the investigation of non-legal pressures tends to be cursory. It may therefore be useful to consider more closely the nature of political enforcement: to enquire how these non-legal norms operate and maintain their normative force.

It is obviously not the organized might of the State—the ultimate sanction of the military—which guarantees the democratic constitution and confers normative force on its standards. Nor could the guarantees derive from the learned authority of the legal Practices. Constitutional guarantees must be real; they are supplied by the institutional fourth estate of the democratic polity: by the Group which I have called the *legitimate opposition* (see *ante*, p. 280).

There is no doubt about the prescriptive character of the constitutional formulations; there is a wide vocabulary which refers to perceived departures from the norms. Recent constitutional history is replete with crises, incidents, affairs, scandals, breaches of convention, unconstitutional and undemocratic acts, improper arrogations and abdications, acts contrary to the rule of law and the spirit of the constitution, allegations of sleaze, and perceived breaches of enacted provisions. It is very important to underline the variety of these types of constitutional default.[61] In understanding political enforcement the media-led populist dimension must be kept firmly in mind. For it is by examining the political responses to the whole range of such departures that we discover the character and use of most constitutional norms.

What forms will the reactions take? The picture is likely to be complicated; departures by bodies or individuals from the norms of the constitution may result in a variety of responses. Serious breaches will be met with calls for positive action: the appointment of Royal Commissions and committees, the convening of conferences, the setting up of enquiries of various sorts, the initiation of debates in the ULP, the commencement of impeachment proceedings, and so forth. Apart from what are essentially *ad hoc* contrivances, we may also find continuous monitoring of particular areas by specialized agencies such as ombudsmen, commissioners, select and standing committees, and so forth. Many of these forms have what is basically an adjudicative function: to make judgments about the propriety of what was done and to decide what action should be taken.[62]

It should be recalled that the constitution is threatened, not only by wrong-doing, but also by social and political developments. How such changes are to be accommodated, the propriety of action in the new and uncharted waters, and the institutional structures required all call for serious and prolonged deliberation.

The legislative and the adjudicative functions in the processes by which the threats and challenges to the constitution are dealt with cannot be clearly distinguished; in those reactions the affirmation of existing norms will be linked inextricably with the production of the new norms. Sometimes adjudication will be unashamedly legislative: an enquiry into wrong-doing may be part of a wider investigation as to whether the understanding and trust of self-regulation should be replaced by enacted rules.

The ULP as an adjudicative Practice

Within the ideal democratic polity the adjudicative and legislative functions in respect of the constitution will be located in the ULP. That is to say that the participants in the legislative Practice are also, and importantly, participants in a very much less structured *adjudicative Practice.* They must decide whether the constitution has been breached, and must sit in final judgement on the findings, recommendations, and reports of the committees, commissions, officers, etc.[63]

Few things could be more important than the insistence that the adjudicative functions with respect to constitutional matters are not within the inherent authority of the legal CS Practice. It can neither demand compliance with constitutional norms, nor review the procedures by which the ULP or its delegates decide to respond to a departure.

We cannot understand the nature of constitutional norms by reference to the text and to our knowledge of the behaviour of legal norms alone. We can only discover their true nature by recognizing that the ULP is the ultimate adjudicatory Practice and taking note of the way in which the norms are employed there.

In considering the adjudicative functions of the ULP it is scarcely necessary to draw attention to the way in which it differs from legal adjudication, or to the fact that the norms which are employed are not at all like legal norms. The norms may sometimes be implicit in the arguments. This sort of adjudication calls for political judgment: for open, informed, democratic debate as to what is permissible in the circumstances. The idea of this ultimate adjudicative Practice is not justice but democratic legitimacy. Since the principles are to be applied to the local circumstances—the prevailing conditions, customs, and mischiefs—they can never supply members with simple, unequivocal answers. The principles—and they are principles and not policies—must be honoured; but the pressures of real life dictate that there can be no right answers. There can at best be only openly and fully deliberated decisions. The reading of the operative constitutional norms is nothing like the interpretation of laws in the courts. As an arbiter, the ULP is not engaged in reading a legal instrument of government—a written constitution—but in creating, reaffirming and remoulding, the norms of the operative constitution.

It may even be a mistake to condemn particular outcomes of constitutional conflicts for being wholly indeterminate: action may be unnecessary; decisions may properly be shelved; wise political counsels may recommend masterly inactivity and underline the virtue of reaffirming the principles while leaving the rules unclear. It is legalism at its most blatant to demand that all constitutional norms should be made plain.

One of the major problems of institutional design in modern polities is how the legislative Practice—the ULP—can be reformed so as to discharge these fundamentally important functions of constitutional oversight and adjudication effectively; to ensure that the ULP delegates only powers of investigation and deliberation, not those of ultimate authority. There will inevitably be awkward problems in attempting to secure a constant and adequate oversight by the ULP as the ultimate arbiter. In constitutional matters bodies with adjudicatory functions have too often been regarded, not as agencies answerable to the ULP, but as flexible instruments of government. The fact that some enquiries are less partisan and more judicial than those made in political debates should not obscure the all-important fact that they should be appointed to investigate, to recommend, and report, not to decide. That must be the prerogative of the ULP.

Political sovereignty

The commonly misunderstood political sovereignty of Parliament is manifested in the exercise of its unbounded adjudicative and legislative powers in respect of the constitution. For lawyers the legal sovereignty of the ULP is solely a matter of the legislative supremacy which is ascribed to all norms affecting individual rights. Yet it is in respect of its legislative power to enact constitutional laws which are *not* capable of being legally recognized or incorporated, and of making consitutional decisions which will not be reviewed by the courts, that we must recognize the ULP's political sovereignty. It is by virtue of its political sovereignty, its authority as the ultimate adjudicative Practice on constitutional matters, that we can recognize the aptness of the phrase 'the High Court of Parliament'.[64] The political sovereignty of the ULP may be described as an inherent authority to control, reaffirm, and remake the constitution.[65]

The relationship between the ULP and the courts is complicated. The legal doctrine of sovereignty means that the courts are subject to the direction of the ULP in respect of their jurisdiction and ground rules. For instance, the ULP is competent to oust the jurisdiction of the courts. However, in adjudicative functions the ULP and the courts are wholly independent of each other; there is here a very clear boundary between the political and the legal fields. Any questions involving judgment, calling for the interpretation of rules, must be decided by the right forum. The political sovereignty of the ULP can be respected by the courts only if they refuse to adjudicate on constitutional matters outside their inherent authority. The ULP must respect the courts in that it must not sit in appeal over legal judgments: over the determination of citizens' rights under the law. The ULP cannot substitute its interpretation of the law for that of the courts. If the ULP wishes to reverse a court's decision it must respect the law by relying on its legal sovereignty; that is, it must enact a new statute to repeal the law expressed in the court's decision.

The principle that no Parliament can bind its successors is as applicable to the political as to the legal sovereign. Statutes of constitutional importance which are not incorporated in the LSS of the legal Practices operate only as possible political constraints. They are by no means immutable or fixed. Their provisions do not have the same permanence as legal norms, which must be deliberately repealed before they drop out of the class of operative norms.

A new look at the constitution

It should be apparent from the above that the democratic constitution is never something imposed on, or adopted by, the members of Society as a package. It is never just the deliverance of tradition, a framework decided on by the founding fathers, or the work of some supreme council on constitutional affairs. A constitution is a structure which must be reaffirmed and recreated daily. Of course at any particular moment it must appear to have stability, for its norms are of fundamental importance, but as a matter of principle the democratic constitution must be seen as a product of contemporary democratic choice. Constitutions are undoubtedly frameworks; they are traditionally based; they do have stability: however, these features must not make us overlook their fundamental character as being, in a democratic polity, the choice of contemporary Society.[66]

The operative constitution of a democracy, including all the particular norms as well as the principles, is not a structure antecedent to democracy; it is rather a product of democratic choice. It does not make democracy possible, but is itself made possible by the choices of democrats. Crucially it is the product of choices made every day, not the outcome of decisions about a fixed framework laid down once and for all.[67] The democratic constitution is not an immutable framework, it is contingent: open to change as its principles are compromised or reaffirmed in changing circumstances.

Inevitably, a host of historical, inherited structures, particular political demands, external pressures, treaty obligations, false perceptions of the extent of legal authority, and the like hinder the full realization of the democratic principles within any particular polity. The answers to questions as to the best forms of government for a particular Society—presidential, parliamentary, monarchical—will not be found in the principles of the ideal constitution. Since democracy represents the triumph of pragmatism, the institutional structure that emerges within a particular country will be the result of choices made, and compromises and accommodations reached, in the political field.

C: Constitutional courts

No review of the constitutional arrangements of modern polities could fail to recognize the immensely important role of constitutional courts. Well established, relatively modern institutions, these courts bring the authority of the law to the resolution of constitutional issues. They have occasionally provided the finality required in constitutional questions which political agreement would have been unable to secure. The impartiality, probity, and competence of the members has in many countries earned courts a respect denied to politicians. Constitutional courts are perceived as bulwarks against arbitrary government, as guarantors of constitutional rights, as the ultimate upholders of the rule of law.[68] The self-image promoted by the judges is unquestionably that of a court of law: they demand the independence and authority appropriate to such a body. The court, as the guarantor of lawful government, will be regarded by many as the keystone of the polity's legal system. No democratic constitution is complete without one.

However, far from being the ideal legal institutional constraint upon government, a powerful constitutional court may—no matter what its virtues—stand as a major obstacle to the achievement of democratic legitimacy. For these courts are hybrid institutions operating on the border between the legal and the political fields. In furtherance of their legal pretensions they bring to the resolution of constitutional problems—problems calling for political judgment and agreement—inappropriate techniques, procedures, articulation, and authority of the law.[69] Such courts would not figure in the ideal constitution; they are to be regarded as being at best pragmatic institutional compromises with legitimacy: compromises made necessary by the manifest shortcomings of political arrangements and activity.

As I have said, Constitutional courts lie on the borders between law and politics; there can be no conceivable objection to the legal resolution by such a court of legal questions: that is, of questions involving vested interests of citizens. In performing this task the constitutional court acts as the ultimate appellate court within the legal CS Practice.

Questions about legitimacy arise where there is an overlap with the political field: where the constitutional courts are asked to make legislative and adjudicative decisions of a non-legal character.[70] In such cases it may be difficult for the court to avoid becoming an essential part of the legislative process.[71] For instance, where enacted rights are so imperfectly defined that they cannot be said to vest any particular interest in individuals, the courts will become involved in the conferral of new, and the extinguishing of existing, rights. Law-making of such a substantial character in defence of rights may well require the conferral or arrogation of the power to veto any legislative provisions which are considered not to conform to the written constitutional norms. Furthermore, although individual rights are not at stake, the courts may be called upon to adjudicate upon the propriety of conduct of both individuals and bodies, according to the uncertain, contested, or unformulated norms of the constitution.

Now this involvement in the political field is not, it is emphasized, attributable without more to the ambition of activist judges. Such involvement is inherent in the nature of the institution itself. It does not matter whether the judges are strict constructivists or activists; they will all have to make decisions which call for political judgement, and which will have important political consequences.[72] It might be thought that a bold activism is then to be preferred; for although it may not conform to the image of perfect neutrality which the court might wish to project, it is, so far as the process of decision-making is concerned, a more appropriate stance than that adopted by judges pretending to do perfect legal justice. It is at least an open and realistic recognition of the non-legal character of the problems to be decided.[73]

The establishment of an institution claiming to be a court of justice to arbitrate fundamental constitutional issues will inevitably legalize the entire constitution, transforming what is essentially a non-legal regime into a structure of legalistically formulated rules. It will encourage members to resort to litigation over constitutional matters; few areas could be said to lie beyond the jurisdiction of this court. The court's authority to declare the rules will enhance the perception of any divergence from them, and the possibility that the court could be persuaded to condemn any unconstitutional act may invest merely technical divergences with unwarranted significance.[74] Politicians who should be aware of their responsibility to maintain the constitution may, when faced with a particular issue, either abdicate responsibility—declaring it to be a matter for the court—or approach it with the inappropriate mind-set of legal adjudication: with that pernicious legalism in which conclusions are justified by reference to rules rather than reasons.[75]

In the court itself, the designation of decisions as legal judgments handed down by a court of justice is honorific; it is a tribute to the authority and finality, of the court's decisions, rather than any belief that they are attained by distinctively legal techniques. In cases where the constitution is silent the judgments can scarcely be said to have a legal character by virtue of being implied or deduced from the written law. Nor, of course, will the decisions be governed by the principles of legal justice.

They will be contrived out of whatever material lie to hand: out of the most proximate written rules, democratic principles, political realities, religious beliefs, and so forth.[76] Any appeal to the intention of constitution-makers or legislators in respect of a particular provision may be regarded as an attempt to divine the political judgment of the past about some matter which calls for the best judgment of our contemporaries.

Nor can it be suggested that, when the rules run out, the court will be able to rely on the soundest constitutional principles of democratic legitimacy, and that this principled calculation gives legitimacy to the newly declared law.[77] This is because the operative constitution which they must interpret is inevitably a set of compromises with the ideal. After all, the constitutional court itself is precisely the creature of such a compromise; and so, in varying degrees, is every other political institution. The compromises they represent are commonly not the outcome of the resolution of conflicts between principles, but of accommodations reached between principles and gross political realities. The operative constitution is the result of an attempt to establish democratic forms of government in the light of conditions, claims, and pressures which cannot be ignored and will not go away. Do not forget that it is a constitution of this sort, founded on compromise, that the court must interpret and apply. For the court to espouse the cause of pure democratic legitimacy, to ignore the political obstacles which shaped existing political arrangements, to strive always towards a perfect framework, would amount to a lack of political wisdom which even a court of justice cannot afford to display. There is no escaping the fact that this is a court which must exercise political judgement; that its value to the polity lies in its political nous rather than its legal knowledge.[78]

The presence of such an adjudicative body claiming to be a court of law presents a challenge to jurisprudence. The opinions of jurists on its activity are likely to be polarized, gravitating either towards the realists who state the unpalatable truth, or towards the foundationalists who deny the legitimacy deficit which the realists reveal. The pre-eminence of a constitutional court in the legal field means that our general perception of law is inevitably coloured by its activity. In fact few things could provide greater impetus for legal foundationalism than the operation of a supreme court running up an acute legitimacy deficit. For the general picture of the law obtained from the realists' view of the highest court makes us question the integrity of the entire legal system.

As a democratic polity always represents a victory for pragmatism it would be impertinent to criticize the operation of those exemplars of pragmatism, the constitutional courts. Within a particular conjunction of political realities such a court may be deemed, by those whose opinions alone are to count, the best solution to otherwise intractable problems. Nor should it be overlooked that the effectiveness of the court may depend upon the vigorous promotion of its legal character: on the idea that it appears to stand with legal impartiality above the political fray and draws on the authority of law which is known to guarantee equality and liberty.[79] In a democratic polity legal foundationalism must be justified not by its truth, but by its utility: by the support it is able to provide to buttress the ill-founded pretensions of the court.

Institutional theory can, however, deny that a constitutional court could ever be the natural, ideal institution for the achievement of legitimacy. While paying tribute to the important role which a particular court may play in a polity, we must also appreciate that the more powerful it becomes, the greater the obstacle it places to progress towards legitimate government. For the very establishment of such a hybrid institution will to some degree emasculate politics and undermine the integrity of law. In any progress towards legitimacy the court, as a hybrid institution, would not flourish but wither away. Progress would entail that its legal function —the protection of individual rights—would be wholly separated from its political function, so that the autonomy it must demand for the former would not be claimed for the latter. In all questions requiring political judgement it should ideally be subservient to the ULP. No amount of judicial hand-wringing over the fact that judges are not elected, no degree of caution and deliberation, no amount of ceremony, can ever give a lawyer's view of political issues a privileged status. This is so even though the questions turn on the interpretation of written rules. At the root of the problem of legitimacy in constitutional matters lies the perception of the constitution itself as a structure of legal rules: a perception inevitably promoted by the constitutional court.

IV: THE LOGIC OF THE RIGHTS OF PUBLIC LAW

Public law rights—the familiar set of rights and freedoms enjoyed in a democracy by citizens against the State—require institutional analysis. The brief account of those rights offered here is designed to clarify their nature and indicate their underlying logic.

The legal recognition of a range of public law rights in modern times does not represent the emergence of a new *species* of legal objects. The basic structure of any constitutional right is the same as that of a private law right. The analysis of the legal right is set out in Chapter 6, *ante.* There the legal right is presented as an entitlement of a special sort: an entitlement to legal assistance—in the shape of an NP of the legal Practice—in respect of some *interest* owned by the citizen which is the object of the right. Each interest is a position of benefit recognized in law.

A legal right is an institutional fact. The interest is not an abstract entity but a real position of benefit, so articulated that every legal right may be said to be *vested* in a legal person. Rights are items in a person's legal account, actual positions of entitlement which are given clarity and force as the judges give the positions ever more precise definition in the variety of practical situations thrown up in the course of litigation.

It is very important to understand that rights can exist as institutional facts only within a legal Practice; they are maintained and protected, not by the enactment of rules, but by the activity of participants in a legal Practice, and can be said to exist only as a consequence of 'the constant will' to protect them. We possess them, not simply because they have been conferred, but because they are protected.

Legal rights are vested, and must be sharply distinguished from the mere *claims*—moral or political—which are commonly called rights.[80] For instance it may be said that, in a society in which illiteracy prevails, education is a right denied; but no matter how strong the *moral* claim of the illiterate to the provision of schools and teachers, they have no *right* to be educated. We move closer to the notion of a right when we say, not that persons ought to receive certain benefits, but that a distinct individual entitlement to them is widely recognized. Only when institutional forms exist which give the claims consistent recognition and protection can we recognize rights. Until that point is reached they are no more the possessions of an individual, capable of being protected, than his claims to charity.[81]

Constitutional rights are narrowly defined here as positions of benefit, protected by the courts, which citizens can claim against the State. These rights do not possess a constitutional character because they appear in a codified body of constitutional and political rights, but because they are recognized by the courts as rights which the individual citizen has against the State.[82]

The identification of constitutional rights by reference to their appearance in a constitutional document, or by a demonstration of their social, economic, or political importance will be, whatever practical advantages may be gained, obfuscating.[83] It will obscure the distinctive logic of the public law rights and militate against the sharp differentiation of the CS and the IE Practices, which must be emphasized if there is to be a fruitful development of the idea of legal justice in the public law domain.

Of course rights which the individual asserts against other citizens, and which are protected in the IE Practice, are also protected in the CS Practice. It is a fundamental principle that, in the absence of express immunity, the State stands in the same position as any other citizen with respect to the private law interests of citizens. The status of the State as a neighbour may be partly concealed by the existence of special regimes instituted to regulate questions arising in connection with the civil liability of the State.

In the absence of specific exemptions the State must respect the property rights of citizens; its officials must prove their authorization for any confiscatory acts.

A: Basic and conferred rights

The rights of citizens have been usefully classified in a number of ways.[84] From the point of view of institutional theory, with its concern for legitimacy, the most important distinction lies between what I shall call basic and conferred rights.

Basic rights

Basic rights are rights to which, in the legal CS Practice, a citizen is automatically entitled by virtue of his subjection to the State; they are entailed in the idea of citizenship with which the law operates. They are every citizen's birthright; the necessary possessions of the member of Society as a legal person. The different types of such rights are briefly discussed in the following section.

The basic constitutional rights of citizens may, in a democratic polity in which the legal Practices are in place, properly be regarded as *natural rights;* they are neither posited nor are they conferred on the citizen; they are rights to which the citizen is entitled by virtue of his or her membership of a democratic Society. However, if they are not conferred it must not be assumed that they exist prior to the emergence of the democratic polity.[85] Their recognition is simply implied from the principles of justice; and such principles are realizable only within well established institutional forms.

Basic rights are not implications from any general—and contestable—conceptions of human nature, or from ideas about the common good or social justice.[86] Nor, importantly, are they framed to promote more perfect forms of democratic government. They are derivations from the specific idea of legal justice which animates a legal Practice occupying its proper place within a democracy: a Practice which has the clearest understanding of the nature and limits of State power. They are the logical entailments of that respect for persons which the State must show. Many of the rights are necessary implications from the conception of the powerless State. Our basic constitutional rights are recognized not because our complaints have been heard by a bench of liberal humanists concerned to implement a new civic deal for citizens, but because the judges are committed to the ideal of legal justice and to the working out of its implications.

Conferred rights

Conferred rights are never natural rights; although some of them may be characterized as being absolutely essential to citizenship, they can only be shown to be necessary by reference to extra-legal ideals. They have a political rather than a legal basis: for many of them the occasion of their enactment and legal recognition represents the successful culmination of a political campaign. Socio-economic rights, such as those to medical treatment, work, housing and welfare, and a number of political rights feature prominently in Charters of citizens' rights.[87]

Yet however widely they are regarded as the fundamental entitlements of all citizens, conferred rights must be seen to derive from conceptions of social justice and of ideal democratic arrangements, rather than from the idea of legal justice.[88] Some are implications from ideas about equality which go far beyond the notion of the citizen's equality before the law.[89] Many of our conferred political rights are misdescribed as being inherent liberties. That they have the support of public opinion and are universally accepted as the unquestionable entitlements of citizens in a civilized society does nothing to alter their status as claims which require legislative action before they become rights.[90]

Since they are not direct implications of legal justice they can be recognized and protected in the legal Practices only if they can be shown to have been expressly conferred upon citizens. They all stand in need of conferral by norms which, importantly, must have the precision and detail necessary to vest them in individual citizens; it is not the business of the courts to work towards the ideal in which all citizens are invested with such rights.[91]

The blanket characterization of the moral claims of individuals to minimal social and economic benefits as rights—rights which are thought to pre-exist their precise conferral—appears to ignore the practical consideration that many benefits are best distributed by non-legal, administrative methods. In the provision of welfare benefits a legislative choice must often be made as to whether legal rights should, or should not, be conferred on those who are to benefit.

The distinction between basic and conferred rights is important since the consequences of overlooking it could profoundly compromise the integrity of the legal Practice. We do indeed have natural rights, but it is imperative that their identification and limits be understood, and that we do not claim for conferred rights, no matter how important, the status of basic rights.

In the first place it is important that basic rights, unlike conferred rights, should not be promulgated. They are natural rights and therefore need no formulation at all. A partisan court committed to legal justice will articulate and give effect to those entitlements wherever the need arises. In many jurisdictions basic rights are of course clearly promulgated. The persistent demands for the promulgation of our basic rights may be partly explained by reference to the influence of the legal positivists who, in their debates with the natural lawyers, were plausibly sceptical about the existence of natural rights. For if natural rights, as Bentham insisted, are nonsense[93] then all our constitutional rights obviously need express conferral by positive laws. Even if their enactment is not strictly necessary, it might be thought that promulgation of our basic rights for the removal of doubt would cause little harm and that it might afford even better protection. However, the promulgation of basic rights in the form of directives to judges must be regarded as an unfortunate development.

The major constitutional objection to the promulgation of charters, which confer constitutional rights, and which are to take effect as legal instruments, is that they will invest the judiciary with powers over matters which should be the concern of the legislature. Whether such a development is regarded as desirable or not, few would question the fact that the promulgation of a charter of rights is bound to result in a sizeable tranche of powers being transferred to the judiciary.[94] In institutional terms the effect of such a transfer will be a serious dislocation of the law. It is likely to result in an arrangement which does nothing to rectify the shortcomings of political processes and activity—which may have motivated calls for change—and guarantees that the courts of law can no longer occupy their proper place within a democratic polity.

Quite apart from this general constitutional objection about the effects of such promulgation on the balance of power within a polity, it will have serious consequences for the protection of those basic rights which we can claim to be ours naturally. In the first place, there is a real possibility that those who frame the Charters may misdescribe or omit important rights, thus making their articulation and recognition a matter which appears to call for a wholly unnecessary judicial activism. In the second place, there is a real possibility that the precise words by which they are conferred will, in the course of litigation, be given an interpretation of such breathtaking ingenuity as to reinforce cynicism about the idea that we are naturally or automatically entitled to any rights.[95]

For many, the advantages of having constitutional rights securely enshrined in a constitutional instruments is of immediate and pressing importance, so that they may be used as a prophylactic against an irresponsible ULP or a careless State.

Charters are to be objected to only insofar as they are introduced, and generally treated, as a set of legal directives. The objections are that they distort what judges should do naturally in respect of basic rights, and that the enacted laws are often not sufficiently well drafted to operate as norms of conferral for any other constitutional rights, thus imposing on the courts the task of making political decisions and administrative arrangements.[96] There can be few objections to the use of such formal reminders, addressed to the players in governmental and political spheres, of the importance of both basic and conferred rights; there may be virtue in the formal declaration of claims for the maintenance and improvement in the conditions of citizens. It may be argued that such an articulation of important claims as rights sensitizes politicians to the importance of establishing and maintaining good legal Practices. As political affirmations they may remind legislators and officials of the interests of individuals, which can so easily be abridged and overlooked in the pursuit of policies.

However, one of the dangers attending the promulgation of constitutional rights, even as a political declaration, is that attention will be distracted from that which, institutionally, needs to be achieved. For the promulgation of rights is no substitute for the development of legal Practices in which alone those rights will have any reality. In some situations what is required is not the conferral of individual rights, but greater institutional integrity.[97] There is little point in proclaiming rights in the absence of an institutional apparatus for their protection. In a democratic polity the realization of the principles of legal justice in courts of law far outweighs the need for the express conferral of rights.

Basic rights are not absolute

If moral claims and political rights may rhetorically be said to be absolute, all legal rights are defeasible. Our basic constitutional rights are clearly not the inviolable, imprescriptible, or inalienable rights of political discourse. That they are natural rights does not make them absolute, as some of their proponents imagine. From the legal point of view all interests can be abridged, destroyed, or ignored under the authority given by well made norms. That is, they can be destroyed by an enactment of the ULP, or by the State under a valid norm created at the end of a chain of authority. It is significant that charters sometimes spell out the exceptional circumstances in which—in the opinion of their authors—the rights may be abridged. So our constitutional rights are possessions which the courts must protect only up to that point where enactments of the ULP, or well made norms created by officials, authorize their abridgement or destruction. The ULP in a democratic polity is sovereign; and the courts are incompetent to declare an enactment of the ULP invalid. They can only invalidate the concretized norms, which are created within the authority delegated by the ULP, for breaches of procedural justice.

Our basic rights have emerged through a process by which the courts have gradually worked out the implications of the idea of legal justice; a process in which confidence has grown as judges have gradually acquired a sounder appreciation of the inherent authority which their commitment to legal justice gives them.[98]

Rights are necessary

The legal CS Practice is something more than an agency for resolving disputes and monitoring official conformity to the rules, and the articulation of the complainant's legal position in terms of individual rights is a necessary part of the protection which the courts can give to the citizen. The rights claimed are not an optional extra in the administration of justice; neither are they a feature of a currently fashionable style adopted in the struggle to subject the executive to legal control. Rights are an indispensable part of the conceptual apparatus employed by judges attempting to secure justice between citizen and State; they are essential, discrete counters in the process of legal reasoning.

Every legal person is treated with respect by being regarded, not as an integral whole, but as the owner of interests which the rights protect. Interests are not aspects of, but things actually possessed by, the legal person. The citizen is seen thus as the possessor of discrete rights because the courts are committed to the doctrine of equality. Interests—rights—are the things in respect of which individuals are to be treated equally. So a legal Practice committed to justice must not only declare the laws but also articulate the individual rights of citizens.

Equality before the law has a different significance in an adjudicatory Practice animated by the idea of mere legality: the idea of ensuring conformity to rules. The participants in such a Practice have no need to articulate rights; they are under no pressure to define the interests of citizens as discrete objects requiring legal protection. If rights do appear in the jurisprudence of such a Practice, the interests may well be elided, and the citizen's rights treated as nothing more substantial than the *correlatives of duties* imposed by the rules. Legality provides no incentive to work out the scope of the interests of individuals. Furthermore, in applying rules, a legality Practice will be more tolerant of judicial discretion than in a Practice committed to justice; we could not be sure that duties imposed on the State by the unclear rules in one case would necessarily have the same normative status and force in a later similar case.

B: The institutional analysis of basic rights

Any analysis of constitutional rights must begin by identifying the different types of interests involved. The basic rights which a citizen in a democracy can claim to possess are manifestly not all of the same type. They are something more than variants of a generalized right in the citizen to be treated justly by the State. They are certainly something more than correlatives of the various duties owed by the State to the citizen. For the *interests* which citizens possess—the objects of the rights—arise out of, and have their meaning within, the citizens' involvement in particular institutional forms. So we must study these rights of citizens in their capacity as *members* of the associational forms of Society, State, Organization, and Group, and also as *participants* in the practical forms of Activity and Practice. The interests arising out of the citizens' involvement in each of these different institutional forms constitute a number of very specific types. In order to understand the nature of the different interests, and the ways in which they can be subject to State action, it is essential to locate them in their precise institutional contexts.

Basic rights associated with Practices

There are three types of constitutional rights arising from citizens' involvement in or connection with the normative Practices of a Society. The first type consists of a power: *the right to participate in a Practice.* Such an entitlement is a capacity—a most important but much neglected species of power—which enables the citizen to alter the normative position of himself or of other members of Society. For every citizen of a Society there are but two basic rights of this sort, and the only two necessary capacities are the capacity to participate in market transactions—which entails the right to own property—and the capacity to participate in legal Practices. No other capacities, not even such important rights as the right to vote and the right to marry, are fundamental constitutional rights: they require conferral. They are not rights entailed in the notion of legal personality.

The second class of interests connected with normative Practices consists of the basic rights possessed by citizens who are *subject to* the NPs of Practices. From the principles of legal justice we must deduce that every citizen has a right to obtain from the courts a review of the validity of the NPs of all State Practices which affect his or her interests. This is a distinct personal interest, not just the application of a principle that the State should act justly towards the citizen. The entitlement to call upon the courts to review the validity of the NPs in the chains of authority is clearly a constitutional right of pivotal importance in CS relations.

The third basic constitutional right, connected with normative Practices, which all citizens possess is *the right to legal justice.* This is the right to appeal against the NP of a legal Practice under which a citizen is ordered to perform some duty. This right is the basis for the familiar constitutional right to a fair trial: an entitlement which obviously depends on the existence of legal Practices.[99]

The interest in lawful administration

Distinct from, but closely allied to, the interests of citizens in ensuring the validity of the NPs of Practices to which they are subject is the constitutional *right to lawful administration.*[100] This is clearly an interest of the citizen implied from the concept of the initially powerless State. The legal person—the citizen of a democracy—is not a communitarian prepared to accept that sacrifices must be made for the common good. As a democrat he or she demands legal justification for all State acts. The courts, committed to ensuring that the State act lawfully towards all citizens, must recognize the citizen's demand for evidence of authority as a distinct basic right. This interest differs from that of the citizen's right to a review of the NPs of normative Practices; it involves proving to the satisfaction of the citizen, not that the norms are well made, but that the State can justify its acts by reference to such authorizing norms. At issue is the extent of the powers conferred. This individual right is founded on the principle that every loss or disadvantage suffered by the citizen at the hands of officials must be authorized by pre-existing legal norms.[101]

Relationships between citizen and State may, in some areas of activity, be governed by rules which are applied by participants in non-legal Practices. Where the ULP has approved the institution of a non-legal regime we must recognize that the citizen's right to lawful administration may be curtailed, and that he or she will have to rely upon the right to procedural justice: to a review of the validity or fairness of the NPs of non-legal Practices. The ousting of the courts' jurisdiction is complete not when the courts are prevented from declaring the rules, but when the right to a review of the procedures under which decisions are taken is denied or abridged.

One recent development may be regarded as an extension of the right to lawful administration: the courts' willingness to protect *legitimate expectations.* Such expectations are essentially no different from any other rights.[102] The interest involved differs from that which founds the right to lawful administration in that the courts demand that, in dealings with the individual, officials must conform not just to legal norms but also to standards of conduct which may not be set out by the rules.

Membership interests

Examining the logic of the legally recognized basic interests of membership in associational forms may lead us to question a number of received ideas. Two sorts of membership—of classes and of Groups—must be considered before we examine the rights of membership.

Classes are not associational forms, so there can be no specific interest in class membership as such. For the citizen, membership of a class, defined by legal rules, confers no benefits or burdens on the member except those for which the class was expressly created. The fact of class membership and all that involves in terms of the prescribed benefits or burdens—the 'is'—cannot become a requirement that the member must benefit or be burdened in any other way—the 'ought'.

Groups are self-selecting fraternities of value and belief. To an extent seldom appreciated, our personal values and beliefs are the product of our membership of Groups (see *ante,* p. 26). It is important to understand that, because they are invincibly fuzzy objects, Groups cannot be given any sort of legal recognition.[103] The membership of Groups is never clear enough to allow for the equality of treatment which justice under the rules requires. Hence no well made legal norm could grasp Group membership. By their very nature Groups may be said to elude the net of legal categories. Nevertheless, although Groups cannot directly be the object of well made legal rules, there is no reason why enacted norms cannot confer upon officials a discretion to decide who is to count as a heretic, a liberal, or a feminist.[104]

From this institutional consideration it follows that our ideas and values are legally untouchable, and that our freedom of conscience cannot be an interest recognized by the law. What the law cannot recognize it cannot protect. Freedom of conscience cannot qualify as a basic constitutional interest since the institutional matrix of our values and allegiances—the Group—cannot be regulated by legal norms. What we regard as an inalienable right, our freedom of conscience, is simply a result of the law's lack of competence to recognize and regulate Group membership by way of legal norms which the courts can declare. All demands to secure the citizen's freedom of conscience must be read as political claims for the maintenance or establishment of legitimate legal administration, and the imperative that officials must not be given discretion to discriminate against individuals on the basis of their beliefs.

The toppling of freedom of conscience from the pedestal of the basic legal right by no means undermines the absolute importance of this fundamental 'right' in a democracy. At all times we must resist demands that the law should control our thoughts, and deny the legitimacy of official action against persons which is based on the sole ground that they entertain certain beliefs and values. Denying that we possess a distinct interest which the law will protect is important because it exposes some of the questionable claims made on the assumption that the law is concerned to protect this so-called freedom as a substantial fundamental right.

Society itself is an artificial associational form. The interest in membership of a particular Society is a profoundly important entitlement and will be protected by the courts as a fundamental constitutional right. This interest is obviously necessary in that legal persons are defined as members of Society. The interest of membership consists of enjoying access to all the manifold benefits available within the country which are not the benefits of other legally recognized interests; and it entails an entitlement to legal protection in respect of all other constitutional interests. The criteria for membership of the artificial form Society must be determined by the ULP.[105] In principle the withdrawal of citizens' rights is a matter for the executive, not for the courts. Non-citizens do not have any constitutional basic interests recognized by law, other than their human rights a (see *post*, p. 350). All questions of disputed citizenship lie on the border between legal determination and political choice; if the claimant satisfies the criteria of citizenship then the law must protect his or her interest; if he or she is not a citizen then he or she cannot claim to possess the constitutional interest.

Every citizen has *a freedom* to join, or to create, *Organizations.* However, that freedom is quite distinct from the interest we are concerned with here: the interest which a citizen may have in the membership of an Organization. A citizen's membership of a private Organization is not enjoyed by permission from the State. However, all memberships are of course subject in various ways to possible limitation and abridgement by the State.

As far as the individual is concerned, Organizations, unlike Groups, are not self-selecting. It follows from the nature of Organizations that qualification for membership of the association is a matter for the existing members. So no citizen has a right to join any Organization he chooses. Furthermore, individual citizens have no basic right—as an implication from legal justice—to demand a review of the Practices by which admission to Organizations is gained. This is an important exception to the citizen's right to judicial review of the procedural justice of normative Practices. Equal opportunity is not a basic right implied from equality before the law. Such a doctrine involves a many-faceted political claim which, if it involves the creation of rights, would require positive enactment by the ULP to ensure that the rights were expressly and effectively conferred.

Similar considerations apply to membership of the organizational structure which is the *State.* There is a facile assumption that all citizens are constitutionally entitled to participate in government.[106] No such basic interest can be recognized in a democracy since administration is difficult and legitimacy demands competent administrators—a competence which not everyone possesses.

Freedoms

A lack of discrimination is apparent in rights discourse which describes a whole range of different interests as freedoms or liberties. Thus our capacities, our memberships, and our human rights are declared to be freedoms, and we are said to have liberties to vote, to marry, and so forth.[107] Such usages are obscuring and encourage false assumptions about the nature of the interests we do possess.

Freedoms or liberties are, in institutional theory, defined as freedoms to engage in *Activities.* Our constitutional freedoms are not freedoms to do particular acts but to engage in particular identifiable Activities (see *ante,* p. 37). Activities are defined as recognizable configurations of human behaviour in pursuit of objectives which we can all understand. Every citizen has a basic constitutional right of freedom to engage in any Activity. This is a substantial interest which the courts must recognize. The recognition of our freedoms is part of the conceptualization of relationships between individual citizens and the powerless State. The State may, with the assent of the ULP, acquire power to control and regulate any Activity; but until that power has been acquired the citizen is free to pursue the ends which define an Activity. The citizen's engagement in an Activity should only be seen to be by permission of the State where the ULP has enacted a blanket prohibition against it and officials are empowered to license individuals to engage in it.

In the eyes of the law political freedoms—the rights of free speech, of assembly, and so forth—are of no greater concern than any other free doms. In a democratic polity they do not need to be expressly promulgated as rights.[108] For any executive control of, or interference with, such Activities requires express authorization, in exactly the same way as regulations for keeping pigeons or breeding pigs.

There is no general right to freedom; there is no general Activity of living wherein we pursue an identifiable end through our engagement in all other Activities. On this view, citizens possess a host of individual freedoms.[109] As an identifiable interest possessed by the citizen, freedom is a concept of public law: an interest enjoyed by the citizen against the State. Our freedoms are not interests which are required in private law. In private law we base our claims to respect upon specific interests other than freedoms. As freedoms exist between individuals and the State there is—*pace* Rawls—no possibility of conflict between freedoms.[110]

Human rights

This is a hugely important and very special class of constitutional rights, and derives from the idea of legal justice as respect for persons. All citizens have a set of clear interests—human rights—which depend on their knowledge that neither their bodies nor their minds may ever be harmed by the State. We may say that each is the recipient of negative services: not to be maimed, tortured, killed, and so forth.

In protecting these interests the courts impose something in the nature of criminal liability on the State. They must be regarded as maintaining, in the only way possible, a criminal code for the State. The courts must approach this task by recognizing individual rights: only in this way can absolute prohibitions on the State be given meaning and force. For there is no possibility of imposing penal sanctions on the State, nor of any enforcement Activity to police the rules.[111] Human rights of this sort are not freedoms enjoyed by citizens: they are stark prohibitions imposed on the State.

So the norms which articulate our human rights must be seen to operate as prohibitions which are absolute. It is important to recognize that, unlike our freedoms, these rights do not arise because the State lacks the power to harm us. There is rather a set of imperatives: the State is forbidden to do certain acts. Yet many usages conceal the character of the prohibitions, for instance the locution that we enjoy a 'freedom from' the use of force.[112] When our human rights are infringed it is more accurate to assert that the State is guilty of an offence to which infamy attaches than to use the mealy-mouthed diplomatic locution that it has abused our rights.

If human rights are not liberties or freedoms from State power, neither are they *immunities* from it.[113] Such a description implies that the State has an underlying power from which, in this respect, citizens are given immunity. As the State has absolutely no such inherent power to curtail our freedoms, *ex fortiori* it has no power to harm us.

Our human rights are a special sort of natural rights. However, it must, once again, be emphasized that, although natural, they do not derive from an extra-legal ideal of the sanctity of human life, nor do they need to be justified in extra-legal terms. The criminal liability of the State is not prescribed by moral codes, international law, or censorious victors; the prohibitions are implied from the posited standards maintained in the legal Practices of the polity. The CS is an embedded Practice, and in respect of our human rights it draws upon the legal material in the penal Practice. So in order to discover the source of the prohibitions on the State we must look to the LS of the penal Practice which, for offences against the person, expresses current conceptions of inexcusable harms. The State must show the same degree of respect for the person as is required of other citizens.

No basic rights are absolute, so exceptions may be made to even these prohibitions, just as exceptions are specified in the penal Practice for offences committed by individuals. It is of central importance to appreciate that the exceptions must be founded upon enacted rules consented to by the ULP; they cannot be justified by good reasons. In a democracy there must be a complete justification; that can be supplied only by the well made norms of the ULP, not by good and pressing reasons given by the State.[114] From the legal point of view charters are thus impertinent in dictating the reasons which are said to justify the abridgement of our human rights.

Conclusion

The limited catalogue of basic rights possessed by all citizens in a democratic polity marks out the boundary of the inherent authority of judges in the ideal CS Practice. Limited though the rights may be, the authority which they entail in the courts is of the profoundest importance. These rights give substance to, and define the limits of, the partisanship of the courts. Judges do not function as the governors of the constitutional motor; nor is it their business to hold the balance between the respective interests of the citizen and the State. Their legitimate task is to protect these basic rights *a l'outrance.* They pertinaciously demand justification for official acts on behalf of the citizen. In demanding precise proofs of lawful government they truly legitimize the State, which they would be unable to do if they were part of that administration.

It cannot be denied that the courts have been somewhat inconsistent in discharging this function. Court records in the USA, Germany, and the UK show, especially in times of emergency, something less than the zealous concern for basic individual rights demanded by legal justice.[115] Although judicial displays of independence from the executive have historically been salutory, their defence of basic rights has been erratic. However, in more recent times the sense that their past record was not wholly laudable has led to an arrogation of powers to protect citizens in respect of desirable but inadequately conferred rights. With encouragement from several quarters, judges have been prepared to assume liberal programmes: a strategy which, however attractive, is simply improper. Some have deemed it their task, not only to fill in political gaps by ascribing rights, but to assume a yet wider function as monitors of executive action in general.

NOTES

1. '[The] most difficult feature of the civil condition to identify and get into place has been the law': Oakeshott (1975: 181).
2. The narrow ambit of public law in institutional theory may be contrasted with the views of both functionalists and normativists: see Loughlin (1992: 60). The functionalists define law as part of the apparatus of government, while the normativists emphasize the separation of powers and the need to subordinate all aspects of government to law. For the view that the proper function of public law is to protect individual rights against excess or abuse see Allan (1992).

3. Whoever hath an absolute authority to interpret any written or spoken laws it is he who is truly the law-giver to all intents and purposes and not the person who first wrote or spoke them': Bishop Hoadley, quoted by Gray (1931: 172).
4. On the inadequacy of the instruments of control see Mitchell (1968: 57). For a call for the establishment of new, non-legal decision-making processes, embodying effective safeguards, and aiming at more open government, see McAuslan (1980: 272).
5. On the dramatic acceleration in the growth of administrative judicial review in the USA see Shapiro (1995: 43–66).
6. There are many strands which lead to the emergence of the centralizing State; it is not to be regarded as the outcome of power-hungry officials making use of new technological advances to extend their powers. The emergence of the centralizing State, with its defining concern for individual conduct, is related to the emergence of the market economy and the establishment of the forms in which democratic ideas are realized. The centralizing State's refusal to allow split allegiances, its opposition to local privileges or religious directions from outside, are the concomitants of the impetus to ensure equality before the law for all its citizens.
7. Religious struggles have been of central importance in the emergence of the democratic polity, especially in the UK. In constitutional history the dissenters, or non-conformists, have played a crucial role in the emergence of the democratic polity. The necessary development must be the achievement of a state of affairs in which political argument is not controlled by religious belief. The requirement of mass legitimation forms the decisive point of difference from the traditional order in which the right to express consent was limited to the privileged and propertied classes; Beetham (1991: 94). See also Macpherson (1966: 10): 'So democracy comes as a late addition to the competitive market society and liberal state. . . . In few countries was anything like it achieved until later in the nineteenth century' (ibid.) The point is underlined in Hall (1949: 87–8).
8. Only within a fairly affluent Society can a State achieve many of the basic functions of centralization. The hyperactive State may be a consequence of affluence. Rawls, as is well known, allows that the principles of justice come into play only at a certain level of economic well-being (1976: 126–7).
9. Dicey (1889: 190).
10. In jurisprudential discussions there is a serious lack of discrimination between the domains. Insufficient attention is paid to the different norms and concepts which are generated in the different Practices. The new CS Practice generates a new discourse: the respect for persons demanded of the State differs from the respect demanded in civil law of other members. Legal Justice has a different logic here. There is asymmetry between the State, initially powerless but acquiring great powers, and the citizen.
11. There are two possible ways in which a CS Practice can emerge. There may be the deliberate institution of special courts or agencies for hearing appeals against the State; see Tate and Vallinder (eds.) (1995: 372). Or there may be a bifurcation from existing ordinary courts, as in the USA and the UK. Under

the doctrine of separation of powers the specialist courts may be regarded as part of the administration, rather than of the judicial system.

12. It may be that, due to the concentration on administrative propriety, the vocabulary of bureaucratic default is more sophisticated in continental jurisdictions than in England.
13. The moral foundation of the rule of law rests securely upon the value we place upon individuals, not on the virtue of conformity to the rules. The concern is, not for mere deontological righteousness, but for persons and Groups. Judges demanding legal correctness in all governmental actions are upholding, not a legal, but a constitutional, a political conception of the rule of law.
14. For the view that to conceive of the person as the carrier of rights is a distinctively modern understanding of social relationships see Dagger (1989). It is frequently asserted that neither the Greeks nor the Romans had a notion of human rights; cf. Gerwith (1978).
15. We may approve of Philip Selznick's idea that legal life 'gravitates towards its own ideas as it evolves over time'; nevertheless it is important to insist that this development depends partly upon the achievement of democratic legitimacy in the other components of the polity; the other forms must also stand in the correct relationship to law. There can, for example, be no such gravitation towards a purer law if the legislature, in its enactments, consistently fails to show respect for the law.
16. This is one of the received ideas of juristic thought. Woolf LJ said: 'Judicial review is all about balance, balance between the rights of the individual . . . and the rights of government . . . to do what it has been elected' *(Observer, 9* May 1993). See also Mitchell (1976: 179) for whom private law remains a jurisprudence of rights while public law is one of interests, and is predominantly concerned to balance public and private interests.
17. 'It has always been one of the pillars of freedom . . . that the judges are no respecters of persons and stand between the subject and any attempted encroachement on his liberty by the executive, alert to see that coercive action is justified in law': *per* Lord Atkin *Liversedge* v. *Anderson* [1942] AC 206 at 489. Cf. Griffith (1977: 203): in the UK the 'judiciary is not placed constitutionally in opposition to the government, but in the overwhelming mass of circumstances, alongside it.' See also Simpson (1992: 25): 'From 1917 onwards British judges have, with the rarest of exceptions, consistently upheld the progressive erosion of British liberty in the name of good government; Zadig's case represents a sort of watershed between the world of Victorian liberalism and the world of the vigilant state.'
18. In the legal world trust is excluded. The law erects barriers behind which trust has its place. The law's relationships are open, clear, articulate, never confidential. This consideration highlights the paramount importance of recognizing within a polity the range of autonomous non-legal regimes in which trust is important. However, trust is absent from constitutional practice. 'Free government,' said Jefferson, 'is founded in jealousy and not in confidence; it is jealousy and not confidence which prescribes limited constitutions, to bind down those whom we are obliged to trust with power':

quoted in Aubert (1983: 42). Yet the fact that trust is absent from constitutional matters does not mean that those matters are legally controlled. Political accountability is a central feature of democratic government; the government must continuously test its representativeness to see that its claim to be supported by public opinion is still valid (Finer 1970: 63–6). Beyond this, it is also accountable for all its actions to the ULP.

19. 'The great growth of administrative law during the latter half of the century has occurred because of the recognition of the judiciary and Parliament alike that it is the function of the high court to ensure that executive action is exercised responsibly and as Parliament intended': *per* Lord Griffith: see Sedley (1994). Implicit in this is the idea of the primordial powerless State. From the standpoint of the functionalist, given the manifold concerns of modern bureaucracies, the notion of the powerless State will certainly be concealed. The growth of the machinery of govermnent, outstripping the law, is seen as an inexorable process, making us overlook the fact that its powers are not extensions of what it already possesses but are all conferred by the ULP. The powerless State is perhaps concealed by talk of limited government. It is the legal requirement that the State provide proof of the requisite power which makes the special safeguarding of the rights of individuals and private associations less urgent than is commonly supposed: cf. Finer (1970: 64).
20. The notion of the powerless state is reflected in Kelsen's efforts to turn it into a juristic fiction. The difference between the discourse of law and other discourses is nowhere more evident than in the law's view of the State. Here we might say that 'legal discourse invents and deals with a juridical hyperreality that has lost contact with the realities of everyday life and at the same time superimposes new realities on everyday life': Teubner, quoted in Cotterrell (1995: 186).
21. The moral motive is a desire to justify one's actions to others on grounds to which they could not reasonably reject. By contrast, the legal motive is to justify by reference to the existing law. This requires explicit justification, never simply an appeal to trust or reasonableness. Valid law is created in such a way that it cannot properly be challenged: it is well made.
22. For a different picture of chains of authority, not considered in the light of power-conferral; see Burton (1992: 152–7). Burton's authorization chain begins with the broad set of all possible *reasons* for action. At a slightly lower stage the lawmaker is authorized to act on a smaller subset of reasons; at a lower stage still, that of law applying and interpretation, the interpretive agencies have a yet narrower subset of reasons for acting. So the higher up the authorization chain one looks, the wider is the set of legitimate reasons for action. In institutional theory the justification for legal acts or NPs, must be found in norms, often rules, not in a subset of reasons. Here I am concerned with power-conferral by way of norms which justify administrative acts of officials. What justifies is a properly deliberated NP, not a limited set of reasons which support it.
23. See Kelsen (1973: 132): 'The legal order is a system of general and individual norms connected with each other according to the principle that law regulates

its own creation.' The normative character of administrative action must be stressed: we must pay attention to the express norms under which action is undertaken. While recognizing that norms can be created by administrative bodies, the distinction between the enactments of the ULP and all other legislated norms is important: the former cannot be judicially reviewed, the latter can. Generally it is the executive rather than the legislature which will threaten breaches of human right, so it is the concretized norms which must be checked to see that they justify what is to be done. See Walkland (1968: 910) on the definition of legislation. He denies that it is possible to identify the different functions in the separation of powers.

24. Cf. von Wright (1963: 198–9).
25. For the courts in the USA after the 1950s ensuring that administrative rules were well made see Shapiro (1995: 52). The courts demanded that rule-making procedures should enable all groups to participate, and ensure that answers were given to group objections and all possible issues considered. The perfectionist demands of the judges turned administrative rule-making into a slow and expensive process. In the UK delegated legislation, subject to parliamentary scrutiny, is less frequently subject to judicial review.
26. In cases where courts have allowed life-support machines to be switched off the emphasis should be less on whether it is permissible to end a vegetative existence, and more on the careful prescription of procedures which must be followed in making that decision in any individual case. Contrast the informality by which 3 doctors in Nazi Germany were empowered to decide who should be sent to gas chambers under a programme of euthanasia. The 'slippery slope' fears are entertained by those for whom procedures are mere procedures.
27. The courts are concerned to ensure 'legitimate processes', not 'legitimate outcomes'; see Ely (1980: 74). Cf. Allan (1988), who regards the distinction between merits and legality as incoherent; it begs the question of the acceptable limits of judicial scrutiny. He makes the important point, however, that adjudication should be distinguished from administration in that the former 'consists in determining the propriety of administrative action in relation to the party aggrieved'. In the CS Practice the courts question the authority of the legal norms, testing them for procedural legitimacy. So when we approach the perennial question 'is there a moral obligation to obey the law?' we might say that in a democracy the individual citizen is scarcely in a position to challenge the laws if they are well made. It is perhaps that character which provides the *prima facie* duty to obey the law. Cf. Greenwalt (1987: 178) who is sceptical about the *prima facie* duty to obey the law; if such a duty exists it must he maintains be based on natural law or utility.
28. It is worth reiterating the need for the emergence of a separate Practice as the focus for a new legal domain.
29. Such a dissonance is to be found in Zadig's Case, R v. *Halliday,* ex parte *Zadig* [1917] AC, where it was unsuccessfully argued that a minister could not create regulation permitting detention without express legislative authority.
30. 'Every time a court declines to interfere with an abuse of state power it legitimises that piece of oppression': Sedley (1991). Courts may properly

decline to interfere with an abuse of power which does not directly affect individual rights; this is not to legitimize the abuse.

31. Dowrick (1961: 176–204) lists the virtues of legal justice.
32. For Kelsen (1973: 181) the state as a juristic entity is a personification of the national legal order.
33. This must be qualified: the human rights are those possessed by individuals as human beings (see *post*, p. 350).
34. It has been argued that the State has rights. In checking official powers the courts may be said to be checking State 'rights'; but even if we adopt this locution, it is never the task of judges to articulate the 'interests' of the State as they do for the citizen. Rights of citizens and 'rights' of the State are not on the same footing, if only because judges are duty-bound to develop the former and to keep the latter strictly within the express law. English courts have been relatively slow to extend their jurisdiction over prerogative powers. There is no reason why the exercise of such powers should not be on the same footing as statutory powers.
35. The court is indeed a law-making body, but not in the style of the Supreme Court of the USA.
36. The norms are at present being whittled away. The new self-image of the judges involves less self-restraint. *Locus standi* rules stand in the way, so they must be replaced. The number of occasions upon which judges remind us that they are not elected is an index of the increasing pressure on the courts to decide matters which require executive or legislative decision.
37. On rules of standing see Cane (1996: ch. 3). See also PL 1987 245 'Understanding Standing' . See also Turr (1982: 135–69) on *actiones populares* and the problems connected with the protection of consumer interests.
38. See Lord Diplock in *IRC* v. *NF of SE;* it is no longer the law that a specific interest is the sole basis for *locus standi.*
39. On the notions of 'justiciability' and 'judicial' see Marshall (1961: 265–87)
40. The unprincipled conception of the rule of law is inadequate; it ignores the individualism of legal justice. For such an account see Goodrich (1986: 156); legal regulation is by way of legal norms, general rules, applied in an impartial fashion to all persons alike. Rules are to be known in advance, and their application is to be placed in the hands of a disinterested and distinct profession.
41. See Herman (1981: 180).
42. See Maddocks (1989: 50–67). In institutional theory a constitution is simply the structure of norms controlling the relationships between the central forms in the polity. It does not involve structures which ensure stability, freedom, or justice (Cicero), nor structures which are in Bolingbroke's words 'derived from fixed principles of Reason'.
43. Dworkin (1986: 432 n. 6). It is no accident that positivist theories were first developed and became most popular in democracies.
44. Austin (1879: 274 5). Historically legal sovereignty depends upon prior claims to political sovereignty or general independence. Democratic sovereigns are legislatures recognized as supreme by the legal Practices. Sovereignty is transferred from an Organization (the State) to a Practice (the ULP).

45. 'A constitution is, first of all, a legal document. It is intended to state the supreme rules of law.... [It should] exclude anything that is not intended to be regarded as a rule of law': Wheare (1966: 50). The non-legal nature of the constitution is concealed by the usage in which commentators refer to the polity as a legal order or a legal system. For example, in referring to Parliament's legislative activity MacCormick says: 'those who exercise power and discretion within a legal system must always at least purport to be acting on the basis of seriously held and seriously considered values' (1981: 144). The view that the academic lawyer expounding constitutional law will provide an overview of all institutions of constitutional importance is widespread. 'Public law deals with legal arrangements which establish the institutions of the state and regulate the exercise of political power': Loughlin (1992: 2). In consequence, constitutional lawyers become involved in political science and the political appraisal of institutions: see de Smith (1980); Wade (1980: 1–2).
46. John Griffith (1989) comments on the divide between a. lawyers who take public law to include all statutes, and b. those who see the primary function of public law as the limitation of governmental power and enforcement of governmental duties. See also Loughlin (1992) on the ideological rift between normativists and institutionalists.
47. A constitution structures and controls all the forms in the polity, not just the executive. The popular view of the constitution as 'a device for limiting the power of the executive' (Pulzer 1992) is far too narrow. See also Wheare (1966: 4–8). Such a view is clearly related to the idea that constitutions are the offspring of the demand for limited government; that they are essentially democratic structures. To moralize the constitution in this fashion is likely to distort our picture of the institutional structures and their ideas.
48. For persisting doubts as to the existence of the British constitution see Ridley (1988: 340–3). Thomas Paine regarded a constitution as the conscious formulation by a people of its fundamental law (1976: 93). If a written constitution is a deliberated structure, an unwritten constitution involves continuous deliberation and decision-making.
49. See Wheare (1966: 50–1), not only for the English view that the constitution is an essentially legal entity, but also for the barely concealed disdain for countries in which it is a political manifesto, creed, or testament.
50. Constitutional law is limited to the determination of the citizen's rights against the State. Dworkin discusses the powers of the Supreme Court in maintaining a constitutional law which goes well beyond the immediate business of taking individual rights seriously (1986: 357). There is virtue in the view that public law is best symbolized, not by a constitutional document, but by a loose-leaf encyclopedia containing sections on housing, planning, social welfare, health, safety, etc.: Loughlin (1992: 241).
51. For the view that the field of study of the public lawyer consists of all these institutional developments see Jennings (ed.) (1993: 71).
52. For the view that English courts do not have the expertise or resources to deal with disputes arising between central and local governments see Loughlin (1991 595–7)
53. In some institutional forms of the polity trust and self-regulation must play

an important part. Public life ought to be dominated by principles of political morality. For an example of the legalistic approach to public life see the USA Ethics of Government Act 1978, which illustrates the delusion that politics can be cleaned up by being subjected to the regulation of legal rules. This does not contradict what I have said above about the need for *norms* to ensure respect for Groups and persons because the principles of legitimacy are operative norms. The self-regulation of courts, the norms of Practice integrity, depend entirely on the restraint and good will of the judges.

54. Something of this is brought out in the description of the constitution as a dialogue; see Fisher (1991). We need to remember always the speed of change and the fact that provisions in a constitution may change substantially from what was first intended. Two centuries of organizational action and judicial interpretation have turned the power of government into something that the founders could never have foreseen.

54a. This is clearly not how the Supreme Court, with its claims to be the ultimate arbiter, is situated. Such a development is, as Mill foresaw, almost inevitable within a federal system.

55. For all norms, meaning is use. At all times the enacted norms of the constitution are the operative norms; they may derive from the written formulations. The reconstituted operative norms may differ markedly from the written norms.

56. Underlying the constitutional rules there is, said Corwin, a body of theory and principle; 'The sum total of ideas of some historical standing as to what the constitution is or ought to be' (see Marshall (1989)). Though institutional understanding is always historical, the emphasis must be on the principles of democratic legitimacy which are not relativist. A constitution will be a set of compromises, but in a democracy those principles are operative norms and must therefore be foundational.

57. The far from powerless State may rely on prerogative powers. It operates today with an accumulation of powers which appear to be indispensable. There is a tendency to believe that old established State powers are constitutional, given by the law. Phrases like the 'hyperactive State' give it a mind of its own as if it relies on inherent powers. The State does not have an organic development; it is not a growth to be nurtured and honoured, but a collection of powers to be restricted.

58. Indeed also for the maintenance of old laws. We should recall the celebrated remark of Holmes that it is absurd that a law should be followed only because it was laid down a hundred years ago.

59. Utopianism is the impulse to promote the ideal at the expense of the practical. We may instance the doctrinaire imposition of ideals concerning property in socialist regimes, and their refusal to countenance practical objections or compromises.

60. Gough (1955: 212) describes the situation in which 'customary forms of legislative procedures and the constitutional principles they may be supposed to safeguard are in the last resort no more fundamental than the contents of the legislative enactments themselves'. The fact that the procedures for constitutional amendment in the UK are no different for those required to

reform the Dogs Act is commonly remarked upon. The constitution is not fundamental or sacred, but is constantly altered.

61. The distinction between moral and political values and norms is worth preserving. The moral touches on the conduct of individuals; the political involves wider questions involving collectives, and relationships between the forms of life.
62. The relation to Parliament is often expressed in terms of accountability. Although accountability and enforcement are distinct, the provisions for ensuring accountability for past acts are intended to maintain or enforce constitutional standards in the future.
63. It is commonly assumed that the maintenance of constitutional propriety is a matter for the executive; that it is for the government to set up commissions, institute enquiries, and so forth. Although this is indeed a governmental responsibility—it is an aspect of good government—the final say, and the responsibility, rest not with the State, but with the ULP.
64. Locke in the Second Treatise declared the legislative to be supreme; and for Bentham Parliament was the supreme operative power. For the view that in the Middle Ages the English Parliament was not primarily a legislature or law making-body but a court see McIllwain (1910).
65. A written constitution interpreted not by the ULP but by a Supreme court can present obstacles to constitutional reform. The authority of the ULP stems from its legitimacy rather than from any legal claim to power; cf. Beetham (1991) for whom authority is regarded as according with the law. The legal authority of the 1688 Parliament may be questionable, but the doubts are unimportant.
66. Procedures for constitutional amendment are commonly prescribed, e.g. requirements for a two-thirds majority, entrenched clauses, new procedures, calls for referendums and plebiscites, etc. If the courts are satisfied with the democratic character of the ULP procedures they will be prepared to ignore the procedural requirements of some prescribed new Practice. It is not within their authority to decide, for instance, whether a referendum is required: that decision calls for the exercise of political judgement. Any new legislative procedure prescribed by statute will be a political not a legal requirement. Parliament's decision that a procedure is no longer required is itself a clear political judgment. It is mistaken to suppose that all enactments are legally operative and legally binding simply because they are formally enacted; many are of political rather than legal significance.
67. The political revolution—the establishment of democracy—ousted the medieval idea that the King, Parliament, and the courts held indefeasible powers defined by custom. Within a democracy the powers of institutions are to be defined and redefined by the sovereign body. In modern Society all powers are no longer fixed and customary, but open to continuous reform and redefinition. The constitution—now the outcome of contemporary choice —does not replace the old custom with a new custom, but specifies the institutional forms for an ongoing revolution. The demand of democrats for an ideal fixed constitution is self-contradictory. The continuous revolution

breeds awareness of the importance of the ULP. Politics which focus on the legislative sovereign are not thereby diminished, but enhanced.

68. The European Court of Human Rights may be regarded as a court of law, but its legal character is qualified: the Convention consists of principles as well as rules; the court is involved in weighing and balancing; its decisions are not technical exercises in interpreting texts but judgments of political appropriateness and morality. There is a willingness to second-guess the judgments of democratic ULPs.
69. A constitutional court's authority lies, not in its ability to command, but in the willingness of other political actors and ultimately public opinion to obey. In a democracy, where accountability is the touchstone of political legitimacy, the authority of the constitutional court may be precarious, especially at the beginning; see Morton (1988: 93).
70. See Friedman (1990: 40) on the arrogation of power by constitutional courts and the undemocratic nature of their deliberations.
71. 'Partly because rights are neither self-evident nor self-actualising constitutional courts are at times led to balance contending rights claims and therefore to legislate': Stone (1995: 224).
72. The wording of the German constitution on defence policy is so vague that it can be interpreted to mean quite different things according to one's political point of view. Of equal vagueness is the 14th Amendment to the US Constitution which guarantees the equal protection of the law.
73. A non-activist, conservative constitutional court faced with questions which manifestly do involve political choices, one which feels it is bound by particular 'legal' doctrines with respect to a constitution—doctrines about the cohesive interrelationship of the provisions and a hierarchy of Articles—may be regarded by many as failing to do justice to the issues which it is to determine. See Wallach (1995: 328).
74. There is also the possibility that courts will be prepared to criminalize violations of Bills of Rights; see Kaczorowski (1989: 565–83)
75. It will mean that politicians will deliberate in the language of constitutional law and make reasoned decisions about the constitutionality of legislation; see Stone (1995: 225).
76. Although some American commentators see the internally divided and plural nature of the US constitution as a valuable resource, rather than a weakness, the main beneficiaries of such plurality are the judges. Written provisions often do not achieve what was intended of them: for instance, they do not confer rights on citizens, but instead confer on the judges legislative powers to confer rights. Problems arise not over vested interests but over imperfectly realized rights. Note Stone's view that 'in judicialised environments, courts do not protect rights better than do legislatures' (1995: 23).
77. E.g. *United States* v. *Nixon* 418 US 682 (1974). The answer to the question in dispute between the President and the special prosecutor over the presidential tapes was not to be found in the existing legal material.
78. The legal landscape in the USA was transformed by the capitulation of the Supreme Court in 1937. The vacuities of New Deal statutes permitted the judges to declare the lawyers' independence from traditional legalisms. To

this date we can trace the 'transformation of legal discourse' in the USA; see Ackermann (1984: 9). The claim that law, which possesses an internal logic, can be reconstituted to suit American aspirations and needs resembles the claims that there is a distinctively African way of doing mathematics or logic.

79. See Dworkin (1986: 154–5) on the pragmatic case for a judge pretending to make decisions in accordance with legal conventions. Morton (1988: 106) observes that the judicialization of constitutional control renders it more legitimate and thus more effective by suppressing, or at least camouflaging, the political discretion of those who exercise it: the judges.
80. On the shift from 'natural' to 'human' rights see Dagger (1989: 305). If natural rights are derived from the idea of self-possession, human rights rest upon a conception of a person as having needs that must be met. 'Thus the right *against* others of the natural rights theorists tend to become claims *upon* others of the human rights theorists.'
81. See Campbell (1983: 18) for a similar emphasis on the positive nature of rights.
82. The relationships between citizen and State are wholly different from relationships between citizens *inter se*. If legal justice is to be done to citizens a distinct legal Practice must emerge in which the new logic of basic public law rights can be worked out; see Martin (1993: 88). Democratic legitimacy requires that important citizen–State disputes are given a legal articulation—not informal settlement by government agencies—so that citizens can have knowledge of their legal rights against the State.
83. The conduct of politics in terms of rights is encouraged by such promulgation. Political argument is distorted where matters such as abortion, pornography, euthanasia—which manifestly call for democratic debate, compromises between Groups, investigation of social consequences, and so forth—are treated as questions about human rights. On the emptying of political life see Gray (1992).
84. See Dagger (1989: 304) on the superabundance of distinctions.
85. Cf. Locke (1956). Locke licenses the identification of mere claims as rights, or as ghostly possessions. If rights are to be treated as institutional facts they must be vested. We have in Locke the origins of an industry which, without concern for institutional realities, seeks to discover what each person ought to be able to claim. It is important to exclude from the class of basic rights all claims to equality which exceed the fundamental claim to equality before the law. So despite the intuitive appeal of, say, the claim for equal pay for equal work, the claim is not a deduction from legal justice. Any such right, interfering as it does with freedom of contract, would have to be conferred. Yet claims of this sort are commonly regarded as having their foundation in the principle of equality before the law. See Friedman (1990: 163).
86. J. A. G. Griffith has doubts about rights: rather than speaking about human rights we should recognize that individuals and groups make claims on society. This approach makes clear that 'law is not and cannot be a substitute for politics' (1979: 16–17).

87. As a general rule basic rights do not, as many conferred socio-economic rights do, have resource implications.
88. On the perception that the rule of law favours the haves rather than the havenots, that it is of more assistance to businesses than to underprivileged groups, see Aubert (1983: 559.
89. See Nagel (1991: ch. 7) on Egalitarianism. See also Martin (1993: 67) on the derivation of the right not to suffer segregation in schooling from the equal protection of the law (cf. *Brown* v. *Board of Education* 347 US 486 (1954).
90. The philosophical basis for the rights declared by statesmen and enshrined in declarations is far from clear. Seighart (1986), like many others, merely accepts the conventional wisdom of statesmen about rights as they appear in charters. Although declared to be unquestionably 'a good thing', their foundations are obscure. There is of course a recognition that in some countries declared rights have a fictive character: Martin (1993: 56).
91. The Italian courts have treated the social rights declared in the Italian Constitution as 'programmatic' norms, norms which, though morally, constitutionally, or politically binding, do no} import legal obligations; see Mandel (1995: 272). By contrast, in *Francowich and Bonifaci* v. *Italy* [1991] ECR 1 5857 the European Court of Justice decided that a directive requiring member states of the EU to protect the wages of employees whose employers became insolvent conferred rights on individuals.
92. For the view that many compensation problems are best resolved by administrative agencies, that there should be less 'reliance on judicial action as a means of dealing with problems of compensation', see Michelman (1967: 1167).
93. 'Natural rights is simple nonsense, natural and imprescriptible rights, rhetorical nonsense—nonsense upon stilts': Bentham in Melden (ed.) (1970).
94. For the view that a Bill of Rights is not law in the traditional sense but 'a broad authorisation for judges to do as they see fit to secure certain outcomes' see Minogue (1986: 213).
95. For illustrations of such breathtaking interpretation see Hart (1983) on the 'due process' provision in the US Constitution. See also Haskell (1987).
96. Constitutional rights may not be vested; there may be no 'explicit, literal, authoritative recognition of what is being claimed': Martin (1993: 67).
97. I have in mind the right to a fair trial; here what is required is the establishment of legal Practices. Until the requisite institutional forms—the legal Practices—are securely established, there is little point in the conferral of rights on citizens.
98. The confidence threatens to become over-confidence. Senior judges increasingly express opinions on matter which properly lie within the scope of executive discretion or legislative judgment.
99. I mean strict legal appeals, which involves a legal Practice with two tiers. Every citizen must have the *capacity* to engage in the legal Practices, a right recognized in many Charters; see e.g. German Constitution, Art.19(4); Italian Constitution, Art. 24; and Art. 6 of the European Convention of Rights. The right of *equal access* is problematic. If the ideal of equal access for all citizens is required for the civil and public law legal Practices, it can be no part of the

business of the participants to secure access for citizens; nor, if access is denied, would the participants be in a position to protect the right. The right would then have to be protected by a non-legal, international body demanding that the State should mend its ways. Furthermore, alternative non-legal Practices may be established to deal with some citizen-State disputes; emphasis on a right to sue may encourage actions which are best dealt with informally.

100. Allan (1992) recognizes such a right: the right to fair treatment at the hands of the State.
101. Cf. Hayek (1944). Principles and the exercise of discretions are of the utmost importance in dealing with Groups.
102. On the nature of legitimate expectations see Cane (1996: 142-67).
103. In Ohio the Court of Appeal for the sixth Circuit upheld as constitutional a Bill banning protective rights for homosexuals and lesbians on the basis that no law can confer rights or impose duties on a group whose identity is defined by 'subjective characteristics'.
104. Legal justice is characterized by an absolute individualism. The propriety of the legal recognition of Group rights must be questioned. The legal articulation of relationships between members of Society should not be influenced by what is known, or believed, about the Groups to which individuals belong; sexism, racism, nationalism, etc. are characterized by such beliefs. Campaigners for racial *equality* dig a pit for themselves when they insist on the rights blacks as a Group, instead of pressing for the protection of the rights of individuals who happen to be black.
105. Should the rules laying down membership criteria be interpreted by the State or the courts? Against the assumption of the courts that all laws are their province must be set the fact that membership of Society is a grant. The exercise of executive discretion, subject to accountability to the ULP, seems to be legitimate here. The ULP has the power to divest a citizen of his or her membership. The Nazi decree depriving Jewish citizens of their nationality might be refused recognition because it was not well made, rather than because it constituted an infringement of human rights so grave that courts could not recognize it as a law at all; *per* Lord Cross in *Oppenheimer* v. *Cattermole* 1976 AC at 249. Practical considerations apart, there is little to recommend such an approach to the norms of a regime lacking democratic legitimacy; it is an approach which suggests that the body of its badly made norms is, like the curate's egg, good in parts.
106. See e.g. Art. 21, Universal Declaration of Human Rights (1948); Art 20, American Declaration of the Rights and Duties of Man (1948); Art. 25, International Covenant on Civil and Political Rights. Cf. Raphael (1976: 143). Such an assumption of pure democracy is wholly impracticable.
107. Rawls is a notable offender, using 'liberties' to include quite other interests. Such usages are not confined to the USA.
108. If we have a right to freedom of speech because the State is not inherently empowered to silence us, is there any need to list the advantages of having free speech? Cf. Raz (1994: 146). We do not need to make out a case for this right; we need only argue for its virtue when its abridgement is threatened

As against other citizens we may question the rectitude of talking about 'protecting' the right of free speech in the civil practice. In civil law we are free to say what we choose against others unless it constitutes an injury to their IE. In civil law that liberty is not a specific interest, but part of our general freedom to do what is not prohibited.

109. As there is no general right of freedom, so there is no right to life which could found such a freedom. There is a right not to be killed—a human right—but that is more like a legal prohibition on the State than a personal freedom. So the right to life cannot be raised as a banner against the right to choice, or a right of privacy. A supposed right to life, interpreted to mean something other than the prohibition against killing, can lead to absurd claims and, because of its visceral appeal, to uncompromising fanaticism.

110. Cf. Rawls (1973: 20). Our basic rights are our individual possessions. We all have them. They do not conflict: i.e. they do not give rise to inter-personal conflicts. If those interests are disputed in private law, the legal articulation of the position will be in terms, not of our freedoms, but of our specific civil and economic rights. Public law freedoms are out of place in private law. Interests defined in terms of desires will obviously conflict; but interests defined as socially recognized entitlements will do so infrequently.

111. Officials can of course be punished as members of Society. At law they may not rely on a defence of following orders which involve breaching the criminal code unless they have been authorized to do so by a well made norm.

112. 'Freedom from' is a common locution which has no relation to individual freedom to act but which refers to the conditions prevailing within the polity. It is a sociological fact that my house has not been burgled, that I am not starving, etc. The norms which guarantee such freedoms are prohibitions, and duties to provide.

113. To view individual freedom as an immunity from State power, is mistaken, and encourages the view that the law recognizes the *de facto* power of the State against which we can be inoculated. The law's starting-point must be that the State is powerless.

114. For a discussion of the view that human rights—a wider class than that which is defined here—are moral rights which do not depend upon constitutional or legal embodiment see Martin (1993: 74–92).

115. See Simpson (1992: 25). The English courts' record of controlling prerogative powers is unimpressive. In times of emergency courts are feeble, in times of peace sometimes governmental in their approach. The attitudes of the courts to the internment of American Japanese during World War II, and of German courts to the *Berufsverbot* against Communists, are instances to be noted with regret. See Elster and Slaagstad (eds.) (1988: 8–9).

9

Legal Foundationalism

I. FOUNDATIONALISM IN GENERAL

For the present purposes, foundationalism is described as the effort to establish the existence of a basic structure of values and norms which are implicit in the very condition of man as a social animal.[1] From the premiss that no man is an island, as a social being with certain capacities, limitations, and needs, the foundationalists say that we can work out minimal moral standards to govern his interactions with his fellow men, and also the political goods and values implicit in his position as a member of a coercive associational form. Any acts or norms which are not consistent with these 'natural' moral and political foundations will be wrong: a corruption of the very fabric and meaning of social life.

In the West the foundationalism of the Middle Ages was undertaken, under the banner of natural law, within the framework of Christian belief. The secular foundationalism of the Enlightenment generated ambitious projects to establish moral and political foundations by reference to ineluctable truths about human beings in society, from which we could deduce moral standards as unchallengeable as the theorems of Euclidean geometry. Despite fundamentally damaging criticisms of the idea that we could discover such foundations, the persistence of the quest has been remarkable.[2] The widespread contemporary perception of the impossibility of the projects of the Enlightenment has certainly not led to the disappearance of all foundationalist enquiry. On the other hand, some have responded to the prevalence of ethical relativism with a pessimistic nihilism: a conviction as to the futility of all enquiry into moral and political foundations. From the institutional point of view, that conviction is an absurdity.

For institutional theory the failure of foundationalist projects to establish truths for all mankind was partly the result of a failure to appreciate the *associational form* for which a foundationalist enquiry is appropriate. The truth that no man is an island should lead us to consider him, not in his contingent condition as a member of a *polis* or a civil Society—which admittedly he almost invariably is—but in his essential character as a member of Groups: those associational forms existing apart from the individual, in which alone human beings can achieve consciousness and establish their identity.[3] Human beings are indeed social animals;

members of associations: in other words they are always Group members, a fact which renders their treatment as atomic individuals, as members of the class of the human race in general, wholly obscuring.[4] Can we really believe that an isolated individual would be able, without recourse to the linguistic, conceptual, and axiological resources maintained by a Group, to make sense of the world, or be in a position to act as an agent? Nihilism appears to be a denial of any such Group membership; it is a denial of both the reality and the necessity of the associational forms upon which the language, consciousness, and humanity of the nihilist depends.

For the members of any significant Group foundationalism is a supremely important enquiry. The foundationalists articulate the goods and values of that Group; they give them clarity, order, and coherence, work out the implications of commitment to them, and generally provide the semantic framework for the Group. Philosophers rationalize, strengthen, and maintain the inter-subjective armature of the Group upon which members draw to make sense of their experience.[5] The domain of the foundationalist is that which is constituted and bounded by the language of the Group. Important contributions to the resources of a Group are made by poets, artists, novelists, journalists, and so forth as they provide images, narratives, prototypes, metaphors, connections, and slogans which have resonance for its members.

Groups are in conflict. I have described how the dissensus which characterizes civil Society consists of the conflict between such Groups (see *ante*, p. 258). In that competitition for members and influence, the work of the foundationalist who strengthens the claims of any Group to provide the most authentic and coherent explanatory framework for our experience of the human predicament will, in the long run, give that Group an advantage.[6]

Society must never be conceived of as a Group. All political philosophers who would go beyond the examination of the principles of legitimate government—who would establish the ends of government, and specify the common good or the principles of substantial justice—should be seen to be establishing Group foundations, not the foundations for a civil Society.[7] They are preparing to legislate, not for the members of a civil Society, but for a people who speak their language. The artificial form civil Society simply does not possess such a language, or such moral foundations: for institutional theory political philosophy of this sort is dead. Yet many commentators do conceive of Society as a Group: a conception which does violence to our awareness that our membership of Society, unlike our membership of any Group, is not the result of self-determination.

II: LEGAL FOUNDATIONALISM

Legal foundationalism, the enemy of legitimacy, is that part of jurisprudence which attempts to establish the values by which the laws of a country should be judged and the ends to which the law should aspire.[8] As a distinct academic discipline, legal philosophy is somewhat coy; there is some diffidence about acknowledging its character as political philosophy. Its practitioners are represented as standing apart from political philosophy, so that when the bell tolled for political philosophy it did not toll for jurisprudence. This sense of surviving the deluge perhaps derives from seeing the law as a distinctive and isolable segment of social life. In view of the law's distinctiveness, the ideological recommendations of distinguished lawyers and academics may appear to carry particular force by reason of their specialized knowledge of the law.[9] Or it may be suggested that the values and ends of the law are capable of being discovered by methods which are not available to political philosophers who, while making no claim to expert knowledge of the law, would establish the ends of government. It seems plausible that legal concepts, such as those of rights, duties, and personality, unlike political concepts can be analysed in a way which is wholly impartial and general. May the ends of law, of which those concepts are an integral part, not then be equally susceptible to neutral and detached investigation? The concept of law, unlike, say, the concept of the state, does not have a history.

Any suggestion that legal foundationalism stands apart from political philosophy, that the ends and values of the law differ from the ends of government, must be scouted.[10] Juristic incursions into political philosophy are not privileged; extrapolation from existing legal norms and activity gives the recommendations of legal philosophers no sort of priority.

The law with which foundationalists are concerned is manifestly substantive law: that body of norms which imposes duties and confers rights, powers, and interests on members of Society. The foundationalist sets out the principles of substantive justice—distributive principles—which should govern legislative activity. Any existing body of law is praised or criticized to the extent to which it reflects, promotes, or stands in the way of this unchallengeable conception of the ends of justice and the principles of right.[11] In order that we are able to sleep undisturbed by our knowledge of the inequalities and pains which the application of the legal rules must entail, we require a single theory establishing a coherent structure of values and arguments to which all members can subscribe.

For foundationalists, questions about the design and operation of the machinery for making, enforcing, and applying law are of secondary importance.[12] They assume that we need to determine the good before we can design the institutions for achieving the right. Priority must be given to working out the principles of social justice, to the ends of law, before we can start devising the institutional means for achieving them. So how far the foundationalist concerns himself with institutional requirements is a matter of personal taste.[13]

The broad sweep of history encompasses a great variety of legal philosophies, in which different types of legal foundational thought are distinguishable.

First there are the *critical foundationalists,* who attempt to set out standards applicable to all legal systems. The master-plan which they would produce has, if not universal, then very general application. Among this class of foundationalists are the various schools of natural law, the advocates of natural rights, Kantians, neo-Hegelians, utilitarians, and liberals.[14] It is a class which includes political theorists as well as lawyers. Although many schools of natural law found their inspiration in the idea of a universal Christian Church, later critical foundationalists relied on the Enlightenment promise that reason and scientific methods could provide foundational plans valid for all Societies. Indisputable truths about the nature of Man and society provided the starting-points from which theorists could proceed to find the minimal standards which should govern the laws of all peoples. The teleological strand has always been very strongly emphasized in the works of the critical school. The concern of the critical foundationalist is not to describe any particular legal system but to prescribe the minimal standards to which all positive law should aspire.

A quite distinct class consists of the *immanent foundationalists,* a class in which jurists outnumber the political scientists. These writers do not seek transnational standards, but try instead to discover the coherent structure of values and ends which are present in the social life of a particular Society. An actual system of law is taken to embody a consensus, a particular set of ethical principles which that Society or people possesses as a common heritage. The moral foundations are immanent in the existing laws and social norms of the country; they are there, waiting to be unearthed and theorized. The job of the foundationalist is to order the values and purposes of a particular Society, to clarify the concepts, to work out the implications and strengthen the arguments; to excise the false consciousness of Society and construct in its place a truer one. The purpose of the law is merely to give effect to the true morality of that Society. From that standpoint the laws, and other normative structures of the society, constitute a text to be pieced together and interpreted. In the work of the immanent foundationalists the descriptive element—wholly lacking in the approach of the critical theorists—appears interwoven with the prescriptive framework.[15] As refined by the foundationalist, the ideological structure is presented as the true morality, the community's moral sense, the general will, the common consciousness. Not for this school of thought the universalist ambition of the critical philosophers to provide metaphysical foundations; nor have its members placed the same reliance upon science and reason; in fact, many have been profoundly sceptical of the projects of the Enlightenment. For these schools the law must be defined in terms of the shared values of the community, and the purpose of the law is to render faithful service to them.

The search for immanent foundations has been variously pursued in the works of continental jurists such as Savigny, Puchta, Gierke, Ihering, Schmidt,[16] Krabbe, Geny, Duguit, and Durkheim. In America the search is most notable in the writings of Pound and Dworkin. It is an approach found in common law theory: the job of the common law theorist has been to seek, in both the cases and the institutions, certain in-dwelling purposes, ends, and values, which can then be ascribed to the community.

In addition to the critical and immanent schools we must recognize the existence of *declared* or *positive* foundations. Apart from times of war or other emergencies, the impetus towards establishing a consensus—towards nation-building—is strongest when a new Society is created. It is in order to promote such unifying ideas that the founders of a Society are likely to specify in the written constitution the values upon which the new Society is to be built. They will draw upon critical philosophy—principles are more weighty if they appear to be timeless—and they may borrow from the immanent philosophies of other Societies to show that they are mindful of the value of experience.[17] So a new Society may be presented with a moral charter in whose light its laws are to be enacted; a declaration of principles standing only in need of application, refinement, and exposition. Declared foundations are to be found in Charters and Bills of Rights. In some Societies such foundations are treated with respect; in others they are regarded as mere rhetoric.[18]

The rough conspectus of the foundationalist schools should remind us of the profound and irreconcilable disagreements between the schools. This is itself of signal importance, for although it does not prove that legal foundationalism is impossible, it does underline both the perennial demand for foundations and the reality of the persisting dissensus.

A: The dangers of legal foundationalism

In the battle of the books authors are profoundly critical of each other; that is part of their business. We can generally rely upon legal philosophers themselves to undermine or weaken the claims to universality, completeness, or validity made by any competing school. I am not here concerned with any particular schools or their critics, but with the question of whether legal foundationalism itself, in any of its forms, is a legitimate enquiry. Some legal positivists have been entirely sceptical about the possibility of providing such moral foundations; we need only look at the works of the positivists such as Kelsen or the Scandinavian realists to find scepticism of a thoroughgoing character. Yet other positivists, while they may have been adamant that, for purposes of study, the law must be kept apart from morality, have been less sceptical, and have shown no aversion to making general ideological recommendations.[19]

The institutional theory of law is immune from such an attack; relying solely upon the values of legal justice, it offers absolutely no conception of substantive justice, or of the ends to which the positive laws ought to be directed. Instead it takes as its starting-point the probability that the schools promoting such values and ends will never converge. This is a theory for a chronic and incurable dissensus.

As an effort to determine the ends and values for the laws of a Society, legal philosophy is to be condemned, not simply because of the misguided nature of the enquiry, but because it is profoundly corrupting. In the very place where we need the judgment of good government it erects the idol of the law. To suppose that it is possible to set out Society's moral foundations has deleterious consequences for our attitudes towards the decision-making Practices of a democracy and may poison the wells of political argument. Claims that law should seek the ends and adopt the values advocated by only one school are even more damaging when supported by claims that, in our existing legal system, we are already committed to them. The claim that pursuing a particular set of values represents no more than fidelity to the values of the existing law is like a toxic additive to a powerful drug.[20]

Now these strong words against legal philosophy must be set against our recognition of the supreme importance of the efforts of philosophers and ideologues to strengthen the foundations of Groups. Few things can be more important than the investigations by philosophers of the language of ideological Groups, or the efforts of writers and artists to reassure us of the worthiness and authenticity of the values to which we as Group members are committed. Philosophers help to articulate the world for us, and point out the implications of our moral and political intuitions.[21]

There is no denying that legal philosophers—despite their latent hegemonic claims—have contributed to that Group differentiation and under standing. There is nothing corrupting about efforts to strengthen the heritage of a Group which recognized that there are other languages and Groups. Dangers arise when writers claim privileged access to what they present as the official, if unrecognized, policy of a Society, and assert that the law itself embodies or supports the particular Group values which they advocate.

B: The basic fallacy

Legal philosophers can be accused of failing to understand the nature of the institutional form which is civil Society. It is a mistake embodied in a well established intellectual tradition: a working framework of ideas about the nation state in which the essential *legal* character of the civil Society is imperfectly understood. Writers insist on attributing an overriding moral significance, or an end, to an association which is just an empty, artificial form; they treat civil Society as a form which could give meaning to life. Yet it is not only a mistake, in the nature of a category mistake, to give such significance to Society or to search for its purpose or end: it is dangerous.[22]

Hegel provides an illuminating illustration of the confusion of Society with Group. Few thinkers provide a more perceptive description of the importance of the Group and of the objectivity of the language and values which it maintains; of the significance of individual self-determination, and of the dependence of persons on social—i.e. Group—life. Yet nowhere is the characterization of Society as a Group more evident. As a result, the tributes which should be paid to the Groups are offered to Society, with all the dangers which attend that glorification.

A realistic view of the world reveals civil Society as an artificial associational form, held together by coercive activity in which general social norms are enforced. Yet legal philosophers tend to ascribe to this manifestly artificial form the characteristics either of a Group or of a Community.[23] If they do not assume, or construct, an immanent communitarian consensus, they advance the claims of the armature of a particular Group as one to which all members of a Society, as rational individuals, must assent.

The writings of legal foundationalists are dominated by the false picture of Society as a morally meaningful association. In many discussions Society takes on, almost imperceptibly, the features of a community: an associational form which can only survive if all members recognize the same fundamental values. The literature is replete with references to the true morality of the community, the common consciousness of society, the instinctive sense of right of the people, social solidarity, and so forth.[24]

There is no doubt that this picture of Society, or of the ideal Society, as a community still retains a powerful hold on the imagination.[25] There is a strong suspicion that its attractions derive from poring over a scrap-book of postcards from the *Gemeinschaft,* the Greek *polis,* Polynesian islands, the societies of the High Middle Ages, and of late eighteenth-century America, but from which dire communications from even purer forms of political community, such as Utopian communes and theocratic and ultra-nationalistic regimes, have been ripped out.

The search for foundations, so important for Group life, is a project which has no relevance for Society because Society's normative foundations are not moral but political, legal, and coercive.[26] Neither the effectiveness of Society's norms in keeping the peace, nor the members' acceptance of those norms as valid will be dependent upon a congruence between the positive norms and a generally held, if minimal, conception of the good. Since we cannot ascribe to Society any purpose, end, or set of values, we cannot decide in advance the content of its legal system.

If in an ethically pluralist Society there is, by definition, no common consciousness on private matters of conduct, or about policies to be pursued by the government, is it not possible to discover a different sort of consensus in the values attending the workings of the institutions and practices which dominate the public life of Society? Do not the public institutions of a democracy in some sense embody or manifest a view of man in his relationships to others which can stand as the moral and political foundations of that Society? Cannot the ideas they embody be regarded as terms of a social contract to which we are all party? An examination of the governing ideas of the public institutions of a democratic polity will reveal that the ideal forms certainly do not embody objectives—such as substantial justice, freedom, personal autonomy, and prosperity—which the legal foundationalists would have us accept as the ends of civil Society.[27] In the first place, neither of the forms Society and State can be said to be animated by ideas of this sort. Although the ideas of the legislative and the legal Practices—with their commitment to respect for Groups and persons—may initially appear more promising, they can hardly help the foundationalist cause, since the governing ideas of these forms apprehend as their necessary concomitants the contingency of all laws, the precariousness of all rights, and an absolute refusal to privilege the values of any particular Group.

C: The foundationalists' image of law

Legal foundationalism reinforces an image of the law which is inappropriate for modern democratic polities. It is a many-faceted conception which misrepresents the distinctive character of legal norms and which, because it gives an inflated picture of the extent of the legal field, does nothing to curb the imperialism latent in legal philosophy. Some of the assumptions behind this image of the law are worthy of note.

Meta-law

Legal philosophers unearthing the foundations are often regarded as setting out, if not the law, then something more important than the law: an ideal law or meta-law against which the formulations of positive law can be appraised.[28] Although the higher law has nothing of the precision of positive law, it is nevertheless part of the law in that judges resort to its deliverances when filling the gaps in the positive law, or apply it to invalidate laws which do not conform to its standards. Since the meta-law occupies such an important place in the administration of justice, the precise definition of positive law becomes less important. Too precise a distinction between the positive rules and the higher principles might even be thought to prejudice the integrity to the law. So foundationalism may encourage a relatively fuzzy picture of that positive law which is founded upon the true morality of Society. There are attractions in this image, which allows growth of the positive law, and does much to promote flexibility in the administration of justice.[29]

The legal backbone of society

Another assumption of common-sense jurisprudence which legal philosophy does nothing to weaken is the idea that law is the normative framework at the very centre of social life; that it is a system of social control supported by the coercive power of the State: in other words, that it is the cement of society.[30]

The cohesion of the artificial form Society is admittedly achieved by enforcement Activity which guarantees the effectiveness of general social norms needed to counter the disruptive effects of individual lawlessness and the conflict between Groups. However, although the existence of Society does indeed depend upon State enforcement of such general social norms, it does *not* follow that these norms necessarily have a legal character.[31]

In democratic polities institutional theory requires that we accord law a secondary role in the business of achieving social control. It is no concern of the judges to maintain the normative backbone of Society; their responsibility is to do legal justice to individuals.[32] Only those rules which have been transformed by their incorporation in the LSS of the legal Practices are to be regarded as valid laws. Of course within a democratic polity the legal Practices will be enormously influential, and since a large number of the social norms will indeed have been transformed, many norms which can be said to be central in social control will have a legal aspect.

This image of law as the cement of Society is often associated with the notion that our laws reflect a framework of shared moral belief. From that viewpoint the breakdown of Society will be heralded by a weakening of the moral foundation of consensus. That image may be appropriate for pre-democratic communities, but in democratic polities it encourages the imperialism of the law and reinforces false conceptions of the legal norm and the legal system.

The assumption of unity or coherence

A further assumption, the subject of much criticism in recent years, is that the substantive positive laws possess, or ought to possess, systematic unity and coherence, and that the legal system either is, or ought to be, working towards the realization of an ideal condition.[33] By contrast, institutional theory would emphasize the disunity of the norms comprising the legal system, and insist that we should expect the legal system, at any given date in the future, to be little better than the 'mess' which Austin perceived the common law of the nineteenth century to be.[34] The most we can hope for is that it is not a disgusting mess. The principles of legal justice dictate that legal norms must not conflict; but we must not assume from that requirement that the LSS of the penal, civil, or public law Practices must, either separately or together, display any more substantial coherence and unity.[35]

Against the claims of the immanent foundationalists who assert that the legal system embodies a coherent set of moral values—or, for that matter, the radical critics of the legal field who are disappointed that it does not—we need to bear in mind not only the undeniable heterogeneity of intentions behind the norms in the LSS, but also their moral neutrality (see *ante*, p. 198).

Furthermore, we need to appreciate the enormous attractiveness of the self-appointed quest for the elusive silver thread which runs through the system as a whole and gives it a satisfying unity.[36] The claim that there is a moral coherence, or unifying principles, within the positive law is, after all, very easy to make. For some workers in this field the demonstration of the existence of such unifying principles is clear and simple, calling for little more than the persuasive powers of rhetoric. For others it is a superhuman task, calling for Herculean efforts of synthesis and casuistry. Unlike the efforts of historians to explain a historical event, where the research of opposing schools adds to our understanding of the circumstances and events, the conflicts between those seeking to demonstrate the moral foundations of the LSS illuminates only the Group values of the parties. For we cannot assume that the hotchpotch of norms in the legal field possesses a meaning or significance independently of the views of the commentator.

Our existing legal system is a miscellany of rules which happen to have survived to the present.[37] They are maintained and created by a ULP, under the influence of a succession of governments which can scarcely be represented as having taken a consistent moral or political stance over the years. Any consideration of the origins of the laws, of the arguments attending their creation, will show a great diversity of political and moral intentions. Today some laws are cures for ancient mischiefs, some are immensely partisan, some wholly technical, some are counter-productive, some enacted only after violent contest, some are marked down for reform, some have produced wholly unforeseen consequences, and so forth.[38] From the legal point of view our laws do not express, or stand for, any coherent set of moral purposes; they are simply a heterogeneous collection of legal presciptions. Neither the history of a statute nor the moral and political arguments for and against it are part of the law. The law consists of the norm formulations in the LSS of the legal Practices. Most enacted laws do not represent the simple achievement of one objective; many are unsatisfactory settlements enacted in the language of compromise.[39]

That courts and legislatures are continually adding to and subtracting from the corpus of the law is no evidence that, as the law matures, there will be a convergence towards, or the working out of, some moral order. That suggestion of a gradual progress towards maturity and coher ence is—given the rate of change in the social world—a romantic myth. Savigny's attack on codification and condemnation of the unsystematic French and Prussian Codes was based on the view that law must aspire to become a coherent and unified body of norms.[40]

The concept of fundamental law

The heterogeneity of our positive law must be considered alongside their contingent character. Although within a Society the positive laws appear to provide a fixed framework for the members' expectations, they are nevertheless all renegotiable in the political arena. In the legal field, in enforcement Activity and the legal Practices, the laws must operate as non-negotiable constraints upon and requirements for action; but that does not mean that, in the political field, any laws lie beyond challenge, reform, or repeal, no matter how important they may be in securing goals prized by nearly all significant Groups. Yet it is central to some foundationalist theory that there are a number of fundamental or basic laws which stand as non-negotiable axioms of political association.[41] In a legitimate polity the promulgation of fundamental laws, which reflect the views of a dominant Group, will inevitably result in conflicts with the principles of institutional integrity which require that respect be shown to all other Groups.[42]

That all laws are politically renegotiable must be regarded as a condition for the acceptance by members of Society of the compromises which are enacted, and which are to be coercively enforced, and which some may violently oppose. All laws remain open to challenge, renegotiation, and repeal. Our disappointment at the enactment of a law, our dislike of its provisions, is tempered by our knowledge of the possibility of future amendment or repeal. The apparently innocuous idea that we can enact and entrench a set of fundamental laws should be qualified by the experience that written formulations can generate wholly unforeseen interpretations.[43] There are good reasons for arguing that the members of Society within a democratic polity must be prepared continuously to renegotiate the boundaries of their freedoms unimpeded by the dead hand and fixed formulas.

D: Manifestations of foundationalism

The demotion of politics

Perhaps one of the most serious charges against legal foundationalism is its disdain for democratic politics.[44] The disdain arises because it is manifestly not in the nature of the legal foundationalist to respect other Groups—to give equal attention to other articulations of the world in which we live. Foundationalist philosophers are concerned mainly to strengthen the foundations, clarify the language, enrich the doctrines, and supply the symbols of just one Group. They believe that they are impartially setting out the foundations, not for a Group but for all mankind, or for Society as a whole.[45] However, the political activity of a democratic Society is a competition between all significant Groups; and only in the ULP will we find a procedure in which respect for significant Groups can be achieved.

In the writings of the foundationalists a subtle denigration of politics follows from the employment of a distinction between high-flown principles—by which all laws must be judged—and the sectional interests and policies of Groups which are the stuff of vulgar politics.[46] It would appear that the self-interested claims made by particular Groups do not themselves embody valuations worthy of attention.

There is, of course, no hint of a hegemonic intention in the foundationalists' assertion of goods, purposes, or principle; they are regarded as self-evidently valid. Foundationalists need to be reminded that their intuitions of the apodictic nature of, say, basic goods arise within a particular articulation of the world, within a particular language and the world-view it provides.[47] Other Groups, other languages. In any one Society there will exist many competing languages; complexes of meaning and experience arising from qualitatively different structures of belief and value. Marxist Groups, with their critiques of the language of capitalism, and feminist Groups with their critiques of the language of masculine liberalism provide useful illustrations. Liberal counter-attacks on the authenticity of the language of such Groups, demanding integrity to truth, and stressing the 'ethics of words', clearly assume that there is but one language of truth.

The legal foundationalists' indifference towards political activity is demonstrated by their willingness to emasculate, by-pass, or denigrate the normative Practices by which, in a dissensus, the general rules are to be created.[48] Within a dissensus all law-making and maintenance must be undertaken either within the ULP or in legislative Practices subject to the ULP, as it is only in these forms that respect for Groups can be guaranteed.

A country's laws must clearly reflect the practical conditions of the ways of life of the inhabitants; but in a democratic polity we can scarcely talk of the general social rules as being spontaneously generated. While customs in traditional communities can arise without conscious mediation, social rules in modern Societies must be very deliberately created if we are to assent to them. In the legitimate polity the paradigm of the social rule must be the enacted norm; and such rules, and any other general norms not so enacted, must all be susceptible to reform or repeal in the ULP.

One of the most misleading assertions about the common law is that the courts experienced difficulty in accommodating legislation. Although there were judicial caveats and qualifications up to the nineteenth century, the subsequent declarations of parliamentary sovereignty by the courts expressed unqualified acceptance of the rule that a common law provision would be trumped by legislation. Those who agonized over the problems supposedly presented to the common law by legislation were not the common lawyers, but those who theorized the common law: immanent foundationalists who conceived of the common law as being founded upon the common consciousness of the people. For them the ideal law was not a democratically enacted measure; it was rather a derivation from the meta-law behind custom—complete, coherent, and organic. The assertion of the common lawyer's difficulty in accommodating democratic legislation provides a singular illustration of foundationalists' myopia.

The judicial review of legislation

The foundationalists' contempt for politics is manifest in their approval of the judicial review of legislation.[49] For foundationalists the products of political activity which emerge as enactments of the ULP but which are judged not to conform to foundational standards should not to be recognized as general social rules, and ought not to be incorporated into the LSS of the legal Practices.[50] This corrupting constitutional innovation—which in vulgar jurisprudence is thought to support the doctrine of the rule of law—has great appeal for some Groups who see in it opportunities for increasing their influence. The obvious attractions of imposing legal restraint on uncontrolled political activity explains the 'explosion' in the numbers of constitutions which, in the immediate post-war years, incorporated provisions for judicial review of legislation.

However, bad politics cannot be cured by bad law; political legitimacy is not obtained by empowering courts to control the legislature. Nor, realistically, can the courts alone be supposed to constitute any sort of bulwark against political oppression. As constraints against ruthless anti-democratic tyrannies the courts are pathetically weak; more significantly, even in democracies courts of law, for all their concern for individuals' rights, have been remarkably ineffectual in preventing political witch-hunts.[51] Political evil must be countered by a politically active opposition.

Those who would empower the courts to act as defenders of the foundations against the 'majoritarian monster' of the ULP need to be reminded that, because the foundations may need to be reconstructed in every case, promulgated foundational principles can be used as easily to obstruct as to further policies of which we approve. The remarkable history of the 'due process' clause in the US Constitution must give the reflective food for thought. We might approve of the exercise of such great power by the courts if the judges were in a position to apply foundational standards clearly and with consistency; but where the declared foundations themselves are as contestable as the policies behind the enactments which the courts may invalidate, it can hardly be supposed that the judges' decisions are the necessary implications of the meta-law.

In place of the complicated procedures of compromise which attend the democratic Practices of legislation, the foundationalists may well provide alternative methods by which the legal scientist, the professor, or the judge can discover the laws. As legislator, the foundationalist stands as a philosopher king, as a Supreme Court judge, or as a mandarin: a decision-maker untroubled by the aggravations, bigotries, paranoias, and in-fighting of political life.[52]

The legal foundationalists would provide for Society a constitution containing a code: a master plan within which political argument is to be conducted.[53] For the legal philosopher the social contract is something more than an agreement between conflicting Groups about the constitutional devices whereby their differences can in future legitimately be compromised. It is often a charter in which many fundamental disputes are pre-emptively compromised. For the legislators it may settle distributive questions in advance of political storms; and for judges it is thought to provide the material from which they can discover the right answers to the hard cases.[54]

Judicial legislation

From Austin to Dworkin, many have believed that judges possess the authority to make law, and ought to do it better. Much of modern legal foundationalism may be read as an attempt to legitimate this practice which is widely perceived to be insecurely based.[55] If we were in possession of Society's master plan it might be plausible to suggest that judges should work towards its embodiment in the LSS rules—which would give the judges a very extensive authority. As the express LSS rules are inferior to the meta-law almost all cases will be hard cases, in which the LSS rules must be checked against higher norms. So within a legal system the extent of law reform by the judges will be limited by their self-restraint.

Deny the foundations, emphasize the dissensus, remove any prospect of a master plan for Society, and any authority of judges to unmake the law disappears, and their authority to make new law will be restricted to those occasions when they genuinely cannot find justification in the existing legal material.[56]

Although it is widely conceded that awkward questions arise about the democratic credentials of judicial legislation, there is confusion about the exact nature of the democratic principles which are breached by it. For instance, there is a certain innocence about the familiar assertion that, when legislating, judges must step carefully because they are not elected. Given the nature of legal Practices, it would not advance the cause of legitimacy by a centimetre if judges did sit in some sort of representative capacity, if they were installed to popular acclaim, or could prove that they enjoyed the confidence of the public. The related suggestion that the legitimacy of judicial law-making would be increased if judges were in some way made more accountable shows a willingness to dispense with the ideal of judicial independence altogether.[57]

The legitimacy deficit of which judges are aware stems from the *informal* and wholly inadequate process by which law must be made in an adjudicatory Practice. The blanket condemnation of formalism does much to conceal the necessity for the achievement of legitimacy of formal Practices of legislation. Democratic law-making requires an established Practice—the ULP—in which the ground rules ensure respect for all significant Groups. Procedures, intimately linked to the popular legislative processes, need to be hammered out to allow for the adequate consideration of all factors, objections, and interests which are relevant to the enactment of any law. The product of such Practices will resemble settlements or compromises reached as a result of negotiation and debate.[58] The all-important respect for Groups can hardly be guaranteed by relying on legislators to listen and tolerate; tolerance is simply not in the nature of Group advocates. Legislative legitimacy is achieved, not because legislators are democratically disposed to listen to others, but because they are forced by *the ground rules of the legislative Practice* to take account of them.[59]

Informal, uncontested legislative power—of which the enactments of Caligula are the paradigm—frees the legislator from any obligation to consider political inputs from Society; there is no requirement that the legislator should consider practical, awkward, or partisan objections of the various significant Groups. Whatever authority informal legislation possesses must depend upon the personal virtue of the legislators: on the perception of their charisma, gifts, knowledge, experience, expertise, access to divine will, or superior understanding. In the well-meaning polity members may accept such informal laws as the prescriptions of the great and the good. The laws are valid because they are good; and they are good because they conform in some measure to a master plan known to the ruler. It is this understanding, this access to the common morality, this knowledge of the real needs and values of the community, this expertise, which legal foundationalists claim to provide.

Where all legislation is created in a well designed ULP there is no need for judges to question the content of the laws. However, where legislative Practices are defective and are not governed by the principle of respect for Groups, or where law-makers are not accountable to a ULP, there will almost inevitably be a call for substantial judicial review. Being sent out into the world without the legitimation of adequate democratic scrutiny and debate, the enacted laws will only be subject to challenge—if at all—in the courts.[60]

To advocate the informal creation of general, coercively backed rules, to which many might object if they were given the chance, has, in a democracy, all the logic of one hand clapping. In a democracy a piece of legislation must by definition be a product of negotiation and debate under conditions in which formal ground rules prescribe that respect is paid to all Groups. The claims of legal foundationalists to be able to provide the meta-law which would legitimate informally made laws are spurious.[61] The legitimation of informal laws, such as judges are forced to make, never comes from theory; it derives from the acceptance of the rules as workable, from the fact that they are not repealed, that they are taken up into the Practices of Society, and above all that they adopted in the LSS by other judges.

Proposals, made in the light of embarrassing exposures of the political nature of legal judgments in some jurisdictions, that judges should be more open about the ideological character of the choices they are making would seem to overestimate the therapeutic effects of candour.[62] Such frankness would certainly go no way to legitimating judicially made laws. To give reasons for a new law does nothing to remedy the failure to meet the democratic requirement that those reasons must before its enactment have been open to the most searching scrutiny and challenge. Any suggestion that it would be possible within a legal Practice to recapitulate the conditions necessary for political contestation, which alone can legitimate, verges on the ludicrous.[63]

The impact of foundationalist theory on the legal Practices is disastrous. It positively encourages judges to stray from legal justice in order to do substantial justice; it undermines the respect for individuals which is the law's singular virtue; and, under the guise of impartiality, it can move to the implementation of policies advocated by a particular Group. The jurisdiction of the courts, no longer limited to securing respect for individuals, is extended to cover all of Society's general norms, and the courts inevitably become part of the political life of Society.

Since the judges are, courtesy of the foundationalists, privy to the ends of the law, there is no good reason why they should not be involved in regulation and administration;[64] discounting in the process, if need be, any calls for individual justice. For instance, if the purpose of law is to achieve the most efficient use of Society's resources, then past injury is of secondary importance, since what has been done cannot be undone, and the real concern of the courts must be to prevent similar injury happening in future. In suggesting that regulatory functions of this sort are the primary business of the courts we see legal foundationalism at its most arrogant. For it is no part of the job of judges to govern: for example, to determine what is the most efficient use of resources. The institution of regulatory structures requires careful consideration, especially since the most appropriate and effective regulatory systems may, in many areas, be of a non-legal nature.[65] The decision whether to introduce legal or non-legal methods of control is not a question which the judges are in a position to answer.

The foundationalism of private law

In a democracy the laws will be justified by reference not to foundations but to the fact that they have been well made; that they have been agreed to. It is significant that in penal and public law, in which the coercive power of the State is most obtrusive and questions of legitimacy are most pressing, the legal norms prescribing punishments for members of Society and conferring powers on the State are entirely statutory. We do not expect developments concerning the prescription of punishments or the conferral of State power to be spontaneous growths; we prefer that they should be the products of careful deliberation in the ULP. In these two domains legal foundationalism misdescribes the purpose of punishment and grossly misrepresents the nature and extent of legal constraints on State power.

Legal foundationalists are perhaps more confident of their influence on judges than on legislators. So it is not surprising that immanent foundationalism derives its sustenance primarily from private law, where the norms govern relationships between members of Society and where questions of legitimacy are secondary.[66] And it is in this domain that the idea of law growing spontaneously in accord with a changing but shared conception of social life does not seem out of place. Here, the idea that law should conform to the foundations is most attractive.

I have already argued (see *ante*, p. 256) that the fact that we are all members of an SE Society—a market economy—cannot provide the moral foundations upon which the law is based. If we cannot find a meaningful moral consensus stemming from our common engagement in SE activity —as we all buy, sell, lend, mortgage, invest, and so forth—neither can we hope to find a consensus in any other activities or areas of social life. The very complexity of social life, the manner and rate of the changes within it—the new discoveries made, the new inventions and technologies introduced, the increasing influence of Groups in other Societies, the presence of ethnic minorities, and so forth—all militate against the emergence of any common conception of the good.

Against this background of change and diversity the law's articulation of the relationships between members might appear to provide the materials from which we could uncover the lowest common denominator of right. Yet there is no reason at all to suppose that the norms of private law constitute any sort of moral cement of Society; nor that they represent a coherent picture of social life, or a defensible scheme of social association. These are not the functions of the law. The sole virtue of laws is in providing stability and clarity; they are a framework of rules doing very disparate jobs by means of which, in very diverse circumstances, the expectations of members can be satisfied. Though we may have the gravest doubts about the justification of the rules by which entitlements are conferred, and although our views may be diametrically opposed to others who also object to the existing rules, we all have to accept them as the rules according to which we must plan and act. Their legal validity does not entail our approval.

Appeals to a history of Society which would provide the basis for a consensus upon which law is supposed to be founded are likely to refer to the positive norms which governed social life in the past. In this connection we need to be sensitive to what E. P. Thompson called 'the enormous condescension of posterity' towards dissenters; to remember that many ancient laws were norms which, even if observed, were bitterly opposed by many of the subjects whose lives they regulated; that they did not then stand as any expression of a contemporary consensus. Savigny's account of the reception of Roman Law in Germany provides a clear example of the condescension of history in the assertion of an ancient consensus. In practical life we need general rules; and at any given time the laws are the only general norms to which we can refer. In dealing with other members we simply cannot govern our conduct by reference to the normative ideals of legal philosophy; we can only look to the positive law. Our private laws are the heterogeneous survivors of a thousand and one contingencies and perceived social mischiefs. They are certainly not the unconscious reflections of an underlying liberal philosophy.

E: The pressures leading to foundationalist activity

A number of factors in the activities and affairs in contemporary polities promote the cause of legal foundationalism. As a result legal foundationalists may, with some justice, feel that they are philosophers by appointment; that they are engaged in performing a real service, and fulfilling a long-felt need.

Foundationalist ideas gain powerful support from those who have experienced the emergence and working of tyrannical and arbitrary States.[67] To counter the absolutist tendencies of States fundamental laws are passed, values declared sacred, and courts are positioned in the front line to check the exercise of State power. The interpretation of such fundamental laws calls for a profound understanding of the foundations of the Society.

Though they subscribe to the doctrine of the separation of powers, and despite their denials, judges clearly are involved in making new law.[68] In the USA the extent of the courts' political involvement—exposed by Realists and members of the Critical Legal Studies movement—has prompted a call to legal philosophers to provide principles which should govern that involvement.[69] Although the legislative activity of judges in the UK has been more modest, the admission by some eminent judges of its reality has been accompanied by their recognition of the need for guidance.

Within the practice of law itself there is inevitably a demand from lawyers for greater coherence. Given the wilderness of cases, statutes, and customs, those who would apply, understand, or teach the law cannot fail to recognize the contribution which judges, adjudicating in the Grand Manner, have made in bringing out general principles which can be found in the legal material. The value of such contributions suggests the possibility that a body of principles—the meta-law—resides in the legal system as a whole. However, the virtues of coherent and principled laws, admired by all codifiers since the time of Gaius, and so much appreciated by those who have to find and apply the laws, or teach them, do not justify the assumption that the ideal legal system could ever display such unity.

One of the most influential factors encouraging legal foundationalists today is the existence of Federal political structures.[70] In such political structures the legislative Practices of Societies are unable to claim sovereignty. So parties to the Federation must turn to the courts for declarations about the validity of any enactments which are said not to conform to Federal norms. The basic values of the Federation cannot be spelled out fully in its constituting instruments, and the judges, who must give meaning to those instruments, will have to rely upon foundationalist ideas. Whatever claims may be made for the virtues of federal structures, they do not have the potential to reduce the legitimacy deficits of member States.

In preaching the need to put law in its place we have to reckon with the fact that legal foundationalism is deeply embedded in the practices and arrangements of our public life.[71] If legal foundationalism is corrupting, should we not look more closely at the possibility of reforming the practices and institutions of public life in order to diminish the pressures which promote it? Certainly, the way to legitimacy does not involve constructing bigger and better theories, nor appointing judges with a better grasp of foundationalist philosophy. The major task in democratic polities today is to institute more effective legislative procedures and Practices, not to make the courts more effective institutions for making decisions about matters where legal justice is not required.[72]

NOTES

1. Foundationalism has been defined variously as: the attempt to set political and moral norms in some kind of metaphysical groundwork (Barber 1994); as a kind of transcendental reduplication of social arrangements (Gellner 1964: 193); and as a quest for an objective morality which justifies a moral absolutism. The foundationalist assumes that the world has an essential normative structure, identifiable by those equipped with the means to discover it. Essentially it is an Enlightenment project: to found a social and political order in conformity with universal principles. See Hampshire (1989).
2. Among the impressive cast of critics of foundationalist projects may be counted Dewey, Pierce, Berlin, Popper, MacIntyre, Raz, Hampshire, Fish, Oakeshott, and Gray.
3. Some aspects of the sort of problem set out by Gauthier may be clarified by the recognition that there are quite different planes of discourse in which the person has a different character. He poses the question: if we admit that individuals are socially caused, that persons are social products, then must we not reject the idea that persons are autonomous (1992: 157)? The legal person, i.e. the member of Society, who is an autonomous individual demanding justification for all the rules of Society, is a wholly different being,

belonging to another level of discourse, from the socialized being who is the product of the normative structures of social life.

4. 'Althusser and Rawls concur in conceiving the liberal political subject as one produced by, rather than being prior to, the institutions, practices and discourses of the liberal state.... Indeed like Althusser, Rawls acknowledges that there may be a split between the public identity which is attributed to the person in law and his/her lived experience': Barron (1993: 95).
5. On the divergent and incompatible uses to which natural law has been put see Ross (1958: 258–68). For Friedman (1960: 95-7) natural law 'has been the chief though not the only way to formulate ideals and aspirations of various peoples and generations with reference to the principal moving forces of the time'. One persistent objective was the justification of government and the legal order in a Christian world; another the assertion of the rights of man: see Shklar (1964: 68). Such Group articulations may have a greater value than Rorty allows, in keeping the rhetoric up to date, or giving useful formulas and working out the implications for us; see Rorty (1994). The strengthening of our beliefs, i.e. the structuring and authentification to our experience, is of the utmost importance.
6. For the view that liberalism elevated one set of values over all other contenders while offering no reason to endorse those values that can survive its own inherent scepticism, see Gray (1995). The borrowings of liberalism from the experience and articulation of the legal field require to be underlined.
7. Fisk (1989) emphasizes social improvement and the common good. For Nagel the main question of political theory is: 'How should we live together in society?' (1991: 6). In a democratic polity there can be no definitive answer; the denizens of a civil Society cannot be provided with such foundations, they can only be encouraged to argue rationally, and with respect for other Groups, about immediate decisions and arrangements to be made in a rapidly changing world.
8. Legal philosophy is often regarded as a branch of jurisprudence apart from political philosophy; see Simmonds (1984: ch.1). The impetus to seek foundations may derive in part from the lawyer's habit of seeking answers to practical issues in legal advice Activity. In dealing with novel situations, with messy and indeterminate norms, the possibility arises of discovering a source from which a systematic and complete system could emerge. Foundationalists supplement the immediate and inadequate normative resources with principles which lie beyond the written law, and on which the lawyer can draw. For institutional theory there is *no right answer;* there are manifestly choices to be made. We should demand only that legal questions should be fully deliberated in a legal framework. Foundationalism is most evident in discussions of constitutional law. There the assumption that the constitution is fundamental law, that the law must give effect to basic constitutional principles, is taken as a licence for lawyers to pontificate on matters which require political decision. It is not for lawyers to determine where the limits of freedom of speech should lie. See, however, Lloyd (1964: 155). Many books purporting to deal with constitutional law are really concerned with non-legal matters. The only concern of lawyers should be to articulate the legal

components of the constitution, not to tell us what the constitution should be or to advocate reforms.

9. Special expertise is claimed. Stammler, whose legal science is concerned with law as a set of rules formulating means to fundamental human purposes, had no doubt about the scholarship involved: 'Whoever would be a philosopher of law must first breathe the dust of legal archives': in Jennings (ed.) (1933: 39). A related tactic is to maintain that the judges are not representatives of society's consciousness but of its *legal* consciousness: see Cotterrell (1989: 30); Aubert (1983: 46). For a cynical appraisal of the work of jurists—'the priesthood whose duty it is to expound the science unmoved by the irrelevancies of practical day to day governmental action'—see Arnold (1935: 33–77).
10. On Natural Law as political ideology see Shklar (1964: 64–88)
11. The concern of feminists to reform the law to reflect womens' interests and experience results in a determination to rethink and redefine the law itself. See Lacey (1993: 196).
12. The solution for Ackerman is not the devising of new institutional structures but the emergence of a new legal discourse: Ackerman (1984: 24). It has been suggested that the problem of constitutional design for Rawls is either very simple or insoluble. 'If people pursue justice single-mindedly it scarcely matters how the rules for decision making are drawn up, since the results can hardly fail to be good; if they don't then all is lost': Barry (1973: 143).
13. Acknowledgement is made to the writers who have emphasized procedural natural law; see Covell (1994). There is great value in Hampshire's (1989) analysis of procedural justice as an index of rationality.
14. On the foundationalist character of liberalism—'the universalist component of the liberal syndrome'—see Gray (1996: 299–306). Liberals assume the universality of values of equality, autonomy, value-pluralism, and rights. They employ the juridical vocabulary outside the legal field.
15. For an attack on the pretensions of detachment and universalizing of philosophers of justice see Walzer (1970). For Walzer all distributions are just or unjust in relation to the social meanings of the goods at stake.
16. Fascism stressed pre-industrial community values rather than universal values; see Jones (1956: 272–84)
17. See Oakeshott (1977: 26) for an account of a society—the USA—called upon at short notice to devise its own political arrangements, and relying upon rationalist ideas. They believed that the proper organization of society and the conduct of its affairs were based upon distinct principles, and not tradition: principles which were natural, and not the product of civilization.
18. The Israeli Declaration of Independence cites freedom, liberty, justice, and peace as envisaged by the Prophets. It has no legal force but is used by the courts as a source to expand rights. The reverential respect for the constitution displayed by subsequent generations gives it a unifying force: Murphy (1993: 10). Such an approach gives the creative foundationalists a field-day: they can find whatever they want within the ambiguous provisions of the constitution. The vice of declared foundations lies in the width of the principles which they lay down, principles which do not decide cases but empower judges; see Rodger (1995: 22).

19. See Kelsen's attack on *soi-disant* positivists whose writings were political tracts (1967: 1). Luhmann, one of the contemporary critics of legal foundationalism, denies that the legal community is grounded in or permeated by moral or political values (1985). He insists that there is a lack of sociological perspective in supposing that laws are so grounded.
20. Cf. Dworkin: 'The Constitution is foundational of other law, so Hercules' interpretation of the document as a whole . . . must be foundational as well. It must fit and justify the most basic arrangements of political power in the community, which means it must be a justification drawn from the most philosophic reaches of political theory. Lawyers are always political philosophers because jurisprudence is part of any lawyers' account of what law is . . .' (1986: 380). This is integrity not to democratic law but to a liberal vision of society. It is no part of the judge's business to determine philosophical issues; such forays are incompatible with the doing of legal justice. Only if philosophical enquiry were productive of unchallengable answers could the judges rely upon them.
21. Many philosophers attempt to steer clear of programmes, being concerned to work out and criticize the implications of particular positions or assertions. This is a crucially important investigation. One of the most important ser-vices of philosophy is to question Group assumptions and to deny Group hegemony; to reveal the plurality and mutual incompatibility of principles of distributive justice. Charles Taylor suggests that philosophers ought to identify the principles and give them a weighting appropriate for the particular society given its history, economy, degree of integration, etc. (1985: 312). Something of this approach is discernible in the works of Walzer, MacIntyre, and Feinberg. Nowhere has the importance of theory been more fully understood than among Marxists, who conceived of theoretical analysis as a form of political activity designed to bring about social change. 'To define a group, delineate its boundaries, and articulate its aspirations, enables the members of the group to develop a higher degree of group consciousness. Individuals can better identify with a corporate body once it has been rendered visible through descriptive writing and polemics': Collins (1982: 7).
22. Nationalists seldom speak the language of democracy; they posit a coherent moral outlook, a shared sense of right; and may seek the establishment of a political carapace for their *Kulturstaat*. One of the dangers of nationalism is that the reliance upon consensual feelings and values diminishes reliance on fixed social rules. Nazis abandoned the principles of legality in 1935: precedents could be ignored; punishments were to be imposed for acts which, though not legally prohibited, ran counter to the 'shared feelings of the people'. See Hall (1949: 54); Jones (1956: 270–300).
23. Societies must be distinguished from both Communities and Organizations. The assertion that Organizations have a structure identical to a legal system (Lyons 1993: 54) is to neglect the democratic character of the artificial form Society in which a legal system exists. It is to neglect, as all legal pluralists do, the distinctive nature of legal language.

24. Accepting Dworkin's observation (1986: 196) that '(p)eople need to identify with', we must nevertheless recognize that the institutional forms with which they identify are Groups and *not civil Society.* Our moral identity is a wholly different matter, on a quite different plane, from our legal personality. Foundationalists, aliens, and politicians would identify individuals by reference to the Societies of which they are members. It is important to appreciate that, in times of peace, Societies do not matter in quite that way. Cotterrell observes that Dworkin postulates a community which either does not exist or is so loosely conceived that the word 'community' lacks any substantial meaning (1993: 191). Group membership involves the evaluation of members' preferences against the axiological armature of the Group. The commmunitarians' view of Society as a Group finds its expression in demands for politics of the common good; see Kymlicka (1990: 206).
25. On changes in the concept of the community see Avineri and de-Schalit (eds.) (1992: 1–5). See also Kymlicka (1990: 199–237).
26. Democracy involves a disposition shared among political antagonists to contract about particulars, rather than a united effort to achieve the common good. Its keystones are, in law, the procurement of respect for individuals, and in politics, respect for Groups. Its institutions are geared to securing that respect, not to the implementation of policies which are thought to serve the interests of the voters or of a large class of them; cf. Martin (1993: 138).
27. Rawls' theory of justice 'tries to draw solely upon basic intuitive ideas that are embedded in the political institutions of a constitutional democratic regime'. See Raz (1994: 64).
28. The vocabulary of higher, meta-, supra-, and ideal law is part of the language of the Ionians. 'The idealistic theories of law . . . are characterised by a dualism of two legal orders, one ideal and one real, whereas the realistic theory of law recognises only one form of law—positive law': Kelsen (1960: 24). For Weber the codification of the law amounted to a loss of its 'metaphysical dignity' (1978: 875). Courts may be directed to rely upon a higher law, e.g. the Higher Law of the Catholic Church, expressed in the Constitution of Ireland. Or they may feel constrained by the principles of a higher law, as in *Madison* v *Marbury* 1803 5 US 137 2. 'Supra-positive' principles have been called upon by the German Constitutional Court to invalidate a 'simple' constitutional norm; see Friedman (1960: 45).
29. Among the attractions of the higher law is the possibility of reforming the law by litigation; appeals against the positive law.
30. That assumption is nowhere more evident than in Cotterrell (1995). Law expresses and channels power; the legal system is power concentrated through structures of government. The view of law as a social control mechanism is a central feature of sociological jurisprudence; lawyers must participate in government, the law operating as a mediator between conflicting needs and demands. Rudolph von Ihering gave law a governmental role; Pound regarded law as an integrating mechanism, interpreting the legal process 'as a form of social control whereby all the competing interests in society are scrutinised, compared and accepted or rejected': Lloyd (1964: 207). Although law is essentially coercive and hence must inevitably be seen as

having a controlling *function,* control is not its *end.* Law is but one style in which a coercive system can work. Law involves legal coercion; its individualism marks it off from other forms of social control. Its only end is legal justice, not some conception of the common good. What the courts enforce is not 'the law' but a norm or set of norms.

31. The regulatory norms of standard maintenance are, I have suggested, not legal norms. Unconnected with legal justice, they must be understood in a different conceptual framework. We need also to recognize the ability of a government to control and influence, not by way of creating norms, but by witholding resources and denying opportunities for action. See Porn (1970: 52–3).
32. To see the law as instrumental in achieving social goals does not entail a view of the law as a coherent body of norms: 'Instrumentalism largely replaces the image of the law as *ratio* with one of *voluntas*': Cotterrell (1995: 253). Devlin (1965) referred to 'the seamless web' of shared standards. He maintained that a degree of shared morality is essential to the minimum of social cohesion and that the weakening of moral belief may reduce it below this minimum. Cf. Hart (1963: 71), for whom only the values of individual freedom, safety of life, and protection from deliberately inflicted harms need be protected. See also Mitchell (1970).
33. A view castigated by Arnold (1935: 65), who described the science of law as 'the effort to construct a logical heaven behind the courts, wherein contradictory ideals are made to seem consistent'. Normative legal theory portrayed law as an integrated structure of ideas, a body of distinct esoteric knowledge: see Cotterrell (1989: 214). However, the modern image of legality puts the unity of law, or its systematic character, in issue; Cotterrell (1995: 283). Postmodernists assert the incoherence; they study the rhetorical devices by which lawyers continue to convince themselves of the law's unity. The law is not philosophical but pragmatic; from the pragmatic point of view it is the inconsistency of legal doctrine which enables it to work; see Fish (1993: 169). The lack of coherence is embarrassing only if we entertain foundationalist longings.
34. Austin (1879, Lecture XXXIX, 703). In 1567 Francois Hotman said of law that 'The discipline is disputatious because it rests on nothing more complete than a collection of fragments, reports, pieces themselves representing uncertain conjectures and incomplete derivations': quoted in Douzinas *et al.* (eds.) (1994: 1). The common law is a complicated patchwork of precedents and statutes. 'The imperfect and complicated state of our fragmentary legislation and complicated case law has been so obvious that Englishmen have never been in danger of believing in the existence of an artificial logical paradise where the law is applied by the exercise of reason': Wortley (1995). The calls for greater coherence in the law are of course endemic; they come from professionals who benefit from consolidation and codification. This provided the impetus for the restatement of the law in the USA. 'By now almost every important common law field has undergone two restatements one typically prepared before, one after, the Second World War': Ackerman (1984: 12). See

Smith (1983) for a plea for greater coherence in the criminal law. Coherence is a legislative rather than an adjudicatory value.

35. On the jurists' urge to formulate principles, see Rodger (1995). For them the life of the law is logic, not experience. 'And yet we know that precisely because the law has evolved in thousands of cases, there may be no completely satisfying principles to be discovered. Indeed it appears that a legal system may work for centuries without such principles ever being fully elucidated by its practitioners.' Rodger quotes Otto Lenel as asserting of the Roman law that 'the greatest and most innovative lawyers who ever lived never formulated the principles which underlay the system'. As the Roman and English legal systems were so successful Rodger wonders whether the work of formulating statements of principle is necessarily the highest priority for a living legal system. For the American realists the life of the law was found in particularistic rules, not in generalizations beyond the rules: 'In both public and private domains lawyers would learn to look upon organising abstractions . . . with deep scepticism' Ackerman (1984: 18). For a rejection of descriptions of the law as necessarily systematic see Sampford (1989) who emphasizes the labyrinthine morass of the law and challenges the systematic theories of law. From the rather different perspective of legal history, Kelley (1991) contrasts the ancient wisdom of *nomos,* which accepted the idiosyncratic, unsystematic nature of the law, with the pipe-dream of law as a rational order: an approach which he calls 'physis'.
36. Foundationalist theorizing commonly takes the form, not of a philosophy for the whole of the legal system, but of theories for a particular area such as property, contract, or tort law. An understanding of contract, tort, or property law is, for jurists, not a working knowledge of the rules, but a search for an underlying order among the rules: for a philosophical basis. For examples see Richardson (1990; Adams and Brownsword (1987). These theories of the rationale of contract or tort law are as foundationalist as general theories of the end of the law. The need to tidy up the laws for the purposes of doing justice does not mean that we must seek for a unifying theory, or work out the most general principles, the silver thread which will guide future development. For the view that '(t)here is no real theory of contract in practice because statutes and precedents—the formal materials—do not contain one' see Price (1989).
37. Karl Jaspers denied that questions of right and wrong were to be settled by argument: 'I can only argue against a law with a new law . . . such argumentation among legal generalities is intrinsically arbitrary.'
38. For Hobbes law was essentially the will of the sovereign; even the deliverances of natural law were not law until interpreted by the sovereign. On the pragmatism of English law, and its concern for remedies rather than principles, see Allan (1988).
39. It is the survival of a rule that is important, rather than the rightness or 'validity' of the reasons given for its promulgation. It is the fact of survival which validates. The reasons for a decision which does not survive may be entirely defensible. *Hepburn* v. *Griswold* 75 US (8 Wall.) 603 (1870). See Christie (1982: 58–9). It was a perfectly defensible decision which was overruled for

practical reasons. In overturning it, it was quite superfluous to attempt to show that the reasoning for the earlier decision was flawed. See Christie (1982: 58–9). That another rule is chosen does not mean that the reasoning for the first rule is bad. Dissenting judgments are not wrong; they are not adopted.

40. The perception of the white waters of legal indeterminacy in a world of rapid change led to its ready acceptance by the realists, and to renewed efforts by foundationalists to build dams and channels to control it. On the former approach see Gilmore (1961). The massive growth of case-law and the proliferation of law reports, which made it difficult to rationalize and organize the law into a systematic and consistent body of knowledge, resulted, in the early twentieth century, in 'a crisis of confidence' in the idea of the law as a coherent body of knowledge; Cotterrell (1995: 279). Llewellyn (1962: 55) asserted that the realists had a very clear conception of law in a constant state of flux; of moving law and of judicial creation of law; of society in flux, and in flux typically faster than the law.
41. The American preference for fundamental law stems, it has been suggested, from their revolutionary origins: the urge to assert rights with which the colonisers could not interfere. See Gough (1955) and Clark (1993).
42. In a world of social change the fixed laws, enacted to create permanent and inalienable rights, can cause major difficulties when fashionable doctrines and ephemeral concerns are given permanent effect.
43. On the ambiguities of Constitutional provisions: e.g. the 14th Amendment to the US Constitution: 'No State shall deny any person within its jurisdiction the protection of its laws', see Lyons (1993: 154).
44. Ackerman says that legal process scholars were perfectly aware that legislatures and bureaucracies made bad mistakes (1984: 39). It appears that they are specially privileged to know what those mistakes are. It is perhaps worth recalling that supreme courts can make mistakes. See Tate and Vallinder (eds.) (1995: 13–26).
45. Of the claims of the two types of foundationalists, the critical and the immanent, the claim to discover the immanent values of a Society has greater potency and is the more dangerous. Immanent foundationalists claim to find the higher law latent *in the law of Society,* embedded as its very backbone and value system; they are especially concerned to find it in the constitutional arrangements of a Society. Rawls' theory of justice 'tries to draw solely upon basic intuitive ideas that are embedded in the political institutions of a constitutional democratic regime': Raz (1994: 64). Liberalism generally borrows its individualistic values from the law and, like the law, has no concern with Groups; this makes for a politics dominated by rights. See Kymlicka (1990: 216).
46. See Crick (1964: 34–55).
47. See Finnis (1980). The basic goods, forms of human flourishing, may appear to be self-evident in the English language, but in other languages different lists of human flourishing might be derived. Religion and art may not be categories which are employed by those whose first language is, say, Swahili, Hausa, or Tamil.

48. Foundationalists underrate, not only the institutional torms, but especially the adversarial procedures; they would put primacy on calculation rather than debate. Bentham, the archetypal rationalist, proposes adjudicatory structures which do not favour democratic inputs. Savigny would substitute historical understanding. Nor did the Interest jurisprudence of Ihering and Pound emphasize the procedures. The modest requirement that laws be justly made and applied is replaced by the idea that they are tools for social engineers .
49. Misrepresentation of the foundations of judicial authority is one of the great obstacles to legitimacy. The idea that judicial authority is rooted in the community has been described as one of the 'most vibrant contributions of common law thought': Cotterrell (1989: 32). However, in a democratic polity it is a false perception, likely to licence judicial activism. The modest requirement that decisions be justified by reference to existing legal materials is liable to be replaced by a duty to engage in law reform.
50. 'What is justifiable in a democratic society' is a criterion by which judges are to appraise legislation; it appears in the European Convention and the Canadian Charter; see Tarnopolsky and Beaudoin (eds.) (1982). The effect of such a directive is to transfer decisions about the public good from the legislature to the courts, who will determine what an enacted legislature may or may not do. For a democrat it might seem to involve a self-contradiction: what is justifiable can only be what the democrats agree in the appropriate forums, not what the courts deem to be justifiable.
51. Courts can of course do nothing in the face of ULP authorization; but they have sometimes proved insufficiently partisan against executives claiming state necessity; see Simpson (1992: 25). Their failures stem from an inadequate commitment to respect for persons; only if that fundamental democratic principle is upheld can the necessary security be guaranteed to all citizens. It is an indictment of the work of the courts of justice that specialist Courts of Human Rights are considered necessary.
52. The rationale of democracy is the securing of respect for individuals and Groups, not securing the interests of majorities, cf. Martin (1993: 138).
53. See Ackerman (1984: 69). There was a fundamental provision of the New Deal '. . . that American lawyers can indeed keep the law responsive to the changing facts of society in a way which promotes the activist careers of their fellow Americans.' Ackerman looks forward to 'a new kind of dialogue that seeks to explicate the complex character of the struggle for social justice in a liberal activist state' (ibid. 72). For Rawls the negotiation in the original position is to decide upon a set of principles once and for all (1971: 33). In a rapidly changing world our rights, if they are something more than basic rights, will need to be reaffirmed, and continuously renegotiated. In a democracy the institutional forms do not require negotiation by persons in the original position; everything else requires negotiation and renegotiation by our contemporaries in the ULP. Perhaps the clearest area of foundationalist thinking is about the constitution. Such thinking is commonly based on a pre-democratic conception of the State as possessing inherent powers, rather than the legal conception of the powerless State. So, we must deter-

mine in advance what the limits are. 'I believe that there are substantive moral rights that exist outside government which will in large part set the task for, and constrain the legitimate activity of, political authority': Sartorius (1987: 58). However, in a democratic polity the issue for the courts is always the extent of the powers conferred, rather than the limits on the governmental powers which can be conferred. Constitutionalism which calls for the protection of a catalogue of rights is a profoundly distorting political doctrine.

54. In a democracy questions about the toleration of the intolerant, about capital punishment, about whether individual interests should prevail over corporate or aggregate interests, and so forth, can only be answered by the ULP. They are not to be found in a theory.
55. Nowhere more than in the USA. Bork (1991) maintains that Dworkin and Tribe represent an elite which, because it 'cannot win elections has undertaken to win law suits instead'.
56. Rehnquist (1975: 678–701) castigates those who suggest that 'non-elected members of the federal judiciary may address themselves to a social problem simply because other branches of government have failed to do so'. He goes on to attack federal judges with 'a roving commission to second guess Congress, State legislatures, and state and federal administrative officers, concerning what is best for the country' (ibid. 698).
57. See Brazier (1991: 161) and the proposal for a Bill of Rights; if Parliament were to be confident that the judges would interpret a Bill of Rights properly it would be important that the judges' views were publicly known and their acceptability tested prior to their appointment.
58. Foundationalists fail to grasp the legitimacy of the well made rule. 'Past political decisions justify coercion because, and therefore only when, they give fair warning by making the occasions of coercion depend on plain facts available to all rather than to fresh judgments of political morality, which different judges might make differently. This is the ideal of protected expectations': Dworkin (1986: 117). To suppose that decisions are justified merely because there are conventions governing the recognition of laws is to neglect the substantial legitimacy which the well made norm can claim as being the best possible decision for that Society.
59. There is a trace of romanticism in the views of Oakeshott and Rorty that public life is a conversation rather than an argument. Voices are raised, doors slammed, tables thumped, shots are fired. Politics may indeed be civil war carried on by other means.
60. See Asimow (1983: 253). Subordinate legislation in USA is governed by the Administrative Procedure Act; as the making of such laws is not subject to democratic processes, there are frequent challenges in the courts.
61. In Kenneth Minogue's words, they would 'claim to give a philosophic stiffening of a process perennially riddled with unreflective political prejudice' (1986: 224).
62. For a realist's view of the judge as policy-maker, and the need for more reasoned policy grounds for decisions see Cohen (1935).
63. The deliberative debate about individual rights might appear to licence the introduction of political and philosophical arguments. However, it does not

licence the introduction of supra-positive principles. The debate is not about the validity of the enactments of the ULP, but the rights of individuals under the existing laws.

64. For which the *locus classicus* must be *Brown* v. *Board of Education* 349 US 294 (1955). For a defence of the court's arrogation of administrative functions see Dworkin (1986: 392) On the recent changes in judicial review in the UK see Ehrman, *Daily Telegraph* 6 Apr.1995. Expressly conferred powers in the courts to issue directions, orders, or writs enforcing constitutional rights are found in the constitutions of India, Nigeria, Germany, and Canada; see Tarnopolsky and Beaudoin (eds.) (1982).
65. See *ante*, p. 120. Note the establishment of regulators of privatized industries. The non-legal direction of such agencies is a useful addition to the control of socially important bodies; their job is not to punish individuals for breaches of legal rules but to secure conformity to standards and to protect the interests of consumers.
66. Criminal foundationalism would emphasize the distinction between *mala in se* and *mala prohibita;* between true crime, defined in relation to the morality of the community, and regulatory crime; see Leigh (1992: ch. 6).
67. For an account of Radbruch's change of heart see Hart (1983). On the variety of factors supporting the expansion of judicial power in many countries see Tate and Vallinder (eds.) (1995: 2–6).
68. Cf. McLachlin (1994: 260). Under the Canadian Charter of Rights and Freedoms there is no doubt that the judges see themselves as having an important new role in deciding matters of social policy.
69. See Ackerman (1984: 3) on the birth of legal constructivism.
70. Federalism is the institutional setting for Supreme Courts. See J. S. Mill's essay 'Of Federal Representative Governments', (1948: 298–307) in which he maintained that the logic of federations, the division between federal and state governments, requires an arbiter independent of both. See also Friedman (1960: 408–16). Federalism may be the solution to the intractable problems of securing peace in areas of the world where well defined ethnic groups exist in a state of tension and are not territorially divided. A unitary Society may be impracticable when significant Groups are not prepared to recognize the sovereignty of a ULP which they perceive to be a majoritarian monster; power has to be diffused.
71. See Cotterrell (1995: 282) on the increasing willingness of lawyers to criticize law and policy. It accompanies an instrumentalist view of the law; each legal rule is to be coupled with specific social or economic goals.
72. Nor does it necessitate lawyers becoming more involved in public life: cf. Lord Radcliff (1978: 139–59).

BIBLIOGRAPHY

ABEL, Richard L. (ed.) (1982) *The Politics of Informal Justice* 2 vols. (New York: Academic Press)

ABEL-SMITH, Brian (1989) *The Legal Profession in England and Wales* (Oxford: Basil Blackwell)

ABERCROMBIE, Nicholas, HILL, Stephen, and TURNER, Bryan S. (eds.) *The Penguin Dictionary of Sociology* 2nd edn. (Harmondsworth: Penguin)

ACKERMAN, Bruce A. (1984) *Reconstructing American Law* (Cambridge, Mass.: Harvard University Press)

ACTON, H. B. (ed.) (1969) *The Philosophy of Punishment: A collection of papers* (London: Macmillan)

ADAMS, John and BROWNSWORD, Roger (1987) 'The ideologies of contract' (1987) 7 *Legal Studies* 205–23

ALLAN, T. R. S. (1988) 'Pragmatism and Theory in Public Law 104 *Law Quarterly Review* 1988 422 –47

—— (1992) *Law, Liberty and Justice* (Oxford: Oxford University Press)

ALLEN, C. K. (1945) *Law and Orders: An enquiry into the nature and scope of delegated legislation and executive powers in England* (London: Stevens & Sons)

—— (1958) *Law in the Making* 5th edn. (London: Oxford University Press)

ALTHUSSER, Louis (1971) *Lenin, Philosophy and Other Essays* tr. Ben Brewster, 2nd edn. (London: NLB)

ANDERSON, Benedict (1991) *Imagined Communities; Reflections on the origins and spread of nationalism* 2nd edn. (London: Verso)

ANSCOMBE, G. E. M. (1958) 'On Brute Facts' *Analysis* vol. 18, no. 3 (1958) 69–72

—— (1978) 'Rules, Rights and Promises' *Midwest Studies in Philosophy* 3 1978 318–23

ARNOLD, Christopher (1978) 'Analyses of Right' in: Eugene Kamenka and A. E.S. Tay (eds.) (1978) 74–86.

ARNOLD, Thurman W. (1935) *The Symbols of Government* (New Haven, Conn.: Yale University Press)

—— (1937) *The Folklore of Capitalism* (New Haven, Conn.: Yale University Press)

ARTHURS, H. W. (1985) *Without the Law: Administrative justice and legal pluralism in nineteenth century England* (Toronto: University of Toronto Press)

ASHWORTH, Andrew (1992) *Sentencing and Criminal Justice* (London: Weidenfeld & Nicolson)

ASIMOW, Michael (1983) 'Delegated Legislation: United States and United Kingdom' 3 *Oxford Journal of Legal Studies* 253–76

AUBERT, Vilhelm (ed.) (1969) *Sociology of Law: Selected readings* (Harmondsworth: Penguin)

—— (1983) *In Search of Law: Sociological approaches to law* (Oxford: Martin Robertson)

AUSTIN, John (1879) *Lectures on Jurisprudence* 2 vols., 4th edn., ed. Robert Campbell (London: John Murray)

AVINERI, Shlomo and de-SCHALIT, Avner (eds.) (1992) *Communitarianism and Individualism* (Oxford: Oxford University Press)

BALANDIER, Georges (1970) *Political Anthropology* tr. A. M. Sheridan Smith (Harmondsworth: Penguin)

BALDWIN, Robert (1995) *Rules and Government* (Oxford: Clarendon Press)

BALL, Terence, FARR, James, and HANSON, Russell L. (eds.) (1989) *Political Innovation and Conceptual Change* (Cambridge: Cambridge University Press)

BANKOWSKI, Zenon (1981) 'The Value of truth: Fact scepticism revisited' (1981) 1 *Legal Studies* 257-66

—— and MUNGHAM, G. (1976) *Images of Law* (London: Routledge & Kegan Paul)

BANTON, Michael (1964) 'Law Enforcement and Social Control' in: Aubert (ed.) (1969) 127–41

BARBER, B. (1988) *The Conquest of Politics: Legal philosophy in democratic times* (Princeton: Princeton University Press)

—— (1994) 'Democracy and the Philosophers' *History Today* August 1994

BARKER, Rodney (1990) *Political Legitimacy and the State* (Oxford: Clarendon Press)

BARRON, Anne (1993) 'Citizenship and the Politics of Identity' in: Norrie (ed.) (1993) 80–100.

BARRY, Brian (1965) *Political Argument* (London: Routledge & Kegan Paul)

—— (1973) *The Liberal Theory of Justice: A critical examination of the principal doctrines in A Theory of Justice by John Rawls* (Oxford: Clarendon Press)

—— (1989) *A Treatise on Social Justice* vol. I (London: Harvester Wheatsheaf)

BECKER, T. L (1970) *Comparative Judicial Politics: The political functioning of the courts* (Chicago: Rand McNally)

BEETHAM, David (1991) *The Legitimation of Power* (Basingstoke: Macmillan)

BENDA-BECKMAN, F. von (1984) 'The Law Out of Context' *Journal of African Law* (1984) 28

BENN, S. I. and PETERS, R. S. (1959) *Social Principles and the Democratic State* (London: George Allen & Unwin)

BENNION, F. A. R. (1992) *Statutory Interpretation: A code* (London: Butterworths)

BENTHAM, Jeremy (1970a) *On Laws in General* H. L. A. Hart (ed.) (London: Athlone Press)

—— (1970b) 'Anarchical Fallacies' in: Melden (ed.) (1970)

—— (1979) *An Introduction to the Principles of Morals and Legislation* (Oxford: Clarendon Press)

BERESFORD, Peter (1993) *Celt and Saxon: The struggle for Britain AD 410-937* (London: Constable)

BERMAN, H. J. (1977) 'The Origins of Western Legal Science' 90(2) *Harvard Law Review* 894–942

BEVAN, Aneurin (1961) *In Place of Fear* (London: McGibbon Kee)

BIRKS, Peter (1996) 'Harrassment and Hubris: The right to equality of respect' John Maurice Kelly Memorial Lecture (Dublin: University College)

BLACK, Donald and MILESKI, Maureen (eds.) (1973) *The Social Organisation of Law* (New York: Academic Press)

BLAKEMORE, Steven (1988) *Burke and the Fall of Language: The French Revolution as a linguistic event* (Hanover, NH and London: University Press of New England)

BOGDANOR, Victor (ed.) (1988) *Constitutions in Democratic Politics* 'Introduction' (London: Dartmouth)

BOLGAR, Vera (1953) 'Why No Trusts in the Civil Law' *American Journal of Comparative Law* (1953) 204–19

BOORSTIN, Daniel J. (1973) *The Mysterious Science of Law: An essay on Blackstone's Commentaries* (Boston Mass.: Beacon Press)

BORK, Robert H. (1991) *The Tempting of America: The political seduction of the law* (New York: Simon & Schuster)

BOSCO, Andrea (ed.) (1991) *The Federal Idea* 2 vols. (London: Lothian Foundation Press)

BOURDIEU, Pierre (1977) *The Outline of a Theory of Practice* tr. Richard Nice (Cambridge: Cambridge University Press)

—— (1988) *Homo Academicus.* tr. Peter Collier (Cambridge: Polity Press)

BRAZIER, Rodney (1991) *Constitutional Reform: Reshaping the British Political System* (Oxford: Oxford University Press)

—— (1994) *Constitutional Practice* 2nd edn. (Oxford: Clarendon Press)

BRITTAN, Samuel (1995) *Capitalism with a Human Face* (London: Edward Elgar)

BRONAUGH, Richard (ed.) (1978) *Philosophical Law: Authority, equality, adjudication, privacy* (London: Greenwood Press)

BRYDE, Brun Otto (1976) *The Politics and Sociology of African Legal Development* (Frankfurt am Main: Metzner)

BURROWS, P. and VELJANOWSKI, Cento G. (1981) *The Economic Approach to Law* (London: Butterworths)

BURTON, Steven J. (1992) *Judging in Good Faith* (Cambridge: Cambridge University Press)

CALABRESI, Guido and MELAMED, Alexander (1972) 'Property Rules, Liability and Inalienability: One view of the cathedral' 85 *Harvard Law Review* (1972) 1089–128

CAMPBELL, T. D. (1983) *The Left and Rights: A conceptual analysis of socialist rights* (London: Routledge & Kegan Paul)

CANE, Peter (1996) *An Introduction to Administrative Law* 3rd edn. (Oxford: Clarendon Press)

CARRITHERS, Michael (1994) *Why Humans Have Cultures: Explaining anthropology and social diversity* (Oxford: Oxford University Press)

—— and COLLINS, Steven and LUKES, Steven (eds.) (1985) *The Category of the Person: Anthropology, philosophy, history* (Cambridge: Cambridge University Press)

CHAMBLISS, W. J. and SEIDMAN, R. B. (1982) *Law, Order and Power* 2nd edn. (Reading, Mass.: Addison-Wesley)

CHAYES, Abram (1976) 'The Role of the Judge in Public Law Litigation' 89 *Harvard Law Review* 1976 1281–316

CHRISTIEJ G. C. (1982) *Law, Norms and Authority* (London: Duckworth)

CLARK, J. C. D. (1993) *The Language of Liberty 1660-1832: Political discourse and social dynamacs in the Anglo-American world* (Cambridge: Cambridge University Press)

CLARK, Lorenne M. G. (1978) 'Privacy, Property, Freedom, and the Family' in: Bronaugh (ed.) (1978) 167–87

CLEGG, Stewart R. (1990) *Modern Organisations: Organisation studies in the post-modern world* (London: Sage Publications)

COADY, C. A. J. (1992) *Testimony; A Philosophical Study* (Oxford: Clarendon Press)

COHEN, F. S. (1935) 'Transcendental Nonsense and the Functional Approach' reprinted in L. K. Cohen (ed.) (1960) *The Legal Conscience: Selected papers of Felix S. Cohen* 33–76 (New Haven: Yale University Press)

COHEN, Morris Raphael (1950) *Reason and Law: Studies in juristic philosophy* (Glencoe, III.: Free Press)

COHN, Norman (1970) *In Pursuit of the Millenium: Revolutionary milennarians and mystical anarchists of the Middle Ages* (London: Paladin)

COLEMAN, Jules (1988) *Markets, Morals and the Law* (Cambridge: Cambridge University Press)

COLLINS, Hugh (1982) *Marxism and the Law* (Oxford and New York: Oxford University Press)

COMMONS, John (1924) *The Legal Foundations of Capitalism* (New York: Macmillan)

COOK, W. W. (1964) 'Introduction' in W. N. Hohfeld *Fundamental Legal Conceptions* (1964)

CORBIN, Arthur L (1919) 'Legal Analysis and Terminology' in: Hall (ed.) *Readings in Jurisprudence* 471–85

COSER, L. A. (1956) *The Functions of Social Conflict* (London: Routledge & Kegan Paul)

COTTERRELL, R. B. M. (1983) 'English Conceptions in Legal Analysis' 46 *Modern Law Review* 1983 681–99

—— (1989) *The Politics of Jurisprudence: A critical introduction to legal philosophy* (London: Butterworths)

—— (1992 *The Sociology of Law: An introduction* 2nd edn. (London: Butterworths)

—— (1993) 'Sociological Perspectives on Legal Closure' in: Norrie (ed.) (1993) 175–93

—— (1995) *The Law's Community: Legal theory in sociological perspective* (Oxford: Oxford University Press)

COUSINS, Martin and HUSSAIN, Athag (1984) *Michel Foucault* (London: Macmillan)

COVAL, S. C. and SMITH, J. C. (1977) 'The Causal Theory of Law' 36 *Cambridge Law Journal* (1977) 110–51

COVELL, Charles (1994) *The Defence of Natural Law: A study of the ideas of law and justice in the writings of Lon L. Fuller, Michael Oakeshott, F. A. Hayek, Ronald Dworkin and John Finnis* (London: Macmillan)

CRAIG, P. P. (1990a) *Public Law and Democracy in the UK and the USA* (Oxford: Clarendon Press)

—— (1990b) 'Dicey: Unitary, self-correcting democracy and public law' 106 *Law Quarterly Review* (1990) 105–43

CRANSTON, Maurice (1976) 'Jean-Paul Sartre: Solitary man in a hostile universe' in: de Crespigny and Minogue (eds.) (1976) 209–27

CRESPIGNY, Anthony de and MINOGUE, Kenneth (eds.) (1976) *Contemporary Political Philosophers* (London: Methuen)

CRICK, Bernard (1964) *In Defence of Politics* (Harmondsworth: Penguin)

CROSS, Rupert (1995) *Statutory Interpretation* 3rd edn., eds. J. Bell and G. Engle (London: Butterworths)

DAGGER, Richard (1989) 'Rights' in: Ball *et al.* (eds.) (1989) 292–308

DANDEKER, Christopher (1994) 'War and the Military Establishment' in: Freedman (ed.) (1994: 109–11)

DAVIS, Michael H. (1986) 'The Law/Politics Distinction in the French Conseil Constitutionnel and the US Supreme Court' 34 *American Journal of Comparative Law* (1986) 45–92

DAWKINS, Richard (1976) *The Selfish Gene* (Oxford: Oxford University Press)

DAWSON, Sandra (1996) *Analysing Organisations* 3rd edn. (Basingstoke: Macmillan)

DELETANT, Dennis and HANAK, Harry (eds.) (1988) *Historians as Nation Builders: Central and South-East Europe* (Basingstoke: Macmillan)

DEVLIN, Patrick (1965) *The Enforcement of Morals* (Oxford: Oxford University Press)

DIAS, R. W. M. (1985) *Jurisprudence* 5th edn. (London: Butterworths)

DICEY, A. V. (1889) *Introduction to the Study of the Law and the Constitution* 3rd edn. (London: Macmillan)

DIETZ, Mary (1989) 'Patriotism' in: Ball *et al.* (eds.) (1989) 177–93

DOUGLAS, Mary (1987) *How Institutions Think* (London: Routledge & Kegan Paul)

DOUZINAS, Costas, GOODRICH, Peter, and HACKAMANOVITCH, Yfat (eds.) (1994) *Politics, Postmodernity and Critical Legal Studies: The legality of the Contingent* (London: Routledge & Kegan Paul)

DOWRICK, F. E. (1961) *Justice According to the English Common Lawyers* (London: Butterworths)

DRAPER, Theodore (1990) *New York Review of Books* vol. XXXVII, no. 8, p. 50

DUFF, R. A. (1986) *Trials and Punishments* (Cambridge: Cambridge University Press)

DUNCAN, Alan and HOBSON, Dominic (1994) *Saturn's Children: How the state devours liberty and prosperity* (London: Sinclair-Stevenson)

DURKHEIM, Emil (1947) *The Division of Labour in Society* tr. George Sampson, 2nd edn. (Glencoe: Free Press)

DWORKIN, Ronald (1977a) *Taking Rights Seriously* (London: Duckworth)

—— (1977b) 'No Right Answer' in: Hacker and Raz (eds.) (1977) 58–84

—— (1986) *Law's Empire* (London: Fontana Press)

—— (1987) 'Legal Theory and Problems of Sense' in: Gavison (ed.) (1987) 9–20

—— (1993) *Life's Dominion: An argument about abortion and euthanasia* (London: Harper Collins)

EDGEWORTH, Brendan (1986) 'Legal Positivism and the Philosophy of Language: A critique of Hart's "descriptive sociology" ' 6 *Legal Studies* 115

EHRLICH, Eugene (1936) *Fundamental Principles of Sociology of Law* tr. Walter L. Moll (Cambridge, Mass.: Harvard University Press)

EISENBERG, Melvin Aron (1988) *The Nature of the Common Law* (Cambridge, Mass.: Harvard University Press)

EISENSTADT, S. N. (1968) 'Institutions: The concept' in: D. L. Sills (ed.) *International Encyclopedia of the Social Sciences* vol. 14, 421–9 (New York: Free Press)

ELDRIDGE, J. E. T. (ed.) (1971) *Max Weber: An interpretation of social reality* (London: Nelson)

ELSTER, Jon (1990) 'Introduction' in: Elster and Slagstad (eds.) (1990) *The Cement of Society: A study of social order* (Cambridge: Cambridge University Press)

—— and SLAGSSTAD, Rune (eds.) (1988) *Constitutionalism and Democracy* (Cambridge: Cambridge University Press)

ELY, J. (1980) *Democracy and Distrust: A theory of judicial review* (Cambridge, Mass.: Harvard University Press)

EMMET, Dorothy and MacINTYRE, Alasdair (eds.) (1970) *Sociological Theory and Philosophical Analysis* (London: Macmillan)

ENTREVES, A. P. d' (1970) *Natural Law* (London: Hutchinson)

ETZION, Amitae (1995) *The Spirit of Community: Rights, responsibilities and the communications agenda* (London: Fontana Press)

EVANS, E. P. (1987) *The Criminal Prosecution and Capital Punishment of Animals: The lost history of Europe's animal trials* Introduced by Nicholas Humphrey (London: Faber)

EVANS, Jim (1981) 'Mandatory and Directory Rules' (1981) 1 *Legal Studies* 227–56

EWING, K. D. and GEARTY, C. A. (1990) *Freedom Under Thatcher: Civil liberties in modern Britain* (Oxford: Clarendon Press)

FEDERICO, Guiseppi di (1995) in: Tate and Vallinder (eds.) (1995) 233–42

FEINBERG, Joel (1970) *Doing and Deserving: Essays in the theory of responsibility* (Princeton NJ: Princeton University Press)

—— (1980) *Rights, Justice and the Bounds of Liberty* (Princeton: Princeton University Press)

—— (1990) *The Moral Limits of the Criminal Law* 4 vols. (Oxford: Oxford University Press)

FINER, S. E. (1970) *Comparative Government* (London: Allen Lane)

FINNIS, John (1980) *Natural Law and Natural Rights* (Oxford: Clarendon Press)

FISH, Stanley (1989) *Doing What Comes Naturally: Change, rhetoric and the practice of theory in literary and legal studies* (Oxford: Oxford University Press)

—— (1993) 'The Law Wishes to have a Formal existence' in: Norrie (ed.) (1993)

FISHER, H. A. L. (1936) *A History of Europe* (London: Arnold)

FISHER, Louis (1991) *Constitutional Dialogues: Interpretation as political process* (Princeton: Princeton University Press)

FISK, Milton (1989) *The State and Justice: An essay in political theory* (Cambridge: Cambridge University Press)

FISS, Owen (1984) 'Against Settlements' 93 *Yale Law Journal* (1984) 1073–90

FLATHMAN, Richard E. (1984) 'Moderating Rights' in: Paul, Miller, and Paul (eds.) (1984) 149–71

FLECK, Ludwick (1979) *The Genesis and Development of a Scientific Fact* ed. Thaddeus J. Trenn and Robert K. Merton (Chicago and London: University of Chicago Press)

FLETCHER, George P. (1978) *Rethinking Criminal Law* (Boston: Little, Brown)

—— (1993) *Loyalty* (Oxford: Oxford University Press)

FLEW, Anthony (ed.) (1966) *Logic and Language* 2nd Series (Oxford: Basil Blackwell)

—— (ed.) (1983) *A Dictionany of Philosophy* 2nd edn. (London: Macmillan)

FOUCAULT, Michel (1976) *History of Sexuality* tr. Robert Hurley (London: Allen Lane)

—— (1977) *Discipline and Punish: The birth of the prison* tr. Alan Sheridan (London: Allen Lane)

FRANK, Jerome (1930) *Law and the Modern Mind* (London: Stevens & Sons)

FREEDMAN, Lawrence (ed.) (1994) *War* (Oxford: Oxford University Press)

FREIDRICH, Carl J. (1958) 'Authority, Reason and Discretion' in: *Nomos 111; Authority* 28–48

—— (1974) *Limited Government: A comparison* (Engleward Cliffs NJ: Prentice Hall)

FRIEDMAN, Lawrence M. (1990) *The Republic of Choice: Law, authority and culture* (Cambridge Mass.: Harvard University Press)

—— (1993) *Crime and Punishment in American History* (New York: Basic Books)

FRIEDMAN, W. (1960) *Legal Theory,* 4th edn. (London: Stevens & Sons)

FUKUYAMA, Francis (1992) *The End of History and the Last Man* (London: Hamish Hamilton)

—— (1995) *Trust* (London: Hamish Hamilton)

FULLER, Lon L. (1958) 'Positivism and Fidelity to Law: A reply to Professor Hart' 71 *Harvard Law Review* (1958) 630–72

—— (1964) *The Morality of Law* (New Haven and London: Yale University Press)

—— (1971) *The Anatomy of Law* (Harmondsworth: Penguin)

GALANTER, Marc (1981) 'Justice in Many Rooms' 1 *Journal of Legal Pluralism* (1981) 1–22

GARTH, Bryant (1982) 'The movement towards procedural informalism in North America and Western Europe: A critical survey' in Abel (ed.) (1982) 183–211

GAUTHIER, David (1992) 'The Liberal Individual' in: Avineri and de-Schalit (eds.) (1992) 151–64.

GAVISON, Rachel (ed.) (1987) *Issues in Contemporary Legal Theory* (Oxford: Clarendon Press)

GELLNER, Ernest (1959) *Words and Things: A critical account of linguistic philosophy and a study in ideology* (London: Gollancz)

—— (1964) *Thought and Change* (London: Weidenfeld & Nicolson)

—— (1970) 'Concepts and Society' in: Emmett and MacIntyre (eds.) (1970) 115–49

—— (1983) *Nations and Nationalism* (Oxford: Basil Blackwell)

—— (1994) *Conditiions of Liberty: Civil society and its rivals* (London: Hamish Hamilton)

GERWITH, Alan (1978) *Reason and Morality* (Chicago: Chicago University Press)

—— (1984) 'The Epistemology of Human Rights' in: Paul, Miller, and Paul (eds.) (1984) 1–24

GIDDENS, Anthony (1978) *Durkheim* (London: Fontana/Collins)

—— (1984) *The Constitution of Society: Outline of a theory of structuration* (Cambridge: Polity Press)

—— (1985) *The Nation State and Violence* (Cambridge: Polity Press)

—— (1987) *Sociology* (Cambridge: Polity Press)

GILBERT, Margaret (1989) *On Social Facts* (Princeton, NJ: Princeton University Press)

GILMORE, Grant (1961) 'Legal Realism: Its causes and cure' 70 *Yale Law Journal* 1960–61 1073–48

GINSBURG, Morris (1993) 'Stammler' in: Jennings (ed.) (1933) 38–51

—— (1965) *On Justice in Society* (Harmondsworth: Penguin)

GLUCKMAN, Max (1953) *The Judicial Process Among the Barotse of Northern Rhodesia* (Manchester: Manchester University Press)

GOLDING, Martin (1978) 'On the Adversary System of Justice' in: R. Bronhaugh (ed.) (1978) 98–121

—— (1984) 'The Primacy of Welfare Rights' in: Paul, Miller, and Paul (eds.) (1984) 119–36

GOODRICH, Peter (1986) *Reading the Law: A critical introduction to legal methods and techniques* (Oxford: Basil Blackwell)

—— (1987) *Legal Discourse: Studies in linguistics, rhetoric and legal analysis* (London: Macmillan)

GOODY, Jack (1986) *The Logic of Writing and the Organisation of Society* (Cambridge: Cambridge University Press)

GOUGH, J. W. (1955) *Fundamental Law in English Constitutional History* (Oxford: Clarendon Press)

GRACE, Clive and WILKINSON, Philip (1978) *Sociological Interpretation and Legal Phenomena* (London: Collier Macmillan)

GRAY, John (1992) 'Against the new Liberalism: Rawls, Dworkin and the emptying of political life' *Times Literary Supplement* 3 July 1992

—— (1995a) *Enlightenment's Wake* (London: Routledge & Kegan Paul)

—— (1995b) 'Our Way' review of Ernest Gellner's Conditions of Liberty *Times Literary Supplement* June 1995

—— (1996) *Post-Liberalism: Studies in political thought* (London: Routledge & Kegan Paul)

GRAY, John Chipman (1931) *The Nature and Sources of Law* 2nd edn. (New York: Macmillan)

GREENBERG, D., KATZ, S. N., OLIVIERO, M. B., and WHEATLEY, S. C. (eds.) (1993) *Constitutionalism and Democracy* (New York: Oxford University Press)

GREENWALT, Kent (1987) 'Comment' in: Gavison (ed.) (1987) 156–79

GREGOR, Mary J. (1963) *The Laws of Freedom: A study of Kant's method of applying the categorical imperative in the Metaphysik der Sitten* (Oxford: Basil Blackwell)

GREISMAN, H. C. (1976) 'The Disenchantment of the World' 28 *British Journal of Sociology* 499

GRIFFITH, J. A. G. (1977) *The Politics of the Judiciary* (London: Fontana)

—— (1979) 'The Political Constitution' Chorley Lecture, 42 *Modern Law Review* 121

—— (1989) Review *Times Literary Supplement* 10 Nov. 1989

—— (1991) *The Politics of the Judiciary* 4th edn. (London: Fontana)

—— and RYLE, Martin (1989) *Parliament: Functions, practices and procedures* (London: Sweet & Maxwell)

GROSS, Hyman (1979) *A Theory of Criminal Justice* (New York: Oxford University Press)

GUEST, A. G. (ed.) (1961) *Oxford Essays in Jurisprudence* (Oxford: Oxford University Press)

GURVITCH, G. (1947) *Sociology of Law* (London: Routledge & Kegan Paul)
HABERMAS, Jurgen (1973) *Legitimation Crisis* (London: Heinneman Educational Books)
—— (1986) 'Law as Medium and Law as Institution' in: Teubner (ed.) *Dilemmas of Law in the Welfare State* (Berlin: de Gruyter)
HACKER, P. M. S. and RAZ, Joseph (eds.) (1977) *Law, Morality and Society: Essays in Honour of H. L. A. Hart* (Oxford: Oxford University Press)
HALEY, John Owen (1982) 'The Politics of Informal Justice: The Japanese experience 1922–1944' in: Abel (ed.) (1982) 125–49
HALL, Jerome (ed.) (1938) *Readings in Jurisprudence* (New York: Bobbs Merrill)
—— (1949) *Living Law in a Democratic Society* (Indiana: Bobbs Merrill)
—— (1982) *Law, Social Science and Criminal Theory* (New York: Rothman)
HAMPSHIRE, Stuart (1960) *Thought and Action* (London: Chatto Windus)
—— (1989) *Innocence and Experience* (Cambridge Mass.: Harvard University Press)
HARE, R. M. (1963) *Freedom and Reason* (Oxford: Clarendon Press)
HARLOW, Carol (ed.) (1986) *Public Law and Politics* (London: Sweet & Maxwell)
HARRUP, Cynthia (1988) *The Common Peace* (Cambridge: Cambridge University Press)
HART, H. L. A. (1954) 'Definition and Theory in Jurisprudence' 70 *Law Quarterly Review* 37–60
—— (1955) 'Are There any Natural Rights' 64 *Philosophical Review* 175–91
—— (1957) 'Positivism and the Separation of Law and Morals' 71 *Harvard Law Review* 593–629
—— (1959) 'Prolegomenon to the Principles of Punishment' in: Laslett and Runciman (eds.) (1962) 158–82
—— (1963) *Law, Liberty, and Morality* (London: Oxford University Press)
—— (1965) *The Morality of the Criminal Law* (Jerusalem: Magnes Press)
—— (1968) *Punishment and Responsibility: Essays in the philosophy of law* (Oxford: Oxford University Press)
—— (1982) *Essays on Bentham: Studies in jurisprudence and political theory* (Oxford: Oxford University Press)
—— (1983) *Essays in Jurisprudence and Philosophy* (Oxford: Clarendon Press)
—— (1994) *The Concept of Law* 2nd edn. (Oxford: Clarendon Press)
HARVEY, B. W. (ed.) (1978) *The Lawyer and Justice: A collection of addresses by Judges and Jurists to the Holdsworth Club of the University of Birmingham* (London: Sweet & Maxwell)
HASKELL, Thomas (1987) 'The Curious Persistence of Rights Talk in "The Age of Interpretation" ' 74 *Journal of American History* 984–1012.
HAWKINS, Keith (1984) *Environment and Enforcement: Regulation and the social definition of pollution* (Oxford: Clarendon Press)
—— and THOMAS, John M. (eds.) (1984) *Enforcing Regulation* (Boston: Kluwer-Nijhoff)
HAY, Douglas, LINEBAUGH, Peter, RULE, John G., Thompson, E. P., and WINSLOW, Carol (1979) *Albion's Fatal Tree* (London: Allen Lane)
HAYEK, F. A. (1944) *The Road to Serfdom* (London: Routledge & Kegan Paul)
HEGEL, Georg William Friedrich (1942) *Hegel's Philosophy of Right* tr. T. M. Knox (Oxford: Oxford University Press)

HENRY, Stuart (1983) *Private Justice: Towards integral theorising in the sociology of law* (London: Routledge & Kegan Paul)

HERMAN, Shael (1981) 'Quot Judices tot Sententiae' (1981) 1 *Legal Studies* 165–89

HERODOTUS (1972) *The Histories* tr. Aubrey de Selincourt, revised with introduction and notes by A. R. Burn (Harmondsworth: Penguin)

HERRENSTEIN, Richard and MURRAY, Charles (1995) *The Bell Curve* (Cambridge, Mass.: Harvard University Press)

HILSON, C. and Cram, I. (1996) 'Judicial Review and Environmental Law: Is there a coherent view of standing ?' (1996) 16 *Legal Studies* 1–16

HOBBES, Thomas (1960) *Leviathan: or The matter forme and power of a Commonwealth ecclesiastical or civil* ed. Michael Oakeshott (Oxford: Basil Blackwell)

HOBSBAWM, E. J. (1990) *Nations and Nationalism since 1780: Programme, myth and reality* (Cambridge: Cambridge University Press)

HOHFELD, W. N. (1964) *Fundamental Legal Conceptions as Applied in Judicial Reasoning* ed. W. W. Cook (New Haven and London: Yale University Press)

HOLLAND, T. E. (1924) *The Elements of Jurisprudence* 13th edn. (Oxford: Clarendon Press)

HOLMES, O. W. (1881) *The Common Law* (Boston: Little, Brown)

HOLSTI, Kalevi J. (1991) *Peace and War: Armed conflicts and international order* (Cambridge: Cambridge University Press)

HOMANS, G. C. (1950) *The Human Group* (London: Routledge & Kegan Paul)

HONORE, Anthony (1973) 'Groups, Law, and Obedience' in: Simpson (ed.) Oxford Essays in Jurisprudence (1973) 1–21

HOOK, Sidney (ed.) (1964) *Law and Philosophy: A symposium* (New York: New York University Press)

HUBER, Peter (1988) *Liability: The legal revolution and its consequences* (New York: Basic)

HUGHES, John (1980) *The Philosophy of Social Research* (London: Longman)

HUIZINGA, J. (1976) *The Waning of the Middle Ages* tr. F. Hopman (Harmondsworth: Penguin)

HUNT, Alan (1989) 'The role and place of theory in legal education: Reflections on foundationalism' 9 *Legal Studies* 146–64

HUTCHINSON, Allan C. (1985) 'The Rise and Ruse of Administrative Law Scholarship' 48 *Modern Law Review* (1985) 293–324

JENNINGS, Ivor (ed.) (1933) *Modern Theories of Law* (Oxford: Oxford University Press)

JOHNSON, David (1994) *The Ideal of Liberal Democracy*

JOHNSON, Mark (1993) *The Moral Imagination: Implications of cognitive science for ethics* (Chicago: Chicago University Press)

JONES, J. Walter (1956) *Historical Introduction to the Theory of Law* (Oxford: Clarendon Press)

JOSEPH, Philip A. and WALKER, Gordon R. (1987) 'A Theory of Constitutional Change' (1987) 7 *Oxford Journal of Legal Studies* 155–81

KACZOROWSKI Robert J. (1989) 'Enforcement Provisions of the Civil Rights Bill 1866: A legislative history in light of *Runyon* v. *McCrary* 98 *Yale Law Journal* (1989) 565–95

KAGAN, Robert A (1984) 'On Regulatory Inspectorates and Police' in: Hawkins and Thomas (eds.) (1984)

KAMENKA, Eugene, BROWN, Robert, and TAY, Alice Erh-Soon (eds.) (1975) *Law and Society: The crisis in legal ideals* (London: Edward Arnold)

KAMENKA, Eugene and TAY, Alice Erh-Soon (eds.) (1978) *Human Rights* (London: Edward Arnold) (eds.) (1980) *Law and Social Control* (London: Edward Arnold)

KANTOROWICZ, Hermann (1934) 'Some Rationalism About Realism' *Yale Law Journal* (1934) 1240–53

—— (1958) *The Definition of Law* ed. A. H. Campbell (Cambridge: Cambridge University Press)

KATE, Jan Ten and KOPPEN, Peter J. van (1995) 'The Netherlands: Towards a form of judicial review' in: Tate and Vallinder (eds.) (1995) 370–80

KELLEY, Donald R. (1991) *The Human Measure: Social thought in the Western legal tradition* (Cambridge Mass.: Harvard University Press)

KELLY, David (1984) 'Life Liberty and Property' in: Paul, Miller, and Paul (eds.) (1984) 108–18

KELSEN, Hans (1934) 'The Pure Theory of Law: Its methods and fundamental concepts' 50 *Law Quarterly Review* (1934)

—— (1960a) *What is Justice? Justice, Law and Politics in the Mirror of Science* (Berkeley: University of California Press)

—— (1960b) 'Plato and Natural Law' *Vanderbilt Law Review* 24

—— (1967) The *Pure Theory of Law* tr. M. Knight (Berkeley: University of California Press)

—— (1973) *General Theory of Law and State* tr. Anders Wedberg (New York: Russell & Russell)

—— (1990) 'On the theory of interpretation' in: 10 *Legal Studies* (1990) 127–35

KENNEDY, Duncan (1976) 'Form and Substance in Private Law Adjudication' (1976) 89 *Harvard Law Review* 1687–94

KEPEL, Gilles (1994) *The Revenge of God: The Resurgence of Islam, Christianity and Judaism in the modern world* tr. Alan Braley (University Park, Pa.: Pennsylvania State University Press)

KING, M. (1981) *The Framework of Criminal Justice* (London: Croom Helm)

KINGDOM, Elizabeth F. (1993) *What's Wrong With Rights: Problems for feminist politics of law* (Edinburgh: Edinburgh University Press)

KIRALFY, A. K. R. (1962) *Potter's Historical Introduction to English Law and its Institutions* 4th edn. (London: Sweet & Maxwell)

KLEINIG, John (1978) 'Human Rights, Legal Rights and Social Change' in: Kamenka and Tay (eds.) (1978) 36–47

KNESS, Ken (1989) 'Legal Indeterminacy' *California Law Review* 77 (1989) 283–337

KYGGIER, Martin (1976) 'Anthropological approaches' in: Kamenka and Tay (eds.) (1980) 27-59

KYMLICKA, Will (1989) 'Liberal Individualism and Liberal Neutrality' in: Avineri and de-Schalit (eds.) (1992) 165–85

—— (1990) *Contemporary Political Philosophy* (Oxford: Clarendon Press)

—— (1991) *Liberalism: Community and culture* (Oxford: Clarendon Press)

LACEY, Nicola (1989) *State Punishment: Political principles and community values* (London: Routledge & Kegan Paul)

—— (1993) 'Closure and Critique in Feminist jurisprudence' in: Norrie (ed.) (1993)

—— and WELLS, Celia and MEURE, Dirk (1990) *Reconstructing Criminal Law: Text and materials* (London: Weidenfeld & Nicolson)

LARMORE, Charles E. (1987) *Patterns of Moral Complexity* (Cambridge: Cambridge University Press)

LASKI, Harold J. (1933) 'M. Duguit's conception of the state' in: Jennings (ed.) (1933) 52–67

LASLETT, Peter (ed.) (1963) *Philosophy, Politics, and Society* (Oxford: Basil Blackwell)

—— (1963) 'The Face to Face Society' in: Laslett (ed.) (1963)

—— and RUNCIMAN, W. G. (1962) *Philosophy, Politics and Society* 2nd Series (Oxford: Basil Blackwell)

—— (1969) *Philosophy, Politics and Society* 3rd Series (Oxford: Basil Blackwell)

LASOK, D., JAFFEY, A. J. E., PERROTT, D. L., and SACHS, Christina (eds.) (1980) *Fundamental Duties* (Oxford: Pergamon Press)

LEACH, Edmund (1982) *Social Anthropology* (London: Fontana)

LEIGH, G. (1992) *Legal Hermeneutics: History, theory and practice* (Berkeley: University of California Press)

LENHOFF, P. (1949) 'On Interpretive Theories: A comparative study of legislation' 27 *Texas Law Review* 312–35

LEVY, Leonard (1992) *Blasphemy: Verbal offenses against the sacred from Moses to Salman Rushdie* (New York: Knopf)

LEWIS, Norman D. (1996) *Choice and the Legal Order: Rising above politics* (London: Butterworth)

LI, Victor (1978) *Law Without Lawyers: A comparative view of law in China and the United States* (Boulder Col.: Westview Press)

LIENHARDT, Godfrey (1966) *Social Anthropology* 2nd edn. (London: Oxford University Press)

LIPSET, S. H. (1958) 'Some Social Requirements of Democracy' *American Political Science Review* 99–105

—— (1960) *Political Man* (London: Heineman)

LLEWELLYN, Karl (1960) *The Common Law Tradition: Deciding appeals* (Boston: Little, Brown)

—— (1962) *Jurisprudence: Realism in theory and practice* (Chicago: University of Chicago Press)

LLOYD, Dennis (1964) *The Idea of Law* (Harmondsworth: Penguin)

LOCKE, John (1894) *An Essay Concerning Human Understanding* 2 vols., ed. A. C. Fraser (Oxford)

—— (1956) *The Second Treatise of Government* ed. J. W. Gough (Oxford: Basil Blackwell)

LOMASKY, Loren (1984) 'Personal Projects as the Foundation for Basic Rights' in: Paul, Miller, and Paul (eds.) (1984)

—— (1987) *Persons, Rights, and the Moral Community* (Oxford: Oxford University Press)

LOUGHLIN, Martin (1991) 'Innovative Financing in Local Government: The limits of legal instrumentalism' *Public Law* (1991) 568–99
—— (1992) *Public Law and Political Theory* (Oxford: Oxford University Press)
LUCAS, J. R. (1993) *Responsibility* (Oxford: Clarendon Press)
LUHMAN, Nicholas (1985) *A Sociological Theory of Law* tr. Elizabeth King and Martin Albrow (London: Routledge & Kegan Paul)
LUKES, Steven (1970) 'Methodological Individualism Reconsidered' in: Emmet and MacIntyre (eds.) (1970) 76–88
—— (1973) *Individualism* (Oxford: Basil Blackwell)
—— (1974) *Power: A radical view* (London: Macmillan)
—— (ed.) (1986) *Power: Readings in social and political theory* (Oxford: Basil Blackwell)
—— and SCULL, Andrew (eds.) (1983) *Durkheim and the Law* (Oxford: Robertson)
LYONS, David (1984) *Ethics and the Rule of Law* (Cambridge: Cambridge University Press)
—— (1993) *Moral Aspects of Legal Theory* (Cambridge: Cambridge University Press)
McAUSLAN, Patrick (1980) *The Ideologies of Planning Law* (Oxford: Pergamon Press)
—— (1983) 'Administrative Law, Collective Consumption and Judicial Policy' (1983) 46 *Modern Law Review* 1–20
MacCORMICK, D. N. (1977) 'Rights in Legislation' in: Hacker and Raz (eds.) (1977) 189–209
—— (1981a) 'Law, Morality and Positivism' 1 *Legal Studies* 131–145
—— (1981b) *H. L. A. Hart* (London: Edward Arnold)
—— (1982a) *Legal Rights and Social Democracy* (Oxford: Clarendon Press)
—— (1982b) 'Legal Obligation and the Imperative Fallacy' in: Simpson (ed.) (1982) 100–30
—— (1993) 'Reconstruction and Deconstruction: Closing in on critique' in: Norrie (ed) (1993) 142–56
—— and WEINBERGER, Otto (1986) *The Institutional Theory of Law* (Dordrecht: D. Reidel)
MacELDOWNEY, John F. (1994) *Public Law* (London: Sweet and Maxwell)
MacFARLANE, Alan (1978) *The Origins of English Individualism: The family, property and social transition* (Oxford: Basil Blackwell)
McGRADE, Arthur Stephen (1980) 'Ockham and the Birth of Individual Rights' in: Tierney and Linehan (eds.) (1980) 149–65
McILLWAIN, C. H. (1910) *The High Court of Parliament and its Supremacy: An historical essay on the boundaries between legislation and adjudication in England* (New Haven: Yale University Press)
MacINTYRE, Alasdair (1971) 'Is a Science of Comparative Politics Possible?' in: Ryan (ed.) (1973) 171–88
—— (1985) *After Virtue: A study in moral theory* (London: Duckworth)
MacIVER, R. M. (1933) *Society: Its structure and changes* (New York: Long & Smith)
—— and PAGE, Charles H. (1950) *Society: An introductory analysis* (London: Macmillan)

McLACHLIN, Beverly (1994) 'The Role of the Judge in Modern Commonwealth Society' (1994) 110 *Law Quarterly Review* 260–9

McLELLAN, David (1975) *Marx* (London: Fontana/Collins)

MACPHERSON, C.B. (1966) *The Real World of Democracy* (Oxford; Oxford University Press)

MADDOCKS, Graham (1989) 'Constitution' in: Ball *et al.* (eds.) (1989) 50–67

MAINE, H. S. (1905) *Ancient Law: Its connection with the early history of society and its relation to modern ideas* 10th edn. (London: John Murray)

MAITLAND, F. W. (1908) *The Constitutional History of England* (Cambridge: Cambridge University Press)

MANDEL, Michael (1995) 'Legal Politics Italian Style' in: Tate and Vallinder (eds.) (1995) 261–286

MANDELBAUM, Maurice (1955) 'Societal Facts' in: Ryan (ed.) (1973) 103–18

MANSFIELD, Harvey C. Jr. (1990) *America's Constitutional Soul* (Baltimore, Md.: Johns Hopkins University Press)

MARSHALL, Geoffrey (1961) 'Justiciability' in: Guest (ed.) (1961) 265–87

—— (1977) 'Positivism, Adjudication and Democracy' in Hacker and Raz (eds.) (1977) 132–44

—— (1989) 'Limitations on Legislators' *Times Literary Supplement* 30 June 1989

MARTIN, Rex (1993) *A System of Rights* (Oxford: Clarendon Press)

—— and NICKEL J.W. (1980) 'Recent Work on the Concept of Right' 17 *American Philosophical Quarterly* (1980) 165–80

MARX, Karl (1990) *Capital: A critique of political economy* vol. 1, tr. Ben Fowkes (Harmondsworth: Penguin)

MELDEN, A. I. (ed.) (1970) *Human Rights* (Belmont Ca.: Wadsworth)

MICHELMAN, Frank I. (1967) 'Property, Utility and Fairness: Comments on the ethical functions of "just compensation" law' 80 *Harvard Law Review* 1165–258

MILIBAND, R. (1969) *The State in Capitalist Society* (London: Weidenfeld and Nicolson)

MILL, John Stuart (1948) *On Liberty: Considerations on Representative Government* ed. R. B. McCallum (Oxford: Basil Blackwell)

—— (1962) *Utilitarianism, On Liberty, Essay on Bentham, together with selected writings of Jeremy Bentham and John Austin* ed. Mary Warnock (London: Collins)

MILSOM, S. F. C. (1985) *Studies in the History of the Common Law* (London: Ronceverte)

MINOGUE, Kenneth (1978) 'Natural Rights, Ideology and the Game of Life' in: Kamenka and Tay (eds.) (1978) 13–35

—— (1986) 'What is Wrong With Rights?' in: Harlow (ed.) (1986) 213

MITCHELL, Basil (1970) *Law, Morality, and Religion in a Secular Society* (Oxford: Oxford University Press)

MITCHELL, J. D. B. (1968) *Constitutional Law* 2nd edn. (Edinburgh: Edinburgh University Press)

MORTON, F. L. (1988) 'Judicial Review in France; A comparative analysis' *American Journal of Comparative Law* 36 (1988) 89-110

MUNDLE, C. W. K. (1954) 'Punishment and Desert' 4 *Philosophical Quarterly* 216–28, and the Postscript in: Acton (ed.) (1969) 81–2

MURPHY, Jeffrey and HAMPTON, Jean (1990) *Forgiveness and Mercy* (Cambridge: Cambridge University Press)

MURPHY, Tim (1994) 'As if: Camera juridica' in: Douzinas *et al.* (eds.) (1994) 69–106

MURPHY, W. F. (1993) 'Constitutions, Constitutionalism and Democracy' in: Greenberg *et al.* (eds.) (1993) 1–21

NAGEL, Thomas (1991) *Equality and Partiality* (New York and Oxford: Oxford University Press)

NICHOLAS, Barry (1962) *An Introduction to Roman Law* (Oxford: Clarendon Press)

NORRIE, Alan (1983) 'Freewill, Determinism and Criminal Justice' (1983) 3 *Legal Studies* 60–73

—— (1993) 'Closure Critique: Antimony in modern legal theory' in: Norrie (ed.) (1993) 1–21

—— (ed.) (1993) *Closure and Critique: New directions in legal theory (Edinburgh:* Edinburgh University Press)

NORTH, P. (1985) 'Is Law Reform too Important to be left to Lawyers?' 5 *Legal Studies* 119.

NOWELL-SMITH, P. H. (1978) 'On Legitimate Authority: A reply to Joseph Raz' in: Bronhaugh (ed) (1978) 32A4

NOZICK, Robert (1974) *Anarchy, State, and Utopia* (Oxford: Basil Blackwell)

OAKESHOTT, Michael (1933) *Experience and its Modes* (Cambridge: Cambridge University Press)

—— (1975) *On Human Conduct* (Oxford: Clarendon Press)

—— (1977) *Rationalism in Politics and Other Essays* (London: Methuen)

O'CONNOR, James (1973) *The Fiscal Crisis of the State* (New York: St Martin's Press)

OLIVECRONA, Karl (1939) *Law as Fact* (London: Humphrey Milford)

OLSON, Mancur (1971) *The Logic of Collective Action* (New York: Schoken Books)

OUTHWAITE, W. (1978) *New Philosophies in Social Science* (London: Macmillan)

PACKER, Herbert L. (1968) *The Limits of the Criminal System* (Stanford: Oxford University Press)

PAGDEN, Anthony (1995) *Lords of All the World: Ideologies of empire in Spain, Britain and France 1500-1800* (New Haven: Yale University Press)

PAINE, Thomas (1976) *The Rights of Man* ed. Henry Collins (Harmondsworth: Penguin)

PARKER, C. F. (1980) 'The Fundamental Duty of Magistrates' in: Lasok *et al.* (eds.) (1980) 96–103.

PARSONS, T. and SHILS, E. A. (eds.) (1951) *Towards a General Theory of Action* (Cambridge Mass.: Harvard University Press)

PASHUKANIS, E. B. (1978) *Law and Marxism: A general theory* tr. B. Einhom (London: Ink Books)

PATERSON, Alan (1982) *The Law Lords* (London: Macmillan)

PATON, G. W. and DERHAM, D. P. (eds.) (1972) A *Textbook of Jurisprudence* 4th edn. (Oxford: Clarendon Press)

PAUL, Ellen Frankel, MILLER, Fred D. Jr, and PAUL, Jeffrey (eds.) (1984) *Human Rights* (Oxford: Basil Blackwell)

PEIL, Margaret (1977) *Consensus and Conflict in African Societies* (London: Longmans)

PERELMAN, Chaim (1963) *The Idea of Justice and the Problem of Argument*, Introduction by H. L. A. Hart tr. John Petrie (London: Routledge & Kegan Paul)

PHILLIPS, Derek L. (1993) *Looking Backwards; A critical appraisal of communitarian thought* (Princeton: Princeton University Press)

PLAMENATZ, John (1969) 'Responsibility, Blame and Punishment' in: Laslett and Runciman (eds.) (1969) 173–93

PLUCKNETT, Theodore F. T. (1956) *A Concise History of the Common Law* (London: Butterworths)

PODGORECKI, Adam (1962) 'Attitudes to Workers' Courts' in: Aubert (ed.) (1962) 142–9

POPPER, Karl (1962) *The Open Society and Its Enemies* 4th edn., 2 vols. (London: Routledge & Kegan Paul)

—— (1976) *The Unended Quest* (London: Fontana)

PORN, Ingmar (1970) *The Logic of Power* (Oxford: Basil Blackwell)

POSNER, Richard A. (1963) *The Economic Analysis of Law* (Boston: Little, Brown)

—— (1995) *Overcoming Law* (Cambridge, Mass.: Harvard University Press)

POSPISIL, Leopold (1971) *Anthropology of Law* (New York: Harper & Row)

POSTEMA, Gerald (1986) *Bentham and the Common Law Tradition* (Oxford: Oxford University Press)

POULANTZAS, N (1978) *State, Power, Socialism* tr. P. Camiller (London: New Left Books)

POUND, Roscoe (1922) *An Introduction to Legal Philosophy* (New Haven: Yale University Press)

—— (1943) 'A Survey of Social Interests' 57 *Harvard Law Review* 1–39.

PRICE, Christopher (1989) 'Taking Rights Cynically: A review of critical legal studies' 48 *Cambridge Law Journal* 283–91

PRIMORETZ, Igor (1987) 'The Middle Way in the Philosophy of Punishment' in: Gavison (ed.) (1987) 193–220

PULZER, Peter (1992) 'Do we need a Constitution?' *Times Literary Supplement* 8 January 1992

PUSEY, Michael (1987) *Jurgen Habermas* (Chichester: Ellis Horwood)

QUINTON, Anthony (ed.) (1967) *Political Philosophy* (Oxford: Oxford University Press),'Introduction' 1–17

RADCLIFF, Lord (1978) 'Law and the Democratic State' in: Harvey (ed.) (1978) 139–59

RAPHAEL, D. D. (1976) *Problems in Political Philosophy* (London: Pall Mall Press)

RAWLS, John (1955) 'Two Concepts of Rules' 64 *Philosophical Review* 3–32

—— (1958) 'Justice as Fairness' in: Laslett and Runciman (eds.) (1962) 132–57

—— (1964) 'Legal Obligation and the Duty of Fair Play' in: S. Hook (ed.) (1964) 318

—— (1973) *A Theory of Justice (Cambridge:* Cambridge University Press)

—— (1987) 'The Idea of an Overlapping Consensus' 7 *Oxford Journal of Legal Studies* 1987 1–25

—— (1993) *Political Liberalism* (New York: Columbia University Press)

RAZ, Joseph (1970) *The Concept of a Legal System* (Oxford: Oxford University Press)

—— (1975) *Practical Reason and Norms* (London: Hutchinson)
—— (ed) (1978) *Practical Reasoning* (Oxford: Oxford University Press)
—— (1978) 'On Legitimate Authority' in: Bronaugh (ed.) (1978) 6–31
—— (1979) *The Authority of Law: Essays in law and morality* (Oxford: Clarendon Press)
—— (1987) 'Autonomy, Toleration and the Harm Principle' in: Gavison (ed.) (1987) 313–33
—— (1994) *Ethics in the Public Domain: Essays in the morality of law and politics* (Oxford: Clarendon Press)
REHNQUIST, William (1975) 'The Notion of a Living Constitution' 54 *Texas Law Review* 678–701
REID, Lord (1972) 'The Judge as Lawmaker' *Journal of the SPTL vol.* 12 NS 1972
RENNER, Karl (1949) *The Institutions of Private Law and Their Social Functions* tr. A. Schwarzchild, ed. Otto Kahn-Freund (London: Routledge & Kegan Paul)
RHEINSTEIN, Max (1954) *Max Weber on Law in Economy and Society* (Chicago and London: Chicago University Press)
RICHARDSON, Megan (1990) 'Contract Law and Distributive Justice Revisited' 10 *Legal studies* 259–70
RIDLEY, F. F. (1988) 'There is no British Constitution: A dangerous case of the Emperor's clothes' 41 *Parliamentary Affairs* (1988) 340
RIKER, William (1982) *Liberalism against Populism: A confrontation between the theory of democracy and the theory of social choice* (San Francisco: W. H. Freeman)
ROBERTS, Simon (1979) Order and Disputes: *An introduction to legal anthropology* (Harmondsworth: Penguin)
ROBINSON, Paul H. (1982) 'Criminal Law Defences: A systematic analysis' 82 *Columbia Law Review* (1982) 199–291
RODGER, Allan (1995) 'Savigny in the Strand' Inaugural John Kelly Memorial Lecture, University College, Dublin (Dublin: Faculty of Law)
RORTY, Richard (1994) 'Towards a Liberal Utopia' interview, *Times Literary Supplement* 10 June 1994.
ROSEN, Lawrence (1989) *The Anthropology of Justice: Law as culture in Islamic society* Lewis Henry Morgan Lectures (Cambridge: Cambridge University Press)
ROSS, Alf (1958) *On Law and Justice* (London: Stevens and Son)
—— (1968) *Directives and Norms* (London: Routledge & Kegan Paul)
ROYAL COMMISSION ON CRIMINAL JUSTICE (1993) *Report of Viscount Runciman of Doxford et al.* Cm. 2263 (London: HMSO)
RUNCIMAN, W. G. (1986) 'On the Tendency of Human Societies to Form Variations' Radcliff-Brown Lecture on Social Anthropology (British Academy), *London Review of Books* 5 June 1986
—— and Others (1993) *Report of the Royal Commission on Criminal Justice* Cm. 2263 (HMSO)
RYAN, Alan (ed.) (1973) *Philosophy of Social Explanation* (London: Oxford University Press)
SAGAN, Eli (1986) *At the Dawn of Tyranny: The origins of individualism* (London: Faber & Faber)
SALMOND, John (1957) *Salmond on Jurisprudence* 11th edn., ed. Glanville Williams (London: Sweet & Maxwell)

SAMPFORD, Charles (1989) *The Disorder of Law* (Oxford: Basil Blackwell)
SAMUEL, Geoffrey (1994) *The Foundations of Legal Reasoning* (Antwerp: Metro)
SANDEL, Michael (1982) *Liberalism and the Limits of Justice* (Cambridge: Cambridge University Press)
—— (1984) 'The Procedural Republic and the Unencumbered Self' 12 *Political Theory* 1
SARTORIOUS, Rolf (1971) 'Hart's Concept of Law' in: Summers (ed.) (1971) 131–61
—— (1987) 'Positivism and Legal Authority' in: Gavison (ed.) (1987) 43–61
SAWYER, G. (1965) *Law in Society* (Oxford: Oxford University Press)
SCHAAR, John H. (1981) *Legitimacy in the Modern State* (New Brunswick and London: Transaction)
SCHURR, Edwin M. (1968) *Law and Society: A sociological view* (New York: Random House)
SCOTT, W. Richard (1995) *Institutions and Organisations* (London: Sage Publications)
SEARLE, John (1969) *Speech Acts* (Cambridge: Cambridge University Press)
SEDLEY, Stephen (1991) 'Free Speech for Rupert Murdoch' *London Review of Books* 19 Dec. 1991
—— (1994) 'The Sound of Silence: Constitutonal law without a constitution' 110 *Law Quarterly Review* (1994) 270–91
SEIGHART, Paul (1986) *The Lawful Rights of Mankind* (Oxford: Oxford University Press)
SELZNICK, Philip (1973) 'Sociology and Natural Law' in: Black and Mileski (eds.) (1973) 1–34
—— (1992) *The Moral Commonwealth: Social theory and the promise of community* (Berkeley and Oxford: University of California Press)
——, NONET, Philippe, and VOLLMER, Howard M. (1969) *Lazo, Society and Industrial Justice* (New York: Russell Sage Foundation)
SHAPIN, Steven (1994) *A Social History of Truth: Civility and science in seventeenth century England* (Chicago: Chicago University Press)
SHAPIRO, Martin (1981) Courts: *A comparative and political analysis* (Chicago: Chicago University Press)
—— (1995) 'United States' in: Tate and Vallinder (eds.) (1995) 43–66
SHKLAR, Judith (1964) *Legalism* (Cambridge Mass.: Harvard University Press
SIMMEL, Georg (1978) *The Philosophy of Money* tr. David Frisby and Tom Bottomore (London: Routledge & Kegan Paul)
SIMMONDS, N. E. (1981) 'Legal Validity and Decided Cases' 1 *Legal Studies* 24–36
—— (1984) *The Decline of Judicial Reason* (Manchester: Manchester University Press)
SIMPSON, A. W. Brian (ed.) (1973) *Oxford Essays in Jurisprudence* 2nd Series (Oxford: Oxford University Press)
—— (1992) *In the Highest Degree Odious: Detention without trial in wartime Britain* (Oxford: Clarendon Press)
SINGER, Peter (1973) *Democracy and Disobedience* (London: Oxford University Press)
SKINNER, Quentin (1989) 'The State' in: Ball *et al.* (eds) (1989) 90–131

SMART, Barry (1985) *Michel Foucault* (Chichester: Ellis Horwood)

SMART, Ninian (1971) *Religious Experience of Mankind* (London: Collins)

SMITH, A. T. H. (1983) 'The Prerogative of Mercy: The power of pardon and criminal justice' *Public Law* 398–439

—— (1985) 'Comment' *Public Law* (1985)

SMITH, J. C. (1983) 'Towards a Rational Criminal Law' (Holdsworth Club: Birmingham University)

SMITH, Stanley de (1960) 'The Lawyers and the Constitution' Inaugural Lecture, London School of Economics

—— and BRAZIER, Rodney (1989) *Constitutional and Administrative Law* 6th edn. (Harmondsworth: Penguin)

SOPER, Philip (1984) *Theory of Law* (Cambridge Mass: Harvard University Press)

—— (1987) 'The Obligation to Obey the Law' in: Gavison (ed.) (1987) 127–55

SPERBER, Dan and WILSON, Dierdre (1989) *Relevance: Communication and cognition* (Oxford: Basil Blackwell)

STEIN, Peter and SHAND, J. (1974) *Legal Values in Western Society* (Edinburgh: Edinburgh University Press)

STERNE, Lawrence (1967) *The Life and Opinions of Tristram Shandy* ed. Graham Petrie (Harmondsworth: Penguin)

STONE, Alex (1995) 'Co-ordinate Construction in France and Germany' in: Tate and Vallinder (eds.) (1995) 205–29

STONE, Christopher D. (1981) 'From a Language Perspective' 90 *Yale Law Journal* 1156–97

STRATHERN, Marilyn (1989) *The Gender of the Gift* (Berkeley: University of California Press)

SUMMERS, L. W. (1987) *The Moral Foundation of Rights* (Oxford: Oxford University Press)

SUMMERS, R S. (ed.) (1971) *More Essays in Legal Philosophy* (Oxford: Basil Blackwell)

—— (1978) 'Comment: "On the Adversary System and Justice" 'in Bronaugh (ed.) (1978) 122–6

TARNOPOLSKY, Walter S. and BEAUDOIN, Gerald. A. (eds.) (1982) *The Canadian Charter of Rights and Freedoms: Commentary* (Toronto: Carswell)

TATE, C. Neal (1995) 'Why the Expansion of Judicial Power?' in: Tate and Vallinder (eds.) (1995) 27–37

—— and VALLINDER, Torbjorn (eds.) (1995) *The Global Expansion of Judicial Power* (New York: New York University Press)

TAWNEY, R. H. (1926) *Religion and the Rise of Capitalism: A historical study* (London: Murray)

TAYLOR, Charles (1985) *Philosophy and the Human Sciences: Philosophical Papers* 2 vols. (Cambridge: Cambridge University Press)

TEIWES, Frederick C. (1976) 'The Origins of Rectification' *China Quarterly* (1976) 1–23

TERRY, Henry T. (1924) 'Duties, Rights and Wrongs' in: Hall (ed.) 457–71

TEUBNER, Gunther (1993) *Law as an Autopoietic System* tr. Anne Bankowska and Ruth Adler, ed. Zenon Bankowski (Oxford: Basil Blackwell)

THOMPSON, E. P. (1975) *Whigs and Hunters: The origins of the Black Act* (London: Allen Lane)

—— (1980) *The Making of the English Working Class* (Harmondsworth: Penguin)

THOMSON, George (1961) *Studies in Ancient Greek Society: The first philosophers* 2nd edn. (London: Lawrence & Wishart)

THOMSON, Janice E. (1994) *Mercenaries, Pirates and Sovereigns: State-building and extra-territorial violence in early modern Europe* (Princeton: Princeton University Press)

TIERNEY, Brian and LINEHAN, Peter (eds.) (1980) *Authority and Power: Studies in medieval law and government* (Cambridge: Cambridge University Press)

TIMASHEFF, N. S. (1974) *An Introduction to the Sociology of Law* (Westport: Greenwood Press)

TITUS, C. H. (1931) 'A Nomenclature in Political Science' *American Political Science Review* (1931) 4540

TOULMIN, Stephen Edelston (1961) *An Examination of The Place of Reason in Ethics* (Cambridge: Cambridge University Press)

TRIBE, Lawrence H. (1978) *American Constitutional Law* (New York: Foundation Press)

—— and DORF, Michael C. (1991) *On Reading the Constitution* (Cambridge Mass.: Harvard University Press)

TURR, Richard (1982) 'Litigation and the Consumer Interest: The class action and beyond' 2 *Legal Studies* 135–69

TWINING, William and MIERS, David (1982) *How to Do Things with Rules* 2nd edn. (London: Weidenfeld & Nicolson)

UNGER, R. M. (1976) *Law in a Modern Society: Towards a criticism of social theory* (New York: Free Press)

—— (1983) 'The Critical Legal Studies Movement' (1983) 96 *Harvard Law Review* 561–675

URMSON, J. O. (1966) 'On Grading' in: Flew (ed.) (1966) 159–86

VALLINDER, Torbjorn (1995) 'When the Courts go Marching in' in: Tate and Vallinder (eds.) (1995) 13–26

VILLA, Vittorio (1984) 'Legal Science between natural and human sciences' 4 *Legal Studies* 243–70

WADE, E. C. S. and BRADLEY A. W. (1985) *Constitutional and Administrative Law* 10th edn., ed. A. W. Bradley (London: Longman)

WADE, H. W. R. (1980) *Constitutional Fundamentals* (London: Stevens)

WALDRON, Jeremy (ed.) (1984) *Theories of Rights* (Oxford: Oxford University Press)

—— (ed.) (1987) *Nonsense upon Stilts: Bentham, Burke and Marx on the Rights of Man* (London: Methuen)

WALKLAND, S. A. (1968) *The Legislative Process in Great Britain* (London: Allen and Unwin)

WALLACH, H. G. Peter (1995) 'Reunification and Prospects for Judicialisation in Germany' in: Tate and Vallinder (eds.) (1995) 325–42

WALSH, V. C. (1961) *Scarcity and Evil* (Englewood Cliffs NJ.: Prentice Hall)

WALZER, Michael (1970) *Spheres of Justice: A defence of pluralism and equality* (New York: Basic Books)

WATSON, Alan (1977) *The Nature of Law* (Edinburgh: Edinburgh University Press)

WEBER, Max (1948) *The Protestant Ethic and the Spirit of Capitalism* tr. T. Parsons (London: Allen and Unwin)

—— (1954) *On Law in Economy and Society* tr. E. Shils and M. Rheinstein (Cambridge Mass.: Harvard University Press)

—— (1971) *Max Weber: An interpretation of social reality* ed. with an Introduction by J. E. T. Eldridge (London: Nelson)

—— (1978) *Economy and Society: An outline of interpretive sociology* 2 vols., ed. G. Roth and C. Willick (Berkeley: University of California Press)

WELLS, Alan (1970) *Social Institutions* (London:

WESTEN, Peter (1981) 'The Empty Idea of Equality' 95 *Harvard Law Review* (1981–82) 537–96

WHEARE, K. C. (1966) *Modern Constitutions* 2nd edn. (Oxford: Oxford University Press)

WHITE, Alan (1984) *Rights* (Oxford: Clarendon Press)

WHITTAKER, Ben (1964) *The Police* (Harmondsworth: Penguin)

WIGGINS, D. (1978) 'Deliberation and Practical Reason' in: Raz (ed.) (1978) 14452

WILLIAMS, Bernard (1962) 'The Idea of Equality' in: Laslett and Runciman (eds.) (1962) 110–31

—— (1994) 'Freer than Others' review of Amartya Sen's *Inequality Examined*, in *Times Literary Supplement* 17 Aug. 1994

WILSON, John (1966) *Equality* (London: Hutchinson)

WINCH, Peter (1958) *The Idea of a Social Science and its Relation to Philosophy* (London: Routledge & Kegan Paul)

—— (1967) 'Authority' in: Quinton (ed.) (1967) 97–111

WINKLER, John J. (1990) *The Constraints of Desire: The anthropology of sex and gender in ancient Greece* (London: Routledge & Kegan Paul)

WOOTTON, Barbara (1981) *Crime and the Criminal Law: Reflections of a magistrate and social scientist* 2nd edn. (London: Stevens)

WORTLEY, B. A. (1955) *Modern Theories of Law* (Manchester: Manchester University Press)

WRIGHT, Georg Henrik von (1963) *Norm and Action: A logical enquiry* (London: Routledge & Kegan Paul)

ZANDER, Michael (1985) *The Law Making Process* 2nd edn. (London: Weidenfeld & Nicolson)

ZANE, John M. (1918) 'German Legal Philosophy' in: Hall (ed.) (1938) fn. 1, p. 365

INDEX